Ebenezer Erskine

The Whole Works of the Late Rev. Ebenezer Erskine

Vol. III.

Ebenezer Erskine

The Whole Works of the Late Rev. Ebenezer Erskine
Vol. III.

ISBN/EAN: 9783337160777

Printed in Europe, USA, Canada, Australia, Japan

Cover: Foto ©Lupo / pixelio.de

More available books at **www.hansebooks.com**

THE
WHOLE WORKS

OF THE LATE

REV. EBENEZER ERSKINE

Minister of the Gospel at Stirling

CONSISTING OF

SERMONS AND DISCOURSES

ON THE

MOST IMPORTANT AND INTERESTING SUBJECTS

A NEW EDITION

IN THREE VOLUMES

VOL. III.

EDINBURGH
OGLE & MURRAY; WM. OLIPHANT & CO.; OLIVER & BOYD.
GLASGOW: J. PRYDE.
LONDON: HAMILTON, ADAMS & CO.
1871

CONTENTS OF THE THIRD VOLUME.

I. A LAMP ordained for God's Anointed.
Psa. cxxxii. 17.—*I have ordained a lamp for mine Anointed.*   1

II. The Angel's seal set upon God's faithful servants, when hurtful winds are blowing in the church militant.
Rev. vii. 1, 2, 3.—*And, after these things, I saw four Angels, standing on the four corners of the earth, that the wind should not blow on the earth, nor on the sea, nor on any tree. And I saw another Angel ascending from the east, having the seal of the living God; and he cried with a loud voice to the four angels, to whom it was given to hurt the earth and the sea, saying, hurt not the earth, neither the sea, nor the trees, till we have sealed the servants of our God in their foreheads.*   36

III. Christ considered as the nail, fastened in a sure place, bearing all the glory of his father's house.
Psa. xx. 5.—*In the name of our God, we will set up our banners.*
Is. xxii. 24.—*And they shall hang upon him all the glory of his Father's house, the offspring and the issue, all vessels of small quantity: from the vessels of cups, even to all the vessels of flagons.*   61

IV. A robbery committed, and restitution made, both to God and man.
Psa. lxix. 4.—*Then I restored that which I took not away.*   111

V. Worthless man much regarded by the mighty God.
Psa. cxliv. 3.—*Lord, what is man, that thou takest knowledge of him? or the son of man, that thou makest account of him*   126

VI. The human nature preferred unto the angelical.
Heb. ii. 15.—*For verily he took not on him the nature of angels? but, he took on him the seed of Abraham.*   146

VII. The broken law magnified and made honourable.
Is. xliii. 21.—*The Lord is well pleased for his righteousness sake; he will magnify the law, and make it honourable.*   159

VIII. The wise Virgins going forth to meet the Bridegroom.
Matt. xxv. 6.—*And at mid-night there was a cry made, behold, the Bridegroom cometh: go ye forth to meet him.*   186

IX. The New Testament Ark opened against the deluge of divine wrath.
Heb. xi. 7.—*By faith Noah, being warned of God of things not seen as yet, moved with fear, prepared an ark to the saving of his house.*   249

CONTENTS.

X. The plant of renown.
Ezek. xxxiv. 29.—*And I will raise up for them a plant of renown.* — 265

XI. God's doves flying to his windows.
Is. lx. 8.—*Who are these that fly as a cloud, and as doves to their windows.* — 302

XII. Christ set up from everlasting.
Prov. viii. 23.—*I was set up from everlasting, from the beginning, or ever the earth was.* — 322

XIII. Abraham rejoicing to see Christ's day afar off.
John viii. 56.—*Your father, Abraham, rejoiced to see my day: and he saw it, and was glad.* — 337

XIV. Christ, as the breaker, opening all passes to glory that were impassible.
Micah ii. 13.—*The breaker is come up before them; they have broken up, and have passed through the gate, and are gone out by it; and their king shall pass before them, and the Lord (or Jehovah) on the head of them.* — 358

XV. Ethiopia stretching out her hands to God.
Ps. lxviii. 31.—*Ethiopia shall soon stretch out her hands unto God.* — 390

XVI. The kingdom of God within the soul of man.
Luke xvii. 21.—*For behold, the kingdom of God is within you.* — 403

XVII. Gospel treasure in earthen vessels.
2 Cor. iv. 7.—*But we have this treasure in earthen vessels, that the excellency of the power may be of God, and not of us.* — 436

XVIII. The character of a faithful minister of Christ.
Col. i. 7.—*Epaphras, who is for you a faithful minister of Christ.* — 457

XIX. Christ in the clouds, coming to judgment.
Matt. xvi. 37.—*Then shall he reward every man according to his works.* — 467

XX. The word of salvation.
Acts xiii. 16.—*To you is the word of salvation sent.* — 474

SERMONS.

A LAMP ORDAINED FOR GOD'S ANOINTED.

Being the substance of two Sermons. The first preached at the admission of the Rev. Mr James Fisher, late Minister of the gospel at Kinclaven, to be Minister of the Dissenting Associate Congregation in and about Glasgow, October 8, 1741; the other preached at Stirling, the third Sabbath of October, 1741.

Psalm cxxxii. 17, "I have ordained a lamp for mine Anointed."

THE FIRST SERMON ON THIS TEXT.

I SHALL not consume time in introducing myself into these words. It is thought by some interpreters, that this psalm was penned by Solomon, upon the occasion of the dedication of the temple unto God. The first part of the psalm, viz., from the beginning of it to ver. 10, consists of petitions. The second part, viz., from ver. 11 to the close, consists of a bundle of great and precious promises relating to David and his family in the type, but mainly and ultimately to Christ and his New Testament church in the antitype.

God promises, (1.) To fix his residence in his church, ver. 13, 14, "For the Lord hath chosen Zion: he hath desired it for his habitation. This is my rest for ever: here will I dwell, for I have desired it." God's gracious presence in his church, and amongst his people, makes her the perfection of beauty, and the praise of the whole earth. (2.) He promises to bless the provision he makes for them, ver. 15, "I will abundantly bless her provision: I will satisfy her poor with bread." He will supply all their needs, according to his riches in glory, by Christ Jesus. He will feed them with the hidden manna, &c. (3.) He promises to give her faithful and successful ministers, ver. 16, "I will clothe her priests with salvation." Ministers are then clothed with salvation, when, by the power of God resting upon them and their ministrations, they are the happy instruments of bringing many to Christ, in whom they find salvation from sin and wrath; and when the arm of the Lord is revealed, then the servants of Christ, and all true believers, do "shout aloud for joy." (4.) He promises, that however low the interest of Christ may be brought, though, like himself, it may appear a root in a dry place, yet, like a tree well rooted in the ground, sore lopt and hacked by man and Satan, it will sprout again, as in the first part of the verse, "There will I make David's horn to bud." The meaning is, I will bring forth a glorious and renowned King out of the rotten stump of the family of David in the fulness of time. Christ himself is the principal bud of that tree, and all believers are the buds of that bud. (5.) He promises, that the lamp of gospel light shall still shine in his true church, for manifesting the glory of Christ: *I have ordained a lamp for mine Anointed.*

Where remark, (1.) The designation given unto Christ by God his Father; he is *mine Anointed.* Though he be despised and rejected of men; though an unbelieving world see no form or comeliness in him, why he should be desired, yet I own him, and challenge him as mine Anointed, the Prophet, Priest, and King of my church. "I have found David my servant: with my holy oil have I anointed him. With whom my hand shall be established: mine arm also shall strengthen him," Psalm lxxxix. 20, 21. (2.) The great mean of God's appointment for manifesting the glory of Christ to a lost world; he has provided a *lamp* for his Anointed. The use of a lamp is to give light to people in the darkness of the night; so the word of God, particularly the gospel, is a light shining in a dark place, until the day of glory dawn, when the Lord God and the Lamb will be the light of the ransomed for endless evermore. (3.) The authority by which this lamp is lighted and carried through this dark world; it is *ordained* of God; and by his commandment it is that we preach and spread the light of the gospel, Mark xvi. 15, 20.

OBSERVE. "That the dispensation of the everlasting gospel is a lamp which God has ordained for manifesting the glory of Christ unto a lost world lying in darkness."

In discoursing this doctrine, through divine assistance, I shall pursue the following method:—

I. Speak a little of Christ as God's Anointed.
II. Of the lamp ordained for him.
III. Of the ordination of this lamp.
IV. Offer some reasons why God has ordained it.
V. Make application.

I. The *first* thing proposed is, to *speak a little of God's Anointed.* "God, thy God, hath anointed thee with the oil of gladness above thy fellows," Psalm xlv. 7. Hence his name *Messiah* in the Hebrew, and *Christ* in the Greek, both of them signify properly, *The anointed One* of God. This designation imports,

1. That he is a Redeemer and Saviour of God's choosing; for none were anointed unto any office under the law, but such as God particularly designed and elected: and such an one is Christ.

"Behold my servant whom I uphold, mine elect in whom my soul delighteth: I have put my Spirit upon him, he shall bring forth judgment to the Gentiles," Is. xlii. 1.

2. This designation intimates, that he was called, "the called and sent of God: I the Lord have called thee," Is. xlii. 6. He did not take this honour to himself, but was "called of God, as was Aaron." When faith embraces him, it hath this in its eye, it takes him up as the sent of God.

3. This designation likewise implies his investiture into his offices as the great Prophet, Priest, and King of his church. He was invested into his offices with great solemnity; the solemnity of a decree, "I will declare the decree," Psalm ii. 7, &c., the solemnity of an oath, "The Lord hath sworn, and will not repent, Thou art a Priest for ever," Psalm cx. 4; yea, with the solemnity of an open and audible proclamation from the excellent glory above, when the heavens were opened, and the Spirit descended upon him in the likeness of a dove.

4. This designation also connotes his being thoroughly fitted and furnished for his work, by an unmeasurable effusion of the Holy Ghost. "Grace was poured into his lips." There is a twofold grace given unto Christ as Mediator, namely, (1.) The grace of personal union, when the human nature, consisting of a true body and a reasonable soul, is taken into the person of the eternal Son of God, which is the great mystery of godliness. (2.) There was a created habitual fulness of grace bestowed on him for the discharging of his mediatorial work, and for the use of his mystical body: he "received gifts for men, that out of his fulness, we might receive grace for grace." Thus you see what is imported in Christ's anointing.

For the further illustration of this anointing, I shall only add,

1. Christ and all his members, all believers, are anointed with the same oil of the Holy Ghost, although in a very different measure. He is anointed with that oil above his fellows; he received not the Spirit by measure: "It pleased the Father, that in him should all fulness dwell." Our anointing is but a drop in comparison of the ocean; yet it is with the self-same Spirit; for "he that is joined to the Lord, is one Spirit." As it is the same human soul that is in the head and in the members of the natural body; so it is the very same Spirit that is in the head and in the members of the body mystical. He is "the head, from which all the body by joints and bands having nourishment ministered, and knit together, increaseth with the increase of God," Col. ii. 19.

2. The anointing of Christ was gradual, according to the different stages or advances in his work. He "increased in wisdom and stature, and in favour with God and man," Luke ii. 52. This anointing began in the first moment of the union between the divine and the human natures. He had a greater measure of the Spirit and the gifts of the Holy Ghost bestowed on him at his baptism; a still larger measure at his death, when, "through the eternal Spirit, he offered up himself without spot to God," Heb.

ix. 14: a greater measure yet was poured upon him at his resurrection, when he was "declared to be the Son of God with power, according to the Spirit of holiness, by his resurrection from the dead:" and when he ascended up on high, he poured out the Spirit like the rushing of a mighty wind, Acts ii. 1–4.

3. The anointing of Christ extends to all his offices, Prophet, Priest, and King. As a Prophet he says of himself, "The Spirit of the Lord God is upon me, because the Lord hath anointed me to preach good tidings unto the meek," Is. lxi. 1, &c. He is an anointed Priest: the human nature which was sanctified, were as it were perfumed with the oil of gladness, which made it savoury to God through the eternal Spirit. "He offered up himself a sacrifice to God for a sweet smelling savour," Eph. v. 2. This anointing extends unto him likewise as a King: "But unto the Son, he saith, Thy throne, O God, is for ever and ever; a sceptre of righteousness is the sceptre of thy kingdom:—therefore God, even thy God, hath anointed thee with the oil of gladness above thy fellows," Heb. i. 8, 9. And again, "I have anointed (as it may be translated) my King upon my holy hill of Zion," Psalm ii. 6. I shall finish this head, when I have told you,

4. That Christ himself, and the whole of his gifts, graces, and qualifications, is ordained for our use, who are sinners of Adam's race. He is "made of God unto us wisdom, and righteousness, and sanctification, and redemption." He is God's gift unto you: "For unto us a child is born, unto us a son is given:—and his name shall be called Wonderful, Counsellor, The mighty God, The everlasting Father, The Prince of peace. God so loved the world, that he gave his only begotten Son, that whosoever believeth in him might not perish, but have everlasting life. Verily, verily, I say unto you, My Father giveth you the true bread from heaven. God sent his only begotten Son into the world, that we might live through him. Herein is love;" and therefore let every lost sinner come unto him, receive and employ this anointed Saviour; take Christ's counsel unto Laodicea, for the same advice and counsel comes to every one of you: "I counsel thee to buy of me gold tried in the fire, that thou mayst be rich; and white raiment, that thou mayst be clothed, and that the shame of thy nakedness do not appear; and anoint thine eyes with eye-salve, that thou mayst see," Rev. iii. 18.

II. The *second* head proposed was, to *discourse a little of the* lamp *that God has ordained for his Anointed.*

By the *lamp* then I understand the word of God, and particularly the word of the truth of the gospel. You know the use of a lamp is to give light to men in the dark, and to let them see their way. All mankind, ever since the fall, are in darkness, yea darkness itself. They have lost their way, and are walking upon the ridge of hell and utter destruction. Now, the gospel, or word of faith which we preach, is a light or a lamp as it were, which God hath set up to discover to the children of men how they have lost their way, and let them see that new and living way of his own devising, by which they may come back again to God and glory. "We have a more sure word of prophecy: unto which we do well that we take heed, as unto a light that shineth in a dark place, until the day dawn, and the day-star arise in our hearts," 2 Peter i. 19. The dark place that the apostle is speaking of, is this dark world, and the heart of man is the darkest place in the world. God who is the Father of lights, he has given his word, the scriptures of truth, as a lantern or lamp, to direct us how we are to glorify God, and to enjoy him for ever. To this light, or lamp, we do well to take heed, as David did, the man according to God's own heart: "Thy word (says he) is a light to my feet, and a lamp unto my paths." Now, the lamp of the word of God casts a twofold light among the children of men, namely, a law light and a gospel light. A law light, to discover sin and misery; for by the law is the knowledge of sin: The law was added because of transgression. I had not known sin (says Paul), except the law had said, Thou shalt not covet. And when the law or commandment came (says he), sin revived, and I died." But then there is a gospel light, which serves to discover the remedy. And this I take to be principally understood in the text: *I have ordained a lamp for mine Anointed.* I, the eternal JEHOVAH, hath appointed the preaching and publication of the gospel as the great mean for bringing lost mankind unto the knowledge of that mighty One on whom I have laid their help. "It hath pleased God by the foolishness of preaching to save them that believe. Go ye into all the world, and preach the gospel to every creature," Mark xvi. 15.

Now, concerning this lamp of gospel light, which God has ordained, for the glory of his anointed, if time allowed, I might 1. Premise a few things about it. 2. Tell you of some great and glorious discoveries that are made by it. 3. Give a few of its properties.

First, I would offer you two or three propositions about it.

1. This lamp was first set up in the purpose of God from eternity, or in the council of peace, when the whole plan of salvation through Christ was laid. "I was set up from everlasting, from the beginning, or ever the earth was: before the mountains were settled: while as yet he had not made the earth, nor the highest part of the world. When he prepared the heavens, I was there: when he set a compass upon the face of the depth: when he appointed the foundations of the earth (says Christ), I was by him,—rejoicing in the habitable part of his earth, and my delights were with the sons of men," Prov. viii. 23–31.

2. This lamp was first lighted in this lower world, immediately after the fall in paradise; when a dark and dismal night of wo and misery was spreading itself over our first parents, then a gleam of light began to break out in the first promise, Gen. iii. 15: and afterwards unto Abraham; "In thy seed shall all the nations of the earth be blessed."

3. The lamp of the gospel shone typically and prophetically during all the Old Testament period, before the coming of Christ in the flesh. It shone, as it were, under a vail, and only among the Jews. As for the Gentiles, except a few proselytes, they were aliens and strangers to the covenant of promise; they sat in darkness, and in the regions of the shadow of death.

4. After the coming of Christ in the flesh, and his resurrection and ascension into heaven, the lamp of gospel light was brightened, and the light of it was made more general and extensive. The vail of types, ceremonies, and prophecies, was rent, and by the commandment of the everlasting God, carried unto all nations for the obedience of faith, Christ being given of God for " a light to enlighten the Gentiles, and for salvation to all the ends of the earth."

5. Ministers of the gospel are, as it were, the lamp bearers. They are commissioned by Christ to preach the gospel, to teach all nations. To them the word of reconciliation is committed; and as the heralds of the great King, they are to lift up their voice like a trumpet, and proclaim the salvation of God to the ends of the earth.

Secondly, I shall tell you of some discoveries that are made by the light of the gospel-lamp. Only in general, remember that all the discoveries it makes are wholly supernatural; the world by all its wisdom could never have found them out. Here vain man would be wise, yet he is born as void of gospel wisdom, as the wild ass's colt. Proud men may, and no doubt will, boast of their natural or acquired wisdom and penetration, as though, by the means of these, they could ransack and unfold the secrets of heaven; and yet even when they are revealed, they cannot know, cannot receive them; the things of the Spirit of God are foolishness to them; hence is that of Christ, "I thank thee, O Father, Lord of heaven and earth, because thou hast hid these things from the wise and prudent, and hast revealed them unto babes. Even so, Father, for so it seemed good in thy sight," Matth. xi. 25, 26.

I shall only mention a few things among many, that the gospel discovers, which nature's light could never have discovered, and which proud nature cannot receive when revealed.

By the gospel-lamp then, 1. We have discovered a Trinity of persons in one God, Father, Son, and Holy Ghost, three distinct persons, and yet but one God: " There are three that bear record in heaven, the Father, the Word, and the Holy Ghost: and these three are one," 1 John v. 7. This is such a hard doctrine to human reason, that Arians, Socinians, and Deists, they will reject the whole scriptures of truth before they entertain it; or if they acknowledge the scriptures, they fall awork to prevent scripture-light, in order to bring Christ down from his supreme Deity in among the rank of created beings; for between the Creator and a creature there is no middle being: and if Christ be a creature, I would ask what way any creature can make itself, seeing " without him was not any thing made that was made?" John i. 3. So then, I say, the gospel-lamp discovers the mystery of the Trinity; and how each person acts his part in the glorious work of our redemption.

2. By the light of this lamp we can look back to eternity past, and see what God was a-doing before the foundations of the world were laid; how a council of peace was held with reference to the recovery and salvation of fallen men; how an overture being made, that the Son of God should undertake the work of our redemption, that the different claims of mercy and justice might be fully satisfied in the salvation of fallen man; and how the Son of God heartily agreed, saying, "Lo, I come: I delight to do thy will, O my God. He rejoiced in the habitable parts of the earth, and his delights were with the sons of men." Without the gospel men could never have known this; but the Lion of the tribe of Judah, he opened the book, and disclosed the grand secret, and orders it to be published unto the ends of the earth.

3. The gospel-lamp discovers the glorious mystery of the incarnation of the Son of God in the fulness of time. In consequence of this glorious transaction, angels they admire and adore a God in our nature. "When he bringeth in the first-begotten into the world, he saith, And let all the angels of God worship him," Heb. i. 6.

4. By the gospel-lamp we have another mystery opened, even the substitution of the Son of God in the room of the guilty sinner, by which means our iniquities come to be laid upon him. "The just suffered for the unjust." He is the ram caught in the thickets, and sacrificed in the room of the sinner. The sword of justice awakes against the man that is God's fellow, who thinks it no robbery to be equal with God. "He was wounded for our transgressions, bruised for our iniquities, the chastisement of our peace was upon him, and by his stripes we are healed."

5. By the gospel-lamp only we know of a law-fulfilling righteousness brought into this world, where "there is none righteous, no, not one. Seventy weeks are determined—to finish the transgression and to make an end of sins,—and to bring in everlasting righteousness," Dan. ix. 24. "What the law could not do, in that it was weak through the flesh, God sending his own Son, in the likeness of sinful flesh, and for sin condemned sin in the flesh; that the righteousness of the law might be fulfilled in us," Rom. viii. 3, 4. "Christ is the end of the law for righteousness to every one that believeth," Rom. x. 4. "For he hath made him to be sin for us, who knew no sin; that we might be made the righteousness of God in him," 2 Cor. v. 21. O what a high discovery is this for us, especially considering, that this righteousness of the surety Christ is brought near to every one in the everlasting gospel, that they may put it on, and improve it for their justification before God! "Hearken unto me, ye stout-hearted, that are far from righteousness. I bring near my righteousness: it shall not be far off, and my salvation shall not tarry," Is. xlvi. 12, 13.

6. By the gospel-lamp, we shall see great and glorious mysteries in the death and blood of Christ. As Samson found a honey-comb in the lion that he had slain, so may we find the great and soul nourishing mysteries of the grace, love, mercy, and wisdom of God in the death and blood of the Lamb of God. Here we may see the justice of God satisfied for the sin of man, by a sacrifice of infinite value, the anger of God turned away, and God declaring himself to be a God of peace through the blood of his eternal Son. Here we see the head of the old serpent bruised, that leviathan slain, and given to be meat to those who inhabit the wilderness of this world. O meat indeed, and drink indeed! Here we may see a new and living way opened and consecrated, that we may enter into the holiest with full assurance of acceptance, &c.

7. The gospel-lamp discovers a mystery in the resurrection of Christ from the dead. There is more of God, and of his infinite power and wisdom, in the resurrection of Christ, than if all Adam's posterity were raised out of their graves, in the twinkling of an eye. Christ is said, by his resurrection, to be " declared to be the Son of God with power," Rom. i. 4. And that power of the Father, whereby he was raised, had an " exceeding greatness " in it, and was a " mighty power," Eph. i. 19. The load of sin and wrath that lay upon the grave of our Surety, would have sunk all the angels in heaven, and men upon earth, to the lowest hell; yet Christ, by his divine power, rises from under this load, and so bears away our iniquities, and leaves them buried in his grave behind him, and death itself swallowed up in victory, &c.

8. The gospel-lamp lets us see a mystery in his ascension into heaven, the most glorious solemnity that ever the inhabitants of the spiritual world saw, which made them all cry out, and shout, " God is gone up with a shout, the Lord with the sound of a trumpet," &c. This world saw little solemnity in Christ's returning to heaven after he had finished the great work of man's redemption. But, O! angels and glorified saints, who were then arrived at heaven, they saw his chariots of state attending him. " The chariots of God are twenty thousand, even thousands of angels: the Lord is among them as in Sinai, in the holy place. Thou hast ascended on high, thou hast led captivity captive: thou hast received gifts for men," Psalm lxviii. 17, 18.

9. The gospel-lamp lets us see a mystery in his appearance for us in heaven; how he appears there as our Representative and High Priest within the vail, with much incense offering up the prayers of all saints, &c.; how he states himself as our Advocate with the Father, to plead our cause, and to agent our business for us, and to repel all complaints given in against us by the accuser of the brethren. " He is able to save to the uttermost, seeing he ever liveth to make intercession for us," Heb. vii. 25. " And if any man sin, we have an Advocate with the Father, Jesus Christ the righteous." He appears for us before the bar, not as a suppliant, but as one having authority: " Father (says the Advocate), I will that they also whom thou hast given me, be with me where

I am; that they may behold my glory which thou hast given me," John xvii. 24.

10. By the gospel-lamp there is a discovery made of a new and better covenant established in Christ as a second Adam, than that which was made with the first Adam, even a covenant of grace and promise; which being confirmed by the death of Christ, is now set out in its last and best edition, viz., as a testamentary deed. Everything in and about this covenant is wonderful and mysterious. The Trinity transacted in it with Christ as a second Adam from eternity: "I have made a covenant with my chosen; I have sworn unto David my servant," Psalm lxxxix. 3. The gradual manifestation of this covenant unto us, and the variety of dispensations that it has undergone under the Old and New Testament, and yet still the same covenant. The absolute freedom of this covenant unto us, no conditions or qualifications required on our part to interest us in it, the proper condition of it being already fulfilled in the obedience and death of Christ, it comes out to us absolutely free, "I will be their God. I will sprinkle them with clean water, and they shall be clean. I will take away the heart of stone," &c. The way how a sinner is brought within the bonds of this covenant is only owing to the gospel-lamp or light, namely, by faith, not of the operation of man, but of the operation of God in a day of power. He just makes the sinner willing to be saved without money and without price, upon the footing of free grace reigning in and through an imputed righteousness, &c.

11. By the gospel-lamp we come to know the mystery of regeneration, or the new birth; which so started and confounded Nicodemus, a teacher in Israel, that he babbles and speaks stark nonsense, when Christ proposes it to him. "Can a man (says he) be born when he is old? can he enter the second time into his mother's womb, and be born?" John iii. 4. The case is just the same with a great deal of men in our day, who set up for wits. They are ready to brand the doctrine of conversion and regeneration with the character of enthusiasm: but let such remember, that the God of truth has said it, with a *verily, verily, except* they know and feel it on their own souls, they "cannot enter into the kingdom of heaven."

12. The gospel-lamp discovers the way of justification for an ungodly sinner, by an imputed righteousness. This discovery is wholly supernatural, which the apostle Paul valued so highly, and gloried so much in, that when compared with the knowledge hereof, he reckoned everything else as so much dross and dung, &c.

13. The mystery of sanctification is discovered by the gospel-lamp; how Christ is made of God unto us sanctification; and how, by the great and precious promises, we are made partakers of the divine nature; and by beholding the glory of the Lord in the glass of the gospel, we are changed into the same image; how the heart is purified by faith in Christ, our old man crucified in him, and the body of sin destroyed, &c.

In a word, to shut up this head, by the light of the gospel-lamp, we may see in through the vail of death and mortality, and behold life and immortality brought to light: "For (says the apostle), we look not at the things which are seen, but at the things which are not seen: for the things which are seen are temporal; but the things which are not seen, are eternal." By the gospel-lamp, and the eye of an enlightened understanding, we may see the Jordan of death divided, and a passage opened for the Israel of God into the promised land of glory, where we shall be for ever with the Lord. By this lamp we may look to the end of time, and see Christ coming to judge the world. He will "descend from heaven with a shout, with the voice of the archangel, and with the trump of God. Behold he cometh with clouds; and every eye shall see him, and they also which pierced him; and all kindreds of the earth shall wail because of him. Verily, verily, I say unto you, The hour is coming, in the which all that are in their graves shall hear the voice of the Son of man, and shall come forth," &c. By this gospel-lamp we may see all that sleep in their graves raised up again, some to the resurrection of eternal life, and others to the resurrection of everlasting damnation; some are seen like condemned prisoners, brought out of jail unto the place of execution, and whenever they see the Judge upon his white throne, crying to the rocks and mountains to fall on them, to hide them from his angry face; whilst others are beheld lifting up their head, because the day of their redemption is come, and crying to one another, "Let us be glad and rejoice; for the marriage of the Lamb is come," Rev. xix. 7. By this lamp we may see the righteous like so many suns shining in the kingdom of their Father, with robes made white in the blood of the Lamb, crying, "Salvation to our God that sits upon the throne, and to the Lamb for ever and ever."

Thus I have told you of some great and glorious discoveries that are made by the light of the lamp of the everlasting gospel. I come now,

Thirdly, To give you a few of its properties and qualities.

1. Then, It is a *divine* lamp, a lamp of God's making and preparing; hence the gospel is called "the gospel of the blessed God." It comes down from the Father of lights. All scripture is given by inspiration of God; hence we are to receive it with a divine faith, &c.

2. It is a *dazzling* lamp. There are such things in the gospel, or discoveries made by it, as dazzle the eyes of men. Some are totally struck blind with it: "For judgment I am (says Christ) come into this world: that they which see not, might see; and that they which see (or imagine they see) might be made blind," John ix. 39. As for real believers, when gospel-light shines into their hearts, and discovers the method of salvation through Christ, they fall a wondering at everything they behold, crying, "O the depth of love, grace, and wisdom! Without controversy, great is the mystery of godliness, God manifest in the flesh!" But

why do I speak of man? The clear-sighted angels, they cover their faces with their wings at the brightness of that glory that shines in the person and mediation of Christ; "which things the angels desire to look into;" and one cries unto another, and says, "Holy, holy, holy is the Lord of hosts, the whole earth is full of his glory," Is. vi. 3. I say, it is a dazzling lamp; and, like light, it is of a piercing and penetrating nature. Both the law and gospel light of the word are penetrating; "For the word of God is quick and powerful, and sharper than any two-edged sword, piercing even to the dividing asunder of soul and spirit, and of the joints and marrow, and is a discerner of the thoughts and intents of the heart," Heb. iv. 12. It shines in through the head, down into the heart, and, like the candle of the Lord, pierces into the belly or bottom of the soul.

3. The light of this lamp is of an assimilating nature. "But we all with open face (says the apostle), beholding as in a glass the glory of the Lord, are changed into the same image, from glory to glory, even as by the Spirit of the Lord." It purifies the soul, and makes it holy: "Now ye are clean through the word which I have spoken unto you," John xv. 3.

4. It is a *glorious* lamp; hence called "the glorious gospel of the blessed God." The author of it is the God of glory; the object of it is Christ the brightness of the Father's glory; and the end of it is the glory of all God's attributes in the everlasting salvation of the lost sinner, &c.

5. It is a most *pleasant* lamp; truly the light of it is sweet; when it shines into the heart, it fills the soul with the light of knowledge, the light of joy and comfort; the consolations of it are strong, and fill the soul with "joy unspeakable, and full of glory," &c.

6. It is the most *profitable* lamp that ever the world saw, because it shews unto us the path of life, and leads the soul into an immense treasure of soul-riches, that makes the man up for an endless eternity, even the unsearchable riches of Christ, &c.

7. It is an *infallible* lamp. We have a great deal of new-lights got up in our day, which like *ignis fatuus*, or wild fire, leads men into the bogs and pits of Deism, Arminianism, Quakerism, and other errors in which men are drowned in perdition. But here is a sure light, which we may follow with full assurance of faith. It is the "sure word of prophecy, to which ye do well that ye take heed. The testimony of the Lord is sure, making wise the simple. And as many as walk according to" the light of this lamp, "peace shall be upon them, as upon the Israel of God," &c.

8. It is an *ancient* lamp, as you heard. It has been shining in the orbs of the church militant since it was first lighted in paradise. And this lamp, instead of waxing dim, as other lamps do, it has shone brighter and brighter in every gradual dispensation of it. Hence,

9. It is a *lasting* and *durable* lamp. It will shine to the world's end, let men and devils do their utmost to have it smothered and

extinguished. All that men have done hitherto on design to put out the lamp, through the hand of God over-ruling their wrath and corruption, has only served to snuff the lamp, as you snuff the candle to make it give better light. "As we have heard, so have we seen this in the city of the living God."

10. It is a *common* lamp to all men. You know the sun in the firmament is a common lamp to this lower world; everybody, rich and poor, has the privilege of the light of the sun, and pays nought for it. Just so the lamp of the gospel, the light of the Sun of Righteousness, Jesus Christ himself, who is "the light of the world, and the day-spring from on high," is a common good to all mankind, that will but take the benefit of his light; they shall pay nothing for it. That the gospel is a common good to mankind, is very evident from the words of the angel at his birth. "Behold (says he), I bring you good tidings of great joy, which shall be to all people." It is also very plain from the commission Christ gives unto his ministers to "go into all the world, and preach the gospel unto every creature" under heaven.

11. It is a *moveable* and *portable* lamp, like the tabernacle of old, and the pillar of fire and of cloud, which moved from one place to another. God has not, in all the word, bound himself to fix his gospel-lamp so in any nation or congregation, as never to take it away from them, and give it unto others. No, Christ plainly tells the Jews, that the gospel of his kingdom was to be taken from them, and to be given to another people bringing forth the fruits thereof. The same, we see, Christ tells the church of Ephesus, that he would take away his candlestick from them, except they did repent, and reform, and do their first works, &c.

Thus I have given you some account of the lamp which God has ordained for his Anointed.

III. The *third* general head laid down in the method was, to *speak of the* ordination *of this Lamp.*

Remember, Sirs, it is God's authority in any ordinance of his, that gives it value, efficacy, and validity; just as the stamp of the king upon the coin makes it to pass current. Nothing will pass current in the church of Christ, with his loyal subjects, that does not bear the stamp of the authority of the King of Zion. What is the reason that the subjects of Christ, that desire to be faithful to him at this day, run away from the generality of pretended ministers? Why, it is because they do not carry the King's commission; they run unsent; they do not hear the voice of Christ in them; they do not see them coming in by the door of the fold; and therefore they will not follow them. Why do we Protestants reject the doctrines of the Romish church, their mass, breviaries, and idolatries? Why it is because they do not bear the stamp of God's authority. And for the same reason we reject Episcopal and Independent government, and the superstition and ceremonies of the English church; it is because they are only the inventions of men, and have no authority from God; and therefore we cannot expect his blessing to accompany them. And, on the other hand, why do we sprinkle water in baptism in the name of the Father, Son, and Holy Ghost? Why do we eat and drink at the table of the Lord a little simple bread and wine, which to carnal reason are inconsistent things? Why do we preach the gospel, which to the wise of this world is foolishness? Why do we pray, and praise, and go about other duties? It is because they are commanded and ordained of God. The gospel is a lamp of God's ordaining; and therefore it is "the power of God unto salvation, mighty through God to the pulling down of strongholds," &c.

The weakest and most insignificant things, when appointed of God, are the only means that will produce the desired effects. What made the sound of rams horns to overthrow the walls of Jericho? What made the waters of Jordan more effectual for curing Naaman's leprosy, or spittle and dust mixed together effectual for opening the eyes of the blind man? Just this. These were the means of God's appointment; and therefore his own power went along with them. So here the gospel, and a gospel-ministry, however contemptible and insignificant in the eyes of the world they may appear; yet, being a lamp of God's ordination, therefore his power is to be looked for by it for the salvation of souls. "It hath pleased God by the foolishness of preaching to save them that believe." By these means it is that sinners are gathered unto the blessed Shiloh.

To let you see how much God is concerned about this lamp of the everlasting gospel, I shall tell you of several things that God has ordained about it.

1. He has ordained the places and parts of the world where it shall be set up and shine. "He gave his statutes unto Jacob, and his testimonies unto Israel; he dealt not so with any nation." If you ask me, Why doth God send the gospel to Scotland, and not to many rich and populous nations who sit in darkness? Why, the reason of it is, "Even so, O Father, for so it hath pleased thee," &c. Hence Paul, viewing the severity of God in taking the gospel from the Jews, and sending it to the Gentiles, he cries out [Gr. ωβαθος, &c.], "O the depth of the riches both of the wisdom and knowledge of God! how unsearchable are his judgments, and his ways past finding out!" Rom. xi. 33.

2. As he ordained the places where the lamp shall be set up, so he ordained how long it should shine, before it be lifted to another part of the earth. He ordained how long it should shine among the Jews, viz., until Christ came. He ordained how long it should shine in the churches of Asia, before he came and removed his candlestick. He has ordained when, and how long, the gospel shall continue in Scotland, and there is but too just ground to fear, that God is about to take away his kingdom from us also, and to give it unto the American world, who are receiving it with joy and gladness. He has ordained how long the gospel and a faithful ministry shall stay in any parish or congregation also.

3. He has ordained what souls or persons shall be converted, edified, or built up, by the gospel: when he sends it unto any nation or congregation of Zion (that is, the place where the gospel-lamp is set up), "it shall be said this man and that man was born there," &c. The election of grace shall obtain, when others are hardened. To the one it is the favour of life unto life, and to others the favour of death unto death. He will order a beam of this lamp to shine into one heart, in hearing the gospel, when it passes by twenty, thirty, or an hundred, or a thousand, who lie as fair as to the external means as others.

4. He ordains by what instrument or minister the gospel-lamp shall be brought unto a people or particular person. Paul is ordained for the Gentiles, Peter for the Jews, and every one of the apostles and other ministers, led by the ruling hand of the sovereign Lord, to labour in this, or that, or the other spot of his vineyard; for the stars are all in his right hand; and he ordains them to shine in this or the other orb of his church; and, whenever he pleases, he removes them from one place to another of his church militant, where he has any work for them; or else, when their work is ended upon earth, he removes them to the church triumphant, where they that have "turned many to righteousness, shall shine like the brightness of the firmament, and like the stars for ever and ever."

5. He ordains what fruit and success a minister with his lamp shall have, what number of souls shall be edified, and who shall be hardened and blinded by his light. It is not always the greatest and brightest ministers that are most successful; for Christ and his apostles, when lifting up the lamp amongst the Jews, were put to complain, "We have laboured in vain," &c. "Who hath believed our report? and to whom is the arm of the Lord revealed? We have piped unto you, and ye have not danced," &c. So much for the *third* thing proposed, namely, concerning God's ordination of this lamp.

IV. The *fourth* thing in the method was, to *give the reasons why God has ordained this lamp for his Anointed*. And,

1. In the *first* place, it is ordained for the honour of God's Anointed; for it is the will of God, "That all men should honour the Son, even as they honour the Father. He that honoureth not the Son, honoureth not the Father which hath sent him," John v. 23. He will have him highly exalted both on earth and in heaven.

2. God has ordained this lamp for his Anointed, that his name may be remembered through all nations, and to all generations. God has ordained that, "his name shall endure for ever, that his name shall last like the sun." When Paul got his commission, the Lord tells him, that he was to "carry his name among the Gentiles and kings," Acts ix. 15. It is by the gospel-lamp, that the church causes his name to be remembered to all generations.

3. He has ordained the gospel-lamp for his Anointed, that the **gathering** of the people may be unto the blessed Shiloh, according

to the ancient prediction of Jacob upon his death-bed, "The sceptre shall not depart from Judah, nor a lawgiver from between his feet, until Shiloh come, and unto him shall the gathering of the people be," Gen. xlix. 10. The perfume of the name of God's Anointed has such a drawing and gathering virtue with it, that whenever sinners get the smell of it about their hearts, they " fly as a cloud, and as doves unto their windows."—Other reasons might be added; but I do not insist further upon the doctrinal part. I proceed now to,

V. The *fifth* thing in the method, which was the *Application*.
Use *first* shall be in two or three *inferences* at present.
Inf. 1. See how dear Christ is in his Father's eye, how warmly and affectionately he speaks of him here, and everywhere in scripture. He, as it were, glories in him, and in his relation to him before all the world. Oh! says he, he is *mine Anointed;* he is *my servant;* he is *mine elect;* he is *my fellow*, and *mine equal*. Why doth God speak so affectionately of him unto a world of lost sinners, but that they may fall in love with him, and say as he says, by an applying faith, as the spouse doth, " My beloved is mine, and I am his? This is my beloved, and this is my friend, O daughters of Jerusalem?" or, as Thomas, " My Lord, and my God?"

Inf. 2. See from what has been said, the amazing love of God towards lost sinners of the tribe and family of Adam, in giving and sending the Son of his love to be our Mediator and Redeemer, and in his anointing and fitting him for the service of our redemption with an unmeasurable measure of the Holy Ghost: and then in ordaining the lamp of the gospel, for displaying his glory and excellency through all the world, and unto every creature. Does not this argue strange love that God has unto lost man? " God so loved the world, that he gave his only begotten Son," &c. O Sirs! admire the height and breadth, and length and depth, of this love.

Inf. 3. See hence the melancholy and deplorable condition of these who want the lamp of the gospel, or who have provoked God to lift his lamp, and to leave them in darkness. Solomon tells us, that " where no vision is," *i.e.*, where the gospel-lamp is not, " the people perish." Their destruction is unavoidable, seeing they want the only means of salvation, there being "no name given under heaven among men whereby to be saved, but by the name of Jesus." Thus the apostle argues. It is only they that " call upon the name of the Lord, that shall be saved. But how shall they call on him in whom they have not believed? and how shall they believe in him of whom they have not heard? and how shall they hear without a preacher? and how shall they preach except they be sent?" Rom. x. 14. 15. By all which the apostle seems plainly to make it appear, that the salvation of sinners is impossible, without the lamp of gospel-light to shew them the way to it. This should stir our bowels on the behalf of the blinded nations who inhabit the dark places of the earth, which are full of the habitations of horrid cruelty, where poor souls are just slaughtered and butchered by the roaring lion for want of the gospel, &c.

Inf. 4. See hence what reason we have to contend earnestly for the faith once delivered unto the saints, and to be valiant for the truth. Why, if the gospel-lamp be taken away out of the land, we are unchurched, and left among the dark places of the earth, and our house is left unto us desolate. What would this earth be, if that great luminary, the sun, were taken out of the heavens? We would be stumbling and breaking our necks upon everything in our way; it would be a most doleful and melancholy habitation. But far better want the sun out of the firmament, than the gospel-lamp out of the land. Strong efforts have been used by hell and earth in all ages, to put out the lamp of God's Anointed, that his soul-captivating glory might not be seen by the sons of men. This is, and has been, the design of all the errors that were ever broached since the Christian church and the gospel-lamp was set up in the world. The Arian heresy is designed to darken the glory of his supreme Deity. The Socinian error agrees with the Arians, and also overclouds, or rather obliterates, his satisfaction. The Arminian error darkens the freedom and efficacy of his grace, by exalting the freedom of man's will in his depraved state. Papists and Legalists, of whatever denomination, they impugn and disparage his everlasting righteousness, by substituting something of their own legal workings, doings, or personal qualifications, in the room of it. And now-a-days, the idol of self-love is substitute in the room of the glory of God, &c. All these, and the like errors, are just like so many damps or mists cast out of hell, through the malice and subtlety of the old serpent, in order to darken and obscure the lamp of gospel-light, that men may not perceive the glory, fulness, and suitableness of Christ, and so believe in him, to the salvation of their souls. However, through the over-ruling hand of God, these mists and clouds have only served in the issue to make the gospel-lamp, and the glory of God's Anointed, to shine with the greater lustre; like the clouds in the air, which you observe have just now overcast the sun in the firmament, they obscure his light for a while, and yet serve only, in the event, as a foil to set off the glory of the sun, when he breaks through these clouds, and darts his beams down upon this earth among the children of men, &c.

Inf. 5. See from this doctrine, what we are to think of the conduct of the judicatories of the Established Church at this day, and for many years by-past, who seem to be upon a conspiracy to put out the gospel-lamp, which God lighted at our reformation from Popery. Perhaps some hearing me may think this charge both heavy and calumnious, and say, Now you are turned very uncharitable. But if it be not so, I would have you to solve these few plain questions. What means the bleating of the sheep? What means that swarm of lax, legal, and erroneous ministers that are to be found almost through all the corners of Scotland? What means that violent way in which men are obtruded upon Christian congregations by presentations or sham calls, without the call, and against the inclinations, of the Christian people? What means the abuse of church discipline, whereby the erroneous are screened from censure, truth falls in the streets, and error patronized? What means their suspending, outcasting, and deposing seven men from the holy ministry, for no other cause but there bearing up the gospel-lamp, and witnessing for God's anointed Prophet, Priest, and King, in opposition unto the prevailing defections and corruptions of the day? What can we think of these things, especially when they have slain the witnesses, and condemned their testimony, but conclude that they have rejected the stone which God has ordained to be the head stone of the corner? And because they have rejected him (I do not speak of every individual), therefore God has rejected them, and is saying of the judicatories and ministry of Scotland, "Because ye have rejected knowledge, I will also reject you, that ye shall be no priests to me; seeing ye have forgotten the law of your God, I will also forget your children," Hos. iv. 6.

Inf. 6. See what good reason we of the Associate Presbytery have for the work we are about at this day, in licensing and ordaining ministers through several corners of the land, in a way of secession from the present judicatories, however irregular it may appear in the eyes of some men. Why, the gospel-lamp must by no manner of means be lost or extinguished. By the attempts that have been made to put it out, or make it useless, we are driven to preserve it in a way of secession from the judicatories, and we can see no other way of keeping up the gospel-lamp in the land, than by fulfilling that command given by Paul unto Timothy, "The things that thou hast heard of me among many witnesses, the same commit thou to faithful men, who shall be able to teach others also," 2 Tim. ii. 2.

And in regard the lamp-bearer at Kinclaven is thurst out of his station there, through ecclesiastical and civil violence, therefore we are this day to change his station, and set him up at Glasgow, upon a call given him by the dissenting congregation in and about this place.

After psalms, proceeded to this purpose.

"You in this correspondent congregation having a considerable time ago petitioned the Associate Presbytery for the moderation of a call, they accordingly appointed myself. Which appointment I accordingly obeyed. And you may remember by a great majority of votes, the call came out for the Reverend Mr James Fisher, minister of the gospel at Kinclaven, and was most harmoniously subscribed for him even by the few who had voted otherwise.

"His call being attested, was presented unto the presbytery, and sustained as orderly proceeded in. Together with the call, reasons of transportation were offered by you of the correspondence of Glasgow. The parish of Kinclaven were summoned, compeared, and heard, and the matter fully reasoned on both sides. After some considerable delay, the presbytery, which met at Abbotshall, taking to consideration the whole affair, together with the conduct of holy providence, which plainly cleared their way, they transported him to be minister of this correspondent congregation, and appointed this day for his admission. His edict being served, was returned, and no objection offered against the designed transportation and admission." And therefore,

We now proceed to fix the relation between you and him.

Here Mr James Fisher was called up, and proceeded.

"Reverend Sir, although both I, and all the reverend brethren and members of the Associate Presbytery are fully convinced of your orthodoxy and soundness in the faith, and of your firm attachment unto the covenanted reformation of Scotland, both as to doctrine, discipline, worship, and government: yet I suppose it will be expedient and necessary, for the satisfaction of the people here, that you give answer unto a few questions, which the Reverend Presbytery appointed me to put to you."

Here the usual questions were read one by one.

After which proceeded thus.

"Now, I suppose you who are the people, are fully satisfied with the answers given by the Reverend Mr Fisher unto these questions. You have, it is true, already signed and consented, that he should be your minister, by the call which you have given him. However, I suppose it will be encouraging to him, and satisfying to the presbytery, that you discover your adherence to your call, by the χειροτονια, or *lifting up of the hand.*

"So many of you as can conveniently come near, may come forward, and take him by the hand; others who cannot, may do it upon the dismissing of the congregation."

Now I shall conclude this work by offering a few words of advice to minister and people.

First, To the minister. Reverend Sir, God, in his adorable providence, who has the stars in his right hand, has seen fit to move you from another place, and to fix you here, in order to bear the lamp for his Anointed to this people, upon a very public and conspicuous tower. And, in order to the right management of the gospel-lamp, there are only a few advices that I would offer; and what advice I offer unto you, I take to myself, and I make no doubt but my Reverend brethren will also listen unto them.

1. Let us study to be well satisfied in our own minds, that we carry the call and commission of God's Anointed, to bear the gospel-lamp before him, so as to be in case to say to our people, as Moses was ordered to say to Israel, "I AM hath sent me unto you," Exod. iii. 14, or with the apostles, "We are ambassadors for Christ, as though God did beseech you by us: we pray you in Christ's stead, be ye reconciled to God," 2 Cor. v. 20. It inspires a minister's heart with courage, and harnesses his spirit against the slavish fear of man, and all that man can do, it makes him bold as a lion in delivering his commission, when he is confident that he stands in Christ's stead, and speaks in his name.

2. It is necessary, in bearing the gospel-lamp, that we remember we are in the very sight and presence of our great and glorious Master, Jesus Christ, "the King of kings, and Lord of lords," whose eyes are as a flame of fire, and observes the motives, ends, and principles, from which we were acted, and will shortly call us to give up an account of our stewardship, &c.

3. It is necessary we remember for what end we carry the lamp of the everlasting gospel to our people, namely, to shew unto them the way of salvation, by presenting both their lost condition by nature in the first Adam, and how they may be delivered by a second Adam. In order to the salvation of poor souls, both law-light, and gospel-light, is necessary to be scattered among our hearers, &c.

4. In holding up the gospel-lamp, let us be frequently trimming our lamps before God's holy oracle, much in studying the scriptures of truth; for these are they that testify of Christ, God's anointed dear. We need to follow that advice given by the apostle Peter to all in common, ministers and Christians: "We have a more sure word of prophecy; unto which we do well that we take heed, as unto a light that shineth in a dark place, until the day (of grace) dawn (in the souls of our hearers), and the day-star arise in their hearts," 2 Pet. i. 19. "The word of God is like a lamp unto our feet, and a light unto our path," Psal. cxix. 105.

5. In order to the successful management of the gospel-lamp, we need frequently, by faith and fervent prayer, to fetch new oil for our lamps from God's Anointed, who had the oil of gladness poured upon his head above his fellows. However we may preach, and bring forth to our people, the pure truths of the gospel; yet without the oil of the Spirit come along therewith, the lamp of the gospel shines dim, and will not make its entrance into their hearts, &c.

6. In bearing the gospel-lamp, and preaching the everlasting gospel, let us study to have our hearts fired with love to God's Anointed, zeal for his glory, and the good of souls. It is observable, when Christ is re-installing Peter into his ministerial office, John xxi. 15, he says unto him three several times, "Simon, son of Jonas, lovest thou me?" And when Peter three several times had appealed to him as the heart-searching God, "Lord, thou that knowest all things, knowest that I love thee," he just requires this as a proof of his love to him, that he would feed his lambs and sheep. The love of Christ, and the love of souls, is like a cord by which a minister is drawn to be faithful, active, and diligent in his work; "for the love of Christ constraineth us," 2 Cor. v. 14.

7. It is fit that we turn the light of the gospel-lamp in the very face of these errors and corruptions, whether in principle or practice, that begin to broach in the land or place we live in. Many pestilential and soul-ruining errors have come abroad from our seminaries of learning, and particularly that which is next adjacent.

Now, I know no better way to prevent their infection, than by bringing them as quickly as possible to the light of the word; for as the birds and beasts of prey creep into their holes when the light of the sun spreads itself along the face of the earth, so all error and corruption, in principle and practice, evanishes before the light of the word.

But I come *next* to speak a word unto the people, who are under the inspection of the minister of Christ now planted and settled among them. Time will not allow me to go on in the improvement of the doctrine I was insisting upon; and therefore I shall conclude at present, with two or three advices, how you are to behave with respect to your minister, who bears the lamp of God's Anointed before you.

1. Remember that there is a covenant between you and him. As he is engaged to fulfil all the parts of the ministerial office towards you, so ye are engaged, on your part, to fulfil all the duties that the word of God, and laws of the King of Zion, require of you toward him. Not only covenants between God and man, but covenants between man and man are secret things, and God resents the violation of them, as you see Ezek. xvii. You are not now at liberty to throw up and desert his ministry, or to turn your back upon him, particularly by running back unto these of the corrupt body, from whom both you and he have made a secession, &c.

2. In order to your fulfilling your part of this day's transaction between you and him, I advise you to attend carefully and diligently upon his ministry, particularly upon the preaching of the gospel in public, the dispensation of the seals of the covenant, diets of catechising, and when he teaches from house to house. When you come to hear the word, remember that the word you hear will take hold of you, and issue either in the life or death of your immortal souls; and what will all the world profit a man if he lose his soul? O then attend diligently, incline your ears, hear, that your souls may live, and the covenant may be made and established with you, &c.

3. Mingle faith with your hearing of the word preached by your minister; take his message, and receive his Master, God's Anointed. We are told that "the word preached did not profit some, not being mixed with faith in them that heard it," Heb. iv. 2. Let not your minister have occasion to take up that complaint against you, "Who hath believed my report? and to whom is the arm of the Lord revealed?" He comes to offer "a Saviour and a great One," to deliver you from sin and wrath. O, be aware of rejecting the offered remedy, for in so doing you despise God's herald or messenger, and him that sent him. When Christ is sending his apostles abroad to preach the gospel, he says, "He that despiseth you, despiseth me; and he that despiseth me, despiseth him that sent me," &c.

4. I advise you to submit to your minister and elders, in the administration of the key of discipline, they, being a radical court of Christ, constitute in the name of Christ for that very end. This is expressly commanded of God: "Remember them which have

the rule over you, who have spoken unto you the word of God: whose faith follow, considering the end of their conversation.—Obey them that have the rule over you, and submit yourselves: for they watch for your souls, as they that must give account: that they may do it with joy, and not with grief: for that is unprofitable for you," Heb. xiii. 7–17. Obedience in the Lord is the indispensible duty of people towards these that have the keys of the kingdom of heaven committed to them; "for what they bind on earth shall be bound in heaven; and what they loose on earth shall be loosed in heaven," Matth. xviii. 18.

5. I advise you to pray much for your minister that is come to bear up the gospel-lamp among you: "Brethren (says the apostle to the Hebrews), pray for us."

Query, What should we pray for? *Answ.* Pray that the soul of your minister may be refreshed daily with the oil of God's Anointed, that so the lamp may be brightened, and he may come forth to you daily in the demonstration of the Spirit and with power; and that, like a scribe instructed in the mysteries of the kingdom, he may bring forth things new and old for the edifying of your souls. Pray that a door of utterance may be given him, that he may declare the mysteries of the gospel, that he may feed in the strength of the Lord, and in the majesty of the name of his God. O pray that he may not only get furniture, but be blessed with success in his work; for although Paul were to plant, and Apollos water, yet their ministry would be ineffectual, unless God gave the increase. Pray that God may give him the art of winning souls, and that his Master may direct him so to cast the gospel net, as that a multitude of souls may be gained. Pray that he may be made "as a sharp threshing instrument having teeth, to thresh the mountains, and beat them small, and to make the hills as chaff," Is. xli. 15.

6. Another advice I give you is, to encourage God's lamp-bearer among you. *Query,* How should we encourage him? *Answ.* (1.), By receiving his Master and his message, as has been said. (2.), By strengthening his heart and hand in his preaching and witnessing work, particularly at this time, when there are many adversaries, and many arrows of reproach and calumny may be cast at him. (3.), By "maintaining the unity of the Spirit in the bond of peace" among yourselves. Jars, divisions, and animosities among a people, are a heart-break to a minister of the gospel of peace, whereas it is his great comfort to find them of one heart and way in the Lord. (4.), By providing a suitable maintenance for your minister, and a place of worship where you and he may meet and attend ordinances without being exposed to hazard from the injuries of the weather. But I know you have these things at heart, and therefore do not insist upon them.

And now, my brethren, suffer me again to renew the word of exhortation. O remember what a valuable blessing the gospel is unto a land or people. Why, it is a lamp to discover the way how you may come to God's Anointed, and so get your souls for a prey. They that know the worth of their souls, and have any concern about their salvation, cannot but prize the gospel in its purity, above all their other concerns in a world; for it is "better than gold, yea, than much fine gold; sweeter also than honey from the honey-comb," Psal. xix. 10.

Beside what was said in the doctrinal part, I might offer many other considerations, to raise your esteem of the glorious gospel.

1. The gospel-lamp lets men see where they are, and how far they have departed from God, how near they are unto utter ruin, like the prodigal in a far country, without God, without Christ, without hope, without help, without light, without life, no eye to pity, no hand to help, &c., in a state of distance, darkness, enmity, every moment liable to wrath and condemnation, yea, *condemned already*, &c.

2. The gospel-lamp discovers "a Saviour and a great One," Is. xix. 20, who is "able to save to the uttermost. I have laid help upon one that is mighty: I have exalted one chosen out of the people, even David my servant: with my holy oil have I anointed him," Psal. lxxxix. 19, 20.

3. In the light of this lamp the sinner may see a ransom found, that he may not go down to the pit, even the blood of Jesus, that sacrifice of a sweet smelling savour, whereby the wrath of an angry God is turned away, &c.

4. By this lamp we may see an angry God reconciled and declaring himself a *God of peace*, and that *fury is not in him*. Here we may see the white flag, and the olive branch of peace held up, and God saying, "I create the fruit of the lips; peace, peace to them that are afar off, and to them that are nigh," Is. lvii. 19.

5. By the light of this lamp, sinners that are beggared and bankrupted by the fall of Adam, are led to a mine of unsearchable riches, which they may lay hand upon, and make their own without theft or vicious intromission. "Unto me (says Paul), who am less than the least of all saints, is this grace given, that I should preach among the Gentiles the unsearchable riches of Christ," Eph. iii. 8. The cry of the gospel is, "I counsel thee to buy of me gold tried in the fire, that thou mayst be rich," &c.

6. By this gospel-lamp, we may see a house of mercy reared and opened, and all manner of provision in plenty, made ready for the poor, the halt, the withered, and lame. "I have said, Mercy shall be built up for ever," Psal. lxxxix. 2. "Wisdom hath builded her house, she hath hewn out her seven pillars. She hath killed her fatlings, she hath mingled her wine; she hath also furnished her table. She hath sent forth her maidens, she crieth upon the highest places of the city. Whoso is simple, let him turn in hither: as for him that wanteth understanding, she saith to him, Come, eat of my bread, and drink of the wine which I have mingled," Prov. ix. 1–5. "In this mountain, shall the Lord of hosts make unto all people a feast of fat things, a feast of wines on the lees, of fat things full of marrow, of wines on the lees well refined," Is. xxv. 6.

7. By this gospel-lamp we may see not only meat, but medicine prepared for the poor diseased soul, that is ready to perish of its wounds and leprosy. Here you will see *balm in Gilead*, and a *physician there*. Here you will see the mystical *brazen serpent*, by a look of which the venom of the old serpent is stayed, and the hurt of it prevented. Here is to be seen the "tree of life, which bears twelve manner of fruits every month, and whose leaves are for the healing of the nations."

8. By this lamp is to be seen the Rock that follows Israel through the wilderness to Canaan; you may see the clefts of the Rock that were made by the rod of God's anger; you may see living water gushing out of the smitten Rock, and a cry made, "Whosoever will, let him come and drink of the water of life freely." You may see the Rock having a shadow, to refresh the weary traveller in his way to glory; you may see God's doves lodging " in the clefts of the Rock, and in the secret places of the stairs," &c.

9. By this lamp you may see and find the chariot of the wood of Lebanon, with its golden bottom, purple covering, paved with love for the daughters of Jerusalem. By which I understand the covenant of grace and promise, which is everlasting, well ordered, and sure. The gospel lets you see, that you have free access into this chariot of salvation, in which you may ride in safety, through all dangers, unto glory: "Thus saith the Lord—unto them that take hold of my covenant, even unto them will I give in mine house, and within my walls, a place and a name better than of sons and of daughters: I will give them an everlasting name that shall not be cut off.—Even them will I bring to my holy mountain, and make them joyful in my house of prayer," Is. lvi. 5-7.

10. By this lamp we may see a ladder reaching between heaven and earth, by which you may have access to that heaven of glory which we fell from, when we broke the first covenant in Adam; but here is a new and living way into the holiest of all.

11. Here you may see and find a city of refuge from the avenger of blood, &c.

12. Here you will find the true ark in which you shall be saved from the deluge.

13. Here you may see chambers where you may hide yourselves in a day of wrath, until the indignation be overpast.

14. Here by this lamp we discover a confirmed testament, securing us to the inheritance of eternal life, which was lost in the first Adam, and much more than ever we lost. Here we may find our God saying, "I am the Lord thy God;" which is more than ever eye saw, or ear heard, &c.

Thus you see what great, glorious, and beneficial discoveries are made by the lamp of the everlasting gospel. And do not all this make it evident, that they are a privileged people, who have the gospel-lamp lighted, and set up among them? It was not without ground, that the psalmist cried out, in the view of these things, "Blessed are the people that know the joyful sound: they shall walk, O Lord, in the light of thy countenance," Psal. lxxxix. 15.

I conclude by reading a portion of scripture to you containing a bundle of necessary duties, both toward yourselves, your minister, and elders, and one another, 1 Thess. v. 12–28. " And we beseech you, brethren, to know them which labour among you, and are over you in the Lord, and admonish you; and to esteem them very highly in love for their works' sake. And be at peace among yourselves. Now we exhort you, brethren, warn them that are unruly, comfort the feeble-minded, support the weak, be patient toward all men. See that none render evil for evil unto any man: but ever follow that which is good, both among yourselves and to all men. Rejoice evermore. Pray without ceasing. In everything give thanks: for this is the will of God in Christ Jesus concerning you. Quench not the Spirit. Despise not prophesyings. Prove all things: hold fast that which is good. Abstain from all appearance of evil. And the very God of peace sanctify you wholly: and I pray God your whole spirit and soul and body be preserved blameless unto the coming of our Lord Jesus Christ.—Brethren, pray for us.—The grace of our Lord Jesus Christ be with you."—Amen.

Psalm cxxxii. 17.—" I have ordained a lamp for mine Anointed."

THE SECOND SERMON ON THIS TEXT.

I PROCEED now to make some further improvement of the doctrine.

A *third* use of the doctrine may be by way of *Trial* and *Examination*. Sirs, we in this land, and you particularly in this place, have had the gospel-lamp for a long time shining among you: but the great question is, Has ever the light of it led you to God's Anointed, and discovered his glory to your souls.

I offer the few following marks for trial in this matter:—

1. Has ever the light of the gospel-lamp discovered the plagues of your heart unto you, so as to fill you with an abhorrence of yourselves, saying, with David, " who can understand his errors? Psal. xix. 12, or with Jeremiah, " The heart is deceitful above all things, and desperately wicked, who can know it?" Jer. xvii. 9. Whenever Job's eyes saw the Lord, he cries, " I abhor myself, and repent in dust and in ashes."

2. The light of the gospel-lamp lets a man see that all the ways and methods of salvation that he hath proposed unto himself, while in a natural state, are nothing but a mere delusion. The man was imagining, that he might be saved by the general mercy of God, by the works of the law, by a profession of religion, or some good thing or other: but whenever the light of this lamp enters into his heart, he sees that it is in vain to look to these hills and mountains; and that to stay where he is or has been, he but walks in the light of his fire, and sparks of his own kindling, and must lie down in

sorrow at the end; and therefore casts away all these cob-web coverings, and accounts them but loss for Christ.

3. I ask you, What think you of God's Anointed? for the gospel-lamp is ordained to discover the glory of God's Anointed. What think you of his person, righteousness, fulness, glory, and salvation, love and grace? I am sure the glory of his person and mediation has put your souls to an everlasting stand, that you know not what to say or think, but are swallowed up in a silent wonder at him, crying with the church, "Who is this that cometh up from Edom, with dyed garments from Bozrah? this that is glorious in his apparel, travelling in the greatness of his strength. Wherefore art thou red in thine apparel, and thy garments like him that treadeth in the wine-fat?" Is. lxiii. 1, 2.

4. If ever the glory of God's Anointed was discovered unto you in the light of this lamp, your hearts have been fired with love to him, and zeal for his glory; so that you know not how to express your esteem of him, and desire after him: O! "Whom have I in heaven but thee? and there is none upon earth that I desire besides thee." Many waters cannot quench love, neither can all floods drown it. Indeed the devil, and the world, and a corrupt heart, are frequently casting water upon this fire; but yet where it is genuine, it gets ay up again; the flame rises, and breaks through all opposition, and sends the sparks of it heavenward.

5. Has ever the lamp of the gospel dropt some of the oil of God's Anointed upon your souls? The gospel is as it were a golden pipe, through which the oil of the Holy Ghost is conveyed into the vessels of the sanctuary from God's Anointed: Gal. iii. 2. "We receive the Spirit by the hearing of faith, not by the works of the law." Now, I ask you, Have you got an unction from the Holy One? *Query*, How shall I know that? *Answ.* In the following particulars. This oil has had the same effect, in some measure, that it had upon Christ. As,

1*st*, Christ's anointing, it made him of *quick understanding*, or of a *ready scent*, as it is in the margin, Is. xi. 3. The same effects, in some measure, has it had upon you; it has given you a quick understanding and uptaking of the things of God, the secrets of his covenant: "Unto you it is given to know the mysteries of the kingdom of heaven," says Christ unto his disciples; "but unto others it is not given. We have an unction from the Holy One, whereby we know all things," 1 John ii. 20. "He that is spiritual, judgeth all things:" he has another discerning than other men have of the things of God and eternity. "We have not received the spirit of this world, but the Spirit which is of God; that we may know the things that are freely given to us of God," 1 Cor. ii. 12.

2*dly*, Christ's anointing made his face to shine. "Oil maketh the face to shine." Hence the spouse cries out, "His countenance is as Lebanon, excellent as the cedars." So if you have shared of this anointing, you will, in your way, and walk, and talk, adorn the doctrine of God your Saviour: you will be changed into the same image with God's Anointed, by beholding of his glory; your light will shine before men, so that others, seeing your good works, will glorify God, your heavenly Father.

3*dly*, Christ's anointing made him active and agile in the work of our redemption; so that he never rested till he could say, "It is finished." So if you be partakers of his anointing, you will be active and diligent in the great work of your salvation, that you may finish your course with joy. O! says David, "I will run the way of thy commandments, when thou hast enlarged my heart," viz., by anointing the wheels of his soul with the oil of the Spirit's influences.

4*thly*, Christ's anointing made his heart glad; therefore called "the oil of gladness." This was it that rejoiced his heart under all the discouragement and opposition he met with in his work. So, if you be anointed with the same oil, your hearts have been made glad therewith. The Holy Ghost is called frequently *the Comforter*, because he gladdens the hearts of Christ's followers, under all the troubles and trials in their way in this weary wilderness. Hence Christ says to his disciples, speaking of the Spirit, "Your hearts shall rejoice, and your joy no man taketh from you." Now, try yourselves by this; know you anything of the consolation of the Spirit? O! says David, "thou hast put more gladness in my heart, than they, when their corn, wine, and oil, did abound."

Use *fourth*, Has God ordained a lamp for his Anointed? then my first advice or exhortation is, to answer the end of the gospel-lamp, by coming to God's anointed Saviour and Redeemer by a true faith. This is the end and design of God in the whole revelation that he has made of Christ in the word. "These things are written, that ye might believe in the name of the Son of God, and that believing ye might have life through him," John xx. 31. This is the end and design of a gospel ministry, and of all the ordinances of the gospel, that ye might behold the glory of God's Anointed, and by coming to him, ye might be built up in the holy faith.

Motives to engage you to come unto God's Anointed.

1. The light of the lamp of the gospel points you directly to him; for it is "Christ whom we preach; and we preach not ourselves, but Christ Jesus the Lord, and ourselves your servants for Jesus' sake." Every gospel-sermon leads to Christ, and lands you in him, if the design of it be answered. O! says Paul to the Corinthians, "I desire to know nothing among you, but Christ, and him crucified."

2. Christ was anointed for your sakes. "He received gifts for men; yea, even for the rebellious, that the Lord God might dwell among us." His oil is for your use. He himself, and all his offices to which he was anointed, are intended for the salvation of lost sinners of Adam's family. Why was he anointed to be a Prophet, but for your illumination in the knowledge of God and his will? Why anointed to be a Priest, but for your reconciliation with God, and justification before him? Why anointed King in Zion, but to deliver us from our captivity to sin and Satan, and to sanctify us,

and write his law in our hearts? Hence he is "made of God unto us wisdom, righteousness, sanctification, and redemption," 1 Cor. i. 30. Now, seeing it is so, why then should we stand off from him by unbelief, and, by following lying vanities, forsake our own mercy?

3. O come unto God's Anointed through the light of the gospel-lamp; for there is an immeasurable measure of the oil of the Holy Ghost with God's Anointed, and all to be communicated unto them that come unto him. "It hath pleased the Father, that in him should all fulness dwell; that out of his fulness we might receive grace for grace." There is no fear of want here. His fulness is not exhausted or diminished by all that is given out. No, he is as full as ever, and as ready to communicate. We read of the widow's pot of oil, 2 Kings iv. 4, 5, &c., that did fill all the vessels that were brought to it, and never stopt till no more vessels were brought. This is the case here; Christ never ceases to communicate of his grace and Spirit, as long as empty vessels are brought to him. The only thing that stops the communication of his grace is, that we do not come to him by faith to receive of his fulness.

4. God's Anointed calls, invites, and beseeches you to come unto him for his grace and fulness. "Ho, every one that thirsteth, come; and he that hath no money, let him come, and buy wine and milk without money and without price," Is. lv. 1–3.

5. God's Anointed has promised you welcome; "Come to me who will, I will in no wise cast out. He that cometh to me shall never hunger; and he that believeth on me shall never thirst. He satisfieth the longing soul, and filleth the hungry soul with good things."

6. If you do not come to God's Anointed, you lose the benefit of the gospel-lamp, and incur the displeasure of that God who ordained the lamp for his Anointed. "This is the condemnation, that light is come into the world, and men choose darkness rather than light, because their deeds are evil. How shall we escape, if we neglect the great salvation" of God's Anointed.

7. Unless you come to God's Anointed, and buy oil, your vessels and lamps will be found empty at the coming of Christ. My friends, before it be long, the midnight cry shall be heard, "Behold, the Bridegroom cometh, go ye forth to meet him." You know what became of the foolish virgins that wanted oil at the coming of the Bridegroom; they go to seek oil when it was out of time; "the door is shut" upon them, and they are shut up in eternal woe and darkness. O take care that it do not fare so with you against the coming of Christ at death, or judgment. And, therefore, while the market of grace lasts, take Christ's counsel, "I counsel thee to buy of me gold tried in the fire, that thou mayst be rich; and white raiment, that thou mayst be clothed, and that the shame of thy nakedness do not appear; and anoint thine eyes with eye-salve, that thou mayst see," Rev. iii. 18.

8. When a people privileged with the lamp of the everlasting gospel, do not answer the design of it by coming to God's Anointed,

God in that case is provoked to remove the lamp, and give it to others that will improve the light of it to a better use: Matth. xxi. 43. "Therefore say I unto you, The kingdom of God shall be taken from you, and given to a nation bringing forth the fruits thereof," says Christ there unto the Jews. By the kingdom of God there, we are to understand the same thing with the gospel-lamp, by which we enter into the kingdom of grace here, and of glory hereafter. Now, says Christ, this shall be taken from you, and then the door of the kingdom of God will be shut up against the Jewish nation, and given unto the Gentiles, which accordingly was done. The Jews were cut off for their unbelief, and the gospel church and lamp set up among the nations of the earth. Now, if God spared not the natural branches, we need to take heed lest he treat us after the same manner, who are wild olives of the Gentiles by nature, Rom. xi. 21. You have a word to the same purpose, John xii. 35, 36. "Then Jesus said unto them, Yet a little while is the light with you: walk while ye have the light, lest darkness come upon you: for he that walketh in darkness, knoweth not whither he goeth. While ye have light, believe in the light, that ye may be the children of light." By all which you see that we are in hazard of losing the light of the gospel-lamp, and of being left in darkness, if we do not come unto God's Anointed.

And here I will tell you of several kinds of darkness that will follow upon the removal of the gospel-lamp.

1st, The darkness of gross ignorance; which is so far from being the mother of devotion, as the Papists teach, that it is the mother of destruction; "My people are destroyed for lack of knowledge," Hos. iv. 6. If we but look through the world, or through this island, or the land wherein we live, and take a view of these corners of it where the gospel-lamp does not shine, or where another thing is substituted in the room of it, we shall find nothing but gross ignorance of supernatural truths, and the people no better than a company of baptized heathens.

2dly, The darkness not only of unbelief, but of infidelity, follows upon the removal of the gospel-lamp. Unbelief may be, and, alas! too frequently is, where the gospel-lamp shines: "Who hath believed our report?" But when the gospel-lamp is taken away because of unbelief, then the people turn infidels. An unbeliever may come to be a believer, because the object of faith is still revealed and presented unto him by the gospel-lamp; but an infidel cannot become a believer, because the object of faith is removed; the things that belong to his peace are hid from his eyes and ears. "How shall he believe in him of whom he has not heard? (as the apostle argues); and how shall they hear without a preacher?" Rom. x. 14. When both lamp and lamp-bearers of God's sending are taken away, how then shall they believe? Men in that case can no more believe, than the eye of the body can see without the light of the sun in the firmament.

3dly, The darkness of idolatry and superstition in worship, follows upon the removal of the gospel-lamp, as we see in these lands or nations where the gospel-lamp once was, but are now covered with Popish and Mahometan delusions and abominations.

4thly, As the gospel-lamp removes, so gradually the darkness of error prevails. Deistical errors, rejecting supernatural mysteries in the word; Arian and Socinian errors, derogating from the glory of God's Anointed, either in his person, offices, or satisfaction; Arminian errors, striking at the freedom and sovereignty of the grace of God both in election and effectual calling, and the perseverance of the saints; legal errors, overturning the doctrine of justification by the righteousness of Christ alone, and foisting in something else in its room, that men may have something to glory in: these and the like errors prevailing in a land where the gospel has been preached in purity, argues a setting, not a rising sun, because the shadows are growing long.

5thly, The darkness of a dead, lifeless, blasted, profane, or ignorant ministry, prevails upon the withdrawing of the lamp of God's Anointed. Indeed, God may leave something in the land called the gospel, and a set of men who call themselves ministers of the gospel. But what sort of a lamp is it that is left, when the true gospel-lamp is taken away? It is the devil's lamp; it is not the narrow way, but a broad-way lamp, to set folk straightway to the bottomless pit. And what sort of ministers or lamp-bearers are left? Why, they are blind guides leading the blind, and both fall into the ditch together.

6thly, The darkness of a departed God and glory follows upon the removal of the gospel-lamp. The name of that nation or congregation then becomes *Ichabod*, i.e., "The glory is departed." And then innumerable woes take place: "Woe also unto them, when I depart from them." Utter destruction and desolation takes place: "Behold your house is left unto you desolate," Matth. xxiii. 38. "And now go to; I will tell you what I will do to my vineyard: I will take away the hedge thereof, and it shall be eaten up; and break down the wall thereof, and it shall be trodden down. And I will lay it waste: it shall not be pruned, nor digged, but there shall come up briers and thorns: I will also command the clouds, that they rain no rain upon it. For the vineyard of the Lord of hosts is the house of Israel, and the men of Judah his pleasant plant: and he looked for judgment, but behold oppression; for righteousness, but behold a cry," Is. v. 5, 6, 7. Thus you see what darkness follows upon the removal of the gospel-lamp for rejecting and refusing to come unto God's Anointed. O then let me beseech you, as though God did beseech you by me, "be ye reconciled unto God," by receiving him, resting upon him alone for salvation from sin and wrath, as he is offered to you in the gospel.

O that I knew how to prevail with you to accept of God's Anointed! Come and let us reason together upon this important matter. Sirs, when you reject God's Anointed, you reject God himself, that God in whom every moment you live, move, and have your being; for God is in Christ his anointed dear; but when you receive him, you receive God to be your God and portion in time and through eternity; his Father becomes your Father, and his God your God.

Pray tell me, What ails you at God's Anointed, that you will not come unto him? Do you reject him because he is an insufficient Saviour? Why, the gospel-lamp discovers the contrary, and that the very reverse is true: "I have laid help upon one that is mighty," says God. Do you reject him on a pretence that he is unwilling to receive you? The gospel-lamp confutes this thought; for you may see him complaining of sinners, that they will not come unto him; swearing by his life, that he is willing, and has no pleasure in the death of the wicked; appealing to the heavens and earth, to bear testimony for him against sinners for their folly and obstinacy, "Be astonished, O ye heavens, at this, and be horribly afraid, be ye very desolate, saith the Lord. For my people have committed two evils: they have forsaken me the fountain of living waters, and hewed them out cisterns, broken cisterns, that can hold no water," Jer. ii. 12, 13. And again, he says, "Hear, O heavens, and give ear, O earth: for the Lord hath spoken, I have nourished and brought up children, and they have rebelled against me," Is. i. 2. Do you stand off from God's Anointed, because you have no claim or right to him? Let not this be pretended; for you have as good a right to him, and as good a warrant to employ him for your salvation, as any of the saints, either in heaven or earth, ever had, before they actually believed in him. Ye have a right to him by virtue of the human nature that he wears, whereby he is related to all the human kind. Ye have a right and claim to him by virtue of his office; he is the Saviour of all men that are willing to be saved. As every man in Israel had access to the brazen serpent, which was a common good to all the camp; so has every sinner a right to look unto Christ, and be saved. Ye have a right to him by the revelation, the offer, the gift, and grant, of the gospel: "Then Jesus said unto them, Verily, verily, I say unto you, Moses gave you not that bread from heaven; but my Father giveth you the true bread from heaven. For the bread of God is he which cometh down from heaven, and giveth life unto the world," John vi. 32, 33. "For unto us a child is born, unto us a son is given," Is. ix. 6. And again, "Ho, every one that thirsteth, come ye to the waters," &c. Is. lv. 1. "And the Spirit and the bride say, Come. And let him that heareth say, Come. And let him that is athirst, Come: And whosoever will, let him take the water of life freely," Rev. xxii. 17. Do ye stand off from God's Anointed for want of power and ability to come to him? Why, God's Anointed in the gospel is reaching forth his saving arm to help every impotent soul, saying, "I give power to the faint, I increase strength to them that have no might." Do you decline to come to God's Anointed, because you are uncertain if God ordained him for you, or you for him, in his eternal purpose or decree? Why, Sirs, I have often told you, and now I tell you again, that in the **matter of believing, you have nothing at all to do with the decrees** of God: "Secret things they belong unto the Lord; but things revealed to us, and to our children." Now, it is among things revealed, that ye should believe in God's Anointed, "This is the work of God, that ye believe in him whom God has sent;" and that moment you believe with the heart, thou mayst read thy name in the Lamb's book of life; and never can or shall any man find out the decree of God as to himself in another way or method. O then come and close immediately with God's anointed Saviour, and the way of salvation through him, whereby you shall at once both give glory to God in the highest, and secure your own salvation for ever. But if you continue to reject God's Anointed, and the lamp he has ordained for him, your light shall be put out in obscurity, and you shall lie down in everlasting sorrow with hypocrites and unbelievers. "Behold, all ye that kindle a fire, that compass yourselves about with sparks; walk in the light of your fire, and in the sparks that ye have kindled. This shall ye have of mine hand, ye shall lie down in sorrow," Is. l. ult.

Query, What advice do you give us, in order to our right improvement of the gospel-lamp as to win a saving interest of God's Anointed? Unto this I answer in these particulars.

1*st*, Be much in viewing yourselves in the light of the holy law of God, which requires no less than an absolute and sinless perfection in every man and woman sprung of Adam, in order to fix a title to life and glory, and which dooms every one to hell and destruction from the presence of the Lord, who cannot produce a personal and perfect obedience thereunto. The language of the law is, "He that doth these things shall live by them:" but "Cursed is every one that continueth not in all things which are written in the book of the law to do them."

2*dly*, Consider seriously whether you be capable to produce what the law requires of you. There are three things demanded of you by God from the bar of the law, to which, if you cannot give a satisfying answer, sentence must pass against you. (1). God will demand of you, Where is that innocent nature you received from me at your creation: for I made you upright? (2). Where is that sinless obedience of life which the law requires? Have you done all that the law requires? None of Adam's race can answer these two; for "all have sinned, and come short of the glory of God." And therefore, (3). A third demand follows: What satisfaction do you give unto my justice? To this the sinner, ignorant of the gospel, is ready to answer, "O will God be pleased with thousands of rams, or with ten thousands of rivers of oil? will he accept of our first-born for our transgression, or the fruit of our body for the sin of our souls?" But will God be pleased with this? No, he no more values all these large proffers, than the cutting off of a dog's neck, or the offering of swine's blood upon his altar: Such "sacrifice and offering I desire not," says God. Well, seeing the sinner cannot give a satisfactory answer to these questions, seeing his nature is vitiated and corrupted, every thought of his heart is evil, seeing he has broken the law, in thought, word, and deed, times without number, what must follow on this, according to the tenor of law and justice, but that the sword of justice awake against the criminal, and that he be hewn in pieces before the Lord, like Agag? Now, I say, my advice unto you is, O take a serious view of this state of matters between God and you. While you are upon a law-bottom, "indignation and wrath, tribulation and anguish, unto every soul of man that doth evil."

3*dly,* Having thus pondered how matters stand between God and you in the light of the law, I advise you next to take the lamp of the gospel, and see what relief is provided by God in his Anointed for you in this dismal situation. See if there be not a suitable and sufficient answer to these posing and silencing questions in God's Anointed as a second Adam, a new covenant-head. When the question is put, Where is that pure and holy nature that we had from God at our first creation? view God's Anointed by the lamp of the gospel, and you will hear him answering, Here it is in my person as their public head and representative, and I present their nature to God as holy and pure as ever it was at its creation. Again, when the question is put, where is that perfect, personal, and sinless obedience they owe to my holy law, which was the condition of life, according to the tenor of my covenant I made with them? why the gospel-lamp will let you see God's Anointed as your Surety, answering, I have fulfilled all righteousness that the law required in their room; I was made sin for them, that they might be made the righteousness of God in me; I am the end of the law for righteousness unto every one that believeth in me; I have magnified the law, and made it honourable, and the righteousness of the law is fulfilled by imputation, in all that come unto me by faith. Again, when the question is put, What satisfaction will the guilty sinner give unto my justice? God's Anointed answers, I was wounded for their transgressions, I was bruised for their iniquities, the chastisement of their peace was upon me; I was made a curse for them, the just suffered for the unjust, to bring them unto God; I bore their sins in my own body on the tree, and therefore justice cannot have recourse upon them. Thus you see how the gospel-lamp discovers a way of relief for the poor sinner standing condemned at the bar of the holy law, how this answers all these questions, to which, all finite understandings, whether among men or angels, were utterly unanswerable.

4*thly,* Having thus viewed how things stand in the light of the law, and in the light of the gospel-lamp, consider deliberately where you will take up your standing before God's tribunal, and for an awful eternity; whether will you take your hazard to answer God to these questions in your own person, by presenting to him the works of righteousness that you have done, for the satisfaction of his justice? or will you quit and renounce all these as filthy rags, and betake yourselves to God's Anointed, as "the Lord your righteousness," saying, "In him alone will I be justified, and in him will I glory? I am sure, if you have any uptaking of God in his infinite tremendous holiness and justice; any uptaking of the holiness, equity, perfection, and extent of the law; any uptaking of your own lost, wretched, and miserable condition; any value for your precious souls, that are condemned already by the law; any view of God's Anointed in the light of the gospel-lamp, you will not be long in determining the matter, what foundation you will venture upon. O, will the soul say, with Paul, "Yea, doubtless, I count all things but loss, for the excellency of the knowledge of Christ Jesus my Lord; for whom I am ready to suffer the loss of all things, and do count them but dung that I may win Christ, and be found in him, not having mine own righteousness, which is of the law, but that which is through the faith of Christ, the righteousness which is of God by faith." This is just the language of faith submitting unto the righteousness of God's anointed Saviour and Surety. The soul just sinks itself, and all its own works and righteousness, into nothing, and states itself before God in Christ, and says, "Behold, O God, my shield, and look upon the face of thine Anointed," Psal. lxxxiv. 9. It is in this way that the soul closes with Christ, and is interested savingly in him; and it is in this way that the infinite power of God is exerted and put forth, when he fulfils the work of faith with power.

5thly, In regard the gospel-lamp discovers Christ not only as an atoning Priest, but also as a teaching Prophet, and a ruling and a governing King, therefore at the same time that we submit unto his righteousness for justification, we must take care to submit to the whole will of God revealed by him, setting to the seal to all the promises of God, as yea, and amen in him, yea to the whole of the gospel revelation; submitting also at the same time to the law as in the hand of a Mediator, and saying, "The law is holy, and the commandment holy, and just and good;" thou hast delivered me out of the hand of mine enemies, therefore rule thou over me. Thus the man gets the law written in his heart, the kingdom of God is set up within him, and every thought brought into captivity unto the obedience of Christ, God's Anointed. So much for advice how to improve the gospel-lamp, in order to your sharing salvation by God's Anointed.

I conclude with a word of advice to believers, who through the light of the gospel-lamp, and the power of God accompanying it, have been determined to come by a true faith unto God's Anointed, for all the ends of his mediation.

1. O bless God for his Anointed, and for the lamp he has ordained for his Anointed; and that he ever made the lamp discover his glory to your souls, and to drop down the oil of his Spirit upon you. All is of grace: "By grace are ye saved, through faith; and that not of yourselves: it is the gift of God: not of works, lest any man should boast." And therefore, O celebrate the praises of that God, whose name is *gracious*, saying, "Not unto us, not unto us, but unto thy name be the glory."

2. Has the gospel-lamp led you unto God's Anointed? Then abide in him, and with him; says Christ to his disciples, "Abide in

me, and I in you," John xv. 4. Abide in him by a life of faith, and let his Spirit abide in you, without grieving his Spirit, or quenching his operations and motions. It is not enough, that ye have once believed, but you must live in him, and upon him, by faith. "The life, I live (says holy Paul), is by faith upon the Son of God, who loved me, and gave himself for me," Gal. ii. 20. It is in this way of a continual coming unto Christ, that we are "built up a spiritual house, an holy priesthood, to offer up spiritual sacrifices unto God, acceptable through Jesus Christ." It is in this way that the life of grace is maintained, until it issue in a life of glory. Faith is always receiving out of his fulness, grace for grace; and thus we are anointed as with fresh oil, and wax stronger and stronger, till we come to appear before God in the heavenly Zion, where we shall receive the end of our faith and hope, the salvation of our souls.

3. Put honour on God's Anointed, for this is the will of him that sent him, "that all men should honour the Son, as they honour the Father." We are commanded to honour our earthly parents, because they are the instruments of our natural being in this world; but how much more should the seed of Christ put honour on him as their everlasting Father, who is the Author of their spiritual being in the world of grace here, and the world of glory hereafter? "For we are his workmanship, created in Christ Jesus unto good works."

Query, How shall we put honour on God's Anointed?

Answ. In these few particulars.

1st, By employing and trusting him in all his saving offices to which he is anointed, and casting all our cares upon him. God the Father, who anointed him, has made him both his own and our great Trustee. He has entrusted him with all the concerns of his glory, and he requires us to trust him with all the concerns of our salvation; and therefore "trust in him as the Lord JEHOVAH, for with him is everlasting strength."

2dly, Put honour upon him by putting away all his rivals, everything that would usurp his room. There are many false Christs in the heart of man. Sometimes the law as a covenant usurps his room, by self-righteousness. Sometimes carnal reason usurps his room, by bringing the mysteries of the gospel, revealed by him, unto its bar. Sometimes the world usurps his room, by stealing away the heart from him. Sometimes the vile idol of self usurps his room, by preferring our own ends unto his glory. Sometimes we are ready to put created grace in his room, by living more upon created grace, than the grace that is in Jesus Christ, and are not content with a life hid with Christ in God, unless we find our life in our hand. These, and many other false Christs, usurp the room of the Christ of God. Now, I say, if we would honour God's Anointed, let him have the principal room in our hearts, and lay all these under his feet, that he may tread them down, and he alone be exalted.

3dly, Put honour upon him, by imitating him both as to the temper of his mind, and tenor of his walk. "Let the same mind be in you, which was also in Christ Jesus. Be ye holy as he who hath called you is holy." He hath left us an example, that we should follow his steps; and therefore "let us run our race, looking unto Jesus," &c.

4thly, Be frequently crying for new drops of the oil of the Spirit from God's Anointed; for the seven Spirits which are sent unto all the saints on earth, flow from the Lamb, as it were slain, in the midst of the throne. It is his promise, "If I go away, I will send him." O cry that he may come like the rushing of a mighty wind upon your own souls, and upon the dry bones in our valley of vision, and upon all the churches.

5thly, When you get any drops of the oil from God's Anointed, study to be dropping of your oil into the empty vessels that you will find everywhere round about you. And this you are to do, by spreading the light of the gospel-lamp as far as you can, and by speaking to the praises of God's Anointed. When the heart indites a good matter concerning God's Anointed, your tongue will be like the pen of a ready writer, to proclaim his praises. The woman of Samaria, whenever she came to know God's Anointed, and to get the oil of his Spirit, she runs to her neighbours, saying, "Come, see a man that has told me all things that ever I did: is not this the Christ?" John iv. 29. *i.e.* the anointed One of God. And thus others are drawn to Christ, through the smell of Christ's ointment upon her.

6thly, Study by all means to preserve the lamp of the everlasting gospel in safety and purity among us, against all that are attempting to rob and spoil us of such an unspeakable mercy; for if the lamp of the gospel go, God's Anointed will go with it; he will not manifest himself by any lamp of man's devising or forming, but only by the light of the lamp that God has ordained for him, viz., the gospel in the purity and simplicity of it. And therefore be aware of following any pretended lamp-bearers, who preach another gospel, and bring out a strange light, not lighted at the Sun of Righteousness, but by some wild-fire of man's imagination. "Try the spirits whether they be of God." Try them by "the law and testimony; for if they speak not according to these things, it is because there is no light in them."

7thly, 'If you would preserve the gospel-lamp and put honour upon God's Anointed, study to be his witnesses, and to bear testimony for him, and for his covenanted doctrine, worship, and government in the land, as founded upon the revelation of the word. Many injuries are done to God's Anointed, both by church and state in our day. O take up his cause and quarrel, and confess him before men, as ever you expect that he should confess you before his Father, and the holy angels, at the day of his appearing.

Lastly, If trouble and persecution come on the land for Christ's sake, and for the gospel, be ready to seal your testimony for him with your blood, like those who "loved not their lives unto the death, and took joyfully the spoiling of their goods" for his sake.

Study to say with Paul, "I am ready not to be bound only, but to die for the name, truth, and testimony of the Lord Jesus."

THE ANGEL'S SEAL SET UPON GOD'S FAITHFUL SERVANTS, WHEN HURTFUL WINDS ARE BLOWING IN THE CHURCH MILITANT.

Being the substance of three Sermons preached in the new Church of Bristo, at Edinburgh, at, and after the celebration of the Sacrament of the Lord's Supper there, October 10, 11, and 17, 1742.

Rev. vii. 1, 2, 3, "And after these things I saw four angels standing on the four corners of the earth, holding the four winds of the earth, that the wind should not blow on the earth, nor on the sea, nor on any tree. And I saw another angel ascending from the east, having the seal of the living God; and he cried with a loud voice to the four angels, to whom it was given to hurt the earth and the sea, saying, Hurt not the earth, neither the sea, nor the trees, till we have sealed the servants of our God in their foreheads."

IT is agreed amongst the generality of interpreters whom I have consulted, that in those three verses I have now read, there is a prediction of some awful spiritual judgments to fall upon the visible church, together with the care that the Lord takes of his own faithful remnant, by separating them from others, that they might not be hurt thereby.

These spiritual plagues are expressed under the notion of *four winds*, ver. 1, which drive away unstable professors, who are not rooted by faith in Christ, just as the wind drives loose and light things before it. Those *winds* are said to be *four*, with allusion to the four quarters of heaven, east, west, north, and south; implying, that the devil sets upon the church of Christ from all airths at once, so that she is like a city besieged by enemies from all quarters. The instruments in the hand of God, for plaguing the visible church with those spiritual judgments, are *four*. Some say they were four evil angels, like those that were sent to be a lying spirit in the mouth of Ahab's prophets, to persuade him to go up to Ramoth Gilead, to his destruction. Others think that they were good angels, because they restrained the winds until the saints were sealed. But we need not insist to determine this difference, seeing we find God, the great Lord and Sovereign, sometimes making use of good, and sometimes of bad angels, as the executioners of his wrath.

But now in the 2d and 3d verses follows the consolation of the saints of God, his little remnant, who are keeping their garments clean, and keeping the word of his patience. The eyes of the Lord are running to and fro through the whole earth to shew himself strong in their behalf, and his care about them is thus expressed. *And I saw another Angel ascending from the east, having the seal of the living God: and he cried with a loud voice to the four angels to whom it was given to hurt the earth and the sea, saying, Hurt not the earth, neither the sea, nor the trees, till we have sealed the servants of our God in their foreheads.* Where, for explication, we may notice these following particulars.

1. The great agent that interposes for the safety of the saints, when the four noxious winds are blowing away the generality of professors: and that is *another Angel:* not any created angel, like the four mentioned in the 1st verse, but the glorious Angel of the covenant, Jesus Christ, who was sent before Israel to open the way into the land of Canaan, concerning whom God says to Israel, Exod. xxiii. 21. "Beware of him, and obey his voice: for my name is in him." This I say is the Angel here spoken of, for he is the head that looks to the welfare of his members, "And he is given to be head over all things unto the church, which is his body;" and all the saints are in his hand, and none shall pluck them out of his or his Father's hand.

2. We may notice from what airth this Angel doth arise and appear; he *ascends from the east,* with allusion to the natural sun in the firmament, who arises from that airth, and spreads his light and influences toward the west. The coming of Christ is compared to lightning coming from the east. He is "the light of the world; the true light, which lighteth every man that cometh into the world." Some observe that the entry of the temple, by which the prince was to ascend, was upon the east; and so it may signify, that when Christ comes, for the help and relief of his church, he appears in a princely and sovereign way; and when he doth so he acts like himself, "the Prince of the kings of the earth."

3. This Angel is the Lord-keeper of the privy seal of heaven, for *he had the seal of the living God.* This shews that he is his Father's great Trustee, who has all power in heaven and in earth committed unto him. On the same account the keys of the house of David, or the government is laid upon his shoulders: Is. xxii. 24, "He shall hang upon him all the glory of his Father's house, the offspring and the issue, all vessels of small quantity: from the vessels of cups even to all the vessels of flagons." The care of God's particular kingdom, of his chosen generation, royal priesthood, peculiar people, and holy nation, is committed to him.

4. We may observe how Christ executes his authoritative trust; *he cries with a loud voice to the four angels, to whom it was given to hurt the earth and the sea.* His *crying* may signify Christ's authority, the eminency of the danger, and his care to have the hurtful winds restrained for a season. Those to whom he directs his cry, are *the four angels, to whom it was given to hurt the earth and the sea;* whereby we are made to understand, that all the angels, both good and bad, are subject to the authority and command of him, who is "the head of all principalities, and power, and might, and dominion," &c. None of them all can act but by orders from him. Christ in heaven is looking to the welfare of his church and people upon earth in time of danger, when they themselves have no thought about their own hazard.

5. We have the particular charge given to the angels by Christ, which I have mainly in view, ver. 3, he said to them, *Hurt not the earth, neither the sea, nor the trees, till we have sealed the servants of our God in their foreheads.*

Where we have, 1*st*, A prohibition. 2*dly*, The party immediately concerned in the prohibition. And, 3*dly*, The reason thereof.

1*st*, The prohibition: *Hurt not the earth, neither the sea, nor the trees, for a time.* Where you see the judgment is not absolutely averted nor discharged, but only suspended, until provision be made for the safety of God's peculiar people. Observe, that any favour shewed unto the wicked, or any suspension of divine vengeance with respect unto them, is owing unto the truly godly that live among them; if it were not for the elect's sake, God would make short work with the rest of mankind: "Except the Lord of hosts had left unto us a very small remnant, we should have been as Sodom, and we should have been like unto Gomorrah."

2*dly*, We have the party immediately concerned in the prohibition; *the earth, the sea, and the trees.* By whom in general we are to understand professors of different kinds, against whom the bensil of those hurtful winds was levelled, and who were to sustain great hurt and injury thereby to their souls, when God's time of loosing them should come. What sort of professors of religion are particularly pointed at by *the earth, the sea, and trees*, shall be declared afterwards.

3*dly*, We have the reason of the restraint that is laid upon the hurtful winds, that they are not suffered to blow for a while, viz., *Until we have sealed the servants of our God in their foreheads.* Where we have,

(1.) The objects of the divine care, *the servants of our God.* It is Christ that is speaking, and he speaks in the capacity of a public head, in his own name, and in the name of all his faithful friends and followers, saying, *our God*, because he is the head of the whole mystical body, and stands in a joint relation to God with his members and people, according to John xx. 17, "I ascend unto my Father and your Father, and to my God and your God." The character that he gives them is, that they are *the servants of God;* and the reason of this designation is, because they were such as feared *his name*, Neh. i. 11, and because they "kept the commandments of God, and the testimony of Jesus," when the flood cast out of the mouth of the old serpent was sweeping away the bulk of visible professors unto a course of apostacy.

(2.) We may notice what was to be done to or for the servants of God; why, they are to be *sealed, i. e.,* they are to be separated or distinguished from others that were to be doomed to distruction; much like that, Ezek. ix. 4–6. Says the Lord to the man who had the writer's inkhorn by his side, "Go through the midst of the city, through the midst of Jerusalem, and set a mark upon the foreheads of the men that sigh, and that cry for all the abominations that be done in the midst thereof;" and then, it is added, "Come not near any man upon whom is the mark." In short, this discovers the particular care that God has of his own remnant, and the special providence that God exercises about them, when his judgments are in the earth.

(3.) Notice the visibility of this seal; they are sealed on their *foreheads.* Thus, Rev. xiv. 1, the hundred forty and four thousand who stand with the Lamb on mount Sion, they are said to "have his Father's name written in their foreheads;" *i. e.*, they had a visible profession of the name of God in the world, and were not ashamed to confess him before men. So here this seal is set on the foreheads of the servants of God; *i. e.*, as they had been faithful to his cause and interest, when others had deserted him and his truth; so he would visibly own them as his before the world, and would not be ashamed of them, and would make his regard for them evident to all men, by the singular care he took of them, when his destroying judgments were in the earth.

(4.) The reason of their being thus sealed is here implied, viz., that they *might not be hurt, i. e.*, that they might be preserved from the danger and hazard of these pestilential winds that were to blow in a little upon the visible church. Thus I have endeavoured to open the text and context a little.

From the 2d and 3d verses we may observe these few things.

Observ. 1. That Christ, the glorious uncreated Angel of the covenant, is the protector and guardian of his church and people. He is that other Angel, who has a watchful eye upon his remnant, that they may not suffer hurt by the winds that were to blow, Psal. xci. "The angel of the Lord encampeth round about them that fear him, and delivereth them," Psal. xxxiv. 7. "The Angel of his presence saved them: in his love and in his pity he redeemed them, and he bare them, and carried them all the days of old," Is. lxiii. 9. In which the prophet refers to Exod. xxiii. 20, 21, where God says to Moses, "Behold, I send mine Angel before thee to keep thee in the way, and to bring thee into the place which I have prepared. Beware of him, and obey his voice:—for my name is in him." This is he that was with the church in the wilderness, and this is he that is with the New Testament church, even he who "rideth upon the heavens by his great name JAH, for the help of his people, and in his excellency on the skies;" and therefore will make all things, even the most cloudy dispensations, " work together for good to them that love God, and who are the called according to his purpose."

Observ. 2. That Christ's appearances for his church make day to break from under the darkest night. Hence here likened unto the sun ascending from the east, dispelling the darkness of the night. Luke i. 78. "Through the tender mercies of our God, the day-spring from on high hath visited us." He brings healing in his wings.

Observ. 3. That however the glory of Christ may be clouded and obscured by the errors of man, and the mists of hell, yet, like the sun in the firmament, he is always in the ascendant. This prophecy here is thought to have a particular respect unto that period of the church, when, after the ten Romish Heathen persecutions, a swarm of heresies brake out in the church, calculated for obscuring the glory of his person and righteousness; and yet at the same time he is ascending, and, in the issue, all these mists serve only as a foil to set forth his glory with the greater lustre. Thus the wrath of men and devils, and all their errors and delusions, shall praise him; and what will not answer this end he will restrain. And therefore "let the children of Zion be always joyful in their King," he will prevail.

Observ. 4. That our glorious Redeemer is a person of the highest interest, credit, and authority, in heaven; for here we are told, that he *hath the seal of the living God.* God has " hung upon him all the glory of his house;" he hath "highly exalted him, and given him a name which is above every name, that at the name of Jesus every knee should bow." O what unspeakable consolation is here, especially considering that he got this authority, and executes it, for the good of his church!

Observ. 5. That such is the power and authority of our Redeemer, that all the executioners of the divine anger against the children of men, or the rotten professors of the visible church, are under his empire and command; for here we see he restrains the four angels, to whom it was given to hurt the earth, and the sea, and the trees. Angels and principalities and powers in heavenly places do obeisance unto him, and are his winged messengers, and as a flame of fire to obey him: and as for wicked men and devils, they are under the chains of his power and providence; he rules in the raging of the sea, and when the waves thereof roar, he stilleth them, and says, "Hitherto shalt thou come, but no farther."

Observ. 6. That when the danger is great and most imminent toward his church and people, that is the season wherein he most readily interposes for help and deliverance. When the four angels were just ready to let loose the four hurtful winds, whereby good and bad, chaff and corn, might have been swept away together, then he gives the cry to stop until the servants of God were sealed, and provision made for their safety. "Now will I arise, saith the Lord," viz., "when their strength is gone, and none shut up, or left."

Observ. 7. That in the times of the greatest defection and apostacy in the visible church, God has still a remnant that are cleaving to him and his way and cause. This is clearly implied here; he has servants that must be sealed, when the winds of error and corruption are hurling away the rest of visible professors: Rev. iii. 4. "Thou hast a few names even in Sardis, which have not defiled their garments," &c. When all Israel was carried away with a flood of idolatry, God had his seven thousand in Israel that had not bowed the knee unto Baal. God will keep his hand about these, come of the rest of the world what will.

Observ. 8. God's remnant in this world, they are mingled with the rest of mankind; they live promiscuously together in the same land, in the same parish, and in the same families. So much is imported in the staying of the winds until the servants of God were sealed. They are just like the wheat and chaff lying in the same barn floor; or like the tares and corn which grow in the same field, and yet are of a quite different nature, and therefore cannot but be a great grievance to one another; the godly are a burden to the wicked, and the wicked are a burden to the godly. Hence is that melancholy sonnet of David's, "Wo is me, that I sojourn in Mesech, that I dwell in the tents of Kedar."

Observ. 9. That although godly and wicked be as it were jumbled together, yet the Lord knoweth them that are his, and his eyes are running to and fro, to shew himself strong on their behalf. Hence you see here the Angel who is their guardian, Jesus Christ, he cries to stop the winds till they be sealed; which implies, that he knows them that were to be sealed, and was exercising a particular providence about them. He that calls forth the stars by name, he knows all his jewels by name and surname; and no wonder, for he bears their name on his breast, their names are written in the Lamb's book, that none of them be lost.

Observ. 10. That when once provision is made for the safety and welfare of God's faithful servants and people, he then gives a loose unto his awful and terrible judgments against a wicked world, the generation of his wrath. You see here that the restraint is only until the servants of God be sealed; which implies, that whenever they were sealed, the restraint was taken off, and the angels loosed the four hurtful winds against the rest of mankind. So soon as Noah and his family were shut up in the ark, the fountains of the great deep, and the windows of heaven, opened, a loose is given unto the waters of the deluge upon the old world. So soon as Lot is gone out of Sodom, snares, fire, and brimstone, are rained down from heaven upon the rest of the wicked inhabitants. Whence we see, that the truly godly, though they be the objects of the world's hatred, yet they are the pillars of the land where they live, to keep off the judgments of God from them: Is. i. 9. "Except the Lord of hosts had left unto us a very small remnant, we should have been as Sodom, and we should have been like unto Gomorrah."

Observ. 11. That God's particular interest in his people is their safety and security in an evil day. They are *the servants of our God,* and therefore they must be *sealed.*

Observ. 12. That Christ and believers they have one common God and Father; and therefore here he takes them in with himself when he speaks of them, *Our God;* hence is that new Testament name, "The God and Father of our Lord Jesus Christ." He and they are included in one covenant, wrapt up in the same robe. But, passing all these, the doctrine I intend to insist upon is that which follows.

OBSERV. "That whatever pernicious and hurtful winds may be allowed to blow in the militant church, Christ, her glorious head and guardian, will take a distinguishing care for the safety of those that are found faithful to him in an evil day, that they do not sustain any real hurt thereby."

The foundation of the doctrine is clear and obvious; for here, when the four winds are just ready to blow, Christ, the great Angel, that has the seal of the living God, ascends from the east, arises as it were out of obscurity, and gives the cry, saying, *Hurt not the earth, neither the sea, nor the trees, till we have sealed the servants of our God in their foreheads.* See for proof Ezek. ix. 4. "Go through the midst of the city, through the midst of Jerusalem, and set a mark upon the foreheads of the men that sigh, and that cry," &c.

In discoursing this doctrine, I shall, through divine assistance, endeavour the order and method following.

I. I shall take notice of a few of those hurtful winds that are suffered to blow in the church militant, and who they are that are hurt by them.

II. I would inquire who are those servants of God for whose sake the hurtful winds are restrained for a time.

III. I would speak a little of the seal that he sets upon them for their security against hurtful winds.

IV. Why he doth set a seal upon them.

V. Apply the whole in some uses.

I. The *first* thing is, to *take notice of some of those pernicious winds wherewith the church of Christ is infested while here in a militant state.*

1. Then, There is the wind of open violence, persecution, and bloodshed. The roaring lion he delights in blood, especially the blood of the saints, who are the true seed of the woman, and therefore commonly this is the first thing that he essays in order to ruin the church of Christ. Hence he instigated Cain to slay his brother Abel. He instigated the Jews to crucify the Lord of glory, and to persecute his apostles: and the Romans, by ten several persecutions, to raze the Christian church if possible from the face of the earth. And it is well known how he did instigate malignant men in power under some reigns before the late revolution, to essay, by persecution and bloodshed, to raze a covenanted reformation, and all that owned it, from off the face of the earth. And we see the same spirit of enmity at this day raging against that same work and cause under another denomination; only the great Angel of the covenant does not allow as yet that wind to blow; but how soon the permission is given, I make no doubt but we may see the Grassmarket, and other places through Scotland, reeking as fast as ever with the blood of the saints.

2. Sometimes, and very frequently, the hurtful wind of error in doctrine is suffered to blow in the barn or field of the visible church. "There must be heresies (says the apostle), that they which are approved, may be made manifest," 1 Cor. xi. 19. Those heresies

are compared to the wind; hence that, Eph. i. 14. "Be not like children, tossed to and fro, and carried about with every wind of doctrine." It galls and torments the devil, to see the church of Christ possessing the pure truths of God. He himself abode not in the truth, and therefore cannot endure to see any abiding in it; and therefore studies by all means to sow the tares of error and corruption in doctrine, whereby the food of the church may be poisoned, and people perverted from the simplicity of the gospel. And, indeed, when once it has entered, it flies like a pestilential wind, corrupting the minds of men. Manifold melancholy instances might be adduced, both in former ages, and in our own day; but I must not enlarge, that I may win forward to the application. I shall only add, that truth in its purity is such a valuable commodity, that every man is to contend for it as in an agony; for if but the least hoof of it be parted with, we are in danger of loosing the whole, because of the necessary connection of truth in the system of our holy religion.

3. Another hurtful wind is the wind of strong delusions as to everlasting soul concerns; and this is consequential unto the former. It is very common and ordinary, when God has given his statutes and testimonies unto a people in purity, as a light unto their feet, and a lamp unto their paths, and, instead of taking heed unto the sure word of prophecy, as unto a light shining in a dark place, they embrace, countenance, and patronize error; God, in that case, chooses their own delusions, suffers them to feed upon ashes, a deceived heart to turn them aside that they cannot deliver their souls, nor say, "Is there not a lie in my right hand?" Is. xliv. 20. Thus he dealt with Israel, Psal. lxxxi. 11, 12. "My people would not harken to my voice: and Israel would none of me. Therefore I gave them up unto their own hearts' lusts: and they walked in their own counsels." Thus he dealt with the abettors and supporters of antichristian errors, 2 Thess. ii. 11, 12, they received not the truth in the love of it; therefore God gave them up unto strong delusions, to believe lies. And this is the very case with multitudes both of ministers and people in our own day. They have forsaken the reformation doctrine, principles, and covenants, in many instances, which are made known to the world: they have rejected a testimony for that glorious work, and killed the witnesses, and cast them out; for which cause God is giving many of them up in this generation to such strong delusion, as to believe a lie, and to cry up that for a saving work of God, which looks like that judgment we read of, Is. vi. 9–12. "And he said, Go, and tell this people, Hear ye indeed, but understand not; and see ye indeed, but perceive not. Make the heart of this people fat, and make their ears heavy, and shut their eyes: lest they see with their eyes, and hear with their ears, and understand with their heart, and convert and be healed," &c.

4. There is the wind of temptation that blows in the visible church. This was a wind that blew hard on the glorious Head and Captain of our salvation, as you see Matth. iv. He was

tempted to a distrust of providence, to self-murder, and to call in question his own supreme Deity. And, therefore, none of his friends and followers need be surprised when they meet with the like attacks; and never is the enemy more ready to make an attack upon the Christian, than when he has been admitted unto fellowship with, and nearness to, the Lord, as you see in the case of Peter, after he had been at the first supper where Christ himself was personally present, Luke xxii. 31, 32, "Simon, Simon, behold Satan hath desired to have you, that he may sift you as wheat," &c. And therefore, you that have been at a communion table, and enjoyed anything of the Lord, take heed to yourselves, for you may expect a winnowing wind from hell to blow ere it be long: O look by the eye of faith to your Advocate with the Father, that he may pray that your faith fail not.

5. Another hurtful wind is the wind of profanity and open ungodliness. Usually when men espouse errors, and lax toleration principles, God gives up with them, lays the reins upon their necks, and suffers them to run into all excess of riot, saying, "Let us eat and drink, for to-morrow we shall die;" let us make the best of the world and the pleasures of it that we can. Thus God dealt with the very heathen, when they did not walk up to the light and law of nature, Rom. i. 25, 26, 28, 29. Now, if God thus punished the abuse of nature's light, how much more will he not punish the abuse of gospel-light, by giving a people unto all manner of impiety? which is the case with multitudes among us at this day, who are given up to the same abominations with heathens.

6. All these winds are commonly followed with the winds of sweeping and desolating judgments, such as sword, famine, and pestilence, whereby the wicked are turned off the stage of time into a miserable eternity. Many awful beacons of God's severity and justice this way are left upon record to us in the scriptures of truth, such as the old world, Sodom and Gomorrah, the Jewish church and nation; and truly I am afraid, yea, I may be pretty positive, that God is saying to us in this land, upon the account of perjury, covenant-breaking, apostacy, contempt of the truth, persecution and church tyranny, profanity, and the like, "How shall I pardon you for these? shall I not visit for these things? and shall not my soul be avenged on such a nation as this?" The rumour of war is begun, but where it shall end, God knows. Perhaps God is saying, as in Is. vi., when the prophet puts the question, When, or *how long*, shall these spiritual judgments last? the Lord answers, ver. 11, 12, "Until the cities be wasted without inhabitant, and the houses without man, and the land be utterly desolate," &c.

Thus I have told you of some of those hurtful winds that God lets blow in the visible church. But now you may ask me, What are we to understand by *the earth, the sea, and the trees*, that shall be hurt by these winds, particularly the winds of error, defection, and delusion, &c.? I shall just give you the opinion of the judicious Durham upon the place.

1. Then, By the *earth*, we are to understand earthly-minded professors, who suppose gain to be godliness. They have some shadow of a profession, and some form of godliness; but yet the world is set in their hearts, their God is their belly, they mind earthly things, such as wealth, ease, credit, preferment, and the like. Such professors are swept away like chaff when the above winds are let blow, Phil. iii. 19, 2 Pet. ii. 15, Jude 10. Hence also, 1 Tim. vi. 10, the love of money is called "the root of all evil; which, while some coveted after, they have erred from the faith." I am afraid earthly considerations and worldly gain, keep many men back from owning the truth and testimony of the day; it would not stand with their employments, Acts xix. 25.

2. By the *sea*, the same commentator understands, light unstable professors, who are fixed in nothing, but, like Reuben, their motto is, " Unstable as water, thou shalt not excel." The apostle Jude calls them, ver. 13, " Raging waves of the sea, wandering stars, and clouds that are carried with a tempest:" like some among ourselves, that are keen Presbyterians one day, the next day Independents, and the next day joining hands with Prelacy; one day keen for supporting a testimony, for the covenants and reformation, and the next day for burying it. Such unstable professors, they are "like the sea, driven with the wind, and tossed."

3. By the *trees*, he understands professors, who, for their gifts of knowledge, learning, utterance, and the like, are high above others, both in their own conceit, and in the opinion of other men; but not being rooted in Christ by faith of God's operation, when the wind blows, they are like the lofty trees plucked up by the root, and overthrown by the winds of error, delusion, or persecution. And do not we see this also fulfilled in our own day, men that seemed once in a day to be pillars in the church, and like tall cedars in Lebanon, overthrown with the present winds of error and delusion.

II. The *second* thing was, to *inquire who are those servants of God for whose sake the hurtful winds are restrained, that provision may be made for their safety when they do actually blow.* I shall not stand much upon this, but only refer you unto a description given of them in two particulars in this same book of the Revelation, chap. xii. 17, where the apostle, by the Spirit, is describing these against whom the dragon makes war, and casts out the flood of malice and enmity; they are " the seed of the woman, that keep the commandments of God, and have the testimony of Jesus Christ."

1. The servants of God are such as " keep the commandments of God;" *i. e.* (1.), They are holy persons; the " sanctified and preserved in Christ Jesus." They have the law of God in their hearts, and therefore have a respect unto all his commandments, Psal. cxix. 6. Although they cannot in this life attain to perfection in holiness, yet it is what they aim at; and therefore forget things behind, and reach forth unto perfection; like these that shall attain unto the resurrection of the just. Holiness is the badge and

distinguishing motto of all the true followers of the Lamb, therefore called "an holy nation, and the people of his holiness. Holiness becometh thy house, O God, for ever." Or (2.), as Durham observes, they "keep the commandments of God," it is to be understood of a keeping the laws, ordinances, and institutions of Christ, in opposition to a set of men in the antichristian church, who, through their traditions, were making void the commandments of God. Observe, That it is the character of Christ's faithful servants, whether ministers or Christians, to observe and do all things whatever he has commanded them in his word. It is not what kings, parliaments, or assemblies, command, but what God commands, is the rule by which they walk; the laws of man must be tried by the law of God. There is a generation of men in our day called ministers, who, instead of keeping the commandments of God, are very careful to keep the commandments of men, though even cross to the command of God: if they be commanded by men to profane the Sabbath, to profane the pulpit, and ministerial character, and to prostitute the headship of Christ, and turn heralds to another head than Christ, they will do it, and defend the deed when they have done. Such servants of men cannot be the servants of Christ Jesus, but they serve their own bellies. And yet such men at this day, though we hear nothing of their repenting of their evil deeds, and though they be holding fast deceit, and refusing to return, some would have us to believe are honoured of God as great instruments of the conversion of souls. I shall only say, that I cannot help thinking, that as such ministers do only carry a counterfeit commission, so the seals of their ministry are but counterfeit seals. For my part, I shall never believe these noisy conversions to be of the right stamp, until I see both ministers and converts following the practice of Judah, and Israel, when returning to the Lord after a course of defection, Jer. l. 4, 5. "In those days, and in that time, saith the Lord, the children of Israel shall come, they and the children of Judah together, going and weeping: they shall go, and seek the Lord their God. They shall ask the way to Zion with their faces thitherward, saying, Come, and let us join ourselves to the Lord, in a perpetual covenant, that shall never be forgotten. The reason is set down in the two following verses, which are applicable in the present case of the church of God in this land; "My people hath been lost sheep: their shepherds have caused them to go astray, they have turned them away on the mountains: they have gone from mountain to hill, they have forgotten their resting-place. All that found them have devoured them, and their adversaries said, We offend not, because they have sinned against the Lord, the habitation of justice, even the Lord, the hope of their fathers." And thereupon they depart out of Babylon, and their ministers or shepherds become as he-goats before the flock.

2. The faithful servants of God, are said to be such as "have the testimony of Jesus." By the testimony of Jesus, we are to understand the gospel of Christ, or the doctrine of faith in its

purity, which only is "the power of God unto salvation," Rom. i. 16. The whole word of God is divided into law and gospel; and sometimes the whole word is called by the one, and sometimes by the other, as you see frequently in the 119th Psalm. Now, the question is, What is it to "have the testimony of Jesus?" *Answ.* (1.), It implies a firm faith of the record of God concerning his Son Jesus Christ; this is called a "believing the report, and setting to the seal that God is true." (2.), A firm trust in Christ as the only Saviour, upon the testimony of God. They credit and trust him for the execution of all his saving offices, as a Prophet, Priest, and King, for wisdom, righteousness, sanctification, and complete redemption. (3.), A holy care to preserve the doctrine, worship, and the government of Christ's house, in its purity, and according to the pattern shewed in the mount; together with a steady contending for the faith, and a standing fast in the liberties wherewith Christ has made his people free, in opposition to error in doctrine, corruption in worship, and all tyranny in government and discipline. Now, these are the servants of God that are here intended to be sealed, in order to their being preserved from those hurtful winds that blow in the visible church; these are they against whom the rage of the great red dragon and his angels is levelled, against these the flood cast out of his mouth doth run. But now I proceed to,

III. The *third* thing proposed in the method, which was, to *speak a little of the seal that is set upon the servants of God.* And here I shall propose and answer two or three questions.

Query 1. Who is he that seals them?

Answ. It is Christ, the great Angel that hath the seal of the living God. He himself was sealed as God's Secretary and Plenipotentiary unto this lower world, John vi. 27. And he hath the seal of the living God committed to him; for he hath "given him power over all flesh, that he might give eternal life to as many as he hath given him," John xvii. 2. He hath the roll of election committed to him, that he may put his mark, his own name, and his Father's name, upon them: Rev. iii. 12. "Him that overcometh, will I make a pillar in the temple of my God, and he shall go no more out: and I will write upon him the name of my God, and the name of the city of my God, which is the new Jerusalem, which cometh down out of heaven from my God: and I will write upon him my new name." There you see that Christ makes the overcomer a pillar in the temple of God; but that is not all, he writes his name upon them, and the name of his God, he puts his own image and Spirit in and upon them, as he is the express image of the Father. Thus you see that it is Christ that seals the servants of our God.

Query 2. What is implied in the sealing them?

Answ. It implies, 1. That he is their great owner and proprietor; for a man seals his own goods, that it may be known they are his. "The Lord's portion is his people, and Jacob is the lot of his inheritance." They are his by election, and his Father's donation, by purchase, and by covenant, and by the inhabitation of his Spirit: and "the foundation of God standeth sure, having this seal, The Lord knoweth them that are his."

2. A seal is for distinction, to distinguish one man's goods from another. And so it implies, that God will have a difference put betwixt his own people and others; for they are his gold and coin of his own mint, the rest of the world are but the dross; they are his wheat, and others are the chaff; and "what is the chaff to the wheat? saith the Lord." He has his fan in his hand, and will thoroughly purge his floor, &c.

3. A seal is for confirmation. The king's seal appended unto a charter establishes and confirms it. And so it may import, that, before the winds are suffered to blow, Christ will have his own servants established and confirmed in the faith of these truths, which were to be most exposed to the winds, that they might not be carried about like children with every wind of doctrine, but might be like mount Zion, which cannot be removed for ever.

4. A seal is sometimes for secrecy. We read of a book, Rev. v. 1, which was sealed with seven seals, because of the great secrets and hid mysteries contained in it. No man can warrantably break up a sealed letter, but he to whom it is directed, because it is hid and secret to any other. And so it may import, that God's people are his hidden ones, and that his secrets are imparted to them, and not to others. God's people they are a hidden people: "They have consulted against thy hidden ones," says the psalmist. God's doves they abide in the clefts of the rock, and in the secret places of the stairs. He has them hid in the secret of his presence as in a pavilion; he has his secret chambers in which he hides them, until the indignation be overpast, Is. xxvi. 20. And then as they are secret hidden persons, so he imparts his secrets unto them, which he hides from the rest of the world: "The secret of the Lord is with them that fear him. Unto you it is given to know the mysteries of the kingdom, but to others it is not given."

5. A seal is a badge of honour, love, and esteem. And so it implies, that his servants are honourable persons, precious in his sight: Is. xliii. 4, "Ever since thou wast precious in my sight, thou hast been honourable," &c.

6. A seal is for custody and preservation. So the saints and servants of God, they are "the preserved in Christ Jesus, kept by the power of God through faith unto salvation."

Query 3. When and how are they sealed?

Answ. 1. From all eternity, they were sealed with his electing and everlasting love. "I have loved thee with an everlasting love," &c. "He hath chosen us in him, before the foundation of the world." He predestinates them unto the adoption of children.

2. In their conversion and effectual calling, they are sealed in their own persons with the image of the second Adam, being predestinated thereunto from eternity; they are renewed in knowledge after the image of him that created them; they are

separate from the rest of the world, and become "a chosen generation, a royal priesthood, an holy nation, a peculiar people, that they should shew forth the praises of him who hath called them out of darkness into his marvellous light."

3. They have a seal of blood set upon them in their redemption and justification; for as you see, ver. 14 of this chapter, "they have their garments washed, and made white in the blood of the Lamb."

4. They have the seal of the Spirit of promise set upon them: Eph. i. 13, "After that ye believed, ye were sealed with that holy Spirit of promise, which is the earnest of our inheritance." The Spirit of God dwells in them as in a temple; he sanctifies them by the truth, he, as a Spirit of adoption, teaches them to cry, *Abba, Father,* and comforts them in all their tribulations with the consolations of God, with the oil of gladness, wherewith he was anointed above his fellows.

Query 4. But why are they said to be *sealed in their foreheads?*

Answ. The forehead, you know, is the upper part of the face, the most conspicuous part of a man's countenance; and I conceive the seal upon the forehead it may import two things.

1. Their visible profession of Christ, and their open owning of the Lord, and his way and cause, in the time of the greatest opposition, when error, and delusion, and persecution, was most rampant in the visible church. Sirs, it is not enough to be night-disciples, when Christ is calling us to confess him before men; no, we must come forth to the open field, when called up to the help of the Lord against the mighty. He did not hide his face from shame and spitting, but openly endured the cross, and despised the shame; and yet shall we be ashamed of him, or afraid to own him before the world? It is dangerous to come near the borders of denying him and his cause before men, lest he should deny us before his Father, and before his angels. Christ's plough, his cause, and testimony, drives heavily for many professors in Scotland at this day; and because they have been so slack-handed this way, God is leaving some, both ministers and people, to put hand to another sort of plough, which will produce a melancholy crop ere all be done.

2. Their being marked or sealed in the forehead implies, that, in the time of common calamity, God will make such a visible difference between his own faithful servants and others, that he that runs may read, according to that, Mal. iii. 18, "Then shall ye return and discern between the righteous and the wicked; between him that serveth God, and him that serveth him not." The righteous and the wicked they live together now (as I was saying); but ere it be long, God will put such a visible mark of favour upon the one, and of vengeance upon the other, that all men and angels shall know the one from the other, and at the end the separation will be as wide as between heaven and hell.

IV. The *fourth* thing in the method was, to *inquire into the* reasons *why Christ, the Angel of the covenant, will have his servants marked in their foreheads, when the winds are to be let blow?*

Answ. 1. In so many words, he will have them sealed, because they are his Father's gift, "Thine they were, and thou gavest them me;" and for the Father's sake that gave them, he will have them sealed.

2. Because he hath bought them at a dear rate, even with the price of his precious blood, not with silver, or gold, or such corruptible things, &c.

3. Because they are his sheep, his lambs that he carries in his bosom, Is. xl. 11.

4. Because they are his servants, the servants of God, their ear he has bored, they love their Master, &c.

5. Because they are his peculiar friends, "I call you no more servants, but friends," John xv. 14, 15.

6. Because they are his seed, Is. liii. 10, Psal. xxii. 30. "A seed shall serve him," &c.

7. Because they are his spouse and bride, he their Husband and Bridegroom, Is. liv. 5, Hos. ii. 16, &c.

8. Because they are his members, and he their Head, they are his bone and flesh, they "hold the head," &c.

9. He seals them, because they believe in him, Eph. i. 13, "After that ye believed, ye were sealed," &c.

10. He seals them, because they love him, so as to mourn for injury done him, Ezek. ix. 4.

11. He seals them, because they are his faithful witnesses, that confess him, when others deny him.

12. He seals them, that they may not suffer hurt by the destroying winds that blow in the visible church. They keep the commandments of God, and the testimony of Jesus; and therefore he will keep them in the hour of temptation, according to the promise, Psal. xci. 3, 7.

V. The *fifth* thing was the *Application* of the doctrine.

And the *first* use I shall make of it, shall be by way of *Lamentation* over the many hurtful winds that have blown, and are still blowing, in our land. God seems in our day to have given a commission unto his angels, the ministers of his wrath, who fulfil his pleasure, to let loose the winds, that the earth, the sea, and the trees, may be hurt thereby; and much hurt and damage have they done already in our valley of vision.

Query, What are the hurtful winds that are blowing at this day, or in this period of the church? for some tell us that the church of Christ in this land, was never in a better condition. I answer, Whatever some may imagine, yet I am of the mind, and many others with me, that the church of Christ was never in a more dangerous condition since our reformation from Popery. God seems to have given a commission to the four angels to loose the four winds, to hurt the inhabitants of the land. And here I will tell you of several hurtful winds, which, like the pestilence, are walking through the land, and hurting many, both professors and others at this day.

1. The hurtful winds of Infidelity, or Deism, are blowing, which strike at the roots, and deny all supernatural revelation, or at least discard all the supernatural mysteries of the Christian religion, which depraved reason is not able to comprehend, such as the doctrine of the incarnation of the Son of God, and of his satisfaction to justice, of the necessity of regeneration, of justification by his imputed righteousness, of sanctification by his Spirit: these, and the like supernatural doctrines of our holy religion, I say, are exploded by many in our day, insomuch that through many places of Scotland, instead of the gospel of Christ, nothing is to be heard, but the dry sapless harangues of heathenish morality. And what must become of those poor souls that are daily entertained with such food? Why, Solomon answers the question, when he tell us, "Where no vision is, the people perish." The hurtful wind of Arian heresy has been travelling through the land, and appeared before the bar of the Assembly without any becoming censure. The doctrine of self-love also, whereby the creature is exalted above the glorious Creator. We have been long taught, that the chief end of man is, to glorify God, and that whether we eat or drink, or whatever we do, we ought to do all to the glory of God. And, to be sure, that which is the chief end of man, ought also to be the leading and chief motive of all his moral and religious actions. But now it is a doctrine sustained by the National Assembly, that our own delight, pleasure, and satisfaction in glorifying God, is the chief motive of all virtuous and religious actions; whereby the creature's happiness is preferred unto the glory of God, who made all things for himself. And I cannot shun to observe, that God, in a way of righteous judgment, is answering many according to this idol of jealousy set up in the temple of God, by letting them adopt, and embrace a religion that lies all in internal feelings, pleasure, and satisfaction to themselves; while the declarative glory of God, and the honour of the Redeemer's crown and kingdom in the world, is none of their concern; yea, it torments them to hear of a testimony against the indignities done to him in the land wherein we live. I might here also insist on the injuries done to the doctrines of the grace of God, in the Acts of Assembly, 1720 and 1722, with relation to the *Marrow of Modern Divinity*, whereby a bundle of precious truths are condemned, and lie under the rubbish ever since, which I hope shall yet be brought forth unto victory.

2. The hurtful wind of church tyranny and abused discipline, has been for a long time blowing in the church of Scotland, whereby the erroneous have been screened, and ministers of Christ cast out of ministerial communion, and deposed for bearing testimony to the truth, in opposition unto the present current of apostacy and backsliding. And how has the boar of ecclesiastical tyranny laid waste, and scattered the flock of Christ up and down the land, through violent intrusions that have been made upon Christian

congregations, imposing men upon them, contrary to that liberty wherewith Christ has made them free?

3. I might, among other pernicious winds, take notice of the public affront done to the Mediator's crown as the alone King of Zion, when, by reading of the act anent Porteous, ministers changed their holding of Christ, and prostituted his sovereignty, and dipt their hands in that innocent blood shed at the execution of Wilson, by not testifying against him as a bloody murderer condemned in law, when they read that act.

4. How has the wind of profanity and open impiety blown upon all ranks in the land, and hurt many, both in soul, and bodily estate? What heaven-daring impiety abounds, insomuch that the land groans under our provocations against the Holy One of Israel? The very abominations of the heathen are perpetrated among us Christians, like these, Rom. i. at the close.

5. There is another wind that God is suffering to blow at this day, whereby both many ministers and people are staggered, and cast down, and that is the noisy wind that the known foreigner of the Prelatic communion of the church of England has brought along with him unto this land. I know indeed that some deny any connection between him, and that work which we have now among us; but it is in vain to deny this, when it visibly follows him through the world, wherever he goes, and is received into communion as a minister of Jesus Christ.

Query, How doth it appear that this is one of the hurtful winds that God has, by the ministry of angels, whether good or bad, loosed upon the church of Scotland? for many call it, and are very confident of it, that it is a heavenly wind. *Answ.* I cannot stay upon it at present; only, notwithstanding of all the fine things I have read and heard about it, I cannot help thinking, that it is one of the most hurtful winds that ever blew in this covenanted land, and that for these reasons. It appears to me, and many others, to be a hurtful and pernicious wind, by observing (1.), Whence it comes; (2.), Whither it blows; (3.), What are its effects.

1*st*, Let us notice whence it comes. It comes from the Prelatic superstitious church of England; and he that has brought it, owns himself to be still of the communion of that church, abjured by this church in her national covenant, and by the three nations in the solemn league; one who has sworn the oath of supremacy, and so renounced the alone headship of Christ in his church, and, in consequence of this, denies the binding obligation of our solemn covenants. And his own account of his conversion appears to be an evident delusion of the devil.

2*dly*, Let us also observe, whither, and for what, this noisy wind blows. It is evident, that it blows up everywhere through the world, and particularly in this land, for filthy lucre, worldly gain and advantage; the cry of it everywhere is, Who will shew us any of this world's good? Another airth toward which it blows, is, toleration of all sects, plainly founded upon the principle of Catholic love and communion, so much applauded by that foreigner, and all that patronize him and his work. And hence the natural tendency of it is, to overthrow the hedge of government, and to cast down the walls and fortifications of Zion, against which the gates of hell shall never prevail.

3*dly,* Let us notice what are the fruits and effects of this noisy wind. I know indeed that some talk of great and good effects of it, in the conviction, conversion, and consolation of many; but I much doubt if this will stand the trial of the word, which is the light by which all spirits, and works, must be tried: " To the law and to the testimony: if they speak not according to these, it is because there is no light in them." An imaginary conviction produceth an imaginary conversion, and an imaginary conversion produceth but an imaginary consolation. I will only tell you of two or three fruits of it, that I know, and can document.

(1.) A stated enmity and bitterness of spirit against a covenanted work of reformation, and all that bear up or own a testimony for it at this day, notwithstanding of their Catholic love.

(2.) A striking men blind, and deaf, and dumb, as to all the public affronts done to Christ, or injuries done to his mystical body. I dare appeal to themselves, if at their most solemn occasions, where they say there was most of the Lord, anything was spoken for God's declarative glory, in opposition unto the bloodshed, perjury, covenant-breaking, or the violent intrusions and rapes committed upon the spouse of Christ, or the profaning of Christ's crown, his sabbaths, and the ministerial character, by reading of Porteous' act. Nay, so far from this that that spirit goes along with intruders, act readers, and the like, as well as others; but not one word of their professing repentance for their evil deeds.

(3.) Another fruit of this work, is the palliating of all the public defections of the church, and so fostering and hardening men in their evil ways. Hence they wipe their mouths, and cry they are innocent, God is with us, and he has forsaken those that pretend to witness against us and our ways. I have heard with my ears, and read little less in some of their writings, Where is the God of the Seceders? he is not owning their ministry as he is owning us. I shall only say with David, when this profane jeer was passed upon him in his affliction and distress, Psal. xlii. 10, " It is as a sword in our bones, while the enemy says daily to us, Where is your God?" But we desire to follow David's example, and say with him in the words following these now quoted, " Why art thou cast down, O my soul? and why art thou disquieted within me? hope thou in God, for I shall yet praise him, who is the health of my countenance, and my God." This puts me in mind of a passage I have read in *Baxter's Life.* A certain faithful minister of Christ, who being ordered to a prison at some distance, under the custody of soldiers; by the way they halted at the house of a malignant lady, who, when she saw the minister in the hands of his enemies, said, Where is the God of the Whigs now? Upon which he desired a sight of her Bible, which she brought with a taunt; he takes the Bible, and casts up the following text, which I shall read also to those who upbraid us after the same manner; the text you have, Mic. vii. 8–10, "Rejoice not against me, O mine enemy: when I fall, I shall arise; when I sit in darkness, the Lord shall be a light unto me. I will bear the indignation of the Lord, because I have sinned against him, until he plead my cause, and execute judgment for me: he will bring me forth to the light, and I shall behold his righteousness. Then she that is mine enemy shall see it, and shame shall cover her which said unto me, Where is the Lord thy God? mine eyes shall behold her: now shall she be trodden down as the mire of the streets." As this scripture, upon the reading of it, struck that woman with a damp and confusion, so may it do those whose language is the same with hers. Now these, I say, are some of the hurtful winds that blow at this day.

Use *second* shall be by way of *Trial* and *Examination*. Seeing it is so that there are such hurtful winds blowing in the church of Christ, it concerns us to try whether we be among the number of these servants of God, who are secured against any real hurt from those pernicious winds, by having the seal of the living God set upon us.

Query, How shall I know if I be among that happy number? In answer to this question, I shall offer you the few following marks of the faithful servants of our God, who have this seal set upon them.

1. All God's faithful servants they have had their bands loosed: Psal. cxvi. 16, "O Lord, truly I am thy servant, I am thy servant, and the son of thy handmaid: thou hast loosed my bonds." All are by nature held fast in the gall of bitterness, and bonds of iniquity; they are lawful captives. Now, has the Lord in a day of power loosed your bands, and proclaimed liberty to you, and made you free indeed?

2. All God's servants have seen their Master's glory, beauty, and excellency; 2 Cor. iv. 6, "God, who commanded the light to shine out of darkness, hath shined into your hearts," &c. Have you seen the Father in the Son? and has the sight transformed you into his image?

3. The first-born of the family will be very dear unto you, "more glorious than all the mountains of prey;" and that will be the language of your heart, "My beloved is white and ruddy, the chiefest among ten thousand."

4. They are all very sensible of their inability to serve him as they ought; yea, they are ready to acknowledge, that without him they can do nothing; they will not brag of their services, as the proud Pharisee, "God, I thank thee that I am not as other men," &c.

5. They have all a great regard for his authority, and will obey God rather than man, as the apostles of Christ, Daniel, and the three children, &c. Every one of them is ready to say, "Lord, what wilt thou have me to do?" Give strength to obey, and command what thou wilt.

6. They are all for the standing of their Master's house, and stand up for their Master's honour. It goes nearer the hearts of his faith-

ful servants to see him injured, or his crown profaned, than any private interest of their own; it grieves them to see their Master's house invaded by thieves and robbers; and they will not take them by the hand, but bear faithful testimony against them. They cannot part with the least hoof that pertains to their great Master.

7. All God's faithful servants have his seal set upon them, as you see in the text, *Hurt not the earth, neither the sea, nor the trees, till we have sealed the servants of our God in their foreheads.* O, say you, how shall I know if I be among the sealed? *Answ.* You may know it by the print of the seal. You know the print of the seal upon the wax, is an exact transcript of the graving that is on the seal. Just so is it here, when Christ seals, or sets his mark upon the soul, he just by the power of his Spirit puts the print of his own grace upon it, John i. 16, "Of his own fulness have all we received, and grace for grace;" *i. e.*, the grace that is in the believer, just corresponds unto the grace that is in Christ. As in nature, so it is in grace; the child receives from the parent by natural generation, member for member, eye for eye, hands, legs, limbs, just like its parent that begat it; so it is in supernatural things, or in regeneration, we receive from him, who of his own will begat us by the word of truth, grace for grace. The Spirit shews the things of Christ unto us, and we, by *beholding* thereof, are "changed into the same image from glory to glory, as by the Spirit of the Lord."

So then, see whether you have the following prints of Christ's seal upon you.

1*st*, The print of his life: "Because I live, ye shall live also." It is the life of Christ that is in the soul of the believer: "I live; yet not I, but Christ liveth in me; and the life which I now live in the flesh, is by faith in the Son of God." Where notice, the believer does not live upon his own feelings, or grace in him, but on Christ the fountain of life.

2*dly*, The print of his light; "for he enlighteneth every man that cometh into the world." So, then, have you in his light seen light? If so, then you will know the difference between light and darkness, day and night; and when it is night, you will long to see the sun again, and go mourning without the sun, &c.

3*dly*, A print of his love; for "God is love," and he "draws with the cords of love;" he kindles a fire of love in the heart, the sparks of which, are always flying upwards toward heaven.

4*thly*, A print of his holiness; "Be ye holy, as I am holy." And this is it that makes the soul to groan under a body of sin and death, to war against it, and to long to be fully like him in holiness.

5*thly*, A print of his faithfulness in the word of truth; "Of his own will begat he us by the word of truth." What is faith, but just the impression of God's faithfulness made on the soul by the word of truth; insomuch that, whenever the soul hears the record of God concerning Christ, it cries, O "this is a faithful saying, and worthy of all acceptation!"

6*thly*, The soul gets a print of his seal for the honour and glory of God, so that the man cannot but stand up for the house of God, and the concerns of his glory. "The zeal of thine house hath eaten me up," says Christ; and therefore, like him, the man that is sealed, he cannot endure to see the house of God turned into a den of thieves, robbers, and hirelings, buyers and sellers, and he is far from joining hand with them.

7*thly*, The man carries the print of Christ's seal upon his forehead, in a way of a visible profession of Christ, and his cause and truth, in opposition to the corruption of a wicked world. Hence it is, that as the world hated Christ, so it hateth them also; for as the world knows its own, so it soon knows the followers of Christ, that keep the commandments of God, and the testimony of Jesus. And this is one thing among others, that gives me a very bad notion of these new conversions so much talked of, that if they know a man to be either a formal or practical acceder, they will not enter upon a religious conversation with him, or give any account of the Lord's way of dealing with them, contrary to the command, "Be ye ready always to give an answer to every man that asketh you a reason of the hope that is in you."

Use *third*, of *Consolation* unto those that are sealed; for we are commanded to speak comfort unto you. And therefore know for your comfort,

1. That Christ, the Angel of God's presence, has the charge of you: "All the saints are in his hand." He has power over all flesh, to give you eternal life.

2. He is ascending from the east, like the sun in the firmament; even when the clouds are thickest and darkest, it does not hinder his arising, and he will break through to the salvation and comfort of all his sealed ones, that keep the commandments of God, and have and contend for the faith delivered to the saints. "His goings forth are prepared as the morning."

3. He is a person of great power and authority; for he hath the seal of the living God, he hath the keys of the house of David, he opens, and no man shuts, and shuts, and no man opens, yea, the keys of hell and death do belong unto him.

4. All the executioners of the divine wrath against a wicked world are under his command; you see here, that the angels that loose the winds, they are at his beck, and fulfil his will and pleasure. Good angels are his ministering spirits, and they minister for good to them that are the heirs of salvation; and the bad angels are in his chains, which he lengthens out, or shortens at his pleasure.

5. It is his opportunity to help his church, and to interpose, when the danger is most threatening, for here he gives the cry, when the winds are at the point of being loosed.

6. All his administrations are calculated for your good, Rom. viii. 28. He rides in heaven for your help.

7. He will guide you with his counsel, and bring you to glory.

Use *fourth*, of *Terror* to all an unbelieving Christless world; who, instead of being the servants of God, are serving divers lusts and pleasures; who, instead of having the seal of heaven, have the seal of hell upon them: all carnal unstable professors, who are already wandering with the winds, giving up with the truth, and the tradition we have received from the Lord in this land. What shall I say to you? your condemnation is awful and terrible, God's soul hath no pleasure in you. Perhaps indeed you may imagine otherwise, and that, in giving up with the covenanted cause of Christ in this land, you have now fallen upon a new way which God approves of, and your own soul delights in; but read these three scriptures, Is. xliv. 20, "He feedeth of ashes: a deceived heart hath turned him aside, that he cannot deliver his soul, nor say, is there not a lie in my right hand? Is. l. 11, "Behold, all ye that kindle a fire, that compass yourselves about with sparks: walk in the light of your fire, and in the sparks that ye have kindled. This shall ye have of mine hand, ye shall lie down in sorrow." Is. lxvi. 3, 4. "He that killeth an ox, is as if he slew a man: he that sacrificeth a lamb, as if he cut off a dog's neck: he that offereth an oblation, as if he offered swine's blood: he that burneth incense, as if he blessed an idol: yea, they have chosen their own ways, and their soul delighteth in their abominations. I also will choose their delusions, and will bring their fears upon them; because when I called, none did answer; when I spake, they did not hear: but they did evil before mine eyes, and chose that in which I delighted not." The winds when loosed to the full, whether will they drive you? especially you that have had the knowledge of the truth, made a profession of it before the world, and yet have turned away from the testimony of Christ in this land? You may see and read your doom, if infinite mercy do not prevent, Heb. vi. 4-6; Heb. x. 26-29; 2 Pet. ii. at the close, &c. Perhaps you may think this very hard, but it is no harder than God has made it, for whom it is impossible to lie.

Use *fifth* shall be of *Exhortation* unto all in general, even to all that are afar off, to come to Christ before the wind be fully loosed, that perhaps shall blow you out of this world into an unalterable state of eternal woe and misery: O come to Christ, I say, in order to your being sealed with his seal, for he is the Angel which hath the seal of the living God. His Father commands you to come to him, 1 John iii. 23, "This is his commandment, that we should believe on the name of his Son Jesus Christ." He himself invites you to come, yea, not only invites you, but importunately solicits you to come, Is. lv. 1-3, "Ho, every one that thirsteth, come ye to the waters, and he that hath no money, let him come; come, buy wine and milk without money, and without price," &c. He passes his word that he will make you welcome, and that you shall not be put away, "Come to me who will, I will in no wise cast out;" he hates putting away: he complains of your backwardness to come, John v. 40, "And ye will not come to me, that ye might have life." His Father sealed him, and he hath the seal of the living God, that he may seal all that come to him in a way of believing: John vi. 27, he makes it an argument to press sinners to come to him for life and salvation, "because him hath God the

Father sealed." If you be sealed by him, you are the preserved in Christ Jesus, the winds shall never hurt you, no evil shall come near your dwelling, Christ himself shall be your hiding-place from the storm. The curse of the law, the storm of vindictive wrath, the sting of death, the malice of Satan, the rage of men and devils, shall never hurt you, "he shall cover you with his feathers," &c. If you be sealed by him, you shall be guided by his counsel, he will lead you in the way you know not, until he bring you unto glory. If you do not come to him to get his seal, the wrath of God abideth on you, and will pursue you through all the ages of eternity, "He that believeth not, is condemned already;" and the day comes, when it shall be said to you, "Depart from me, I never knew you," for you have not my seal on your hearts or foreheads.

Do not say, I am a sinner, and therefore he will not receive me; for it is only sinners he deals with: "He came not to call the righteous, but sinners to repentance."

Do not say, I am a great and grievous sinner, he will not put his seal upon me; for he says to the greatest of sinners, "I am mighty to save," Is. i. 18. Remember Paul, Manasseh, Mary Magdalene, for they all obtained mercy, and are triumphing in heaven.

Do not say, I have nothing to recommend me to him; for he wants nothing but poverty, misery, blindness, &c.

Do not say, I fear the door is shut; for he says, John x. 9, "I am the door: by me if any man enter in, he shall be saved," &c.

Do not say, I am not elected, and do not belong to his commission; for neither you, nor all the devils in hell, can say you do not belong to the election of grace. Come to him by faith, and get his seal, and then you may read your name in the Lamb's book of life.

Do not say, His bowels are shut up against me, I have sitten his call so often; for he says, Jer. iii. 1, "Thou hast played the harlot with many lovers; yet return again to me, saith the Lord." Ver. 22, "Return, ye backsliding children," &c.

Do not say, I want power; for "he gives power to the faint, and increases strength to them that have no might."

Do not say, He is angry with me; for that moment you come to him, his anger turneth away, and he says to the soul that comes, "Thou art my dear son, my pleasant child," like the father of the prodigal, Luke xv. It is the delight of his soul, to see a prodigal coming home to him.

Direct. 1. Be convinced, that by nature you have the seal of hell upon you, and that you belong to the devil: study to know and be convinced that God is angry with you every day, that you are condemned already, dead in sins, upon the very borders of eternal wo and misery.

2. Be convinced and persuaded that Christ is "a Saviour, and a great one, mighty to save," Psal. lxxxix. 19; Is. lxiii. 1.

3. Be persuaded that you have a title to him, to employ him as your Saviour: a right by his wearing the human nature: a right to him by office; a Saviour is for a lost sinner, a Mediator to make peace, a Redeemer to set captives at liberty, a Prophet to

teach the ignorant, a Priest ordained for men: a right by the command of God, by his own invitation, and the free grant and gift of him to sinners in the gospel.

4. In the persuasion of all this, cast thy perishing soul into his arms, lie down at his door, and say, If I perish, I shall perish here, where never one perished.

5. In a dependence on the divine power, and in obedience to the divine command, 1 John iii. 23, mint at believing, and be persuaded upon his own faithful promise, that through his grace, ye shall be saved as well as others.

Use *sixth* shall be in a word to God's sealed ones, that have come to him in a way of believing. And all I shall say to you, shall be in a few advices, in order to your being established, and preserved from any hurt or danger, by the pernicious winds that blow in our day.

1. then. As you have come to Christ the Angel that hath the seal of the living God, so study to be always renewing your acts of faith upon him, that he may renew and brighten his own seal upon your souls: 1 Pet. ii. 4, 5, "To whom coming, as unto a living stone,—ye also as lively stones, are built up a spiritual house," &c. Let the life you live, be by faith on the Son of God; for "by faith ye stand. He that trusteth in the Lord shall be as Mount Zion, which cannot be removed, but abideth for ever."

2. Cry that the wind of heaven may awake, and come and blow away the hurtful winds of hell: Cant. iv. ult., "Awake, O north-wind, and come, thou south, blow upon my garden, that the spices thereof may flow out." Ezek. xxxvii. 9, "Come from the four winds, O breath, and breathe upon these slain, that they may live." And then the dead and dry bones will stand up as a numerous army to fight the battles of the Lord. And learn to distinguish the winds that come from heaven, and those that come from another airth. And particularly remember, that every wind, however specious, that blows against the present truth or testimony, is a hurtful wind. A testimony is lifted up for the covenanted doctrine, discipline, worship, and government of the church of Christ, which the greatest enemies are not able to disprove, being so evidently founded on the word of God. Now, every wind that blows against the truth, though it appear like a heavenly wind, yet it must be rejected, as coming from a bad airth; Is. viii. 20, "To the law and to the testimony: if they speak not according to this word, it is because there is no light in them."

3. In order to your being preserved from all hurtful winds, hide the word of God in your hearts: Psal. cxix. 11, "Thy word have I hid in mine heart, that I might not sin against thee." It is said of the righteous man, "The law of his God is in his heart, none of his steps shall slide." And therefore, take heed to the sure word of prophecy, as unto a light shining in a dark place, for by it you shall be throughly furnished unto every good work, and secured against the wind of error, delusion, temptation, profanity, or apostacy from the truth.

4. Hold fast what you have received, that no man take your crown. Have you received Christ Jesus the Lord, and been determined to embrace him who is the unspeakable gift of God? hold fast the gripe you have gotten of him, as the spouse did, "I held him, and would not let him go." Have you received any of his love-tokens on this occasion? lay them up, and hold them fast, for Satan will do his best to spoil and rob you of them. Have you received the testimony of Jesus, and made a profession of your faith? then hold fast the profession of your faith without wavering, stedfast unto the end; be stedfast and immovable in your profession, particularly in your profession of the present truth, against which the main bensil of the present winds are levelled. If a thief or robber enter a house, and be carrying away any part of your furniture or goods, your present care is to preserve or recover that part of your furniture which is in greatest hazard of being lost. "God hath given Jacob for a spoil, and Israel to the robbers, even he against whom we have sinned." The house of God is in danger of being quite plundered, and spoiled, much of his valuable furniture is carried off; study then to recover what is lost, and hold fast what remains of the covenanted doctrine, worship, discipline, and government of the church of Christ in this land.

5. Keep a strict and watchful eye upon all the enemies of Christ, and of your own salvation. You have enemies both within and without doors. Take heed, in the first place, of an evil heart of unbelief, that it do not turn you away from the living God; for when you are turned away from God, you cast yourselves out of his protection, and then you are an easy prey to all your other enemies, and are fair to be driven away like chaff before the wind. "Watch and pray, that ye enter not into temptation." Be not ignorant of Satan's devices, and wiles, who casts himself into every shape in order to catch the prey, and who at this day is transforming himself into an angel of light, by counterfeit convictions, conversions, and raptures of joy, which (it is well known through the land) leave men and women just where they were, if not worse; because, imagining themselves to be in a state of grace, they are proof against all that can be said to the contrary, until God come and sweep away the refuge of lies.

6. *Lastly,* Take care what ministers you own and hear as the ambassadors of Christ. This is as necessary a caveat in our day, as it was in the days of the apostles, 1 John iv. 1, "Beloved, believe not every spirit, but try the spirits whether they are of God: because many false prophets are gone out into the world." And if you ask, How shall we try them? Christ answers the question, Matth. vii. 15, 16, "Beware of false prophets, which come to you in sheep's clothing, but inwardly they are ravening wolves. Ye shall know them by their fruits." But, say you, what are their fruits by which they may be known? *Answ.* Do you see any of them fishing up and down for worldly gain? do you see them strengthening the hands of those that are pulling down the carved

work of reformation, and weakening the hands of those that are minting to build it up? do you see them tormented by a testimony for the Lord's work in the land, and siding with these that are carrying on a course of backsliding? do you see them entering any other way than by the door of the house? depend upon it, they are not the true prophets of Christ, but inwardly they are ravening wolves. And therefore do not own them as the ambassadors of Christ; they do not carry Christ's commission; and therefore, though they shall say, "Lo, here is Christ, or lo, he is there," whatever pretensions they may make to the Spirit of Christ, yet go not after them, because these fruits are not the fruits of the faithful prophets of Christ's sending; and if he never sent them, they cannot profit their hearers, however, perhaps, they may have the art of touching the imagination, or raising passions unto strange and unaccountable effects.

CHRIST CONSIDERED AS THE NAIL FASTENED IN A SURE PLACE, BEARING ALL THE GLORY OF HIS FATHER'S HOUSE.

A Sermon, preached at Stirling, December 28, 1743, immediately before the Renovation of our solemn Covenants, by the Ministers of the Associate Presbytery. And some other Sermons preached afterwards upon the same subject.

Psal. xx. 5, "In the name of our God we will set up our banners."

PREFACE.

MY friends, we are met together this day about a very great and weighty work, namely, renewing of our solemn covenant-engagements to the Lord, which, for a great many years back, have been lying buried in oblivion, by the generality of the inhabitants of the land. Many grave-stones have been cast upon them, since they were last renewed by authority, both civil and ecclesiastical. Their obligation was rescinded by act of the Scots parliament: they were ignominiously burnt at Edinburgh, by the hand of the public executioner; many have suffered upon scaffolds and gibbets, in the fields and cities, for asserting the obligation of these covenants, under some reigns before the Revolution; and, since that period, they have lain much neglected, yea, measures gone into, both by church and state, inconsistent with a covenanted reformation. However, we, the ministers of the Associate Presbytery, are this day met together, in order, through grace, to renew these solemn covenants, in a suitableness unto the circumstances wherein we stand in holy providence, and, in the Lord's strength, to essay the rolling away the stones from the grave, in which they have been so long buried, and to bring them forth again to the light. We that are ministers are only concerned in the work of this day, that we may, like the he-goats, lead the way to the Lord's flock, who, I hope, in due time shall follow.

There are two things which I judge somewhat remarkable, with respect to the work we have in view, namely, the time, and the place of it. 1*st*, As for the time, I judge it pretty remarkable, that this same time hundred years, the Solemn League for reformation was sworn by persons of all ranks through the three kingdoms of Scotland, England, and Ireland; and that, nothwithstanding of the strong efforts of hell and earth, since that time, to have them buried in utter silence, yet this day, God, in his adorable providence, is making these covenant-engagements with him to peep from under the ground. 2*dly*, I judge the place of their begun resurrection somewhat remarkable, namely, in the town of Stirling, where that faithful witness, Mr James Guthrie, minister of the place, was stoned, and otherwise maltreated and abused, by a malignant party, for his faithful adherence unto the covenanted reformation, and who also suffered martyrdom in the same cause, in the Grassmarket of Edinburgh. And although we be shut out of the legal synagogue of the place, have not access to speak in the pulpit of that eminent light of our Israel, yet, it is worthy of our observation, that God has, in his holy providence, brought a place of worship out of the old quarry, where we may worship him, even in Stirling, and set about the renovation of our solemn covenant-allegiance unto the exalted King of Zion.

Perhaps some may say, as in Neh. iv., "What will these feeble associates do? will they make an end in a day? will they revive the stones out of the heaps of the rubbish, which are burnt?" I answer, It is all one with God to work by many or by few; by the weak things of the world, or by the great and mighty, who appeared for this cause at our reformation. I remember a scripture or two that has been comfortable to myself since the first beginning of the work that God has been employing us in for some time past. One you have, Mic. ii. 13, "The Breaker is come up before them; they have broken up, and have passed through the gate, and are gone out by it, and their King shall pass before them, and the Lord on the head of them." The other is, Matth. xxviii. ult., being Christ's parting word of promise to his disciples immediately before he ascended up on high, "Lo, I am with you alway even unto the end of the world." In the faith of his faithful word of promise, though our hands be weak and few, we are to set forward in this great work. The apostles were but twelve poor fishermen, sent out to build the kingdom of Christ, and to encounter hell and earth, principalities and powers, and the rulers of the darkness of this world; and yet, the Breaker going up before them, the Jewish economy is unhinged, the idolatries of the Gentile nations fallen down, and the power of the Roman empire is made to stoop to the obedience of Christ, the Prince of the kings of the earth. And what do we know, but the Lord may so far countenance the little mint we are making to own the royal authority of Zion's King this day, as to determine all the inhabitants of Britain and Ireland, in his own time to do the same, and again, like Ethiopia, to stretch out their hands to God, and to return to him, from whom they have so far departed. His blessing upon this essay will do it effectually; for "his hand is not shortened, that he cannot save; neither his ear heavy, that he cannot hear."

Is. xxii. 24, "And they shall hang upon him all the glory of his Father's house, the offspring and the issue, all vessels of small quantity: from the vessels of cups, even to all the vessels of flagons."

THE FIRST SERMON ON THIS TEXT.

IN this chapter, from ver. 20, we have an illustrious prophecy of the kingdom and government of the glorious Messiah, under the type of Eliakim's preferment and promotion in the kingdom and government of Judah, as appears by comparing ver. 22 with Rev. iii. 7, where Christ applies this passage to himself. More particularly we have,

1. Eliakim's call unto his honourable employment, whereby is represented Christ's call unto his mediatory work and office: ver. 20, "And it shall come to pass in that day, that I will call my servant Eliakim the son of Hilkiah." Christ did not run unsent, like many in our day, who intrude themselves into the office of the ministry, Is. xlii. 6; Heb. v. 4, 5, he did not take the honour unto himself, but was called of God, as was Aaron.

2. We have the badges of honour bestowed upon him in consequence of his call: ver. 21, 22, "And I will clothe him with thy robe, and strengthen him with thy girdle, and I will commit thy government into his hand, and he shall be a father to the inhabitants of Jerusalem, and to the house of Judah. And the key of the house of David will I lay upon his shoulder: so he shall open, and none shall shut, and he shall shut, and none shall open." (1.) He is clothed with a royal robe. So Christ is clothed, Rev. i., with a garment down to the foot, that serves to cover and adorn himself and all his members; and his robe is so odoriferous, with the holy anointing oil of the Holy Ghost, that they perfume the ivory palaces, Psal. xlv. 8. (2.) He is strengthened with a girdle, a girdle of truth and faithfulness; he is always ready girded for the execution of his work. (3.) He hath the keys of the house committed to him, and the sole government; he opens, and none shuts, &c., the keys of the heart, and the keys of hell and death are in his hand.

3. We have his confirmation in his honourable office and station; he is "fastened as a nail in a sure place;" ver. 23, "And I will fasten him as a nail in a sure place," &c. Christ is nailed in his mediatory work and office by an eternal decree, Psal. ii. 6, and by

the oath of God, Psal. cx. 4; and all the powers of hell and earth shall never loose this nail. Many attempts have the powers of hell and earth made to loose this nail, but the gates of hell could never, and never shall accomplish their design.

4. We are here told to what advantage he should discharge his trust: "He shall be for a glorious throne to his Father's house." God manifested in the flesh, or God reconciling the world to himself in Christ, is the throne of grace to which we are called to come with boldness, that we may obtain mercy, and find grace to help in time of need: and this may well be called *a glorious throne*, because there is, in this dispensation of grace, the brightest display of the glory of God; the views of which made the angels, Is. vi., to cover their faces with their wings, and Luke ii., to tune their harps at his incarnation and birth, crying, "Glory to God in the highest." Christ is the ornament of his Father's house, the brightness of his glory, and the brightest crown that ever adorned the human nature. Heaven and earth has credit by him. Solomon tells us, Prov. xxvi. 6, that "he who sends a message by the hand of a fool, cutteth off the feet, and drinketh damage;" *i. e.*, he sullies his own character, ruins his business, and is a reproach to him that sent him. But Christ, the Sent of God, the great Apostle and High Priest of our profession, he managed the affair of redemption, in which he was employed, to such advantage, that all parties concerned in his embassy to this lower world, reap advantage and honour by him; he restores what he took not away, even glory to God, and salvation and happiness to lost mankind.

5. We have Christ's pre-eminence in God's family, and the dependence of all the domestics upon him: ver. 24, *And they shall hang upon him all the glory of his Father's house*, &c.

Where we have, 1*st*, The designation given unto the church of God; it is called, "The house of the God and Father of Christ." God has a higher and a lower house. His higher house is heaven, where is the residence of the church triumphant, Is. xiv. 2. His lower house is the church militant: 1 Tim. iii. 15, we read "of the house of God, which is the church of the living God." See IIeb. iii. Christ was sent and received gifts for men, that the Lord God might have a house wherein he might dwell with men, Psal. lxviii. 18.

2*dly*, We have the nature and quality of the house: it is *glorious*, there is *glory* in it: Is. iv. 5, where the prophet, speaking of the church of Christ under the New Testament, says, "The Lord will create upon every dwelling-place of Mount Zion, and upon her assemblies, a cloud and smoke by day, and the shining of a flaming fire by night: for upon all the glory shall be a defence." And Psal. lxxxvii. 3, "Glorious things are spoken of thee, O city of God." There is a visible glory in the church visible, of which we read, Rom. ix. 4. "To them belonged the adoption, and the glory. Some view of this glory and majesty made Balaam, when he saw the comely order of the tents of Israel and God's tent, or tabernacle, in the midst of them, to cry out, "How goodly are thy tents, O Jacob, and thy tabernacles, O Israel! The Lord his God is with him." There is such a divine majesty in the church of Christ, when her doctrine, discipline, worship, and government are ordered according to the pattern shewed in the mount, and so much of a divine lustre, as strikes beholders both with terror and admiration; for then it is that "she looks forth as the morning, fair as the moon, clear as the sun, and terrible as an army with banners," unto all the enemies of Christ; so was it in our own land, in our reforming period. And as there is a visible glory in the church visible, so there is an invisible glory in the church invisible. God communicates something of the divine glory and image unto every one of his children: "The King's daughter is all glorious within." Through justifying and sanctifying grace, they who had "lain among the pots," become like "the wings of a dove covered with silver, and her feathers with yellow gold."

3*dly*, We have the high and honourable station that Christ hath in his Father's house; he is the great Master-household, and the whole family is committed to him, and is said to "hang upon him as a nail fastened in a sure place." Of which more afterward.

4*thly*, We have the common consent of the whole family unto his management; *They shall hang upon him all the glory*, &c.; *i. e.*, the Father of the family, and the whole offspring of the house, concur amicably that he should have the sole management. God the Father cries, "He is mine elect in whom my soul delighteth; and I have laid help upon one that is mighty;" and all the family in a day of conversion, having the light of the knowledge of the glory of God in the face of Christ darted into their hearts, unanimously cry, every one, Approve, approve, approve!

5*thly*, We have some account of the furniture of the house committed to the management of the great New Testament Eliakim. (1.) The *glory*. (2.) The *offspring and issue*. (3.) The *vessels of small quantity, from vessels of cups, even to all the vessels of flagons*. By which we are to understand believers, for they are the children of God, and the seed of Christ by regeneration; and likewise called *vessels*, because they are the recipient subjects of divine grace, which is the wine, milk, and honey of the house. But of these things more afterward, if the Lord will.

The doctrine that offers from the words is this:

DOCT. "That as the church is the house of God, so Christ is the sole manager of it, and all its concerns hang upon him as upon a nail fastened in a sure place." *And they shall hang upon him all the glory*, &c.

In discoursing this doctrine, through divine assistance, I incline to observe the following method:

I. I would shew that the church is the house of God, and shew somewhat of its glory.

II. That Christ is the great manager of the house.

III. That he is fastened in the management like a nail in a sure place.

IV. Shew that all its concerns hang upon him, all the glory, all the offspring, and all the vessels of a lesser and greater quantity.

V. Why the management of the house is committed to him.

VI. Make some application and improvement of the whole.

I. The *first* thing in the method is, to *shew that the church is the house of God*.

This is clear from the whole current of scripture; I only quote two or three texts to this purpose. Is. ii. 2, 3, where there is a prophecy in the church of God in the days of the New Testament, "And it shall come to pass in the last days, that the mountain of the Lord's house shall be established in the top of the mountains, and shall be exalted above the hills; and all nations shall flow unto it. And many people shall go and say, Come ye, and let us go up to the house of the Lord, to the mountain of the house of the God of Jacob," &c. Heb. iii. 6, Christ is said to be "faithful as a Son over his own house; whose house are we, if we hold fast the confidence, and the rejoicing of the hope firm unto the end." Heb. x. 21, Christ is called "the high priest over the house of God." 1 Pet. ii. 5, Believers "are built up a spiritual house." Now, how fitly the church is called the house of God, will appear by the following particulars.

1. He is the founder of the house: Is. xiv. ult., "What shall one answer the messengers of the nation? God hath founded Zion." And like a wise builder, he doth not lay his foundation upon the sand, but upon the rock, against which the gates of hell shall never prevail. He hath founded the earth upon the seas, a fluctuating and unstable element; but when he builds a house, wherein he might dwell among men, he builds it upon a rock, and upon the holy mountain of the divine perfections as they are manifested in Christ. And as he lays the foundation, so he rears up the superstructure. It is God that doth build up Jerusalem; he it is that digs the stones out of nature's quarry, and joins them to the foundation that he hath laid in Zion.

2. He is the purchaser of the house; he hath bought it with an immense sum, not of silver and gold, but with the red gold of the blood of his eternal Son, Acts xx. 28; 1 Pet, i. 18, 19. All the vast sums expended in building the temple of Solomon were but a mere trifle in comparison of what was laid out in the purchase of the New Testament church.

3. Having purchased the house, it follows that he is the sole proprietor of it, and of everything in it or about it: "The Lord's portion is his people: Jacob is the lot of his inheritance." His treasure, his peculiar treasure, is kept here: Here he hath his jewels, his crown, and diadem : "Thou shalt be a crown of glory in the hand of the Lord, and a royal diadem in the hand of thy God." The house, I say, and all its valuable furniture, are his property.

4. It is fitly called his house, because here he hath his abode and

residence; he shews himself present in his church, both in a symbolical, gracious, and providential way: Psal. cxxxii. 13, 14, "The Lord hath chosen Zion: he hath desired it for his habitation. This is my rest for ever: here will I dwell, for I have desired it." Thus you see that the church is a house, "whose builder and maker is God."

And hence it naturally follows, as is here supposed, that it must be a very glorious structure. The plan of it was laid by Infinite Wisdom from all eternity: Prov. ix. 1, "Wisdom hath builded her house, she hath hewn out her seven pillars." There being a joint concurrence of all the Three Persons of the glorious Trinity, it must needs be a consummate piece of workmanship.

I give you at present a little glimpse of the glory of this house in a few particulars, because I may have occasion afterwards, if the Lord will, to insist on these at greater length, when I come to shew how all the glory hangs upon the Nail fastened in a sure place.

1. The foundation of the house is glorious; the stones are laid with *fair colours*, and its foundations with *sapphires*. When God is to lay the foundation of his church, he invites all the world to come and behold its glory: Is. xxviii. 16, "Thus saith the Lord God, Behold, I lay in Zion for a foundation, a stone, a tried stone, a precious corner-stone, a sure foundation." This foundation is none other than Christ, the brightness of the Father's glory, as the apostle Paul declares, 1 Cor. iii. 11, "Other foundation can no man lay, than that is laid, which is Jesus Christ." Such is the glory of the foundation, that it transmits a divine glory upon all the inhabitants, all the vessels of the house.

2. The form of the house is glorious, when moulded according to the pattern shewed in the mount of divine revelation. A house must needs have a form; to deny this is to make it like the primitive chaos, Gen. i. 2, "without form, and void." The Old Testament church had a certain form both of doctrine, worship, discipline, and government; much more must the New Testament church, considering that the whole Mosaic œconomy was but like a porch to lead the world in to the greater glory of the New Testament dispensation. This the apostle argues at length, 2 Cor. iii., from ver. 7 to the close. Of this form of the house the prophet Ezekiel speaks as a thing most sacred, chap. xliii. 10, 11, "Thou son of man, shew the house to the house of Israel, that they may be ashamed of their iniquities, and let them measure the pattern. And if they be ashamed of all that they have done, shew them the form of the house, and the fashion thereof, and the goings out thereof, and the comings in thereof, and all the forms thereof, and all the ordinances thereof, and all the forms thereof, and all the laws thereof: and write it in their sight, that they may keep the whole form thereof, and all the ordinances thereof, and do them." Where you see that the form and fashion of the church of the New Testament, among the Gentile nations, is reckoned by God such a sacred thing, and of so great importance, that the prophet, and

consequently all ministers of Christ, are commanded expressly to shew the form and fashion of it, from the pattern described in the mount of divine revelation; and not only so, but to write it in a book, that they may keep the whole form thereof, and all the ordinances thereof, and do them. I do not know if, in any nation under heaven, this precept has been more literally and expressly obeyed and fulfilled. The form of doctrine, and of sound words, is drawn out of the scriptures, in the Confession of Faith; the form of worship, in the directory for the public worship of God through the three kingdoms; the form of church government, the ordination of ministers, and books of discipline, all drawn out of the scriptures of truth, and written or printed in a book, and the whole land brought under the bond of a solemn covenant to observe and do accordingly; which covenant we that are ministers are about to renew this day. And seeing this is the case, what shall we think of the doctrine of Mr George Whitefield, who lately traversed up and down the land with so great applause and disseminated his latitudinarian principles, as if the church of Christ had no form of government established by Christ, and therefore non-essential, and a matter of indifference whether the church of Christ be of the Episcopal, Presbyterian, or Popish form, providing that people were acquainted with the essentials of Christianity, and were good men in the main? All this poisonous doctrine he hath propagated under the specious pretence of advancing a catholic love and communion among good men of all denominations. Who does not see this to be a battery raised against the covenanted form of doctrine, discipline, worship, and government of the church of Christ in the three kingdoms, and particularly the last, viz., the Presbyterian form of government? which yet is so clearly founded upon the word of God, that when the articles of government, and the scriptures that support them, were read to him (Mr Whitefield) by a company of ministers here present, he had not a mouth to object against any one of them. And yet how lamentable is it to see such a number of professed Presbyterian ministers, and others, blown away from their covenanted Presbyterian principles, into the latitudinarian and sectarian camp, by the breath of an English priest, whom they took into full church communion with them? No wonder though they were left to adopt that awful delusion that has followed upon his ministrations in this land, agreeable unto the threatening denounced against those who do not receive the truth in the love of it, 2 Thess. ii. 10–12. It is true, they who have been left to adopt his ministrations, and to partake of that delusive influence that has attended it, they cry it up as an excellent work of the Spirit of God; but some of us have not wanted opportunity to know the contrary, that instead of being a spirit of truth and love, it is a spirit of malignancy and enmity against the truth, and covenanted cause of God in this land, and that it inspires the convicts and subjects of it with an inveterate prejudice against those who bear up the testimony of Jesus, and do not strike sail unto the corrupt established church, and the course of defection she is carrying on in opposition to solemn covenants for reformation. The walls and ramparts of Presbyterian church-government have endured many a blast of the wind of hell in this land, and no wonder, because it is founded upon a rock; and I make no doubt but it shall stand this effort of the gates of hell also. The form of the house of God, I say, is glorious, as is the form of every work of his hand. And therefore let us still "walk about Zion, and go round about her, and mark her towers and bulwarks, that we may tell it," in a way of testimony and solemn covenanting, "unto the generations following; for this God," who has set up the towers and walls of his church among us, "is our God in covenant for ever and ever, and he will be our guide even unto death," Psal. xlviii. at the close.

3. The door or entry of the house is glorious. And if you ask, What is the door of the church visible or invisible? I answer, Christ answers the question, John x. 9, "I am the door: by me if any man enter in, he shall be saved, and shall go in and out, and find pasture." This is the gate of God, by it the just shall enter in; and by it the sinner may enter in, and become just: no sooner doth he enter this door by faith, but he is clothed with the garment of salvation, and covered with the best robe of the imputed righteousness of Christ; yea, becomes the righteousness of God in him, he being "the end of the law for righteousness unto every one that believeth."

4. The pillars of the house are glorious: Prov. ix. 1, "Wisdom hath builded her house, she hath hewn out her seven pillars." These pillars are the perfections of the divine nature, as they are displayed and manifested in Christ, his wisdom, power, holiness, justice, mercy, love, and faithfulness; all which do, with a pleasant harmony, combine to support the fabric of the house of mercy, which God has said shall be built up for ever.

5. The ordinances of the house are glorious; there Christ and his family do meet, and have fellowship one with another. David, Psal. lxxxiv., cries out, "How amiable are thy tabernacles, O Lord of hosts! One day in thy courts is better than a thousand: I had rather be a door-keeper in thy house, than dwell in the tents of sin." And when he was, through the fury of Saul, and other persecuting enemies, driven to the wilderness of Judea, and so deprived of access to those galleries of the King of glory, where he used to enjoy communion with him, how doth his heart and flesh cry out after the living God? Psal. lxiii., and Psal. xlii. And they that have David's experience of fellowship with God in his ordinances, will be ready to say with him, "I love the habitation of thy house, and the place where thine honour dwelleth."

Not to multiply particulars, all the offspring of the house are glorious: "The King's daughter is all glorious within; her clothing is of wrought gold." The servants of the house are glorious in the eye of the church: "How beautiful upon the mountains are the feet of them that preach the gospel of peace!"

Thus I have given you a short hint concerning this house and its glory; neither time nor strength will allow me to go on to the other particulars proposed in the prosecution of the doctrine, and therefore must refer them till God shall give another occasion; and because the great work of the day is before us, therefore I shut up at present with two or three inferences from the text and doctrine.

1. See hence what happy and privileged persons believers are, who are the offspring and issue of this family, being born of God, and having a name and a place in his house, even an everlasting name which shall never be cut off. "O," says David, "Blessed are they that dwell in thy house, for they are still praising thee. Happy art thou, O Israel: who is like unto thee, O people saved by the Lord!" Only let it be remembered, there is a great difference between a free-born son, and a servant in the house, who is working for his lawful wages; for the son abideth in the house for ever, but the servant at term-day is turned to the door. There is a difference between a coming into the house for a while, and a being planted there by regeneration; for " they that are planted in the house of the Lord, shall flourish in the courts of our God," &c. They are the trees of righteousness, the planting of the Lord, in whom he will be glorified.

2. See what a dangerous risk they run who do injury to this house; instead of building the house of God, do their utmost to pull it down, and raze it to the foundation. There are a generation of men in our day, who turn the house of Christ's Father into a den of thieves, who plunder the house of its valuable furniture, and spoil the offspring and issue of the house of their valuable privileges. They call themselves the servants of the house, and yet, contrary to the laws of the house, they beat and cast out their fellow-servants, for no other cause but for contending and witnessing against them in giving away the rights of the church, and of the Lord's little ones, unto the world's great ones, particularly in the important affair of electing ministers, that are to have the charge of souls. In a word, truth falleth in the streets, equity cannot enter, error in doctrine is patronised, the keys of discipline perverted; they go to, as with axes and hammers, to break down the carved work of reformation, which, by the authority and oath of God, we are bound to maintain, preserve, and defend. Well, but shall they always trample on the divine authority, and break God's covenant, and escape? No, they shall not, says God, Ezek. xvii. 18. Jerusalem will yet be a burdensome stone; and the head-stone of the corner, which they reject, will in the event fall heavy upon their heads, and grind them to powder, Zech. xii. 1–3; Psal. ii. 1–4; Dan. ii. 44, 45, &c.

3. If Christ be the sole manager of his Father's house, and doth all the glory of it hang upon him? then it ill becomes any crowned head to wear the jewel of supremacy in and over the church, which is the house of the living God, save he only whom God hath anointed King over his holy hill of Zion. The Pope, or Antichrist, pretended to this supremacy; and when King Henry VIII. of England renounced the Pope's jurisdiction, he took that jewel of the crown of Christ, and set it in his own crown, and got himself

proclaimed head in all causes, not only civil, but ecclesiastic, and the oath of supremacy imposed in consequence thereof upon the subjects of England, and there it stands to this day. This supremacy, at the restoration of King Charles, was extended to Scotland, and an absolute power granted to the king, to mould the church of Christ according to his pleasure. Upon which, contrary to the oath of God, lying upon himself and the whole land, the whole covenanted work of reformation from 1638, and the obligation of our solemn covenants for reformation, were rescinded by acts of parliament, some of which are not to this day abrogated. Our forefathers witnessed against these things, and many of them sealed their testimony with their blood. Their testimony, for Scotland's reformation and solemn covenants, has never been fairly adopted by the church of Scotland, since the deliverance God wrought for us at the Revolution; but, on the contrary, a conspiracy has been found among the prophets of our Israel, for burying that testimony, and our solemn covenants for reformation, in utter silence and oblivion. However, God, who takes the wise in their own craftiness, and turns the counsel of the froward headlong, has, in his overruling providence, raised up that testimony, and a judicatory upon the footing of the covenanted reformation, who are this day met together, on design to revive and renew our covenant-allegiance unto the exalted King of Zion, after the example of our worthy forefathers, and the precedents thereof which stand upon record in scripture, particularly, Deut. xxix. 10-16; Neh. ix. 38. But these things I cannot insist upon at present.

I shall only add another inference from the text, though I have not yet insisted on the doctrinal part from which it flows. Is it so, that all the glory of the house of God, the offspring, issue, and all the vessels of the house, hang upon Christ, *as upon a nail fastened in a sure place?* This serves to shew where the stress of our covenanting in a way of duty doth lie, namely, upon the great Manager: for without him, we can do nothing, and without faith in him and a single dependence upon him, it is impossible to please God; he is the strength of Israel, and the horn of salvation, upon whom all our engagements to duty must hang. And therefore let us set about this work with the eye of faith fixed upon him, as the glory of our strength, saying, with David, "We will go in the strength of the Lord God, making mention of his righteousness, even of his only." But neither time nor strength allows me to go farther at present. The Lord bless what has been said.

The author not having time or strength to overtake the main purposes of the text in his first discourse, and considering, that, through the divine blessing, his other discourses on that subject may be edifying to the body of Christ, he consented to their being transcribed also from his notes for the press.

Stirling, April 27, 1744. E. E.

Is. xxii. 24, "And they shall hang upon him all the glory of his Father's house, the offspring, and the issue, all vessels of small quantity: from the vessels of cups, even to all the vessels of flagons."

THE SECOND SERMON ON THIS TEXT.

HAVING discoursed the *first* general head in the prosecution of the doctrine, I proceed now to,

II. The *second* thing proposed, which was, to *shew, that as the church is the house of God, so Christ is constituted the great Manager of his Father's house, all the concerns of it are committed to his care.* There is nothing clearer than this from the scriptures of truth. Is. ix. 6, "Unto us a child is born, unto us a son is given, and the government shall be upon his shoulder." Mic. v. 2, "Out of Bethlehem shall he come forth unto me, that is to be ruler in Israel: whose goings forth have been from of old, from everlasting." But this will be farther cleared in the induction of the following particulars.

1. In the council of peace, from eternity, he was chosen to be the builder of the house. It was enacted at that council-table, from eternity, as in Zech. vi. 12, 13, "Behold, the man whose name is the BRANCH, he shall grow up out of his place, and he shall build the temple of the Lord, and bear the glory, and sit and rule upon his throne." As by him, who is the wisdom of God, and the power of God, he brought a beautiful world out of the barren womb of nothing; so by him he rears up a beautiful habitation for himself among men, out of the vilest of materials, which were good for nothing but to be faggots for the fire of hell.

2. As he is the builder, so he is the Father, and the everlasting Father of the family; Is. ix. 6, "His name shall be called, The everlasting Father." The first Adam was but a short-lived father unto his family; although he lived a long natural life, nine hundred and thirty years, yet he soon died as a covenant-head, and left his family like a company of fatherless orphans cast out to the open field, without any eye to pity them among men or angels. But when God, in his infinite love, is to take up a new family among the sons of men, he provides also a new Father, an everlasting Father, for them. God had promised to his beloved Son a seed to serve him, Psal. xxii., and that he should see his seed: and that they might never more be orphans again, he constitutes his own Son, the Son of his love, God blessed for ever, to be their everlasting Father, and through him the Father of Christ becomes their Father also.

3. He is the great Oracle and Counsellor of the house; Is. ix. 6, "His name shall be called the wonderful Counsellor." And O what happiness is it to the offspring and issue, that they have such a Counsellor to go to in all their perplexing cases, who hath all the treasures of wisdom and knowledge hid in him, and therefore can never give the counsel that causeth to err! There is no searching

out of his understanding; he was never bemisted, or nonplussed, with difficult cases; yea, he is, both by office and promise, engaged to lead the blind in the way they know not, to make darkness light before them, and crooked things straight. The faith of this made David sing, Ps. lxxiii. 24, "Thou wilt guide me by thy counsel, and afterward thou shalt bring me to thy glory."

4. He is the great Priest over the house, Heb. x. 21. As the high priest under the law was over the temple, so Christ is the great High Priest over the house of God, and as such he is entered within the vail of the visible heavens, to appear in the presence of God for us, to represent our persons, and to offer up the prayers of the church with the much incense of his intercession.

5. He is the great Lord-treasurer of the house; yea, he himself is the treasury of the house; for "it hath pleased the Father, that in him should all fulness dwell, that out of his fulness we all might receive grace for grace." As all the stores of Egypt were in the hand of Joseph, so all the stores of grace are in the hand of our Jesus. The whole blessings and gifts of the covenant of grace lie ready in his hand for the use of the offspring; and whenever the children or servants of the house want furniture, either for work or warfare, they have no more ado but to come unto him for it, and whoever comes unto him, he will in no wise cast out. For,

6. He is the great Lord-steward or Dispenser of the house; it is he that gives the offspring and issue their food in due season; there is not a crumb of the children's bread but passes through his hand, and his very hand perfumes the food to the true-born children of the family, for his fingers drop sweet-smelling myrrh; and whenever they get a meal from him, their hearts are so cheered with it, that they are ready to sing, as Eph. i. 3, "Blessed be the God and Father of our Lord Jesus Christ, who hath blessed us with all spiritual blessings in Christ Jesus."

7. He is the Lawgiver of the house: Is. lv. 4. "I will give him for a commander to the people." Which may be understood not only in a military but forsenic sense, because all the laws of a God-Creator are issued to the offspring of the family through him; for " we are not without law to God, but we are under the law to Christ;" and as such, all the children of the house cry out with one consent, Is. xxxiii. 22, "The Lord is our judge, the Lord is our king, the Lord is our lawgiver," or, as it is in the Hebrew, " our statute-maker:" and this is it that makes the law to the believer a law of love, and a law of liberty; his yoke is easy, and his burden light; and his commandments are not grevious;" the love of Christ constrains them to obey, and run like the chariots of a willing people." So I say, he is the Lawgiver of the house, and we that are ministers are expressly ordered to "go and teach all nations, to observe and do whatsoever he has commanded us," Matth. xxviii. at the close. And therefore, whatever ministers or church officers teach or act in the house of God, that is inconsistent with his orders, they have him to reckon with. And what sort of a reckoning they will meet with, at the coming of the great

Master, see Luke xii. 45.-47, "But and if that servant say in his heart, My Lord delayeth his coming; and shall begin to beat the men servants, and maidens, and to eat and drink, and to be drunken: the lord of that servant will come when he looketh not for him, and at an hour when he is not aware, and will cut him in sunder, and will appoint him his portion with the unbelievers. And that servant, which knew his lord's will, and prepared not himself, neither did according to his will, shall be beaten with many stripes."

III. The *third* thing in the method was, to *shew that Christ is fixed, in the management of the house of God, as a nail in a sure place.* This will appear, if we consider,

1 That there is an irreversable decree passed in heaven for it, that he should be the sole manager and governor of the house: Ps. ii. 6. 7, "I will declare the decree: the Lord hath said unto me, Thou art mine only Son, this day have I begotten thee. I have set *or* anointed him King in my holy hill of Zion." And therefore they who go about to dethrone him, as head and King of Zion, or to invade his sovereignty, as some have done of late, they make but as vain an attempt, as one who with his hand attempts to remove mountains of brass; yea, these mountains of brass, I mean the divine purpose establishing Christ's government, will crush and grind them to powder in the issue, however light an account they make of it at present.

2. He is fixed in the administration of the house, with the solemnity of a covenant transaction: Ps. lxxxix. 3, "I have made a covenant with my chosen:—Thy throne shall be established for ever." In the council of peace, between the Father and the Son, it was concluded, agreed, and finally ended, that the Son of God should reign over the house of Jacob for ever: and, for further security, this is recorded in the volume of God's book.

3. With the solemnity of an oath taken by the great JEHOVAH. This is one of the immutable things wherein it is impossible for God to lie: Ps. lxxxix. 4, "Once have I sworn to build up thy throne, and perpetuate thy seed." And if God hath interposed his oath, all controversy should be at an end about Christ's supremacy in the house of God.

4. In his oath he pledges the brightest jewel of the crown of Heaven, the most dazzling perfection of his nature: "I have sworn by my holiness, I will not lie unto David," &c. He will as soon cease to be a holy God, as suffer his Son's authority in his house to be overturned.

5. He is fixed in the management by a solemn call and investiture: "I the Lord have called thee," Is. xlii. 6, Heb. v. 4. he was "called of God, as was Aaron." And as for his inauguration into his mediatory offices of Prophet, Priest, and King of his church, we read of it in the context: and Matth. iii. at the close, when the heavens were opened, a voice heard from the excellent glory, "This is my beloved Son, in whom I am well pleased;" and the

Spirit, at the same time, descending upon him in the likeness of a dove.

6. He is fixed in the government by an actual possession of the throne, he is set down at the right hand of the Majesty on high: Ps. cx. 1, "The Lord said unto my Lord, Sit thou at my right hand, until I make thine enemies thy footstool." See this actually fulfilled, Phil. ii. 9.-11, "Wherefore God also hath highly exalted him, and given him a name which is above every name: that at the name of Jesus every knee should bow, of things in heaven, and things in earth, and things under the earth; and that every tongue should confess, that Jesus Christ is Lord, to the praise and glory of his eternal Father."

7. He is fixed in the government of the church, by a complete victory over all his and his church's enemies, so that none of them are capable to give him the least disturbance. The head of the old serpent is bruised, sin, that first-born of the devil, is finished, and transgression ended, the world is overcome, death is unstinged, the curse of the broken law is abolished, torn, and disannulled, hell and death bound and cast into the lake that burneth with fire and brimstone.

Thus you see that our great Immanuel is fixed in the government of his Father's house, like a nail fastened in a sure place.

IV. The *fourth* thing in the method was, to *shew that the whole house, with all its appurtinances, hang or depend upon this blessed nail that is fastened in a sure place.* I shall confine myself to the text; and there we find three things mentioned, that are said to hang upon our blessed Eliakim. 1. *All the glory.* 2. *All the offspring and issue.* 3. *All the vessels of the house, from vessels of cups, to vessels of flagons.* A word to each of these.

First then, *All the glory* of the house hangs upon our Lord Jesus Christ. I gave already a hint to prove that the house is glorious; but now I would enlarge it a little, in order to let you see, that every glorious thing in the house of our God hangs upon the nail that he has fastened in a sure place; and you may take up this in the following particulars.

1. God's presence in a church is that which makes her glorious: Ps. l. 2, "Out of Zion, the perfection of beauty, God hath shined." Ps. lxxvi. 1. 2, "In Judah is God known: his name is great in Israel, in Salem, also is his tabernacle, and his dwelling-place in Zion." When God withdraws from a church, the ways of Zion do mourn, and a dismal *Ichabod* is to be read in every corner of her streets, "The glory is departed." Well, this glory hangs upon Christ, for it is owing to him that the tabernacle of God is with men. Unless God were in Christ reconciling the world to himself, if he had not been well pleased with his person, his mediation, and smelt a sweet savour in the sacrifice of his death, the Lord God had never taken up house again with men, no more than with the angels that fell. It is owing to Christ's appearing in the

presence of God for us in heaven, that God's delights are with the sons of men upon earth.

2. The revelation of the mind and will of God in the scriptures of truth, is the glory of the church, and as necessary for her as the light of the sun in the firmament is unto this lower world. This is "as a light shining in a dark place, to which we do well to take heed, until the day dawn, and the day-star arise in our hearts." This was the glory of the church of Israel, that God gave his statutes and testimonies unto them when he dealt not so with every nation. This makes the church a *Goshen*, a land of light, when the rest of the world are the dark places of the earth, full of the habitations of horrid cruelty. Now, this revelation hangs upon the nail fastened in a sure place; for Christ is the Alpha, and Christ is the Omega of the whole scriptures. He is the glorious Author of it: "The only begotten Son, who is in the bosom of the Father, he hath revealed him," John i. 18. It is only the Lion of the tribe of Judah that opens the book, and looses the seven seals thereof. He is the subject matter of the scriptures, for "to him bear all the prophets and apostles witness;" they are just the record of God concerning Christ; hence Christ declares, John v. 39, "These are they which testify of me." He is the end of the scriptures; they are pointed to him, as the needle in the compass points to the pole star; the very design and end of the Bible is, what the star in the heavens was to the wise men of the east, to shew them where Jesus the King of the Jews is to be found, John xx. 31. "These things are written, that ye might believe that Jesus is the Christ, the Son of God, and that believing ye might have life through his name."

3. A faithful ministry is the glory of a church; for where these are wanting, the house of God is turned into a den of thieves, and grievous wolves, that plunder the house instead of preserving or defending it. Faithful ministers are the watchmen, that give warning when the house is in danger by invading enemies; they are the stewards that dispense the bread of life unto the children of the family: they are the lights of the house, which are not to be under a bushel, but upon the candlesticks, that they may scatter the light through the house, for the benefit of the whole: hence they are called *the glory of Christ;* much more are they the glory of the church. Now this glory hangs on the nail fastened in a sure place, for it is he that gives the church pastors according to his heart, to feed his people with sound wisdom, Jer. iii 15, and Eph. iv. 11, 13, "When he ascended up on high, he gave some apostles, prophets, evangelists, pastors, and teachers, for the edifying of the body." They have their commission from him; for "no man taketh this honour unto himself, but he that is called of God, as was Aaron." They have their furniture for work and warfare from him, and he sends none a warfare upon their own charges; it is he that puts the treasure in earthen vessels. They have their success from him; he makes them able as well as successful ministers of the New Testament; he teaches them to be

fishers of men; and Paul himself may plant, and Appollos water, but he gives the increase. He it is who creates the fruit of the lips, and gives the tongue of the learned.

4. The ordinances of the gospel, dispensed in purity by faithful ministers of Christ, are the glory of a church. These are "the gates of Zion, which God loves more than all the dwellings of Jacob;" these are God's *tabernacles*, which David knew to be so *amiable*, that he envied the sparrows and swallows that had access there, while he was excluded from attending them, Ps. lxxxiv. 3, and xxvii. 4. It is in the ordinances of the gospel that the saints enjoy fellowship with God, and receive communications of his grace; hence compared to *pools* that afford water to the weary traveller, and *wells* out of which they draw water with joy, and *breasts* at which the babes of grace are suckled. Well, all the ordinances of the gospel hang upon the great Manager, such as word and sacrament, prayer and praise. The preaching of the word is of his appointment, Mark xvi. 15, "Go ye into all the world, and preach the gospel to every creature." Our authority to baptize is from him, Matth. xxviii. at the close, "Go teach all nations, baptizing them in the name of the Father, and of the Son, and of the Holy Ghost." The sacrament of the Lord's supper carries evidently his stamp, " What I have received of the Lord, that do I deliver unto you," 1 Cor. xi. 23, &c. And as they are of his institution, so it is he, by his own presence, and the influence of his Spirit in them, and with them, who gives them their success and sweetness. Through him it is that these ivory palaces smell of myrrh, aloes, and cassia, whereby he and his people are made glad. He fills the pools with water, by causing the rain to come down, even the former and latter rain of his quickening and comforting influences; and without him these ordinances are but as dry breasts, and miscarrying wombs.

5. The judicatories of a church, higher and lower, constitute in his name, and moulded according to his appointment, for the government and for the exercise of the keys of discipline; these I say, are the glory of a church, for these are "the thrones of judgment, the thrones of the house of David." When these courts, constituted in the name of the King of Zion, proceed in their management with an eye to the honour of Zion's King, and according to that complete system of laws that he has given in his word, then it is that a church "looks forth as the morning, fair as the moon, clear as the sun, and terrible as an army with banners," unto all ignorant, erroneous, or scandalous persons; and her very enemies are obliged to say of her, as Balaam said of Israel, "How goodly are thy tents, O Jacob!" &c. Now, all this glory hangs upon the nail fastened in a sure place, for he alone is King in Zion, the government is upon his shoulders. He it is that gives the keys of the kingdom of heaven unto his office-bearers, and promises that "what they bind on earth, shall be bound in heaven; and what they loose on earth, shall be loosed in heaven;" and where they assemble in courts for discipline, he "will be in the midst of them."

6. The covenants of a church are her glory; God's covenant of grace and promise, and their covenants of duty and gratitude, Rom. ix. 4, it is said of the Old Testament church "To them belonged the adoption, the glory, and the covenants." God's covenant of grace and promise is the glory of a church. It was the misery of the poor Gentiles under the Old Testament, before the coming of Christ, that they were "strangers to the covenants of promise." This is the church's charter for all her immunities and privileges, visible or invisible, for the life that now is, and that which is to come: and it is "an everlasting covenant, well ordered in all things and sure:" and him that takes hold of this covenant, "even him will God bring to his holy mountain, and make joyful in his house of prayer," Is. lvi. Now, this covenant hangs upon Christ, the nail fastened in a sure place; for God has "given him for a covenant unto the people;" it was made with him as a second Adam, and with his seed in him; he has fulfilled the condition of it, by the holiness of his nature, the obedience of his life, and the satisfaction made by his death; his fulfilling the commands and demands of the broken covenant of works, is the very condition of the covenant of grace, and by virtue of his doing so the cry comes out, Is. lv. 1, "Ho, every one that thirsteth, come ye to the waters; he that hath no money, let him come; come, buy wine and milk without money, and without price." The covenant, and all the blessings and promises of it, hang upon this blessed nail; they are all in him, and "in him yea and amen."

Again, our covenants for duty, obedience, and gratitude, they hang upon this blessed nail. These are the glory of a church and land, as they were unto the church of Israel. God avouched them to be his peculiar people, and they avouched him, by solemn covenant, to be their God; on which account they are called *Hephzibah*, and *Beulah;* a people *married* to the Lord. This was the glory of this land, and of the three nations, though perfidiously broken, burnt, and buried. Blessed be God there is some small degree of a resurrection of these solemn covenants, by what has been lately transacted in this place.

But now, I say, the glory of all our covenants, and engagements unto personal or public reformation and obedience, must needs hang upon this nail fastened in a sure place. When men engage to duty in a legal way, in the strength of their own covenants, vows, promises, and resolutions, without fastening faith's gripes upon the nail in a sure place, for righteousness and strength, they do only make to themselves ropes of sand, that will fall asunder as fast as they can make them. Christ only is "the strength of Israel;" all our funds of grace lie in him, "in whom it has pleased the Father that all fulness should dwell." And whatever duty we engage to should be in the strength of promised grace for assistance, and in the faith of his righteousness and intercession for acceptance: Is. xlv. 24, "Surely, shall one say, In the Lord have I righteousness and strength. I will go (says David) in the strength of the Lord God: I will make mention of thy righteousness, even of thine only." And it is in this way that his commandments are not grievous, his yoke easy, and his burden light.

7. The multitude of real converts is the glory of a church; for they are called "a crown of glory in the hand of the Lord, and a royal diadem in the hand of our God." It is spoken of as the glory of Zion, that "this man and that man was born there," for then "the Highest himself doth establish her;" and it is prophesied and foretold of the New Testament church, that "more should be the children of the desolate, than of the married woman; that a willing people shall be made in the day of his power;" and that these should be "like the drops of dew from the womb of the morning; that the city shall flourish like the grass" for multitude of converts. Well, this glory of the church hangs upon Christ; for it is by the rod of his power that this is effected and brought about; of his own will he begets us by the word of grace. And when he makes us fishers of men, and directs us when and where to let down the net, a multitude of fishes are enclosed; a seed is begot to serve him, which shall be counted to him for a generation, who shall declare his righteousness to a people who are not yet born?

8. The purity, holiness, and faithfulness of church members is the glory of a church, when that motto is written upon the conversation, walk, and talk of professors, "Holiness to the Lord." Well, this glory of the church hangs upon this blessed nail; for it is by virtue of their union with him, the living root and head of influences, that they derive sanctifying influence from him; for except we abide in him, and he in us, we cannot bring forth much fruit; yea, without him we can do nothing. "I am (says the Lord) like a green fir tree, from me is thy fruit found." Let men talk of their moral virtues as they have a mind, they will make never a saint, or a holy person, until he be lopt off from the first Adam, and his covenant of works, and be planted in Christ by regenerating grace: for "can a man gather grapes of thorns, or figs of thistles?" The tree must be made good, otherwise no good fruit can be expected. It is only they that are planted in the house of the Lord, by regenerating grace, that shall flourish in the courts of our God, and be called the trees of righteousness, the planting of the Lord, in whom he will be glorified.

Thus you see that the whole glory of the house of God hangs upon the nail fastened in a sure place.

I thought to have proceeded to inquire who are the offspring and issue of the house of God; and how they, and all that concerns them, do hang upon the nail fastened in a sure place. But this I must refer to another occasion.

Allow me only to deduce an inference or two from what has been said.

1. See hence that the church of Christ is the most dignified and honourable society in the world, that has so much of the divine glory in her. "Glorious things are spoken of thee, O city of God!" She has a glorious King in the midst of her, even "the holy One of Israel, the King of glory, the Lord of glory, the Prince of the

kings of the earth." She has glorious walls: "Salvation is appointed for walls and bulwarks," Is. xxvi. 1, Ps. xlviii. A glorious river to defend and refresh her: Is. xxxiii. 21. "The glorious Lord shall be unto her a place of broad rivers and streams," &c. A glorious trade and traffic: Phil. iii. 20, "Our conversation is in heaven," or, our traffic is with the land afar off. Glorious riches and treasures are in this house, even "the unsearchable riches of Christ;" glorious immunities and privileges, freedom from sin, the law, Satan, the world, death and hell; and all the true inhabitants have an interest in the city's stock, free access to the King's throne, and to all the blessings of the covenant.

2. See whence it is that God exercises such a care about his church, that he rides in the heavens for her help, and turns about the whole wheels of providence for her benefit. Why, his glory is there: Is. xlvi. 13. "I have placed salvation in Zion for Israel my glory."

3. See hence how much it is our concern to contend for the house of our God, against all those that would spoil her. Why, God's glory, and our glory, is in the house. And therefore let us plead with God, that glory may still dwell in our land, and that he may create upon our Zion, and her assemblies, a cloud by day, and the shining of a flaming fire by night; and that upon all the glory there may be a defence; and that he may yet recover the spoils of the house, that the uncircumcised Philistines have carried away.

4. See hence, that when a church departs from Christ, either in point of doctrine, worship, discipline, or government, she is off from her proper hinge, and therefore is fallen from her purity; her crown is fallen from her head, her glory is departed. The glory of that church is at a low pass, which hangs upon the nail of legal securities, by kings and parliaments, instead of the nail which God hath fastened in a sure place. This, alas! is the case with the church of Scotland at this day. What have the judicatories to support them, in their screening the erroneous, suspending, ejecting, and deposing men for bearing testimony to the truth? in tyranizing over the Lord's people, by wresting from them their Christian rights and liberties, and the like? The word of God cannot support them in such proceedings; they do not hang upon the nail in a sure place; no, such things stand in a flat contradiction unto the authority and will of the King of Zion. The only thing that supports and emboldens them in such proceedings, is the nail of a legal security and establishment, which one time or other will give way, and then all that hangs on it falls to the ground. As it is said of Eliakim, personally considered, or of Shebna his predecessor, upon his removal by death, or otherwise, from his high station in the court of Hezekiah, he and all his dependents should fall together, in the verse following the text, "And in that day, saith the Lord of hosts, shall the nail that is fastened in the sure place be removed, and be cut down and fall;

and the burden that was upon it shall be cut off:" Thus will it fare with churches that hang only on legal securities from men; Jer. xvii. 5, 6, " Cursed is the man that trusteth in man, and maketh flesh his arm, and whose heart departeth from the Lord," &c.

Is. xxii. 24.—"And they shall hang upon him all the glory of his Father's house, the offspring and the issue, all vessels of small quantity, from the vessels of cups, even to all the vessels of flagons.

THE THIRD SERMON ON THIS TEXT.

I AM yet insisting upon the *fourth* general head proposed in the prosecution of the doctrine, viz.— *What is it that hangs upon our blessed Eliakim, Jesus Christ?* And here we are told of three things that are said to hang upon this nail. 1. All the glory of his Father's house. 2. The whole offspring and issue. 3. All the vessels of the house, from the least to the greatest. And these two, namely, the offspring of the house, and the vessels, are a great part of its glory, also mentioned in the first part of the verse. I have already mentioned several glorious things in the house of our God, which do all hang upon the nail fastened in a sure place.

I proceed, *secondly*, to speak a little of *the offspring and issue* of the house, which are also said to hang upon Christ. By *the offspring and issue*, I understand all true believers, who are so called upon several accounts.

1. Because they are born or brought forth in the house: Ps. lxxxvii. 5, " Of Zion it shall be said, This man and that man was born in her." And ver. 6, " The Lord shall count when he writeth up the people, that this man was born there." The church is the mother that bear them; for " Jerusalem, which is from above, is the mother of us all," Gal. iv. 26.

2. Because the Father of the house or family begat them; James i. 18, " Of his own will begat he us by the word of truth. John i. 13, " Which were born, not of blood, nor of the will of the flesh, nor of the will of man, but of God;" hence commonly designed the children of God, being in a day of power begotten by the incorruptable seed of the word.

3. Because the first-born of the family, Jesus Christ, the only begotten of the Father by eternal generation, he owns them for his brethren, and is not ashamed to do so, saying to his Father, " I will declare thy name unto my brethren; in the midst of the congregation will I praise thee," Ps. xxii. 22, compared with Heb. ii. 12.

4. They are fitly called the offspring and issue of the house, because, like new-born babes, they are suckled and dandled there: 1 Pet. ii. 2. "As new-born babes drink in the sincere milk of the word, that ye may grow thereby." The ordinances of the gospel, particularly the preaching of the word, and administration of the sacraments, are, as it were, the breasts which the church, like an indulgent mother, draws out unto all the babes of the family: Is. lxvi. 11. "That ye may suck, and be satisfied with the breasts of her consolations:" and in the verse following, believers are said to be "borne upon her sides, and dandled upon her knees." What shall we think of that church that dandles the bastards, and neglects the true begotten of the family, and is more concerned to encourage and cherish the world's great ones, than Christ's little ones, and that yields the corrupt and unsound milk of error unto the children of the family, which has an evident tendency to poison instead of nourishing them? Surely she must be an adulterous mother, for the natural mother is more careful of the children.

5. They are called the offspring and issue of the house, because they have their education and nurture there: "All thy children shall be taught of the Lord:" and they are trained up in the knowledge of the mysteries of the kingdom. The Father of the family takes pains upon their instruction; and all that have heard and learned of the Father, come to the Son to be taught by his word and Spirit more and more: and thus they know the Lord, and follow on to know him; and his goings forth to them are prepared as the morning. Upon this, and other accounts, believers are called the offspring and issue of the house.

And now I come to let you see that the offspring and issue do all hang, with every thing that concern them, upon the New Testament Eliakim, who is fastened as a nail in a sure place.

1. Then, their very being, as they are new creatures, hangs upon him: Eph. ii. 10. "Ye are his workmanship, created in Christ Jesus." The expression is remarkable; they are "created in Christ Jesus." As the branch has its being in the root upon which it is grafted, so has the believer his spiritual being, as a new creature in Christ, insomuch that, if you take Christ from the believer, or the believer from Christ, he is not, his being ceases. A true Christian is a creature in Christ Jesus.

2. Hence it follows, that their life hangs upon Christ. The second Adam is called a *quickening spirit*, because he is the resurection and the life of his whole mystical body. The law of the Spirit of life, which is in Christ Jesus, makes them all free from the law of sin and death: and it is not so much they that live, as Christ that lives in them: hence the life that they live is "by faith in the Son of God." He it is that quickens them at first, when dead in trespasses and sins; and he it is that holds their souls in life; the fountain of life is not with them, but with him. The life of the believer is just bound up in the life of Jesus: "Because I live (says he) ye shall live also." Whenever the spiritual life of

the believer begins to languish, they run to him, and cry, "Wilt thou not revive us again, that we may rejoice in thee?"

3. Have the offspring and issue of the house any thing of the light of saving knowledge of God? Why, this hangs upon Christ; for he is their everlasting light, the true Sun of Righteousness, the day-spring from on high, that gives light to them that sat in darkness, and in the regions of the shadow of death: 2 Cor. iv. 6, "God who commanded the light to shine out of darkness, hath shined into our hearts, to give us the light of the knowledge of his glory, in the face of Jesus Christ." He it is that translates them from the power of darkness unto his marvellous light. It is in his light that they are made to see light; and through him it is that the path of the just is as the shining light, that shines more and more unto the perfect day. His absence makes night, and thence they go mourning without the sun; but by his return the shadows of death are turned into the morning.

4. The offspring and issue of the house of God enjoy a glorious liberty: Rom. viii. we read of "the glorious liberty of the sons of God." Well, this hangs upon Christ; for "if the Son makes us free, then are we free indeed; and, Gal. v. 1. we are enjoined to "stand fast in the liberty wherewith Christ hath made us free;" which has a respect both to our ecclesiastic liberty, as we are members of the visible church, and our spiritual liberty, as we are believers, or members of the church invisible. All sinners, that are out of Christ, are prisoners in chains, captives to the mighty, under the power of sin, under the curse of the law, led captive by Satan at his pleasure; but Christ comes in a day of power, and says, let the lawful captive be delivered, and the prey be let go from the terrible; and it is done. He says to the prisoner, go forth; it is the Lord that looses the prisoners, and gives liberty from the power of all their enemies, that they may serve him in holiness and righteousness all the days of their lives. In a word, he gives liberty, and he maintains it.

5. The offspring and the issue of the house have all the best robe put on them, when they return from a far country to their Father, I mean, a justifying and law-bidding righteousness, whereby they are enabled to stand before God with acceptance, so as the shame of their nakedness shall never appear. Well, by whom, or from whom, have they this? It is from Christ, who is "the end of the law for righteousness to every one that believeth. He was made sin for us, who knew no sin, that we might be made the righteousness of God in him." Our blessed Eliakim clothes all the children of the family with his own livery; through him it is that the righteousness of the law is fulfilled in them. Hence every one of the genuine children of the family will be ready to say, "Surely in him have I righteousness, and in his righteousness I am exalted; in him will I be justified, and in him alone will I glory." He it is that hath "clothed me with the garments of salvation, and covered me with the robe of his righteousness."

6. Have the offspring and issue of the house any thing of the

beauty of holiness within, or shining out in their way and walk before the world? Why, this they have from Christ, who is made of God unto them, not only righteousness, but *sanctification.* It is the beauty of the Lord their God that is upon them; he takes them from among the pots, and makes them like the wings of the dove covered with silver, and her feathers with yellow gold.

7. Have they any strength for work or warfare? Why, he is "the glory of their strength;" they are *strong,* not in themselves, but "in the Lord;" not in their own might, but "in the power of his might." He it is that makes the feeble, as David, and as the angel of God. He it is that teaches their hands to war, and their fingers to fight; by him the arms of their hands are made strong to do exploits, and to break through troops, and break bows of steel in pieces; through him it is they wax valiant in fight, and turn to flight the armies of the aliens: and when their faith in a lively way is acted upon him, they can speak like little omnipotents, with Paul, "I can do all things through Christ strengthening me."

8. Are they heirs of God and of glory? It is through him that they are so: "If children, then heirs; heirs of God, and joint heirs with Jesus Christ." By faith the believer serves himself heir to the God of Christ, as his God, and to the Father of Christ, as his Father; and upon Christ's title he adventures to take up the words of the Head, saying, with the confidence of faith, "Thou art my God, my Father, and the rock of my salvation. God is the portion of my cup, and of mine inheritance; thou maintainest my lot. The lines are fallen unto me in pleasant places, and I have a goodly heritage."

I might enlarge this head in a great many particulars. I only add, in so many words, whatever we can name in and about the believer, it all hangs upon Christ. Hast thou any faith, believer? Why, Christ is the author and finisher of it. Hast thou any spark of true love to God? It is Christ that kindled it; he it is that sheds abroad the love of God in our hearts by the Holy Ghost. Hast thou the lively hope of a glory to come? Why, he is our hope; and it is Christ in us that is the hope of glory. Hast thou any delight in the law, and in the ways of holiness? Well, he puts his Spirit in us, causing us to walk in his statutes. Hast thou any thing of that peace which passes all understanding? Well, Christ is our peace with God, for he made peace by the blood of his cross; and his blood, applied by faith, yields peace like a river; "Peace I leave with you, my peace I give unto you." Hast thou a joy that is unspeakable, and full of glory? Christ is the fountain of it; the river that makes glad the city of God, takes its rise from under the throne of God, and of the Lamb. Thus you see that the offspring and the issue, and every thing about them, hangs upon the blessed nail, &c.

Thirdly, But now I am come to a *third* thing in the text which hangs upon the nail fastened in a sure place, and that is the *vessels of the house, from vessels of cups to vessels of flagons.* Now, for clearing this clause of the text, I would, 1. Shew what we are to understand by the *vessels* of the house. 2. Shew that these vessels are of different sizes, some *vessels of cups*, other *vessels of flagons*. 3. Make it appear that they all *hang* upon Christ, and by what bonds they do so.

1. I would shew what we are to understand by the *vessels* of the house. I answer, by the *vessels* of the house we are to understand believers, who, under different considerations, are sometimes called the *house* itself, Heb. iii. 6.; sometimes the *seed* and *offspring* of the house, as here, and Ps. xxii. at the close; sometimes the *vessels* of the house, 2 Tim. ii. 20. 21. " But in a great house there are not only vessels of gold and of silver, but also of wood and of earth; and some to honour, and some to dishonour. If a man therefore purge himself from these, he shall be a vessel unto honour, sanctified and meet for the Master's use, and prepared unto every good work." I find several epithets or designations given in scripture unto believers, under the notion of *vessels*. Sometimes they are called *chosen vessels*, Acts ix. 15. says the Lord to Ananias concerning Paul, " He is a chosen vessel unto me." They were all chosen in Christ before the foundation of the world. Sometimes *vessels of mercy*, Rom. ix. 23. because it is not according to the work of righteousness that they have done, but according to his mercy, that he saves them. Sometimes " prepared vessels, fitted for the Master's use," 2 Tim. ii. 21. because he forms them for himself, to shew forth his praises. Sometimes " vessels of honour and glory," because he draws a greater revenue of honour and glory to himself from them, than from all the world beside. In a word, they are called *vessels*, because the milk, the wine, the honey, and the oil of divine grace, is bestowed and laid up in them; out of the fulness of Christ they are daily receiving grace for grace. And as the vessels of a house are its ornament, so are fruitful believers the ornament of the church, and of the great owner thereof, for he calls them his *crown* and *diadem*.

2. We are here told that these vessels are of different sizes; some are *vessels of cups*, others are *vessels of flagons;* plainly intimating, that in God's family there are saints of different stature; there are babes, young men, and fathers; for " unto every one is given grace according to the measure of the gift of Christ." Some are like the smoking flax, others like a flaming lamp; some like the bruised reed, others like the tall cedar of Lebanon.

And if you ask me, why God will have it so, that the vessels of the house shall be of different sizes? I answer, (1.) For the manifestation of his own sovereignty. He is the Lord of the house, and he will do all his pleasure; and it is the good will and pleasure of God to give more of his grace unto one, and to another less; " and who may say unto him, What dost thou?" He is no man's debtor, but may do with his own what he pleases. (2.) Because this is for the beauty and ornament of the house. It serves not a little to ornament and adorn a house, that there are different vessels in it, some more, and some less, for different services; the least vessel, like the least member in the natural body, has its proper usefulness in the body, so that the one cannot say to the other, " I have no need of thee." (3.) God will have it so, that there may be room for the edifying exercises of the fellowship of the saints. If every saint had the same degree of faith, love, knowledge, and other graces, the one could not be edified by the other; but it is otherwise ordered, that the strong may be useful to the weak in strengthening; and that those who have more knowledge and experience than others, may communicate of their gifts to the benefit and edifying others, until they all come to a perfect man, to the measure of the stature of the fulness of Christ. But I do not insist on this at present. I come,

3. To shew that all the vessels of different sizes, from vessels of cups to vessels of flagons, do *hang* upon the great Manager, Jesus Christ, as upon a nail fastened in a sure place. This is what is commonly called the mystical union between Christ and believers, and is in scripture set forth to us by a variety of metaphors: sometimes by the union that is between the branches of a tree and the root of it; for as all the branches hang upon the root, and receive their sap and nourishment, growth, and fruit from it, so doth every believer, whether of a higher or lower stature, receive life, grace, and growth from Christ, Hos. xiv. 8, " I am like a green fir-tree, from me is thy fruit found." John xv. 5, " I am the vine, ye are the branches: He that abideth in me, and I in him, the same bringeth forth much fruit: for without me ye can do nothing." Sometimes this union is represented by the union betwixt the building, and the foundation upon which it stands. As the whole building, and every stone of it, hangs and rests on the foundation, and receives their support and stability from it; so doth the whole house of God, and every spiritual stone thereof, hang upon Christ by faith of his operation, 1 Pet. ii. 4, 5, " To whom coming, as unto a living stone,—ye also as lively stones, are built up a spiritual house," &c. Sometimes this union is represented to us by the union betwixt head and members of the natural body, for which I refer you to two texts of scripture, Eph. iv. 15, 16, Col. ii. 19, from which you see, that the whole body, and every particular member, greater or lesser, hangs upon Christ as by joints and bands. But here arises the main question to our present purpose.

Quest. What are these bands by which all believers, from the least to the greatest, hang upon Christ?

Answ. These bands are principally two. (1.) The Spirit. (2.) Faith of the Spirit's operation.

1st, I say, the Spirit is one, and the principal band whereby believers do hang upon Christ: 1 Cor. vi. 17, " He that is joined unto the Lord, is one spirit with him." By the Spirit the union is made up between Christ and his members, Eph. ii. 22. " We are built up an habitation of God through the Spirit;" yea, the Spirit himself is the band, 1 John iii. 24. " We know that he (viz. Christ) abideth in us, because of the Spirit that dwelleth in us." The Spirit of life that is in Christ Jesus, by the means of the word, in a day of conversion, enters into the soul, and quickens it; and in the very quickening by the Spirit, it becomes a member of Christ; and so for ever after it hangs upon him as a nail in a sure place.

2dly, Another band, by which they all hang upon the nail, is faith of the Spirit's operation Not a mere historical, temporary, partial, or legal faith; but a living, working, justifying, and sanctifying faith, which applies and appropriates Christ by the means of the word of grace and promise; such a faith as eats the flesh, and drinks the blood of Christ, and so lives in and upon him, according to that of the apostle, Gal. ii. 20, " I am crucified with Christ: Nevertheless I live: yet not I, but Christ that liveth in me: and the life I live is by faith on the Son of God." In a word, faith hangs all its everlasting concerns upon the nail fastened in a sure place, and there it stays and rests all its cares and concerns; and in this way the soul is kept in perfect peace, knowing that the nail being well fastened will not yield and give way. And thus you see how it is that all the glory, the whole offspring and issue, and all the vessels of the house, greater and lesser, hang upon our blessed Eliakim.

V. The *fifth* thing in the general method is, to *inquire into the reasons of the doctrine.* Why is Christ constituted sole Manager of his Father's house? why doth he hang the offspring and issue, and all the vessels, upon him, as upon a nail fastened in a sure place?

I shall not stay in answering this question, the reasons of it will naturally occur from what has been already said; only, therefore, in so many words, the management of the house, and of all its concerns, are committed unto Christ, because it was the good pleasure of God that it should be so. But though sovereignty is enough to satisfy us upon the head, yet there are some ways of Infinite Wisdom to be observed in this constitution of things in the church which is the house of the living God; as,

1. He only had ability for bearing such a weight; " I have laid help (saith the Lord), upon one that is mighty."

2. Because Christ voluntarily undertook it in the council of peace, saying, " Lo, I come: I delight to do thy will, O my God." Whereupon JEHOVAH, the Father, said and determined, " He shall build the temple, and bear all the glory."

3. Because hereby a new revenue of glory is brought in to the God and Father of our Lord Jesus Christ, even glory to God in the highest, higher glory than what comes in by creation and providence.

4. Because hereby all men are brought to honour the Son, as they honour the Father. " Every knee shall bow unto him, and every tongue shall confess, that he is the Lord, to the glory of God the Father."

5. Because this was for the safety and comfort of the saints and children of God. All their everlasting concerns hang upon him, that they may warble out that song through eternity, Rev. v. 12, 13, " Worthy is the Lamb that was slain, to receive power, and

riches, and wisdom, and strength, and honour, and glory, and blessing. And every creature which is in heaven, and on the earth, and under the earth, and such as are in the sea, and all that are in them, heard I, saying, Blessing, and honour, and glory, and power be unto him that sitteth upon the throne, and unto the Lamb, for ever and ever."

Is. xxii. 24.—"And they shall hang upon him all the glory of his Father's house, the offspring, and the issue, all vessels of small quantity: from the vessels of cups, even to all the vessels of flagons."

THE FOURTH SERMON ON THIS TEXT.

THE *sixth* thing is the *Application* of the doctrine.
 First, For *Information* and *Instruction.* I have deduced several inferences already, intermingled with the doctrinal part, and therefore I shall mention the fewer at present.

 1. See hence, why it is that the eyes of the Lord run to and fro, to shew himself strong on the behalf of his people in this world; why he rides in the heavens for their help, and makes all things work together for their good. There is good reason for it; they are the offspring and issue of his family; they are the gold and silver vessels of his house; and you know, if a man have power and ability, he will not suffer his offspring to be hurt, or his house to be plundered of its valuable furniture, which perhaps he has bought at a dear rate. Hence it is that he watches his house by day and night, lest any hurt it. All his saints are in the hand of the great Manager, and he defies hell and earth to pluck them out of his hand.

 2. See hence, what trust and credit our glorious Kinsman-Redeemer has with his Father. Why, you see how that he puts the whole family under his hand; he hangs the whole glory upon him, all the offspring and issue, and all the vessels, &c. He has made him to be head over all things to the church, which is his body. "All power in heaven and in earth is given unto me," says Christ. "The Father judgeth no man, but hath committed all judgment unto the Son." And seeing he has such trust and credit with his Father, what an indignity is done to the Father, and Son also, when a sinner, through unbelief, declares him to be unworthy of any credit, and says, practically, that the nail that God has fastened is loose, weak, or insufficient, and therefore will not venture the weight of his salvation or justification upon it, but will choose rather to hang upon some nails of his own fastening, such as the nail of an empty profession, the nail of God's general mercy,

the nail of legal duties and obedience, and the like, which are all but rusty, weak, or broken nails, that will give way, and ruin all that do depend upon them.

3. See hence what great ground and reason of the perseverance of the saints, and why they cannot fall totally or finally away from a state of grace; why, they hang upon the nail fastened in a sure place. The great Manager of his Father's family, he has them in his custody, and is to give an account of the offspring and issue, and every vessel of the house unto his Father, and he will make a good account of every one of them, and say to his Father, that intrusted him with them, "Of all that thou hast given me, I have lost none. Here am I, and the children which thou hast given me." If a believer can fall totally or finally away, it is either because the nail may break or be loosed, or because the bands, by which they hang upon the nail, may be broken or cut. But none of these can fall out. The nail, as you heard in the doctrinal part of this discourse, is fixed so, that heaven and earth will sooner be dissolved than that it should yield or give way in the least. And as for the bands, by which they hang upon the nail, they are so firm, strong, and well fastened, that the soul, when it has a view of its security in the light of the Lord, is able to give that charge of Paul's, Rom. viii. 35, 37, 38, 39, " Who shall separate us from the love of Christ? shall tribulation or distress, or persecution, or famine, or nakedness, or peril, or sword? Nay, in all these things we are more than conquerors, through him that loved us. For I am persuaded, that neither death, nor life, nor angels, nor principalities, nor powers, nor things present, nor things to come, nor heighth, nor depth, nor any other creature, shall be able to separate us from the love of God which is in Christ Jesus our Lord."

4. See the great difference between the state of a believer, now under a covenant of grace, and the state of Adam under a covenant of works. Adam, the first covenant-head and representative, though an innocent, yet was but a fallible creature, and being left unto the liberty of his own will, that nail gave way, and he and all his posterity, fell into a horrible pit of sin and misery, from which the whole creation could not recover them. But the case of the believer is not so, he hangs on a nail in a sure place, he stands on the foundation God has laid in Zion, against which the gates of hell shall never prevail. Many a pull and pluck has the devil and the world given at the vessels that hang upon this nail, and yet by all their power and policy, they were never able to carry off a cup, let be a flagon, that did hang upon the nail fastened in a sure place. To this purpose is that of Christ, John x. 28, 29, " None shall pluck them out of my hand: none shall pluck them out of my Father's hand."

5. See hence, that the saints have no cause of boasting or glorying in themselves, but only in Christ; for he is the nail in a sure place, upon whom all the glory, and all the offspring and issue do hang. "Where is boasting? It is excluded, By what law, of works? Nay; but by the law of faith." Now, the law of faith is,

to lay the whole weight of our salvation and justification upon Christ, to receive him, and to rest upon him alone for eternal life, and all the purtenances of it; to " receive out of his fulness, grace for grace." And therefore, " He that glorieth, let him glory in the Lord," saying, " The Lord is my strength and song, he also is become my salvation." When the believer finds pride of gifts or grace begin to stir in his heart, he should presently check it, by putting these, or the like questions, to himself, " What hast thou, O man, that thou hast not received? and if thou hast received it, why dost thou boast as though thou hadst not received it?" Let none of the branches that grow upon the true vine boast, as though they had their standing, strength, or righteousness in themselves. " If thou boast, remember that thou bearest not the root, but the root beareth thee," Rom. xi. 18. All hang upon the nail.

6. See hence a good reason for that solemn work and duty of covenanting, by stretching out the hand unto the Lord, as it is said of Ethiopia, Ps. lxviii. 31. This duty is warranted by scripture example, and scripture prophecy concerning the days of the New Testament, and the example of our worthy forefathers in the three kingdoms, and this land in a particular manner. As God the Father, by solemn oath, has constituted his own Son the great Manager of his house, hanging all the offspring and issue upon him; so it is highly reasonable that all the offspring and issue of the family should homologate his deed, by solemn oath and covenant, before the whole world, because this is for his declarative glory, upon whom all the glory hangs. It is requisite that we not only believe with the heart unto righteousness, but confess him with the mouth unto salvation, Rom. x. 10. And this is in a particular manner necessary in a day like this, when the prophets are become such fools, and the spiritual men so mad, as to derogate from the glory of the great Manager of his Father's house, both in his prophetical, priestly, and kingly offices, by tolerating the erroneous, foisting in moral virtue in the room of his everlasting righteousness; and by throwing up his alone headship, and enacting laws, and inflicting censures, inconsistent with his authority in his holy oracles: I say, what more just and reasonable, in such a case, than that all that love our Lord Jesus Christ, and regard his honour and glory, should, in the most solemn manner imaginable, declare their adherence to him in the presence of angels and men, saying with Joshua, " Whatever others do, we and our house will serve the Lord." There are a generation of men in our day, who set up only for a private, selfish kind of religion. If they believe with the heart, they think they have done enough. If they enjoy raptures and ecstasies of love to Christ, they are easy what come of Jerusalem, what come of the ark of God, or a covenanted reformation. Let error in doctrine, corruption in worship, tyranny in government, prevail as much as they will, it is all a matter; these are not the essentials; all is well with them if they have what they call the Spirit. But what sort of a spirit is that which

follows, cleaves to, and coalesces with abjured prelacy, a corrupt backsliding ministry, and judicatories that deny the obligation of solemn covenants, and at the same time inspire men with enmity against a testimony for a covenanted reformation, and all that own it? Surely such a spirit must be the spirit of the old serpent transforming himself into an angel of light; the old malignant spirit that persecuted our forefathers unto death, for cleaving to a covenanted reformation, although now indeed, it has put on the name and vizard of Presbyterian. They that boast of such a spirit, as if it were a spirit of conversion, they boast themselves in a thing of nought; yea, in a thing that is worse than nought, even of a spirit of strong delusion. A deceived heart, and a subtle devil, has turned them aside from the truth, that they " cannot deliver their souls, nor say, Is there not a lie in my right hand?

Use *second* of the doctrine may be by way of *Trial* and *Examination*. Is it so, that believers are the offspring and issue of the house of God? Then it concerns every one to try himself, whether he be of that blessed progeny. We read, Heb. xii. of bastards in the visible church, which cannot be reckoned among this number. They are indeed called the children of the kingdom; but they are such as do not inherit the kingdom of God, because they will be cast into utter darkness. And therefore it concerns us to see, whether or not we be the lawfully begotten children of Zion, the true offspring and issue of God's household and family. I remember, in the doctrinal part, I told you why they are called the offspring and issue; and now I would offer you two or three marks whereby they may be known.

1. All the offspring and issue of God's family, they have passed through the strait gate of regeneration, or the new birth; for, says Christ, " Except a man be born again, he cannot enter into the kingdom of God." But, say you, how may I know if I be a partaker of the new birth? I answer, The new birth brings a new state or standing with it. You have quit your standing upon the law bottom of works, and all foundations of sand, and taken up your only stand upon the foundation laid in Zion, which is Christ Jesus. The new birth brings a new heart along with it: Ezek. xxxvi. 26, " A new heart will I give them," &c. The new birth brings with it new principles of action, a principle of life, of faith and love; new motives and ends; self-love constrains the sinner, but the love of Christ, and the glory of God, constrains the true convert to duty. The new birth makes a man to affect the new covenant, even a covenant of rich grace and promise, " saying, this is all my salvation." The new birth makes a man to affect new laws. He was formerly under the law of sin and death; but now he delights in the law of the Lord, and approves of it, as holy, just, and good; he delights in the law of the Lord, after the inner man. The new birth brings a new language along with it; the man gets a new tongue; formerly he spoke the language of Ashdod, but now the language of Canaan. The new birth produceth new views, both of things temporal and eternal. So then,

try yourselves by these whether you be among the true offspring and issue of the house of God: for "he is not a Jew, who is one outwardly; neither is that circumcision, which is outward in the flesh: but he is a Jew, who is one inwardly; and circumcision is that of the heart, in the Spirit, and not in the letter, whose praise is not of men, but of God."

2. All the offspring and issue of the house have seen their Father's countenance; and they are always glad at the sight of it, like David, "Thou hast put more gladness in my heart by thy countenance, than they when their corn, wine, and oil did abound."

3. All the offspring of God's family, each one of them resembles the children of a king, because they bear a likeness unto their Father, and his first-born Son: "By beholding his glory, we are changed into the same image." And they hate themselves, because of their dissimilitude through remaining sin and indwelling corruption; saying, with Paul, Rom. vii. 24, "Wretched man that I am, who will deliver me from this body of sin and death!

4. All the offspring of God's family, they have great trust and faith to put in Christ the great Manager of the family: hence called *believers*, because they believe in, and believe on his name: John i. 12, "But as many as received him, to them gave he power to become the sons of God, even to them that believe on his name." The very name of Christ is so sweet to them, that it is like ointment poured forth; and if they had all the souls that ever sprang of Adam dwelling in their bodies, they could commit the keeping of them all to him.

5. All the offspring of the house are acquainted with the Manager's voice, the voice of his word, and the voice of his rod, "My sheep know my voice." When they hear his promising voice, they are filled with joy and peace in believing it. When they hear his commanding voice, they are ready to say, I will run the ways of thy commandments; only give grace to obey, and command what thou wilt. When they hear his threatening voice, they tremble at his word. When they hear his correcting voice, in worldly trials and crosses, they are ready to say with David, "I was dumb with silence, I opened not my mouth, because thou didst it."

6. All the offspring and issue of the family, they love to lisp out their Father's name, crying, *Abba, Father*, Rom. viii. It is true, through the prevalency of unbelief, and a sense of guilt and filth, they blush when they speak to him as a Father; but yet, now and then, as faith gets up its head, they will be ready to cry, as the church, Is. lxiii. 16, "Doubtless thou art our Father, though Abraham be ignorant of us, and Israel acknowledge us not: thou, O Lord, art our Father, our Redeemer, thy name is from everlasting."

7. If you be the true offspring of this family, your Father's presence will be your delight, and his absence, hiding, and frowns will be an intolerable affliction. Christ, the first-born of the family, he never complained so much of all his other troubles, as when

his Father looked down upon him, Ps. xxii. 1, " My God, my God, why hast thou forsaken me?" Just so is it with all the genuine offspring, as you see in David, Asaph, Heman, and others.

8. You will dearly love all that bear their Father's image, and the image of him who is the express image of the Father; and the more resemblance they have unto him, you will love them the better: 1 John iii. 14, " By this we know that we have passed from death unto life, because we love the brethren." You will esteem them, as David, the excellent ones of the earth; with them will be all your delight.

Lastly, All the offspring and issue of God's house, they have a zeal for the standing of their Father's house; they "love the habitation of his house, and the place where his honour dwells; and therefore will have something of the Spirit of the first-born, of whom it is said, " The zeal of thine house hath eaten me up." Is it possible that a true child of a family can be unconcerned, when he sees robberies committed on his house, or the house of his father turned into a den of thieves? Or will a true born child herden and associate himself with such, without opposing them, and witnessing against them? A true child of the family will be ready to say of such, as Jacob said of Simeon and Levi, " They are brethren in iniquity: O my soul, come not thou into their secret," &c. Thus I have given you some marks which have a relation to the first character given to believers in the text.

I come next to pursue a trial, with an eye toward the second character or designation of vessels of different sizes, vessels of cups, and vessels of flagons, all hanging upon the nail fastened in a sure place. In the church, which is the house of the living God, there are vessels of mercy and vessels of wrath, vessels of honour fitted for the Master's use, and vessels of wrath fitted for destruction.

Now, here some may readily put the question, How may I know if I be a vessel of mercy and honour? For clearing the way to the answering of this question, you will consider, that all the children of men sprung of Adam by natural generation, the elect of God as well as others, are, in the eye of the law, vessels of wrath fitted for destruction, through the pollution and guilt of original or actual sin. And until God come in a day of power, and dig the vessel of mercy from under the filth and rubbish of the fall of Adam, no man can make a difference betwixt the vessels of mercy, and of wrath, because this is among secret things that belong to the Lord.

But if the question be, How may a person know if he be yet a vessel of mercy fitted by regenerating and sanctifying grace for the Master's use? Hath God yet formed me for himself? Hath he taken me out of nature's quarry, out of the miry clay, and washed, and justified, and sanctified me in the name of the Lord Jesus, and by the Spirit of our God? Now, I say, if this be the question, I will give you a few marks of the vessels of mercy and honour.

1. Every vessel of mercy in the house of our God, (whether they be vessels of cups, or vessels of flagons), has seen himself to be a vessel of wrath by nature, condemned already, full of the vermin of sin and corruption, treasuring up to himself wrath against the day of wrath. Hence all God's Israel are ready to take up that melancholy song, "A Syrian ready to perish was I: At that time I was afar off, an alien to the commonwealth of Israel, a stranger to the covenant of promise, without God, without Christ, and without hope in the world." Hence,

2. All the vessels of mercy are taken up in admiring the rich and free mercy of God, in taking up the like of them from among the pots." "Not by the works of righteousness, but according to his mercy he saved us, by the washing of regeneration," &c. Oh, says Paul, "I was a blasphemer, a persecutor, an injurious person, but I obtained mercy. He took me (says David) out of the horrible pit, and miry clay, and set my feet upon a rock, and put a new song in my mouth, even praises unto our God."

3. All God's vessels of mercy have undergone the hammer of the law in a greater or lesser measure: "Is not my word as a hammer, saith the Lord, that breaketh the rock in pieces?" The law is a school-master, to lead us unto Christ. So much hammering by the law is necessary, and no more, as serves to beat the heart and hands of a sinner off from the broken nail of the law, in point of righteousness. "I through the law (says Paul), am dead to the law." So much of this hammer is needful, as to beat down the vain and towering imaginations of our own goodness, holiness, wisdom and righteousness; the Dagon of self, in all the shapes and forms of it, must be broken down for ever. The vessel of mercy shall never more say with the proud Pharisee, God, I thank thee, that I am not as other men;" or, with Laodicea, "I am rich, and increased with goods, and stand in need of nothing."

4. All the vessels of mercy are made heartily content to change their holding. All mankind have their holding either on the first or second Adam: they are either hanging by the broken nail of the covenant of works, or by the gospel-nail of the covenant of grace; they are either seeking life and righteousness by the works of the law, or by the grace of the gospel. Now, in a day of conversion, the sinner having his hands knocked off from his first holding, he by the hand of faith, which is God's gift, receives Christ, and takes hold of that covenant whereof he is head, saying, "In him will I be justified, and in him will I glory; for in him have I righteousness and strength; he is to me the end of the law for righteousness; for he was made sin for us, though he knew no sin, that we might be made the righteousness of God in him;" so Paul, Phil. iii. 8. 9.

5. All the vessels of mercy are melted in the fire of gospel grace and love, and made pliable to the will of God. The heart of stone is melted into a heart of flesh, Ezek. xxxvi. 26. The iron sinew of the obstinate will, through the heat of divine love, is made to give way, and yield unto the divine will, Ps. cx. 3.; the

language of every vessel of mercy, is " Lord what wilt thou have me to do?" The adamantine heart is dissolved into evangelical repentance, so that the man now looks on him whom he had pierced, and mourns, Zech. xii. 10.

6. All the vessels of the house are washed, and will be frequently washing themselves in the fountain of a Redeemer's blood, from sin and from uncleanness, Zech. xiii. 1. The vessels of the house, through remaining corruption, temptation, and frequent falls into the puddle of actual sin, gather dust, and become dim and unfit for the use and service of the great Father and Manager of the house; and therefore he will have them sprinkled with clean water; he will have their hearts sprinkled from an evil conscience, and their bodies washed with pure water: " Except I wash thee (says Christ to Peter), thou hast no part in me." And this washing is what they themselves cry for, especially when defiled with any fall: hence they cry, with David, Ps. li. 2, " Wash me throughly from mine iniquity, and cleanse me from my sin." And, ver. 7, " Purge me with hyssop, and I shall be clean: wash me, and I shall be whiter than snow."

7. All the vessels of the house, from the least to the greatest, have the name of the Father of the house, and of the Manager of the house, and of the house or city they pertain to, engraven upon them. It has been, and still is, the custom of great men, to have their names and arms graven on their gold and silver vessels; so is it in the house of our God. All the vessels of mercy have his name and motto engraven upon them: Rev. xiv. 1, " Lo, a Lamb stood on the Mount Sion, and with him an hundred forty and four thousand, having their Father's name written in their foreheads." They have the name of Christ, the great Manager of the house, written on them, particularly that name, Jer. xxiii. 6, " The Lord our righteousness;" and in this name of his do they rejoice all the day long, for in his righteousness are they exalted. And then, as we are told, Rev. iii. 12. the name of the new Jerusalem, which cometh down from God out of heaven, is engraven on them; for they prefer Jerusalem unto their chiefest joy. In a word, God's name, his glory, honour, and authority, his truth, his worship, his cause, and interest, the word of God, the testimony of Jesus, the prerogatives of his crown and kingdom, every true believer hath these, as it were, engraven on his heart, and will study to profess and maintain them before the world.

8. If you be the vessels of mercy and honour, the Master of the house will now and then be making use of you, by pouring the wine, the oil, the water, or milk of his grace and Spirit into you: " For out of his fulness do we all receive, and grace for grace." Every vessel of the house is anointed with the fresh oil of the Holy Ghost: " We have an unction from the holy One." And they that want this anointing of the Spirit, in one degree or another, the Manager of the house will not own them as his: " If any man have not the spirit of Christ, he is none of his." They will be

found among the foolish virgins, whose vessels had no oil, when the mid-night cry was heard, " Behold, the bridegroom cometh, go ye out to meet him." But, I say, all the vessels of mercy have a greater or smaller measure of the anointing of the Spirit; and every anointing of the Spirit, enlargeth the vessel to hold more, insomuch, that, through the frequent communications of the Spirit. a cup vessel at first becomes a large vessel, or a vessel of flagon, until it be ready to be transported from the lower to the upper storey of the house, where every vessel shall be filled brimful of God.

Quest. Some exercised soul may be ready to say, O how happy would I be, if I knew that I were but the least vessel in the house of God, hanging on the nail fastened in a sure place! but, alas! I am such a poor, worthless, useless creature, that I am afraid I am none of them.

Answ. It is the nature of all the vessels of mercy in the house of God, yea, of the great flagons, to esteem themselves worthless, and among the least, yea, less than the least of all the vessels of the house. Eph. iii. 8. says the great apostle Paul, " I am less than the least of all saints." And the lower that they sink in their own eyes, the higher do they rise in the esteem of the great Lord of the house, Is. lvii. 15. and the more of his grace and favour do they receive, for " he giveth grace unto the humble."

Object. 2. May another say, I am so broken and tossed with worldly trials, that I am ready to think I am none of the offspring or vessels of his house. *Answ.* " Many are the afflictions of the righteous, and through many tribulations we must enter into the kingdom." Christ himself suffered before he entered into his glory, and so have all the cloud of witnesses, Heb. xi. And therefore it is a false conclusion to think you do not belong to the Lord, because of multiplied roots of affliction: for "if we be without chastisement, whereof all are partakers, then are we bastards and not sons. Whom the Lord loveth, he chasteneth." God's gold and silver vessels go frequently into the furnace, and there is a *need be* for it, to purge away their dross; and therefore learn to say with Job, " When thou hast tried me, thou shalt bring me forth as gold."

Object. 3. I am such a vile polluted creature, that I cannot think am one of his offspring by regeneration, none of the vessels of honour, but rather a vessel of wrath, fitted for destruction. *Answ.* God will not cast away his gold and silver vessels, because of the dross and alloy of sin and corruption that is about them. A man will take up a vessel of his house, though it be lying in a dunghill. So here; David, Solomon, Peter, and many others of the saints, fell into the mire of sin, and yet the Lord took them from the dunghill, and made them like the wings of a dove. And therefore, seeing God will not cast off for ever, do not you cast off yourself.

Object. 4. I am so harassed with Satan and his fiery darts, that I am afraid I am none of God's children, none of his vessels; I am tempted to evils and abominations that I am afraid to name to any in the world. *Answ.* Christ himself was tempted in all things as we are, that he might be a merciful high priest, to sympathize with them that are tempted. Again, consider, for thy encouragement, that usually the devil gives the sorest pulls and pushes at the offspring of God's house, at the gold and silver vessels of his family: and if you did not belong to God, Satan would not pursue you so much. When Israel came out of Egypt, then Pharoah and his host pursued most vigorously. Again, "The God of peace shall bruise Satan under your feet shortly."

Object. 5. I am none of the offspring or vessels: for God is hiding, and carrying to me as an enemy, insomuch that the very remembrance of him is a terror to me. *Answ.* This is no unprecedented case among God's children. David, when he "remembered God, he was troubled;" Asaph cries, "Is his mercy clean gone?." Heman, Ps. lxxxviii. "While I suffer thy terrors, I am distracted." Yea, Christ, the first-born and beloved Son, is under such agony of soul, that he cries out "I am exceeding sorrowful, even unto death. It is hard to tell how far fatherly displeasure and chastisement may be carried; but this is an uncontroverted truth, that the foundation of God standeth sure, and God will never disinherit any of the offspring and issue, or cast away any of the vessels that hang, by a faith of his operation, upon the nail fastened in a sure place.

Use *third* may be of *Consolation* to the offspring and issue, and all the vessels of cups and flagons. This doctrine may yield comfort to you.

1. In case of public reelings and commotions in the world. The abounding sin of all ranks, and the present aspect of providence, gives just ground to fear, that some shaking judgment is not afar off, such as sword, famine, or pestilence, to avenge the quarrel of a broken covenant, a contemned gospel, and the blood of those whose souls are crying from under the altar. But whatever calamities may be a-coming, though the world should be unhinged, heaven and earth mingled, and nothing to be heard or seen but the confused noise of the warriors, and garments rolled in blood, yet verily it shall be well with the righteous; the great Manager of the house is given to be head over all things to the church, which is his body; and he, being at the helm, will take care that the least cup of his Father's house shall not be lost, though the mountains should be removed and cast into the midst of the sea, Is. xxvi. Ps. xlvi. at the beginning.

2. Here is comfort in case of personal afflictions. Sometimes the Lord sees fit to take the vessels of his house, and to cast them into a hot furnace, or to plunge them into the deep and bitter waters of Marah; deep may call unto deep, one wave making way for another: but here is comfort, the great Manager sits at the side of the furnace, to see that the dross be purged, but the vessel preserved. He treads upon the waves, and the wind and the seas obey him, and at length he will say, "Peace, be still;" and then there shall be a great calm, Ps. xlii. 7, 8, "All thy waves and

thy billows are gone over me. Yet the Lord will command his loving-kindness in the day-time, and in the night, his song shall be with me."

3. Here is comfort in case of rents, divisions, and manifold disorders in the visible church, as there is at this day: men beating there fellow-servants, and putting them out of the house, for their faithfulness to the Master of the house; their maltreating the offspring and issue of the family, misplacing the vessels, preferring the man with the gold ring, to the man that is rich in faith, and an heir of the kingdom; these, or the like evils, take place in the visible church, and have a melancholy appearance. But here is comfort, that the great Manager of the house is looking on; he permits and overrules all these confusions and disorders, for his own holy and wise ends, for the trial of faith and patience, and to shew his own skill in bringing order out of confusion: and when he has performed his whole work, in Mount Zion, and in Jerusalem, he will reign among his ancients gloriously.

4. Here is comfort to the Lord's remnant, when there are few or none of the rulers, nobles, or gentry of the land to own the cause of Christ, or to put to their hand to the rebuilding of the walls or gates of Jerusalem, lying in rubbish, as in the days of former reformation in this land. The great New Testament Zerubbabel can carry on his work, either with them or without them, even though great mountains be standing in the way; for it is "not by the might or power of man, but by my Spirit, saith the Lord of hosts, that the work is effected. The man whose name is the BRANCH, he shall come out of his place; he shall build the temple, and bear all the glory." This use might be enlarged in many particulars, wich I wave at present, that I may go on to a fourth use.

Is. xxii. 24.—"And they shall hang upon him all the glory of his Father's house, the offspring and the issue, all vessels of small quantity: from the vessels of cups, even to all the vessels of flagons."

THE FIFTH SERMON ON THIS TEXT.

THE *fourth* use, namely, of *Exhortation*. 1. To all in general. 2. To believers in particular.

First, I would offer a word of exhortation to all in general. Is Christ the great Manager of his Father's house, and has God the Father hung all the glory, all the offspring and issue, all the vessels greater and smaller upon him, as upon a nail fastened in a sure place? Then let every man and woman, that has a soul to be saved, come to him in a way of believing, and lay the stress of their eternal salvation upon the great Manager of the house. This is a business of everlasting concern, and therefore allow me to enforce the exhortation a little.

There is no help for you in heaven, or in earth; all other nails are weak, broken, or crooked, but this of God's fastening; and therefore to the bottom of eternal woe and misery you must go, unless you hang your salvation upon it. No name given under heaven whereby to be saved, but by the name of Jesus; neither is there salvation in any other; all refuge fails, and proves only a refuge of lies: "In vain is salvation expected from the hills, or multitude of mountains:" and therefore I may put that question to you in this case, "Whither will you flee for help? or where will you leave your glory," if you do not "commit the keeping of your souls unto him as unto a faithful Creator."

This Manager is a person of great skill and experience in the business of saving souls that are lost by the fall of Adam; it is his trade and business upon which he came into the world; no case is desperate to him, for he is able to save to the uttermost, and he has been occupied in the work of saving the lost, ever since sin entered into the world. Many, many have gone through his hands, and he has made a good account of every one of them; the innumerable company that are about the throne, singing the song of Moses and the Lamb, are all standing monuments of his skill and experience; every one of them cries, "Worthy is the Lamb that was slain: for thou hast redeemed us, and thou hast washed and saved us by thy blood."

The great Manager has not only skill, ability, and experience, but he is most willing to be employed. "To you, O men, doth he call, and his voice is to the sons of men. Come to me who will, I will in no wise cast out. Come, and let us reason together, saith the Lord: though your sins be as scarlet and crimson, I will make them white as snow and as wool." And to put the matter out of doubt, and beyond all controversy, he assures you of his willingness with the solemnity of an oath, Ezek. xxxiii. 11. "As I live, saith the Lord, I have no pleasure in the death of the wicked, but rather that they turn unto me, and live," &c. He is so willing and desirous of having the management of thy salvation committed to him, that it is the joy of his heart when a lost sinner comes to him for this end, as you see cleared in the three parables, Luke xv.

You are well warranted to hang your all upon this nail, for it was fixed in a sure place. For this very end he was set up from everlasting, from the beginning, to be the Saviour of lost sinners; he is ordained for men in things pertaining to God: and it is the command of God, that you believe in him to the saving of your souls, that you receive and rest upon him, 1 John iii. 23. And therefore you must either trust this great Manager with your salvation, otherwise you counteract the authority of Heaven in the greatest command that ever was issued out from the excellent glory.

Let nothing then scare you from coming to the great Manager by faith, or from hanging your justification, sanctification, and salvation, upon this nail fastened in a sure place. "Take heed, brethren, lest there be in any of you an evil heart of unbelief, in turning you away from the living God; and let us fear lest a promise of salvation being left us, any of us should seem to come short of it;" the consequence thereof will be fatal through all eternity.

Do not say, I am not prepared for coming to him; for I know of no preparation a sinner can make for Christ, but that of his seeing himself lost and undone without him. What preparation had the man-slayer, besides danger from the avenger of blood, when he fled to the city of refuge? What preparation has a drowning man to make for taking hold of a strong rope cast in to draw him ashore? Is not the sick man prepared for the physician? the man starving through want prepared for meat?

Do not say, that the fiery law, and its curse, stands in your way; for the law condemns you because you do not improve the remedy presented to you in the gospel. The thunders of the law are hushed into a pleasant calm, whenever the sinner comes unto mount Zion, and to Jesus the Mediator of the new covenant. Christ is "the end of the law for righteousness to every one that believeth; and therefore no condemnation to them that are in him."

Do not say, that the decree of God is any obstacle in your way of coming unto Christ, and hanging your eternal salvation upon him; for as the decree of God is secret, and does not belong to us, so, in the decrees of Heaven, the end and the mean are connected together, and the one made subservient unto the other. Does any man concern himself with God's decrees in the ordinary affairs of life? Does the merchant argue, if God has decreed that I shall be rich, it shall come to pass, though I never go to the market and buy and sell? Or doth the husbandman argue, I shall have a plentiful crop, if God has ordained it, although I neither plant nor sow? Men will not venture their worldly affairs upon such a foolish way of arguing; why then should any argue at that rate in matters wherein their precious souls are concerned, and lie at stake?

May some poor soul say, O, gladly would I come to the great Manager Christ, and hang my soul's eternal salvation upon him, as on a nail fastened in a sure place; but, alas! I find such an utter impotence and inability to believe in him, that all exhortations are in vain, until the power of God be put forth to enable me; "No man can come to Christ, unless the Father which sent him, draw him." *Answ.* (1.) The soul that is truly sensible of its own inability to believe, or do any thing for itself, is in the fairest way of believing; for faith springs out of a thorough conviction of its own impotence and inability, either to will or to do. And therefore, (2.) From a sense of your own impotence, look up to him that giveth power to the faint, and increaseth strength to them that have no might; for he who commands you to believe, is the Author and Finisher of faith, ready to fulfil in you all the good pleasure of his goodness, and the work of faith with power. (3.) I would say to you that are in good earnest in making this objection, and complaining of inability to believe, that the power of God is exerted in a very silent and imperceptible way in bringing the sinner to believe in Christ, therefore likened unto the falling of the dew, the growth of the corn, or a grain of mustard seed, or the gradual working of leaven in a measure of meal, which are best known by the effects; and therefore observe and see if you can perceive any of the effects of the Spirit of faith in or about you, such as, a prizing of the word and ordinances, a drinking the sincere milk of it, a valuing of Christ, a renouncing of our own, and a leaning only to a Surety's righteousness, heart-love to all that bear the image of God; these, or the like fruits of faith, may be sometimes found in the soul that is complaining of its own inability to believe; and if so, it is a hopeful evidence that the good work is begun, and so you may be "confident of this very thing, that he who hath begun the good work, will perform it against the day of Jesus Christ."

I shut up this exhortation with two or three advices, in order to your committing your all into the hand of the great Manager of the house of God.

1. Study to be in good earnest in the matter of believing; for it is with the heart that man believes unto righteousness. Faith is not a dreaming, sleeping work, as you see in the case of Peter's hearers, Acts ii. the jailor, Acts xvi.

2. Consider well the worth of the soul, and what danger it is into of being lost for ever. "What is a man profited, if he gain the whole world, and lose his soul?"

3. Be frequently viewing the majesty of that infinite God, with whom you must have to do for ever and ever, and what a fearful thing it is to fall into the hands of an implacable and eternal enemy. "Who knows the power of his wrath? Who can dwell with devouring fire?" &c.

4. Be convinced, that, by the breach of the holy law in Adam, your federal head, and also in your own persons, you are liable to the wrath and displeasure of God, yea, *condemned already.*

5. Be convinced of the utter insufficiency of all those nails that you have been formerly trusting to. Perhaps you have been trusting to the nail of a general mercy in God. But this will not hold; for God himself has declared, that he who "made *sinners,* will have no mercy on them; that he will by no means clear the guilty," without a satisfaction to his justice, and faith's improvement of that satisfaction set forth in the gospel-revelation. Perhaps you are leaning to the nail of gospel-church-privileges, or receiving the seal of the covenant in baptism, or the Lord's supper. But this nail will give way: "Unless you be baptized with the Holy Ghost, and eat the flesh, and drink the blood of the Son of man, you have no life in you." Perhaps you are leaning to the nail of a blazing profession. But, alas! this will fail you, as you see in the case of the foolish virgins, and those Matth. vii. 22. to whom Christ says, "Depart from me, I never knew you." Perhaps

you are leaning your weight upon the nail of some common attainments under the drop of the gospel, such as, a common knowledge, a common faith, a common reformation, a common zeal for the public cause of Christ, without an actual taking hold of God's covenant of grace and promise. All these will give way. That knowledge that does not humble and sanctify, that faith that is not accompanied with a humble sense of unbelief, that reformation of life that does not begin at the heart, that zeal that is not founded on knowledge, will never abide the trial. Perhaps you are laying your weight upon the law, or the works of it, either in part or in whole; your morality, civility, delight in duties, or your own good meanings and endeavours. But, alas! this nail will break also: for the law is weak through the flesh, and there is no law given, since the fall of Adam, that can give life, otherwise righteousness would come by the law. The Jews leaned to this nail, and went about to establish their own righteousness, as it were by the works of the law. But what came of it? The nail broke, and they fell under the condemnatory sentence of that law to which they leaned; and there they lie, and will lie till their eyes be opened. Now, I say, study and be fully persuaded of the utter insufficiency of all these, or other nails you are venturing your salvation upon. The hail shall sweep away all these refuges of lies.

6. Turn away your eyes from all these, and take a view of the strength, sufficiency, and excellency of the nail that God has fastened in a sure place. Study the excellency of Christ in his person as Immanuel, God man; the validity of his commission as the sent of God; the sufficiency of that righteousness he has brought in for justifying of the ungodly by his obedience unto the death; the stability and freedom of the covenant whereof he is Head, Surety, and Mediator; the prevalency of his intercession, by virtue of which he is able to save to the uttermost all that come to God by him: I say, be much in viewing and meditating upon these things.

7. With these join earnest and importunate prayers in the name of Christ, that he, who is Father of light. the Author of every good and perfect gift, may send forth his light and truth, that in his light you may see light; that it may be given you, by his word and Spirit, to know the mysteries of the kingdom of heaven, particularly that leading mystery of a God in our nature, "God manifested in the flesh, justified in the Spirit," &c. And while you are praying for these things, study to believe, and be confident toward him, that he will hear you, and that he doth hear you, because these things are agreeable to his will, Mark xi. 24. 1 John v. 14.

8. In obedience to the command of God, and in a dependence upon his power, make the mint at resting upon the nail fastened in a sure place: commit your eternal all into the hands of the great Manager of his Father's house, saying, "I believe, Lord, help thou mine unbelief:" I believe that through the grace of our Lord

Jesus Christ, I shall be saved, as well as others that have taken the same course: and thus he that believeth entereth into his rest. And in this way wait on the Lord; for " he that shall come will come, and he will not tarry."

I proceed now to offer a word of exhortation and advice to believers, who are here designed the *offspring* and *issue* of the house, and likewise the *vessels of cups* and *of flagons*. I shall offer a few advices unto you, suited unto these different characters given you in the text.

First, then, Considering you under the character of the *offspring* and the *issue* of God's family, I have the following advices to offer you.

1. Bless God that ever put you among the children, and gave you the pleasant portion and the goodly heritage. The question that is put, as to this matter, Jer. iii. 19, " How shall this be done ?" plainly implies, that there were such insuperable difficulties in the way of its accomplishment, as no created power was capable to remove. Although a general assembly of angels and archangels had been convened to answer this question, How shall these sinners of Adam's family, being heirs of hell and wrath, lawful captives to the god of this world, under sentence of eternal death; how shall they, in a consistence with the honour of the law, justice, and holiness of God, be put among the children, and become heirs of God, and be possessed of the inheritance that is incorruptible, undefiled, and that fadeth not away? they had been all put to an eternal stand, they behoved to own that it was a question too high for them to resolve. But behold the knotty and unanswerable question solved by Infinite Wisdom and Sovereignty, inspired with infinite grace and love, in the close of that verse, " And I said, thou shalt call me, My Father, and thou shalt not turn away from me." As if he had said, Although this question puts the whole creation to silence, yet I myself will answer it. My own beloved and eternal Son, having, in the council of peace, promised as a second Adam to satisfy justice, and to repair the honour of my law, by his obedience unto the death, I have determined to put them among the children, and by the power of my Spirit, they shall, upon the footing of the ransom I have found, cry, *Abba, Father*, unto me, and I will keep them by my power through faith unto salvation. O how should the consideration of all this grace and love, manifested in your adoption, fill your hearts with wonder, and your mouths with the highest praises of God, saying with the apostle, 1 John iii. 1, " Behold, what manner of love the Father hath bestowed upon us, that we should be called the sons of God! O what is man that thou art so mindful of him? or what is the son of man that thou shouldst be so kind unto him? Bless the Lord, O my soul, and all that is within me, bless his holy name," &c. O levy a tribute out of the whole creation, and invite all creatures in heaven and earth to concur with you in celebrating his praises, as David doth under a sense of redeeming love and grace, Ps. ciii. through the whole.

2. Let the whole offspring and issue of God's family be much employed in beholding and admiring the nail upon which they and all their privileges hang; for all the glory and offspring hang on Christ as the great Manager of his Father's house, as you heard in the doctrinal part. Believer, thou hast thy very being as a new creature in him; and all thy privileges, in time and through eternity, they have their conveyance to thee through him. Hence is that doxology of the offspring and issue of God's house, Eph. i. 3, "Blessed be the God and Father of our Lord Jesus Christ, who hath blessed us with all spiritual blessings in heavenly places in Christ Jesus." It is the will of the Father, that "all men should honour the Son, as they honour the Father; that every tongue should confess, that Jesus Christ is Lord, to the glory of God the Father." And therefore, I say, let every one behold and admire the glory of his person as Immanuel, the glory of his mediation; for through him it is that your relation to God, as your God and Father, doth come: John xx. 17, "I ascend unto my Father and your Father, and to my God and your God."

3. Let all the offspring and issue of the family give a firm credit to their Father's word, set to their seal unto this word of promise, and believe the record of God concerning the great Manager and Priest over the house of God. It were a thing criminal among men, and an iniquity to be punished by the judge, for a child to say to the father that begat him, Thou art a liar. But is it not much more criminal for the offspring of God by regeneration, to say so to him that begat them by the word of truth? And yet this is the way that God is treated by his own children, under their fits of unbelief, despondency, and discontent; for "he that believeth not, hath made God a liar." Alas! how often do we contradict our everlasting Father to his face, by saying either with the heart or tongue, "His promise fails for evermore; he hath forgotten to be gracious; his mercy is clean gone?" Is not this flatly opposite to what he hath declared in his word, that "his mercy is from everlasting to everlasting; that his grace never faileth; that he is ever mindful of his covenant; his promise he will not break?" O beware of the sin of unbelief, for it is a reproaching and contradicting your Father, "Why sayest thou so, O Jacob? Why speakest thou so, O Israel? Is he not thy Father, that begat thee? Beware of him, and provoke him not; for he will visit these thine iniquities with the rod, and thy transgressions with stripes." Well then, credit your Father's word, for faithfulness is the girdle of his loins, and truth the girdle of his reins. Man may lie, and the son of man may repent, but it is impossible for God to lie. Imitate Abraham, the father of the faithful, who, "staggered not at the promise through unbelief, but was strong in faith, giving glory to God."

4. Let all the offspring and issue of the family trust the blessed Manager, and rest upon him in all cases with assured confidence. Hath God the Father intrusted him with all the glory, all the offspring, and all the vessels of his house; and shall not all the

members of the family, particularly his own offspring and issue, trust him also with every thing that concerns them in time and through eternity? This being the leading duty called for from the text and doctrine, allow me to enforce it with some few motives, and then to illustrate it by answering a question or two.

First, I would enforce the duty with a few weighty considerations. Consider, then, in the first place, that as God the Father reposes a full trust and confidence in him, and has hung upon him all the glory of his house, so he calls and commands all mankind, particularly the children of the family, to do the like, and to write after his example, "This is my beloved Son, in whom I am well pleased; hear ye him." He hath my ear, let him have yours also. He cries from heaven, "Behold my servant whom I uphold, mine elect in whom my soul delighteth." And for what end doth he thus commend him, but that we may make him the object of trust and confidence, as he doth? There is not one duty in all the word of God, that is so much, or so frequently inculcated, as that of faith in Christ, or a firm trust in him, for all the ends of his incarnation; yea, this is the great end of the whole revelation, John xx. 31. "These things are written, that ye may believe in the name of the only begotten Son of God."

There is no pleasing of God, no way to avert his wrath and displeasure, but by trusting the great Manager of his house; without faith in Christ it is impossible to please him, even though you were capable to perform all the other duties enjoined in the holy law, which yet is impossible through the want of faith in the promised Messiah. All the splendid services of Israel were rejected as an abomination, Is. i. 10-12. although commanded in the law. But, on the other hand, the weakest mint at commanded duty, though attended with many infirmities, is accepted of God, if done in faith. And the reason of this is, because faith hangs the whole glory of the soul's acceptance upon the nail fastened in a sure place, and not upon any work or duty done by us. The language of it is, "I will go in the strength of the Lord God, and I will make mention of thy righteousness, even of thine only."

Trust the great Manager, for he is "the mighty God," Is. ix. 6. Take his own testimony as to this, Rev. i. 8. "I am Alpha and Omega, the first and the last, saith the Lord, which is, and which was, and which is to come, the Almighty." He is the man who is God's fellow, neither is it any robbery for him to be equal with God, for he and his Father are one, the same in substance, equal in power and glory. Let this engage your trust in him, for this he gives as the ground and reason why he should be the confidence of all the ends of the earth, and of them that are afar off upon the seas: Is. xlv. 22. "Look unto me, and be ye saved, all the ends of the earth: for I am God, and there is none else."

The great Manager is your near Kinsman, bone of your bone, and flesh of your flesh, and has acted the Kinsman's part, by avenging your blood upon the head of the old serpent, and by redeeming the mortgaged inheritance of eternal life; and therefore it is natural and kindly to put your trust in him: "How excellent is thy loving kindness, O God! (says David), therefore the sons of men put their trust under the shadow of thy wings." He is not only God, but man; the man of God's right hand, whom he hath made strong for himself, *i.e.* for the purposes of his glory in our redemption. As he hath authority and ability to manage our affairs, so he is gone to his Father to appear in the presence of God for us. As he died for our offences, and rose again for our justification, so he hath stated himself, before the high bar, as our Advocate with the Father. And whatever business we have in dependence before the high court, he is always present to look after it, and never absent when the cause is called; and he hath the concerns of his clients so much at heart, that he reckons them his own. Being touched with the feeling of our infirmities, he agents and manages the cause of the offspring and issue of the house *gratis*, without any money or price. "He shall deliver the needy when he crieth: the poor also, and him that hath no helper," Psa. lxxii. 12. "He standeth at the right hand of the poor, to save him from those that would condemn his soul," Psa. cix. 31. Let these or the like considerations engage your firm trust in the glorious Manager.

But, besides all these, consider what advantage shall accrue to yourselves, by putting all your trust and confidence in him. Hereby you shall be kept in perfect peace amidst all the shakings of this world, Is. xxvi. 3. You shall hereby be filled with joy and peace, yea, "with joy unspeakable, and full of glory." You shall be rendered immoveable like the rock, when storms of trouble and temptation are overthrowing others who build upon the sand. In a word, your trust in and upon the great Manager, shall be followed with an exceeding and eternal weight of glory; none perish that trust in him: "Whosoever believeth in him, shall not perish, but have everlasting life."

I conclude at present with that word, Is. lxiv. 4. "From the beginning of the world men have not heard, nor perceived by the ear, neither hath the eye seen, O God, besides thee, what he hath prepared for him that waiteth for him."

Is. xxii. 24.—" And they shall hang upon him all the glory of his Father's house, the offspring, and the issue, all vessels of small quantity: from the vessels of cups, even to all the vessels of flagons."

THE SIXTH SERMON ON THIS TEXT.

YOU may ask me first, when, or in what cases are we to trust the glorious Manager? I answer, in general, there is no case unseasonable: "Trust in him at all times; yea people, pour out your hearts before him." More particularly,

1st, When you are in any concern about the salvation of your souls, roll this weight upon the nail fastened in a sure place. Are you in any doubt or fear anent your eternal state? Put it out of doubt, by committing this unto him, who came to seek and save that which was lost, saying with David, "Into thy hands do I commit my spirit, O thou JEHOVAH, God of truth, who hast redeemed me." The direct actings of faith on Christ, is the surest and shortest way of securing the one thing needful, for "none perish that trust in him."

2dly, When pressed with manifold charges of guilt, from the devil, from the law, from conscience; in that case trust in the Manager, for "his blood cleanses from all sin." We have redemption in his blood; and under this covering you may say, "Who can lay any thing to *my* charge?" It is the voice of the great Manager to the offspring and issue, "I, even I am he that blotteth out thine iniquities for mine own name's sake."

3dly, When indwelling sin is molesting thee with its insurrections, trust him that he may destroy the works of the devil in thy heart, that he will, according to his promise, "subdue your iniquities," Mic. vii. 19. Rom. vi. 14. "Sin shall not have dominion over you."

4thly, When Satan is molesting you with his fiery darts, act faith upon him; fear nothing from that enemy, whose head he has already bruised; and, in this case, improve his atoning blood, for it is said of saints in former ages, that "they overcame him by the blood of the Lamb." When you are afraid of falling or stumbling, take hold of the Manager, for "he keeps the feet of his saints, and holds up their goings." When called to any work or duty that is above your strength, remember that he is "the strength of Israel. Be strong in the grace that is in Christ Jesus, for he sends none a warfare upon their own charges." When engaged either in personal or public covenanting work, do all in the name and strength of the great Manager, and with an eye to the sacrifice of his death for acceptance Psa. l. 5. "Gather my saints together unto me; even those that have made a covenant with me by sacrifice." When the world is reeling and staggering, seas roaring, tempests of personal or public trouble blowing, then trust the Manager, for "he doth whatever he pleases in the heavens above, in the earth, in the seas, and in all deep places." Study to see all things in his hand, and all things working together for good to them that love him; and then you will sing, as Is. xii. 2. "Behold, God is my salvation: I will trust, and not be afraid." Or, Psa. xcvii. 1. "The Lord reigneth, let the earth rejoice," &c. When Jacob is brought low, and men pointing at the true church of Christ, and saying, "This is Zion whom no man careth for;" in that case, look to the Manager, for it is he that builds up Jerusalem, and gathers the dispersed of Israel into one. "What shall one answer the messengers of the nation? The Lord hath founded Zion, and the poor of his people shall trust in it." When there is a famine of bread trust him; for he that feedeth the ravens, will not starve the offspring and issue of the family: Psa. xxxvii. 3. "Trust in the Lord, and do good, so shalt thou dwell in the land, and verily thou shalt be fed." Is there a great scarcity of the word, the bread of life, and few faithful hands to dispense it? Trust him, for the stars are in his right hand; he gives apostles, prophets, evangelists, pastors, and teachers, for edifying of his body; and it is his promise, "I will give them pastors according to mine heart." Are the sheep and the shepherds scattered? Well, trust him, for he that hath scattered Israel will gather them again: "He shall gather the lambs with his arms, and carry them in his bosom," &c.

Thus you see there is no case in which the offspring and issue are not to hang by faith upon the blessed Manager, as a nail fastened in a sure place.

I conclude this exhortation with two or three advices. (1.) Be much in studying your own weakness and insufficiency for work or warfare, that you may be denied to your own strength; for it is *the poor* that "commits themselves to him." (2.) Be well acquainted with his name, I mean, the glory of his person; for it is "they that know his name that will put their trust in him." (3.) Study to know the near relation he stands under to you, both by his human nature, and by his offices as Mediator, Redeemer, Prophet, Priest and King, Head and husband, for the knowledge of these breeds trust and confidence. A wife trusts in her husband, a child in his parent, the members trust their head. (4.) Be well acquainted with the great and precious promises of the covenant of grace, and how the condition of them all is fulfilled to your hand by Christ, as a second Adam, in his fulfilling the *do* and *die* of the covenant of works. Legal conceptions of the covenant of grace, as if our faith, love, obedience, repentance, were the condition of the covenant, brangles faith in the free actings thereof on Christ and the covenant of grace. We must come without money or price to take hold of the covenant, and to apply the blessings thereof, because Christ has already paid the money and price that justice demanded. (5.) Pray much for the Spirit of faith; and, under the conduct of the Spirit, habituate yourselves to a frequent acting of faith, that so the life you live in the flesh may be "by faith on the Son of God."

I come now to offer a word to believers, under the notion of *vessels* hanging upon the nail which God has fastened in a sure place. And here I might, (1.) Offer a word to the *vessels of cups*. (2.) To the *vessels of flagons*, or believers of a higher stature. (3.) A word to both in common.

1. A word to weak believers, who are designed *vessels of cups*. I only suggest these two or three things unto you. (1.) It is a high privilege to occupy the least room in the house of our God. The prodigal son, when he came to himself, only begged of his father, that he might have the place of a hired servant; he was glad to be under his father's roof, and to eat in his father's house, at any rate. (2.) God has service for the least vessel of his house, as well as for the largest. God never made an useless creature,

and he does not form any useless vessels; no, every vessel is formed of himself, to shew forth his praise. (3.) The least vessel is God's property, and he will not disown, but maintain his property, and own it before men and angels, saying, "They are mine," in the day when he makes up his jewels. (4.) The bands, by which you hang upon the nail fastened in a sure place, are as strong as those by which the vessels of flagons are secured; for he has said as to both, "They shall never perish, neither shall any pluck them out of my hand." (5.) The weakest measure of grace is a pledge of more; for "to him that hath shall be given." What grace you have got is the arles-penny of more a-coming, for "his goings forth are prepared as the morning," as the break of day is a pledge of more light to follow: "The path of the just is as the shining light, that shineth more and more unto the perfect day." The least measure of grace has glory connected with it, according to the order of the covenant, Ps. lxxxiv. 11, "The Lord God is a sun and shield, he will give grace and glory;" first grace, and then glory.

I next offer a word of advice unto the vessels of cups, I mean weak believers. Although you are not to envy or grudge at God's bounty or liberality to others, in making them vessels of flagons, yet you may and ought earnestly to covet more grace than you have yet received; and therefore we are commanded to "grow in grace, and in the knowledge of our Lord and Saviour Jesus Christ." In order to which, be humble under a sense of your own weakness and emptiness; for "he giveth grace to the humble." Be diligent in the improvement of what grace you have received; for "the hand of the diligent maketh rich." Be frequently coming to the Manager of the house for more grace: "To whom coming, as unto a living stone,—ye also as lively stones, are built up," &c. Improve all the means of God's appointment for your edification, such as, the word, sacraments, prayer, Christian conference, that you may "add to your faith, virtue; to virtue, knowledge; to knowledge, temperance; to temperance, patience; to patience, godliness; to godliness, brotherly kindness; and to brotherly kindness, charity; for if these things be in you, and abound, they make you that ye shall neither be barren, nor unfruitful in the knowledge of our Lord Jesus Christ, 2 Pet. i. 5-8.

2. A word to the *vessels of flagons*, believers of a higher stature. To you I would say,

1*st*. Be not proud of grace received, but walk humbly with your God. "Who made thee to differ? and what hast thou that thou hast not received? His soul that is lifted up is not upright in him." True grace, where it is genuine, the more a man receives of it, he is always the more humble and empty, as you see in Paul, Eph. iii. 8, "Less than the least of all saints." To keep your sails low, consider that the most eminent saints have discovered the greatest weakness, even in the graces wherein they most excelled; as we see in the case of Abraham, Moses, David, Peter, and others. They that have the greatest measure of grace, they get as much to do with it; strong corruption, strong temptation, and strong trials to grapple with: and the more talents that a man doth receive, the more hath he to account for, as to the improvement of them; for "to whom much is given, of them much shall be required."

2dly, Instead of despising others that are not come your length, study to be helpful and serviceable unto them. The vessels of cups are ordinarily filled out of the flagons; so study to impart and communicate of your grace, of your faith, love, hope, knowledge, under their graces, unto those that are weak in grace. The strong children in a family are helpful to the young and weak. Thus it is in the natural body, the strong member is helpful unto the weak and infirm; so ought it to be in the mystical body of Christ. And when you see any fall through weakness, do not triumph over them; but "strengthen the weak hands, and confirm the feeble knees; say to them that are of a fearful heart, Be strong; restore such an one with a spirit of meekness.

3dly, Whatever grace you have received, be not strong or confident therein, like Peter; but be strong in the grace that is in Christ Jesus, and let the life you live be by faith in the Son of God. Grace received will soon give way in a day of trial and temptation. An innocent Adam, left with the stock in his hand, soon turned bankrupt, and ruined all his posterity. And therefore, I say, do not trust to the life or grace you have in hand, but in the grace and life you have in your head Jesus Christ, the glorious Manager and Steward of his Father's house. Still remember, that all the vessels hang upon him; and therefore let all the weight lie where God has laid it.

3. A word of advice unto vessels of all sizes, whether they be *vessels of cups,* or *vessels of flagons.*

1st, Adore the riches of divine grace and mercy, that put a difference between you and others, for naturally you were as bad as others.

2dly, Let every one possess his vessel in sanctification and honour. Do not debase or defile the vessel of thy soul or body, by prostituting it unto the service of sin, satan, or any abominable lust. You was once lying in the miry clay of nature, but God has washed, justified, and sanctified you; and therefore study to keep yourself clean and holy in heart, life, and in all manner of conversation. If you defile yourselves with sin, the Manager of the house will be fair to cast you into a furnace of affliction, or, like Jonah, to plunge you into deep waters, till you acknowledge, "Mine own iniquities correct me, and my backslidings do reprove me."

3dly, When you find any defilement of sin cleaving to you (which you will never miss while in the body), flee to the fountain opened for sin and for uncleanness in the house of David. Be often bathing thy soul in the blood of Jesus, which cleanseth from all sin.

4thly, Come to the fountain for supply under all wants, that you may obtain mercy, and find grace to help in time of need.

"Out of his fulness do all we receive, and grace for grace." Let thy vessel just lie under the flowing of this blessed fountain, that it may never be found empty when the midnight cry is made, "Behold the Bridegroom cometh, go ye forth to meet him."

Lastly, Pray for a plentiful outpouring of the Spirit, according to the promise, Is. xliv. 3, "I will pour floods upon the dry ground," that so all the empty vessels of the land, that are destitute of the waters of God's grace, may be filled; and those that are hanging upon the first Adam, and under the curse of the law, may, by the power of grace, change their holding, and hang upon the nail that God has fastened in a sure place.

A ROBBERY COMMITTED, AND RESTITUTION MADE, BOTH TO GOD AND MAN*.

A SERMON,

Preached upon a thanksgiving day, after the Sacrament, in Dunfermline, Monday, August 11, 1746.

Ps. lxix. 4,—"Then I restored that which I took not away."

IT is abundantly plain, that there are several passages in this psalm applied unto Christ in the scriptures of the New Testament; particularly that in the 9th verse of the psalm, "The zeal of thine house hath eaten me up," we find it applied to Christ, John ii. 17; and likewise that immediately following, "The reproaches of them that reproached thee are fallen upon me," Rom. xv. 3; so likewise in the 21st verse, "They gave me also gall for my meat, and in my thirst they gave me vinegar to drink," applied to Christ, Matth. xxvii. 48, and Mark xv. 23. But I need go no further to prove this, than the first word of the verse where my text lies, "They hate me without a cause," Christ applies it to himself, in John xv. 25. We find our Lord here, in the verse where my text lies, he is complaining of his enemies; he complains of their causeless hatred in the first clause of the verse, "They

---

* I have perused the following notes of my sermon, preached at Dunfermline August last, taken from my mouth in the delivery. My other work cannot allow me time to transcribe it. However, I have corrected and amended what I thought might mar the sense. If the doctrine of the gospel here delivered be understood, I am not anxious about the wisdom of words, lest the gospel should be of none effect.

Stirling, Dec. 27, 1746.   E. E.

hate me without a cause;" he complains of their multitude, "They are more than the hairs of mine head;" he complains of their implacable cruelty, "They that would destroy me, being mine enemies wrongfully, are mighty." Now our blessed Lord is thus treated by the world, whom he came to save. When there is such a powerful combination of hell and earth against him, one would have been ready to think, that he would have stopped, and gone no further; but he did not faint, nor was he discouraged, for all the opposition that was made against him; for you see, in the words I have read, what he was doing for lost sinners, when he was meeting with harsh entertainment from them. *Then*, even *then*, says he, *I restored that which I took not away.*

In which words you may notice these following particulars. (1.) You have hear a robbery disclaimed; a robbery was committed, but it is disclaimed by the Son of God; *I took not away.* There was something taken away from God and from man; by whom it is not said, but it is easy to say, that surely an enemy did it. But then, (2.) We have a restitution made of that robbery that was committed: *I restored*, saith Christ, *I restored what I took not away.* The work of man's redemption, it is a restitution both unto God and unto man of what was taken away by sin and by Satan. When once the work of redemption is completed, there will be a restitution of all things; for we read, Acts iii. 21, of the "restitution of all things." Again, (3.) We have an account of the person restoring. Who made the restitution? It was *I*, saith the Lord; *I restored what I took not away.* I who speak in righteousness, and who am mighty to save, I the child born, and the son given to the sons of men, whose name is "Wonderful, Counsellor, The mighty God, The everlasting Father, and The Prince of peace;" I, even *I restored what I took not away.* Again, (4.) You have the voluntariness and frankness of the deed. No man is obliged to make restitution of what is taken away by another, unless he does it of his own accord. Well, says Christ, though I took it not away, yet I made restitution of the robbery and stealth that was committed; I engaged to do it in the council of peace, "Lo, I come: I delight to do thy will," &c. Again, (5.) We have here the time when our glorious Immanuel made this restitution of what he took not away. It was, *Then I restored what*, &c., when his enemies were destroying him; when they were robbing him of his name, and robbing him of his very life, he restored what was taken away by robbery from men. You will see how low our blessed Lord descended to make this restitution, and when it was; it was, in the first verse, when the waters of God's wrath were coming into his soul, even *then*, says he, *I restored that which I took not away.* Now, from the words thus briefly opened, the doctrine that I take notice of is shortly this.

DOCT. "That it was the great design of the Son of God, when he descended into a state of humiliation here, in this lower world, to make restitution both unto God and unto man, of what he never took away." For as there was a robbery committed upon God and upon man by sin and Satan; so our glorious Redeemer, he makes a restitution of the stolen goods, he restores both to God what was his due, and unto man what he had lost.

Now, in the prosecution of this doctrine, if time and strength would allow, the method that I propose is,
I. To premise two or three things for clearing of the way.
II. To inquire into the stolen goods, what it was that was taken away both from God and man.
III. I would make it appear, that our glorious Immanuel, he makes restitution of what was taken away both from God and from man; he restores unto God his due, and unto man his loss.
IV. I would shew when it was that our Lord did this; for it is said here, *Then I restored.*
V. I would give the reasons why Christ made this restitution, when he was under no manner of obligation to it, but his own free will. And then,
VI. *Lastly,* I would make some application of the whole.

I. The *first* thing proposed is, to *premise two or three things for clearing of the way.* For clearing of it you would consider,
1. That when God made man, he made him a rich man: he bestowed all manner of goods upon him, that were necessary to make him live comfortably here, and to make him eternally happy hereafter.
2. You would consider, that Satan, by this time, having fallen, like a star, from heaven to earth, when he lighted upon this world, upon this earth, he presently saw man standing and acting in the capacity of God's viceroy, bearing his image, and having the whole creation in subjection to him. This filled the enemy with envy, and therefore he enters into a resolution, if it were possible, to commit a robbery upon man, and to strike at God's sovereignty through man's side; and accordingly,
3. Satan prevailed upon our first parents, and beguiled them into an eating of the tree of knowledge of good and evil, which God had discharged them to eat upon the pain of death; and thereby the paction betwixt God and man (I mean the covenant of works) was broken.
4. The covenant of works being broken, and man having entered into a rebellion against God with the devil, he justly forfeited all the spiritual and temporal goods that God bestowed upon him, and likewise lost his title to a happy eternity, and became the enemy's vassal; and thus the enemy robbed him of all the goods that God bestowed upon him.
5. *Lastly,* The eternal Son of God having a delight in the sons of men, and beholding them in this miserable plight, he enters upon a resolution that he will take on man's nature as a coat of mail, and that he will in man's nature be avenged upon that serpent that hath beguiled our first parents, and spoiled them of their

patrimony. And accordingly, in the fulness of time, he comes, and is manifested to destroy the works of the devil, and to recover all the stolen goods; he spoiled principalities and powers, and triumphed over them in his cross, and then divides a portion with the great, and the spoil with the strong; and, with a view to this, it is said in this text, *Then I restored that which I took not away.* And so I come to,

II. The *second* thing I proposed, and that was, to *inquire a little into the robbery that was committed by sin and Satan, both upon God and upon man.*

And, *first,* To begin with the robbery that was committed upon God. It was the devil's great drift, by tempting man to sin against God, to rob God of his glory. God made all things for his glory, and for his pleasure they are and were created. The whole earth, before sin entered into it, was full of his glory; and whenever Adam opened his eyes, and looked abroad through the creation, he saw the glory of God sparkling, as it were, in every creature he cast his eyes upon. Well, the enemy's design was to despoil and rob God of his glory. There is a question put, Mal. iii. 8, " Will a man rob God?" will a creature adventure to rob his Creator? And yet this wickedness is perpetrated. God is invaded, and his glory is in a great measure taken away, I mean his declarative glory, for it is impossible his essential glory can be invaded.

I will tell you of several things relative to the glory of God, which were attempted to be taken away, and quite obscured and sullied by the sin of man.

1. There was an attempt made to rob God of the glory of his sovereignty, as the great Lord and Lawgiver of heaven and earth. Man, when he sinned against God, and brake the law in compliance with the motion of the enemy, what was the language of the deed? It was, " We ourselves are lords, and will come no more unto thee;" we will make our own will a law: " Let the Almighty depart from us : for we desire not the knowledge of his way."

2. There was an attempt to rob him of the glory of his wisdom. The wisdom of God was impeached by the sin of man as a piece of folly, namely, in giving a law to man, that was not worthy to be observed. Sirs, depend upon it, every sin you are guilty of, charges God with folly, and exalts the will and wisdom of the creature, above the will and wisdom of God expressed in this holy law. And what a capital crime is it for poor men to charge God with foolishness!

3. By sin there is an attempt to rob him of the glory of his power, in regard the sinner gives a defiance to the Almighty, and, upon the matter, says, he is not able to revenge his quarrel on us, the arm of his power is withered. That is the language of sin. And then,

4. There is a robbery upon God's holiness, which is one of the most orient and bright pearls of his crown. When the holy law is

violated and transgressed, the language of that action is, God is like ourselves, he approves of our ways. Again,

5. There was an attack upon his justice, and a denying his rectoral power and equity. God says, "The soul that sinneth shall die, that he will by no means acquit the guilty." Well, but the language of sin is, "God will not require it," or he may be pleased or pacified with this or the other petty atonement.

Not to insist: there was a despising of God's goodness. God gave man a great estate; he gave him the whole earth, and would have given him the heavens also, if he had continued in his integrity; but yet all that goodness of God was trampled under foot by the sin of man.

Also, there was a denial of the faithfulness of God in the threatening that was denounced against the sin of man, "In the day that thou eatest of it, thou shalt surely die." But the language of sin is, God is not true to his word, he will not surely do it; said Satan, "Thou shalt not surely die." Thus you see there was an attempt made to rob God of the glory of all his perfections at once.

Secondly, Let us inquire a little into the goods that were stolen from man by sin and Satan. Here we may see a melancholy scene. The glory of the human nature was quite marred by sin. Man was made the top of the creation; but by sin he was brought below the very beasts that perish, so that, "The ox knoweth his owner, and the ass his master's crib, but my people know not me, saith the Lord; and they do not consider" their obligations to me.

Sin, it robbed man of his light and sight. You know what befel Samson when he was taken captive by his enemies, they put out his eyes; so when we fell into the enemies hands, they put out our eyes, and all mankind have been born blind since that time. Again, sin hath robbed us of our very life, and laid us among the congregation of the dead. All mankind are a dead and putrified company, "dead in trespasses and sins," Eph. ii. 1. And then, sin hath robbed man of his liberty unto any thing that is spiritually good; and ever since we have become captives to the devil, the world, and our lusts. Again, sin hath robbed us of our wisdom, and brought us to prefer folly to the wisdom of God. Every man by nature is playing the fool. Who but a fool would spend his money upon that which is not bread, and his labour upon that which profiteth not? Sin robbed us of our righteousness, and rendered us a company of guilty criminals before God, and brought us under the sentence of the broken law, *condemned already*, John iii. 18. Sin robbed us of our beauty, of the beautiful image of God, consisting in holiness and conformity to the great Creator, and it hath brought the hue of hell upon all mankind, lying among the pots. Again, sin hath robbed us of our health. Man was a healthy creature both in soul and body before the entry of sin; but sin hath robbed us of that, so that, "from the crown of the head to the sole of the foot, there is no sound part about us." Sin hath robbed us of our peace, and set us at war with God, with ourselves, with one another, and at war with the whole creation. Sin hath robbed us of our beautiful ornaments that God put upon us at our creation, and stript us naked, as it is said of Laodicea, Rev. iii. 18. Sin hath robbed us of our treasure, insomuch that we are become beggars, poor, and naked. In short, sin hath robbed us of our God, so that we are become " without God in the world." There is a robbery for you that cannot be paralleled! You see what was taken away from God and man, by the sin of man. I might likewise tell you that sin robbed man of that paradise of pleasure in which God set him at his creation. No sooner had man sinned through the instigation of Satan, that old serpent, but he was turned out of the garden of Eden, Gen. iii. 24, and a flaming sword placed, that turned every way, to keep him from having access to the tree of life in the midst of the garden. Sin hath robbed us of heaven, and made us heirs of hell and wrath. In short, sin hath disordered and disjointed the whole creation. Whenever man sinned, there came such a load upon the earth, through the curse of God, that ever since the whole creation hath been crying in pain, seeking deliverance from that dead weight that hath been lying upon it. So that, I say, by the sin of man there is a robbery committed, there are goods stolen from God and man, and the good creatures of God.

III. The *third* thing proposed was, *to make it appear that our glorious Immanuel, he makes a restitution of what was taken away both from God and from man.* He restores unto God his due, and restores unto man his loss.

And, 1. He makes restitution of glory to God, and that in the highest measure and degree, as was intimated by the angels, at the nativity of our Lord, Luke ii. 14. The first note of the song of the angels is, "Glory to God in the highest," &c. It is just as if they had said, Glory hath been taken away from God, by the sin of the first Adam and his posterity; but now there is a higher revenue of glory to be brought in to the crown of heaven, than the whole creation in innocency could afford. Accordingly, our blessed Lord he declares, when his work was finished, after he had gone through his course of humiliation, he comes to his Father, John xvii. 4. and he says, Now, Father, " I have glorified thee on the earth." Observe the phraseology, for there is something remarkable in it, " I have glorified thee on the earth:" the *earth* was the theatre of rebellion where God was affronted, his law violated, and his sovereignty contemned; but, says he, " I have glorified thee on the earth," where thou wast dishonoured. I ought to go through all the perfections of God, that were leased by the sin of man, and tell how Christ restores glory to every one of them.

He restores glory to the divine *sovereignty*, bowing his royal neck to take on the yoke of the law which we had broken. He was made of a woman, and made under the law, that he might magnify it, and so maintain the honour of the great Lawgiver.

He restores glory likewise to the divine *wisdom ;* for Christ himself, in his person and mediation, is just " the wisdom of God in a mystery," even his " hidden wisdom, the manifold wisdom of God." O Sirs! never were the treasures of divine wisdom and knowledge so much expended as in the person and mediation of our Lord Jesus Christ.

And then, he restores glory likewise to the divine *power ;* for Christ is " the power of God : " and when he went forth to the great work of man's redemption, he went forth armed with infinite power to manage it; therefore he is called " the arm of God, and the man of God's right-hand, whom he hath made strong for " the purposes of his glory. How gloriously was the power of God displayed, when he came from Edom, with dyed garments from Bozrah, glorious in his apparel, travelling in the greatness of his strength ; spoiling principalities and powers, who had spoiled God of his glory, and man of all that was valuable unto him !

He restores glory to the *holiness* of God. This attribute was injured by the sin of man, but its glory is restored by Christ ; and there is such a brightness of divine holiness shines in the person and mediation of Christ, that when the Angels look upon him, Is. vi. they are dazzled, they are overwhelmed, not being able to behold it, they cover themselves, and cry, " Holy, holy, holy is the Lord of hosts : the whole earth is full of his glory."

And then, he restores glory to the divine *justice ;* for in the work of man's redemption, justice gets a complete, and full satisfaction, till it cry, It is enough. And the justice of God manifested in the execution of the penalty of the law upon the Surety, is laid as the very foundation of the throne of grace, that we are called to come to for grace and mercy to help in the time of need, Ps. lxxxix. 14, " Justice and judgment are the habitation, or establishment, of thy throne," viz.—justice satisfied, and judgment executed upon the glorious Surety.

Again, he restores glory to the divine *goodness.* God was good to man, but man trampled it under foot : But Christ makes a higher display of the divine goodness than ever was seen by men or angels ; for in his person, and mediation, and sufferings, the goodness of God breaks out like an ocean, in amazing streams of love, grace, and mercy. The love of God, O how does it shine in the giving his only begotten Son into the world ! " Herein is love, not that we loved God, but that he loved us, and gave his own Son to be a propitiation for our sins." And then for grace, *grace* is made to " reign through righteousness unto eternal life, by Jesus Christ our Lord." And for mercy, it is " built up for ever." Thus I say, their is a restitution of glory to the divine goodness.

And likewise there is a restitution of glory to the divine *faithfulness.* The faithfulness of God engaged in the penalty, was trode upon by man and the devil ; but the faithfulness of God is maintained in the execution of that penalty threatened against man in the person of our glorious Immanuel : and not only so, but the faithfulness of God comes to be *established* in the new covenant "in the very heavens:" for all the promises come to be "yea and amen in Christ, to the glory of God." Thus you see, that Christ restores what he took not away from his Father; he restores "glory to God in the highest," which he never took away.

2. Let us see next what restitution he makes to man; for man was robbed of all that was valuable to him, either for time or eternity.

First, The human nature was debased by sin, and sunk below the beasts that perish. Well, but the Son of God comes and takes the human nature into a personal union with himself, and thereby exalts the human nature above the angelical nature: Heb. ii. 16, "Verily he took not on him the nature of angels: but he took on him the seed of Abraham." And, chap. i. 5, "Unto which of the angels said he at any time, Thou art my Son, this day have I begotten thee?" And see what follows, "When he bringeth in the first-begotten into the world, he saith, And let all the angels of God worship him." Thus the glory of the human nature is restored and advanced to a far higher pinnacle of glory and honour, than when it stood in the first Adam before his fall, adorned with all its embroideries, in a state of innocency. O Sirs, look up and see your nature exalted, taken out of the dunghill, and set on the throne of God. The throne of God is called "the throne of the Lamb," because our nature is there in a personal union with the great God.

But this is not all: he not only restores the glory of the human nature; but, to all who believe in him, he restores to advantage all the losses we sustain, either by the sin of the First Adam, or our own personal transgression; as will appear by running over the particular losses mentioned upon the former head.

First, then, Did sin robe us of our sight and light, and leave us in darkness? Well, Christ makes a restitution of that; for he comes forth as the bright and morning star, to give light to the darkened world, which may make us all sing and say with Zacharias, Luke i. 78, "Through the tender mercy of our God; whereby the day-spring from on high hath visited us." Ps. cxviii. 27.-29, "God is the Lord, which hath shewed us light; bind the sacrifice with cords, even unto the horns of the altar. Thou art my God, and I will praise thee; thou art my God, I will exalt thee. O give thanks unto the Lord, for he is good: for his mercy endureth for ever."

Again, Hath sin robbed us of life, and left us among the congregation of the dead? Christ makes restitution of that; for he is "the resurrection and the life:" and having recovered life by his own death, John xiv. 19. He keeps it in his hand and heart, and binds up our life with his "Because I live, ye shall live also. Our life is hid with Christ in God."

Again, Did sin rob us of our liberty? Christ makes restitution of that; he buys our liberty at the hand of justice, and then takes the executioner and binds him, and spoils him of his power over the poor captive; and having purchased liberty, he goes forth and "proclaims liberty to the captives, and the opening the prison-doors to them that are bound."

Again, Did Satan and sin spoil us of our wisdom, insomuch that ever since we are infatuated, and like fools, spend our money for that which is not bread, and our labour for that which cannot profit us? Well, Christ restores wisdom unto fools and babes; he is "made of God unto us wisdom;" and when we are determined to come to him, he makes us wiser than our teachers; wise to know the mysteries of the kingdom that are hid from the wise and prudent of the world, and revealed unto babes: "Unto you it is given to know the mysteries of the kingdom of heaven," &c.

And then again, Did sin spoil and robe us of our original righteousness? Christ makes restitution of that; for he himself is "the Lord our righteousness, and he was made sin for us, he who knew no sin, that we might be made the righteousness of God in him."

Did sin spoil us of the beautiful image of God? Christ makes restitution of that; for that very moment that a poor sinner looks unto him with the eye of faith, he gets the print of the second Adam drawn again upon his soul, and it is by beholding his glory that we are changed into the same image.

Did Satan and sin rob us of, and take away our health? Well, Christ, he comes to make restitution of that: for he is the Physician of value, and there is no disease so obstinate as is able to stand the virtue and healing power of this Physician; so that, if we perish with our diseases, we need not do it with that word in our mouth, "Is there no balm in Gilead, and no physician there?"

Did Satan spoil us of our peace? Well, Christ makes restitution of that; for "he is our peace." Peace on earth was one of the articles of the angels praise, "Peace on earth, and good will towards men." Sin robbed us of our peace with God. Christ restores that; for "God is in Christ, reconciling the world unto himself." Did sin rob us of our peace of conscience? Christ restores that; "Peace I give unto you: not as the world giveth, give I unto you," &c.

Did sin kindle a fire of war and of strife betwixt man and man? Well, when Christ comes with the sceptre of his power, he makes them beat their swords into ploughshares, and their spears into pruning hooks; he makes the wolf dwell with the lamb, and the leopard lie down with the kid.

Did sin rob us of our ornaments? Christ restores these, he makes the King's daughter all glorious within; he brings us a far better garment, even the garment of salvation, and a robe of righteousness to adorn us.

Did sin take away our riches and treasures? Christ opens up a far better treasure, even *unsearchable riches;* and he tells us, that "riches are with him, yea, durable riches and righteousness."

Did sin rob us of our God, and leave us without God in the world? Christ makes restitution of that; for what is Christ? He is *Immanuel*. And what is that? He is *God with us.* That may make our hearts rejoice indeed; our God is come back to us, and is saying, "I am the Lord thy God; I will be their God, and they shall be my people." It is a God in Christ that speaks in such a dialect to poor sinners. Thus you see, that Christ restores to man, what he took not away from him. I might enlarge much on this subject.

Sin robbed us of our title and charter to eternal life; whenever the covenant of works was broken, our charter was gone. But Christ restores a better charter, even the covenant of grace; he himself is "given for a covenant to the people," and is the Alpha and Omega of the covenant; all the promises and blessings of it are "in him yea and amen." The covenant of works was a frail covenant, a slippery security; but the covenant of grace, and the charter granted unto us in Christ, it is a lasting charter: Is. liv. 10, "The mountains shall depart, and the hills be removed, but my kindness shall not depart from thee, neither shall the covenant of my peace be removed, saith the Lord, that hath mercy on thee."

In short, Christ restores beauty and order again to the whole creation. Whenever man sinned, there fell such a dead weight upon the creation, that the whole creation was like to crumble to its original chaos; but the thing that prevented it was, the Son of God bought this earth as a theatre, on which his love to sinners might be displayed; therefore he will uphold the theatre till the scene be acted; and when it is acted, he will commit it to the flames: there is a word to that purpose, Is. xlix. 8, "I will preserve thee, and give thee for a covenant of the people, to establish the earth, to cause to inherit the desolate heritages." The theatre of this earth was giving way under the weight of the wrath of God; but Christ being given as a covenant of the people, he upholds the earth and all things by the word of his power, as it is, Heb. i. 3.

Thus much for the *third* thing, which was, to let you see how Christ makes restitution of these good things which he never took away from God or from man.

IV. The *fourth* thing proposed was, to *inquire into the time when Christ did all this: when did he restore that which he took not away?*

I shall not stay upon this; I pointed at it in the explication. I told you that it was in a state of humiliation that he made this restitution. I cannot stand to tell you of the several steps of his humiliation whereby he restored what he took not away. We have a summary description thereof, in that question of the Catechism, "Wherein did Christ's humiliation consist?" The answer is, "In his being born, and that in a low condition, made under the law, undergoing the miseries of this life, the wrath of God, and the cursed death of the cross; in being buried, and continuing under the power of death for a time." By these steps of his humiliation, he brought about the blessed project of redemption. Then was it that he restored what he took not away: Gal. iv. 4, 5, "In the fulness of time, God sent forth his Son made of a woman, made under the law, to redeem them that were under the law, that we might receive the adoption of sons." But I do not stay upon this; I hasten forward.

V. The *fifth* thing proposed was, to *inquire a little into the reasons of the doctrine.* Why was it that our Lord restored what he took not away? Why did he restore these goods that sin and Satan took away both from God and from man? In answer to this, I only suggest these few particulars.

1. Christ made this restitution, because it was his Father's pleasure that he should do it; he did always these things that pleased his Father: "No man taketh my life from me (saith he), but I lay it down of myself. This commandment have I received of my Father."

2. He restored what he took not away, because it contributes very much to enhance his mediatorial glory. Gen. xiv. there you read of what Abraham did, he armed his men, and went in quest of the five kings that had plundered Sodom; he pursues them, takes them captives, and recovers the spoil, and restores what not he, but the enemy, had taken away; and this was much for Abraham's honour. So it is to the immortal honour of our glorious Immanuel, that he pursued, and spoiled principalities and powers, who had robbed God and man; and then restores unto both what they, not he, had taken away. Upon this account, " God hath highly exalted him, and given him a name which is above every name," &c.

3. Christ restored what he took not away, out of regard that he had to the holy law of God. The holy law was violated, and the sovereignty of God in it was trode down: but Christ had a mind to maintain the dignity of the law, it being an emanation of the holiness of God; therefore he will restore a perfect obedience to the law, and bring in an everlasting righteousness that answers it to the full, that so a foundation may be thereby laid for our legal investiture in the privileges of children we had lost by sin.

4. Because his delights were with the sons of men. Sirs, Christ had a bride in Adam's family to espouse to himself for ever. God the Father gave him a bride. And when he saw her in the devil's clutches, he arms himself with divine power, and rescues the bride: " He loved me, and gave himself for me." And then, Christ restores what he took not away, that so the glory of grace might be exalted in the salvation of lost sinners; and that none glory in themselves, but that they that glory may glory in the Lord. It is not we, but he only, that makes the restitution, and grace reigns to us through that restitution that he made.

5. and *lastly,* Christ restores what he took not away, that he might " still the enemy and the avenger," as the expression is, Psa. viii. 2.; "the enemy and the avenger," that is the devil. Sirs, when the devil robbed man, he thought the day was his own, and triumphed as if the world and the glory thereof were his own, and men led as captive prisoners. But Christ stills the enemy,

he stills his boasting; for he spoils the spoilers, takes the prey from the mighty, and delivers the captives from the terrible.

VI. The *sixth* thing proposed was the *Application*.

1. Is it so, as you have been hearing, that Christ restores what he took not away? Then, hence see, what a generous Kinsman we have of him; he never took away any thing from us, and yet he restores all to the spoiling of his own soul, and pouring of it out unto death. O! how hath the kindness of God to men appeared! What reason have we to adore the achievements of our renowned Redeemer, who went forth conquering and to conquer!

2. This doctrine serves to let us see into the meaning of that word, Rom. viii. 3, "He condemned sin." Why, or how did he it? Why, sin is a robber, it committed a robbery on God and man; and is it not just that a robber should be condemned to die? Well, Christ condemns sin, and yet he saves the sinner: the sinner deserved to be condemned; but he manages the matter so dexterously, that he kills sin, and preserves the sinner.

3. Hence see what a criminal correspondence it is that the generality of the children of men have with sin. It is dangerous to haunt and harbour robbers; and yet will you keep a robber in your bosom. Sin is a robber; and every time you sin, it is committing robbery upon God and your own souls; therefore do not harbour it, "Stand in awe, and sin not."

4. If sin be such a robber of God and man, then see how reasonable the command is, to crucify sin, and to mortify the deeds of the body, "Mortify the deeds of the body; crucify the flesh, with its affections and lusts." Why crucify them? Why kill and destroy them? They are robbers. Therefore let us wage war against all manner of sin, whether within us or without us; let us "resist even unto blood, striving against sin," because sin is a robber, and deprives us of all the good you are hearing of.

5. From this doctrine see what way Christ takes in order to carry on his mediatory work of making peace betwixt God and man. There was a robbery committed upon God and man; and unless there was a restitution to both parties, there could be no peace. Well, Christ restores what he took not away; he restores glory to God, happiness to man; and so he carries on his mediatory work; for when both parties have restitution, then there is peace. Christ, he makes an end of sin, for he is the Lamb of God that taketh away the sin of the world." And why takes he it away? It is, that so peace may be restored betwixt God and man, restitution being made to both.

6. From the doctrine we may likewise see, that the believer in Christ is the wisest man in the world, however the world may look upon him as a fool. Why? because he comes to Christ, and gets restitution of all the losses he suffered either by the sin of the first Adam or his own. No wonder he be a thriving man, because he gets his losses made up in Christ; for he comes, and out of his fulness receives grace for grace, and gets wisdom, righteousness, sanctification, and redemption, from the Lord Jesus.

7. See the folly and madness of the sin of unbelief. The generality of the hearers of the gospel will not come to Christ to get restitution of what they lost by Adam and their own sin; John v. 40, "Ye will not come to me, that ye might have life." O what folly is this! If you had lost any of your worldly goods at the last rebellion, how readily would you seek restitution, if it were to be had? And yet such fools are the most part of sinners under the gospel, that though Christ counsels, calls, and beseeches them to come and get restitution of their God, of their life, and all losses, yet they will not hear, Ps. lxxxi. 11, "My people would not hearken to my voice," &c.

8. See the folly of the legalist, that goes about to make restitution to God, and to himself, of what was taken away by sin. The legalist, like the proud Pharisee, comes to God with his filthy rags, and thinks to please God with this and that obedience. But, O Sirs! consider, that "by the works of the law no flesh living can be justified;" you will never repair your own losses, nor the dishonour you have done to God, but only by coming to Christ, who is "the end of the law for righteousness to every one that believeth."

I should next improve the doctrine by an use of *Trial.* Try whether you have ever come by faith to a second Adam, and found in him a reparation of your losses by the sin and apostasy of the first Adam. They who find Christ himself, they have found all, for "Christ is all, and in all. All things are yours; whether Paul, or Apollos, or Cephas, or the world, or life, or death, or things present, or things to come; all are yours; for ye are Christ's; and Christ is God's." They who find him, they find the goodly pearl, a treasure of unsearchable riches; and therefore cannot but reckon all their losses made up to wonderful advantage. And if so, whatever appeared gain to you formerly, will be esteemed loss for Christ; yea, doubtless, you will count all but dung and loss for Christ, that you may know him, win him, and be found in him. You will be dead to the law, and the works of it, being married to a better husband, whose name is, "The Lord our righteousness;" for "in him shall all the seed of Israel be justified, and shall glory." Again, if you have found reparation in Christ, you will wage a continual war with sin and Satan; you will resist the devil, and resist even unto blood, striving against sin. These robbers, they never come but to spoil you of some good, whatever disguise they may appear in. And if you have received any love-tokens from the Lord on this occasion, you may lay your account with an attack; the pirates pursue and attack the ship with the richest cargo. Lastly, Whenever the enemy has prevented and twin'd you of your comforts, you will fly to Christ for restitution, saying, with David, "Restore unto me the joy of thy salvation," for he it is who restores what he took not away.

I close with a word of *Exhortation.*

Sirs, I have a proclamation to issue forth in the name of the Lord Immanuel. Be it known unto men, by these presents, That whereas two great robbers have entered into the world, viz. sin and Satan, and have stolen away all the valuable goods which once pertained to Adam and his family, whereby they are all reduced to the utmost poverty and misery; it has pleased God the Father, from the love he bears to mankind-sinners, to send his only begotten Son into the world, to repair all their losses, and to restore what he took not away. Accordingly, the eternal Son of God hath come into the world, and having armed himself with the human nature and divine power, he hath gone forth and pursued the robbers, and taken Satan captive, and bruised his head, and destroyed that destroyer of mankind; he hath finished transgression, and made an end of sin, and hath brought in a robe of righteousness, and hath recovered all the goods that the robbers had taken away, all the goods and gear men lost; hath recovered them with wonderful advantage; and the goods are all in his hand, and he hath sent out us, who are his ambassadors, to cause all mankind to see what losses they have sustained; and whoever have lost any thing, their God, and their souls, heaven and happiness, he is willing to restore it to mankind, and that without any safer; for he will do it without money and without price. Come, and get your own again; for Christ hath received gifts for men, for the sons of men. O come, come, come, Sirs, and get from the glorious Restorer what you have lost, what you stand in need of, through time and eternity! O come and get your life, your God, and your souls again for a prey!

Since the rebellion commenced, many a man has lost very much; some have lost their land, some their houses, some their legs, and some their arms, and many their lives. And now, if the Duke of Cumberland, the King's son, should issue forth a proclamation, to every man to come and get his losses repaired, in his father's name, I believe you would not be shy to put in your name, and tell that you have lost this and that. Well, the Son of the King of heaven, the great JEHOVAH, he hath all his Father's treasures in his hand, and he hath sent us to tell you to come and get your losses repaired. O Sirs, what are men's temporal losses in comparison with their soul losses! "What is a man profited, though he should gain the whole world, and lose his own soul?" Well, come and get your souls for a prey from the Son of God.

I might make use of many motives to persuade you. Pray you, consider only the goods you lost are in Christ's hand, and that they are in his hand that they may be restored again to you. He invites you to come, "Incline your ear, and come unto me," &c. He not only invites you, but counsels you, "I counsel thee to buy of me gold tried in the fire," that is, I counsel you to get your losses restored. He not only counsels you, but commands you, "This is his commandment, that ye believe in his Son," &c. He not only commands, but he promises; he gives all manner of security that your losses shall be made up, if you come to him for a reparation, Ps. lxxii. 4, "He shall judge the poor of the people, he shall save the children of the needy." Come then, poor and needy sinner. He is grieved to the heart when sinners will not come and get their losses repaired; he was grieved when Jerusalem would not be gathered as a hen gathereth her chickens under her wings. I will tell you, many a man have got their losses repaired; an innumerable company have got restitution from him, Rev. vii. 9, " I beheld, and lo, a great multitude, which no man could number, of all nations, and kindreds, and people, and tongues, stood before the throne, and before the Lamb, clothed with white robes, and palms in their hands." Now, when others have come and got reparation, will not ye come and get reparation too?

O Sirs, consider what you are doing. Mind, there is no hope of reparation after death; but if you come for reparation, you must come now to the King's Son; therefore, " To-day if ye will hear his voice, harden not your hearts, as in the provocation."

Upon this last day of the feast, I cry to all mankind, if my voice could reach them, to come and get their losses repaired by the Son of God, who *restores that which he took not away.* Do not say, " I am rich, and increased with goods, and stand in need of nothing;" for I can assure you, that he who is infinitely wise, and knows you better than you do yourselves, declares, that you are " poor, miserable, wretched, blind, and naked," through the robbery that sin hath committed. Say you, I cannot get time to come, because of worldly business. But let me tell you, that your worldly business is but mere trifles in comparison with this; therefore make all other business but by-business in comparison with this one thing needful. Says another, I will get time enough afterwards. I will tell you, delays are dangerous; what know you, man, what a day may bring forth? Death may come, and then you are gone for ever through eternity. Says another, I am afraid the time is gone already, and that he will not make a reparation of my losses. No, Sirs, I will tell you, that while there is life there is hope, and the Son of God is at the back of your heart, crying, " Behold, I stand at the door, and knock: If any man (out of hell) hear my voice, and open to me, I will come in to him, and will sup with him, and he with me." But O say you, I fear my losses are irreparable. I will tell you, poor sinner, as broken a ship has come to land, as we use to say; as great sinners as you have got a reparation of their losses, and a full pardon to the boot. What think you of Manasseh, and Mary Magdalene, and Paul? The same hand that repaired their losses is ready to repair yours; " his hand is not shortened, that it cannot save," &c. Says another, What if I be not among the number of the elect? I answer, You have nothing a-do with election; for " secret things belong unto the Lord, but that which is revealed unto us and our children." Election does not belong directly and immediately to the business of believing, but only things revealed: and if revealed things belong unto us, then put in your claim: for " the promise is to you and your seed." Say you, I am impotent, and cannot come. I answer. That was one of the losses Christ came to restore; " he gives strength to the weak, and to them that have no might he increaseth strength." Say you, My will is an iron sinew, it will not answer. *Answ.* He that restores that which he took not away, offers to restore your good heart and your will, "Thy people shall be willing in the day of thy power." Ezek. xxxvi. 26, "I will take away the heart of stone, and give the heart of flesh." Says another, I would fain come to get my losses repaired, but I think when I come to him he boasts me away. Do not think so; for he says, "Whosoever will come to me I will in no wise cast out." When he frowns upon you, and calls you a dog, be as the Syrophenician woman, do not give over, and you shall prevail, "Truth, Lord, I am a dog, yet the dogs eat of the crumbs that fall from the master's table;" the Lord repaired her losses, and granted her all the desires of her heart.

I should conclude with a word to believers, who have got their losses repaired by the glorious Immanuel. I only say two or three things to you by way of advice. (1.) O sing praises to the blessed Restorer, "O my soul, bless the Lord, who hath redeemed thy life from destruction, and crowned thee with loving kindness and tender mercies," Ps. ciii. 1-4. (2.) Whenever you meet with new losses, come back to the blessed Restorer. Satan will be about with you, he goes about like a roaring lion, seeking whom he may devour, and to take away any good you have got on this solemn occasion; but when the enemy has robbed you, I say, come back to Christ by faith, and you will find restitution again. Again, my advice to you is, O love the Lord with your heart, strength, and mind; let him have the strength and flower of your affection, lay nothing in the balance with him; and, as an evidence of your love, keep his commandments, walk worthy of the Lord, to all well pleasing; contend for the faith once delivered to the saints; study, with the church, to cause his name to be remembered to all generations, that the people may praise him for ever and ever, who *restored what* he *took not away*.

WORTHLESS MAN MUCH REGARDED BY THE MIGHTY GOD.

A SERMON,

Preached upon a thanksgiving day, after the Sacrament, in Dunfermline, Monday, July, 1737.

PSALM CXLIV. 3.—"Lord, what is man, that thou takest knowledge of him? or the son of man, that thou makest account of him."

HERE is a question put, that is both answerable and unanswerable; it is both easy and difficult: it is easy to tell what man is, for the end of his perfection is soon discovered; but why

God takes knowledge of man, or makes so great account of him, as to heap his favours on him, is a thing that God only can best account for. David, in the two preceding verses, declares, *first*, what a reconciled God in Christ was to him and makes it the ground of his praise and triumph : 1. Says he, My God is my strength ; he is the strength of Israel, the glory of their strength. However feeble and weak the saints be in themselves, yet "their Redeemer is strong, the Lord of hosts is his name. O blessed is the man whose strength is the Lord Jehovah, with whom their is everlasting strength ; for he shall go from strength to strength, till he appear before the Lord in Zion," &c. 2. His God was his goodness ; for "there is none good but one, that is, God ;" who, as he is the chief good himself, so he is truly good to Israel ; good to them that wait upon him, and to the soul that seeks him. And whatever goodness is in any of the sons of men, or saints of God, he is the glorious source and fountain of it ; "for every good and perfect gift cometh down from above," from an infinitely good God, &c. 3. His God was his fortress and his high tower. David saw himself in God, as a man is in his castle, that can look down on all his enemies with contempt ; and hence we find him frequently expressing himself with the greatest confidence of safety, "I will not be afraid of ten thousands of mine enemies against me round about:" O! who can hurt them that have "the eternal God for their refuge, and his everlasting arms underneath them?" 4. His God was his deliverer. Many a danger David had been in, from Saul, from Absalom, and his other enemies ; but his God had always interposed for his preservation ; probably he may have his eyes upon the great deliverance that God wrought for him, and all his saints, by Jesus Christ, in finding a ransom for him, that he might not go down to the pit, &c. 5. His God was his shield : as a shield in the day of battle defends against darts and arrows that are shot against a man's body, and wards off the blows that are levelled against him ; so his God had protected him against the malicious arrows of reproach and malice, &c. 6. His God had made him a skilful and successful soldier ; his hands had been used to the shepherd's crook, and the musician's harp ; but God had taught "his hands to war, and his fingers to fight," and to lead and head the armies of Israel, &c. 7. His God had taught him not only to manage the sword, but to sway the scepter ; in the close of verse 2. "He subdueth my people under me." He who had ordained him to be king of Israel, in the room of Saul, swayed the hearts of all the tribes to acknowledge him as their king and ruler ; just so he, in a day of power, bends and bows the wills and minds of men to submit to the government of the Son of David, Christ Jesus, every one crying, Thou hast delivered us out of the hands of our enemies, therefore rule thou over us.

Well, David having thus viewed the goodness of God unto him, and remembering the greatness, glory, and majesty of his Benefactor, who had done all this for him ; he extends his views unto the goodness of God to mankind in general, and especially to the saints, and cries out, in a rapture of wonder, in the words of my text, *Lord, what is man, that thou takest knowledge of him! and the son of man, that thou makest account of him!* So then the words are a question of admiration. And more particularly we may note, 1. The subject-matter of the question, and that is man; earthly man, as some read it; man that is "sprung of earth, and whose foundation is in the dust;" man who was "made a little lower than the angels," but who is now sunk into the greatest ignominy and contempt, by his apostasy from God. 2. We have a question of contempt put, concerning this creature, man, or the son of man, what is he? or wherein is he to be accounted of? We may hear the solution of this question afterwards. 3. Notice to whom this question is proposed; it is to the Lord: *Lord, what is man?* The Lord is a God of knowledge, and there is no searching of his understanding: he needs not that any should testify of man to him; he knows the inward value of persons, things, and actions: God has balances in which he weighs all mankind, and therefore he can well tell what man is; "he searches the hearts, and tries the reins of the children of men," and knows far better what you and I are, than we do ourselves. 4. We have the ground and reason of this enquiry concerning man; it is the knowledge that God takes, and the account God makes, of such an inconsiderable creature, that "the high and lofty One, who inhabits eternity, and who dwells in the high and holy place," that he should "bow his heavens, and come down," to visit man in a way of love.

OBSERVE, "That the regard that God shews unto man is truly wonderful and surprising."

This I take to be the plain import of the question. We have the like question put, Job vii. 17-18, "What is man that thou shouldst magnify him? and that thou shouldst set thine heart upon him? and that thou shouldst visit him every morning, and try him every moment," Ps. viii. 3, 4, "When I consider the heavens the work of thy fingers, the moon and the stars which thou hast ordained, what is man that thou art mindful of him? and the son of man, that thou visitest him." These are down-bringing questions. It is observable in scripture, that questions, when they are put concerning God, they are intended to raise our affections and admiration to the highest. So Exod. xv. 11, "Who is like unto thee, O Lord, among the Gods?" and Micah vii. 18, "Who is a God like unto thee?" These are uplifting questions. But when the question is concerning man, it brings him down in his own eyes unto nothing, "that no flesh may glory in the presence of God."

Now, in discoursing this doctrine, through the Lord's assistance, I shall endeavour,

I. To give a scriptural solution of this diminutive and down-bringing question, *What is man?*

II. What is imported in God's regarding man, or making account of him.

III. Wherein doth God discover his regard unto man?

IV. Shew that this is truly wonderful and surprising.

V. Apply.

I. The *first* thing is to give a scriptural solution of this question, *What is man?* for we can never wonder at and admire the regard that God shews unto man, until we know what man is. Come, then, Sirs, let us weigh ourselves in the balances of the sanctuary, and see what we are; 1*st*, As creatures; 2*dly*, As fallen creatures.

1*st*, What is man, as he is a creature of God? Why, trace him to his first original, he is but a piece of modified dust, enlivened with the breath of God: Adam signifies earth, and red earth, Gen. ii. 7, " The Lord God formed man of the dust of the ground." Hence is that of the apostle, 1 Cor. xv. 47, " The first Adam was of the earth, earthly;" also that of the prophet Jeremiah, who, addressing himself to Israel, cries out, " O earth, earth, earth, hear the word of the Lord," &c. Again, *What is man?* He is in scripture reckoned a *potter's vessel*, that is easily dashed and broken; " Hath not the potter power over the clay of his hand, to make one vessel unto honour, and another unto dishonour?" Rom. ix. 21, and Ps. ii. 9. Christ " will dash all his enemies in pieces, as a potter's vessel." If you ask further, *What is man?* the prophet Isaiah will tell you that he is but grass; Is. xl. 6, 8. " The voice said, Cry. And he said, What shall I cry? All flesh is grass, and the goodliness thereof as the flower of the field. The grass withereth, the flower fadeth, because the Spirit of the Lord bloweth upon it: surely the people is grass." What is all this multitude here present, but just a pickle grass: for as grass springeth out of the earth, and falls down again to the earth, so shall we and all living; and then the place that knows us shall know us no more. If you ask again, *What is man?* the Spirit of God will tell, Is. xl. 15. That " all mankind is before God but as the drop of the bucket, and the small dust that will not turn the scales of a balance," no body regarding it; and yet all mankind before the Lord is no more. O then, *What is man, that God should take knowledge of him?*" If you ask yet again, What is man before the Lord? Why, you have an answer that reduces man and all nations of men, into nothing. Is. xl. 17, " All nations are before him as nothing." Can any thing be less than nothing? yea, it is added in the close of that verse, " They are accounted before him less than nothing and vanity." And thus you see an answer to that question, What is man, considered as a creature? But,

2*dly*, What is man as a fallen creature? Man, even in his best estate, is altogether vanity before God: what then is he in his worst estate? " God planted him a noble vine, but he is become the degenerate plant of a strange vine." Let us consider what he is in this respect: a creature he is indeed; but then he is the worst of all creatures through sin; for if we search out his character from the record of God, we shall find him described, 1. To be a diseased creature, over-run with a loathesome leprosy, from the crown of the head to the sole of the foot: the disease of sin has invaded the very vitals, insomuch that the very mind and conscience is defiled and wasted, &c. Hence it follows, 2. That man, fallen man, is become an ugly and a loathesome creature, Job. xv. 16, "How much more abominable and filthy is man, which drinketh iniquity like water? Sin is called the abominable thing that God's soul hates. O! how abominable then is man, who is nothing else than a mass of sin, a compound of all manner of iniquity? 3. What is man? He is an impotent and a helpless creature, without strength, "like the helpless infant cast out into the open field," Ezek. xvi. Men may talk of the power of nature, and of their ability to convert and turn themselves, as they have a mind; but, if we believe the Spirit of God, speaking by the Son of God, he will tell us that "no man can come unto him, except the Father who sent him draw him." What can a new born infant do for its own help, cast out into the open field? Of all creatures it is the most helpless and impotent; and yet this is man's condition in his natural state. 4. *What is man?* Why, the Spirit of God will tell you that he is a rebellious creature; that he has lifted up arms against his great Lord; broken his allegiance to God, and joined in a confederacy with the devil against God. With proud Pharaoh, "we have disowned God, saying, Who is the Lord, that I should obey him?" Numb. xx. 10, "Hear now, ye rebels, must we fetch you water out of this rock?" &c. 5. *What is man, fallen man?* Why, he is a condemned creature, under sentence from the great Judge of heaven and earth: "He that believeth not is condemned already, and the wrath of God abideth on him," &c. Condemned by God, condemned by the law, condemned by conscience, &c. 6. *What is man, fallen man?* Why he is a noxious and a hurtful creature; (he has hurt the creation of God; "Cursed is the ground for thy sake," says the Lord to Adam); a cumberer of the ground; "Yea, the whole creation groaneth and travaileth in pain, under the burden of his sin." 7. He is a noisome creature, that hath a filthy smell in the nostrils of God, angels, and saints; and therefore compared to the stench of a green opened grave, that is ready to raise the pestilence: "Their throat (says David, speaking of the wicked) is an open sepulchre, and the poison of asps is under their tongue." Yea, we find fallen man compared unto those creatures that are most hurtful unto us; he is compared unto a toad, a serpent, an asp, a tiger, a lion, and the like hurtful beasts. 8. *What is man, fallen man?* Why, he is a dead creature, Eph. ii. 1. "And you hath he quickened who were dead in trespasses and sins." Now, what account do we make of the dead? They are buried out of the sight of the living; "Bury my dead out of my sight," said Abraham of Sarah; so what account should God make of dead sinners, who are destitute of the life of grace? but bury them out of his sight in hell. Thus I have told you some things in answer to that question, *What is man?* and told you what he is, as he is a creature, and as he is a sinner, or a fallen creature. And, after all, is there not good ground for this question in my text, *What is man, that thou takest knowledge of him? or the son of man, that thou makest account of him?*

II. The *second* thing, What is imported in this regard that God shews unto man, and the son of man? He is here said to take knowledge of him, to make account of him. *Answ.* It implies, 1. That, for as low, mean, and miserable a creature man is, yet he is not beyond God's notice and observation. "I saw thee," says the Lord, "when no eye pitied, when thou wast cast out and polluted in thy blood." When Adam hid himself in the bushes of paradise, "the eyes of the Lord were upon him." He saw what a pitiful pickle he was in, and all mankind in him. So Gen. vi. 5, "God saw that the wickedness of man was great in the earth, and that every imagination of the thoughts of his heart was only evil continually." 2. *What is man, that thou takest knowledge of him?* It implies that the regard God shews unto man does not flow from any thing in himself, that there is no excellency whatever in him, to recommend him unto God, neither birth nor beauty, nor riches, nor wisdom, no qualification at all that is desirable. When God takes knowledge of his elect in a way of mercy, what are they, but children of wrath, as well as others? dead in sin: and therefore, "it is not of him that willeth, nor of him that runneth, but of God that sheweth mercy." 3. *What is man?* &c. It implies, that, whatever regard God shews unto man, it is the fruit of his own free grace, and sovereign will and pleasure: "By grace are ye saved through faith, and that not of yourselves, it is the gift of God. I will heal their backslidings; I will love them freely," Hos. xiv. 4. Hence all the promises of the covenant, they run in the tenor of sovereignty, no other reason being given for them, but that of his own sovereign will. "I will be their God, and they shall be my people. I will sprinkle them with clean water, and they shall be clean; from all their filthiness and idols will I cleanse them. A new heart also will I give you," &c. 4. *What is man?* It implies, that God has no need of man, or of any of his services; Job xxii. 2, "Can a man be profitable unto God, as he that is wise may be profitable unto himself? Is it any pleasure to the Almighty that thou art righteous? or is it gain to him that thou makest thy ways perfect?" From whence it is plain, that God maketh not account of man, as that he could be profitable or advantageous to him. O, Sirs! let us not fancy that God is obliged to us for our praying, reading, hearing, obedience, or communicating: no, no; God needs neither us nor our services, &c. 5. *What is man?* It implies, that God's mercy and love unto man, and the son of man, is of a preventing nature: man is not seeking after God when he takes knowledge of him in a way of mercy. What knowledge was the poor infant taking of the Lord, when the Lord took knowledge of it, Ezek. xvi. 4, 6, Is. lxv. 1, "I am sought of them that asked not after me, I am found of them that sought me not." O Sirs! none of Adam's race would ever look after God, did not God look after us: yea, so far are we from seeking after God, that we are running further and further away from him, until he seek and find us, Is. lxii. 12, "Thou shalt be called sought out." God sought out and prevented Paul in the way to Damascus, when he had little thoughts of the Lord: he sought out Zaccheus, and every soul is sought out by preventing grace, &c. 6. *What is man?* It implies, that whatever man be, however despicable, low, and inconsiderable, yet God treats him as if he were some great and considerable person. Hence he is said to magnify him in that forecited Job. vii. 17, "What is man that thou magnifiest him?" he makes an account of him, as if he were something worth. But this leads me to

III. The *third* thing in the method, which was to show, wherein doth God discover such a regard to *man,* and the *son of man?* And here, a matter of praise upon a thanksgiving-day; let us consider, *first,* The regard that God shews unto all men in common; *secondly,* The regard he shews to his chosen generation, his peculiar people.

First, I say, let us take a short view of the regard that God shews in common unto all men, and that both in creation and providence. 1*st,* Let us observe what regard God shewed unto man, that petty poor creature, at his creation. He builds a stately house, and provides it with all necessary furniture, before he gave him a being. He rears up the beautiful fabric of heaven and earth for his use. He "gives the sun to rule by day, and the moon to rule by night," that by these luminaries he might see about him, and behold the other works of God. He spreads out the heavens as a curtain and canopy over his head, and studs and embellishes it with an innumerable multitute of glittering stars, like so many stones of fire. He plants the garden of Eden with all manner of trees, and plants, and fruits. He calculates and adjusts the creation, to gratify both his sensitive and rational appetite: he makes colours to please his eye, sounds to please his ear, delicious fruits and meats to gratify his taste, and savoury smells his scent: he frames wonders in heaven above, and earth below, for his reasonable soul to pry and wade into with pleasure and delight. Thus, I say, God discovers his regard unto man, by building and furnishing a lodging for him, before he had given him a being. But, 2*dly,* let us consider the regard God shews unto man in the course of his common providence, and that notwithstanding his apostasy from the state in which he was created. 1. Then, although we be all transgressors from the very womb, yet he continues a succession of men upon the face of the earth: what a wonder was it, that upon the first sin of Adam, he did not hew down the root of mankind, and throw him into hell, in order to prevent the sprouting up of so many branches that have sprung off him, bearing the bitter fruits of sin and rebellion against God? and yet, in his wonderful patience and long suffering, he continues a race of mankind upon earth, when he could, with so much ease, rid himself of his adversaries, and avenge himself of his enemies. O! *what is man?* 2. Let us see the wonderful care that God has in and about the formation of man in the womb. What accession had you, or I, or yet our parents, in giving us these hands and feet, and other bodily members? how came it about, that these members and bodly parts are so well shaped, and that we were not born monsters? why, it is the hand of Providence that moulded and fashioned us after this manner. David, Ps. cxxxix. 14. observes this with praise and gratitude; "I am fearfully and wonderfully made." 3. Whenever man is brought into the world, although he is the most helpless creature in himself, yet he has provided the best of help to cherish and preserve him. He not only helps us into the world, and keeps us from being stifled in the birth, but he provides the knees to dandle, and the breasts to suckle us. He not only inspired our parents with tender care and affection towards us in our non-age and infancy; but he himself, as a tender parent, nourished and brought us up, preserving and providing for us, giving us our daily bread, and all the necessaries and conveniencies of life. Have any of us comfortable dwellings in a family capacity? why, it is God that sets the solitary in families. Have any of you a stock of children like olive plants round about your table? why, children are God's heritage, and the fruit of the womb is his reward. Have you riches and worldly substance? why, this is of the Lord, as he tells Israel; "It is his blessing that maketh rich?" it is the Lord that giveth you to be rich. Has he given to any worldly honours and preferments? it is "God that sets up one, and casts another down." O! how doth God follow man with goodness and mercy every year, and every day and moment! How quickly would all flesh be starved to death, if he did not open his large granaries every year, causing the earth to produce the grain that nourisheth us, and other creatures! The psalmist David observes this as matter of praise, Ps. cxlv. 15. 16. "The eyes of all wait upon thee, and thou givest them their meat in due season; thou openest thy hand, and satisfiest the desire of every living thing." O, how wonderful is it, to behold the connection of causes that God has established! how he has linked heaven and earth together, by his powerful hand, in order to the maintaining of man upon earth! Hosa. ii. 21. 22. "And it shall come to pass in that day, I will hear, saith the Lord, I will hear the heavens, and they shall hear the earth, and the earth shall hear the corn, and the wine, and the oil, and they shall hear Jezreel." O! *what is man? or the son of man,* that the great wheels of the creation should be carried about for his benefit and sustenance. And, to conclude this head of common providence, and the kindness God shews unto man there, let us observe, how the innocent creatures that never sinned against God, or violate the laws of their creation, are every day slaughtered for the use of rebel nothing man; the fishes of the sea, the fowls of the air, the beasts of the field, their lives sacrificed to sustain the life of man, who has forfeited his title unto all good things, either in this world or the world to come. O, what a favourite must man be above the rest of the creatures? And so valuable is the life of man, that he has made it one of the ten commandments of the moral law, binding to all generations, that none shall kill man, or take away his life, till his own immediate hand put an end and period to it. Life shall go for life; "Whosoever sheddeth man's blood, by man shall his blood be shed:" and that for this good reason, because that "after the image of God created he him." O, may not this short hint of the kindness of God to man, running out in the channel of common providence, make us to cry with David, here in the text, *Lord what is man?* &c. But to pass this head of God's common goodness to man, in creation and providence.

Secondly, Let us next take a view of the good of his *chosen* that we may triumphantly praise with his inheritence upon a day of thanksgiving. And here, believers, worthy communicants, let me turn even the doctrine into a word of exhortation, and call you in the words of the psalmist, upon a thanksgiving day: "Sing unto the Lord, O ye saints of his, and give thanks at the remembrance of his holiness." And to excite and engage you to this duty, you will consider with me a little, what knowledge the great God has taken of you, and what account he has made of you by the outgoings of his love. 1. Before time. 2. In time. 3. After time ends, in eternity.

1. I say will you take a view of his love and kindness towards you *before time,* and let that engage you to cry, What is man that thou takest knowledge of him, and of me in particular? (1.) Then I say, Let us run back to the ancient years of *eternity,* and see how the kindness and love of God to man, did appear then; "when God looked upon you in your blood, he said unto you, Live, and your time was a time of love." Oh! is it not wonderful to see electing love, passing by the fallen angels, and resting upon such a poor pitiful creature as fallen sinful man? And when he passed by kings and princes, noble, and wise, and rich, and many thousands that the world would think would been the objects of his love, he passed by them, and pitched upon thee, a poor creature that no body regards. Oh! is not thy soul saying, "What am I, that God hath taken such knowledge of me? that he should have loved me with an everlasting love? that he should have chosen me before the foundations of the world? and predestinated me to the adoption of children, by Jesus Christ to himself?" (2.) The decree of electing love being past, a method must be found out for thy salvation, consistant with the honour of the law and justice of God: and therefore, as if *man,* and *the son of man,* had been some great creature, and thou in particular, believer, a council of the Trinity must be called to advise the matter; and thus the plan of thy salvation was laid.—'Oh, says the eternal Father, my love is set upon a remnant of Adam's family, and I have proposed to save

them, and to bring them to glory: but oh, how shall I put them among the children? I see that they will violate my law, and become liable to my wrath and justice, and my love to them cannot vent in a prejudice unto justice: and therefore, O Son of my eternal love, I set thee up, and ordain thee to assume their nature in the fulness of time; a body for this end have I prepared for thee, that thou mayest, as their Surety and Redeemer, fulfill my law in their room, and satisfy my justise, by the sacrafice of thy death; and I hereupon promise, that I will stand by thee in the work; mine arm shall strengthen thee; I will raise thee from the dead, and set thee on my right hand; and I will give them as a seed to serve thee, thou shalt be their Head, their Husband, their Advocate, and Mediator, and thou shalt reign over them as a peculiar kingdom, for ever and for ever.'—' I agree with my whole heart to the overture, says the eternal Son; " Lo, I come; in the volume of thy book it is written of me: I delight to do thy will, O my God;" yea, this law of redemption is within my heart; it is seated in the midst of my bowels.'—' Agrees to it, says the Holy Ghost: I will form his human nature, by my overshadowing power, in the womb of the virgin: I will sanctify his human nature, and make it a fit residence for the fulness of the Godhead to dwell in, that, out of that fulness, they may receive grace for grace: I will take of the things that are his, and shew them unto them; and carry on the work of sanctification in them, till they be brought unto glory.'—Thus, I say, the plan and method of thy salvation was laid, believer, in eternity, before the foundations of the world was laid. O then, shall not the consideration of all this make us cry, *Lord, what is man, that thou takest knowledge of him? or the son of man, that thou makest account of him?*

2. Let us come down from *eternity* to *time*, and see what work is made, in the execution of this glorious project of free grace and love towards *man*. This world being created, as a theatre upon which the glorious scene was to be acted; *man* is brought forth into the stage; a covenant of works transacted between God and him, by the breach of which *man* is plunged into an abyss of misery and sin. But no sooner is he fallen, but the eternal purpose and project of infinite love and wisdom begins to break forth; and so the scene of grace begins to be acted. When man is trembling at the apprehensions of being stricken through with the flaming sword of justice, a promise of relief and deliverance breaks out from under the dark cloud of wrath, " That the seed of the woman should bruise the head of the serpent." An angry and offended God on a sudden becomes IMMANUEL, God with us, to avenge the quarrel upon the old serpent, for the hurt he had done his viceroy and representative in this lower world. This grace contained in the first promise, is gradually opened in promises, types, and prophecies, during the Old Testament economy; until, according to the concert in the council of peace, and declared resolution in paradise, the great and renowned Champion, the Son of God, actually takes the field: and having put on the coat of

the human nature that his Father had provided for him, he works wonders in it for that petty creature man, that he might bring about his salvation. What did he? say you. *Answ.* O! What did he not, that was necessary to break up the way, and clear the passage to glory and eternal life, for man? Why, in so many words (for I cannot insist on particulars), by his obedience to the death, " He finishes transgression, and makes an end of sin; he makes reconciliation for iniquity: he brings in an everlasting righteousness." He " confirms a new covenant with many: he makes the sacrifice and oblation to cease," and unhinges the Mosaic economy, he reveals the counsel of God anent redemption; opens up the mystery of salvation in his doctrine; confirms it from heaven by a multitude of miracles; " he magnifies the law, and makes it honourable; he spoils principalities and powers, and triumphs over them in his cross; through death he destroys death, and him that hath the power of death;" he wrests the keys of death out of the devil's hand, and takes them into his own custody, that he might make it a passage to glory, instead of being a passage to hell: he dies for our offences, and rises again for our justification; he ascends up to heaven with a shout of triumph and victory; and sits down on the "right hand of the Majesty on high," as the public Head and Representative of his friends on earth, and to " appear in the presence of God for them." A little after he is set down upon the throne, he pours down his Spirit, like " the rushing of a mighty wind, upon his disciples at Pentecost; and gives gifts unto men, gives some apostles, some prophets, some evangelists, some pastors, some teachers;" and sends them abroad, with a power of working miracles, and of speaking all languages; to proclaim the glory of his finished salvation to every creature under heaven; " That whosoever believed in him might not perish, but have everlasting life." And Oh! may not a reflex view of all this work about *man* make us cry, *Lord, what is man, that thou takest knowledge of him? or what the son of man, that thou makest so great account of him?*

Well, is that all? No; for he doth yet more for man in time. Having finished the salvation of man in a way of purchase, his voice is unto men, and the sons of men; he proclaims his salvation unto the ends of the earth, and causes the joyful sound of the gospel-trumpet to be heard to the world's end. And Oh! what wonders doth he work here to make way for the salvation of poor man! A throne of grace is reared, to which man may have recourse with boldness, " that he may obtain grace, and find mercy to help him in every time of need." Acts of grace are emitted from this throne, indemnities, promises, and proclamations of grace: " Ho, every one that thirsteth, come ye to the waters: and he that hath no money, let him come, &c. Heralds are sent abroad to proclaim the grace of God through Christ to man, and to lift up their voice in the tops of the high places; a word of reconciliation is committed unto them; and they, as ambassadors for Christ, pray men, and the sons of men, to be reconciled unto

God: "because Christ was made sin for us, that we might be made the righteousness of God through him." The great storehouses of grace are opened; his righteousness and salvation brought near to every one's door in a dispensed gospel, with a voice from heaven, Come and welcome to Christ, and all his fulness. He stands with the outstretched arms of redeeming love, crying, "Behold me, behold me! O how would I gather you, as the hen gathers her chickens under her wings!" O what is man that he is thus mindful of him!—But then, what work is he at with man after all this, in order to the effectual application of the purchased and exhibited salvation? The hammer of the law must be applied, in order to break the rocky heart in pieces; the fallow ground must be plowed up, to prepare it for the reception of the incorruptible seed of gospel truth; the strong holds of Satan must be pulled down; the high imaginations of the heart levelled: Satan and proud self must be dethroned. The sinner is dead, buried, and stinking in the grave of sin; the "stone must be rolled away from the sepulchre, and wonders must be showed unto the dead, the Spirit of life must breathe upon the dry bones:" the sinner is blind, and he must have his eyes opened: he is a prisoner, and his chains of captivity must be loosed; the obstinate iron sinew of his will must be bended by the almighty power of God, and "he persuaded and enabled to embrace Christ, and salvation through him, as he is freely offered in the gospel." The sinner being thus translated from death to life, from darkness to God's marvellous light, in effectual calling, O what work doth the Lord make about the poor inconsiderable creature! how doth he heap favours and privileges, one after another upon him! He betrothes the poor forlorn creature to himself, as if it had been a chaste virgin, makes it the bride, the Lamb's wife, and says to it, Now, "thy Maker is thine Husband, the Lord of hosts is his name," &c. He takes away the filthy rags, and clothes it with change of raiment, even the white linen of his own everlasting righteousness, and makes it to sing that song, Is. lxi. 10, "I will greatly rejoice in the Lord, my soul shall be joyful in my God; for he hath clothed me with the garments of salvation, he hath covered me with the robe of righteousness, as a bridegroom decketh himself with ornaments, and as a bride adorneth herself with her jewels;" he takes the burden of all the debt it owed unto justice upon himself, and stands between it and all charges that law and justice had against it, enabling it to say, "Who can lay any thing to my charge? it is God that justifieth, who is he that condemneth? it is Christ that died, yea, rather that is risen again, who is even at the right hand of God, who also maketh intercession for us:" he becomes an everlasting Father to the poor creature, and puts it among the children, making it an heir of God, and a joint heir with himself, and says to it, "Wilt thou not from this time cry unto me, My Father," &c. He puts the beauty of his own holiness upon the soul, and makes it like "the king's daughter, all glorious within," like the embroideries of needlework; he maketh it "like the wings of a dove, covered with silver, and her feathers with yellow gold:" he visits the soul frequently, and manifests himself to it, so as he does not manifest himself to the world; he waters it with the dew of his Spirit, like the vineyard of red wine: he breathes on it by his Spirit, makes the north and south wind to awake, come and blow on it, whereby the graces of the Spirit, like so many spices, are made to send forth a pleasant smell: he bears it company through fire and water, and never leaves it: he makes the man to dwell in the secret of his presence and under his shadow, and as the mountains are round about Jerusalem, so his attributes pitch their tents on every hand of it for its defence; he plants a guard of angels about his bride, for her honour and safety, as a lifeguard, Heb. i. 14. and in a word, he "keeps it by his power through faith unto salvation; makes goodness and mercy to follow it;" and at last divides Jordan, and brings it home, under a guard of angels, to the promised land of glory, and presents it before his Father "without spot or wrinkle, or any such thing." And upon a review of all this that he doth before time, and in time, may we not justly cry out in a rapture of admiration, *Lord, what is man!*

3. If we follow the Lord's way with men, from an eternity past, through time, to an eternity to come, we shall see just cause to cry, *what is man?*—But here a vail lies between us and that glory and happiness that God has ordained and designed for man in the world to come. And the things there ordained for man are so great, that "eye hath not seen, nor ear heard, neither hath it entered into the heart of man to conceive, the things which God hath prepared for them that love him," 1 Cor. ii. 9. What thinkest thou, believer, of being "for ever with the Lord," and of having "places among them that stand by," and beholding the glory of God and of the Lamb? what thinkest thou of coming in person to "Mount Zion, the city of the living God, the heavenly Jerusalem" above described, Rev, xxi. whose "wall is of Jasper, and the city itself of pure gold, like unto transparent glass; where there is no need of the sun or moon," or of these ordinances, word and sacraments, and ministers, because the glory of the Lord doth lighten it, and the Lamb is the light thereof?" what thinkest thou, believer, of coming to the "general assembly, and church of the first-born, which are written in heaven?" what thinkest thou of joining an "innumerable company of angels, and the spirits of just men made perfect," who sing a new song, crying. "Salvation to our God, and to the Lamb, for ever and ever." Rev. vii. 10, "Worthy is the Lamb that was slain, to receive power, and riches, and wisdom and strength, and honour, and glory, and blessing?" what thinkest thou of coming to God the judge of all, as thy God and Father? what thinkest thou of coming to Jesus the Mediator of the new covenant; and of seeing him no "more darkly as through a glass, but face to face, seeing him as he is, and beholding the glory that his Father hath given him?" what thinkest thou of sitting down at the table that shall never be drawn, and of eating

and drinking with him, and the ransomed company, in the kingdom of heaven? Matth. xxvi. 29, " I will not drink henceforth " said he, at the institution of the supper, before he died, " of the fruit of the vine, until that day when I drink it new with you in my Father's kingdom." What thinkest thou of these new scenes of glory, wisdom, power, holiness, justice, mercy, grace, and love, and faithfulness, that will be opening through eternity, in the immediate vision of God, and in the works of creation, providence, and redemption; every one of which will fill thy soul with a new rapture of wonder and praise? what thinkest thou of sitting down with Christ victoriously upon his throne, as he also overcame, and is set down with his Father upon his throne? what thinkest thou of possessing these thrones in glory, that became vacant by the apostacy of the angels that fell? what thinkest thou " of ruling the nations with a rod of iron? of binding their kings with chains, and their nobles with fetters of iron? yet this honour have all the saints," 1 Cor. vi. 2, " Do ye not know, that the saints shall judge the world?" ver. 3, " Know ye not that we shall judge angels?" what thinkest thou of eating of the hidden manna, and the fruits of that tree which grows " in the midst of the paradise of God: which beareth twelve manner of fruits every month, and whose leaves are for the healing of the nations?" what thinkest thou of entering into these ivory palaces of glory with joy and triumph, on every side, the house of many mansions, the house of Christ's Father, " whose builder and maker is God?" thou shalt be satisfied then, to the full, with the fatness of his house, and drink of the rivers of his pleasures. What thinkest thou of becoming a pillar in the temple of God, where thou shalt go no more out, and having Christ's name, his Father's name, and the name of the city of our God written on thee for ever? what thinkest thou of being for ever freed and delivered of all these burdens under which thou groanest? of all these fiery darts whereby thou art now harassed? of all these oppressing fears and challenges? of all these tears, sorrows, and afflictions, which make thee to go through the world, with a bowed down back, hanging thy " harp upon the willows?" what thinkest thou of these eternal things, that are shortly to be possessed? of an eternal God, an eternal life, an eternal light, eternal love, eternal rest, eternal vision and fruition, eternal likeness and conformity to the Lord, that are abiding thee? what thinkest thou of the " crown of glory that fadeth not away?" what thinkest thou of " a kingdom that shall never be moved: an inheritance that is incorruptible, and undefiled, and that fadeth not away?" what thinkest thou of having these twilight blinks of glory through the vail, turned into an eternal day of glory? for there the Sun of righteousness shall never set, never, never, be eclipsed. O Sirs. all this, and ten thousand, thousand, thousand, times more than I can tell you, is prepared for you on the other side of death; and after all, have we not reason to sing and say, as in the text. *Lord, what is man that thou takest knowledge of him? or what the son of man, that thou makest such account of him?*

IV. The *fourth* thing in the method was, to *shew, That it is truly wonderful and surprising, that God, the great God, should have such a regard to man, that he should take such knowledge, and make such great account of him.*

I need not stay upon this, after what has been said; only in a few words. (1.) 'Tis surprising, if we consider God's infinite and amazing greatness and glory. Oh! who can think or speak of him in a suitable manner? He that shows such a regard to man, is " the high and lofty One that inhabits eternity, and dwells in the high and holy place, to which no man can approach; he that dwells in light that is inaccessible, and full of glory." He whose " throne is high and lifted up," above all the thrones of heaven and earth: He before whom angels and archangels are standing, with their " faces and their feet covered with their wings," crying, " Holy, holy, holy is the Lord God of hosts:" he who " stretched out the heavens, and laid the foundations of the earth:" he who " weighs the mountains in scales, and the hills in a balance, takes up the waters of the ocean in the hollow of his hand, and doth whatsoever he pleaseth in the armies of heaven, and among the inhabitants of the earth." O! is it not surprising and wonderful, that this great and infinite Jehovah, who hath all being, life, light, glory, and perfection, inherent in himself, and stood in no need of man nor angels, that he should take such knowledge of man, or the son of man? *Lord, what is man?*

(2.) It is surprising, if we consider what man is, what a poor inconsiderable, contemptible creature he is, both as a creature, and as a sinner, of which I spake in the entry upon the first head, in answer to that question, *What is man?* &c.

(3.) It is surprising and wonderful, because it cannot be conceived or expressed, it runs beyond all thought and all words; " Eye hath not seen, nor ear heard, neither hath it entered into the heart of man to conceive," of the kindness and condescension of God to man: so much is clearly imported in the psalmist's way of speaking, of the goodness of God in the text; *Lord, what is man, that thou takest knowledge of him?* Hence are these or the like expressions of wonder and amazement, " How excellent is thy loving-kindness, O God! How great is thy goodness which thou hast laid up for them that fear thee? Oh! the height, the depth, and length, and breadth, of the love of God, which passeth knowledge!" These expressions, they are just a posing and putting our finite minds to an eternal stand: and therefore we must stop, for what can we say more?

V. The *fifth* thing was the *Application.* And because I have been all along practical in the doctrinal part, therefore I shall conclude with a few inferences.

1st, See hence the folly of all such as are taken up in admiring any created excellency, either to be found in themselves, or others of the human race, without running up to the fountain head, an infinite God, from whom all being, beauty, glory, and excellency doth flow. The spirit of God speaks of it as a piece of brutish folly, for man to look at the creature, without tracing it and all its excellency to God, as its original: Ps. xciv. 8, "Understand, ye brutish among the people; and, ye fools, when will ye be wise? he that planted the ear, shall he not hear? he that formed the eye, shall he not see?" ver. 10, "He that teacheth man knowledge," shall not he know? These are questions that may confound all the atheistical fools in the world, who say in their hearts or practice, "There is no God;" and at the same time discover to us, that man is but a poor dependant creature, deriving all his powers in soul and body from an infinite God: hence is that challenge, Is. ii. at the close, "Cease ye from man, whose breath is in his nostrils; for wherein is he to be accounted of?" This challenge, together with the words in my text, are enough to stain the pride of all gloriation in man; *Lord, what is man, for wherein is he to be accounted of?* Especially when balanced with the excellency of his glorious Creator, he just evanishes into nothing. You heard upon the first head of doctrine, what man is in general, as a creature and as a sinner. Now, let us take a view of him in his best excellencies and qualifications, and see what they will amount to in God's reckoning, or compared with the infinite excellency of his infinite creator? What account is to be made of his being before God? why, he is not, for 'tis God only whose name is, I AM. What account is to be made of man in his pedigree, which some, like the princes of Zoan, boast of? why, he is the "degenerate plant of a strange vine." What account is to be made of his riches? why, these take the wings of the morning, and fly away, and cannot "profit man in the day of wrath." What account is to be made of his honours? they cannot "descend to the grave after him." What account is to be made of all his projects and schemes? why, that day "his breath departs his thoughts perish," and are all disconcerted and dashed in pieces. What account is to be made of his beauty? it is quickly turned into rottenness and deformity. The wisdom of man before God is but folly; his knowledge specious ignorance, his strength and power is but impotency. What is his life in the world, but a vapour which the wind of sickness and death blows away, out of time into eternity? upon the whole, then, may we not well cry, *Lord, what is man, and wherein is he to be accounted of?* Let us cease from trusting in man; for "cursed is the man, that trusteth in man, and maketh flesh his arm, and whose heart departeth from the Lord: but blessed is the man, that trusteth in the Lord, and whose hope the Lord is," Jer. xvii. 5, 6.

2*dly*, See hence the horid ingratitude of sinners, in waging war against that God, who is so good and so kind unto man. Oh! what tongue can express, or what heart can conceive, the monstrous ingratitude of sinners, in rejecting his laws, trampling on his authority, affronting him every day to his face? May not the Lord say to us, "Do ye thus requite the Lord, Oh ye foolish and unwise? Oh my people, what have I done unto thee? and wherein have I wearied thee? testify against me; was I ever a barren wilderness, or a land of darkness" unto you?

3dly, See hence the way and method that God takes to "lead sinners to repentance: why, he just pursues them with his kindness, and draws them "with cords of a man, with bands of love; knowest thou not, O man, that the goodness of God leadeth thee to repentance?" The first thing that melts and thaws the heart of a sinner, in a kindly way, is an uptaking of the love and kindness of God to man, especially as it vents through the death and blood of Christ, in the free pardon of sin, and acceptance through Christ. Whenever the soul comes to see that love, that grace, that mercy and bowels, that it has been spurning against, it begins to smite upon its thigh, with Ephraim, saying, "What have I done?" and with David, "Against thee, thee only, have I sinned, and done this evil in thy sight." And it is this that influences the turning of the soul from sin unto God, with full purpose and endeavour after new obedience; saying with Job, "That which I see not, teach thou me, if I have done iniquity, I will do no more:" the soul is just killed and melted with a sense and uptaking of the love of God.

4thly, Is God so good and so kind to worm man? then see hence, what a reasonable command the first command of the law is, "Thou shalt have no other gods before me:" that is, 'Thou shalt know and acknowledge me as God, and as thy God, and shalt worship and glorify me accordingly.' Oh! shall we give any thing, any creature, any lust, any idol, that room in our hearts, that is due unto such a kind Lord? shall we not say with Ephraim, "What have I to do any more with idols? O Lord, our God, other lords besides thee have had dominion over us, but by thee only will we make mention of thy name. All people will walk in the name of their God; and we also will walk up and down in the name of the Lord our God. Whom have *we* in the heavens but *him?* and there shall be none in all the earth whom *we* desire besides *him*."

5thly, See hence the criminal nature of the sin of unbelief, which is a saying upon the matter, God is not to be trusted, notwithstanding all his kindnesses, pity, and love to man. He calls him *a liar:* and says there is no good to be got at his hand; that he is a *hard master*, and his words are no indications of his mind: an evil heart of unbelief turns us away from the living God: why, what way doth it this? It just acts the part of the false spies that went up to Canaan, and brings up an ill report of a good God, of a true and faithful God: it says, "His mercy is clean gone, he will be favourable no more, his promise fails for evermore:" and as Israel turned back to Egypt, when they heard the ill report that the false spies brought of Canaan; so the soul, when it hears the ill report, that unbelief brings up of God, the heart turns away from him. O Sirs! take heed of an evil heart of unbelief, especially after that you have been at a communion table. There is nothing that the devil more cherishes and fosters folk in, than in their unbelief: this was the way that he ruined man at first; he made our first parents, first to conceive harsh thoughts of that good God who had been so kind to them, and then quickly he ruins them; and this is the very way that he still goes to work with his posterity; he tells you, that whatever God has done in sending his Son, whatever he has said in his word, whatever experience of his love you have met with, yet you have no ground upon which to trust him, his promise fails, he has forsaken and forgotten. If he once brings you this length, I no not how far God may be provoked to give you up to the will of the roaring lion.

6thly, Is God so kind to man? worm, worthless man? Is the regard that he shews to us so surprising and wonderful? then let us discover a regard to him, and to every thing that belongs to him.

I shall instance in a few particulars, wherein we are to discover our regard to him and for him.

1. Let us regard him even in the works of nature; the works of creation in heaven above, and in the earth below. This is a large volume, opened and spread out before all mankind: it was a book in which David was frequently reading, and he took great pleasure to see God there, "O Lord my God, how great and manifold are thy works? In wisdom hast thou made them all." The whole 104th psalm is a lecture upon the works of creation, and the order God has established among the creatures. See also psalm 8th beginning, and psalm 19th beginning, &c.

2. Let us regard him in his *works of providence*, in the government of the world, and in the government of his church, through all periods of time; and let us regard him in all the dispensations of his providence towards the land we live in, and to our families and ourselves in particular, Ps. cvii. at the close, "Whoso is wise, and will observe these things, even they shall understand the loving-kindness of the Lord." When he is trysting us with favourable dispensations, let us observe this with praise: and when he is trysting us with afflicting dispensations, let us humble ourselves under his mighty hand, that he may lift us up, &c., Ps. xxviii. 5, "Because they regard not the works of the Lord, nor the operation of his hands, he shall destroy them, and not build them up."

3. Let us regard him in *his Christ*, and the glorious work of redemption through him, and, beholding him, lift up the everlasting doors of our hearts unto "the Lord of hosts, the Lord mighty in battle." It is the great sin of Scotland, for which the Lord is contending, that Christ has not been received and regarded, either in his prophetical, priestly, or kingly offices. You know what came of them who did not regard the Lord, and reverence him, in the person of his Son: he "sent forth his armies, and miserably destroyed them:" I fear armies of men, whose language we do not understand, shall travel through our land, and avenge the quarrel of a despised, contemned, and affronted Christ, &c.

4. Let us regard him in his *book of the scriptures*. We call the scriptures the book of God; and so it is, for it is given by the

inspiration of the Holy Ghost; and therefore let us regard it, by reading and searching and diving into it, till we find the pearl; John v. 39, "Search the scriptures, for in them ye think ye have eternal life; and they are they which testify of me." And to encourage a regard to it, see Prov. ii. 2-4, God observes what regard is paid to his book among folk; "take heed to it, as unto a light shining in a dark place."

5. Regard him by attending his courts, I mean the ordinances of his worship, word and sacraments, especially the word preached, where his heralds are sent to proclaim and intimate his mind "in the high places to men, and to the sons of men." David, though a great king, looked on it as his honour, to attend the courts of the King of kings, and esteemed " a day in his courts better than a thousand in the tents of wickedness. God's way is in his sanctuary:" these are the galleries where he has many a sweet interview with his subjects. "One thing (says David) have I desired of the Lord, that will I seek after, that I may dwell in the house of the Lord all the days of my life, to behold the beauty of the Lord, and to enquire after him in his temple." These are the banqueting-houses, where he entertains them with "fat things full of marrow."

6. Shew a regard to his *great name*. This is one of the ten commandments of his moral law, "Thou shalt not take the name of the Lord thy God in vain; for he will not hold him guiltless that taketh his name in vain." Oh! "sanctify that great name, the Lord your God," and make it "your fear and your dread." Be aware of profaning it either in your common conversation, or by your unnecessary customary swearing by it, or by a slight mentioning of it even in religious duty; and ay when ye go to mention that name in any duty of worship, study to fill your minds with a holy awe and dread of it, &c.

7. Shew a regard of *his day*, and put respect upon him, by remembering it, "to keep it holy." See a sweet and encouraging promise to them that regard God's day, Is. lviii. at the close; "If thou turn away thy foot from the Sabbath, from doing thy pleasure on my holy day, and call the Sabbath a delight, the holy of the Lord, honourable; and shalt honour him, not doing thine own ways, nor finding thine own pleasure, nor speaking thine own words; then shalt thou delight thyself in the Lord, and I will cause thee to ride upon the high places of the earth, and feed thee with the heritage of Jacob thy father: for the mouth of the Lord hath spoken it." I am ready to judge, that folk's acquaintance with God himself is known by the regard they shew to his holy day.

8. Shew a regard unto his *voice*: the voice of his word; the voice of his Spirit; the voice of his providence; the voice of mercies, and the voice of afflictions: for the Lord's voice crieth in all these, and it is the man of wisdom that hears his voice, "To-day if ye will hear his voice, harden not your hearts: be not like the deaf adder stopping her ear at the voice of charmers, charming

never so wisely." Whenever he comes, say, "Speak, Lord, for thy servant heareth." His voice is sweeter than the melody of angels and archangels to the soul that knows him: "It is the voice of my beloved, behold he cometh, leaping upon the mountains, skipping upon the hills."

9. Shew a regard to all *his laws* and *commandments;* get them engraven upon your hearts, that they may be a lamp to your feet, and a light to your paths.

10. Shew a regard to his *promises* and *words of grace,* and any word of grace that he seals, and sends home by his Spirit upon thy heart; let that be a *michtam* or *golden word* to thee; and say of it, "It is better to me than gold, yea, than much fine gold: God hath spoken in his holiness, I will rejoice:" roll it like a "sweet morsel under thy tongue."

11. Shew a regard to his *members,* by esteeming them as the "excellent ones of the earth," and doing all the offices of kindness to them that ye are capable of: for what says he, Matth. xxv. 40, "Inasmuch as ye have done it unto one of the least of these my brethren, ye have done it unto me." Cultivate fellowship and acquaintance with these that belong to the Lord, and let them be the men of your counsel, and your intimates. My "delight is with the saints." Tell them that fear the Lord, what he hath done for your soul.*

12. Regard him in his *messengers* and *ambassadors,* his *sent servants,* who act for their great Master; and faithfully declare his mind, and contend for his cause in a day of defection and backsliding, especially any that he has set, as it were, in the front of the battle, to bear the shock of the enemy; they have many against them, and therefore they need your sympathy and countenance, who "love the Lord." A kindly word or look from a member of Christ will do more service to a minister of Christ than folk are aware of: Paul, in his bonds, was refreshed and comforted with the sympathy of believers.

13. Shew a regard to *him,* by espousing his cause, the interest of his house and kingdom. Sirs, the cause of Christ is upon the field at this day; the covenanted standard of Scotland is displayed, in opposition to that course of defection which the whole land is gone into, and which the judicatories of the established church are carrying on, with might and main. The cry is given, "Who is on the Lord's side?" let them "come up to the help of the Lord, to the help of the Lord against the mighty." Some, both ministers and Christians, profess friendship unto the cause of Christ, his covenanted doctrine, discipline, worship, and government: but they love to dwell at ease, and, like Issachar, to crouch under the burden: but I have little skill if that be the Lord's way, and the Lord's call, when others are jeoparding themselves "in the high places of the field," for the cause and testimony of Jesus.

---

* But let it be done in a judicious way, that they may be excited to join with you in celebrating his praises.

I may say to such, be who they will, as the prophet said to Israel, in a day of defection from the Lord, "How long halt ye between two opinions? If Baal be God, serve him, and if Jehovah be God," then serve and follow him. If the judicatories of the church be fighting the cause of Christ, and building the Lord's house, then cleave to them, and good reason: but if they be building Jericho, instead of Jerusalem; if they be pulling down the work of God, instead of building it up; if the ark of God, his covenanted cause and testimony, be carried without the camp, it is time to follow it; let "us go out therefore unto him without the camp, bearing his reproach." And if folk shift following Christ, his cause and sworn testimony, especially when it is espoused by a handful upon all hazards, they need to consider upon it in time, lest that sentence go against them; "Curse ye Meroz, curse ye bitterly the inhabitants thereof, because they came not to the help of the Lord, to the help of the Lord against the mighty." Christ and his cause will carry the day without you; but take heed that he don't resent it, ere all be done; his frowns and down-looks are heavier than the frowns of all the men on earth, or angels in heaven, or devils in hell.

ACTION SERMON.

THE HUMAN NATURE PREFERRED UNTO THE ANGELICAL.

HEBREWS ii. 16.—"For verily he took not on him the nature of angels; but he took on him the seed of Abraham."

THE apostle, ver. 10, had spoken of Christ as the Captain of our salvation: he shews, ver. 14 and 15, how, according to the first promise, Gen. iii. 15, he had taken the field, and bruised the head of the old serpent; why, says he, ver. v. 14, "He took part of the children's flesh, that through death he might destroy him that had the power of death," &c. The legal power of death fell, by virtue of the sentence of a broken law, into the hand of the devil, as God's executioner; and it had continued there, unless law and justice had been satisfied by the death of the Surety; but Christ, "through death, destroyed him that had the power of death;" i.e., he sapped the foundation of his authority and power, by his justice-satisfying blood: he, as it were, wrung the keys of hell and death out of the devil's hand, upon Mount Calvary, and so "spoiled principalities and powers, and made a shew of them openly." The use that we, law-condemned sinners, are to make of this, is (ver. 15), to pull up our sinking spirits, and triumph over death as a conquered and slain enemy, saying, "O death, where is thy sting? O grave, where is thy victory?" for he did all this "to deliver them, who, through fear of death, were all their lifetime subject to bondage." Now the apostle, in the words of my reading, gives a good reason why Christ, as the Captain of our salvation, destroyed death, "and him that had the power of it," and delivers poor men from the sting and fear of it. Why, says he, he is our kinsman, unto whom the right of redemption did belong; *for verily he took not on him the nature of angels*, &c.

Where we have, *first*, a negation or denial of a great dignity unto the angelical nature; *he took not on him the nature of angels*, or, as it reads in the margin, *he taketh not hold of angels:* when an innumerable company of them fell from the state wherein they were created, he took not hold of their nature, to recover them from woe and misery; it is plainly supposed, that they were not the objects of his love, and therefore he did not become a God-angel, as he became a God-man.

In the words following, we have, *secondly*, an affirmation of this honour to the human nature, which he denied to the angelical; *he took on him the seed of Abraham*, in the margin, *of the seed of Abraham he taketh hold*, *i.e.*, he joined the human nature, in the seed of Abraham, to himself, in a personal union, that so, being our Kinsman, he might become our Redeemer and our Husband. The apostle, when he is writing to the Galatians, who were Gentiles, tells them, Gal. iv. 4. That he was "made of a woman," according to the first promise, Gen. iii. 15, but when he writes to the Hebrews, he speaks in the style of the promise made to Abraham, "in thy seed shall all the nations of the earth be blessed;" by telling them, that according to that promise, he took on him *the seed of Abraham*, that so they might be encouraged to believe in him; for ministers, in preaching Christ, are to bring the sinner and the Saviour as near to one another as possible.

Thirdly, In the words we have a strong asseveration, shewing the certainty and importance of this matter, that *he took not on him the nature of angels, but the seed of Abraham:* Verily, says he, it is so; it "is a faithful saying, and worthy of all acceptation;" and therefore, let all the seed of Israel, or Abraham, believe it, and set to their seal of faith to it.

OBSERVE "That it is a truth of the greatest certainty and moment, that the Son of God, when he passed by the nature of angels, took on him the human nature, in the seed, or family, of Abraham."

The doctrine is clearly founded upon the words, *For verily he took not on him the nature of angels, but he took on him the seed of Abraham.*

In discoursing the doctrine a little, I shall, through divine assistance, make it evident,

I. That the Son of God took not on him the nature of *angels*.

II. Make it appear, that he hath taken unto him the *human nature*, and is become one of our tribe and family.

III. Shew what may be imported in his taking on *him the seed of Abraham*, or his taking *hold* of it, as in the margin.

IV. Shew what is the importance of this truth implied in the asseveration *verily*.

V. Apply.

I shall endeavour brevity on these heads.

I. The *first* thing is, to make it evident, that Christ, the Son of God, *took not on him the nature of angels*.

Of all created beings, *angels* are the most excellent, they being pure immaterial spirits, approaching nearest to the nature of God, who is the infinite, eternal, and uncreated Spirit, Ps. civ. 4, " He maketh his angles spirits, his ministers a flaming fire;" and yet when they fell from their first state, and so needed a Saviour as much as fallen man, yet the apostle here tells us, with a *verily*, that *he took not on* their nature, or did not *catch hold of* them, to save them from ruin. This is clear and evident from the terms in which the first promise is uttered, Gen. iii. 15. where, at the same time that the remedy and relief is promised to fallen man, vengeance and wrath is denounced against Satan, " It shall bruise thy head," says the Lord to Satan, viz., the " seed of the woman." This is upon the matter repeated, Is. lxiii. 4, " The day of vengeance is in mine heart, and the year of my redeemed is come;" as if he had said, 'The old quarrel with Satan, the enemy of man's salvation, is still in mine heart, I am to execute vengeance upon him when I come in the flesh, to redeem my people from his slavery and bondage.' And accordingly, we are told, Col. ii. 15. That he " spoiled principalities and powers," and triumphed over them in his cross. Eternal war is proclaimed from heaven against the fallen angels: hence we are told, Jude 6. " The angels which kept not their first estate, he hath reserved in everlasting chains under darkness, unto the judgment of the great day." From all which it is clear, that he is so far from showing such a regard to the fallen angels, as to take their nature upon him, that he hath taken up, and will pursue an everlasting quarrel against them. And I make no doubt but it fills those evil spirits with horror and torment, to hear these tidings told in this assembly, where we are met together to commemorate the love of God, in taking on the human nature, and giving it a sacrifice for the sin of man.

I know some divines pretend to assign some reasons, why God passed by the nature of angels, when he took on him the human nature: but seeing the Spirit of God is silent as to this matter, it is safest for us to resolve it into the will of that sovereign Lord, " who doth in the armies of heaven, and amongst the inhibitants of the earth," what pleaseth him ; and to say with Christ, Matth. xi. 26, " Even so, O Father, for so it has pleased thee." And therefore I proceed to

II. The *second* thing proposed, which was, to prove, that the glorious Son of God, who thinks it not "robbery to be equal with God," hath indeed taken upon him the human nature, although he hath passed by the nature of angels.

Sirs, we need all much to be established in the faith of this glorious and fundamental truth. A flaw in our faith as to this, makes the whole building totter; and I am afraid that they who think it an easy matter to believe it, never yet saw the infinite distance between the nature of God and the nature of man; for, without controversy, this is a great mystery, "God made manifest in the flesh." And the truth and certainty of it may be cleared and confirmed.

1*st*, From scripture prophecy concerning him, Ps. xxii. where he speaks of his hands and his feet being pierced; of his being cast upon his Father's care from the womb: Thou art he that took me out of my mother's belly. So Is. liii. through the whole, the prophet speaks of his being wounded and bruised for our iniquities, of his death and resurrection, which all plainly suppose his taking on our nature.

2*dly*, Scripture history makes it evident, that he took on him our nature in the seed of Abraham, particularly his genealogy, Matth. i. and Luke iii. Yea, the whole history of the four evangelists concerning his birth, life, death, resurrection, and ascension, in our nature, into heaven, prove, that *verily he took on him the seed of Abraham:* how could his hands and his feet be pierced with nails, and his side with a spear? how could blood and water issue forth at the wound? if he had not *verily taken on him the seed of Abraham.*

3*dly*, This is clear from plain scripture testimony. I only mention these two or three: The testimony of the apostle here, in the 14th verse of this chapter: "Forasmuch then as the children are partakers of flesh and blood, he also himself likewise took part of the same. Rom. i. 3. "Jesus Christ, who was made of the seed of David, according to the flesh." Rom. ix. 5. "Of whom, as concerning the flesh, Christ came who is over all God blessed for ever." John i. 14, "The Word was made flesh, and dwelt among us," &c.

4*thly*, Take the testimony of angels unto this great truth: the angel Gabriel attests it, when he said to the virgin Mary, Luke i. 30-32. "Fear not, Mary, for thou hast found favour with God: and behold, thou shalt conceive in thy womb, and bring forth a son, and shalt call his name Jesus; he shall be great, and shall be called the Son of the Highest." So in the 2d. chapter, 10th verse, the angels tell the shepherds, "We bring you good tidings of great joy; for unto you is born, in the city of David, a Saviour, which is Christ the Lord."

5*thly*, He goes yet higher, and gives you the testimony of the "three that bear record in heaven, the Father, the Word, and the Spirit." The Father attests it by preparing a body for him. The Son attests it by putting it on; *he took on him the seed of Abraham;* he wore it on earth for about thirty-three years, and from hence has carried it away to heaven with him, and from heaven declares the tuth of his incarnation and death, saying, "I am he that liveth and was dead, and behold I am alive for evermore, and have the keys of hell and of death," Rev. i. 18. The Holy Ghost attests it, by his forming the human nature in the womb of the virgin, by his overshadowing power. But I do not insist. The titles that are everywhere given him from his human nature, make this evident: he is called a Man, and the Son of Man, a title in which he himself delights, and repeats every now and then; he is called frequently the seed of the woman, the seed of Abraham, the seed of David, a branch that sprung out of the root of Jesse. From all which we may conclude, with the apostle, in the words of my text, that *verily he took on him the seed of Abraham.*

III. The *third* thing was, what may be imported in the expression of the text, of his taking *on him the seed of Abraham.*

I cannot enlarge upon such a subject; only it imports,

1*st,* That the human nature was upon the point of perishing with the fallen angels, till Christ took hold of it.

2*dly,* It implies his pre-existence, as God, unto his actual incarnation, whereby the Socinian error falls, who assert, that he had no being till he was born of the virgin; for if so, how could he take to him the human nature? Sirs, let Arians and Socinians be for ever confounded: for our Immanuel was God, co-equal with his Father, from eternity; and, in the fulness of time, seventeen hundred and forty-two years ago, was "made of a woman: In the beginning was the Word, and the Word was with God, and the Word was God.

3*dly,* It implies the verity and reality of his incarnation, of which I spoke already. His human nature was no phantom, or appearance, but the real human nature, and the whole nature of man, consisting of a true body and reasonable soul; for, says the apostle, *he verily took on him the seed of Abraham.*

4*thly,* The expression implies, that it was a voluntary deed; *he took on him;* as a man puts on his clothes with his own hands, so the Son of God voluntarily put on the human nature; voluntarily agreed to it in the council of peace, Ps. xl. 8. and, from eternity, rejoice "in the habitable parts of the earth," and he was a volunteer when it came to the execution.

5*thly,* It implies, that the assumption of the human nature terminates in the person of the Son of God. Although the other persons, Father and Spirit, had their own peculiar agency, in forming and preparing the human nature; yet it is the Son, the second person of the glorious Trinity, that wears it: so that it cannot be said of the Father or Holy Ghost, but only of the Son, that he "took unto him the seed of Abraham:" so that is not an essential, but a personal union, between the divine and human nature.

6*thly,* It implies, that though the union be personal, yet it is without any confusion of the two natures: they still remain essentially distinct, although indeed, through the intimacy of the union, the properties of each nature are frequently ascribed to the whole person.

7thly, It implies, that it was an act of amazing love, grace, and condescension, that he took our nature upon him. Hence the apostle cries out with wonder, 1 Tim. iii. 16. " Without controversy, great is the mystery of godliness; God was manifested in the flesh." This is such a depth, that the angels desire to look into it. Hence the cherubims were made with their faces pointing towards the mercy-seat.

8thly, It implies, that the human nature did not constitute the person of Christ: for here we see that he, as a person, took the human nature to himself, or took it into his own person. If the human nature were a person, then he would have two persons, as well as two natures: but this is an error long since condemned; and the expression in the text bears, that it was only the nature, therefore called *the seed of Abraham;* agreeable to this is that, Luke i. 35. " That holy thing which shall be born of thee: " it is not that holy person, but that holy thing, viz., the innocent nature of man, consisting in a true body and reasonable soul. So much for what is imported in the expression.

IV. The *fourth* in the method was, to touch a little at the importance of this matter pointed at in the word of asseveration VERILY, *Verily he took not on him* the nature of *angels but the seed of Abraham.*

It is observed in the history of the evangelists, when our blessed Lord is to declare any doctrine that is of great consequence and moment, to arrest the attention of his audience, he ushers it in with a VERILY; and sometimes he doubles it with a " VERILY, VERILY, I say unto you; " as in his discourse unto Nicodemus, concerning the necessity of regeneration, John iii. 3, " Verily, verily, I say unto thee, except a man be born again, he cannot see the kingdom of God; " so here the apostle, after his example, when he is asserting the doctrine of the incarnation of the Son, ushers it in with a VERILY, that we may advert to it as a thing of the last moment. The importance of it will appear, if we consider that this point of the incarnation, or union of the two natures, was the main leading matter that was upon the carpet, in the council of peace, between the Father and the Son: it was the hardest thing to be determined and effected; and that without it, nothing could be done, for the redemption and salvation of lost sinners of Adam's family. There were three things that justice demanded, in order to the salvation of lost man: 1*st,* That the human nature be presented to God, in its original purity, without spot or blemish. 2*dly,* That the holy law be perfectly obeyed, and the honour of it maintained. 3*dly,* That seeing the law is broken, the penalty of it, or its curse, be endured by one in man's nature, whose blood must be of infinite value for the satisfaction of justice. Well, in this case, the eternal Son of God looked, and " there was none to help or uphold, and therefore his own arm brought salvation."

"Come (says he unto his Father), since there is no sacrifice nor offering that will please, Lo, I come; I delight to do thy will; a body hast thou prepared for me, in *the seed of Abraham;* I will put it on, and satisfy all these hard demands of justice: I, as a second Adam, a public head and representative of the seed thou hast given me, will present the human nature entire in my own person; and will, through my sanctifying Spirit in them, present them also unto thee, at the end of time, without spot or blemish, or any such thing. I also, as their Covenant-head and Surety, will, in their nature, fulfil the whole law as a covenant, and bring in an everlasting righteousness for their justification, and write it as a rule upon their hearts, and, by my Spirit put within them, will cause them to walk in my statutes. And because justice demands that the same nature that sinned should also suffer, therefore I will give my human nature a sacrifice for their sin; I will be wounded for their iniquities, bruised for their transgressions: of my hand shalt thou require the debt that they owe to justice." In a word (for I cannot insist), the incarnation of the Son of God is such a material and important matter, that without it the whole business of man's salvation and redemption ceases for ever; all the other supernatural mysteries of our holy religion turn upon it, as a hinge: take this away, and immediately the doctrine of his obedience to the law, and death upon the cross; his resurrection, ascension, and intercession; all fall to the ground together: but the apostle here, to certify us of it, tells us, *Verily he took not on him the nature of angels, but he took on him the seed of Abraham.*

V. The *fifth* thing was to make some improvement of this doctrine. It would admit of a large application; but I must needs cut short, because of the work that we have before us.

Use *first* shall be of information, in the few particulars following. Is it so, that when God passed by the nature of *angels, he took on him the seed of Abraham?* Then,

1*st,* See hence the wondrous love of God unto mankind sinners, that he preferred our nature unto the nature of angels; he passed them by, and pitched upon the human nature, and joined it to himself, in the person of his eternal Son. There is such an amazing and astonishing love here, as would fill our hearts with wonder, and our tongues with hallelujahs of praise, if we but saw it in the light of the Lord, and had it "shed abroad upon our hearts; surely God is love; for he so loved the world, as to give his only begotten Son, that whosoever believeth in him should not perish, but have everlasting life."

2*dly,* See hence how unjust and unreasonable the enmity of the heart of man against God is. Shall we hate that God who passed by the nature of angels, and took on him *the seed of Abraham?* It cannot be supposed that the fallen angels would have treated him so, if he had passed by our nature, and pitched upon their nature, and become a God-angel, instead of a God-man; yet this folly is in the heart of every sinner by nature; " the carnal mind is enmity against God."

3dly, See hence the monstrous ingratitude of Arians, Socinians, and others, who take occasion from his assumption of the human nature, and becoming his Father's servant in the great business of man's redemption, to disparage him, as if he were but an inferior deity, not one and the same God, in essence and substance with the Father. O! " Tell it not in Gath, publish it not in the streets of Askelon," that such blasphemies have been vented against the great God our Saviour, and so little resentment discovered against the blasphemer, in the supreme ecclesiastical court of this national church, constitute in his name and authority. But whatever others do, let us this day acknowledge, that Jesus Christ is the Lord Jehovah, to the praise and glory of his eternal Father, who sent him, not to take *on him the nature of angels,* but the *human nature, in the seed of Abraham.*

4thly, See hence to what a pitch of honour the human nature is raised, by its standing in a personal union with the infinite Jehovah, in the person of the Son of God. When we take a view of our nature as it stood in the first Adam, even in innocency, why, the spirit of God declares by the psalmist, that even in its best estate it was altogether vanity, being but a fallible creature: but view the nature of man in his fallen state, we see him lying in a " horrible pit, and miry clay," an object of abhorence to God and all his holy angels; he is wholly " corrupt and filthy," fit for nothing but to become fuel for the fire of divine wrath: and yet for an infinitely holy and righteous God to take that nature out of the dunghill, and join it into a personal union with his eternal and only begotten Son, why, this is a brighter crown of glory by far set upon the human nature, than ever Adam wore in innocency; yea, a greater honour than ever was conferred upon the nature of angels. O! how may this make every one of us to cry, " What hath God wrought? O what is man, that thou art so mindful of him? and what the son of man, that thou art so kind unto him."

5thly, See hence the excellency of the person of our glorious Redeemer, whose death we are this day called to commemorate. I remember the daughters of Jerusalem put a question unto the spouse, Cant. v., " What is thy beloved more than another beloved?" Why, Sirs, there is something in the person of Christ, that is not to be seen in any person in heaven or in earth. What is that? say you: Why, in his person is to be seen God and man linked in a personal union; " God manifested in the flesh, is the great mystery" of the Christian religion. Look to God in the person of the Father, look to God in the person of the Holy Ghost, and you see indeed the great God, who is infinite, eternal, and unchangeable in his being, wisdom, power, holiness, &c. But then, look to God in the person of the Son, who is the same God with both, and you see the human nature; there you see " Immanuel, God-man, God with us, God reconciling the world unto himself, not imputing their trespasses unto them, but pardoning iniquity, transgression, and sin." O Sirs, a God in Christ will be the admiration of saints and angels through eternity; and it is a view of this person that fills the mouths of all the saints with praise, saying, "Thou art fairer than the children of men; grace is poured into thy lips; he is white and ruddy, the chief among ten thousand," &c.

6thly, See hence the criminal nature of the sin of unbelief, which rejects him who took *not on him the nature of angels, but the seed of Abraham*. Unbelief upon the matter denies this glorious truth, and says, "No thanks to God for taking hold of the seed of Abraham; he might as well have taken on the nature of angels, for I will not be obliged to him for salvation." The unbeliever chooses rather to go to hell with his lusts, than to go to heaven with Christ: he crucifies "the Son of God afresh, and puts him to an open shame:" he tramples the blood of Christ under his feet; for which reason Christ declares, that he "that believeth not is condemned already, and the wrath of God abideth on him," John iii. 18-36.

7thly, See, from this doctrine, the great difference between the first and the second Adam; the head of the covenant of works, and the head of the new covenant. Why, the first Adam, as the apostle tells us, was but a made creature, and he "was made a living soul; but the last Adam is a quickening spirit: the first Adam was of the earth earthy; but the second Adam is the Lord from heaven:" who *took not on him the nature of angels, but took on him* the human nature, in *the seed of Abraham*. O what a blessed exchange doth the sinner make, when he quits the first Adam and his covenant, and betakes himself to a second Adam, and takes hold of him as the head of the covenant of grace! when he doth so, he quits the foundation of sand, and builds upon that "rock of ages, against which the gates of hell shall never prevail." The first Adam is a fountain of death to all his posterity, Rom. v. 12, "By one man sin entered into the world, and death by sin; and so death passed upon all men, for that all have sinned:" but the second Adam is the fountain of life to all his seed; "I am the resurrection, and the life; and he that believeth in me, though he were dead, yet shall he live:" and this we are assured of by the record of a glorious Trinity, 1 John v. 11, "This is the record, that God hath given to us, eternal life, and this life is in his Son."

8thly, See, from this doctrine, what is the great work and business of those who sit down at a communion table; what it is that makes a worthy or unworthy communicant. That which makes a worthy communicant, is a "right discerning of the Lord's body;" and when this is wanting, a man becomes "guilty of the body and blood of the Lord, and so eats and drinks judgment to his own soul." Now, what is it to discern the Lord's body? It is just an insight into this doctrine, or text, that *the eternal Son of God, he took not on him the nature of angels, but the seed of Abraham*. More particularly, I will tell you two or three things included in discerning the Lord's body.

(1.) It is to have the mind enlightened with a saving knowledge of the mystery of salvation, as the plan of it is laid out before us in the word, or in the person and mediation of Jesus, 2 Cor. iv. 6, "God who commanded the light to shine out of darkness, hath shined in our hearts, to give the light of the knowledge of the glory of God in the face of Jesus Christ."

(2.) It is to see the love and wisdom of the Father, in preparing a body for his eternal Son, in which the fulness of the Godhead should dwell, as in a temple.

(3.) It is to see the Holy Ghost forming that body, by his overshadowing power, in the womb of the virgin, so as that it might be free of original sin, and might be a sacrifice without spot or blemish, to be offered up unto God.

(4.) It is to see the eternal Son of God wearing that body in a personal union with himself, in order to his giving an infinite value unto what he was to do and suffer for us.

(5.) It is to see him offering up that body and blood, which he had thus assumed, in our room and stead, a sacrifice for the satisfaction of justice for our sin; for he offered up himself for us "a sacrifice and offering of a sweet smelling savour;" to see the just suffering for the unjust, to bring us to God. Now, when the soul thus discerns the body of Christ, or the mystery of the incarnation of the Son of God, then faith eats his flesh and drinks his blood, like "fat things full of marrow, wines on the lees, well refined." O Sirs! see if, like Samson, you can this day find the honey-combs of salvation, and the great and precious promises, in the carcase of the slain Lion of the tribe of Judah, for this "is meat indeed, and drink indeed."

Use *second* may be of *Trial*. O Sirs! what think you of him *who took not on him the nature of angels, but the seed of Abraham;* have you given him his errand into the world, by believing in him? Is thy soul crying, "Hosanna to the Son of David;" O! "blessed is he that cometh in the name of the Lord," to save us: O! "this is a faithful saying, and worthy of all acceptation, that Christ came into the world to save sinners, of whom I am chief?" Is thy heart glowing with love to him, who is altogether lovely? and saying, O! "whom have I in heaven" but him? — "yea, doubtless, I count all things but loss for the excellency of the knowledge of Christ Jesus my Lord." Well, if this be the disposition of thy soul, I invite you to come and feast with him. "Eat, O friends, drink, yea drink abundantly, O beloved. Eat ye that which is good, and let your soul delight itself in fatness, and I will make an everlasting covenant with you, well ordered in all things, and sure:" the whole good of the covenant is before you.

Use *third* of *Exhortation*, to all hearing me, young and old, great and small, rich and poor. Whoever you are, if you be of the human kind, men and women, sprung of Adam; O! will ye answer the design of the Son of God, his taking on our nature, when he past by the nature of angels, by believing in him? The Father presents him to you, as the object of his delight, that you may believe in him, Is. xlii. 1, "Behold my servant whom I uphold, mine elect in whom my soul delighteth," &c. Christ himself invites and calls us to this, Is. xlv. 22, "Look unto me, and be ye saved, all the ends of the earth, for I am God, and there is none else."

Quest. What will we behold, or see, in an incarnate God? In him who *took on him the seed of Abraham?* when he passed by the nature of angels? *Answ.* There are wonders to be seen in him, which the standing holy angels behold with admiration and eternal wonder. 1. O come and see an angry God reconciled; God looking out with a smile upon the guilty sinners, through the veil of the human nature, 2 Cor. v. 19, "God was in Christ reconciling the world to himself, not imputing their trespasses unto them;" crying, "Fury is not in me," for the sake of him in whom I am well pleased, Is. xii. 1, 2, Luke ii. 10, 12, &c. 2. In him you may see God dwelling with man upon earth, and "the whole earth filled with his glory." 3. In him you will see the great God, that gives laws unto angels and men, made under his own law, that he might magnify it, and make it honourable, that so "the righteousness of the law might be fulfilled in us," who had broken every command of it. 4. In him you will see "the hand-writing which was against us," and bound us over to wrath, woe, and misery, cancelled and torn; so that you may cry, who can lay any thing to your charge? 5. In him you will see the brandished and flaming sword of justice, that was ready to be soaked in the blood of the guilty sinner, awakening against the man who is God's fellow, Zech. xiii. 7, and having drunk of his royal blood, the sword is again put up in its scabbard, and the white flag of peace cast out with this motto, "He hath made peace by the blood of his cross." 6. Here you will see the head of the old serpent bruised, and the Lamb of God overcoming him by his own blood. "Through death he destroyed him that had the power of death." 7. In him you will see the two insuperable mountains of natural and moral distance between God and man removed, and made as a plain. The natural distance is removed in his incarnation, and the moral distance in his satisfaction. All bars and impediments that stood in our way from law and justice removed, which could never have been effected by all the angels in heaven, or men upon earth; and yet this is done, and done by him, *who took not on him the nature of angels, but the seed of Abraham.* 8. Here you will see "the veil of the temple rent from top to bottom, and the way to the holiest of all opened;" so that we may now "enter in with boldness by the blood of Jesus." The veil of the ceremonial law is rent, the veil of the curse of the moral law is rent, in the rending asunder of the soul and body of Christ upon Mount Calvary. 9. In him you may see God, first marrying our nature into a personal union with himself, and then, having come upon a level with us, or having become one of our tribe, or family, presents himself as a Bridegroom, proffering marriage with our persons; for this is the voice of Immanuel God-man, Is. liv. 5, "Thy maker is thine husband (the Lord of hosts is his name);" or, Hos. ii. 19, "I will betrothe thee unto me for ever; yea, I will betrothe thee unto me in righteousness, and in judgment, and in loving-kindness, and in mercy; I will ever betrothe thee unto me in faithfulness, and thou shalt know the Lord," viz. in a way of conjugal love and communion. 10. Here you will see him confirming the covenant of grace and promise, and turning it into an inviolable testamentary deed, which no man can disannul. Dan. ix. 27, "He shall confirm the covenant with many." Heb. ix. 16, 17, "Where a testament is, there must also of necessity be the death of the testator, for a testament is of force after men are dead: otherwise it is of no force at all while the testator liveth." Sirs, this is what we are to present you with in this holy ordinance of the supper, even the confirmed testament of him who took on him "*the seed of Abraham;*" for Luke xxii. 29, "This cup (says Christ) is the new testament in my blood," Matth. xxvi. 27, "drink ye all of it."

Secondly, Another word of exhortation is this. I call you who are the sons and daughters of Zion, not only to "go forth and behold king Solomon," and the wonders of his person and mediation, but I call you to be his bride and spouse, by giving the heart and hand to him as the bridegroom. Let there be a match this day made up betwixt Christ and your souls. Has the glorious Son of God, "the brightness of his Father's glory," taken hold of your nature in the family of Abraham? O then take hold of him as your kinsman; and say, as Ruth did unto Boaz, "Spread thy skirt over me," and perform the kinsman's part by marrying me. Sirs, I tell you, that our blessed goel and kinsman, as he took part of your flesh, so he wears your nature, that he may wed you, and betrothe you unto himself for ever. O! will you go with the man, "Immanuel, God with us?" His hand is stretched out, while I am speaking, saying to every one in this company, "Behold me! behold me!" O! subscribe the contract with heart and hand, saying, "I am the Lord's; I will be for thee, and not for another, who took not on thee the nature of angels, but took on thee the nature of man, or *the seed of Abraham.* O! that this may be the wedding-day."

"All things are ready, O come to the marriage." 1. The Bridegroom is ready, the matchless Immanuel; behold he standeth behind your wall. "Behold the Bridegroom cometh," yea he is come; he stands at the door and knocks, saying, Open to me, Rev. iii. 20, &c. 2. The Bridegroom's Father is ready; he consents that there should be a match between you and his eternal Son; he cries from heaven, "This is my beloved Son, in whom I am well pleased, hear ye him. This is his commandment, that ye believe in him," and so take him as my unspeakable gift. 3. The Spirit, the third person of the glorious Trinity, is ready, as the minister, to cast the everlasting knot between you and him, Rev. xxii. 17, "The Spirit saith, Come." Heb. iii. 7, 8. The Holy Ghost saith, "To-day if ye will hear his voice, harden not your hearts." Many a kind motion doth the Spirit of God make on your souls, in order to carry on the match. 4. The friends of the Bridegroom, all faithful ministers and Christians, are ready: they rejoice "greatly because of the Bridegroom's voice" in the gospel, offering marriage to you. O to hear the voice of the bride also saying, "My beloved is white and ruddy, the chiefest among ten thousands—His countenance is as Lebanon; excellent as the cedars—My beloved is mine, and I am his; he feedeth among the lilies; until the day break, and the shadows flee away." 5. The contract is ready, I mean the covenant of grace. The draught of it was made at the table of the council of peace from eternity, and the extract of it is in the Bible you have amongst your hands: and we bring it forth to you in the preaching of the gospel, and present it to every one, saying, "To you (and you, and you), is the word of this salvation sent. The promise is to you, and to your seed." O! let us all fear, lest a promise being made, any of us should come short of it through unbelief. 6. The marriage-house is ready, both the lower and the higher stories of it are ready: and that moment you believe, you enter into the rest of the blessed Bridegroom; ye enter into the house which Wisdom hath built with seven pillars, and shall ere long be transported to the upper house of many mansions, where ye shall behold his face, and "be with him for ever." The marriage-supper is ready; for Wisdom has not only builded her house of mercy, but "she hath killed her oxen and fatlings; she hath mingled her wine, and furnished her table," Prov. ix. 2, 5, "Wisdom hath builded her house, she hath hewn out her seven pillars. She hath killed her beasts, she hath mingled her wine; she hath also furnished her table. She hath sent forth her maidens, she crieth upon the highest places of the city. Whoso is simple, let him turn in hither: as for him that wanteth understanding, she saith to him, Come, eat of my bread, and drink of the wine which I have mingled." 7. The marriage-robe of righteousness. and garment of salvation, is ready; for the "righteousness of God is revealed in the gospel." The Lord is crying to this company, "Hearken unto me, ye stout-hearted, that are far from righteousness, I bring near my righteousness,—I have placed salvation in Zion, for Israel my glory."

Well then, Sirs, since all is ready, there is nothing wanting but the bride. O come, and be the bride of the glorious Bridegroom; and let us all cry one to another, as Rev. xix. 7, "Let us be glad and rejoice, for the marriage of the Lamb is come, and his wife hath made herself ready." Amen, Amen, Amen.

THE BROKEN LAW MAGNIFIED AND MADE HONOURABLE,
&c.

Isaiah xlii. 21.—"The Lord is well pleased for his righteousness sake; he will magnify the law, and make it honourable."

THE FIRST SERMON ON THIS TEXT.

THIS chapter, you see, is ushered in with a solemn call from God the father of all the world, both Jews and Gentiles, to take notice of Messiah the Prince, the eternal Son of God, whom he was, in the fulness of time, to send into the world, upon the great errand and business of the redemption of lost sinners of Adam's family: and to arrest their attention and admiration unto this extraordinary person, many great and glorious things are said of him; as that he was his Father's honourary servant, his elect, the darling and delight of his soul; that he is qualified, and fitted, and called to his work. And having spoken of the base treatment he was to meet with from the Jewish nation, the prophet comes, in the words of my text, to declare what account his own Father made of his person and undertaking: Whatever base and low thoughts his friends and countrymen may have of him, yet he "is glorious in the eyes of the Lord;" God's sentiments of him are quite different from theirs, for *the Lord is well pleased for his righteousness sake;* as if he had said, However he be "despised and rejected of men, as a root sprung out of a dry ground," however you may make no more account of him than if he were deaf, blind, and dumb, yet "he is my beloved Son, in whom I am well pleased." Observe, from this connection, that God's thoughts of Christ are very different from the thoughts that an unbelieving world have of him; an unbelieving world, with Herod, and his men of war, set him at nought, but his Father reckons him the "brightness of his glory," and calls him his elect.

The words then in general are, Jehovah's verdict concerning the righteousness brought in by the great Messiah, with the ground thereof; *the Lord is well pleased for his righteousness sake.*

Where we may notice, 1. The great and glorious party here spoken of, and that is *the Lord*, or, as in the original, *Jehovah* the righteous Judge, the offended Lord and Lawgiver, to whose wrath all mankind are obnoxious and liable, through the breach and violation of the first covenant.

2. Something asserted concerning him, which may arrest the attention of all mankind, and fill their hearts with joy, and their mouths with praises, and that is, that he *is well pleased*. Whenever man had sinned, the anger and wrath of God was kindled against him, and his fury was breaking out like fire, and nothing remained for poor man, but a fearful looking for of wrath, and fiery indignation, to consume him and all his posterity, as a company of traitors and rebels; but here is a surprising declaration,

that though he was angry, yet his anger is turned away, his frowns are turned into smiles; *the Lord, Jehovah, is well pleased.* Again,

3. We have the cause and ground of this surprising declaration. Why, what is the cause of his being well pleased? It is *for his righteousness sake;* not for the sake of any ransom, atonement, or satisfaction, that the sinner could make, for no man can by any means redeem his own or his brother's soul, nor give unto God a ransom for it. The redemption of the soul is precious, and ceaseth for ever as to him; but it is *for his righteousness sake,* who finished transgression, and made an end of sin, who makes "reconciliation for iniquity," and so brings in an "everlasting righteousness;" the "righteous Lord loveth righteousness," and without it he cannot look with pleasure on any of Adam's race; while Christ becomes the "end of the law for righteousness," he fulfills the precept, and undergoes the penalty of it, whereupon the Lord declares himself to be *well pleased for his righteousness sake.*

4. We have the reason why the Lord Jehovah sustains the righteousness of the Surety in the room of the sinner, or why he is so *well pleased for his righteousness sake;* why (*he shall magnify the law, and make it honourable*), the holy law of God, given unto man in innocency as a covenant, or an eternal rule of righteousness, was violate and broken, and the authority of the great Lawgiver affronted and contemned by man's disobedience: but Christ, as our Surety, he is "made of a woman, and made under the law;" and, by bringing in everlasting righteousness, he not only fulfilled the law, both in its precept and penalty, but he magnifies it, and makes it honourable; he adds a new lustre and glory unto the law, which it never had before, through the dignity of his person who obeys it.

Some read the latter clause of the verse thus, *He shall magnify the law, and make* (him) *honourable:* and so the meaning is this: 1. Christ shall not only repair the honour of the law, but restore honour to God the great Lawgiver; and, indeed, never was there such a revenue of glory and honour brought in to the crown of heaven, as by the obedience and satisfaction of Christ: "Now (says Christ) is the Son of man glorified, and God is glorified in him." Through Christ, God can save sinners, and give vent to his love, grace, and mercy, upon terms that are honourable to his law, justice, holiness, severity, and other perfections, that were lessed and injured by the sin of man. Or, 2. *He shall magnify the law, and make him (i.e. Christ) honourable;* and so the latter clause of the verse is a promise of the Father unto the Son, that, upon his repairing the honour of the law by his humiliation, he would make him honourable by a glorious exaltation, he would give him "a name above every name." But, in my subsequent discourse, I shall follow the reading in the translation, and the sense already given of it.

From the words thus opened, I observe this comprehensive doctrine, almost the same with the words:

"That Christ, as our glorious Surety, having magnified the law, and made it honourable, the Lord Jehovah declares himself to be well pleased for his righteousness sake."

But I shall divide this doctrine into these two:

First, "That Christ, as our Surety, has magnified the law, and made it honourable, by his obedience to the death."

Secondly, "That however God was displeased and provoked with the sin of man, yet he is well pleased for the righteousness sake of the blessed Surety."

I begin with the *first* of these, viz. "That Christ, as the Surety of lost sinners, has magnified the law, and made it honourable."

I only quote two scriptures for the confirmation of this; the one you have, Rom. viii. 3. 4. where the apostle tells you, that through the sacrifice and satisfaction of Christ, "sin is condemned, and the righteousness of the law is fulfilled in us;" and Rom. x. 4. Christ is there said to be "the end of the law for righteousness unto every one that believeth."

Now, in discoursing this doctrine, or this branch of the complex doctrine, I shall, through divine assistance, observe the order and method following.

I. Suggest a few things concerning the law, and how it was disparaged by the sin of man.

II. Speak a little of the glorious person who undertakes the reparation of it as our Surety.

III. Inquire what may be imported in the expression of his magnifying the law, and making it honourable.

IV. How he magnifies the law, and what way he takes to *make it honourable.*

V. Give the reasons of the doctrine.

VI. Make some application.

I. The *first* thing is, to suggest a few particulars concerning the *law of God*, which is debased and disparaged by the sin of man.

1st then, Ye would know, that the *law* here principally intended is the moral law of the ten commandments, at first engraven upon the hearts of our first parents at their creation, and afterwards, because that edition or copy of it was much obliterated and defaced by the fall, published to Israel from the mouth of God upon Mount Sinai, and written upon tables of stone, and laid up in the ark for the use of Israel. This, I say, is the law here intended. The ceremonial and judicial laws were things peculiar unto the Jews, or commonwealth of Israel; but the moral law had a being so soon as man was created, and is binding upon all nations. For the breach of this law man was condemned, and all his posterity laid under the curse: and therefore this must be the law which Christ, as our Surety, came to magnify and make honourable. And concerning it, I offer,

2dly, That the moral law is nothing else but a transcript of the original holiness and purity of God's nature. God's essential holiness and righteousness was too bright and dazzling a pattern for man, even in a state of innocency; and therefore he transcribes a copy of it, and pictures it out upon the heart of man, that he might make it the rule of his obedience in heart and in life, requiring him to be holy as he is holy.

3dly, The law being a copy or emanation of God's holiness and righteousness, it must be dearer to him than heaven and earth, or the whole frame of nature. Hence is that of Christ, Matth. v. 17, 18, "Think not that I am come to destroy the law and the prophets; I am not come to destroy, but to fulfill. Verily I say unto you, Till heaven and earth pass, one jot or tittle shall in no ways pass from the law, till all be fulfilled." Sirs, whatever mean or low thoughts we may have of the law, through the blindness of our minds, yet I can asure you, that it is such a sacred thing with God, that he will sooner unhinge the frame of nature, and reduce it to its original nothing, than suffer it to be trampled upon by sinners, without shewing a suitable resentment.

4thly, This law was given to our first parents under the form of a covenant; a promise of life being made to them, upon condition of their yielding a perfect obedience; and a threatening of death added, in case of disobedience, "In the day thou eatest, thou shalt surely die." In this covenant Adam stood as the public head and representative of all his posterity: had he continued in his obedience to the law of that covenant, eternal life had been conferred on him, and all his posterity, by virtue of the promise of God; the sum and substance of that covenant being, as the apostle tells us, "the man who doth these things shall live by them."

5thly, Man being left to the freedom of his own will, through the flattering hisses of the old serpent, "did brake the law of God," and so forfeited his title to life by virtue of that covenant; and brought himself, and all his posterity, under the curse or penalty of death temporal, spiritual, and eternal, Rom. v 12, "By one man sin entered into the world, and death by sin; and so death passed upon all men, for that all have sinned."

6thly, The law being broken and violated by sin, the honour of the law, and the authority of God, the great Lawgiver, are, as it were, laid in the dust, and trampled under foot, by the rebellious and disobedient sinner. When man sinned, he, upon the matter, denied that the law was holy, just, and good; and, at the same time, disowned God for a sovereign, saying, with proud Pharaoh, "Who is the Lord, that I should obey him? I myself, am Lord, and will come no more unto thee." In a word, every sin, every transgression of the law, is a breaking God's bands, and a casting his cords from us, and a saying, practically, 'Let the Almighty depart from us, for we desire not the knowledge of his ways.' And what an unsufferable affront and indignity is this, for worm man to offer unto the "high and lofty One that inhabits eternity? and what a wonder is it, that "indignation and wrath, tribulation, and anguish," does not pursue every sinner through eternity?

7thly, The law being violated, and the Lawgiver affronted, in such a way as has been hinted, the salvation of sinners by the law, and the works of it, becomes utterly impossible, unless the honour of the law, and of the great Lawgiver, be repaired and restored some how or other. It is among the irreversible decrees of heaven, that "in his sight no flesh living shall be justified," unless the holiness of the law be vindicated by a perfect obedience to its precept, and a complete satisfaction be given unto justice for the injuries done to the honour of the great Lord and Lawgiver: without this, "he will by no means acquit the guilty." Thus matters stood with Adam before the first promise of Christ, and thus matters stand with all his posterity, until we fly to him, who is "the end of the law for righteousness to every one that believeth."

II. The *second* thing was to enquire, Who he is that undertakes *to magnify the law, and make it honourable,* as our Surety?

I answer, it is none other than Messiah the Prince, of whom you were hearing from Daniel ix. 24, the eternal Son of God, who voluntarily offered himself as a Surety and Saviour of lost sinners, and who gave bond from eternity to his Father, that, in the fulness of time, he would not only assume our nature, but repair the honour of the law, and satisfy justice to the full, saying, as Ps. xl. 7, 8, " Lo I come, in the volume of the book it is written of me: I delight to do thy will, O my God; yea, thy law is within my heart." Now, this is the person who magnifies the law and makes it honourable; and concerning this glorious person we find many great things said in this chapter. As,

1. That he is his Father's servant, as ver. 1, "Behold my servant whom I uphold." He is essentially considered "in the form of God, and thinks it not robbery to be equal with God," and yet "he made himself of no reputation, and took upon him the form of a servant, and, as a servant, he had both his work and his wages appointed him by his Father. His work was, to redeem the lost sinners of Adam's family, by his obedience unto death; and his wages or reward was, his own and his Father's glory, and our salvation; and for this "joy that was set before him, he endured the cross, despising the shame," thinking his thirty-three years' service but a little time, for the love he bore to his Father's honour and our salvation, alluding to Jacob's service for Rachel.

2. We are here told of him, that he is his Father's elect, ver. 1, "Behold my servant whom I uphold," mine elect, that is, my chosen one, according to that, Ps. lxxxix. 19, " I have laid help upon one that is mighty; I have exalted one chosen out of the people." He was elected by his Father, and we are elected in him, Eph. i. 4, "He hath chosen us in him, before the foundation of the world." Oh, Sirs! let God's elect, or chosen redeemer, be

our choice also. The reason why his Father chose him, and set him up from everlasting, was, none other was fit for the undertaking, none other was capable to bear the weight of that service, but he alone.

3. We are told that he is his Father's darling or delight, ver. 1, "Behold my servant whom I uphold, mine elect in whom my soul delighteth." Agreeable to this is that which Christ, under the notion of the wisdom of God, tells us concerning himself, Prov. viii. "I was by him as one brought up with him, and I was daily his delight, rejoicing always before him." Oh, Sirs! let it fill us with wonder and admiration at the love of God to lost sinners, that he should take his beloved Son, his only Son, the Son of his bosom and delight, and give him to the death for us sinners, that he might repair the honour of the law, at the expense of his blood, that so we might be saved in a consistency with the law and justice of God; "this is the Lord's doing," and my justly be "marvellous in our eyes."

4. We are told concerning this person, who magnified the law as our Surety, that he is qualified by his Father for the work and service of redemption, by the anointing of the eternal Spirit, ver. 1, "I will put my spirit upon him, God, even his God, hath anointed him with the oil of gladness above all his fellows." There is a fulness of the Spirit in him, as the head of the mystical body, that out of his fulness we might receive grace for grace, and because of the savour of this good ointment, his "name is as ointment poured forth."

5. He is one whose commission is very extensive; for we are told in the close of ver. 1, that he shall "bring forth judgment to the Gentiles." The eternal counsels of heaven, here called judgment, were to be published, not only to the Jews, but even to the Gentiles, who were "aliens to the commonwealth of Israel," for many hundred years. I will not only give him "to raise up the tribes of Jacob, and to restore the preserved of Israel;" but also to be "a light unto the Gentiles, and to be God's salvation to the ends of the earth." Oh! that now, when this prophecy is turned into history, there may be a flocking of the poor Gentiles into this "ensign that is set up unto the nations; Christ preached unto the Gentiles" is a part of the incredible "mystery of godliness."

6. We are told of him, that he was to be a meek and lowly Saviour, and that he would manage and carry on his work without much noise, ver. 2, "he shall not cry, nor lift up, nor cause his voice to be heard in the street."

7. That he was to be very tender and compassionate towards his poor people, particularly the weaklings of his flock, ver. 3, "a bruised reed shall he not break, and the smoking flax shall he not quench;" he will not discourage or dispise the least degree or beginnings of faith, love, or obedience; no, "he shall feed his flock like a shepherd, he shall gather the lambs with his arm, and carry them in his bosom, and shall gently lead those that are with young."

8. That he would be victorious and successful in his work, maugre all the opposition that should lie in his way, either from heaven, earth, or hell, ver. 3, 4, " He shall bring forth judgment unto truth. He shall not fail, nor be discouraged, till he have set judgment in the earth."

9. We are told of him, that he would bear his Father's commission, and be sustained in his work by the right hand of his power, ver. 6, " I the Lord have called thee in righteous, and will hold thine hand, and will keep thee." He did not intrude himself into the work of the ministry, or run unsent. No, but he was " called of God, as was Aaron," and being called, he was not left alone.

10. We are told of him, that he is the free gift of God unto a lost world, in the close of ver. 6, " and give thee for a covenant of the people," insomuch, that whosoever believes in him, has a saving interest in the covenant of grace and promise, and in all the sure mercies of David. Whosoever believes in him, and trusts and credits him with his eternal all; whosoever receives him as the unspeakable gift of God, may travel through the wide covenant, and pick up there whatever he finds for his use, saying, ' This is mine, and that is mine, and all is mine, because Christ is mine, as the free gift of God.'

11. We are told of him, that he would be the light of the world, and particularly a light to the poor Gentiles, who had so long sitten in the regions and shadow of death, ver. 6. close, I will give him " for a light of the Gentiles," ver. 7, " to open the blind eyes." Christ is the true " Sun of righteousness, the light of the world," and every man has as good a title to make use of him for all the ends of his salvation, as he has to make use of the light of the sun in the firmament, to which every man is born heir, be he rich or poor, noble or ignoble, saint or sinner. O Sirs, take in the light of the Sun of righteousness into your understandings, and you will find " healing under his wings."

12. We are told of him, that he would loose the devil's prisoners, ver. 7. He shall " bring out the prisoners from the prison, and them that sit in darkness out of the prison-house." Sinners, they are the lawful captives of hell, and the devil has law and justice on his side against all mankind, to detain them in the bonds of iniquity, as God's jailor: Well, but Christ he magnifies the law, and makes it honourable, and the great Judge is " well pleased for his righteousness sake; " and therefore he says, in a day of power, to the poor prisoners, " Go free." And thus you see who and what he is, from the context, who is here said to *magnify the law.*

III. The *third* thing proposed, was to enquire what is imported *in his magnifying the law, and making it honourable.*

Answ. There are these few things supposed or implied in the expression.

First, As you were hearing, it supposes that the law is broken, and thereby the greatest indignity done to it, and to him who gave it. Hence sin, which is a transgression of the law, is called a casting of God's counsel behind our backs, as we do with a thing that we nauseate and disdain. The sinner disdains to be under the government of the law of God, but sets up his own lusts and corrupt inclinations in the room thereof, and what greater ignominy and disgrace can be put upon the royal law of heaven.

Secondly, The expression implies or supposes, that God, the great Lawgiver, stands upon reparation; he will have his law vindicated, and the honour of it repaired, otherwise no flesh living can be saved. Oh that this were but duly weighed by sinners who have broken the law times and ways without number! If reparition be not made to the holy law, for the transgression thereof, it stands as an eternal bar in the way of our salvation. Now, are you capable to yield it a perfect obedience after you have broken it? or can you satisfy the penalty of it, and make an atonement unto justice?

Thirdly, It implies, that man, who has broken the law, is utterly incapable to repair its honour, or to satisfy justice. Indeed every legalist is attempting it, but alas he walks in a vain shew, he walks in the light of his fire, and in the sparks that he has kindled, and then lies down in sorrow. He but wearies himself in the greatness of his way, for his webs cannot become garments, neither shall he cover himself with his works; for "by the works of the law shall no flesh be justified."

Fourthly, It implies, that God, the great Lawgiver, admits of the "substitution of a Surety in the room of the sinner," otherwise he could not magnify the law in our room and stead. Sirs, if God had stood to the rigour of his law, according to the tenor of the first covenant, "in the day thou eatest thereof thou shalt surely die, he would have exacted reparation of us in our persons; in which case, we should have fallen an eternal sacrifice into the hands of avenging wrath and justice: but, glory to his name, he dispenses with the rigour of his law, and admits of a Surety, and not only admits of a Surety, but provides a sponsible one too for us. "I have laid help upon one that is mighty: I have found David my servant."

Fifthly, It implies, that Christ, as our Surety, actually put his neck under the yoke of the divine law. Though he was no debtor to the law, either as to its precept or penalty, yet he bowed his glorious head, that that heavy yoke might be wreathed about his neck for us. Hence is that of the apostle, Gal. iv. 4. 5. "made of a woman, made under the law, to redeem them that were under law."

Sixthly, It implies, that the holy law is no loser by Christ's substitution in our room; no, it has all that it demanded in order to its satisfaction. Did the law demand holiness, and perfect holiness, in our nature? Well, it hath its demand in Christ, for he was originally holy; he is without the stain or defilement of original sin: "That holy thing which shall be born of thee shall be called the Son of God," Luke i. 35, " He was holy, harmless, undefiled, separate from sinners." Did the law demand perfect obedience unto its commands? Well, that it hath in Christ; for he fulfilled all righteousness. " He did no violence, neither was guile found in his mouth." Did the law demand satisfaction to justice, or the execution of its penalty? Well, it hath its demand in him: for "he was wounded for our transgressions; the just suffered for the unjust, that he might bring us to God." Thus the law loses nothing by Christ's substitution, but hath all that it required.

Seventhly, It implies, that the holy law, instead of being a loser, gains an additional honour and glory by the righteousness of the Surety. Never had the law such a subject before, as its own Lord who made it. Suppose the sinless obedience of Adam and all his posterity, and the obedience of all the angels in heaven, and of all creatures were put together, and this obedience continued through eternity, yet this could not magnify the law, or make it honourable; because the obedience of creatures is nothing but what they owe in justice to the law of their great Creator: But here we have the great Lord of angels and men, whose will is a law to them all, yielding obedience to the law in our room: This surely adds a new lustre and an additional glory to the law, which it never had before. And thus you see what is implied *in Christ's magnifying the law and making it honourable.*

ISAIAH xlii. 21.—" The Lord is well pleased for his righteousness sake; he will magnify the law, and make it honourable."

THE SECOND SERMON ON THIS TEXT.

IV. THE *fourth* thing in the method was to inquire, *How is it that Christ magnifies the law, and makes it honourable?*

Now, for clearing this matter, I would have you to consider, that the moral law comes under a twofold consideration; it may be considered as a covenant, and as a rule of life. As a covenant, promising the reward of life eternal to every one that yields a perfect obedience to its commandments, and threatening death eternal to every one that fails in the performance of this condition; or it may be considered as a rule of obedience, simply prescribing the duty which the rational creature owes unto God, its great Creator, and Preserver, and Benefactor, without any promise of life or threatening of death annexed to it, which gives it its covenant form. Now, Christ magnified the law, and made it honourable, under both these views and considerations.

First, As a covenant, he magnifies it, and makes it honourable; and this he did, by fulfilling all its demands. As I hinted already, there were three things which the law insists upon from fallen man, by virtue of the covenant-transaction between God and Adam in a state of innocency. 1. Holiness of nature. 2. Righteousness of life. 3. Satisfaction for sin and disobedience: None of which we are in the least capable to afford; but every one of them is completely afforded in Christ.

1. I say, the law, as a covenant, demands of us a perfect holiness and rectitude in our very natures. This God gave unto Adam in innocency; for he made him upright after his own image. This uprightness and integrity of nature was quite lost by the fall; we are "conceived in sin, and shapen in iniquity: the whole head is sick, and the whole heart faint: from the sole of the foot, even unto the head, there is nothing but wounds, and bruises, and putrifying sores." Hence we are "by nature the children of wrath:" so that the law cannot find a holy, pure, and innocent nature, among any sprung of Adam by natural generation. But this demand of the law is fulfilled in Christ, the second Adam, as the public head and representative of his spiritual seed; for "he was conceived by the power of the Holy Ghost, in the womb of the virgin, and born of her without sin:" Luke i. 35. "That holy thing which shall be born of thee." That holy thing, that is, that innocent human nature which shall be born of thee. Heb. vii. 26. He is "holy, harmless, undefiled, separate from sinners." The law requires of every son of Adam, that he should have a nature as upright and holy as that which he received from God, the great Lawgiver, at his creation. This is absolutely impossible for us to give, but it is found in Christ; for in him human nature is also restored unto its integrity and perfection; and every believer being in him, as their public head and representative, they are in the reckoning of the law born holy in Christ, the second Adam, even as they were created holy in the first Adam. Hence believers are said to be complete in him, Col. ii. 10. They have a complete holiness of nature in him. This, according to the demands of the law, is continued in Christ: for the law not only demands that our nature be holy, but that we should persevere and continue in this condition. Now, this demand of the law is fully answered in Christ; for in him our nature continues to be perfectly holy for ever, how ever unholy it may be in us, personally or abstractly considered: and God looking upon our nature, as it is in him, not as it is in us sees us altogether fair and perfect in holiness in him, not in the least marred: according to what we have, Song iv. 7. "Thou art all fair, my love, there is no spot in thee." And thus, this first demand of the law is fulfilled in Christ, as to the perfect holiness of our nature.

2. The law not only demands a perfect holiness of nature, but also a perfect and sinless obedience of life. The language of the law, as a covenant, unto all the sons of Adam, is, "He that doth these things shall live by them. If thou wilt enter into life, keep the commandments." We must "continue in all things which are

written in the book of the law to do them." But now this demand of the law cannot be answered or fulfilled by us; for 'no mere man, since the fall, is able perfectly to keep the commandments of God, but doth daily break them in thought, word, and deed:' Our nature, as you were hearing, being wholly corrupted, every thought and imagination is evil only and continually. Now, although this active, perfect obedience by the law, cannot be yielded by any of mankind, descending from Adam by natural generation, yet it hath its demand from Christ, our glorious Surety, Head, and Representative. The law required of us, that our obedience should be universal, perfect, and constant: these are all to be found in the obedience our Surety yielded unto it. For,

(1.) His obedience to the law as our Surety is universal; all things written in the book of the law must be obeyed: if there be the least failure of obedience as to any one jot, or any the least of its commandments, it lays the man under the curse. Now, I say, Christ did every thing that the law required; he fulfilled all righteousness; he did "no violence, neither was guile found in his mouth."

(2.) His obedience to the law was every way perfect as to the manner. The law required that we not only do every thing that it requires, but that we "love the Lord, *and serve him*, with all the heart, and with all the soul, and with all the strength, and with all the mind, and our neighbour as ourselves." O! who among all Adam's race can obey and love the Lord after this manner? Well, but this is done in Christ: love to God and man shined to its perfection in him, and in the whole course of his obedience.

(3.) His obedience was constant, and continued unto the very end. Thus the law required that we should not only do all things, but "continue in all things which are written in the book of the law to do them." Man "being in honour continueth not;" and in the best state, in his best frames, cannot continue in such an universal and perfect obedience, as the law requires, for one moment; but Christ, our glorious Surety, continued in an universal and perfect obedience to the very end; from his birth to the grave; from his womb to the tomb. Hence we are told, Philip. ii. 8. that he was *obedient to death;* and John xvii. that he *finished the work* which the Father gave him *to do*. Thus you see the law is magnified and made honourable, as to this demand of righteousness of life, in Christ our glorious Surety: and this is what divines commonly call his *active obedience*.

3. Another thing that the law demands of fallen man, is a complete satisfaction unto justice, in consequence of the penalty or sentence of the law; "In the day thou eatest thereof, thou shalt surely die." The veracity and faithfulness of God was engaged in this threatening, and justice stood upon its execution, insomuch that without death, or shedding of blood, there could be no remission of sin. Now, supposing that the threatening of death temporal, spiritual, and eternal, had been executed upon Adam and his posterity for ever, the law and justice of God would have been

glorified in our ruin; but yet it could never have been said, that the law and justice of God were satisfied, far less could they have been magnified and made honourable: but by the death and sufferings of the Son of God in our room and stead, the penalty of the law is so fulfilled, and the justice of God so fully satisfied, that the Lord Jehovah declares himself *well pleased for his righteousness sake*, the *law* being thereby *magnified and made honourable*. It was the man who is God's fellow, and who thinks "it not robbery to be equal with God," who became a curse and a sacrifice for us. The best blood of the whole creation goes for the satisfaction of law and justice. And thus you see how all the demands of the law are satisfied to the full in Christ: and thus he magnifies the law to the full as a covenant.

Secondly, Christ magnifies the law, not only as a covenant, but likewise as a rule of life, and this he doth several ways.

1. By writing a fair copy of obedience to it, in his own example, for the imitation of all his followers. Christ calls the law, as a rule of obedience, his yoke, "Take my yoke upon you;" and to make the yoke easy to his friends, he first wears it, and smoothes it himself, that it might not gall their necks; hence we are told, that he has left "us an example that we should follow his steps;" and we are so to walk even as he walked, to follow him, and to run our race looking unto him, as our glorious Pattern of obedience. We must be holy, "as he that hath called us is holy."

2. By explaining it in its utmost extent, for as David tells us, "it is exceeding broad." The Jewish doctors, in order to establish a righteousness of their own, they pared off the spirituality of the law, and confined the meaning of it to the bare letter; but Christ, in his sermon upon the mount, vindicates the law from these narrow and corrupt glosses, and lays it open in its extent and spirituality, shewing, that the law of God not only concerned the external man, or overt acts of the life, but reached the heart, and the innermost recesses of the soul, as you see, Matth. v. where he tells them, that rash anger was murder in the eye of the holy law, and that a lascivious look towards a woman was heart-adultery, and the like.

3. By establishing the obligation of it as a rule of obedience unto all his followers. Although indeed he dissolves the obligation of it as a covenant to all believers, so as they are neither to be justified nor condemned by it, yet he establishes it, I say, as a rule of duty even to believers, as well as others, "Think not that I am come to destroy the law or the prophets, nay, I am not come to destroy, but to fulfil it," Matth. v. 17. Rom. iii. at the close, "Do we then make void the law through faith? God forbid: yea, we establish the law." The law is now delivered to us in the hand of a Mediator; it has lost nothing of its original authority as coming from a God-creator, but this law of the Creator receives an additional authority, as being issued to us through a God-redeemer.

4. By writing it upon the heart of all his followers, by the finger of his eternal Spirit, according to that promise, Jer. xxxi. 33. "I will put my law in their inward parts, and write it in their hearts,

and will be their God, and they shall be my people." Whenever a soul is called effectually by the word and Spirit of Christ, he, that moment, inlays a principle of holiness, or conformity to the law, in its heart: hence are these breathings of soul after obedience to it, that we find so frequent among the saints; "Let my heart be found in thy statutes: O that my ways were directed to keep thy statutes: Hold up my goings in thy paths, that my footsteps slip not."

5. By enforcing obedience to the law among all his followers, by stronger motives than the law itself abstractly considered, could afford. Death, hell, and ruin are the principal motives that the law makes use of in exacting obedience from fallen man: "In the day that thou eatest thereof, thou shalt surely die: The soul that sinneth it shall die: Indignation and wrath, tribulation and anguish, upon every soul of man that doth evil." But now Christ in the gospel does not drag but draws the soul sweetly into the ways of obedience, by the consideration of redeeming love; he draws them with the "cords of a man, and with the bands of love: The love of Christ constrains me (says Paul): If ye love me, keep my commandments." He sets them at liberty from wrath, and the curse, and then calls them "to serve him without fear, in holiness and righteousness all the days of their life;" and so he makes his yoke easy, and his burden light.

6. By actuating them in their obedience to the law by his own Spirit, according to that promise of the covenant, Ezek. xxxvi. 27. "I will put my Spirit within you, and cause you to walk in my statutes, and ye shall keep my judgments, and do them." Hereby they are made to study holiness "in all manner of conversation," and the light of their obedience and holiness in their walk shines forth, so as others seeing their good works, are made to "glorify their Father which is in heaven."

Thus you see how Christ magnifies the law, and makes it honourable, as a covenant, fulfilling the righteousness of it in his own person, as our Surety, and as a rule of obedience in the hearts and lives of his followers; though indeed I think it is in the first sense that the words are principally to be understood, I mean the law as a covenant, as seems plain from the other clause of the verse compared with this, *The Lord is well pleased for his righteousness sake;* not for the sake of our obedience, but for the sake of *his righteousness, the Lord is well pleased.*

V. The *fifth* thing in the method was, to *inquire into the reasons of this doctrine: why is it that Christ doth magnify the law, and make it honourable.*

Unto this I answer in these particulars.

1st, He did it from the regard he had to his Father's honour and authority, affronted in the violation of the law. The sovereignty, holiness, justice, and other perfections of God, were despised, his government disturbed in the breach of the law. Now, that he might restore that honour to God which he took not away, he would magnify *the law, and make it honourable:* hence he could say to his Father, when he had finished his work, "Father, I have glorified thee upon earth," where he was dishonoured by the sin of man.

2*dly*, He did it out of love that he bore to our salvation, which could not be accomplished, without the penalty of the law had been endured, and the precept of it obeyed. The law and justice of God was ready to fall upon us, but he seasonably interposed, saying, "Lo! I come," &c.

3*dly* Because he was ordained of God from eternity for this work and service, he was set up for it by the decree and ordination of heaven, and he did always these things that pleased his Father.

4*thly*, Because he had given his engagement in the council of peace; he entered his name in the volume of God's book, and had his ear bored as his Father's servant for this work; and having sworn or promised to his own hurt, he would not change. It was upon the credit of this engagement of Christ to satisfy law and justice, that all the Old Testament saints were admitted into heaven; and if he had not fulfilled his undertaking, they had been turned out of heaven again, in among the damned: but his Father knew that he was match for his work, and that he would not "faint nor be discouraged, till he had set judgment in the earth."

5*thly*, He magnified the law as a covenant, that "we might be freed from it," in its covenant-form, and curse, Gal. iv. 4, He was "made under the law to redeem them that were under the law." Rom. vii. 4, "Ye are dead to the law by the body of Christ."

6*thly*, He magnified the law, and made it honourable, as a covenant, that we may obey it as a rule, and serve the Lord without fear of the curse and condemnation, "in holiness and righteousness all the days of our lives." If Christ had not repaired the honour of the law, we had been in bondage through fear of the law's penalty taking place upon us every moment.

7*thly*, To procure and confirm his own right of government as Mediator, Rom. xiv. 9, "To this end Christ both died, and rose, and revived, that he might be Lord both of the dead and living." He was resolved to be Lord, not only by right of creation, but by the right of redemption; not only the Lord that made us, but the Lord that bought us: and therefore he magnifies the law.

8*thly*, That he might still the enemy and the avenger, and outshoot the devil in his own bow. Satan's usurped kingdom and dominion in the world stood upon the violation of the law; the law being broken, the devil got his power from God, as his jailor and executioner over poor man: but now Christ, as a Surety-kinsman, having fulfilled the law, and satisfied justice, the bottom falls out of the devil's kingdom, his head is bruised, and through death he that had the power of death is destroyed. When Satan had got man to break the law, and so brought under the penalty, ("the soul that sinneth it shall die,") no doubt the devil would say, 'Now the day is mine own, God cannot save man in a consistency with his own holiness and faithfulness engaged in the penalty of the law.' He thought, no doubt, that he had God at a disadvantage, being bound to destroy his own viceroy, that bore his own image in this lower world. But Infinite Wisdom outwits the enemy, he "takes the wise in his own craftiness," and turns the counsel of that froward spirit headlong: "My Son (says God) shall take on man's nature, and in his room and stead shall magnify the law and make it honourable, by obeying the commands and enduring the curse; and so, upon that ground, he shall bring about the salvation and freedom of man, in a consistency with my holiness and faithfulness too;" 1 John iii. 8, "For this purpose the Son of God was manifested, that he might destroy the works of the devil." Thus you see the reasons why Christ *magnified the law, and make it honourable*.

VI. I proceed now to the *sixth* thing I proposed, which was the *application of this doctrine*.

And the *first* use I shall make of this doctrine, shall be by way of inference in the particulars following.

1st, Is it so that Christ, as our Surety, has *magnified the law, and made it honourable?* then see hence the excellency of the law of God, and the sacred regard that God bears unto it. Why, if ever man, who had violated the law, be admitted to the presence of God, or the enjoyment of him, either here or hereafter, it shall be in such a way as the honour of the law shall be salved and repaired. O Sirs! beware of diminutive thoughts of the holy law of the ten commandments, for God thinks honourably of it, and will have the honour of it maintained at any rate. If the righteousness of it be not fulfilled in you by imputation, the penalty of it shall be fulfilled in your eternal condemnation. The great plot of Infinite Wisdom, in the work of redemption, was to have the law magnified and made honourable, in the salvation of the lost sinner; and because this could not be done another way, the eternal Son of God must be "made of a woman," that he might be "made under the law," that so the honour of the holy law might be maintained and preserved. O does not this say, that God has a sacred regard unto the honour of it? And yet, alas! how few are they among professed Christians, that discover any regard to its honour, while they trample it every day under their feet, by their disobedience unto it, in thought, word, and deed? No man is a Christian indeed, until he come, in some measure, to have honourable thoughts of the law as God hath, saying, with Paul, "the law is holy, just, and good," David had such honourable thoughts of it, that he meditated in it day and night, and esteemed all its commandments concerning all things to be right.

2*dly*, See hence the evil of sin, and why Christ came to finish transgression, and make an end of it. Why, sin is a transgression of the law, which Christ will have magnified and made honourable. God, the righteous Judge, has such a quarrel against sin, for the violation of his law, that he has denounced "indignation, and wrath, tribulation and anguish, against every soul that doth evil:"

And his quarrel against it will be prosecuted to the lowest hell, against a wicked unbelieving world: He has determined, that the wicked shall be turned into hell, and all the nations of the earth that forget God, and cast his law behind their backs. Yea, when sin was laid by imputation upon him, who had no sin of his own to answer for, even the eternal and beloved Son of God; yet the raging sword of justice awaked against him, and bruised him for our transgressions. Why, Sirs, does not all this discover the evil and malignity that is in sin, as it is a transgression of that law which God will at any rate have magnified and made honourable? O, ye that love the Lord, hate it, for it is the abominable thing that his soul hates, &c.

3dly, Did Christ *magnify the law, and make it honourable?* Then see hence the dreadful situation of every sinner that is out of Christ, destitute of his righteousness. Why, the law of God, which denounces death unto every transgressor, stands in its full force against them: it still insists upon the debt of perfect and sinless obedience against you; and because ye cannot give that, it denounces the curse of God upon you; "As many as are of the works of the law are under the curse," Gal. iv. 10. The law will have its curse executed and fulfilled, either in the Surety or the sinner.

4thly, See hence the wonderful love of God to lost sinners, in sending his own Son to magnify the law, after we had violated and broken it; and at the same time it discovers the grace and love of our Lord Jesus Christ, who, though he be supreme Judge, King, and Lawgiver, yet was willing to be "made under the law," and to obey it as a subject, that we might be delivered from law-vengeance, and have the righteousness of it fulfilled in us through him, Rom. viii. 3. 4, "What the law could not do, in that it was weak through the flesh, God sendeth his own Son, in the likeness of sinful flesh, and for sin condemned sin in the flesh: That the righteousness of the law might be fulfilled in us, who walk not after the flesh, but after the Spirit."

5thly, See hence the ignorance and error of those who are prejudiced against the doctrine of imputed righteousness, and justification by faith, as if it were prejudicial to the holy law, or did any way derogate from its honour and authority. Why, it is so far from derogating from the law, that it is the only way how it can be fulfilled and magnified. Christ does not destroy the law, but fulfills its righteousness, in his own person, by an active and passive obedience, and in all his members, by imputation: hence Christ is said to be "the end of the law for righteousness." The law gets what it seeks in Christ; and whenever a sinner believes in Jesus, the law ceases its pursuit against that man, crying, 'There is no condemnation for him, because I have got what I craved in his Surety, who has brought in an everlasting righteousness, whereby I am honoured.'

6thly, See hence the error of those who assert, that a justified believer is still liable to the curse, or penal sanction of the law.

Seeing the law is satisfied, both as to precept and penalty in Christ the Cautioner, how can the believer be liable still to its curse? This doctrine derogates from the excellency of that law-magnifying righteousness, which is imputed to believers in their justification. If Adam had continued yielding a perfect obedience to the law, neither he, nor any of his posterity, would have been liable to the curse or penalty; how much less is the believer liable, who is adorned with the righteousness of God by imputation? That word may strike terror into those who advance such doctrine, Rom. vii. 33, "It is God that justifieth, who is he that condemneth?" It is God that acquits the believer from the curse, who then dare to make him liable?

7*thly*, See the error and folly of those, who go about to "establish their own righteousness" as the ground of their justification and acceptance, and "refuse to submit unto the righteousness of God," like the Jews, Rom. x. 3. Oh how much do men disparage the law, and despise the righteousness of Christ, who do so! for in effect the self-righteous person says, 'That he is more capable to magnify the law by his own obedience than Christ.' For this slight the Jews put upon the righteousness of Christ, God slighted and rejected the whole Jewish nation; and for this sin every self-righteous person shall be rejected of God.

8*thly*, This doctrine lets us see the error of those, who, though they will not absolutely reject the righteousness of Christ, yet will adventure to mingle something of their own with it. Oh, say some, 'Christ and my faith, Christ and my good works, Christ and my prayers, my repentance, my tears and good qualifications, will justify me.' Why, this way, whatever you may think of it, is a disparaging of the righteousness of Christ, as though it alone did not fully answer the law. Sirs, remember that faith is a resting on Christ alone, and his righteousness, to the exclusion of every thing in you, and about you, as the ground of your acceptance: it is Christ's righteousness alone, that magnifies the law; and therefore there is no need of anything of ours: yea, if you seek righteousness but in part by the law, you are fallen from grace, and Christ shall profit you nothing; and therefore say with the Church, Is. xlv. 24. "In the Lord alone have I righteousness," and with David, Psal. lxxi. 16, "I will go on in the strength of the Lord God, I will make mention of thy righteousness, even of thine only."

9*thly*, See the error of those who deny Christ's active obedience to the law to be any part of our justifying righteousness; alleging, that it is only his passive obedience, or his suffering the penalty, that is imputed to us for justification. Why, when it is said here, that Christ magnified the law, and made it honourable, it must needs be understood of his obedience to the precept, and that principally, because the precept or command only is the law; the penalty is not essential to it, but only a thing consequential in case of disobedience: so that his magnifying the law must needs have a respect to the precept; and his obedience to the precept of the law, is properly his righteousness, which is imputed to us,

Rom. v. 19, "By the obedience of one shall many be made righteous;" and it is upon this that our title to life doth stand, as Adam's title in the covenant of works stood upon his own perfect and personal obedience to the command.

10*thly*, See hence how little reason, even believers, who are justified before God, have to be proud of what they are to come to. They are indeed accepted in the Beloved, and they are highly dignified and exalted; but then it is not in their own, but in their Surety's righteousness, that they are exalted; it was he, not they, that magnified the law, and made it honourable: Hence the saints in glory will cast their crowns at his feet, saying, "Thou hast loved us, and washed us—in thy blood;" and therefore, "worthy is the Lamb that was slain."

ISAIAH xlii. 21.—"The Lord is well pleased for his righteousness sake: he will magnify the law, and make it honourable."

THE THIRD SERMON ON THIS TEXT.

USE *second* of this doctrine may be of *Trial*, whether the righteousness of the law be fulfilled in us, through the imputation of his righteousness, who has magnified the law, and made it honourable.

For your *Trial* as to this matter, I offer the few following marks.

1*st*, I ask, has the law slain you, and put you out of conceit of your own righteousness? Paul, before his conversion, was a mighty man for the law, and he thought himself alive because of his obedience to the law, and his zeal for it, being "touching the law blameless:" But O! when the commandment came, in its spirituality, sin revived, and he died; he saw that, notwithstanding all his pretended obedience to the law, and his zeal for it, he was but a dead man; and then, what things were gain to him, these he counted loss, and particularly he saw that his own righteousness was but dung and loss. Oh! says he, "I through the law am dead to the law," and to all righteousness by the works of the law. Now, try yourselves by this; has the law come with such power upon thy conscience, as to break all these rotten planks of the covenant of works to pieces, on which you were swimming for your life?

2*dly*, I ask you, Where have you set down your stand for eternity, and for an awful tribunal? I am sure, if the righteousness of the law be fulfilled in you through faith in Christ, you have set it down only upon the foundation of the law-magnifying righteousness of Christ, saying with the church, "Surely in the Lord only have I righteousness;" and in this only will ye be confident, as the ground of your acceptance here, and of your through-bearing before the bar of the great God. When you look to the holy law, and your own personal obedience to it, you will be ready to cry, 'Away with it, it is but as filthy rags;' if "thou, Lord, shouldst mark iniquities, O Lord, who shall stand?" But when you look to the law, as magnified and made honourable by Christ, you will be ready to say, 'In this, and in this alone, will I be confident; in him will I be justified, and in him alone will I glory, as the Lord my righteousness.' And whenever the law or conscience charges you with the debt of obedience to it, as the condition of life, you will be ready to say, 'I indeed own myself a debtor to thee in point of obedience, as a rule, but in point of righteousness and justification, I owe thee nothing at all; no, I am dead to the law, through my better husband, who has in my name magnified and made it honourable, and therefore to him thou must go for payment of that debt.'

3dly, If you be under the covering of that righteousness which magnifies the law, I am sure you will put all the honour you can upon the law, as a rule of obedience; and your gratitude to him who fulfilled the law for you as a covenant, will be as oil to your chariot wheels in running the ways of his commandments. Your hearts will be so enlarged in love and gratitude, that his commandments will not be grievous to you; no, but you will "delight in the law of the Lord, after the inward man." His yoke will be easy, and his burden will be light to you.

You to whom the way of holy obedience is a burden, and who are never in your element but when you are "fulfilling the lusts of the flesh," by lying, swearing, drinking, Sabbath-breaking, do not imagine that ever you have come in under this law-magnifying righteousness: Why? because the law, as a rule, is none of your delight.

4thly, You will be concerned to magnify him, who magnified the law as your Surety. The high praises of the Redeemer will be much in your mouth; you will think and speak honourably of him, upon all occasions, like these who are clad with the white livery of his righteousness. In Mount Zion they cry, "Worthy is the Lamb that was slain. Salvation to our God, and to the Lamb, for ever and ever." Oh, men are blessed in him with a perfect righteousness, and therefore let all nations and generations call him blessed, Psal. lxxii., at the close.

5thly, You will be on all occasions improving the righteousness of Christ by faith, for all the ends and uses of it which I mentioned, when discoursing of the excellency of this righteousness. You will improve it as a ransom unto justice, to deliver you from going down to the pit; you will improve it as a laver, to wash you from sin and from uncleanness; as a spiritual banquet, on which you will feed your hungry souls, for it is meat indeed and drink indeed; as a robe to cover your nakedness, and the best robe whereby to appear in the presence of God; as a shade to defend you from the scorching heat of the fiery law, or an awakened conscience; as a refuge to shelter you when pursued by avenging justice; as a ladder by which you will ascend unto communion with God, here and hereafter; and as the only title and foundation of your claim to eternal life. Thus, I say, you will be constantly improving the righteousness of Christ by faith, for some of these ends and uses; and in this sense we may understand that word of the apostle, Rom. i. "The righteousness of God revealed from faith to faith." It is that which faith fastens upon at first for justification, and it is that which faith is continually afterwards applying for some good use or other, in the soul's progress in the way to glory.

6*thly*, If the righteousness of the law be fulfilled in you, through the righteousness brought in by the Messiah, you will have many an inward battle with sinful and legal self. The apostle Paul, who gloried in the righteousness of Christ, and preached the mystery of justification to others, more than ever any mere man did, yet we find he has many an intestine combat with self, Rom. vii. 23, "But I see another law in my members warring against the law of my mind, and bringing me into captivity to the law of sin which is in my members: O wretched man that I am, who shall deliver me?" You, who say that ye submit and trust to the righteousness of Christ, as the only ground of your justification and acceptance, and yet have no struggle with this home-bred enemy, and are not laid in the dust before the Lord because of its prevalency, I dread, whatever orthodox heads you may have, yet your hearts are not soundly settled upon the foundation of the law-magnifying righteousness of Christ; and my reason for it is, because in every believer there is, through the remains of indwelling corruption, such a strong bias towards the law as a covenant, and towards sin, as gives him continual matter of exercise, insomuch that his heart is just like a field of battle, where two armies meet, and contend for the victory one against another? "What will you see in the Shulamite? as it were the company of two armies? the flesh lusting against the spirit, and the spirit against the flesh, and these are contrary, the one to the other. The motions of sin which a man finds in his members are continual matter of humiliation to him, and set him a-work to mortify the deeds of the body, to crucify the flesh, with the affections and lusts thereof; and the strong bias that he finds in his soul towards the law as a covenant fills him with fears and jealousies, lest he never yet in reality submitted to the righteousness of Christ, which sets him a-work to examine and prove himself, whether he has ever yet won Christ, and is found in him, having that "righteousness which is through the faith of Jesus Christ." You that never knew anything of this, and the like exercise of spirit in your souls, I dread that you are yet strangers to a real closing with the righteousness which is brought in by the great Messiah.

7*thly*, When conscience is bleeding through some wound that you have got from an arrow of law-terror, or when the guilt of sin is staring you in the face, and an angry and frowning God, "whither do you fly, or run for ease and relief?" As for the desperate sinner, he drowns the voice of conscience with diversions and recreations. They will, like Saul, sometimes take up the timbrel and harp; or, like Cain, when God and conscience were crying for vengeance against him for the blood of his brother Abel, he goes into the land of Nod, and diverts himself with building cities and houses. As for the hypocrite, he wraps himself up in his profession, and feigned graces, and there he finds case. As for the legalist, when he is wounded with the terrors of God, being married to the law, he runs to the duties and works of the law, and studies to please God, and satisfy the cry of his conscience with these. But as for the believer, the whole creation cannot give him case, till, by a renewed act of faith, he get in under the shadow of that everlasting righteousness, by which the law is magnified and made honourable, and till he see God well pleased for his righteousness sake, and sensibly smiling on his soul again through this righteousness; this, and nothing but this, can yield comfort. And O! when he sees God smiling on him through this righteousness, this puts gladness in his heart more than when corn, wine, and oil did abound. Try yourselves by this.

In a word, if the righteousness of the law be fulfilled in you through the righteousness of the Messiah, the life you live in the world will be by faith in the Son of God, and ye will not reckon so much that ye live, but that Christ liveth in you. Many a flight will thy soul be taking to him upon the wings of faith and love, as the Lord thy righteousness. Whenever you look towards the majesty of God, and view his unspotted holiness and unbiassed justice; whenever thou looks upon the fiery law, or hears a thunderclap from Mount Sinai; whenever thou looks into another world, or an awful tribunal; whenever thou looks to the depravation of thy nature, and the innumerable evils that compass thee about; whenever thou looks to the melancholy aspect of providence, thy soul will ay be taking the other flight by faith unto Christ, as thy Surety and Redeemer; and the viewing the law magnified, and justice satisfied, and God reconciled in the person and undertaking of Christ; and whenever thou looks to him, thou wilt find thy Spirit lightened and eased, and be ready to say with David, "Return unto thy rest, O my soul; for the Lord hath dealt bountifully with thee." So much shall serve for an use of *Trial*. I proceed now to,

III. The third use of this doctrine, which may be of *terror to all the ungodly world, that are living in the open or secret violation of the holy law of God.*

Hath God magnified the law, and made it honourable, at the expense of the humiliation, incarnation, obedience, death, and sufferings of his eternal Son? O how dreadful and dismal is the condition of these, who, instead of yielding the obedience of faith unto this law, are daily in their practice trampling the authority of the law under their feet, breaking God's bands, and casting the cords of his law from them, and yet will needs pretend to and profess the name of Christ, as if Christ had magnified the law and made it honourable, that they might have a liberty to break it, and to follow the swing of their own carnal and corrupt hearts. The apostle Jude, ver. 3d of his epistle, when speaking of such licentious Christians, he calls them ungodly men; turning the grace of our Lord Jesus Christ into lasciviousness, of old ordained to this condemnation. O Sirs! do not mistake it, Christ has *magnified the law, and made it honourable*, not to loose but to establish the obligation of it as a " rule of obedience, he gave himself for us, that he might redeem us from all iniquity, and purify unto himself a peculiar people, zealous of good works," Tit. ii. 14, He hath delivered us from the hand of all our enemies, that we "might serve him without fear, in holiness and righteousness before him all the days of our life," Luke i. 74, and that we may by his grace be taught to deny all " ungodliness and worldly lusts, and to walk soberly, righteously, and godly in this present world," Tit. ii. 12, So that ye who draw encouragement from the doctrine of Christ's magnifying the law, and making it honourable, to violate and dishonour the law of God, ye are just counteracting the design of the obedience of Christ unto the death, and, like the filthy wasp, sucking poison out of the gospel of salvation. And do you expect to be justified by the righteousness of Christ, and eternally saved by his blood in such a way as this? no, no; ye have "neither part nor lot in this matter." As sure as God lives, ye are under the law as a covenant, and therefore under the dominion of sin, and the curse of the broken law is upon you; ye are " condemned already, and the wrath of God abideth on you." And unto you God saith, " What hast thou to do to make mention of my righteousness, or that thou shouldst take my covenant in thy mouth, seeing thou hatest instruction, and castest my words behind thee." And therefore consider your danger in time, before you come in before the awful bar of God, lest, when you arrive there, he tear you in pieces, when there is none to deliver you out of his hand. But I turn me again from Mount Sinai to Mount Zion, and go on to,

IV. Fourth use of this doctrine, by way of *encouragement to convinced* and *awakened sinners*, and to *doubting* and *trembling believers*.

We have a commission " to bind up the broken hearted, to comfort them that mourn in Zion, to strengthen the weak hands, and confirm the feeble knees, to say to them that are of a fearful heart, Be strong, fear not; we bring to you good tidings of great joy," tidings that may make your hearts triumph, and leap for joy within you, as the babe leapt in Elizabeth's womb, at the salutation of Mary. Here, I say, are the best news that ever were heard to law-condemned sinners, that Christ, as our blessed Surety, has brought in everlasting righteousness, by which he has *magnified the law, and made it honourable*.

There are these following topics, or grounds of *Encouragement* and *Consolation*, springing out of this doctrine.

1st, Is the law magnified by the Surety, which was broken by the sinner? Hence it follows, that the great Lawgiver is satisfied and well pleased, as it follows in the text, *The Lord is well pleased for his righteousness sake ;* that which displeased and provoked the majesty of God, was the breach of his law, but since the law is again magnified, surely he cannot but be a well pleased Deity.

Upon this ground it is, that such declarations are issued out, " Fury is not in me," I was angry, but mine " anger is turned away : As I live, I have no pleasure in the death of the wicked, but rather that the wicked turn from his way and live. Turn ye, turn ye, why will ye die ? " O Sirs ! that which scares you from coming back to God is the apprehension, that, because of the breach of the law, God is implacable, and will never be reconciled. But we will tell you, for your encouragement, that a God in Christ is *well pleased for his righteousness sake, because he hath magnified the law, and made it honourable.* God was in Christ, not pursuing the world as an avenging enemy, but reconciling the world to himself. And therefore let not an evil heart of unbelief turn you away from the living God, as though he were not *well pleased for Christ's righteousness sake.* It was not for nought that that proclamation was made three times with an audible voice from heaven, "This is my beloved Son, in whom I am well pleased." O it is glorious encouragement to a lost sinner, hanging over the mouth of hell, that God is well pleased in his Christ.

2dly, Is the law *magnified and made honourable?* then it follows, that the great bar that lay in the way of our salvation is removed. Upon the first Adam's violation of the holy law, mountains of wrath were rolled in the way of salvation; the way was so filled with briars and thorns, woes and curses, that it became altogether impassable for any of Adam's race. Hence came that horror and despair that was seated in the hearts of our first parents immediately after they had sinned. The sight of the cherubim, and the flaming sword turning every way, to keep the way of the tree of life, had a dismal signification : Well, but Christ, the second Adam, he has *magnified the law, and made it honourable,* and therefore it must needs follow, that all these impediments and bars in the way of our salvation are now removed, and the way is clear to every soul that has a mind to enter in by faith, John x. 9, " I am the door : by me if any man enter in, he shall be saved, and shall go in and out and find pasture." All legal impediments arising from law and justice, in the way of salvation are now taken out of the way, and there is a free call to every man to enter in and be saved ; in which case nothing can hinder but unbelief, which is a refusing to enter in by Christ, and they that do so, how shall they escape ?

3dly, Is the law *magnified and made honourable?* Then here is encouragement, that " sin is finished, and transgression ended." The very essence of sin lies in a transgression of the law. Well, but if the law be again magnified, then where is sin ? It is surely buried in the obedience of Christ to the death, by the righteousness of the Surety. The guilt of it is taken away, and the power and dominion of it is broken in every believer, and the very being of it shall be destroyed, ere it be long. So that I may say, to believers under the covert of Christ's righteousness, as Moses said to Israel, with respect to the Egyptians, that were pursuing them for their lives, Exod. xiv. 13. "Fear ye not, stand still, and see the salvation of the Lord, which he will shew you to-day, for the Egyptians whom ye have seen to-day, ye shall see them no more again for ever." Poor believer, thou art afraid of these innumerable sins, which compass thee about, lest they pursue thee, and take away thy life, but stand still, and see the salvation which God hath wrought; all thy sins are buried for ever out of God's sight, and shall be buried out of thy sight also, in the Red Sea of a Redeemer's blood, and under the covert of his law-magnifying righteousness, whereby he hath made an end of sin.

4thly, Is the law *magnified and made honourable?* Then the handwriting of the curse that was against us, and contrary to us, is cancelled and discharged. Upon the footing of the righteousness of Christ, which magnifies the law, it is, that that gracious declaration is issued out, John iii. 17. "God sent not his Son into the world to comdemn the world, but that the world through him might be saved." Christ has retired the bond that lay in the hand of justice, and had it discharged in his resurrection from the dead; and upon this ground it is declared, that "there is now no condemnation to them that are in Christ Jesus." And if you ask the reason of this interlocutory. Here it is, Christ has magnified the law, and made it honourable: therefore the penalty of the law cannot take place against any soul under the covert of his righteousness. No, no; "Christ hath redeemed us from the curse of the law, being made a curse for us."

5thly, Is the law *magnified and made honourable?* Then it follows, that grace and mercy reign through righteousness, and that the law and justice can be no impediment in the way of pardoning mercy. The poor sensible sinner, whose eyes are fixed upon his own sin, and the holiness of the law, is many times ready to say and think with himself, 'O! God can never extend mercy to the like of me, in a consistency with his law and justice. He is obliged to take vengeance on me, by virtue of his justice.' But, Sirs, consider that the Surety Jesus Christ has magnified the law, and made it honourable, that mercy and grace might have an unrestrained current, even towards the guiltiest sinners that believe in Jesus. Hence is that of the apostle, Rom. iii. 24-26. "Being justified freely by his grace, through the redemption that is in Jesus Christ, whom God hath set forth to be a propitiation through faith in his blood, to declare his righteousness for the remission of sins. To declare, I say, at this time his righteousness; that he might be just, and the justifier of him who believeth in Jesus." And therefore let this encourage you to pursue after the pardon and remission of sin on this account, that the law is already magnified and made honourable in the Surety's righteousness. God exalts and glorifies his name gracious, and merciful, when he blots out iniquity, upon this footing; yea, glorifies the law and justice also, more than if he would pursue the quarrel against thee to the lowest hell through eternity.

6*thly*, Is the law *magnified and made honourable?* Then hence it follows, that the condition of the covenant of grace, properly so called, is already fulfilled. Since the fall of Adam, God never entered into covenant with man himself directly and immediately: no, the covenant of grace is made with us in Christ, as our Surety, Head, and Representative. As the covenant of works was made with the first Adam, as our natural and federal head, and with us in him; so the covenant of grace is made with us in the second Adam, as our spiritual Head, and the condition of the covenant was fulfilled by him. And if you ask me, 'What is the proper condition of the covenant of grace?' I answer, 'It is just this, that Christ should be made under the law, and by his obedience unto the death *magnify it, and make it honourable.*' Upon this condition eternal life, and all the purtenances of it, were promised to him and his seed. Now, when any of the lost race of Adam believes in Christ, they do not, by that act of faith, fulfil the condition of the covenant of grace, but only take hold of the condition of it, fulfilled by Christ, and, in so doing, they become "heirs of God, and joint heirs with Christ Jesus." And so they may travel through the large field of the covenant, and pluck this, and that, and the other blessing of the covenant, saying, 'This is mine, and that is mine, and the whole of the covenant is mine, because I have the condition of the covenant in my new spiritual Head, Jesus Christ, he has *magnified the law and made it honourable.*' O! with what courage might the believer go to work, in laying claim to the covenant, and the blessings of it, if he had but this view of matters, in the light of the Lord?

7*thly*, Is the law *magnified and made honourable* by Christ as our Surety? Then it follows, that whatever was lost in the first Adam, is now recovered by the second Adam. By the first covenant, if we had continued in it, we had a title to God as our God, a title to his favour and fellowship, a title to the creatures, all things being put under our feet, and a title to a happy eternity, after the course of our obedience in this world had been fulfilled. By Adam's fall we lost all this, and more than I can name. But all is again recovered in the new covenant Head, by his magnifying the law and making it honourable; and the soul united to him, hath all its losses repaired with advantage, in him; we have God in him as the Lord our God, for God is in Christ, our God, and our Father. "I ascend (says Christ) to my Father and your Father, to my God and your God." We have the image of God fully restored in him, and going on gradually in us. We have a complete stock of knowledge in him, who of God is made unto us wisdom, and a beam of that knowledge that is in the head shines into the heart of every believer. We have a complete righteousness in him, and we are made the righteousness of God in him. We have a complete holiness of nature in him; for, for our sakes he sanctified himself, that we also might be sanctified through the truth; and, through the holiness of Christ the head, God looks upon all the members, and says, "Thou art all fair my love, there is no spot in thee." We have a perfect and complete heaven of glory, and eternal life in him; for he that believes in the Son hath everlasting life: and this we are assured of by the faithful word of the Trinity, 1 John v. 11. "This is the record that God hath given to us, eternal life: and this life is in his Son. He that hath the Son, hath life." Thus, I say, all that was lost in the first Adam is regained in Christ, the second Adam, and all upon this ground, that the second Adam, as our Surety, has *magnified the law, and made it honourable?*

8*thly*, Has Christ *magnified the law, and made it honourable?* Then the intercession of Christ for us, in heaven, goes upon a solid ground, and shall be prevalent on our behalf. Why, it goes upon the ground of that everlasting righteousness which he has brought in, whereby he has *magnified the law, and made it honourable.* Hence he is called "Jesus Christ the righteous," 1 John ii. 1. 2. "If any man sin, we have an Advocate with the Father, Jesus Christ the righteous; and he is the propitiation for our sins." Believer, do not fear, that thy case committed to the hand of thy Advocate, in the high court above, shall miscarry: no, he never lost a poor man's cause, for the Father always hears him. Thy Advocate is not only well skilled in the laws of the court, but in pleading thy cause: he pleads it upon the footing of a law-magnifying righteousness, and therefore he must prevail in thy behalf.

9*thly*, Has Christ *magnified the law, and made it honourable?* Then there is good ground of boldness in coming "to the throne of grace, for mercy and grace to help in time of need." Why, believer, that righteousness that magnifies the law, and makes it honourable, is imputed to thee, and by faith thou shouldst go with this surety righteousness upon thee; and this is the ground of thy confidence in all thy dealings with God. We are ready to think, 'O my prayers will be rejected of God, he will never hear them, because I cannot order my cause before him: I cannot win to this or the other frame or enlargement of heart.' Why, believer, that is but a tang of the old legal Adam in thee, that imagines that God regards thy person, from thy frames and enlargements. No, no; "he hath made us accepted in the beloved." You, and your best frames, graces, and enlargements, would be driven away out of the presence of an infinitely holy God, if it were not for this cause, that Christ has *magnified the law, and made it honourable:* and therefore let this be thy only ground of boldness before the Lord. "Having a great High Priest, who is passed into the heavens, Jesus the Son of God; let us come boldly unto the throne of grace, that we may obtain mercy, and find grace to help in time of need."

10*thly*, Has Christ *magnified the law, and made it honourable?* Then it follows, that failures of obedience, on the believer's part, do not make void the covenant of grace, or the believer's title to the blessings and privileges of the covenant. Why, the whole law as a covenant, and all the righteousness and obedience that it demands is perfectly fulfilled in his head Jesus Christ: and therefore the believer cannot fall out of the covenant, through the imperfections of his obedience. I own, indeed, that a believer should aim at, and endeavour no less than perfect obedience, in his own person, and for failures in obedience he shall smart: "God will visit his transgressions with the rod, and his iniquities with stripes." But observe what follows, "My loving-kindness I will not take from him," viz. Christ, with whom the covenant is made, and who has fulfilled the condition of it by his perfect righteousness; and therefore, "my covenant I will not break" with them, nor alter the word of promise, "that is gone out of my lips."

11thly, Has Christ *magnified the law, and made it honourable?* Then believers have matter of everlasting triumph and rejoicing in Christ, and cannot receive the spirit of bondage unto fear, except in a way of correction. Believers are commanded to rejoice evermore, to shout for joy; and when they see how matters are stated in the new covenant Head, they will accordingly rejoice in Christ always, even when they have no confidence in the flesh. Why, what should discourage them, who have " the righteousness of the law fulfilled in them " through Christ; yea, who are the righteousness of God in him? That which brings the believer at any time under a spirit of bondage again to fear, is the unbelief and legality of his heart, which turns away his eyes from Christ and the righteousness of the law fulfilled and magnified in him; and then indeed the terrors of the law covenant, and of an angry God, fall upon him, " He remembers God, and is troubled," and the arrows of the Almighty are within him. But while the believer can, by faith, see the law magnified in his Head, and the Lord Jehovah *well pleased for his righteousness sake*, his heart will rejoice, and his joy will no man take from him.

12thly Has Christ *magnified the law, and made it honourable?* Then see upon what an advantageous ground the believer stands in encountering his spiritual enemies. Why, through the law-magnifying righteousness of Christ, he has God on his side, he has the law on his side, and justice on his side, yea, Omnipotence on his side, and therefore he may lift up his head in the day of battle, and go on with courage against all his enemies.

To instance, (1.) When he is molested with the insurrection of indwelling sin, or of any particular lust, the believer may take courage in mortifying and crucifying it, because through the righteousness of Christ, sin has no law-right to reign over the believer as it hath in other men, who are under the law as a covenant. "Sin (says the Lord) shall not have dominion over you, for ye are not under the law, but under grace."

(2.) Doth Satan harass and molest thee with his fiery darts? Why, believer, take courage, for through Christ's magnifying the law, Satan's head is bruised, and he has no more right in law to molest or trouble thee, than he has to molest thy glorified Head above; and therefore put on the breast-plate of his everlasting righteousness, and resist him, " stedfast in the faith."

(3.) Art thou assaulted with the law coming into thy conscience, craving of thee the debt of perfect obedience, as the condition of life? Why, here is a ready answer to this enemy. Tell the law and conscience, that the law, as a covenant, has got its due, and more than it demanded, in thy new covenant Head; for he has not only obeyed it to the full, but has *magnified it, and made it honourable.*

(4.) Art thou at any time brought under bondage through fear of death? Why, here is encouragement for encountering with that king of terrors. That which gave death its power and sting, was the violation of the law: but may the believer say, 'Here is the law again *magnified and made honourable,* and therefore, O death, what hast thou to say? It is true, indeed, I must put off this clay tabernacle for a while; but this I do, not as a debt due to the law, or the curse of it, but at the will of my God and Father, I lay down my body in the grave, that I may receive it again, without any tincture or smell of sin or death about it, in the morning of the resurrection. Death, may the believer say, is no death to me; no, to me to live is Christ, and to die is gain; because Christ, my Head, has magnified the law and made it honourable, and therefore has swallowed up death in victory; death and hell, through the righteousness of my Head, are now cast back into the lake from whence they came."

Thus you see what unspeakable encouragement and consolation springs out of this doctrine, *that Christ has magnified the law, and made it honourable.*

THE WISE VIRGINS GOING FORTH TO MEET THE BRIDEGROOM.

MATTHEW xxv. 6.—"And at midnight there was a cry made, Behold the Bridegroom cometh, go ye forth to meet him."

THE FIRST SERMON ON THIS TEXT.

THESE words that I have read are a part of the famous parable of the ten virgins; for clearing of which, you would carefully advert to these two or three things.

1*st*, The Bridegroom here spoken of is none other than Christ Jesus the Lord, the eternal Son of God, who, from all eternity, rejoiced in the habitable parts of the earth, and whose delights were so much with the sons of men, that he first married our nature into a personal union with himself, that so there might be some sort of equality in the bargain; and having made himself of our tribe, comes to betrothe us to himself for ever in a marriage-relation.

2*dly,* The virgins here spoken of are the professors of religion, members of the church visible. The church is called the bride, the Lamb's wife, Rev. xix. 7.-9. particularly professors, saints, and believers, at least in profession, are so called virgins, because of the beauty of holiness that should adorn them.

3dly, The office of these virgins is to *meet the bridegroom.* This alludes unto a common custom among the Jews, who consummated their marriages at night; when the bridegroom was on his way to the place of marriage, the bride with so many virgins that attended her, went forth with lamps to meet him, in order to conduct him to the bride's chamber. Now, with allusion to this custom, professors of religion are said to go and meet the Bridegroom.

4thly, Notice the different characters of these virgins, five were wise, and five foolish. The foolish represent the case of nominal or hypocritical professors, who have the lamp of a profession, and content themselves with a name to live, while destitute of the life and power of religion; and, by wise virgins, we are to understand real saints, or believers indeed, who not only profess Christ and Christianity, but are Christians indeed, having the oil of his grace and spirit within them.

5thly, We have the common fault of both these sorts of virgins, while the Bridegroom tarried, they all slumbered and slept; together with the surprising summons they all get to attend the Bridegroom, ver. 6, *Behold the Bridegroom cometh, go ye forth to meet him.* It is the last clause of this verse that I intend to insist upon, viz. *Behold the Bridegroom cometh, go ye forth to meet him.*

We have a key given us, ver. 13. for opening of the general scope of this parable, "Watch, therefore, for you know neither the day nor the hour wherein the Son of man cometh." Which words, though they chiefly and particularly relate unto the coming of Christ by death, or his coming at the last judgment: yet, as Mr Shephard and other interpreters are agreed, they do not exclude, but include, his other intermediate comings, whether in the dispensation of the word and sacraments, of ordinances, or providences, it is the duty of all to prepare for his reception and entertainment.

The words read, ver. 6. are a surprising summons or advertisement unto the church in general, and every individual member thereof, to make ready for his entertainment, because he is at the door. *And at midnight there was a cry made, &c.*, where we may notice the particulars following.

(1.) To whom the advertisement is given. It is unto all in general, both unto the wise and foolish virgins. The gospel is preached unto a promiscuous multitude of good and bad, gracious and graceless, according to Christ's command, "Go ye into all the world, and preach the gospel unto every creature."

(2.) We have the manner in which the advertisement is given. It is by a cry, so as all might hear and take warning, Is. lvii. 1. "Cry aloud, spare not, lift up thy voice like a trumpet." Ministers, are God's criers or heralds. It is said of John the Baptist, that he was "the voice of one crying in the wilderness," &c. Whatever be the message God puts in our mouth, whether it be of mercy or of judgment, we are not to whisper it in a corner, but to publish it as upon the house top, Prov. i. 20.-24, "Wisdom crieth without the city, she uttereth her voice in the streets, she crieth in the chief place of concourse."

(3.) We have the time when the summons or advertisement is given. *At midnight,* when they all slumbered and slept, and had given over hope and expectation of his coming: both the wise and foolish virgins were saying, "The Lord delayeth his coming;" and therefore, "Yet a little sleep, a little slumber, a little folding of the hands to sleep." In this case, even *at midnight,* in a surprise, the cry is made, *Behold the Bridegroom cometh.*

(4.) We have the summons or advertisement itself, *Behold the Bridegroom cometh, go ye forth to meet him.* These are the words I intend particularly to insist upon, and in them we may notice these following particulars.

1. The solemnity of the warning in the word *Behold,* which may be taken there as a note of attention or admiration. It is like the warnward when the King's proclamation is issued forth by the herald; he cries, *Oyez,* to arrest the attention of the audience, like that, Is. lv. 1, "Ho every one that thirsteth," &c. Or we may take it as a note of admiration, *Behold* and wonder at the glory of the Bridegroom, who is a-coming. We find commonly, when the Messiah is spoken of by the prophets under the Old Testament, they usher in their prophecies anent his coming, with a note of admiration, *Behold!* Is. vii. 14, "Behold a virgin shall conceive, and bear a son, and shall call his name IMMANUEL;" Is. xlii. 1, "Behold my servant whom I uphold," &c.; Is. lv. 4, "Behold I have given him for a witness to the people, a leader and commander to the people;" Zech. ix. 9, "Rejoice, O daughter of Zion, behold thy King cometh unto thee," &c.; signifying that Christ is a wonderful person, and his coming to us in mercy is wonderful.

2. We have the character of the person concerning whom this intimation is made. He is called the *Bridegroom,* and the *Bridegroom* in a way of eminence, because their is none that ever bore this character that can be compared to him. Whenever we hear the name of a bridegroom, we presently conclude there is a marriage in hand; so here when Christ takes this amiable character and title to himself, we should presently conclude there is a match or marriage in hand, that Christ is a lover, and that he hath a bride, and a purpose of marriage with her, according to that you have, Hos. ii. 19. 20, "I will betrothe you unto me for ever," &c. But more of this afterwards, if the Lord will.

3. In the words we have the approach of the Bridegroom, *Behold the Bridegroom cometh.* There are various comings of Christ we read of in scripture. There is his first coming in the flesh, and his second coming unto judgment, either general or particular. There are his typical and prophetical comings to the church, in the Old Testament, and his actual coming in person to fulfil and accomplish the great work of redemption, by his obedience, death,

and resurrection. There is his coming, in the dispensation of the gospel, to a church or nation. There is his coming, in the power of his word and Spirit in a day of conversion to a church, or to a particular soul, as when he said to Zaccheus, "This day is salvation come to this house." And, *lastly*, there is his coming in word or sacrament with the renewed manifestations of his love, or the renewed influences and communications of his Spirit of grace; as when it is said, Ps lxxii. 6, "He shall come down like rain upon the mown grass; as showers that water the earth:" or Hos. vi. 3, "His going forth is prepared as the morning; and he shall come unto us as the rain; as the latter and former rain unto the earth." Now, I do not, in my intended discourse upon these words, exclude any of these comings of Christ that I have mentioned. But at present I understand them of his approach in a way of grace and love, in the dispensation of word or sacrament, or any other ordinance of his appointment, wherein he uses to manifest himself, and impart the fruits of his dying love unto the souls of his people.

And one reason why I choose to discourse the words in this view, is, because he here presents himself in the quality of a bridegroom, coming with a design of marriage or espousal; and so we have a word much parallel unto this, Song iii. 11, "Go forth, O ye daughters of Zion, and behold King Solomon with the crown wherewith his mother crowned him in the day of his espousals, and in the day of the gladness of his heart."

4. We have the duty incumbent upon all the virgins, on the approach of the Bridegroom. *Go ye out to meet him.* This alludes, as was hinted before, unto the practice or custom in marriages among the Jews, in the time of our Saviour's being upon earth. The bride and her maids, under night, went forth to meet him with lighted lamps, in order to attend him to the place of marriage, with some sort of nuptial solemnity. In allusion to this custom, the church in general, and all particular professors, under the notion of *virgins*, are commanded and called to go out and meet Christ, when he is coming in the dispensation of his word and ordinances, or when he comes at death or the last judgment. But the import of this expression may occur afterwards, in the prosecution of the following doctrine.

DOCT.—"That it is the indispensable duty of all and every one, when Christ, the glorious Bridegroom of souls, is a-coming, to go out and meet him, by giving him a suitable reception and entertainment." *Behold the Bridegroom cometh, go ye out to meet him.*

I shall only adduce two places of scripture for proof and confirmation of this doctrine. The one you have, Ps. xxiv. at the close, where Christ, under the notion of some great person, is represented as drawing near unto the gates or doors of some great house or city; and thereupon a summons is issued out, 'Cast open the gates, and make room for his entertainment.' "Lift up your heads, O ye gates, and be ye lift up, ye everlasting doors, and the King of glory shall come in." And when the question is put, "Who is this King of glory?" the answer is made, ver. 8, "The Lord strong and mighty, the Lord mighty in battle." The summons is again renewed: "Lift up your heads, O ye gates, even lift them up, ye everlasting doors, and the King of glory shall come in." Another text you have to this purpose, Song iii. 9. and downwards, where Christ, under the notion of King Solomon, who made to himself a chariot of the wood of Lebanon, the pillars thereof of silver, the bottom of gold, the covering of purple, being paved with love for the daughters of Jerusalem. This chariot of state is none else than the chariot of the everlasting gospel, wherein Christ, like a bridegroom, goes forth, manifesting the glory of his person, and the glorious device of Infinite Wisdom for the salvation of sinners. And in the last verse a cry is made, like this in my text, to all professors of religion, who are designed the daughters of Zion. "Behold King Solomon with the crown wherewith his mother crowned him in the day of his espousals, and in the day of the gladness of his heart."

But now, in discoursing this doctrine, I shall, through divine assistance, observe the following method.

I. I would premise a few things with relation to the spiritual marriage spoken of in this parable.

II. Give some account of the Bridegroom, and his excellent engaging qualities.

III. Give some account of the bride, and the vast disparity of the match.

IV. Speak a little of the comings of the Bridegroom, and his gracious approaches to his people.

V. Speak of the import of the duty required upon his approach, in these words, *Go ye out to meet him.*

VI. Give the reasons of the doctrine, why we are to go out and meet him, and give him suitable reception.

VII. Make some practical improvement of the whole.

I. The *first* thing in the method is, to premise a few things anent the spiritual marriage; for, as I said in the explication, a bridegroom supposes a marriage in hand.

1*st*, God the Father, from all eternity, had a purpose of marriage betwixt his own beloved Son, and a select company of the fallen race and posterity of Adam: hence Christ tells us, Matt. xxii. 2. "The kingdom of heaven is like unto a certain King who made a marriage for his son." The marriage was made in the purpose of God from eternity, and the bride was given unto the Bridegroom before ever she had a being, "Thine they were, and thou gavest them me," John xvii. 8. Psa. ii. "I shall give thee the heathen for thine inheritance, and the uttermost parts of the earth for thy possession." And that they were given him in a design of marriage, is plain from what the Lord says to, and concerning the church of the Gentiles, by the spirit of prophecy, long before their being called by the gospel, Is. liv. 1. 5. "Sing, O barren, thou that didst not bear; for more are the children of the desolate, than the children of the married wife." And ver. 5. "Thy Maker is thine Husband, the Lord of hosts is his name."

2*dly*, This proposal of marriage with a bride of Adam's family was graciously received and entertained by the Son of God before the world was made," Prov. viii. 3. He rejoiced "in the habitable parts of the earth, and his delights were with the sons of men.—I delight to do thy will, O my God," says he, Psa. xl. 8. *q. d.* 'I consent to, and am heartily willing and content; a bargain be it; let it be registrated in the volume of thy book;' *i. e.* Let it be entered into the records of heaven, and an extract thereof be given out in the scriptures of truth unto sinners of mankind, that they may have their thoughts about it.

3*dly*, So much was the heart of the Bridegroom set upon the match, that he undertook to remove all impediments that lay in the way: and indeed the impediments were so great and insuperable, that nothing but almighty power, inspired with infinite and amazing love, could remove them; and yet they are all rolled away by the wisdom and power of the Bridegroom.

The *first* impediment was the inequality of the parties as to their nature. We may easily suppose that the question would be put upon the first proposal of the marriage, how shall God and man, the Creator and the creature, be ever brought unto a conjugal relation? The distance of natures is infinite, and therefore there can be no marriage. 'Well, (says the Son of God, the brightness of the Father's glory, and the express image of his person) [he takes care to remove that], I will assume the human nature unto a personal union; I will become the seed of the woman, the seed of Abraham; I will be God manifested in the flesh; I will become IMMANUEL, God with them, and so that natural impediment shall be removed; I will come upon a level with the bride, and so I will be a help meet for her.'

(2.) There is another impediment arises from the law: O, says the Law, 'I have an action against the supposed bride. She was once married unto me, and I promised her the inheritance of life, upon the condition of her fulfilling perfect obedience to my commands; but she disobeyed, and played the harlot, and she is under the curse; and therefore there can be no marriage.' 'Well but (says the Bridegroom), I will remove this impediment also; I will be made a curse for her, and so redeem her from the curse; I will cancel the hand-writing that is against her, and contrary to her.'

(3.) 'Well but (says justice), I stand upon a complete satisfaction; for without death, and the shedding of blood, there can be no remission of sin.' 'Well (says the Bridegroom), I will die for the bride, and in her room and stead; the sword of justice shall be soaked in my blood instead of hers; my life shall be a ransom for hers; I will be wounded for her iniquities, and bruised for her transgressions; I will be made sin for her.'

(4.) There is another impediment yet that must be removed: The bride hates the Bridegroom; she is wholly averse from the match; and what will be done in this case? 'Well (says the Bridegroom), I will undertake to gain her affection. Psa. cx. 3. Thy people shall be willing in the day of thy power. I will draw with the cords of a man, and with the bands of love; and then her affections shall be gained, and she shall call me *Ishi*.'

(5.) Another great impediment in the way of the marriage is, that the bride is a lawful captive to sin and Satan: "Now (says Satan) shall the lawful captive be delivered; both law and justice have put her in my power; and therefore I will not part with my prisoner.' 'Well but (says the blessed Bridegroom), it is true, Satan, thou hast law and justice on thy side: but I will fulfil the law, and satisfy justice; and, in so doing, thy head shall be bruised, and the lawful captive shall be delivered, and the prey shall be taken from the terrible. I will redeem her by purchase and by power.' And accordingly he spoiled principalities and powers, and took the bride by main force out of the devil's prison, saying to the prisoners, *Go ye forth*, &c.

From what is said, it appears, that the heart of the Bridegroom is exceedingly set upon the match, with desire he desired to be baptised with his own blood, that he might finish her redemption; and, having completed her redemption, he longs for the day of espousals, when he gains the love and affection of the bride. So much was the heart of the Bridegroom set upon the match, that, when he saw the bride in danger of perishing, he flew, as it were, from his Father's bosom, left all the glories of heaven behind him, and travelled through the armies of hell and earth, yea encountered the legions of his Father's wrath, in order to accomplish her deliverance. Hence is that of the church, Is. lxiii. 1. "Who is this that cometh from Edom? with dyed garments from Bozrah? this that is glorious in his apparel, travelling in the greatness of his strength? I that speak in righteousness." And ver. 3. "I have trodden the wine-press alone, and of the people there was none with me."

4*thly*, A *fourth* premise is, That the covenant of grace is the contract of marriage, the plan of which was agreed upon in the council of peace, betwixt the Father and the Son, from all eternity: Psa. lxxxix. 3. "I have made a covenant with my chosen, I have sworn unto David my servant." It was originally made with the Bridegroom, as the Head, Husband, and Representative of the bride, wherein he undertakes, that the grace of God shall reign and be glorified through his own righteousness, to her eternal life and salvation. As Surety of the covenant, he undertakes to fulfil the condition of it, by his own obedience unto death, to buy his bride from the hands of justice, by paying a ransom of his own blood for her, and to buy, at the same time, all the blessings and goods of the covenant for her use; and that, by the power of his word and Spirit, he will make her to take hold of his covenant, bring her within the bond of it, and make an effectual application thereof in due time, according to the order of the covenant; and that he will betrothe her unto himself for ever, in righteousness, and in judgment, and in loving-kindness, and in mercies; yea, that he will betrothe her unto himself in faithfulness, and that she shall know the Lord, Hos. ii. 19, 20.

5*thly*, In the day of his espousals all this is fulfilled. The Bridegroom presents himself to the bride in his divine and human glories, fulness, and excellencies; he makes the "light of the knowledge of the glory of God," in his own person, to shine in her heart; wherewith she is made to see him, and fall so much in love with him, that she cannot but cry out, "O! he is infinitly fairer than the sons of men, he is as the apple-tree among the trees of the wood, the chiefest among ten thousand, white and ruddy, his countenance is as Lebanon, excellent as the cedars; his mouth is most sweet, yea, he is altogether lovely. O! this is my Beloved, this is my Friend: if I had ten thousand hearts and hands to give, he should have them all. I am well pleased with his person; well pleased with the contract he has made, and signed with his blood; well pleased with all the promises, which I see to be yea and amen in him; well pleased with his law: I will follow him whithersoever he goes." And in this way the marriage is concluded and agreed upon, "I will make an everlasting covenant with them, even the sure mercies of David," Is. lv. 3. Jer. xxxii. 40. "I will make (or establish) an everlasting covenant with them. That I will not turn away from them to do them good, but I will put my fear in their hearts, that they shall not depart from me. I will never leave thee, nor forsake thee." So much for the *first* thing.

II. The *second* thing in the method is, to *speak a little of the blessed Bridegroom, who is here said to be a-coming. Behold the Bridegroom cometh.*

But O! Who can speak of him to any purpose? we but darken counsel by words without knowledge, when we speak of him; and no wonder, for he is the unspeakable gift of God. All the saints that ever were on earth, and all faithful ministers, martyrs, and witnesses, that ever appeared in the church militant, have been aye speaking to his commendation, but they always acknowledged he was above all their praises; the most that they could say of him was, that he is altogether lovely, and that there is none in heaven or in earth that is to be in the least compared unto him. Ask the innumerable company of angels, and the spirits of just men made perfect, who see him as he is, and know him as they are known of him, what is their estimate of him? All they can say of him is, Rev. v. 9. "Worthy is he to take the book, and to open the (seven) seals thereof. Worthy is the Lamb that was slain." But how worthy is he they cannot tell; his praise is in all the churches, both militant and triumphant. But their praises are nothing but a profound silence, in comparison of what he is and deserves, Psa. lxxxv. 1. " Praise waiteth (or is silent) for thee, O God, in Zion—Go forth, O ye daughters of Zion, and behold him;" for *behold he cometh, go out and meet him.*

All I shall say anent him, shall be comprised in the answer of a few questions, that some poor soul may be ready to put concerning the blessed Bridegroom. They that love Christ, and have a mind to match with him, have commonly a great deal of questions to put concerning him.

Quest. 1. Will you tell us, what is the Bridegroom's name, if you can tell? *Answ.* That is not easily answered, for it is a part of Agur's confession of faith, Prov. xxx. 4. "Who hath ascended up into heaven, or descended. What is his name, and what is his Son's name, if thou canst tell?" And when Manoah asked the angel what was his name? (that he might do him honour), He (viz. Christ the angel of the covenant) answers, "Why askest thou thus after my name, seeing it is secret?" or, as in the margin, seeing it is Wonderful. Such a secret is his name, that no man can call him Lord, but by the Holy Ghost; you may read his name in your Bibles, and still his name will be a secret, till the Spirit of the Lord open it unto you by glorifying his person in your eyes, and then, and never till then, will you cry out, O! his name is like ointment poured forth; O! he has a name above every name that can be named, whether in this world or that which is to come: Every knee must bow unto this name, and every tongue must acknowledge that Jesus Christ is Lord, to the praise and glory of God the Father.

I will just tell you of a few of the scriptural names of the Bridegroom. And O! look up to him for a glimpse of his glory in them.

His name is Jesus, Matth. i. 21. Now, what think ye of that name? for the sound of salvation is in it: "Thou shalt call his name Jesus, for he shall save his people from their sins." O lost sinner, roll the name of the Bridegroom, as a sweet morsel under thy tongue. His name is Christ, or the renowned Messiah, the Anointed One of God. Grace was poured into his lips, for God, even his Father, anointed him with the oil of gladness above all his fellows. His name is the Lord, for he is Lord of all; Lord of lords. He is God's first-born, whom he hath made higher than the kings of the earth; yea, all the kings of the earth must do homage unto him, some time or other; and no wonder, for by him "kings reign, and princes decree justice." What is his name? His name is Immanuel, God-man, or God with us, to stand in our quarrel; to take our part against the old serpent; and accordingly he has bruised his head, and through death has destroyed him that had the power of death.

See a whole cluster of the names of the Bridegroom together, Is. ix. 6. Where the bride, the Lamb's wife, glorying in her beloved consort, cries out, in a holy triumph, "Unto us a child is born, unto us a son is given, and the government shall be upon his shoulder, and his name shall be called Wonderful, Counsellor, the Mighty God, the everlasting Father, the Prince of peace."

1*st*, His name is a great, glorious, and renowned name, a name above every name, Philip. ii. 9-11. "God hath highly exalted him, and given him a name which is above every name, that at the name of Jesus every knee should bow, of things in heaven, and things in earth, and things under the earth. And that every tongue should confess, that Jesus Christ is Lord, to the glory of God the Father." So Eph. i. 20, 21, 22. God "hath set him at his own right hand in the heavenly places, and exalted him far above all principality, and power, and might, and dominion, and every name that is named, not only in this world, but also in that which is to come."

2dly, His name is a savoury name: Song i. 3. "Because of the savour of thy good ointment, thy name is as ointment poured forth, therefore do the virgins love thee." O Sirs! there is such an odoriferous perfume in the name of Christ, that when once a poor soul gets a scent of it, it can never forget it, and the very remembrance of it, is a feast and banquet to the soul, Is. xxvi. 8. 9. "Yea, in the way of thy judgments, O Lord, have we waited for thee; the desire of our soul is to thy name, and to the remembrance of thee. With my soul have I desired thee in the night: yea, with my Spirit within me, will I seek thee early."

3dly, His name is a medicinal name. If faith be but acted upon his name, it makes the bones that were broken to rejoice; makes the blind to see; the deaf to hear; the lame man to leap like an hart, and the tongue of the dumb to sing, Acts iii. 6. 7. 16. So Acts iv. 12. &c.

4thly, His name is a sheltering and hiding name: when storms are blowing, whether from heaven, earth, or hell, Prov. xviii. 11, "The name of the Lord is a strong tower, the righteous fly unto it, and are safe." It is not only a tower, but a strong and impregnable tower, and the gates of hell shall never prevail against that soul that has fled for refuge unto it.

5thly, His name is an attractive name, it draws the heart and soul to him: it is by the sound of this name that the gathering of the people is unto him as the blessed Shiloh. What is it that makes the gospel the power of God unto salvation? Why, it is just the displays of the glory of his renowned name, "If I be lifted up from the earth (says Christ), I will draw all men unto me."

6thly, His name is an enlightening name to the poor soul that is walking in darkness; hence Is. 1. at the close, "He that walketh in darkness, and hath no light, let him trust in the name of the Lord," &c. plainly intimating, that a glance of the name of Christ, by the eye of faith, will make light to spring out of darkness, to the soul, under the darkest clouds of desertion: and no wonder, for he is the "light of the world, the true light, the Sun of righteousness."

7thly, His name is a quickening and enlivening name: By the name of Jesus the dead are raised unto life; and no wonder, for this is one of his names. *The Life*, John xiv. 6. and John xi. 25. *The Resurrection and the Life.* Let but a languishing saint, when he is crying, with the eunuch, Is. lvi. "I am a dry tree," let him but hear the name of the Lord Jesus, let him but get a glimpse of the glory of his person, he will be ready to cry with the apostle,

Col. iii. 3, I am "dead, but my life is hid with Christ in God." Or with Paul, Gal. ii. 20, I am crucified with Christ; nevertheless I live; yet not I, but Christ that liveth in me: and the life which I now live in the flesh, I live by the faith of the Son of God, who loved me, and gave himself for me."

8*thly*, His name is a prevalent name in heaven, insomuch, that, if this name be set in the front of our prayers and petitions, they will prevail, and obtain a hearing, and a gracious answer and return, John xiv. 13, "And whatsoever ye shall ask in my name, that will I do," &c. This name perfumes our prayers like incense.

9*thly*, It is a worthy name, James ii. 7. speaking of the rich man with the gold ring and gay clothing, tells us, they "blaspheme that worthy name by the which ye are called;" the triumphant company in heaven know it to be so, for they warble forth the praises of his name, saying, "Worthy is the Lamb that was slain," Rev. v.

10*thly*, It is a durable and everlasting name, Ps. lxxii. at the close." "His name shall endure for ever, his name shall be continued as long as the sun: for men shall be blessed in him, and all nations shall call him blessed: and therefore blessed be his glorious name for ever, and let the whole earth be filled with his glory." This name will make sweet melody in heaven, through all eternity.

Now, Sirs, what think you of the Bridegroom, when you hear of his name? will you match with him? will you marry him? if thy heart can say, "O, if I had ten thousand hearts and hands, I would give them all to him." Well, if this be the language of thy heart, it is a done bargain; he is thy Bridegroom, and thou art his bride, the Lamb's wife.

Quest. 2. O I would hear more about him! Will you tell me what is the Bridegroom's pedigree and parentage? of whom is he descended? *Answ.* I can tell you some things anent his genealogy: "He is of the seed of David according to the flesh," he is the offspring of ancient kings, as you may see from his genealogy, Matth. i. and Luke iii. If you ask anent his divine pedigree, he "is the only begotten Son of the Father, and the brightness of his glory, and the express image of his person." But as to the manner of his generation, who can declare it! this is a secret, and secret things belong unto the Lord. Only from this hint you may see, the Bridegroom is so honourably descended, that it is a wonder he should match with any of the fallen tribe of Adam.

Quest. 3. What is the Bridegroom's personal worth and excellency? *Answ.* There is such a divine glory in his person, that the lustre of it darkens the sun in the firmament, that it appears to be as sackcloth and darkness. Such glory is in his person, as dazzles the eyes of angels to behold him, Is. vi. They cover their faces with their wings, crying, one to another, "Holy, holy, holy Lord of hosts," &c. All the perfections of the Deity shine with a meridian lustre and glory in the person of our glorious Bridegroom. The fulness of the Godhead dwells in him bodily. He is "in the form of God, and thinks it not robbery to be equal with God." So glorious is the person of the Bridegroom, that he captivates every eye and heart that beholds him, and imparts his glory, in some measure, to every soul that looks on him by the eye of faith, 2 Cor. iii. 18. " But we all, with open face, beholding as in a glass, the glory of the Lord, are changed into the same image, from glory to glory," &c. The bride, by looking on the glory of the Bridegroom, is made like the " king's daughter, all glorious within, and to look forth as the morning, fair as the moon, clear as the sun, and terrible as an army with banners: O go forth, ye daughters of Zion," and behold his glory.

Quest. 4. What are the endowments and qualifications of the Bridegroom? *Answ.* His qualifications are so rare and singular, that tongue cannot tell them, nor heart conceive them. Only, to commend him to your esteem, love, and affections, there are these few qualifications that may recommend him to any rational soul.

1. " For beauty, he is white and ruddy, the chiefest among ten thousand, his countenance is as Lebanon, excellent as the cedars, fairer than the children of men, and altogether lovely."

2. For wisdom, all the " treasures of wisdom and knowledge are hid in him : " he is wise in heart, and mighty in counsel. So wise, that he has outwitted all the power and policy of hell and earth : although his enemies dig counsel as deep as hell, yet hell and destruction being naked before him, he just takes the wise in their own craftiness, and the counsel of the froward he carrieth headlong ; and he imparts wisdom unto the simple bride, making her wise unto salvation, acquainted with the mysteries of the kingdom, which are hid from the wise and prudent of the world.

3. For riches, the Bridegroom that offers to match with you is immensely rich ; he is a man of substance indeed, and he causes those that love him to inherit substance ; his riches are unsearchable, Eph. iii. 8. his riches are durable, Prov. viii. 18.

4. For honour, he is renowned in heaven and earth, having a name above every name that can be named ; Prov. viii. 18. " Honour and riches are with me." Honour and majesty are before his face: and he makes all that believe on him honourable, Is. xliii. 2, " Ever since thou wast precious in my sight, thou hast been honourable," &c.

5. For strength, he is the man of God's right-hand, whom he has made strong for himself. The strength of omnipotence is in him, for he is the mighty God, Is. ix. 6. and the Almighty, Rev. i. 8, He came from Edom, and from Bozra, " travelling in the greatness of his strength, shewing himself mighty to save."

6. For authority, he has power over all flesh, " that he may give eternal life to as many as the Father hath given him. All power is his in heaven and in earth ; things in heaven, and things in earth, and things under the earth, yea, every knee must bow unto him, and every tongue must confess, that Jesus Christ is Lord, to the glory of God the Father."

7. For meekness and lowliness, he is incomparable, and proposes

himself as the great pattern of it for our imitation, Matth. xi. 29, "Learn of me, for I am meek and lowly."

8. For constancy in his love, in his promises, and in all his amiable excellencies, he is Christ Jesus, "the same to-day, yesterday, and for ever." His name is, "I AM; he rests in his love, and changes not, therefore the sons of Jacob are not consumed." His promises are not like the promises of men, yea to day, and nay to-morrow; no, but "all the promises of God are in him yea and amen; one jot or tittle of what he says shall never pass away; the mountains shall depart, and the hills be removed; but my kindness shall not depart from thee, neither shall the covenant of my peace be removed, saith the Lord, that hath mercy upon thee." These are some, and but a small part, of the qualifications of the blessed Bridegroom: "Go forth, then, ye daughters of Zion, and behold him."

MATTHEW xxv. 6.—"And at midnight there was a cry made, Behold the Bridegroom cometh, go ye out to meet him."

THE SECOND SERMON ON THIS TEXT.

THE *third* thing proposed in the general method was, to speak a little of the *Bride*, for where there is a bridegroom, there must of necessity be a bride. And here the bride of Christ may be viewed in a three-fold situation; either 1. As in a state of nature; 2. As in a state of grace; or, 3. As in a state of glory.

(1.) Let us view her as in her natural state, and so we shall find her in a doleful and deplorable condition (I speak of the elect, whether personally or collectively considered). If we view her in her natural descent and pedigree, she is a corrupt branch, sprung of the rotten root of the first Adam, conceived in sin, brought forth in iniquity, altogether as an unclean thing, black like the Ethiopian, by lying among the pots of hell, Ezek. xvi. Christ there puts his church and people in mind of their natural condition, ver. 3-6, where, by a lively metaphor of a new born infant, the Lord represents the condition of all mankind.

1. "Thy navel was not cut," *i. e.* just feeding and living upon things below, for "that which is born of the flesh is flesh." Man's nature sucks in the poison of carnal things, and to be carnally minded is death.

2. "Thou wast not salted at all." Salt preserves from putrefaction. The spirit and grace of God is sometimes likened unto salt, "have salt in yourselves." Now, man by nature is quite destitute of this salt, and so must be wholly putrefied and corrupted, therefore likened unto a putrefied carcase, Rom. iii. or an open sepulchre.

3. "No eye pitied thee, to do any of these things unto thee,"

&c. Man of all creatures is the most helpless when he is new born, especially if cast out in the open field. What can a sinner do for himself? or what can angels or men do for him? The whole creation stand aloof, and cry, 'We cannot help you out from under the curse of the law, or the wrath of an angry God.' And therefore he must inevitably perish, like the new born infant, cast out to the open field, unless some one take it up.

Now this is the condition of Christ's bride when he set his love upon her, as you see in the 6th and 8th verses of the same xvi. of Ezek. and "when I passed by thee, and saw thee polluted in thine own blood, I said unto thee, when thou wast in thy blood, Live," &c. We have another very clear description of man in his natural state, Eph. ii. 5-12, "And you hath he quickened who were dead in trespasses and sins," &c.; and Titus iii. 3, "For we ourselves also were sometimes foolish, disobedient, deceived, serving diver's lusts and pleasures, living in malice and envy, hateful and hating one another." Thus you see how the Spirit of God describes the natural condition of all mankind. Oh how may it fill us with admiration, to think that such a creature should become a bride to the Son of God! and yet his love surmounts all; "O the height, the depth, the breadth, and length of the love of God."

(2.) Let us view the bride as in a state of grace, and see what a strange alteration free grace makes upon her. This is also set forth in Ezek. xvi. by an elegant metaphor, from ver. 6-14.

1. He quickens her and gives her life, ver. 6, "I said unto thee, Live."
2. He casts the skirt of his everlasting righteousness over her, ver. 8.
3. He takes her unto a marriage-relation with himself, within the bond of the covenant, ver. 8.
4. He washes and cleanses her with the washing of regeneration, ver. 9.
5. He anoints her with the oil of his Spirit.
6. He decks and adorns her with the ornaments of holiness, the graces of his Spirit, ver. 11. 12.
7. He confers royal dignity upon her, ver. 12, at the close; puts a crown upon her head.
8. He makes her perfect and complete in himself, through the comeliness he puts upon her, ver. 14. Thus you see what the love of Christ doth for his bride, while yet only in time of espousals.

(3.) We might also view her in a state of glory, when the marriage shall be consummate at Christ's second coming, but this is what "eye hath not seen, nor ear heard," nor hath it entered into the heart of man to conceive. Only I refer you to two or three texts, that give us a glimpse of the glory that Christ will then confer upon his bride, Matth. xiii. 43, "They shall shine forth as the sun in the kingdom of their Father." Dan. xii. 3, "They that be wise shall shine as the brightness of the firmament, and they that turn many to righteousness, as the stars for ever and ever."

Col. iii. 4, "When Christ also who is our life shall appear, then shall ye appear with him in glory." 1 John iii. 2, "Beloved, now are we the sons of God, and it doth not yet appear what we shall be; but we know, that when he shall appear, we shall be like him, for we shall see him as he is," &c. Thus I have given you a short account of the bride in her natural state, and in a state of grace and glory.

IV. The *fourth* thing was to speak a little of the *coming of the Bridegroom. Behold the Bridegroom cometh.*

Now, to clear this matter, I would have you to know, that I do not at present speak either of Christ's first coming in the flesh, or of his second coming unto judgment. His first coming in the flesh was to purchase a bride for himself by his obedience and death. His second and last coming, at the end of the world, will be to solemnise the marriage, and to fetch the bride home to the royal palace, the house of many mansions that he is preparing for her reception, when she shall be made fully ready. I say, I do not at this time speak of either of these, however the last may be intended in this parable. At present I shall speak a little of these intermediate visits that the Bridegroom makes unto his bride during the time of espousals, before he come at the last day to solemnise the marriage before men and angels.

1*st*, The Bridegroom comes and visits his church and people in the chariot of providence; I understand his favourable dispensations when he comes to build up Zion, he appears in his glory, and regards the prayer of the destitute. Thus when the Lord brought Israel out of their Egyptian bondage, with a high hand and outstretched arm, plaguing Egypt, slaying their first born, and at length bringing his church and people through the Red Sea, while, at the same time, he overthrew Pharaoh and his host, on which occasion Israel sang that song, Exod. xv. through the whole: So likewise, when he turned back their captivity from Babylon, and settled them again in their native land, and caused the city and temple to be rebuilt, and daily sacrifice and oblation to be offered, this was a favourable visit in the chariot of providence. Much like unto this, was the visit the Lord made in his providence to this poor land, when, at our reformation from Popery, he spirited our nobles, gentry, and commons, to shake off the yoke of Popish tyranny and idolatry, and to embrace the gospel of Christ, and authorise the true reformed religion, by laws and acts of parliament, which stand in force to this day, and were adopted by this church in the year 1638, and again authorised by law at the revolution, and since that time. These, I say, were gracious visits that the Lord made to this church, riding in the chariot of providence, with the bright side towards her; and how often doth he visit particular believers, by favourable dispensations of providence, when they expected nothing but death and destruction. He has interposed mercifully for their deliverance, and made them to sing with David, Ps. cxvi. "I was brought low, and he helped me."

And Ps. ciii. "He redeemeth my life from destruction, and crowneth me with loving kindness and tender mercy."

Sometimes again the dark side of the chariot appears in gloomy and wrathlike dispensations, as when he sets up the right hand of the cruel enemy over them, gives them like "sheep to the slaughter, to be killed all the day long." When he breaks them with breach upon breach, and rushes upon them like a giant;" as in the case of Job: when he cast the three children into a fiery furnace, and Daniel into the lions' den. These and the like dispensations have a very black and dismal aspect; and in this case the church and people of God are ready to cry out with Jacob, "All these things are against us." And yet the black chariot of providence is bottomed and lined with love, grace, and mercy, as appeared in the case of Job, Daniel, the three children, and Jacob; and so the scripture comes to be fulfilled, that "all the ways of the Lord are mercy and peace to them that love him," Ps. ciii.; and Rom. viii. 28, "All things work together for good to them that love God, to them who are the called according to his purpose."

But I do not at present speak so much of the visits that the Lord Christ makes unto his people in the chariot of providence, as the visits he makes to them in the chariot of the gospel revelation, and ordinances of his appointment, such as word, sacrament, prayer, meditation, Christian conference, and the like, which are so many trysting places, in which the Bridegroom comes and visits his bride, manifesting forth his glory to her, spreading his banner of love over her. Now, as to the visits that Christ makes to his bride of this kind, in the chariot of the gospel revelation, there are these few things I would remark concerning them.

1*st*, The first visit of distinguishing love that he makes to the bride is in the day of conversion, when he draws by the veils of ignorance, unbelief, error, and prejudice, and manifests himself to her in his divine glory, fulness, suitableness, and excellency, in such a way as ravishes her heart with his love and loveliness. This is called the time of espousals, Song iii. last, because then it is that the consent of the bride is gained, and her heart drawn after the Bridegroom with the irresistible cords of victorious love. Of this the Lord puts Israel in mind, when he says, "I remember thee, the kindness of thy youth, the love of thine espousals, when thou wentest after me in the wilderness, in a land that was not sown," Jer. ii. 2.

2*dly*, The heart of the bride being thus hanked or catched with the glory of the Bridegroom, he, for holy and wise ends, withdraws commonly his sensible presence, and leaves her with a promise of his returning in due time; like that, John xiv. 18, "I will not leave you comfortless; I will come to you;" or that, John xiv. 21. 23, "He that loveth me shall be loved of my Father, and I will love him, and manifest myself unto him," &c., or John xvi 22, "I will see you again, and your hearts shall rejoice," &c. You know it is not usual for the bridegroom to stay or cohabit with the bride, even after the espousals, until the marriage be solemnised, and then they take up house, and dwell together; but until that time come he makes only passing visits, or comes and goes; only when he goes, he leaves her with a promise of coming back. Just so is it in the present case, Christ leaves his people with a promise to support them in his absence.

3dly, I remark, that Christ is many times present with the bride and spouse, when she is not aware of it. An instance of this we have in the case of Jacob, Gen. xxviii. 16. The Lord there appears to him in a dream, and when he awakes, he says, "Surely the Lord is in this place, and I knew it not;" and Mary, John xx. 14. she is weeping, and saying, "They have taken away my Lord, and I know not where they have laid him." She was speaking to Christ himself, but knew not that it was Christ, but supposing him to be the gardener, said to him, "Sir, if thou hast borne him hence, tell me where thou hast laid him, and I will take him away," &c. So we see the same in the case of the disciples going to Emmaus, Luke xxiv. Christ was conversing with them, and opening unto them the scriptures, reproving them for their unbelief; and yet they did not know that it was he, until, upon reflection, they say one to another, "Did not our hearts burn within us while he talked with us," &c.

4thly, Every visit the Bridegroom of souls makes unto his bride is an assured pledge of after visits, until he come to consummate the marriage at the end of the day; for, as we are told, Hos. vi. 3. "His going forth is prepared as the morning." As the break of day is a pledge of the sun's rising, and his rising is a pledge of his ascending to the meridian or mid-day; so every visit that Christ makes to the soul makes way for further discoveries of his glory, until the day of glory break, and all shadows for ever flee away.

5thly, The Bridegroom loves sometimes to surprise the bride with his visits, he comes even at midnight, when she is little looking for him, Song vi. 12. "Or ever I was aware, my soul made me like the chariots of Amminadib;" or, as it reads in the margin, "set me on the chariots of my willing people." So Is. xlix. 14, 15. Zion is there saying, under a dark cloud of desertion, "The Lord hath forsaken me, and my Lord hath forgotten me:" But, all on a sudden, the Lord comes, and says, "Can a woman forget her sucking child, that she should not have compassion on the son of her womb? Yea, she may forget, yet will I not forget thee."

6thly, These sensible surprising visits of the Bridegroom, they are but rare, and of a short continuance: they are like a bright blink of the sun from under the cloud, which in a little is presently overcast with a new cloud, like that of the disciples upon Mount Tabor, at Christ's transfiguration, when they saw his countenance to shine as the sun, his raiment white as the light, and a voice saying, "This is my beloved Son, in whom I am well pleased:" but ere ever they were aware, a dark cloud intercepts all. *Quest.* Why are the Bridegroom's visits so rare, and of a short continuance. *Answ.* The Lord will have it so, to let the bride know that the marriage is not yet consummate, and she is only yet in a state of espousals: cohabitation only follows the consummation of the marriage in heaven. Again, the bride, while here away, in a state of imperfection, is not able to bear a constant fellowship with the Bridegroom, I mean bright sensible manifestations, the old bottles cannot bear much of that new wine. Paul himself was in danger of being lifted up with pride, through abundance of manifestations; and therefore a messenger of Satan was sent to buffet him. And, again, by this way he makes them long for heaven, where the Bridegroom and the bride shall meet, never to part, saying, " I desire to depart, and be with Jesus, which is best of all."

7thly, The Bridegroom may, and frequently doth intermit his visits for a very long space of time; he may absent himself not only for days, or weeks, or months, but for years, and many many years together. It is thought, that long twenty years intervened between Jacob's Bethel visit, Gen. xxxviii. 18, and his visit he got chap. xxxi. 13. When the Lord appeared unto him, saying, " I am the God of Bethel, where thou anointedst the pillar, and where thou vowedst a vow unto me." It is no strange thing for the saints to be walking in darkness, and seeing no light: and, in this case, they are ready to cry with David, Psa. xiii. 1. "How long, how long wilt thou hide thy face from me;" Psa. lxxxix. "Where are thy former loving-kindnesses," &c.; Psa. lxxvii. "Hath God forgotten to be gracious? will he be favourable no more?" &c. The reason of this withdrawing is either some idol harboured, or to hide pride from their eyes, or to quicken the soul's longing after himself, or to teach and train them up unto a life of faith upon the promise; for here " we walk by faith, and not by sight."

8thly, Although the Bridegroom may be long absent, yet he will return at length, when his own time comes, which is aye best both for his glory and her good. He will not contend for ever, neither will he be always wroth, lest the spirit of the poor bride should fail within her: " Weeping may endure for a night, but joy cometh in the morning," Psa. xxx. 5. So Is. liv. 5-8. "Thy Maker is thine Husband. For a small moment have I forsaken thee, and in a little wrath have I hid my face from thee for a moment; but with great mercy will I gather thee, and with everlasting kindness will I have mercy on thee, saith the Lord thy Redeemer."

9thly, Let him come when he will, or how he will, he is aye welcome; for he brings all good with him. *Quest.* What doth he bring with him. *Answ.* 1. He brings his Father with him, John xiv. 23. "My Father will love him, and we will come unto him, and make our abode with him." 2. He brings the Comforter, which is the Holy Ghost, along with him; and then the soul is anointed as with fresh oil, which makes the heart glad, and the countenance to shine. 3. He brings peace and joy with him, a " peace that passes all understanding, a joy that is unspeakable, and full of glory." 4. He brings victory over sin, Satan, death, and hell, along with him; and, in a word, he brings pardon of sin, and all manner of salvation, along with him. And therefore, I say, let him come when or how he will, he is aye welcome. But I pass this, and should now go on to

V. The *fifth* thing proposed in the method, which was to speak to the duty called for in all the virgins, upon the intimation and warning given them, *Go ye out to meet him.* But this I refer unto another occasion.

ACTION SERMON.

MATTHEW xxv. 6.—"And at midnight there was a cry made, Behold the Bridegroom cometh, go ye out to meet him."

THE THIRD SERMON ON THIS TEXT.

HAVING in some former discourses spoken of the Bridegroom and of the bride, and of the coming of the Bridegroom, I now proceed to speak of the call and summons given to the virgins, both wise and foolish, *Go ye out to meet him.* And this I shall endeavour to discourse by resolving the few following questions that may be put by the professed virgins that are hearing me.

1. What is supposed or implied in the duty, *Go ye out to meet him?*
2. What is the motion of the soul in going out to meet him?
3. For what end and purpose are we to go out and meet the Bridegroom?
4. Where may we expect to meet him?
5. Who they are that stand fairest for a meeting with him in love and mercy?
6. What sort of a meeting have the wise virgins with the Bridegroom, when they go forth to meet him in a way of believing?

Quest. What is supposed or implied in the duty, *Go ye out to meet him?*

1*st*, It supposes a present distance between them and the Bridegroom. There was a total distance between him and the foolish virgins; they had heard of him by the hearing of the ear, but their eyes had never seen him, the light of the knowledge of his glory had never shined in their hearts. O! how many such have we in our Christian assemblies, "whom the god of this world has blinded, lest the light of the glorious gospel of Christ, who is the image of God, should shine unto them?" And as there was a total distance between Christ and the foolish virgins, so there was a partial distance between him and the wise virgins, otherwise they had not been slumbering and sleeping.

2*dly*, *Go ye out to meet him.* It supposes, that it is the work and business of God's heralds to prepare the way for a meeting between Christ and sinners, to bring Christ near to sinners, and sinners near to Christ. When Christ was coming, yea actually come in the flesh to the Jewish nation, John the Baptist cried, " Prepare ye the way of the Lord, make straight in the desert a high way for our God." We, as ambassadors for the Bridegroom, come to beseech and intreat sinners to go out and meet the Bridegroom in a way of believing, and saints (wise virgins) to go out and hold communion with him in the renewed actings of faith. Wisdom crieth to all promiscously, " Come, eat of my bread, and drink of the wine which I have mingled."

3dly, Go ye out to meet him. It implies, that the Bridegroom is not afar off, but that he is nigh at hand. It is the way of unbelief, and a deceitful heart to say, " The Lord delayeth his coming ; " he is behind the mountains, while yet he is at the door: Rev. iii. 20. " Behold, I stand at the door and knock ; if any man hear my voice, and open the door, I will come into him, and will sup with him, and he with me." And therefore, " say not in thine heart, who shall ascend into heaven ? (that is, to bring Christ down from above) or, who shall descend into the deep? that is, to bring Christ again from the dead. For the word is nigh thee, even in thy mouth, and in thy heart; that is the word of faith, which we preach," Rom. x. 6-8.

4thly, Go ye out to meet him. It says, that the Bridegroom is a person of note and merit, that he is worthy of all reception and entertainment: 1 Tim. i. 15, " This is a faithful saying, and worthy of all acceptation, that Christ Jesus came into the world to save sinners." Sirs, we tell you, that the Bridegroom is worthy of the greatest welcome : his person is worthy, for he is the Son of God ; and he comes upon a worthy and wonderful errand, even to save sinners, and not only so, but to wed them for a bride ; for he is saying, " I will betrothe thee unto me for ever."

5thly, Go ye out to meet him. It implies that the Bridegroom is not to be found within, but without, *Go ye out to meet him.* Quakers and enthusiasts boast of a Christ within them ; but though Christ, by his Spirit, dwells in the heart of a true believer, yet the first meeting that faith has with Christ, is by going out to meet him : It is a Christ outwardly revealed in the word that true faith deals with : the grace of faith is indeed seated in the soul, as the eye is in the body, but then, like the eye of the body, it is wholly taken up with objects without itself. Faith lies in a continual outgoing toward Christ revealed and exhibited in the word: Israel had never found the manna, unless they had gone out to gather it ; and they had never been healed of the stings of the fiery serpents, except they had looked without to the brazen serpent : so we shall never meet the Bridegroom, except we go out and meet him.

6thly, Go ye out to meet him. It says, that in believing in Christ, in receiving him, there is a disbanding of other lovers ; for " no man can serve two masters." Sin, Satan, and the world, have dominion over the man, while in a natural and Christless state ; he is playing the harlot with other lovers ; some lust or idol he is hugging in his bosom, that is as dear to him as a right hand or right eye. But now, whenever he goes out to meet the Bridegroom, he cries with Ephraim, Hos. xiv. 8, "What have I to do any more with idols?" "O Lord, our God, other lords, besides thee, have had dominion over me; but by thee only will I make mention of thy name," Is. xxvi. 13.

7thly, Go ye out to meet him. It says, that the soul, in believing or receiving Christ, quits all false confidences, and arises out of those beds of sloth and security upon which it was stretching itself. The virgins here, they were all slumbering and sleeping, some of them upon one bed of sloth, and some upon another. But the cry comes *at midnight, Behold the Bridegroom cometh, go ye out to meet him;* which says plainly, that they behoved to quit their short beds, and cast away their narrow coverings, if they would meet the Bridegroom and have fellowship with him. 1. There is the bed of spiritual death and security, Eph. v. 14, "Awake, thou that sleepest, and arise from the dead, and Christ shall give thee light." 2. We must quit the bed of church privileges, and go forth from these; and beware of saying, "The temple of the Lord, the temple of the Lord, the temple of the Lord are these." 3. The bed of civility and moral honesty: the young man in the gospel could say, "All these things have I kept from my youth up," and yet was a stranger to Christ, and to the new birth. 4. The bed of a legal righteousness; we must arise out of that, for by "the works of the law no flesh living can be justified." 5. The bed of evangelical righteousness; this also must be quitted, if ever we would go forth to meet the Bridegroom. Some seek righteousness not directly by the law, but, "as it were, by the works of the law." They make their faith, love, repentance, and obedience, unto a pretended new gospel law, a sort of righteousness to themselves, and thereupon build their faith and hope of the imputation of the righteousness, which is nothing but a subtle way of subverting the whole gospel of Christ, and the method of free justification by the righteousness of Christ alone, a building the imputation of Christ's righteousness upon straw and stubble, and, at best, a profane jumbling of Christ's righteousness and our own together, an error against which the apostle denounceth an anathema, Gal. i. 6. 8.

8thly, Go ye out to meet him. It implies some knowledge of the Bridegroom, accompanied with an assent of the mind unto the report of the gospel, and the record of God concerning him; for we do not go out to meet strangers, of whom we have no knowledge, or of whom we have never heard: the soul that goes out to meet Christ, is made to know him. By "his knowledge shall my righteous Servant justify many:" and, from the knowledge it has of his person and mediation, it assents to what is recorded of him in the word, and reported of him in a preached gospel; and is ready to say, as the Queen of Sheba, when she saw the glory of King Solomon, and heard his wisdom. 'The half (what I heard at a distance) was not told me, to what I now see and know.' "This is life eternal, that they might know thee, the only true God, and Jesus Christ whom thou hast sent."

9*thly*, It implies a high esteem and hearty approbation of the person of Christ, and the method of justification, sanctification, and salvation, through him. O! will the soul say, he is " worthy of all acceptation," indeed: "Whom have I in heaven but thee, and there is none upon earth that I desire besides thee. Yea, doubtless, and I count all things but lost, for the excellency of the knowledge of Christ Jesus my Lord: that I may win Christ, and be found in him; and unto you who believe he is precious."

10*thly, Go ye out to meet him*. It implies an outgoing of the whole soul, in all its powers and faculties, after the Bridegroom, and an actual subscribing the contract of the new covenant, with heart and hand, according to what is prophesied and promised, Is. xliv. 3, "One shall say, I am the Lord's; and another shall call himself by the name of Jacob; and another shall subscribe with his hand unto the Lord, and surname himself by the name of Israel." And, from that time forward, the bride is betrothed unto the Bridegroom, according to that, Hos. ii. 19. 20. She now begins to call him *Ishi;* my husband being the echo of the bride's voice unto the words of the Bridegroom, Is. liv. 5, "Thy Maker is thine husband; the Lord of hosts is his name."

11*thly, Go ye out to meet him*. It implies, that it is the duty, and will be the desire of the soul espoused to Christ to pursue after the enjoyment of him, and fellowship with him, in all the duties and ordinances of his appointment, while in a state of espousals, till the marriage be consummate at the end of time, Ps. xxvii. 4, "One thing have I desired of the Lord, that will I seek after, that I may dwell in the house of the Lord all the days of my life, to behold the beauty of the Lord, and to inquire in his temple." It is but a toom house to the bride when the Bridegroom is absent; and therefore when she misses him, she goes mourning without the sun, crying, "O that I knew where I might find him, saw ye him whom my soul loveth," &c. So much for the first question. I now proceed to,

The *second* question: What is the motion of the bride? or how doth she move when she goes out to meet the Bridegroom? For going out to meet him implies motion. I answer,

1*st*, It is not a carnal or corporeal, but a spiritual and a soul motion: "O my soul, thou hast said unto the Lord, thou art my Lord," Pas. xvi. 2. "Return unto thy rest, O my Soul," Ps. cxvi. 7. Is. xxvi. 9, "With my soul have I desired thee," &c.

2*dly*, It is not a blind, but a rational and understanding motion: he draws with the cords of a man, and with the bands of love. The entrance of God's word having given light to the mind, he has got an understanding to know him that is true. So that the man in going out to meet the Bridegroom, knows well what he is doing, for he knows the Lord, and therefore follows on to know him more and more.

3*dly*, It is not a forced, but a free and voluntary motion the soul hath, when it goes out to meet the Bridegroom, Ps. cx. 3, "Thy people shall be willing in the day of thy power." He rejoices to meet the Lord in his ways, &c.

4thly, It is not a cold, but a most affectionate motion. All the affections of the soul are taken up with the glory of the Bridegroom, such as love, delight, desire, that before were pursuing other lovers, do now centre upon him alone.

5thly, It is not a slow, but a swift and speedy motion: "I made haste, and delayed not to keep thy righteous judgments." Like the flight of a dove to its windows, when pursued by the birds of prey, or that of the man-slayer to the city of refuge.

6thly, It is not a careless, but a careful and resolute motion. The man, in going out to meet the Bridegroom, is resolved to be at him, and with him, whatever bars or impediments be in the way: he will not say, "there is a lion in the way, a lion in the streets:" no; although lions and leopards be in his way; though all the armies of hell, and showers of fiery darts be in his way, he will break through them all.

7thly, It is a praying, importunate, and wrestling motion. The man in going out to meet the Bridegroom, is crying, "O when wilt thou come unto me? And O that I knew where I might find him," &c.

8thly, It is a very mysterious motion: the soul is carried out after Christ, and it knows not how: like the wind which blows where it listeth, we hear the sound of it, "but cannot tell whence it cometh, or whither it goeth."

9thly, It is a joyful and cheerful motion. O with what alacrity doth the soul receive and embrace the Bridegroom, in the day of espousals? the soul is just filled "with joy and peace in believing; yea, a joy unspeakable and full of glory," saying, "Let us be glad and rejoice, for the marriage of the Lamb is come."

The *third* question, for what end and purpose are we called to go out and meet the Bridegroom?

1st, We are to go out and behold him, and contemplate his glory, Song iii. last, "Go forth, O ye daughters of Zion, and behold King Solomon," &c. Is. xlii. 1, "Behold my servant whom I uphold, mine elect in whom my soul delighteth," &c. The Lord, by the prophet, had been reproving the nations for their idolatry, in the close of the preceding chapter, ver. 29, "Behold they are all vanity, their works are nothing, their molten images are wind and confusion." Well, to take their hearts off their idols, he presents them with an object worthy of their looks: It is as if the Lord had said, Turn away your eyes from beholding vanity, and behold "mine elect in whom my soul delighteth," &c. As if he had said, He is worthy to be beheld, and if you knew him, you would think little of all other objects that take up your mind.

2dly, We are to go out, and admire and wonder at the glory of his person and mediation; for one of the names of the Bridegroom is Wonderful, Is. ix. 6. Admire the union of the two natures in him, "for without controversy great is the mystery of godliness, God was manifested in the flesh; admire the height, the depth, the breadth, and the length, of the love of God," in matching with our nature, that he might be a fit Bridegroom for us, and match with our persons: "Verily he took not on him the nature of angels, but he took on him the seed of Abraham." Admire the exploits he has wrought in the great work of our redemption; he has brought over an angry and offended God, to be a God with us. Admire how he has bruised the head of the serpent, finished transgression, made an end of sin, made recouciliation for iniquity, brought in an everlasting righteousness, and confirmed the covenant with many, and made the sacrifice and oblation to cease. O! how should these things make us cry out with admiration, as the church doth, Is. lxiii. 1, "Who is this that cometh from Edom, with dyed garments from Bozrah," &c.

3*dly*, We should go out and meet him so as to match with him, for he is the Bridegroom, and wants a bride among the sons of men, Prov. viii. 30. The day of his espousals with any poor soul is the day of the gladness of his heart; he just rejoices over that poor soul that gives its consent to take him for a Husband, as a bridegroom rejoices over his bride; and the report of it reaching heaven, makes all the angels and spirits of just men made perfect to rejoice with him. O then go out and meet him, and present yourselves as chaste virgins to this one Husband.

4*thly*, Go out and meet him, and feast with him, and feed upon him, for the Bridegroom and his royal Father has provided a banquet for every one that will come to the marriage, and he has sent forth his servants, saying, "Tell them who are bidden, Behold I have prepared my dinner, my oxen, and my fatlings are killed, and all things are ready: come unto the marriage," Matth. xxii. 4. Is. xxv. 6, "And in this mountain shall the Lord of hosts make unto all people a feast of fat things, a feast of wines on the lees, of fat things full of marrow, of wines on the lees well refined," Prov. ix. 1-3, &c.

5*thly*, Go out and meet him, and list with him, for the Bridegroom is a "man of war, and the armies which are in heaven follow him," Rev. xix. 14. Virgin souls are said to "follow the Lamb, whithersoever he goeth," Rev. xiv. 4. and they that follow him, he makes them all conquerors, yea, more than conquerors, and admits them as such to sit with him upon his throne, as he also overcame, and is set down with the Father upon his throne, Rev. iii. at the close. Sirs, we are the recruiting officers of the Bridegroom, the Captain of salvation, who leads many sons unto glory. We want you to take on in the service of the King of kings, and Lord of lords, that under his victorious banner, you may wage war against sin, Satan, and the world, which he came to destroy.

Quest. 4. You call us to go out and meet the Bridegroom, Where may we meet him? O! may some poor soul say, 'That I knew where I might find him. O! tell me where he feedeth, and where he maketh his flocks to rest at noon.' *Answ.* Although the Bridegroom, as to his human nature, be in heaven, and in this respect the heavens are to "receive him until the times of restitution of all things;" yet he is to be found any where upon earth as to his divine, spiritual, gracious presence, by those that are really seeking after fellowship and communion with him by faith, in the ways and means of his own appointment: and this is what he has promised to his church, "Lo, I am with you alway, even unto the end of the world. In all places where I record my name, I will come unto thee, and I will bless thee. Where two or three are gathered together in my name, there am I in the midst of them." So that I say, there is as real communion and fellowship to be had with Christ now, though ascended, as ever his disciples had when he was going out and in among them, in a state of humiliation here upon earth; hence, says the apostle John concerning Christ, after he was gone away to heaven, 1 John i. 3, "Truly our fellowship is with the Father, and with his Son Jesus Christ."

But O, say you, Will you tell me more particularly where I may meet him and find him? *Answ.* He is so fond of a meeting with sinners, that he is sometimes, yea, many times, found of them that seek him not, as in the case of Paul going a black errand to Damascus, and poor Zaccheus upon the sycamore tree, seeking only to satisfy his curiosity: and if so, much more will he be found of them that seek him in the ways of his appointment; for he has said, he meeteth him that rejoiceth and worketh righteousness, those that remember him in his ways.

Quest. What are these ways and means of his appointment where I may meet the Bridegroom, and have fellowship with him?

Answ. He is sometimes found in the mount of secret meditation, "while I was musing, the fire burned," says David. Many a sweet interview have the souls of believers with Christ in meditation, Ps. lxiii. 6, "When I remember thee upon my bed, and mediate upon thee in the night watches—ver. 5. My soul shall be satisfied as with marrow and fatness." He is to be met with in secret prayer, "Then shall ye find me, when ye seek me, and search after me with all your hearts." In this duty Jacob found the Lord, and wrestled for the blessing till break of day, and like a prince prevailed, Hos. xii. 3. 4, "He took his brother by the heel, in the womb, and by his strength he had power with God: Yea, he had power over the angel, and prevailed: he wept, and made supplication unto him: He found him at Bethel," &c compared with Gen. xxxii. 24-26, "And Jacob was left alone; and there wrestled a man with him, until the breaking of the day. And when he saw that he prevailed not against him, he touched the hollow of his thigh; and the hollow of Jacob's thigh was out of joint, as he wrestled with him. And he said, Let me go, for the day breaketh; and he said, I will not let thee go, except thou bless me." He is to be met with in the duty of personal, family, or public fasting and humiliation, "But to this man will I look, who is poor, and of a contrite spirit, and trembleth at my word." He is to be met with in the duty of Christian conference and fellowship, when they that "feared the Lord spake often one to another, the Lord hearkened and heard." He is to be met with in reading and searching the scriptures, John v. 39, " Search the scriptures, for in them ye think ye have eternal life, and these are they which testify of me." While the Ethiopian eunuch was reading his Bible, the Lord met him in the ministry of Philip, insomuch that he " went on his way rejoicing." Many a sweet glimpse of the glory of the Bridegroom has the bride, while she is looking after him, through the glass of the revelation, 2 Cor. iii. last, " We all with open face beholding as in a glass the glory of the Lord, are changed into the same image, from glory to glory, even as by the spirit of the Lord." He is especially to be found in the gates of Zion, the public ordinances of his worship, where his people attend upon him in their assemblies, for prayer, for praise, for preaching and hearing the gospel, and for the celebration of the sacraments of baptism and the Lord's supper in a solemn manner; " the Lord loves these gates of Zion more than all the dwellings of Jacob." These are the streets and broad ways where the spouse sought him, Song iii. It is true she missed him for a while, but, at length, she met the Bridegroom, and was in a case to say, " I found him whom my soul loveth, I held him and would not let him go." David saw his power and glory in his sanctuary; hence Ps. lxxxiv. he declares how amiable his tabernacles were unto him; " A day (says he) in thy courts is better than a thousand; I had rather be a door-keeper in the house of my God, than to dwell in the tents of wickedness."

He is especially to be met with in the breaking of bread at a communion table: for " the cup which we bless, it is the communion of the blood of Christ; and the bread which we break, it is the communion of the body of Christ." Here the blessed Bridegroom is to be seen in his dyed garments; for, out of love to his bride, he trode " the wine press alone, when of the people there were none with him." If that question be put to him, " Why art thou red in thine apparel, as one that treadeth the wine fat? He may well answer, It is no wonder my apparel be red, for I was " wounded for thine iniquities, and bruised for thy transgressions."

MATTHEW xxv. 6.—" And at midnight there was a cry made, Behold the Bridegroom cometh, go ye out to meet him."

THE FOURTH SERMON ON THIS TEXT.

THE *fifth* question was, Who are they that stand fairest for a meeting with the Bridegroom in love and mercy?

Answ. What God may do, in a way of sovereign grace, for Christless, unbelieving, and profane sinners, who are in covenant with death, and at agreement with hell, we know not, for he can pluck a brand out of the fire, and take the prey from the mighty, when and how he pleases. He catches the wild ass in his mouth, that is snuffing up the east wind of sin and vanity. Only when you are running in the broad way to hell, you have no reason to look for anything but that indignation and wrath, tribulation and anguish, that is denounced against every soul that worketh evil. You that are among the rank of the foolish virgins, that are contenting yourselves with the empty lamps of a profession, and sleeping and slumbering away the day of grace, without buying the oil of grace for your lamps; you see, in the close of this parable, what you are to look for, even to meet with a shut door, and when you shall cry out of time, Lord, Open to us, he answers, Depart, I know you not.

But I do not speak of you, or the like of you, at present: but poor souls that are really exercised about soul matters, and are taken up with the Bridegroom and fellowship with him. I will tell you of some that stand fair for a comfortable meeting with the blessed Bridegroom, in the ordinances and means he has appointed for that end and purpose.

1. You who, like the wise virgins, are not satisfied with the lamp of a profession, but are buying oil for your vessels, while the market of grace is standing. You see the wise virgins go out and meet the Bridegroom, and enter into the marriage with him.

2. You who love the Bridegroom, and remember his words with pleasure, rolling them like a sweet morsel under your tongue, he has promised that ye shall have a meeting with him, John xiv. 23, "If a man love me, he will keep my word, and my Father will love him, and we will come unto him, and make our abode with him."

3. You that quit and renounce the covenant of works, made with the first Adam, and are taking hold of a covenant of grace and promise, made with a second Adam, you stand fair for a meeting with the Bridegroom. I give you his promise to lean upon, Is. lvi. 4, 5. "For thus saith the Lord unto the eunuchs that keep my sabbaths, and choose the things that please me, and take hold of my covenant: even unto them will I give, in mine house, and within my walls, a place and a name, better than of sons and of daughters. I will give them an everlasting name, that shall not be cut off." And it is again repeated, ver. 7, "Even them will I bring to my holy mountain, and make them joyful in my house of prayer; their burnt offerings and their sacrifices shall be accepted upon mine altar: for mine house shall be called an house of prayer for all people:" And therefore, *Go ye out and meet him.*

4. You that are waiting with hope and expectation for a visit of the Bridegroom, you stand fair for a meeting with him, "for he is good to them that wait for him," to the soul that seeketh him: He taketh pleasure "in them that fear him; in them that hope in his mercy. It is good for a man to hope," &c.

5. You who are poor and needy, and who are longing for a supply of soul needs, out of the fulness that is in Christ: for he has said, that "the needy shall not be forgotten;" that he will "supply all your need," Is. xli. 17, "When the poor and needy seek water,

and there is none, and their tongue faileth for thirst, I the Lord will hear," &c.

6. The importunate beggar who hangs on at a throne of grace, and the door of the house of mercy, and will not take a nay-say, shall meet the Bridegroom, and get its errand, for he has said, that "to him that knocketh, it shall be opened. Then shall ye find me, when ye seek me with all your heart."

7. The poor wearied and burdened soul, that is crying, "Mine iniquities have gone over my head, O wretched man that I am, who shall deliver me from this body of sin and death,—for it is a burden too heavy for me to bear." The Bridegroom says to such, "Cast thy burden upon the Lord, and he shall sustain thee: Come unto me, all ye that labour and are heavy laden, and I will give you rest."

8. The poor deserted soul that is walking in darkness, and sees no light, crying, "O when will he come unto me, the Lord hath forsaken me, and my Lord hath forgotten me." The Bridegroom hears thy moans after him, and is saying, as Is. xlix. 15, "Can a woman forget her sucking child, that she should not have compassion on the son of her womb? Yea, they may forget, yet will I not forget thee," or Isa. liv. 7, 8. "For a small moment have I forsaken thee, but with everlasting kindness will I have mercy upon thee." Ver. 10, "The mountains shall depart, but my love shall never depart from thee." Thus you see who they are that may look for a meeting with the Bridegroom.

The *sixth* and last question was, What sort of a meeting is it, that is between the bride and the Bridegroom.

Answ. 1. It is a real meeting, though, indeed, it be of a spiritual nature. A graceless world that know nothing of this matter, they look upon all religion, all fellowship with Christ, as a fancy. But they that have the knowledge and experience of it can say, in some measure, "Truly our fellowship is with the Father, and with his Son Jesus Christ." There is a far greater reality in it, than is in all the pleasures of sin and sense. Hence is that of David, Psa. iv. 7. "Thou hast put gladness in my heart, more than in the time that their corn and their wine increased," Psa. lxxxiv. 10. "A day in thy courts is better than a thousand in the tents of wickedness."

2*dly*, It is a most friendly and familiar meeting. The Bridegroom and bride converse and open their hearts to one another, with the most unreserved freedom. Christ imparts his secrets unto the bride; "The secret of the Lord is with them that fear him," Psa. xxv. and John xv. 15. "All things that I have heard of my Father, I have made known unto you." And, on the other hand, the bride imparts her mind with an unhampered freedom to the Bridegroom, and tells him all that is in her heart, even secrets she would not tell all the world besides.

3*dly*, It is a most joyful meeting upon both sides. As for the Bridegroom, it is "the day of his espousals, the day of the gladness of his heart." Whenever he meets his bride, he cries, "Thou hast ravished my heart, my sister, my spouse; thou hast ravished my heart with one of thine eyes, with one chain of thy neck," Song iv. 9. And then he adds, ver. 10. "How fair is thy love, my sister, my spouse! How much better is thy love than wine! Ver. 11. "And the smell of thy garments is like the smell of Lebanon." And, on the other hand, the bride, the Lamb's wife, rejoices with joy unspeakable and full of glory, Rev. xix. 7. "Let us be glad and rejoice, and give honour to him, for the marriage of the Lamb is come."

4*thly,* It is an honourable and dignifying meeting on the bride's part. Believers espoused to the Son of God are highly advanced indeed, to become the Lamb's wife, a greater honour than ever was conferred upon the highest angel in heaven, who are made ministering spirits to the heirs of salvation, Is. xliii. 4. "Ever since thou wast precious in my sight, thou hast been honourable."

5*thly,* It is a meeting that shall never end in a total parting, and is a prelude of that everlasting meeting they shall have with him at his second coming, when the marriage is solemnised before men and angels. I proceed now to,

VI. The *sixth* thing proposed, which was to give the reasons of the doctrine. *Why is it the duty of all the Virgins, both wise and foolish, to go out and meet the Bridegroom?* I answer,

1*st,* Because this is a falling in with the great design of God, in sending his beloved Son into the world. Why did he send him, but that he might be received? He is called the sent of God, to engage us to believe in him.

2*dly,* Because God has commanded it. His authority is interposed, that sinners of mankind entertain him in a way of believing, 1 John iii. 23. "This is his commandment, that we should believe on the name of his Son Jesus Christ," &c. Hear ye him, and that soul that does not hear him, "shall be cut off from among his people, and the wrath of God abideth on him."

3*dly,* Because the Bridegroom himself calls that we should *go out and meet him. Come unto me. Behold me, behold me,* &c.

4*thly,* Because the Holy Ghost calls in the word, and by all his motions and operations, to *go out and meet the Bridegroom.* "The Holy Ghost saith, To-day if you will hear his voice, harden not your hearts," Heb. iii. The Spirit saith, Come, Rev. xxii. 17. And what a dangerous thing is it to resist the Spirit, when he glorifies Christ, and testifies of him?

5*thly,* Because the bride, the spouse of Christ, all true believers, that are best acquainted with him, calls upon all others to come and match with him. She does not love to enjoy him alone; no, she would have all to be as happy in him as herself: hence they cry, "O taste and see that the Lord is good. Come and hear, all ye that fear God, and I will declare what he hath done for my soul," Psa. lxvi. 16. Hence, when the daughters of Jerusalem asked, "What is thy beloved more than another beloved?" She runs out in commendation of him, Song v. 10-16.

6*thly,* This is the design of the record of God concerning him in the word: Why has God set him forth in the word, and given him his testimonial, but to engage the world to fall in love with him, as the Bridegroom of souls? This is the design of all faithful ministers and friends of the Bridegroom, to make a match between Christ and you; and, Sirs, you will never give us our errand, or answer the design of our commission, as ambassadors of Christ, until you go forth and meet him, and give heart and hand unto him, so as we may be in case to say, as Paul did to the Corinthians, 2 Cor. xi. 2. "I have espoused you to one husband, that I may present you as a chaste virgin to Christ." But more of this afterwards. I proceed now to,

VII. The *seventh* thing in the method, which was *the application of the doctrine*.

Use *first*, shall be of *information* in the few following particulars.

1st, See hence the unspeakable and amazing love of God towards lost and undone sinners of Adam's Family: for he had a marriage plot in his mind from all eternity, with our tribe and family. No sooner had God made man, and breathed into his nostrils the breath of life, but he was so much in love with the work of his own hand, that he enters into a contract of marriage with him, upon condition of perfect obedience to the law, saying, "Thy Maker is thy Husband," and all I require of thee is to yield obedience to my commands, which he gave him power to do. Yea, after man had violate this contract, and prostitute himself to the devil, the world, and his own lust, gone astray after other lovers, that God should so love him, even then, as to match, first with his nature, by taking it into a personal union with him, in his eternal Son, and then to come and say, "Thy Maker is thine Husband, I will yet betrothe thee unto me, in righteousness, faithfulness, mercy, and loving-kindness." O who can think of this love but must be stricken with wonder? and cry, O the height, the depth, the breadth, and the length of it! for it passeth the knowledge of men or angels. How excellent is this loving-kindness! Lord, what is man, that thou shouldst thus remember him? or the Son of man that thou shouldst be so kind to him?

2*dly*, See hence, that God's ways are not as our ways, nor his thoughts as our thoughts. We would think it a strange disparagement for a person of high rank and station, suppose a gentlemen, a nobleman, a duke, a king, or great emperor, to fall so much in conceit with a poor forlorn miserable beggar, all full of sores, from the crown of the head to the sole of the foot, as to marry her, and make her his wife, his consort and queen, and set her upon the throne with himself. I say, we would think it very strange, because of the inequality of the match. But O, Sirs, there is an infinitely greater inequality between the Son of God, and a poor filthy guilty sinner, than between the greatest king that ever swayed a sceptre, and the most abject creature that ever sprung from Adam's race. To this purpose is that of the apostle Paul, ye know the grace of " our Lord Jesus Christ, that though he was rich, yet for your sakes he became poor, that ye through his poverty might be rich." And how doth he make us rich, but by taking us unto a conjugal relation unto himself: for all is ours by contract when married to the Heir.

3dly, From this doctrine see the wondrous sibness between Christ and his church, and every particular believer: why, he is the Bridegroom, and they are both collectively and singularly considered the bride, the Lamb's wife: and " as the Bridegroom rejoiceth over the bride, so shall the Lord thy God rejoice over thee." There is a threefold mysterious union we read of in scripture.

1. The mysterious union of the three Persons in one essence, Father, Son, and Holy Ghost, three in one, and one in three.

2. There is the mysterious union of the two natures, viz: God and man in one person, 1 Tim. iii. last, " Without controversy, great is the mystery of godliness, God was manifest in the flesh."

3. There is the mystical, or mysterious conjugal union between Christ and believers, Eph. v. 32, " This is a great mystery (says the apostle), but I speak concerning Christ and the church;" and ver. 30, " We are the members of his body, of his flesh, and of his bones." O what a strange sibness is this, between Christ and us. The apostle, from ver 25, had been discoursing of the relative duties between husband and wife; and enforcing this duty, from the consideration of the close and intimate union between husband and wife; " They are no more twain but one flesh." And then presently adds, " This is a great mystery, but I speak concerning Christ and the church." Whereby he gives us to understand, that the natural marriage between Adam and Eve, or other husbands and their wives, is a faint shadow and representation of the spiritual marriage between Christ and the church.

There is such a depth of infinite wisdom in the works of God in this visible world, that they serve as a glass to lead the spiritual mind unto another world, and the hid mysteries of our holy religion. Hence it is, that the scriptures of truth, which are a revelation of the mind of God, abound so much with parables and metaphors, which are nothing else but a revelation of divine supernatural mysteries, by expressions borrowed from the things of this world, which are obvious to our external senses. The apostle, Rom. v. 14, tells us, that the first Adam was the figure or representation of him that was to come, *i. e.* of a second Adam, and new covenant Head: I might state the similitude, and also the dissimilitude in many respects, which I do not stand upon at present; but I confine myself unto the point in hand, namely, that of marriage between man and woman, particularly between Adam and Eve, as bearing a manifold similitude unto the marriage between Christ and the Church. This I shall endeavour to illustrate in these particulars.

1st. When God made our first parent Adam, he gave this whole earth to him, for his inheritance: he set him in a paradise of pleasure, and made him lord of all the works of his hand, so that he wanted for nothing to make him happy. But it was some abatement and diminution of his happiness, when he wanted one like himself, as a consort to enjoy the same happiness with him. For it is the observation, even of a heathen philosopher, there is no pleasant or comfortable enjoyment of any happiness alone: and therefore God himself said concerning Adam, "It is not good that the man should be alone:" thereby intimating, that it would add to his happiness if he had a creature of his own stamp and mould to converse with, and share of his happiness. Now, in this, the first Adam was a figure of him that was to come; the blessed Bridegroom of souls, Christ Jesus, was happy from eternity, and possessed all divine perfection and glory. But he resolves to have a bride, a consort for himself, that might share with him of the same happiness and glory, that he himself was possessed of. And for this end, he casts his eyes upon the fallen tribe of Adam, lying in their blood, and chooses a bride and spouse for himself there. Hence, Prov. viii. 30. He is said, before the creation of the world, to rejoice in the habitable parts of the earth, his delights were with the sons of men; the desire of his eyes and heart was among them, in prospect of a marriage union with them.

2dly, The first woman, you know, was taken out of Adam's side, when he was cast into a deep sleep: hence, says the apostle, "the man is not of the woman, but the woman of the man." Just so, in the spiritual marriage, the bride and spouse of Christ, is (as it were) taken out of his side, when he slept the sleep of death upon the cross, and in the sepulchre. The church is just founded in the blood of Christ. His death was her life; the price of our redemption is not by "silver or gold, or such corruptible things, but the precious blood of Christ the Lord."

3dly, The man and the woman are of one common nature. Just so is it in this spiritual marriage, Heb. ii. 11, "Both he that sanctifieth, and they that are sanctified, are all of one, wherefore he is not ashamed to call them brethren." The Bridegroom, indeed, as to his divine nature, is the Son of God, the second Person of the glorious Trinity, and so of a nature quite different from ours, and so infinitely above us, that there could be no marriage between him and us; but in the fulness of time he was made of a woman, made under the law, that so, being upon a level with us, he might be made like unto us in all things, and betrothe us unto himself as his beloved spouse and bride.

4thly, We are told, Gen. ii. 22, That when God had formed the woman of a rib taken out of the man's side, he brought her to the man; she did not know that there was such a creature as Adam in the world; and therefore could never have come to him unless she had been brought: Just so the bride and spouse of Christ, the second Adam, is by nature ignorant of God, and his Son Christ Jesus, and would never come to him, unless she were brought to him by the power of God, John vi. 44, "No man (says Christ) can come unto me, except the Father which hath sent me, draw him." To the same purpose is that ver. 4. 5, "Every man, therefore, that hath heard, and hath learned of the Father, cometh unto me."

Quest. What way is that? *Answ.* * 'He enlightens the mind in the knowledge of Christ, renews the will; and so persuades and enables us to receive the Bridegroom, as he is freely presented in the gospel,' Psa. cx. 3.

5thly, Whenever Eve was presented to Adam, he gladly and joyfully received her, and expressed his satisfaction with her, saying, "This is bone of my bones, and flesh of my flesh." Just so, whenever a poor sinner is determined by the Father to come unto Christ, O how doth he rejoice, and how gladly doth he entertain him. This is "the day of his espousals, and the day of the gladness of his heart." "All that the Father giveth me shall come unto me, and him that cometh to me, I will in no ways cast out." This is signified by the reception of the prodigal, Luke xv.

6thly, In marriage between man and woman, both parties quit their former relatives in some respect, that they may cleave to one another; "For this cause shall a man leave father and mother, and shall cleave to his wife;" and the wife, on the other hand, doth the same. Just so is it between Christ and his bride. Christ, the blessed Bridegroom, when he had his bride to redeem and purchase, he left the bosom of his Father, and the glory of the higher house, that he might accomplish our redemption, at the expense of his death; and when he had a mind for a bride among the Gentiles, he forsook his mother's house, namely, the Jewish church, that he might betrothe her unto himself for ever. It is with a particular view unto the Gentiles, that he says, Isa. liv. 6, "Thy Maker is thine Husband." And, on the other hand, the soul truly espoused unto Christ the Bridegroom, is said to forget her own people, and her Father's house, Psa. xlv. 10, "Hearken, O daughter, and consider, incline thine ear; forget also thine own people, and thy Father's house." The meaning is, that she gives up with the devil, the world, and the lusts of the flesh, or the law as a covenant, unto which she had been cleaving, and says, "O Lord, other lords besides thee have had dominion over me;" but now I will be under the law to Christ, as my only Lord and Lawgiver.

Other particulars of this nature might be added, but some of them may occur afterwards; these that I have named are sufficient to show, that there is a wonderful sibness between Christ in heaven, and the church of believers on earth, and that infinite Wisdom has seen fit to paint out and decipher the marriage union between Christ and his church, by the relation between the husband and the wife; which made the apostle say, when discoursing of the relation between husband and wife, Eph. v. 32. "This is a great mystery; but I speak concerning Christ and the church."

Inf. 4. See from this doctrine, what happy and honourable persons believers are, and why they are called the excellent ones of the earth, with whom is all Christ's delight. Why, they are the bride of an honourable Bridegroom. O! who is so well matched? Every believer is married to his Maker, to the Prince of life, the

---

See Shorter Catechism, Q. *What is effectual calling.*

Lord of glory, the Heir of God; and he makes his bride also an heir of God, and a joint heir of all things with himself. There are two or three mysteries, or seeming contradictions, about the bride of Christ, (1.) She is basely, and yet honourably descended. If we view the believer as to his natural birth and pedigree, he is a child of the devil, and an heir of hell; and O! what a wonder is it, that ever the Son of God should match with such a creature? But, by her new birth and adoption, she has the blood royal of heaven in her veins, John i. 13, "Born not of blood, nor of the will of the flesh, nor of the will of man, but of God." (2.) Christ's bride is black, and yet beautiful, "I am black, but comely, O ye daughters of Jerusalem, as the tents of Kedar, as the curtains of Solomon." View her in her natural state, or as she is harassed with Satan, the world, and indwelling corruption, she is black and ill hued; but yet she is comely, through the comeliness of the Lord her God; he says of her, "Thou art all fair, my love, there is no spot in thee." (3.) Christ's bride is naked, and yet well arrayed; naked in herself, quite destitute of all righteousness: "There is none righteous, no, not one." But the Bridegroom decks her with the garments of salvation, and with a robe of righteousness, Isa. lxi. 10. (4.) She is poor, and yet possessed of great riches: In herself considered, she is poor, and has nothing but poverty, wretchedness, and misery, yea, drowned in debt to law and justice; but yet, by virtue of her marriage relation to the Bridegroom, she is possessed of unsearchable riches, and gold better than the gold of Ophir. In a word, she is condemned in the court of law, of justice, of conscience; and yet, by virtue of her relation to Christ the Bridegroom, she is absolved and discharged, and can lift up her head and say, "Who can lay any thing to *my* charge? It is God that justifieth, who is he that condemneth?" Thus you see what happy and honourable persons believers are, by virtue of their marriage relation to Christ.

Inf. 5. From this doctrine we may see the folly, madness, and misery, of a carnal, Christless, and unbelieving world, (who fall in among the ranks of the foolish virgins). Why, although they be called, as well as the wise virgins, to *go out and meet the Bridegroom*, they yet lie still slumbering and sleeping in their beds of sloth, saying, "yet a little sleep, a little slumber, a little folding of the hands to sleep," neglect to buy oil for their vessels, and so do not *go out to meet the Bridegroom*, but lie still in the embraces of some lust and idol or other, which they prefer unto Christ, the glorious Bridegroom: O! "be astonished, O ye heavens, at this, and be horribly afraid, be ye very desolate," at the folly of sinners, who forsake their own mercy for lying vanities that cannot profit them. You prefer a soul-murdering lust to the glorious Bridegroom, like the Jews, who preferred Barabbas unto Jesus. "This is the condemnation, that light is come into the world, and ye choose darkness rather than light." And you have reason to fear, lest the Lord say unto you, as he did unto Ephraim, "He is joined to his idols, let him alone."

Inf. 6. See the good office of the Spirit of God: why? he it is that testifies of the glory of the Bridegroom, and enlightens the eyes of the poor sinner to take up the glory of his person and mediation, and so gains the consent of the bride; yea, he is the leading band of union between the parties, for " he that is joined to the Lord is one spirit."

Inf. 7. See the usefulness of a gospel ministry: why, they are the friends of the Bridegroom, and come, by commission from him, to court a bride for him among the sons of men. A faithful minister travels as in birth till the match be made up; and, O! when the match is made, this is the joy and rejoicing of their hearts, for they are their crown and rejoicing in the day of the Lord. They that are won to consent to the Bridegroom, and to *go out and meet him*, will be ready to say, " How beautiful, upon the mountains, are the feet of them that preach the gospel of peace, and bring glad tidings of good things."

Inf. 8. See the excellency of the grace of faith. It is the band of union, whereby we are married to Christ, as our Husband; for it includes the assent and consent of the soul unto this better Husband, whereby we come to be betrothed unto him for ever. Not to insist upon particulars, it is by faith that we put on Christ as the Lord our righteousness. By faith the bride receives out of Christ's fulness, grace for grace, whereby the heart is purified, the old man crucified, and the body of sin destroyed, that we may not serve sin. By faith we overcome the world, 1 John v. 4, " This is the victory that overcometh the world, even our faith." By faith we resist the devil, and quench his fiery darts, Eph. vi. 12. And if you ask, how it is that faith does this? I answer, (1.) Faith brandishes the sword of the Spirit in the face of the enemy, as Christ did, Matth. iv. saying, Thus and thus it is written. (2.) Faith takes up the blood of the Lamb, and presents it to the enemy; at the sight of which he flies, remembering that by this blood his head was bruised upon Mount Calvary, and therefore cannot endure the sight of it. Hence is that word, Rev. xii. 11. " They overcame him by the blood of the Lamb, and by the word of their testimony." By faith we receive the great and precious promises, whereby we are made partakers of the divine nature. All manner of grace is laid up in the promises, for the babes of grace, like milk in the breast; and faith is the mouth of the soul, which, when applied to the breast, sucks in the sincere milk of the word, and of the grace of God by the word, whereby the soul is made to grow in grace, like a babe thriving upon the breast. But I pass this use.

MATTHEW xxv. 6.—"And at midnight there was a cry made, Behold the Bridegroom cometh, go ye out to meet him."

THE FIFTH SERMON ON THIS TEXT.

I go on to a *second* use of this doctrine, viz., by way of *Trial* and *Examination*. And here there are two questions that naturally arise, 1. Have you matched with the Bridegroom? are you espoused to that one Husband. 2. Have you gone out and met the Bridegroom? has he and you had any pleasant and comfortable interviews?

Quest. 1. Whether are you the bride? are you married unto Christ the blessed Bridegroom of souls? I offer the following marks to clear you as to this.

1st, The true bride of Christ has the Bridegroom in great admiration; her esteem of him is such, that she just admires every thing in him and about him. She admires his personal glory, as IMMANUEL; she wonders that ever the second Person of the glorious Godhead should ever have past by the angelic nature, and joined himself in a personal union to the human nature, out of love to her, that he might be a help meet for her. Hence that word of the apostle is much in her mouth and heart, 1 Tim. i. 3. "Without controversy, great is the mystery of godliness," God was manifest in the flesh. O he is just a Nonsuch! "as the apple tree among the trees of the wood. The chiefest among ten thousand." And when the bride thinks of the love he bore to her before the world was made; and how, in the fulness of time, he came and spent his blood for her redemption; how in time he drew her with the cords of love, conquered her enmity by shedding abroad his love upon her heart; she is just swallowed up with admiration, and is ready to cry out, "O, what am I, or my house, that thou hast brought me hitherto! Is this the manner of men, O Lord God? O, what hath God wrought! O the height, the depth, the breadth, and the length of his love! It passeth all knowledge."

2dly, The true bride of Christ knows the voice of the Bridegroom, and is much delighted with the words of his mouth, "My sheep hear my voice," John x. You see, Song ii. 8. how her heart flighters at the first opening of his lips, "It is the voice of my beloved:" It is sweeter to me than the melody of angels or archangels. Every word of the Bridegroom creates admiration in her heart, and she remembers them with delight and pleasure, Song ii. 10. "My Beloved spake, and said unto me, Rise up, my dove, my love, my fair one, and come away." Such words make her heart to glow and burn within her. O, says Job, "I have esteemed the words of his mouth more than my necessary food;" and O, says David, "the law of thy mouth is better unto me than thousands of gold and silver, more to be desired are they than gold, yea, than much fine gold, yea, sweeter also than honey, and the honey comb." O, says Jeremiah, "thy words were found, and I did eat them, and thy word was unto me the joy and rejoicing of mine heart."

3*dly,* Not only every word, but every thought of the Bridegroom, is a banquet unto the soul of the bride, "How precious also are thy thoughts unto me, O God. My meditation of him shall be sweet: I will be glad in the Lord." So David, Psa. civ. 34. and Psa. lxxiii. 6. "When I remember thee upon my bed, and meditate on thee in the night watches;" ver. 5. "My soul shall be satisfied as with marrow and fatness." Many a sweet interview has the bride with Christ, upon the mount of meditation, which strangers do not intermeddle with.

4*thly,* The true bride of Christ hates all his rivals. She is dead to the law her first husband, and is ready to say, "I through the law, am dead to the law." She is dead to sin, and crucifies the flesh, with the affections and lusts, though as dear as a right hand, or a right eye. She is dead to the world, and counts all its profits, pleasures, and honours, nothing but a mass of vanity. "I am crucified to the world, and the world to me." Thus, I say, the true bride of Christ hates all Christ's rivals; "I count all things but loss for the excellency of the knowledge of Christ, and do count them but dung," &c. Yea, she is ready to part with all relations whatever for him, father, mother, wife, children, let them all go for him; yea, if her life comes in competition with Christ, she will be ready to say, "I am ready not to be bound only, but to die," for the glory of the Bridegroom; "They loved not their lives unto the death," for the love that they bore unto the Lord Jesus.

5*thly,* The bride of Christ has much trust and confidence to put in the Bridegroom, and by trusting in him is kept in perfect peace, and is filled with joy and peace in believing. She dares venture upon the greatest dangers, when called, upon the credit of his word, "Fear not, for I am with thee; be not dismayed, for I am thy God," &c. The very name of the Bridegroom is the ground of her trust, and is to her like a strong tower, whither she flies and is safe. The language of the bride's confidence towards the Bridegroom is that, Psa. xxxvi. 7. "How excellent is thy loving-kindness, O God! therefore the children of men put their trust under the shadow of thy wings;" and Psa. xxvii. 5. For "in the time of trouble he shall hide me in his pavilion; in the secret of his tabernacle shall he hide me," &c.

6*thly,* The bride of Christ has a great regard for his commands, and is ready to follow him whithersoever he goes. The Bridegroom says to the bride, "If ye love me, ye will keep all my commandments," John xiv. 15.; and ver. 21. "He that hath my commandment, and keepeth them, he it is that loveth me." The wise virgins will keep themselves chaste for the service of the Bridegroom and will not defile themselves with "the corruption that is in the world through lust." Hence is that, Rev. xiv. 4. speaking of the hundred forty and four thousand, that stood with the Lamb upon Mount Zion: "These are they who were not defiled with woman (*i.e.* with the errors, idolatry, and abomination of Antichrist), for they are virgins: These are they who follow the Lamb whithersoever he goeth."

7*thly*, The true bride of Jesus holds fast the testimony of Jesus, in opposition to the devil, and the world, and all errors and corruptions that are cast out of hell in order to obscure his declarative glory, Rev. xii. 17. There we are told, that the dragon " was wroth with the woman, and went to make war with the remnant of her seed, which kept the commandments of God, and have the testimony of Jesus Christ." And if it be asked, What is the testimony of Jesus? it is answered, Rev. xix. 10. For " the testimony of Jesus is the spirit of prophecy," *i.e.* the " word of God, which holy men of God speak as they were moved by the Holy Ghost." Now, the true bride of Christ "contends earnestly for this testimony or faith which was once delivered unto the saints," and will receive no doctrine, no practice, no decision, though it were of the general assembly of angels, but what quadrates or agrees with, and is founded upon this testimony and word of Jesus; and this is what Christ hath given in charge to his bride, the church, and every believer in particular, Isa. viii. 20. " To the law and to the testimony, if they speak not according to this word, it is because there is no light in them."

8*thly*, The bride of Christ is very fond to bring forth a seed to serve him; and for this end she studies to bring him to her mother's house, and the ordinances of his appointment. It is only his presence in the church that makes the word effectual for the conversion of sinners and the edification of saints; and therefore they that are married to the Bridegroom are fond to see his power and glory in the sanctuary, that so it may be " said of Zion, This and that man was born in her," Psa. lxxxvii. 5. and " who hath begotten me these," Isa. xlix. 21.

9*thly*, The bride of Christ longs sometimes for the consummation of the marriage at death, especially at the last judgment, when the collective body of Christ shall be made fully up, and when the Bridegroom shall present his bride to his Father, " not having spot or wrinkle, or any such thing," and when she " shall shine forth as the sun in the kingdom of her Father." Paul had this in his eye, when he said, " There is laid up for me a crown of righteousness, which the Lord, the righteous Judge, shall give me at that day, and not to me only, but unto all them also who love his appearing ;" and the church, when she said, Song viii. last verse, " Make haste my beloved, and be thou like to a roe, or to a young hart upon the mountains of spices."

Second question for trial is, Have you had any meeting with the Bridegroom? Has he and you had any pleasant and comfortable interview? Did he draw near and manifest himself to you, as he does not unto the world. I do not insist on this. Only in a few words:

1*st*, A meeting with Christ, the Bridegroom, puts life, new life, into the languishing soul and spirit of the bride; and no wonder, for he is "the resurrection and the life. He that hath the Son hath life."

2dly, A meeting with Christ, the Bridegroom, gives light to the bride when sitting in darkness; and no wonder, for he is the bright and morning Star that brings day with him. He is the true light, and darkness evanishes before him.

3dly, A meeting with the Bridegroom fires the heart with love, that many waters cannot quench, and all floods are not able to drown. His banner is love, and the bride will follow the banner through life and death, Rom. viii. at the close.

4thly, A meeting with the Bridegroom brings liberty and enlargement of soul with it. The soul that was in bonds is made free by the Son; and then the soul sings, as in Psa. cxvi, " O Lord, truly I am thy servant, and the son of thy handmaid: thou hast loosed my bonds: " and then it runs the way of his commandments, he having enlarged it.

5thly, A meeting with the Bridegroom quickens the longings of the soul for another meeting: For the bride never tires of his company; and when he is making as though he would withdraw, she hangs about him to detain him, saying, O ! " Why shouldst thou be as a stranger in the land, and as a wayfaring man that turneth aside to tarry for a night ?" And when he is withdrawing, O, will she say, " that I knew where I might find him ! I charge you, O daughters of Jerusalem, if you find my Beloved, that ye tell him, that I am sick of love."

6thly. If you have met the Bridegroom, you will study to keep his room for him, until he return again. Christ's bride will not play the harlot, or take up with other lovers in his absence ; and when enticed by the devil or the world, to join with them in sin, the true bride of Christ will be ready to say, with David, " Depart from me evil doers, for I will keep the commandments of my God ; or as Joseph, when tempted by his adulterous mistress, " How can I do this great wickedness, and sin against my Lord," my blessed Bridegroom, unto whom I have given heart and hand : And hence the true bride of Christ is ready to resist even unto blood, striving against sin ; she would rather venture upon the anger and displeasure of all the world, than endure one frown of the Bridegroom's face ; and therefore, having presented herself as a chaste virgin unto Christ, she studies to maintain her chastity and purity.

7thly. Every meeting with the Bridegroom adds a new print or lineament of the beauty of the Bridegroom upon the soul of the bride. For, by beholding of his glory, we are changed into the same image. Hence the world about them are ready to take knowledge of them, that they have been with Jesus: the light of Christ's bride borrowed from the Bridegroom's company, shines before men ; so that others seeing her good works are made to glorify the Bridegroom, in the way and deportment of the bride.

8thly, Every meeting with the Bridegroom fills the soul of the bride with a holy blush at the thoughts of her own unworthiness, and the undeserved love and kindness of the Bridegroom; insomuch that she is ashamed, yea even confounded, when she sees that he is pacified towards her, notwithstanding of all her strayings and debordings, Ezek. xvi. at the close; and this makes her to cry out with Job, chap. xiii. when the Lord manifested himself to him in a way of love, "I have heard of thee by the hearing of the ear: but now mine eyes see thee: wherefore I abhor myself, and repent in dust and ashes." So much by way of trial.

Use *third* shall be by way of *Consolation* to believers, who are the true bride of the blessed Bridegroom.

And well may we speak comfort to the bride, for he himself just joys over her with singing, and says, that " her heart shall rejoice, and her joy no man taketh from her."

To help on the joy of the soul espoused unto this one husband, I shall only touch a little upon two scriptural expressions, wherein the closest union and most intimate communion between Christ and his spouse is held forth: in one place, Christ is said to have them, and, in another, they are said to have him. The first you have, John iii. 29, " He that hath the bride is the Bridegroom;" the second you have, John v. 12. where it is said of believers, the bride of Christ, " He that hath the Son hath life;" so that they mutually have one another. And therefore upon scripture ground we may safely say, that the Bridegroom hath the bride, and the bride hath the Bridegroom. But now that I may open this twofold spring of consolation, I shall essay to draw a little water out of them, for the consolation of the bride, the Lamb's wife: I begin with

The *first*, John iii. 29, " He that hath the bride is the Bridegroom." Now Christ hath the bride in these following respects.

1*st*, By eternal donation and gift from the Father. The Father of the Bridegroom gifted the bride unto his beloved Son, John xvii. " Thine they were, and thou gavest them me." They were the Father's by electing love: he chose them from among the mass of corrupted mankind, and he makes a propine of them to his eternal Son, that he might redeem them with his blood, and call them in due time by his grace, justify them freely, sanctify them throughout, and save them eternally.

2*dly*, The Bridegroom hath the bride by purchase. She is by nature the law's debtor, justice's prisoner, and the devil's slave. Christ takes a view of her in this deplorable condition; the justice of God pursuing like the avenger of blood; the devil, as God's executioner, ready to haul her to the prison of hell. 'O (says Christ), I have loved her with an everlasting love, and my heart is so much set upon a marriage with her, that I am content to satisfy the law and justice in her room; let the curse of the law due to them fall upon me; let the awakened sword of justice rage against me, that they may escape; I will be wounded for their iniquities, and bruised for their transgressions.'

3*dly*, He hath the bride by conquest. Although law and justice be satisfied, yet, the devil having got possession he will not quit the prisoner, unless she be taken out of his custody by main force. Well, says the Bridegroom, 'I will lead captivity captive, I will bruise the head of that old serpent the devil, spoil principalities and powers; and so the lawful captive shall be delivered, and the prey taken from the mighty.'

4thly, He hath the bride by her own consent, in a day of power, Psa. cx. 3. He conquers her enmity against him by discoveries of his love and loveliness, Hos. xi. 4. Jer. xxxi. 3, "I have loved thee with an everlasting love; therefore with loving-kindness have I drawn thee:" and thereupon the bride signs the contract, Isa. xl. 3. 4. "One shall say, I am the Lord's, and another shall subscribe with his hand unto the Lord," &c. And so the espousals are made, and the Bridegroom hath the bride. But it may be asked, 'Where hath he the bride?' Answer,

1st, He hath her in his house: for as King Solomon built a house for Pharoah's daughter, so Christ, the true Solomon, builds a twofold house for his bride, a house on earth, and another in heaven. We read of a house that Wisdom hath built, Prov. ix. 5. with seven pillars, for the entertainment of his bride, and the stones thereof are laid with fair colours, and the foundation thereof of sapphire; and this is that house of mercy, which God will have built up for ever: and then he has prepared a house, yea, a "city which hath foundations, whose builder and maker is God;" John xiv. 2. 3. "In my Father's house are many mansions," &c.

2dly, He hath the bride not only in his house, but in his hand; Deut. xxxiii. 3, "All his saints are in thy hand," *i. e.* in the hand of the Bridegroom; John x. 28, "I give unto them eternal life, and they shall never perish, neither shall any pluck them out of my hand." O believer, is not this a glorious spring of consolation, that thou art continually in the hand of thy glorious Husband and Bridegroom? He keeps his bride in the hollow of his hand, the hand of his power and providence.

3dly, What more? I can tell you more yet. The Bridegroom hath the bride in his arms and bosom; Isa. xl. 11, "He shall gather the lambs with his arm, and carry them in his bosom," &c. O what a sweet lodging is this, to lie in the bosom of him, who lay from eternity, and will lie to eternity, in the bosom of the Father, encircled with the everlasting arms of the eternal God! O blessed lodging! Psa. xci. 1, "He that dwelleth in the secret place of the Most High, shall abide under the shade of the Almighty."

4thly, The Bridegroom hath the bride continually in his eye: such is the love that he bears her, that his eye can never be off her; wherever she is, his eye follows her, and his eyes run to and fro through the whole earth to show himself strong in her behalf.

5thly, The Bridegroom hath the bride continually in his very heart. O "says the spouse, set me as a seal upon thine heart, as a seal upon thine arm." As the priest had the tribes of Israel upon his breast, so Christ has his people set as a seal upon his heart; she can never be out of his mind. Now is not this a glorious spring of consolation to the soul espoused to Christ; that thy Bridegroom, believer, has thee in his house, in his hand, in his arms, and bosom, and set in his eye, and on his very heart? But,

Secondly, As the Bridegroom hath the bride, so the bride hath the Bridegroom; for he that hath the Son hath life. If thou be a believer, thou hast the Son, who is the Bridegroom. Take this in these particulars,

1st, If thou be the bride, and hast received him by faith, thou hast the person of the Son for thy Husband and Bridegroom, "Thy Maker is thine Husband." You know, that in marriage the relation is between the person of the man and woman; so, in the spiritual marriage, it is the person of Christ and the person of the believer that are married. And what thinkest thou, believer, of being married to the second Person of the glorious Trinity? To which of the angels did he ever say, Thou art the bride, the Lamb's wife?

2dly, Being married to the Son of God, thou art a partaker of the divine nature, as he is a partaker of the human, 2 Pet. i. 4. The beauty of the Lord thy God is upon thee. The Bridegroom imparts and communicates his beauty to the bride; and then she looks " forth as the morning, fair as the moon, clear as the sun ;" and he says, "Thou art all fair, my love, there is no spot in thee."

3dly, The Bridegroom's Father, is thy Father; John xx. 17, "I ascend unto my Father and your Father, and to my God and your God." Christ, as the second Adam and new covenant Head, says for himself, and all believers who are his bride, Psa. lxxxix. "Thou art my Father, my God, and the Rock of my salvation." And the Father of Christ allows and requires his Son's bride to come to him with holy and humble confidence, and cry, Abba, Father, unto him: "Doubtless thou art my Father, wilt thou not cry unto me, my Father? thou art the guide of my youth."

4thly, The Holy Ghost is thy Comforter, to encourage and comfort the bride in the absence of the Bridegroom; John xvi. 6, "It its expedient (says Christ) for you, that I go away; for if I go not away, the Comforter will not come ; but if I go away, I will send him unto you," and he shall dwell in you, and abide with you for ever. The spirit of the Bridegroom abiding with the bride is far better than if she enjoyed his bodily presence.

5thly, The very life of the bride is hid in the Bridegroom, Col. iii. 3, "Your life is hid with Christ in God. Because I live, ye shall live also." Perhaps, poor believer, to thy own sense and feeling, thou mayest be brought to that pass, as to say, "My life draweth nigh unto the grave, I am free among the dead:" I am a dry tree, and like Ezekiel's dry bones; but remember, that the fountain of life is with thy Head, Husband, and Bridegroom; " because I live, ye shall live also."

6thly, Know for thy comfort, that the contract of the covenant stands fast; he has betrothed thee to himself, not for a day, for a month, or a year, or an age, but for ever: "I will make with them an everlasting covenant." The covenant stands fast with him: "My covenant I will not break, nor alter the thing that is gone out of my lips."

7thly, Having the Son, thou hast all the promises of the new covenant, as so many wells of salvation, out of which thou mayest draw waters with joy; for all the promises of God are in him, and in him they are to the bride of Christ yea and amen. O! how great and precious are these promises.

8thly, Having the Son for thy Bridegroom, the law, nor justice, nor the world, nor life nor death, have any action or process against thee. You know, in law, the wife cannot be pursued for debt: the husband is liable for her debt; and if the husband pay the debt, the creditors have nothing to say against the wife. Well, this is the case with thee, O believer, who hast the Son for thy Husband: he has cleared scores with law and justice, and was discharged of it in his resurrection, wherefore "he was taken from prison and from judgment;" and therefore the soul married and betrothed unto him, being under his cover, may lift up the head and cry, Rom. viii. 33. 34, "Who can lay anything to my charge? It is God that justifieth, who is he that condemneth?"

9thly, Whatever deep seas or Jordans of trouble thou mayest have before thee, the Bridegroom has passed his word for it, that he will be present with thee in them, Isa. xli. 10, Is. xliii. 2 "When thou passest through the waters, I will be with thee," &c. When thou art laid upon a sick-bed, or a death-bed, the Bridegroom will attend thee; for he has said, "I will never leave thee nor forsake thee:" yea, when thou liest down in the grave, thou shalt sleep in his bed and bosom; "Them that sleep in Jesus, will God bring with him."

10thly, Thy Bridegroom, believer, when thou art giving up the ghost, and thy soul departing from thy body; he, with a guard of angels, will be ready to receive thy spirit, John xiv. 3, "I will come again and receive you unto myself, that where I am there ye may be also." O what comfort is it to a dying saint or believer that no sooner is he absent from the body, but he is present with the Lord; and may welcome the waggon of death, that is come to fetch the bride home to the house of the Bridegroom, saying, with dying Stephen, "O Lord Jesus, receive my spirit!"

11thly, Though thou drop the carcase of the body into the grave, where it sleeps quietly until the morning of the resurrection, yet the Bridegroom says, I will raise them up at the last day. This promise he frequently repeats, particularly John vi. "I will raise him up at the last day." O lift up thy head, believer; for the day of thy complete redemption, even the redemption of thy body from the power of the grave, draweth nigh. Thy beloved Bridegroom will, as it were, come to the bed-side of the grave, and cry, "Awake and sing, thou that sleepest in the dust:" and then the dew of the Holy Ghost, that quickened thy soul when dead in trespasses and sins, shall also quicken thy dead body, and thereupon the earth shall cast out the dead, Is. xxvi. 19, compared with Rom. viii. 11. Then, O then, believer, shou shalt "shine forth like the sun in the kingdom of thy Father;" thy vile body shall be made like unto the glorious body of the Bridegroom; and thereupon the nuptial solemnity will begin, which shall never have an end, each one crying to another, as Rev. xix. 7, "Let us be glad and rejoice, and give honour to him; for the marriage of the Lamb is come, and his wife hath made herself ready."

Thus you see what unspeakable ground of consolation and eternal triumph there is for the soul that is espoused unto Christ: but the ten thousandth thousandth part of it cannot be told; for eye hath not seen, nor ear heard, nor hath the heart of man conceived, what is laid up for her in Christ.

Object. 1. O! may some poor soul say, these are great things indeed; but I am afraid they do not belong unto me; I am afraid I am not the bride; he is such a great and glorious person, and I such a poor despicable worm, so guilty, so filthy, that I am afraid the match was never made between him and me; and therefore I am afraid to apply all that comfort that belongs to the bride of Christ.

Answ. It is one of the properties of the bride of Christ, to be humble, and lowly, and self-denied, and to be admiring the infinite distance between the Bridegroom and her: She is never taken up with admiring her own gifts and graces, her own beauty and excellency, but the beauty, glory and excellency of the Bridegroom: She does not boast of what she has received, but all her boasting and glorying is in the Lord: And the more humble and denied the bride of Christ is, the more amiable and desireable she is in the eyes of the Bridegroom, Isa. lvii. 15. and lxii. 2.

Object, 2. I am so pestered with a body of sin and death, carnality, unbelief, and pride, and other heart plagues, that I doubt if my spot be the spot of Christ's bride.

Answ. You see how much the great apostle Paul was distressed with the law of sin which was in his members, Rom. vii. "Wretched man that I am, who shall deliver me from this body of death." Christ says of his bride, Song vi. "What will you see in the Shulamite? as it were the company of two armies;" grace and corruption continually struggling together; the flesh lusting against the spirit, and the spirit against the flesh: and therefore do not draw rash conclusions upon this account.

Object. 3. I thought once in a day my heart could rejoice in him as my beloved; and I thought his left hand was under my head, and his right hand did embrace me, and I could say, "My beloved is mine, and I am his:" But, alas! he is gone; "The Lord hath forsaken me, my Lord hath forgotten me."

Answ. "Why sayest thou so, O Jacob, my way is hid from the Lord? Can a woman forget her sucking child, that she should not have compassion on the fruit of her womb? yea, she may forget, yet will I not forget thee." And therefore wait upon the return of thy Bridegroom, as they that watch for the morning, yea, more than they that watch for the morning:" for as sure as the morning light will arise, after a dark night, as sure will he return to thy soul in a way of grace. And therefore live by faith; and let Israel, the true bride of Christ, hope in the Lord. And I give you his word as the ground of your sure hope, Isa. liv. 7. 8. "For a small moment have I forsaken thee, but with great mercies will I gather thee. In a little wrath I hid my face from thee, for a moment, but with everlasting kindness will I have mercy on thee, saith the Lord thy redeemer."

Use *fourth* of this doctrine shall be by way of reproof and terror unto all these, who, instead of closing the bargain, and going forth to meet the Bridegroom Christ Jesus, continue married unto other husbands. But more particularly,

First, Some, yea multitudes of gospel-hearers, are married to the law as a husband; and this is the case with all legalists, and self-righteous persons, that are seeking life, righteousness, and acceptance with God, by their own personal obedience, their prayers, and repentance, mortification, and this and that good thing that they have done, or some good qualification that they find in themselves. If this be the case with you, you never yet went out to meet the Bridegroom, you were never married to the better Husband, but continue married to the law.

Here I would do two things, *first,* shew who they are that are yet married to the law; *secondly,* discover to you your miserable condition while it is so.

1. I say, I would shew who they are that are married to the law; for all mankind are married unto it in Adam, and all mankind continue under Adam's covenant, until the power of grace make a divorce.

1*st,* If the law never slew you, you are yet married unto it as a husband, Gal. ii. 19. "I through the law am dead to the law;" Rom. vii. 9. "I was alive without the law once, but when the commandment came, sin revived, and I died." Every man by nature sits mounted upon the throne of an imaginary righteousness, he thinks himself a living man, and that he can do well enough by his own endeavours for life; like the Jews spoken of, Rom. x. 3. who were ignorant of the righteousness of God, and went about to establish their own righteousness.

2*dly,* You that never knew what it was to mourn over, and wrestle against the legal set and bias of your hearts towards the law as a covenant, you remain yet married unto it as a husband. A believer that is married unto Christ, through the remaining legality of his heart, is many times looking back unto his old husband, and ready to rest upon duties done by him, and his own frames and enlargements, as the ground of his acceptance with God, which is a putting these things in the room of Christ; and this is sad matter of mourning and humiliation unto him: and if you know nothing of this exercise, it is a shrewd evidence that you are not married unto Christ, but under the law as a covenant.

3dly, When you are in any distress or perplexity of mind, where is it that you find rest, ease, and quiet? For you know it is but natural for a poor woman in her distress to run to her husband for relief. Just so is it with the believer that is married unto Christ; when he is weary and heavy laden, he can never rest till he come to Christ, and then he sits down under his shadow with great delight. But if you find rest in your own works, duties, qualifications, your personal covenants, your vows, repentance, and reformations, it is a sign you are yet married unto the law.

4thly, You that can be grieved for your gross sins and outbreakings, that perhaps wound your reputation before the world, but never yet had a sore heart for the corruptions of your nature, and the internal plagues of your heart, such as unbelief, enmity, pride, ignorance, and carnality; it is a sign that you are yet married unto the law as a husband: and the reason is; because, if ever the law had come home in its extent and spirituality, it would have been "quick and powerful, sharper than any two-edged sword, piercing to the dividing asunder of soul and spirit, and discover the secret thoughts and intents of your hearts, which are only and continually evil.

2. I come to tell you of your misery while married to the law, and not to Christ.

1st, You are married to a very rigorous husband, that demands nothing else than a perfect and every way complete obedience, and that under the pain of death; like the Egyptian taskmasters, the law, to which you are married, requires brick, but neither can nor will afford any straw. My meaning is, that it requires perfect working, but gives no grace, no strength, whereby to obey. Yea,

2dly, You are married to a cursing husband, Gal. iii. 10. "Cursed is every one that continueth not in all things which are written in the book of the law to do them." Observe the expression, if you do not continue in all things, the law curses and condemns you. Some folks fancy if they do as well as they can, they answer the demands of it, and God, the great Lawgiver, will be satisfied with what they do, and forgive their defects and short-comings. Well, you may go on, and foster yourselves up in this fancy: but in the name of the Lord I warn you, "You shall lie down in sorrow."

3dly, You are married to a weak husband, Rom. viii. 3. "What the law could not do, in that it was weak through the flesh." This is not to be understood as if the law had lost any of its authority to require obedience, or to condemn the sinner for disobedience: Not at all, the law is as strong as ever, and as sacred as ever. But the law is weak; it has lost its covenant power to confer life upon the sinner that has once broken it; it is weak to redeem or save the sinner; it cannot justify; it cannot pardon; it cannot afford life unto any springing of Adam by ordinary generation, because "all have sinned, and come short of the glory of God." It is weak through the flesh, *i.e.* through the corruption of our nature, and our inability to obey it; for, if we could yield perfect obedience to the law, the law would be as strong as ever to save us, according to that word, "He that doth these things shall live in them," but he that doth them not shall die.

4thly, You are married to a dead husband, Rom. vii. 6. speaking of the law, says the apostle, "That being dead wherein we were held." What help can a woman's husband, that is dead and buried in the grave afford unto her? She may go and weep upon his grave, and cry; but he no more hears her than the grave-stone. Just so is the case: The law to which we were married in the first Adam is dead, and its votaries may work, and sigh, and cry, and do as they will for help by the works of the law: It no more regards all that they can do, than a dead carcase regards when you speak to it; for "by the works of the law no flesh shall be justified." But still indeed the law is alive to curse and condemn, as was just now said.

Thus you see what a miserable husband you are married to, while married to the law; but that you may yet better know your misery, there are these things I have to tell you from the Lord.

1st, While married unto the law, you are farther off from heaven than the grossest of sinners. Hence Christ tells the Pharisees, who were touching the law blameless, but because they rested upon the works of the law as the ground of their justification and acceptance, Christ tells them, that "publicans and harlots should enter into the kingdom of God before them." *Quest.* Are not publicans and harlots continuing so in the broad way to hell? *Answ.* No doubt of that; but there were more of the publicans and harlots converted by Christ's ministry, than of the Scribes and Pharisees. And how came that about? Why, the publicans and harlots were more easily convinced that they were in the high way to ruin, and so more easily turned from the evil of their ways, than the Pharisee, who wrapt himself up in the garment of his own obedience and righteousness, and so under that covering screened himself against all the arrows of conviction.

2dly, While married unto the law, you are under the dominion and power of sin, Rom. vi. 14, "Sin shall not have dominion over you, for ye are not under the law, but under grace;" plainly importing, that while a man is married unto the law, sin is in its reigning power, for "the strength of sin is the law." The law irritates corruption, but does not mortify it; it condemns a man to lie under the dominion of every lust and idol.

3dly, You are "aliens from the commonwealth of Israel, strangers from the covenants of promise." You have a right of access indeed, by sitting under the drop of the gospel, but no saving interest therein; you have no more right of possession than the devils have.

4thly, All your worship and service is rejected of God, because you reject his beloved Son, whom he has given for a covenant unto the people. While a man is upon a law bottom, all he doth is an abomination to God, Isa. i. 11.-13.

5thly, All the attributes of God are armed against you: His holiness hates you as unclean: his justice condemns you, because all your righteousness is as filthy rags; his wisdom devises an evil device against you; and his power will execute all the threatenings of the law upon you: "They shall be punished with everlasting destruction from the presence of the Lord."

Thus you see what a dangerous condition you are in, while married to the law.

Secondly, I should now speak a word to these who are married to their lusts, and are cleaving unto the world's trinity, the lusts of the flesh, the lusts of the eye, and the pride of life. The prophet Hosea speaks of some who were joined to their idols; they are so wedded to their sinful profits and pleasures, such as the lust of drunkenness, the lust of uncleanness, the lust of covetousness, that they never yet went out to meet the Bridegroom in a way of believing. What shall I say to all such profane sinners, that are hugging their Delilahs in their bosom, and giving them that room that is due to the Lord Jesus Christ? I have only a word or two unto you.

1st, You are in love and league with that which God hates; for every sin and lust in heart or hand, in life or lip, is the abominable thing which God hates.

2dly, You are married to that which Christ came to destroy and condemn. Christ's great errand was to finish transgression, and make an end of sin. "He condemned sin in the flesh," or by the sacrifice of his flesh or human nature. Can you expect to be saved by Christ, while you harbour that condemned traitor.

3dly, You are married unto a foul-murderer, that is stabbing you to your very heart, and the life of thy soul must go for it, if you hold it fast, though as dear as a right hand.

4thly, You are married unto that which the holy law of God condemns. The law pours out its anathemas against every sin, because sin is a transgression of the law, Gal. iii. 10. "Cursed is every one that continueth not in all things which are written in the book of the law to do them,"

5thly, If you continue married to your lusts, you must bed with them in hell, where your present lusts will be found so many vipers to sting you to the heart for ever. Your meat will then be turned into your bowels, and will be as the gall of asps within you. In a word, snares, fire, and brimstone, and a furious tempest of wrath and vengeance, shall be the portion of your cup, if you continue married to your lusts.

Perhaps some may be saying in their hearts, "I hope I am married unto Christ, and shall be saved by him, though I continue in my old way of lying and drinking, cheating and whoring, and over-reaching my neighbours; I hope God will pardon these, and the like failings and infirmities." Well, you may foster yourselves up in these vain hopes; but what says Christ? "No man can serve two masters," he must give up either with the one or with the other. O, shall the throne of iniquity have fellowship with God? and shall sin, and self, and the world, have the throne of your hearts, and the obedience of your lives, and yet think you to have fellowship with God? What communion hath light with darkness? What concord hath Christ with Belial?" And what agreement hath the temple of God with idols? 2 Cor. vi. 14 15. And therefore I say, if ever you go out to meet the Bridegroom, you must let these go, and say with Ephraim, What have I to do any more with idols? So much for reproof.

MATTH. xxv. 6.—And at midnight there was a cry made, Behold the Bridegroom cometh, go ye out to meet him.

THE SIXTH SERMON ON THIS TEXT.

THE *fifth* use of this doctrine I shall endeavour to manage in an address to two sorts of persons: *First,* To all in general. *Secondly,* To believers in particular.

First, I say, I would address myself to all in general.

Sirs, you have been hearing of Christ in the quality of a Bridegroom, and how he is not only come in the flesh, but actually come in the dispensation of the gospel, to court a bride for himself among the sons of men. He who married our nature unto personal union with himself, when he past by the nature of angels, that he might be upon a level with us, is now actually presenting himself to us in this gospel, as the Bridegroom of souls, and saying, with his hand stretched out, " Behold me, behold me ;" I will be for you, if you will be for me, and not for another : " Behold, I stand at the door and knock ; if any man hear my voice, and open the door of his heart to me, and consent to the bargain, I will come into him, and will sup with him, and he with me : I will betrothe thee unto me for ever."

Now, I say, seeing this is the case, my call and exhortation unto all is, to give the assent and consent of faith unto the bargain. I, as a friend of the Bridegroom, have a commission to court for him, and to say to you, as Rebekah's friends said to her, upon a proposal of marriage with Isaac, " Wilt thou go with this man?" the Man IMMANUEL, GOD-MAN ; the man of God's right hand ; the Man whose name is the Branch, who builds the temple, and bears all the glory ; the Man who hath all power in heaven, and on earth ; who is KING OF KINGS, AND LORD OF LORDS. O, will you sign the contract of the new covenant with the hand of faith, and say, " I am the Lord's, my Maker is and shall be my Husband, whose name is the Lord of hosts, and my Redeemer, the Holy One of Israel." O, what a happy day would it be to this assembly, if every individual soul would give Rebekah's answer to the proposal, with the same affection and resolution, ' I will go with the man. I will follow him whithersoever he goes; his God shall be my God, his Father shall be my Father, where he dwells there will I dwell; neither death nor life, nor things present, nor things to come, shall ever separate between him and me.' Now, because it is Christ's way not to drag with violence, but to draw his bride to him with the cords of a man, and the bands of love, therefore I shall essay to enforce the exhortation with a few motives or arguments.

Mot. 1. Shall be taken from the glory and excellency of the blessed Bridegroom. And here it is fit you remember what was said of him in the doctrinal part. As to his name, he has a "name above every name that can be named." As to his pedigree, who can declare his generation? As to his personal worth and excellency, his qualities are every way incomparable. Now, seeing such a Bridegroom offers to betrothe you to himself, O let it be a bargain; give your consent unto him, that the everlasting knot may be cast between you and him.

Mot. 2. To engage you to match with the Bridegroom, O consider how fond he is of the match, how much his heart is set upon it. This will appear, if you consider,

1. That he had it upon his heart from all eternity, before the world was made: "I have loved thee with an everlasting love," Jer. xxxi. 3. Before we had any being, save in his own purpose, when he saw us in our blood, his time, even then, was a time of love, Ezek. xvi.; and the accomplishing of that project of love was the joy of his heart, Prov. viii. 30. He rejoiced in the habitable parts of the earth, and his delights were with the sons of men."

2. He was so fond of the match, that, though he be God's fellow, and thinks it not robbery to be equal with God," yet he consented voluntarily to become his Father's bond servant out of love to us. This is the import of the word, "Mine ear hast thou bored, Lo, I come; I delight to do thy will, O my God! yea, thy law is within my heart." As Jacob became Laban's servant for fourteen years, out of love he had to Rachel; so did Christ become his Father's servant in the great work of redemption, out of love he had to the bride, that his Father promised him, in Adam's family.

3. Because he was none of our kindred, therefore he became our Kinsman, by manifesting himself in the flesh, or taking part of our flesh, Heb. ii. 14. John i. 14. "The Word was made flesh;" he became as one of us, that so the natural distance being removed, the marriage might be accomplished.

4. Because the bride was a bond slave to law and justice, and could not be redeemed but with a ransom of infinite value; therefore the Bridegroom dies for the bride, and redeems her, not with silver and gold, but with his own precious blood: he gave his life a ransom for many.

5. Because she was a prisoner unto Satan, and a lawful captive unto her greatest enemy, who was ready to devour her; therefore he comes in the quality of a victorious and renowned conqueror, and travels in the greatness of his strength, spoils principalities and powers, makes a shew of them openly, and "through death, destroys him that had the power of death," setting the captives of the mighty at liberty.

6. Because the bride was as black as hell, by lying among the pots; therefore he undertakes to wash and cleanse her, and to put his own beauty upon her, whereby she should be as the wings of a dove, covered with yellow gold.

7. Because the bride was naked, the devil having run away with her beautiful ornament of original righteousness; therefore the Bridegroom undertakes to clothe her with white raiment, so as the shame of her nakedness might not appear: the Bridegroom is made of God to her, "righteousness and sanctification," &c.

8. So fond is the Bridegroom of the match, that he despatches his heralds to make open proclamation of his purpose of marriage to her, and he gives it us ministers in our commission, to insist upon it, and not to take a refusal; 2 Cor. v. 20. "Now then we are ambassadors for Christ, as though God did beseech you by us, we pray you in Christ's stead be ye reconciled to God," by embracing his beloved Son, and consenting to him as your Head, Husband, and Bridegroom.

9. So fond is he, that he waits for a good answer from the bride; he waits that he may be gracious, and he exalts himself, that he may shew mercy; he stands at the door and knocks, till his head is filled with dew, and his locks with the drops of the night.

10. He is grieved at the heart when he gets a refusal. How did he weep over Jerusalem, saying, O, "If thou hadst known, even thou, at least in this thy day, the things which belong unto thy peace! How shall I give thee up Ephraim? How shall I deliver thee Israel? Mine heart is turned within me, my repentings are kindled together."

11. How glad is his heart when the consent of the bride is gained? He is so glad, that he calls heaven and earth to rejoice with him: for there is joy in heaven when but one sinner is converted: O then the cry is given, Rev. xix. 5. "Let us be glad and rejoice, and give honour to him, for the marriage of the Lamb is come, and his bride hath made herself ready." The joy of that day is expressed by the joyful solemnity of a king's coronation, Cant. iv. last, "Go forth, O ye daughters of Zion, and behold King Solomon, with the crown wherewith his mother crowned him in the day of his espousals, and in the day of the gladness of his heart."

Now, is Christ so fond of a match with you, and will you be cool, careless, and averse? especially, if you consider by way of

Mot. 3. The vast disparity and disproportion between you and him. Never was there such an unequality in marriage between parties as here; and yet his love and kindness towards the bride makes him come over all inequality. O let heaven and earth, angels and men, stand amazed! He who is the Lord, the Creator of all the ends of the earth, offers to match with his own creature, the work of his own hand, Is. liv. 6. "Thy Maker is thine Husband." He who is the ANCIENT OF DAYS, the EVERLASTING FATHER, offers to match with a forlorn infant cast out into the open field. He who is the most noble Branch of heaven or earth, offers to match with a vile prostitute, who had played the harlot with many lovers, whose father was an Amorite, and her mother a Hittite. He who is the Heir of God, Heir of heaven, the Heir of all things, offers to match with the children of Satan, and heirs of hell. He who is the greatest beauty of heaven and earth, the brightness of the Father's glory, offers to match with a bride, black as the Ethiopian, and spotted like the leopard, who is full of wounds and bruises, and putrefying sores. O let heaven and earth stand amazed at the condescension of the Bridegroom, and the folly of sinners in refusing such a match!

Mot. 4. To win your hearts to the Bridegroom, consider how much it will turn out to your advantage, if you take on with him as your Husband. View this in these following things.

1. The Bridegroom will clear, and ease you of all your debts. As for temporal and worldly debts he has a thousand ways to rid you of these, if he see it for his glory, and your good: for the earth is his, and the fulness thereof, and he bids you cast all your cares upon him, for he careth for his bride; he that paid a ransom for your souls, how will he not with that freely give you all things? But as to the debts you owe to law and justice, which indeed of all are the greatest and heaviest, heavier than you can bear, the least farthing of which you could never have paid, either by an eternity of obedience, or an eternity of punishment, that moment you close with Christ, you are cleared and discharged; the Bridegroom stands between you and all your creditors. You know the wife is not sueable at law while clothed with a husband, he answers for all. Just so when you close with Christ the better Husband, who is raised from the dead, you become dead to the law," Rom. vii. 4. *i. e.* you have no more concern with the law, and the debts you owe to it as a covenant, either for obedience or punishment, than if they had never been; insomuch that, with joy and triumph you may lift up your heads in the presence of all your creditors or accusers, and say, ' Who can lay any thing to my charge? for it is Christ that died for my offences, and rose again for my justification and acquittance; I am under his covering, I am with him in the bride-chamber, where law and justice have no action against me.' O then, poor diver, broken and bankrupt sinner, go out and match with the Bridegroom, and that moment, "It is God that justifies you," saying, "I, even I am he that blotteth out your transgressions."

2. O Sirs, go out and meet the Bridegroom, and take on with him, and all your wants shall be supplied, be they never so great and many, Phil. iv. 19. "My God shall supply all your need, according to his riches in glory, by Christ Jesus," The Bridegroom, as you have heard, has unsearchable riches: all the treasures of wisdom and knowledge, of grace and of glory, are in him; and out of his fulness you shall receive grace for grace; quickening grace, for he is the Resurrection and the Life; enlightening grace, for he is the Sun of righteousness, the bright and the morning Star; strengthening grace, for he giveth power to the faint, and increaseth strength to them that have no might. In a word, he will give grace and glory, and no good thing will he withhold from the soul that consents to marry him.

3. The Bridegroom will heal all your soul maladies: for he is well skilled in physic; he is the Physician of value, and there is no disease so obstinate, but he will cure it with a word speaking. Hast thou a hard heart? he will soften it, and turn it unto a heart of flesh. Hast thou a withered hand, that cannot work? well, he strengthens the weak and withered hand. Hast thou lame feet, that cannot walk? well, he makes the lame to leap like an hart. Hast thou a blind eye? or wast thou born blind? well, he has eye-salve to make the blind to see clearly. In a word, the first moment the soul matches with Christ, he begins the cure, and, against the day of consummation of the marriage, the bride will be fully ready, the good work will be perfected, and the bride will be presented "without spot or wrinkle, or any such thing."

4. O go out and meet the Bridegroom, and match with him, and he will bear all your burdens, let them be never so heavy: "Cast thy burden upon the Lord, and he shall sustain thee." Christ is the most sympathising Husband that ever was: If he see his bride or beloved spouse oppressed in spirit with any sort of trouble, be what it will, he is just afflicted in all her afflictions, and he will be with her in the fire and in the waters, that the fire may not burn, nor the waters overwhelm her. See how he speaks to his beloved spouse in her tossings, Is. liv. 11. "O thou afflicted, tossed with tempest, and not comforted, behold, I will lay thy stones with fair colours, and thy foundations with sapphires."

5. O match with the Bridegroom, and he will subdue all thy enemies, and make thee a conqueror, yea, more than a conqueror over them. They that match and take on with Christ, must indeed lay their account to have the armies of hell upon their top: The old serpent casts out water like a flood against the woman, and the remnant of her seed, that "keep the commandments of God, and have the testimony of Jesus Christ." But be not discouraged, poor soul; thy Bridegroom has already bruised the head of the old serpent, and, ere it be long, will also make thee to tread Satan under thy feet. He that stood between thee and avenging justice, will likewise stand with and for thee, in opposition to all enemies whatever. Let men and devils curse the bride of Christ, he will bless her. Let her be excommunicate, or cast out of the Church unto the devil's common, Christ will not affirm, but make void such sentences. In the ninth chapter of John, we read of a poor man born blind, whose eyes Christ had opened upon the Sabbath day, by making a little clay, and putting it upon his eyes. The Jewish Sanhedrim met; and under a very religious pretence of zeal for the Sabbath day, they convene the man before them, who professed Christ, in as far as he knew him; and thereupon they excommunicate him, and cast him out of the church, and held him as a Heathen man and a Publican. Well, was this sentence bound in heaven? No; so far from that, that ver. 35. when Christ heard they had cast him out (or excommunicated him, as in the margin), Christ seeks him out, and finds him, and manifests himself the more to him, as you may see, ver. 35—38.: and, in the 39th verse, he passes a heavy doom and sentence upon them that had cast him out: "For judgement I am come into this world, that they who see not might see, and that they who see (or imagine that they are the only men that see things, or know them in a better light), might be made blind." Thus Christ will take up and defend his bride, to the confusion of them that do her hurt.

6. O match with the blessed Bridegroom, and he will manage all your concerns for you, and that both in heaven above, and earth below; for he has "all power in heaven and in earth." Thy Bridegroom, believer, will agent all thy business for thee on earth; for all the wheels of providence, they are rolled in a subserviency unto his design of love towards his beloved spouse and bride, Rom. viii. 28. Deut. xxxiii. "He rides upon the heavens in thy help, and in his excellency on the sky." And as for thy concerns in the high court of heaven, he is thy

Agent and Advocate there, 1 John, ii. 1. 2. "If any man sin, we have an Advocate with the Father," &c.

7. O match with Christ the Bridegroom, for he provides his bride in a large jointure. Although she contracts nothing with him but debt, and want, and poverty; yet he, in a way of free grace and love, contracts all things with her. See the tenure of the contract, 1 Cor. iii. 21. "All things are yours, whether Paul, or Apollos, or Cephas, or the world, or life, or death, or things present, or things to come; all are yours, for ye are Christ's, and Christ is God's." Oh! how well is the spouse of Christ provided, by virtue of the contract of the new covenant! He provides his bride of a crown, and "a crown of glory that fadeth not away." He provides her of "a kingdom that cannot be moved, an inheritance incorruptible, undefiled, and that fadeth not away." He provides her of "a city that hath foundations, whose builder and maker is God;" and a jointure house "not made with hands, eternal in the heavens." In a word, he contracts, that his own God and Father shall be her God and Father for ever. What more can the most enlarged heart desire? More "eye hath not seen, nor ear heard, neither hath it entered into the heart of man to conceive."

Mot. 5. To win your hearts to the blessed Bridegroom, consider the excellency of the contract he makes with his bride. I told you in the entry, the contract is the covenant of grace and promise, transacted in eternity between the Bridegroom and his eternal Father, on the behalf of these whom the Father gave him, Psal. lxxxix. 3. "I have made a covenant with my chosen." And, in a day of power, when the bride gives her consent, that same covenant is made and established with her, Is. lv. 3. "I will make with them an everlasting covenant, even the sure mercies of David." I shall name a few properties, and you have them all in a bundle together, Hos. ii. 19. 20. "And I will betrothe thee unto me for ever; yea, I will betrothe thee unto me in righteousness, and in judgment, and in loving kindness, and in mercy. I will even betrothe thee unto me in faithfulness, and thou shalt know the Lord."

1. It is an everlasting contract; for thus saith the Bridegroom, "I will betrothe thee unto me for ever." As the contract bears date from the ancient years of eternity, so it runs forward to an eternity to come; and, Oh! who can form a right thought of never-ending eternity? Oh! it is a great, but comfortable word to the bride of Christ, "I will betrothe thee unto me for ever. I will make an everlasting covenant with them, that I will not turn away from them to do them good." Death breaks all contracts between man and wife, and nullifies the relation; but "neither death nor life, nor things present, nor things to come," shall separate between Christ and his spouse.

2. It is a just and righteous contract; for it stands bottomed upon the everlasting righteousness brought in by the Bridegroom, "I will betrothe thee unto me in righteousness." The righteousness of Christ is the condition of the contract of the new covenant. By his obedience unto death, he confirmed the covenant unto many; and he gifts this righteousness unto his bride as her wedding garment, and puts it on her with his own hand: Hence she sings, Is. lxi. 10. "I will greatly

rejoice in the Lord, my soul shall be joyful in my God: for he hath clothed me with the garments of salvation, he hath covered me with the robe of righteousness, as a bridegroom decketh himself with ornaments, and as a bride adorneth herself with her jewels."

3. It is a wise and well ordered contract; for, says the Bridegroom, "I will betrothe thee unto me in judgement," *i. e.* with great wisdom and understanding. This chariot of the wood of Lebanon, viz. the covenant of grace, was made by a greater than Solomon, in whom "are hid all the treasures of wisdom and knowledge." It was the result of the council of peace, between the Father and the Son, from all eternity, and therefore cannot but be well ordered in all things." It is the wisdom of God in a mystery, even his hidden wisdom, which none of the princes of the world knew. In other contracts between man and wife, there are sometimes very intricate and perplexing clauses, which occasion law-suits and vexations; but no such thing here, every thing is clear.

4. It is a most loving contract; for, says the Bridegroom, "I will betrothe thee unto me in loving-kindness." The love that Christ did bear to his bride from all eternity is the source and original of the whole of the match. The chariot of the wood of Lebanon is just paved with love for the daughters of Jerusalem. Love makes him to choose her for his bride from eternity; "I have loved thee with an everlasting love." Love made him lay down his life a ransom for his bride; "He loved me, and gave himself for me." Love made him draw her within the bonds of that covenant, whereof he is the Head; and love made all the promises of the contract; and love obliges him to fulfil them.

5. It is a gratuitous and free contract that he makes with her; for, says the Bridegroom, "I will betrothe thee unto me in mercies; and it is observable, that is in the plural number, because that there are a multitude of tender mercies with the Bridegroom towards the bride. She was in misery when he looked upon her, wallowing in her blood, without any eye to pity, or hand to help; but his tender mercies made him to spread his skirt over her, and to say unto her, Live; and thus his "mercy is from everlasting to everlasting upon them that fear him." His tender bowels yearn towards his beloved spouse, when he sees her in any distress and trouble; for, "in all her afflictions he is afflicted;" and although her afflictions be many, yet at length he relieves her out of them all.

6. It is a faithful and true contract; for he says, ver. 20. "I will betrothe thee unto me in faithfulness." The very name of the Bridegroom is faithful and true, Rev. xix. 11. He is the Amen, the faithful and true Witness. He is not man, that he should lie, nor the son of man, that he should repent; and therefore the contract of the covenant is more sure than heaven and earth: his "covenant he will not break, nor alter the thing that is gone out of his lips, Is. liv. 10. "The mountains shall depart, and the hills be removed; but my kindness shall not depart from thee, neither shall the covenant of my peace be removed, saith the Lord, that hath mercy on thee."

7. It is an additional clause of the contract, Hos. ii. 20. "(And thou shalt know the Lord.) I will give them an heart to know me,

that I am the Lord." The Bridegroom manifests himself to the bride in another manner than he doth to the rest of the world, Is. xxxiii. 17. "Thine eyes shall see the King in his beauty." Hos. vi. 3 "Then shall we know, if we follow on to know the Lord." This is the leading blessing in the contract of the covenant, and therefore called life eternal, John xvii. 3. "And this is life eternal, that they might know thee the only true God, and Jesus Christ whom thou hast sent." To see the glory of Christ, and to be with him, is just the culminating or consummating point of the happiness of the saints in heaven, John xvii. 24. But that which seems especially to be imported in the expression, "Thou shalt know the Lord," is, that the bride shall be admitted into the most intimate fellowship and communion with the Bridegroom. As, upon the consummation of the marriage, the bride and the bridegroom know one another, in a way of conjugal union and communion; so the bride of Christ shall enjoy the sweetest communion with the Lord, so as to be in case to say, with the spouse, "His left hand shall be under my head, and his right hand shall embrace me; and as a bundle of myrrh is my well-beloved unto me, he shall lie all night betwixt my breasts." Thus you see what an excellent contract it is that Christ makes with the bride. Now, this contract we bring unto you in a preached gospel, requiring you in God's great name to take hold of it, and subscribe it by the hand of faith, according to that prophecy and promise, Is. xliv. 5. "One shall say, I am the Lord's, and another shall call himself by the name of Jacob, and another shall subscribe with his hand to the Lord, and sirname himself by the name of Israel."

Mot. 6. To engage you to go forth and meet and match with the Bridegroom, in a way of believing, consider, that, by the command of the Bridegroom, proclamation is made of the purpose of marriage with the bride, and no lawful objection or impediment is or can be made against the design. O, Sirs, we who are the friends and heralds of the Bridegroom, by commission from the Bridegroom and his eternal Father, have proclaimed, and continue to proclaim, from the tops of the high places, in the chief places of concourse, "Whoever will, let him come, and be the bride, the Lamb's wife. Unto you, O men (says he), I call, and my voice is to the sons of men." And what is his voice? See it, Is. lv. 1—3. "Ho every one that thirsteth, come, &c. Incline your ear, and come unto me; hear, and your soul shall live, and I will make with you an everlasting covenant." Now, shall proclamation of marriage be made, and yet shall the bride draw back, and make the proclamation of none effect.

Mot. 7. Consider, that if you be pleased with the match, all parties are pleased.

1. The Father of the Bridegroom is pleased. The first motion of the bargain was made by him; he first proposed the match for his beloved Son, in the council of peace, saying, 'O my Son, wilt thou match with yon company of Adam's family, and buy them off from the hand of justice, and betrothe them unto thee for ever? Mine they are, and I give them unto thee.' And as the Father proposed the match, so he presents his beloved Son unto the bride, saying, "This

is my beloved Son, in whom I am well pleased; hear ye him. Behold my Servant whom I uphold, mine Elect in whom my soul delighteth." For what end doth the Father thus commend him unto you, if he be not pleased with the match? Yea, he commands and requires you to take him by the hand, 1 John, iii. 23. "This is his commandment, that we should believe on the name of his Son Jesus Christ," &c.

2. As the Father of the Bridegroom is pleased, so is the Bridegroom himself, yea, as you heard in ten or twelve particulars, he is exceedingly fond of it. His delights were and are with the sons of men; he rejoices over the soul that comes to him, "as the bridegroom rejoiceth over the bride."

3. The friends of the Bridegroom, all faithful ministers, are pleased, yea, they travail as in birth, till they gain your consent to take your Maker for your Husband; and that day your consent is gained, they rejoice, and forget their sorrow, like a travailing woman when a manchild is born into the world.

4. Fellow virgins, all true believers, are well pleased and rejoice when a poor soul gives heart and hand to the Bridegroom, Psal. xlv. 14. 15. "The virgins, her companions that follow her, shall be brought unto thee: with gladness and rejoicing shall they be brought." Thus, I say, all parties are pleased. O, then, let it be a bargain, and go forth and meet the Bridegroom.

Mot. 8. As all parties on the side of the Bridegroom are pleased, so all things are ready, and therefore come to the marriage. The Bridegroom is ready, as the words of the text declare, *Behold the Bridegroom cometh, go ye out to meet him;* yea, he stands at the door, and knocks. The Holy Ghost, the Comforter, is ready to cast the everlasting knot, saying, "To-day, if ye will hear his voice, harden not your hearts." He is ready to give the bride "the oil of joy for mourning, and the garment of praise for a heavy spirit." The contract of the covenant is ready, being signed by the Father, saying, Is. xlii. 6. "I will give thee for a covenant unto the people;" and the Bridegroom has signed it with his own blood, Dan. ix. Heb. ix. The marriage house is built, and ready for the reception of the bride, Prov. ix. at the beginning, "Wisdom hath builded her house, she hath hewn out her seven pillars." The marriage supper is ready, "My oxen and my fatlings are killed, Matth. xxii.: and Prov. ix. 2. "Wisdom hath killed her beasts, she hath mingled her wine, she hath also furnished her table," &c. In a word, all the angels and saints in heaven, all ministers and Christians upon earth, are ready to clap their hands, and to tune their harps, and there will be joy both in heaven and in earth, at your going forth to meet the Bridegroom.

Mot. 9. Go forth, and meet the Bridegroom in a way of believing; for sad, sad, will be the event, if you do not, after all that has been said. Why, say you, What will be the event? or what will follow?

1. You will sadden the heart of the Bridegroom, who is the joy of heaven and earth. How sad a heart got he from the Jews, when he grieved for the hardness of their hearts, and when he wept over them! And will you follow their footsteps, and grieve the heart of your God also?

THE WISE VIRGINS GOING FORTH TO MEET THE BRIDEGROOM. 243

2. If you go not forth to meet him, he will depart from you, and give you up, Gen. vi. 3. "My Spirit (says he) shall not always strive with man." Psal. lxxxi. 11. "My people would not hearken unto my voice; Israel would none of me, so I gave them up," &c. Many a sad wo will befall you upon his departure, Hos. ix. 12. "Yea, wo also to them, when I depart from them."

3. He will go to his Father that sent him, and enter a complaint against you, saying, 'O Father, according to thy command, I went and proposed myself as a Bridegroom to such a people or person, but they refused the match, they cast the bargain.' And O how will God the Father resent the indignity? John iii. 18. 36. "He that believeth not, is condemned already, and the wrath of God abideth on him. There remains no sacrifice for such a sin:" For, in so doing, you trample the blood of the Bridegroom under your feet, Heb. x. 26. 29.

4. Heaven and earth, and the whole creation, will be astonished, and horribly afraid at you, in preferring other lovers unto him, who is altogether lovely, Jer. ii. 12. 13.

5. Sin, Satan, and the world, will pick you up, and lead you captive, and God will say, They are joined to their idols, let them alone, Hos. iv. 17. seeing they continue in covenant with death, and at agreement with hell, Is. xxviii. 15. Let them go, and see what the end will be: "I have purged thee, and thou wast not purged, and therefore thou shalt not be purged from thy filthiness any more," Ezek. xxiv. 13.

6. Remember, despised love issues out in flames of **wrath** and resentment, Prov. i. 24. "Because I have called, and ye refused, I have stretched out my hand, and no man regarded;" ver. 26. "I also will laugh at your calamity, and mock when your fear cometh."

Sirs, I am afraid, that some if not many of you in this place, are more taken up in drinking, caballing, and peuthering about your ensuing elections, than you are about this important affair of having your own souls, and the souls of others, matched unto the Son of God. Your heads and hearts are so filled with these sinful and trifling matters, that the Bridegroom cannot get a hearing. Yea, you are "like the deaf adder that stoppeth her ear, which will not hearken to the voice of charmers," Psal. lviii. 4. 5. But, dear friends, allow me to reason the matter with you, in the name of God, Is. lv. 2. "Wherefore do you spend your money for that which is not bread, and your labour for that which profiteth nothing?" What will the gain of the election or the gain of the whole world avail, if you lose your own souls by not going forth from these things to meet the Bridegroom? For the Lord's sake remember, that if you do not go forth, and meet him, and match with him by faith now, you shall meet with him and see him shortly upon the back of death, and at the last judgement, Rev. i. 7. "Behold he cometh with clouds, and every eye shall see him," and you also that pierced his heart by unbelief, and then you will wail because of him: O how will you look him in the face, whose offers of love you despised? What will you do? and what blushing and confusion of face will fly up unto your breast and countenance, when you shall see your despised lover sitting upon his white throne, with all his holy angels, "ten thousand times ten thousand, and thousands of thousands, ministering unto him?" Oh, "to whom then will ye fly for help, and where will ye leave your glory?" Is. x. 3. How will you choose rather, if possible, to be buried under rocks and mountains, than appear before the face of him (Rev. vi. 16.), who once in a day courted your affections and consent to be his bride, but was maltreated, rejected, and despised by you? You said by your practice, we will not go with this man, Gen. xxviii. 58. we will not have him to rule over us, Luke xix. 14. "Let God depart from us, for we desire not the knowledge of his ways; what is the Almighty that we should serve him," Job xxi. 14. Therefore the dreadful and awful sentence shall go forth against you, Matth. xxv. 41. "Depart from me, ye cursed, into everlasting fire, prepared for the devil and his angels," and thereupon you shall be hurried by legions of devils into everlasting torments. O consider these things in time, ye that forget God, and make light of the offers of the Bridegroom's love, lest he tear you in pieces, when there is none to deliver.

2dly. But I do not love to conclude with the thunders and lightnings of Mount Sinai, but choose rather to turn again to Mount Zion, and to cry again, and again, *Behold the Bridegroom cometh, go ye out to meet him.* Go forth, O ye daughters of Zion, and behold the beauty and excellency of the true King Solomon, Cant. iii. 11. "O that this may be the day of his espousals, and the day of the gladness of his heart." Behold how glorious he is in his apparel, and how he comes travelling from Edom, and from Bozrah, in the greatness of his strength, in order to meet you, and will not you go forth and meet him? The Bridegroom began his journey towards you, from the early ages of eternity, Mic. v. 2. For his goings forth were of old, from everlasting. He left the glory he had with his Father before the world was, and travelled up and down this world for his spouse, for about the space of thirty-three years, in poverty, reproach, and persecution; he travelled through seas of wrath, and the Jordan of death, and then back again to heaven, in order to bring about the match; and, since his ascension, he has been travelling in the chariot of the everlasting gospel, first among the Jews, and then among the Gentile nations; and he is come even unto these isles of the seas, and utmost parts of the earth; he has been long stretching out the arms of redeeming love unto Scotland, and unto the inhabitants of Stirling, crying, *Behold me, behold me:* How gladly would I gather you, unto me as the "hen gathereth her chickens under her wings!" Matth. xxiii. 37. How would my soul rejoice over you, as the bridegroom rejoiceth over the bride, if you would but entertain and embrace me as your Bridegroom! I, who am your Maker, will be your Husband, and betrothe you unto me for ever. Well then, Sirs, take on with the best of Husbands, and say with thy whole heart and soul, Thine are we, O David, and on thy side will we be, thou Son of Jesse, 1 Chron. xii. 18. O let it be an everlasting bargain, that shall never be dissolved.

Oh! may some poor soul say, gladly would I go forth and meet the Bridegroom, and present myself as the bride, the Lamb's wife; but when I begin to think of it, there are a thousand obstacles cast in my way, which I know not how to surmount.

Well, let us hear what either the devil, the world, or an evil heart of unbelief, has to say; for there is no objection they can offer, that is of any relevance; the blessed Bridegroom has removed all impediments on the side of law and justice, by his obedience unto death; and he stands ready to answer, and we in his name and authority are ready to answer, whatever may come from any other airth.

Object. 1. Oh! may some poor dejected soul say, 'The distance between the Bridegroom and me is so great and infinite, that I can never think it will be a bargain; he is God's first-born, higher than the kings of the earth; will he ever match with me, a poor despicable worm, who am but nothing, yea, less than nothing and vanity.'

Answ. It is true, the distance between him and you is great as he is the Son of God, God co-equal with the Father; and if he had not removed this bar, by taking the human nature into a personal union with himself, there could never have been any such thing as a spiritual marriage between him and any of Adam's race; "But though he be in the form of God, and thinks it not robbery to be equal with God," yet he has become our equal also, by the assumption of the human nature; that so, being upon a level with us, he might betrothe us to himself for ever. Since he has come over the mountain of infinite distance, both natural and moral, let not the distance of parties be any impediment on your side; but consider the greater the inequality of the match be, the more are the riches, freedom and sovereignty, of the grace of God exalted, and this is the great plot of heaven, Is. lvii. 15. "Thus saith the high and lofty One that inhabiteth eternity, whose name is Holy, I dwell in the high and holy place"—To which no man can approach, 1 Tim. vi. 16. "With him also that is of a contrite and humble spirit, to revive the spirit of the humble, and to revive the heart of the contrite ones." God would have us, and all the world, to know that his ways are not our ways, nor his thoughts our thoughts; but as the heavens are higher than the earth, so are his ways higher than our ways, and his thoughts than our thoughts. It is God's way to pass by the great, the rich, and the wise and noble, and to pitch upon the weak, the poor and contemptible things of the world, "that no flesh may glory in his presence."

Object. 2. May another say, 'I am a poor deformed creature, there is nothing desirable in or about me, I am a transgressor from the womb, conceived in sin, and shapen in iniquity, altogether as an unclean thing; will ever the glorious Bridegroom match with the like of me?"

Answ. If Christ stood upon this objection, he could never have a bride among the race of Adam; he never married any of Adam's race because of their beauty or comeliness, but that he might make them beautiful, through his comeliness, that he puts upon them, Ezek. xvi. 8—12.

Object. 3. But Oh! 'My transgressions are multiplied, innumerable evils compass me about, and my sins have been highly aggravated against light, against love, against covenant vows and engagements: I gave my consent unto Christ, but I have hidden back, and therefore, Christ will never look upon me.'

Answ. Be it so as you say; yet, if you will return, he will receive you graciously, Jer. iii. 1. Though "thou hast played the harlot with many lovers, yet return again to me;" and Is. i. 18. "Come now and let us reason together, saith the Lord: though your sins be as scarlet, they shall be white as snow; though they be red like crimson, they shall be as wool." Remember the example of Manasseh, Mary Magdalene, Paul, and many others; the same mercy and grace that saved them, is as able to save you: his "hand is not shortened that he cannot save," &c.

Object. 4. 'I am lying in a dunghill of sin and misery, the Bridegroom will never look upon me.'

Answ. He raiseth the poor out of the dust, and lifteth the needy out of the dunghill, and sets them with princes: See what a dunghill the poor Israelitish infant was lying in, when the Lord passed by, and said unto it, *Live,* Ezek. xvi. "Though ye have lain among the pots, yet will I make thee as the wings of a dove, covered with silver, and her feathers with yellow gold."

Object. 5. 'I am so miserable, the Bridegroom will never look upon me.'

Answ. That is a mistake, for the Bridegroom's name is merciful, and his mercy is in the heavens.

Object. 6. 'I am blind,' says the sinner. Christ answers, "I recover sight to the blind;" Christ says to blind, " Laodicea, I counsel thee to buy of me eye-salve that thou mayest see."

Object. 7. ' I am naked, have no robe of righteousness to cover me.' Ay, but (says the Bridegroom) give but thy consent, and I will bring forth the best robe in heaven, and cover the shame of thy nakedness that it may not appear.

Object. 8. 'I am poor, and so poor, that I have no desireable qualification to recommend me.' *Answ.* The Bridegroom, "though he was rich, yet he became poor, that, through his poverty, we might be made rich." He has abundance of gold, "gold tried in the fire, unsearchable riches;" and all his riches are thine, that moment you consent to him.

Object. 9. 'I am dead, there is not the least spark of spiritual life in me, and therefore the Bridegroom will never look upon me.'

Answ. "Hear (says the Bridegroom to the dead), and your souls shall live," Isa. lv. 3. "And I will make an everlasting covenant with you, even the sure mercies of David; he that believeth in me, though he were dead, yet shall he live, for I am the resurrection and the life:" And if thou be but groaning under a sense of thy deadness, it is a sign of some life, for the dead do not use to tell any such tales of themselves. See what Christ doth to the dead, Eph. iii. 1. "You hath he quickened, who were dead in trespasses and sins," Ezek. xxxi. "The spirit of life quickeneth the dry bones."

Object. 10. 'I do not know if ever the Bridegroom loved me, or choosed me.'

Answ. He has revealed his love in the proposal of marriage that he makes thee in the gospel of his grace. He has said that he is willing; and he swears on his life, that he has "no pleasure in the death of the wicked, but rather that they would turn unto him and live." He declares, that he hates putting away; and that him that comes to him, he will in no ways cast out, that "the promise is unto you, and to your children, and to all that are afar off."

Now, your way is, to take him by his word, and to judge of his thoughts and purpose by his word; for "those things which are revealed belong unto us, and to our children for ever." I illustrate the case in hand, by a familiar similitude of a proposal of marriage made unto a woman; the man that is in suit of her, not only proposes and profers love to her, but he solicits and courts her consent; he forms the contract to the greatest advantage; he makes over himself and his whole estate unto her, and confirms his ingenuity by his oath, that she may not have any doubt of his love and affection.

Now, if after all, the woman should say, I will not consent to marry this man, because I do not know if he really loves me; would not every body look upon the woman as most ridiculous and unreasonable? and, in this case, does she not charge the man with the most horrid disingenuity? Well, this is the very case: how should you know the love of Christ to you, but by his offers, promises, intreaties, and declarations of his love; and to doubt of his love, is to charge him foolishly with deceitful dealing: and O! do not treat him so any more, but believe, and see his salvation.

Object. 11. 'Oh! God, is angry with me, I think I see frowns in his countenance, when I begin to think of matching with his beloved Son.'

Answ. You are in a great mistake; for the main ground of his controversy with you is, because you do not go forth to meet his beloved Son: And that moment you receive him by faith, you shall find him a well pleased God; for to as many as received him, as their Saviour, Husband, King, Priest, and Prophet, John i. 12. "to them gave he power to become the sons of God."

Object. 12. "You urge me to wed by faith the Bridegroom, and gladly would I do it, but I find an entire impotency, and inability in myself, and it is only the power of God that must do the work; and therefore, all you have said is in vain, till a day of power come.'

Answ. It is true, it is the power of God that must make a sinner willing; but the way that this power is exerted is, by convincing the sinner of his own inability either to will or to do, that so he may put the whole work in the Lord's hand. And if this be your case, the good work is already begun; and he that has begun to convince you, and humble you under a sense of your own impotency, he will carry it on, and finish the matter; for he has said, Psal. cx. 3. "Thy people shall be willing in the day of thy power," Isa. xl. 29. "He gives power to the faint, and to them that have no might increaseth strength."

I conclude this exhortation with two or three advices.

1. Be convinced and persuaded of your dangerous and deplorable

case, while married unto the law, and your lusts; for which see the use of reproof and lamentation.

2. Conceive and entertain hopes of getting the match between Christ and you accomplished and brought about. A hopeless despair as to this matter cuts the sinews of all activity: "There is no hope; no, for I have loved strangers, and after them will I go," Jer. ii. 25. and therefore, "it is good that a man should hope," Lam. iii. 26.

3. Be much in studying the love of God in providing such a help every way meet for you. It was an evidence of God's kindness to Adam, when he said, "It is not good that the man should be alone," Gen. ii. 18. I will make "him an help meet for him." Much more is it an evidence of the love of God to lost man, that he has laid help for him upon one that is mighty, Psal. lxxxix. 19.

4. I recommend to you to be much in studying the love of the eternal Son of God, in marrying the human nature unto a personal union with the divine, that he might act the part of a Kinsman Redeemer. Oh! think what he has done in order to get a bride for himself in Adam's family, for one love kindles another, and "we love him because he first loved us," 1 John iv. 19.

5. Be much in viewing the glorious fulness and suitableness of the Bridegroom through the lattices of the word read and preached; "For all—we beholding as in a glass the glory of the Lord, are changed into the same image, from glory to glory," &c. 2 Cor. iii. last.

6. Oh! cry and plead much for the purchased and promised Spirit, that he may glorify Christ, and testify of him to your souls, according to the promise of the Bridegroom, before he left this world, John xvi. 14. "He shall glorify me, for he shall receive of mine, and shew it unto you."

7. In matching with the Bridegroom, disband all other lovers, saying with Ephraim, Hos. xiv. 8. "What have I any more to do with idols." Is. xxvi. 13. "O Lord my God, other lords besides thee have had dominion over me, but henceforth by thee only will I make mention of thy name." If you be for me (says Christ), let these soul-murdering lusts go; let go your lust of covetousness, your lust of uncleanness, your lust of pride, malice, revenge, your lust of drunkenness and gluttony; for as no man can serve two masters, Matth. vi. 24. so can no man be married unto Christ and these lusts at once; Christ says, Destroy these, crucify them, "Mortify the deeds of the body," Rom. viii. 13. "Fornication, evil concupiscence, and covetousness, which is idolatry," Col. iii. 8. I came to destroy these works of the devil, John iii. 8. And therefore give a bill of divorce to them, if you would follow me.

I shut up this discourse with a word of counsel and advice to believers, who, through the power of grace, have been determined to go forth and meet the Bridegroom.

Oh! bless the Lord that ever gave you counsel to do so, for this was never effected by the power of nature, but only by the power of victorious grace, Psal. cx. 3. "Thy people shall be willing in the day of thy power." Thou wast dead in sin, Eph. ii. 1. but he "passed by thee, and said unto thee, Live," Ezek. xvi. 6. Thou wast full of enmity against God and his anointed, Psal. ii. 2, but he captivated thy heart with his own love, and loveliness. Who made thee to differ from others that are left behind, "in the gall of bitterness, and in the bond of iniquity?" Why, it was the blessed Bridegroom that drew thee to him with the cords of his own love; and therefore let the high praises of the Bridegroom, and of his eternal Father, be continually in thy mouth, Psal. cxlix. 16. John vi. 44. "No man can come to me, except the Father which hath sent me draw him." Let the bride, the Lamb's wife, put much confidence in the Bridegroom; and well may she do it, for he is "the confidence of all the ends of the earth, his name is FAITHFUL and TRUE," Rev. xix. 11.

THE NEW TESTAMENT ARK OPENED AGAINST THE DELUGE OF DIVINE WRATH.

HEB. xi. 7.—*By faith Noah, being warned of God of things not seen as yet, moved with fear, prepared an ark to the saving of his house.*

THE FIRST SERMON ON THIS TEXT.

IN the preceding chapter, the apostle, in the close of it, had exhorted the believing Hebrews to persevere in the faith; and to enforce the exhortation, he demonstrates, in this chapter, the excellency of the grace of faith, and that, *first*, Abstractly in itself considered, ver. 1-3; *secondly*, By laying before them the example of their believing ancestors, both before and after the flood.

This verse which I have read contains the example of the faith of Noah, who was the last patriarch of the old world, and the first of the new world; I mean the last before, and the first after, the flood. More particularly in the words you have these things.

1st, An alarm sounded, (warning is given by God of things not seen as yet.) The party that gives the warning is God. And when God speaks or warns, well doth it become all the inhabitants of the earth to listen, Psal. l. 1, "The mighty God the Lord hath spoken, and called the earth, from the rising of the sun unto the going down thereof." When the lion roars, the beasts of the field tremble. The subject matter of the warning is about *things not seen as yet;* that is, the approach of the general deluge, or destruction of the whole world by water, of which there was not the least visible appearance when the warning was given of God. Sirs, the word of God deals mostly about things that are not seen, things invisible and eternal, which as yet lie behind the curtain; hence faith, that believes the word of God, is called, ver. 1 of this chapter, "the evidence of things not seen;" a setting to the seal to what God says, though not obvious unto sense.

2dly, In the words we have the person, and the only person, that took the alarm in all the old world, viz. Noah, whose character we have, Gen. vi. 9, "a just man, and perfect in his generation." He was a just man, being justified by faith, in the promised seed of the woman; and he was a holy man, whose walk and conversation justified his faith, in the view of the ungodly inhabitants of the old world.

And being such a person as lived near God, God takes him upon his secrets, and imparts that unto him, which was hid from all the world besides. "The secret of the Lord is with them that fear him, and unto them will he shew his covenant." Yea, sometimes he not only imparts to them the secrets of his covenant, and the mysteries of his kingdom; but also the secrets of his providence, what he is about to do in the world: so did he unto Noah; and so did he unto Abraham, when he was about to destroy Sodom: "Shall I hide from Abraham the thing that I do?" The Lord will do nothing, but he will reveal it unto his servants the prophets. It is dangerous to pry curiously into the secrets of God's purpose or providence, but when he is pleased to reveal them, they are welcome.

3dly, We have the way how the warning was taken by Noah. It was by faith; that is, he believed the word of God, that the flood would come: and the ground of his believing was the faithfulness and power of God; his faithfulness, "for it is impossible for God to lie;" and his power, that was able to give being to his word of threatening, as well as his word of promise.

4thly, We have the affection of Noah's soul, that was stirred or exercised by this awful warning of the approaching deluge; he was *moved with fear*. When faith sees a smiling and reconciled God in Christ, it moves the soul with joy and gladness, yea, a "joy unspeakable, and full of glory." But when faith sees a frowning or a threatening God, then it begets fear, not a slavish, but a filial fear; like a dutiful child, that falls a-trembling when he sees the rod in his Father's hand, and anger in his countenance. Such was the fear of Noah; and God declares, that he has a particular regard unto the soul that thus fears him, Is. lxvi. 2, "To this man will I look, who is poor, and of a contrite spirit, and who trembleth at my word."

5thly, We have the wise improvement that Noah made of God's warning concerning the deluge: why, his faith and fear excited him to prepare an ark: "The wise man (saith Solomon) foreseeth the evil, and hideth himself." True faith of God's operation is a sagacious grace; it takes up things not as yet seen, dangers that are out of the view of the rest of a blind world, and provides for safety against approaching dangers. So here, Noah's faith engages him to prepare an ark against the deluge. Noah had not the ark to build when the deluge came; no, it was ready for use, when the windows of heaven, and the fountains of the great deep, were opened; and the fruit and effect of his faith and fear, and diligence in preparing of the ark, was the saving of himself and his house.

Now, I do not stand so much upon the literal, as the mystical and spiritual intendment of all this. The history and mystery of the Old Testament is opened and unveiled in the New Testament. It is granted by all, that the deluge of water, whereby God destroyed the old world, was a typical representation of the wrath of God that is revealed from heaven against all the wickedness and ungodliness of the children of men, which will infallibly sweep away the wicked, and all the nations that forget God, into hell: and that Noah's ark was a type of Christ, and of that salvation that believers have in him, from the wrath of God, and the curse of the broken law; for "whosoever believeth in him, shall not perish, but have everlasting life." The apostle Peter gives us an hint, and that not an obscure one, of what I am saying, concerning this typical design of the deluge and ark, 1 Pet. iii. 19-21, "By which also he went and preached to the spirits in prison: which sometime were disobedient, when once the long-suffering of God waited in the days of Noah, while the ark was a preparing, wherein few, that is eight souls, were saved by water. The like figure whereunto, even baptism, doth also now save us (not the putting away of the filth of the flesh, but the answer of a good conscience towards God), by the resurrection of Jesus Christ." Where, by *the spirits in prison*, we are to understand the souls of the inhabitants of the old world, who, in the days of Peter, were imprisoned in hell, but in the days of Noah, they were alive in their bodies. Noah, by the direction of the spirit of Christ, went and preached to them, and warned them of the approaching deluge; but they never regarded him, but went on in their sinning trade, until the water came, and carried them away, except eight souls that were saved in the ark. Now, there is the type, and then follows the anti-type, ver. 21, "The like figure whereunto, even baptism, doth also now save us," &c.

The main doctrine that I have in view from the words, is as follows.

Doct.—"That Christ is the great New Testament Ark into which sinners must enter, if they would be saved from the deluge of divine wrath."

The method, through divine assistance, shall be as follows.

I. I would speak a little of the wrath of God, with allusion unto the universal deluge.

II. Of the warnings God has given, and is still giving, of the deluge of his wrath.

III. I would speak of Christ as the only ark wherein safety is to be found.

IV. Speak of the access that sinners have to this New Testament Ark.

V. How it is that a sinner enters into this ark, so as to be saved from the deluge.

VI. Deduce some inferences, and make some application of the whole.

I. The *first* thing is, to speak a little of the wrath of God, with allusion unto the universal deluge in the days of Noah.

1*st*, then, The sin and wickedness of the old world was the procuring cause of the deluge, Gen. vi. 5-7, "And God saw that the wickedness of man was great in the earth, and that every imagination of the thoughts of his heart was only evil continually, And it repented the Lord that he had made man on the earth, and it grieved him at his heart. And the Lord said, I will destroy man, whom I have created, from the face of the earth, both man and beast, and the creeping things, and the fowls of the air; for it repenteth me that I have made them."

Now, I say, as the sin of man procured a deluge of water, so doth it procure the deluge of the wrath of God, that is or has been revealed against all the wickedness and ungodliness of the children of men. Before sin entered into the world, God and man lived in perfect amity and friendship; Man was the darling of heaven, God's viceroy; and he gave him a sovereignty over all the works of his hands, Gen. i. 18. But no sooner had man sinned, but a dismal cloud of wrath began to hover over man's head, which had dissolved in a shower of snares, fire, and brimstone, to the destruction of all mankind, had it not been for the interposition of a second Adam, the eternal Son of God, who undertook to take away the sin of the world. For his sake, and upon the account of his satisfaction unto justice, a stop is put to the execution of divine vengeance. But that same flood of wrath will run with the greatest violence against all unbelievers, who reject him, and his great salvation, Heb. ii. 3 and x. 28, &c.

2*dly*, God did not take the inhabitants of the old world in a surprise; but gave them warning before the flood came and destroyed them: he dealt with them by the ministry of Noah for the space of one hundred and twenty years, Gen. v. 32 compare with vi. 11, in order to reclaim them, but all in vain,

Just so, God is long-suffering, and slow to wrath, towards the children of men. He doth not speedily execute judgment, like man, in a fury and rage; no, but he waits to be gracious; he warns of the wrath to come, and beseeches and entreats them to turn from their evil ways: Forty years was his spirit grieved with that generation of Israel in the wilderness, until at length he sware in his wrath that they should never enter into his rest; but many a time he turned away his wrath, Psal. lxviii. 38, before it came to that.

3*dly*, When the appointed time for the execution of the threatening against the old world came, God made the heavens and the earth to combine for their destruction; for both the fountains of the great depth from below were broken up, and the windows of heaven above were opened upon them, Gen. vii. 11.

Just so, God, who is the Lord of hosts, and doth whatsoever he wills in the army of heaven, and among the inhabitants of the earth, Dan. iv. 35, can and will arm the whole creation against impenitent sinners: he can command the earth to open its mouth, and swallow up its inhabitants, as it did Koran, Dathan, and Abiram, Numb. xvi. 31, 32; and he can call for hosts of angels, and celestial luminaries, to avenge his quarrel upon rebellious sinners, as he did in the case of Sennacherib, 2 Kings xix. 35, and the inhabitants of Canaan, Exod. xxxiii. 2.

4*thly*, The waters of the flood were irresistible. All the inhabitants of the old world, with their united force, though many of them were giants, men of huge stature and strength, Gen. vi. 4, yet they were not capable to stop the current of the flood.

Sirs, the wrath of God, when it breaks out upon Christ-despisers, cannot be stopped by all the power of angels or men: "Who hath hardened himself against God, and hath prospered?" Job ix. 4. "Who would set the briers and thorns in battle against him, he would go through them, he would consume them together, Is. xxvii. 4. "The stout-hearted are spoiled, the men of might cannot find their hands," when God contendeth, &c., Psal. lxxvi. 5.

5thly, The waters of the deluge overflowed all the refuges that the inhabitants of the old world fled to for shelter. We may easily imagine, that they would fly to the highest rocks and mountains to save themselves from the waters; but the waters swelled and rose, until it covered all the high hills and mountains on the face of the earth, under the whole heaven, Gen. vii. 18—20, there was no shelter left them.

Just so is it in the case before us. Sinners, when they hear of the wrath and vengeance of God pursuing them on the account of sin, they fly to the hills and mountains of their own making. Some fly to the mountain of general mercy: but God sweeps away that; for "he that made them will not have mercy on them, and he that formed them will shew them no favour," Is. xxvii. 11. Some fly to the refuge of an outward profession of religion, and think to find shelter there; but the water of God's wrath pursues them there, as it did the foolish virgins with their empty lamps, Matth. xxv. 6. Others they fly to the mountain of the works of the law; but the deluge pursues them there, "for by the works of the law shall no flesh be justified," Gal. ii. 16. Thus God makes "the hail to sweep away the refuge of lies," Is. xxviii. 17.

6thly, The flood was universal; it spared none but those that were in the ark. In like manner, the flood of God's wrath will destroy all that are out of Christ; "for there is none other name given under heaven among men, whereby we must be saved, but the name of Jesus," Acts iv. 12.

II. The *second* thing was, to speak of the warnings that God gives of the deluge of everlasting wrath that is to come upon all Godless and Christless sinners; for as God warned the old world of the deluge of water, 1 Pet. iii. 20, so doth he warn the inhabitants of this world, particularly of the visible church, of the wrath to come.

I shall not stay upon this, having lately had an occasion, from Job ix. 4, to present before you a great many beacons of divine wrath, that he has set up in the scriptures of truth, to warn sinners, that they split not on the same rocks on which others dashed their souls into a hell of eternal wrath and misery. No man can read his Bible, or hear the gospel preached, but he must hear of a wrath to come from God upon impenitent sinners: "Except ye repent (says Christ), ye shall all likewise perish," Luke xiii. 3. God "shall wound the head of his enemies, and the hairy scalp of such a one as goeth on still in his trespasses," Psal. lxviii. 21. "The wicked shall be turned into hell, and all the nations that forget God," Psal. ix. 17. And, of all sorts of sinners, the wrath of God will burn hottest against gospel and Christ despisers: "It shall be more tolerable for the land of Sodom and Gomorrah, in the day of judgement, than for such," Matth. x. 15. A notable word to this purpose you have, Heb. x. 28, "If they that despised Moses' law died without mercy, under two or three witnesses of how much sorer punishment, suppose ye, shall he be thought worthy, who hath trodden under foot the Son of God, and hath counted the blood of the covenant, wherewith he was sanctified, an unholy thing, and hath done despite unto the Spirit of grace."

HEB. ii. 7.—By faith Noah, being warned of God of things not seen as yet, moved with fear, prepared an ark, to the saving of his house.

THE SECOND SERMON ON THIS TEXT.

HAVING spoken to the two first heads of the method, I now go on to

III. The *third* thing proposed, which was, to speak a little of Christ, as the great New Testament Ark, that God has provided for saving sinners from the deluge of his wrath.

1st, The ark was a mean of God's preparing for the salvation of Noah and his family. It is true, Noah built the ark; but it was entirely at God's order and direction. It would never have entered into Noah's head or heart to build the ark, if God had not given him the plan of it.

Just so, Christ is a Saviour of God's providing and appointment. The plan of man's redemption by Christ was laid in the heart of God; it is the wisdom of God in a mystery. Men and angels would have been at an eternal stand, if it had been put to them, how man should be saved from the wrath of God, and the curse of the law, in a consistency with the justice, holiness, truth, and faithfulness of God. The whole creation cried, Your help is not in us. Well, but God devises a way; the Son of God shall be incarnate, and be substitute in the room of sinners; and by his obedience to death, justice shall be satisfied, and the honour of the law repaired, and " whosoever believeth in him shall not perish, but have everlasting life," John iii. 16. Psal. cxviii. 23, " This is the LORD'S DOING, it is wondrous in our eyes." We find God glorying in it as the chief of his ways, Psal. lxxxix. 19, 20, " I have laid help upon one that is mighty, I have found David my servant," &c.

2dly, The ark was very large and capacious, as is clear from the account that we have of it, Gen. vi. 14—19. And it was necessary it should be so, considering that it was the common receptacle, not only of Noah and his family, but of all sorts of beasts, birds, and living creatures, that were upon earth, and necessary provision for their subsistence, for the space of about a whole year.

But, Sirs, the New Testament Ark is far more large and capacious than Noah's ark; for he is none other than the infinite and incomprehensible God, in the person of the eternal Son, who made all things, John i. 3, compare with Heb. i. 3, and upholds them by the word of his power. As there was room and provision in the ark for all the living creatures of every kind that entered into the ark; so there is room in Christ for all that will come, be they Jew or Gentile, Barbarian, Scythian, bond or free, male or female, it is all one. Ye are welcome to enter into the New Testament Ark, John iii. 16, and x. 9.

3dly, All that entered into the ark were saved, but all that did not enter in perished, Gen. vii. 21—23. Just so is it here, Mark xvi. 16, " he that believeth in Christ shall be saved, but he that believeth not shall be damned."

4thly, Noah's ark was a piece of grand folly to the wits of the world: no doubt they would flout him and mock him as a fool, while he was a preparing the ark, to the saving of his house. Just so Christ, and the way of salvation through his death, " is to the Greeks foolishness, and to the Jews a stumbling block," 1 Cor. i. 23.

5thly, Hence it came that few, only eight souls, entered into the ark, and were saved, Gen. vii. 18. Just so is it here, Christ " is despised and rejected of men," Is. liii. 3, and therefore few come unto him, Matth. xxii. 14, " Many are called but few are chosen," chap. vii. 14, " Strait is the gate, and narrow is the way that leadeth unto life, and few there be that find it."

6thly, Although there were but few saved in the ark, yet it was a great evidence of God's love and kindness to man, that any of them were spared, when they all deserved to die, Gen. vi. 5. 2. 12. Just so here, although there are but few that are saved, yet his providing a Saviour, and saving a remnant of mankind by Christ, is a wonderful instance of his love and kindness to mankind, 1 John iv. 9, " In this was manifested the love of God towards us, because that God sent his only begotten Son into the world. that we might live through him." See John iii. 16, " God so loved the world that he gave his only begotten Son, that whosoever believeth in him should not perish, but have everlasting life."

7thly, The ark, after it had been tossed upon the waters for about seven months, at length rested upon the mountains of Ararat, Gen. viii. 4, so Christ, our New Testament Ark, after he had been tossed in this world, and torn in his name, person, miracles, and ministry, he rested from his work and warfare, in his resurrection and ascension; after he had suffered, he entered into his glory, Luke xxiv. 26, having finished the work the Father gave him to do, he rested in heaven, and is repossessed of that glory he had with the Father before the world was," John xvii. 4. 5.

8thly, They that were saved in the ark (viz. Noah and his children) became heirs of a new world, Gen. ix. 10, &c. So all that are saved by faith in Christ become heirs of God, and of glory, and are " begotten into the lively hope, to an inheritance incorruptible, and undefiled, and that fadeth not away, 1 Pet. i. 3, 4.

9thly, Noah and his family, after they were saved by the ark, got a promise, *That the water should never more destroy the earth*, Gen. ix. 9—11.; and, in token thereof, the bow was set in the clouds, ver. 12—17.

So all that fly to Christ are secured by God's covenant and promise from the wrath and curse of God, Rom. viii. 1, " There is, therefore, now no condemnation to them who are in Christ Jesus," See Is. liv. 10—12, "For the mountains shall depart, and the hills be removed, but my kindness shall not depart from thee, neither shall the covenant of my peace be removed. O thou afflicted, tossed with tempest, and not comforted, behold I will lay thy stones with fair colours, and lay thy foundations with sapphires. And I will make thy windows of agates, and thy gates of carbuncles, and all thy borders of pleasant stones." We read, Rev. iv. 3, of a rainbow about the throne of Christ, which alludes unto the transaction with Noah anent the flood.

10*thly*, All sorts of creatures, clean and unclean, were admitted into the ark, without distinction, Gen. vii. 8. 9. The ark was open to them all.

Just so is it now, under the New Testament, since the coming of Christ in the flesh, the gospel of the grace of God is preached promiscuously unto Jews and Gentiles, without any distinction. It is true, before the death of Christ, and during his personal ministry on earth, the poor Gentiles were excluded, and the disciples, when sent to preach the gospel, it was only to the cities of the Jews, but they were discharged to go into the way of the Gentiles, or to enter into any of the cities of the Samaritans, Matth. x. 5, But after his death and resurrection, their commission is enlarged, and the door is cast open unto all nations, Mark xvi. 15, "Go ye into all the world, and preach the gospel to every creature." It is true, the apostles, even after the resurrection of Christ, and the down-pouring of his Spirit in his extraordinary gifts, could not receive this commission of preaching the gospel to every creature; they continued preaching it to the Jews only, Acts x. 19, until they were cured of their mistake, by Peter's vision of beasts, clean and unclean, Acts x. 11—16, and the Holy Ghost his falling down upon the Gentiles, as well as upon the Jews, ver. 44; and thereupon they began, according to their commission, to preach the gospel to all without any distinction; and when the Jews refused the gospel, the apostles turned themselves unto the Gentiles, Acts xiii. 43—49. So that I say, as Noah admitted of beasts clean and unclean into the ark, in order to their being saved from the deluge; so our great New Testament Ark is opened to sinners of all sorts and sizes; if they be descended of the first Adam, they are all welcome to a second Adam, Prov. viii. 4, "Unto you, O men, I call, and my voice is to the sons of men." But this leads me to

IV. The *fourth* thing in the method, which was to speak a little of the door of access unto the New Testament Ark.

Noah's ark stood open until all the creatures that could not subsist in the waters had entered in, and until the deluge broke out, Gen. vii. 7—9; for, if it had been shut, no creature could have entered into it, or been saved.

Just so, if there were not a way or door of access unto Christ, no flesh could be saved. But we bring you good tidings of great joy, Luke ii. 10. Christ is a common Ark, a common Saviour, to sinners of mankind: And to encourage poor perishing sinners to come to him, I will tell you of several doors by which entrance by faith is to be had into the New Testament Ark, that you may not perish in the deluge.

1*st*, The door of the revelation of Christ, as a Saviour come into the world. What is the design of the whole scriptures of truth, from the beginning to the ending, but to make Christ known to the sons of men, in order to their believing in him, that they may be saved from the wrath to come, John xx. last, "These things are written, that ye might believe that Jesus is the Christ, the Son of God, and that believing, ye might have life through his name." John v. 39, "Search the scriptures, for in them ye think ye have eternal life, and they are they which testify of me." Sirs, Christ is evidently set forth before you in the world, read and preached, his whole righteousness and salvation is *set before you*, and brought *near to you;* and, pray, for what end? but that you may improve him to all the ends of his saving offices. They that want the bible and a preached gospel, will have far more to say for themselves than you, unto whom the word of God and the gospel of salvation is *sent*, John xv. 22, compared with Matth. x. 15, Rom. x. 14, for "how shall they believe in him of whom they have not heard? and how shall they hear without a preacher?" For this is not the case with you: for Christ is nigh to you, in your mouths and hearts, even in this word of faith which we preach, Rom. x. 8. So that the very revelation of Christ is a door of faith, especially when we declare to you, from Christ's own mouth, "that he came not into the world to condemn the world, but that the world through him might be saved," John iii. 17.

2*dly*, The incarnation of the Son of God, or his assuming our nature into a personal union with his divine nature, is a blessed door of faith for any poor perishing sinner of Adam's family. This we find is set forth for a ground of faith through the whole scriptures of truth: It was the first thing proposed to Adam and Eve immediately after the fall, when they were under awful apprehensions of present death, Gen. iii, 14. 15. (viz. the seed of the woman) shall bruise thy head, (viz. of the serpent). They were to believe that the Son of God, who was speaking to them, would, in the fulness of time, become the seed of the woman, or be incarnate, and avenge their quarrel; and the faith of this eased and quieted their spirits, because in this they saw that God was upon their side. So in the promise made to Abraham, the incarnation of the Son of God presented unto him and his posterity, Gen. xxii. 18, "In thy seed shall all the nations of the earth be blessed." Upon which the apostle, Gal. iii. 16, gives the following commentary, "He doth not speak of seeds as of many, but as of one, and to thy seed, which is Christ." In the rest of the scriptures, where these two promises are more fully opened, we find the incarnation of the Son of God was presented as a ground of faith and hope to the church of God. David, in the Psalms, frequently speaks of him as man, Psal. viii. 4, compared with Heb. ii. 6, the Son of man, and the Man of God's right hand, Psal. lxxx. 17. Isaiah speaks of him as a Child born unto us, although at the same his name is THE MIGHTY GOD, chap. ix. 6, and liii. as a man of sorrows, and acquainted with grief. Jeremiah, as a Branch of righteousness, chap. xxxiii. 15, that was to spring out of the root of Jesse, Is. xi. 1. And every where almost in the New Testament, he is presented as the Word made flesh, John i. 14; made of a woman, Gal. iv. 4; the Seed of the woman, Gen. iii. 16; born of a virgin, Matth. i. 16; Who "took not on him the nature of angels, but the seed of Abraham," Heb. ii. 16. And commonly, when he speaks of himself through the evangelists, he denominates himself by the human nature, rather than by the divine, the Son of man. One special reason of which is, as I think, because the faith of sinners could not terminate or fix upon his divine nature, but by virtue of his human nature. The hand of faith lays hold upon the skirt of the human nature, that it may thereby draw, as it were, the divine nature alongst with it, knowing that the personal union between these two natures cannot be dissolved. Now, that there is here a general ground of faith laid for all mankind that hears tell of this great mystery of godliness, God manifested in the flesh, appears, if we consider, that it was not the person, but the nature of man that Christ assumed. And the nature of man is equally related to every man and woman that possesses a true body and a reasonable soul. Insomuch that every one that hears of him is warranted to say, this is my brother, "bone of my bone, and flesh of my flesh," Gen. ii. 23, as Adam said of Eve when presented unto him, and therefore a help meet for me, ver. 20. O Sirs, consider this, and dwell upon it. Christ, by virtue of his incarnation, is our Goel or Kinsman, he is our blood relation, and he took part of your flesh, that so he might be capable to act a part for you, which none else of the human race was capable to do, even to redeem you by his blood, and by death to bruise the head of the serpent. And is not this a noble ground of faith, trust, and confidence in him? O Sirs! enter in and take possession of the New Testament Ark, by this door of his incarnation, and claim him as yours, by an appropriating faith, saying with the church, Is. ix. 6, to us (or to me) is this child born, &c. This doctrine was delivered by the angels at the birth of Christ, as good tidings of great joy unto all people, Luke ii. 10, 11, where they say to the shepherds, (not to us, but) "To you is born this day, in the city of David, a Saviour, which is Christ the Lord."

3*dly*, Another passage by which faith may enter into the New Testament Ark, is Christ's obedience to the law, which was violate, broken, and dishonoured, by the sin of the first Adam, and of all his posterity. For understanding of this you would know, that the condition upon which life was promised to Adam, and to all mankind in him, was perfect obedience unto the command of the law, "He that doth these things shall live in them," Lev. xviii. 5, compared with Gal. iii. 12. And if Adam had continued in his obedience, he and his posterity might have claimed temporal, spiritual, and eternal life, as a debt due to them (though not upon the account of the intrinsic merit of his obedience, yet) by virtue of the paction in the covenant of works. Well, man being in honour, continued not, Psal. xlix. 12, compared with Gen. iii. 6. He brake the covenant by eating the forbidden fruit; and all his children's teeth ever since have been set on edge against God, their carnal minds being enmity against God, are not subject to the law of God, Rom. viii. 7, by which means they have lost their title to that life promised in the first covenant, and are fallen under the sentence of death; and without the honour of the law, be repaired by a perfect obedience yielded unto it by man, or one in man's nature, it stands as an eternal bar in the way of life and salvation unto all mankind. Well, Christ, the eternal Son of God, as man's Kinsman and Surety, undertakes to repair the broken law, saying to his Father, "Lo, I come, in the volume of the book it is written of me, I delight to do thy will, O my God; yea, thy law is within my heart," Psal. xl. 7, 8, compared with Heb. x. 7, as if he had said, 'Let my ear be bored unto thy service in this matter, for it is the firm purpose of my heart to fulfil all righteousness that the law requires of mankind sinners.' And accordingly, in the fulness of time, he is not only made of a woman, but made under the law, Gal. iv. 4, and in our stead and room magnifies the law and makes it honourable, Is. xlii. 21; by which means, 'all legal bars and impediments lying in the way of salvation and life, from the part of the command of the law is made up again, and the law as fully satisfied as though it had never been broken, and the title to the life promised in the covenant of works comes to stand in the person of our common Kinsman and blood-relation;' upon which account, his righteousness and salvation is published and brought near unto all; yea even unto them that are stout hearted and far from righteousness, Is. xlvi., at the close. And you see in the fortieth psalm, after he had said to his Father, in the council of peace, "I delight to do thy will, O my God, yea, thy law is within my heart," immediately he adds, ver. 9, 10, "I have preached righteousness in the great congregation, I have not refrained my lips, O, Lord, thou knowest, I have not hid thy righteousness within my heart," &c. Thus you see, that all who have the gospel preached unto them have a right of access to his righteousness or perfect obedience, to the law; and whoever they be that believe in him as the Lord, our righteousness, Jer. xxiii. 6, they enter into the New Testament Ark, and are saved from the deluge of God's wrath; "For there is no condemnation to them that are in Christ Jesus," because the righteousness of the law is fulfilled in them, Rom. viii. 1, 3, 4, and x. 4, Christ becomes the end of the law for righteousness to them. Hence is that of the apostle, 2 Cor. v. at the close, "God was in Christ, not imputing their trespasses to them; for he hath made him to be sin for us, who knew no sin, that we might be made the righteousness of God in him.'

HEB. xi, 7,—By faith Noah, being warned of God of things not seen as yet. moved with fear, prepared an ark to the saving of his house.

THE THIRD SERMON ON THIS TEXT.

AFTER resuming of what is above, I go on to tell you,
4thly, The death of Christ, or his atoning blood, is another door by which poor sinners do enter into the New Testament Ark, and are saved from the deluge of divine wrath. We are said to come by faith unto the blood of sprinkling, Heb. xii. 24, "and to enter into the

holiest by the blood of Jesus," chap. x. 19. Christ as crucified is evidently set forth, Gal. iii. 1, before all, in the dispensation of the gospel; hence the apostle Paul tells the Corinthians, "That he determined not to know any thing among them, save Jesus Christ, and him crucified," 1 Cor. ii. 2. Christ says, speaking of his death, "And I, if I be lifted up from the earth, will draw all men unto me," John xii. 32. And accordingly, when the apostles went through the nations preaching the gospel, what was the great thing they continually harped [insisted or dwelt] upon? "We (says he) preach Christ crucified, unto the Jews a stumbling-block, and unto the Greeks foolishness, but unto them which are called, both Jews and Greeks, Christ the power of God, and the wisdom of God," 1 Cor. i. 23, 24.

For clearing this matter of the death of Christ as a ground of faith, you would know that there is a threefold sufficiency in the death of Christ.

1. An intrinsic sufficiency arising from the infinite dignity of his person who suffered, being the infinite God in the person of the Son, clothed with a veil of flesh; and in this respect, there was such a value in his death and blood, that it was sufficient, not only to redeem all mankind, but ten thousand worlds, supposing their existence and fall too, if it had been so ordained. But,

2. There is an ordinate sufficiency, whereby the death and satisfaction of Christ is limited unto the elect, and in this respect Christ declares that he laid down his life for the sheep, John x. 15.

3. There is a legal sufficiency, by which the law and its penalty is fully answered; insomuch that neither law nor justice is any obstruction or bar in the way of a sinner's salvation, that believes in him; but on the contrary, that moment a sinner believes in him, 'all the charges that the law and justice had against the poor sinner, they are all cancelled,' Gal. iii. 10, Col. ii. 14, Rom viii. 1, 33, 34.

Now, when we speak of the death of Christ as a ground of faith, we abstract entirely from the ordinate sufficiency of it for the elect; for that being among the secret things that belong unto the Lord, Deut. xxix. 29, it can never be a ground of faith unto any man, no, not unto the elect themselves, that Christ died for the elect, otherwise a man behoved to know his election, before he adventured to believe, which is a thing absolutely impossible, in regard our election of God is a thing that can only be known by obeying the call of the gospel; hence we are commanded, 2 Pet. i. 10, to give all diligence to make our calling and (then) our election sure. And therefore seeing it is not the ordinate sufficiency of the death of Christ that we are commanded to preach, which would lead us in among the secret decrees of God, which do not belong unto us, it must needs be the intrinsic and legal sufficiency of the death of Christ, that is to be held forth, as the ground and foundation of faith to sinners of mankind. Hence are these universal and extensive expressions in scripture, John i. 29, "Behold the Lamb of God, which taketh away the sins of the world." 1 John ii. 2, "He is the propitiation for our sins, and not for our sins only, but for the sins of the whole world." Tim. iv. 10, "He is the Saviour of all men, especially of those who believe." All mankind have such an interest in the death and satisfaction of Christ, as the devils have not. Yea, considering that it was the human nature, that was the sacrifice, and that all mankind are related to him, through his taking hold of the human nature (as was said), it is impossible to conceive how all mankind, especially gospel-hearers, should not have an interest in his death, I mean, such as warrants them to say, in faith, "He loved me, and gave himself for me," Gal. ii. 20. "He was delivered for our offences," Rom. iv. 25. "He was wounded for our transgressions, bruised for our iniquities," &c., Is. liii. 5. And upon this account I conceive that the death of Christ, and the benefits flowing therefrom, is said to be a feast made unto all people, of fat things full of marrow, of wines on the lees well refined, Is. xxv. 6. This is the carcase unto which all the hungry eagles of mankind should gather, and feed to the full, Matth. xxiv. 28. Hence it is, Luke xiv. 21, 23, "The poor, the maimed, the halt, and the blind, that lie about the hedges and highways, are called, yea compelled, to come in," and feast with him.

5thly, The great and precious promises of the covenant of grace, especially the absolute promises (which have no manner of condition annexed to them), are another door by which faith enters into the New Testament Ark, and saves the soul from the deluge of divine wrath. A promise of Christ was the first door opened to Adam and Eve, immediately after the fall, Gen. iii. 15, It (viz. the seed of the woman) shall bruise thy head (viz. the serpent's) after the same manner the door of faith was opened to Abraham, Gen. xxii. 18, "And in thy seed shall all the nations of the earth be blessed." And (in that promised seed) "I will be a God unto thee, and to thy seed after thee," chap. xvii. 7. All the other promises are so many streams and little rivulets of grace that flow out of the womb of these two promises; such as that, Is. xliv. 3, "For I will pour water upon him that is thirsty, and floods upon the dry ground," Jer. xxiv. 7, "I will give them a heart to know me, that I am the Lord, Ezek. xxxvi. 25-27, "Then will I sprinkle clean water upon you, and ye shall be clean: and from all your filthiness and from all your idols will I cleanse you; a new heart also will I give you," &c., "And I will put my Spirit within you, and cause you to walk in my statutes," Hos. xiv. 4, "I will heal their backsliding, I will love them freely." Now, it is by virtue of these great and precious promises of the new covenant, that we receive and apply Christ, and his righteousness and fulness, as our excellent confession of faith well expresses it; and therefore I call this promise of God a door by which we enter into the New Testament Ark.

For further clearing of this matter, you would know and consider these few following particulars.

1. Ever since the fall of man, and the discovery of his purpose of grace, God has dealt with him in the way of a free and gratuitous promise, as has been just now cleared.

2. The truth and faithfulness of God is engaged in his promise, first, to Christ immediately as the covenant Head, and dispensed and given out to us in him, by him, and through him. God had never made a promise to any of the race of Adam, if he had not undertaken

to fulfil the broken law, and satisfy justice for the sin of man; and upon that condition, God becomes a promising God to Christ, and to us on his account: hence all the promises of God are said to be in him. Christ has fulfilled the condition of all the promises, and hence they come out to us freely, without money and without price, Is. lv. 1.

3. The very end of a promise is, that it may be believed and rested upon as a security to those to whom it is made and granted: if it be believed, and rested upon, we receive the benefit of it, but if it be not believed, it is rejected, and the promiser is not bound, but is loosed from any obligation by his promise. If you or I grant a bond or a bill to another for the payment of a sum of money, in case he to whom the bill or bond is granted, will not have the money, in that case the granter of the bond or bill is free, and is under no more obligation; Just so in the case in hand, God grants us the benefit of his promise, and registrates it in the scriptures for the greater security, and is bound by his faithfulness to fulfil his promise, to every one who accepts of his bill, and sues for payment at a throne of grace, employing Christ as his Advocate for a forthcoming. But the man that refuses God's promise, rejects it as an insufficient security, or neglects to seek payment, or do not state Christ as his Advocate, he loses the benefit of the promise, and affronts a God of truth, and is as if his promise were not worth a button; and is it any wonder that God makes such an one to know his breach of promise? And yet his faithfulness is not made of none effect, God will be true, and every man a liar, Rom. iii. 4.

4. To cut off all handle from unbelief, the promises of God carry a general indorsement or direction to all the race of Adam, and especially to all the visible church, Luke ii. 9, "I bring you good tidings of great joy which shall be to all people." Wisdom's promising voice is to men, and to the sons of men: "To you is the word of this salvation sent." The apostle Peter, Acts ii. 38, when he is preaching to a company of men who had imbrued their hands in the blood of Christ, he calls them to repent, "repent every one of you, and be baptized, in the name of Jesus Christ, for the remission of sins;" and to lead them to repentance, he discovers to them the mercy of God in Christ, by presenting to them the promise of pardon in the blood of the Messiah, which they had shed, saying, ver. 39, "The promise is unto you, and to your children, and to all that are afar off, even as many as the Lord our God shall call." And, what Peter said to his hearers, that I say unto every one of you, "The promise is unto you, and to your children." And as the apostle Paul tells the Hebrews, chap. iv. 1, The promise is left to you as God's charter for the good land of glory, as God's promise was given to Israel as a security or charter for the land of Canaan; so God's promise is our charter for eternal life, and "therefore let us fear, lest a promise being left us of entering into his rest, any of us should seem to come short of it." But as that generation of men that came out of Egypt could not enter in, because of their unbelief; just so, there are many, many, that shall never enter into the land of glory above, because of their unbelief; they have a good right, but they lose the benefit of their right by unbelief, as Israel did, who believed not in God, and trusted not in his salvation, Psal.

lxxviii. 22; so that you see the promise is a door for entering into the Ark. O, do not shut the door of faith upon yourselves, lest God should shut it also, and swear in his wrath that ye shall not enter it, but be left to perish in the deluge, Psal. xcv. 7.

Object. 'I still doubt if I have a right to close with the promise; I am afraid that I be but guilty of presumption.' *Answ.* It can never be presumption to do what God commands you, " and this is his commandment, that we should believe in the name of his Son Jesus Christ." And if the promise does not belong to you, and to all to whom it is revealed, as a ground of faith, it is impossible to conceive, how it is that an unbeliever makes God a liar, John v. 10, by disobeying it,' for no man is obliged to believe a promise that is not made to him.

6thly, Another door by which faith enters into the New Testament Ark, is the Father's gift of Christ unto mankind lost. 'There is such a gift of Christ in the word as warrants any man that reads it, to receive, appropriate, and apply Christ and all his purchased salvation to himself in particular, and to rejoice in him as his own property, Is. lv. 4, " Behold I have given him for a Witness unto the people, a Leader and Commander unto the people," Is. xlii. 6, " I will give thee for a covenant of the people, for a light of the Gentiles," chap. xlix. 6, " I will also give thee for a light to the Gentiles, that thou mayest be my salvation unto the end of the earth;" John iii. 16, " God so loved the world, that he gave his only begotten Son, that whosoever believeth in him should not perish but have everlasting life," John vi. 32, " My Father giveth you the true bread from heaven," Is. ix. 6, " Unto us a child is born, unto us a son is given." From these, and many other places, it appears, there is such an universal gift or grant of Christ unto sinners of mankind, as makes it lawful and warrantable for every one to receive, use, and apply him, for all the ends for which he is given; for wisdom, righteousness, sanctification, and redemption. No man doubts of his right to take or receive a gift when it is held out to him, and he bidden take it; and we have a common proverb among us, Have or take will make a deaf man hear. It argues a very strange infatuation, among men and women, that they should so readily grasp at a gift of this world's good, and yet be backward in receiving God's unspeakable gift, that would make them up in time and through all eternity. If I had this house full of gold and silver to distribute and scatter among you, and were calling every man and woman, young and old, to come and get as much as they want, I am sure there would be few or none in that case that would draw back, every one would be more forward than another, to receive or gather. Well, Sirs, why so forward to receive worldly riches that take wings and fly away? and yet refuse to receive Christ and his unsearchable riches which we are a scattering among you in the dispensation of the word! Here is the great gift of heaven, without money or price. Here is the gift of life, " for he that hath the Son hath life," 1 John v. 12. Here is the gift of righteousness, that will entitle you to God, to heaven, and glory, and all the good of the covenant. Here is given gold tried in the fire, Rev. iii. 18, that moth and rust cannot corrupt. Matth. vi. 20. Here is the best robe, Luke xv. 22. White raiment, Rev. iii. 18, clothing that doth not wax old. Here is the merchandise of wisdom, that is better than the merchandise of silver, and her gain, which is better than fine gold, Prov. iii. 1, 4.

You particularly that are young children and bairns, you are perhaps longing for to-morrow, being the first Monday, and the first day of the new-year 1750, that you may go to your friends and acquaintances to ask your new-year's gift. I would give you my advice before it come, and that is, that before ever you go to man or woman to ask any thing, go first to God, " who giveth liberally to all men, and upbraideth not." James i. 5, and ask your new-year's gift from him. *Quest.* What shall we ask from him? will you put words in our mouth? *Answ.* I will tell you what to say and ask as your new-year's gift from God. Go to God, and say, ' Lord give me grace to improve the new-year to thy glory, and my own eternal good and advantage, if thou spare me, Lord, give me thyself, to be my God and portion for ever, for thou hast said, I am the Lord thy God, Exod. xx. 2, Lord, give me Christ, and let him be my Prophet, Priest, and King, Surety, Mediator, and Advocate. Lord, give me thy Spirit, for thou givest thy Spirit to them that ask him, Luke xi. 19, Lord give me the new heart, and the new spirit, for thou hast promised it, Ezek. xxxvi., Lord give me a heart to know thee, that thou art the Lord. Lord, put thy fear in my heart, that I may never depart from thee, Jer. xxxii. 40. Lord, forgive me all my sins, and lead me not into temptation, but deliver me from all evil, Luke xi. 4, especially from the evil of sin, which is the abominable thing which thy soul hates. Lord, teach me how to answer my chief end, how to glorify thee here, so as I may enjoy thee eternally hereafter.'

Now, I say, go to God in the morning of the new-year's day, and seek these and the like things from him, as your new-year's gift. And to encourage you to be in earnest, consider, (1.) These soul gifts are far better than any thing your friends can give you. (2.) Your God is liberal, and more ready to give than you are to ask. John xvi 24, " Hitherto (says Christ), ye have asked nothing in my name, ask, and ye shall receive." Your heavenly Father has a full hand and a free heart, Matth. vii. 7, " Ask, and it shall be given you; seek, and ye shall find; knock, and it shall be opened unto you." (3.) The Lord loves young children to be about his hand, Psal. xxxiv. 2, " Come, ye children, hearken unto me, I will teach you the fear of the Lord," Prov. viii. 17, " I love them that love me, and these that seek me early shall find me." (4.) God's new-year's gift will make you up for all your days, yea, for all eternity; and what he gives of saving grace, he will never take it back again, " for the gifts and calling of God are without repentance," Rom. xi. 29. Only be importunate with the Lord, and do not take a nay-say; say as Jacob, Gen. xxxii. 27, " Lord, I will not let thee go, except thou bless me;" and whatever you ask of God, seek it all for Christ's sake; for, says Christ, John xiv. 14, " If ye shall ask any thing in my name, I will do it;" and though you get not what you ask at first, yet be not discouraged, but go again, and again, and again unto him. If you get not your new-year's gift the first day, go again the next day, and the next day, and continue in prayer, and ye shall find the Lord; for he has said, Jer. xxix. 12, 13, "Then shall ye call upon me, and ye shall go and pray unto me, and I will hearken unto you, and ye shall seek me, and ye shall find me, when ye shall search for me with all your heart," and with all your soul.

Now, before we part, I have a word to say to you that are old people, and of a riper age.

The first day or first week of the new-year, I understand uses to be very ill spent in eating and drinking, and that perhaps to excess. I would give you that caveat or warning that Christ gave to all that profess his name, Luke xxi. 34, "Take heed, lest at any time your hearts be overcharged with surfeiting and drunkenness, and cares of this life, and so that day (the day of death and judgment) come upon you unawares." It is a bad requital to God for his goodness these bygone years, to begin the next year with an abusing yourselves, and abusing the good creatures of God with any manner of excess; and therefore, let your moderation appear in all things, for the Lord is at hand, Philip. iv. 5.

HEB. xi, 7.—By faith Noah, being warned of God of things not seen as yet, moved with fear, prepared an ark to the saving of his house.

THE FOURTH SERMON ON THIS TEXT.

WE read, Deut. xxvii. 11, 12, and downwards, of two great mountains, viz. Mount Ebal, and Mount Gerizzim; the one was a mount of cursing, and the other of blessing. Upon these two mountains God sets a two-fold throne; upon Mount Ebal he places a throne of justice, and on the other a throne of grace. From Mount Ebal there is an eruption of woes and curses against all mankind, which, like the deluge, overspreads the face of the whole earth, "for all have sinned and come short of the glory of God," Rom. iii. 23, and therefore the wrath of God, like the swelling deluge, pursues them wherever they go, until they fly to the mount of blessings, Mount Gerizzim or Mount Zion, where stands the covenant of grace, the New Testament Ark, Jesus Christ, from which there comes a cry to the poor sinner, that knows not what to do to be saved from the curse of the law, and the wrath of the Lawgiver, "Turn ye to your strong holds," Zech. ix. 12, enter into the Ark; and whosoever doth so, "shall not perish, but have everlasting life," John iii. 16.

I have been essaying to cast up the doors of the New Testament Ark, that poor law-condemned, justice-condemned, and conscience-condemned sinners may take the benefit of it, and be saved from the deluge. I have named and cast open six of them. (1,) The door of the revelation of Christ in the word, for he is revealed that sinners may believe in him and be saved. (2.) The door of the incarnation, whereby God becomes our Kinsman in the person of his Son, that we may take hold of the skirt of him that was a jew, Zech. viii. 23, and go with him and be saved. (3.) The door of his perfect obedience to the law, in the room of the first Adam, whereby the title to eternal life, which was lost by the disobedience of the first Adam, is again recovered; and thus he has power to give eternal life to whom he will, as we see he himself declares, John v. 21, 22. (4.) The door of his satisfaction, whereby the hand-writing of the curse that was against us, and contrary to us, is cancelled, and the bond lying in the hand of justice, which bound us over to wrath, is retired, Gal. iii. 13, " Christ hath redeemed us from the curse of the law, being made a curse for us." (5.) I told you, that the great and precious, especially the absolute unconditional promises of the covenant of grace (every one of them), is a door of entrance into the New Testament Ark; all which promises come indorsed to sinners that are afar off, and to them that are near, Is. lvii. 19, Acts ii. 39, for their encouragement to take hold of them as ropes of salvation, whereby they may be drawn up out of the ruining deluge of wrath, into the ARK Christ, in whom all the promises of God are yea and amen, 2 Cor. i. 20. (6.) The last door that I named was the door of God, the Father's donation or gift of his Son as a Saviour, by price and power; by the price of his blood and the power of his Spirit. He hath given him to be a Saviour, a Witness, Leader, Commander. And for what end is a gift given and tendered, but that it may be received? These I have already spoke to.

7thly, I proceed now to open a *seventh* door by which faith enters into the New Testament Ark, and that is, the name of God, as it is revealed through Christ in the glorious gospel: "The name of the Lord is a strong tower, unto which the righteous runneth," Prov. xviii. 10, and to which the sinner may run and be saved. Psal. ix. 9, "They that know thy name will put their trust in thee:" he that walketh in darkness, and hath no light, he is called to "trust in the name of the Lord, and to stay himself upon his God," Is. l. 10. From these and the like scriptures you see, that the name of a God in Christ is given as a blessed ground of faith, trust, and confidence: and no wonder, considering that God is in Christ reconciling the world to himself, not imputing their trespasses unto them," 2 Cor. v. 19. But I shall at present insist a little on that name of God which he revealed and proclaimed unto Moses, when he condescended, at his request, to make all his glory to pass before him, Exod. xxxiv. 6, 7, "And the Lord passed by before him, and proclaimed, The Lord, the Lord God, merciful and gracious, long-suffering, and abundant in goodness and truth, keeping mercy for thousands, forgiving iniquity and transgression and sin, and that will by no means clear the guilty."

Now, let us consider this name of the Lord a little, and see whether there be not enough in it to put unbelief for ever out of countenance.

It is a most certain truth, that ignorance of God, and of what he is in Christ, is the very mother of unbelief, by which we are turned away from the living God as an enemy. Satan knows this very well; and therefore his great slight and cunning is, to fix the eye of a sinner, whose conscience is awakened, upon its sinful, miserable, and deplorable condition, and represent God unto him as a God of inexorable justice, an avenging enemy, a consuming fire, that so he may fill it with desperation, and put it in the same case with himself; and he endeavours with might and main to hide and conceal the revelation that God has made of his name through Christ, according to what the apostle says, 2 Cor. iv. 4, "The God of this world hath blinded the minds of them that believe not, lest the light of the glorious gospel of Christ, who is the image of God, should shine unto them." But in spite of the devil, and all his art and cunning, to smother the name of God in Christ, let us study to display the name of the Lord, as he has himself proclaimed it in that place just now cited, and see if there be not a noble and glorious ground of faith and confidence for the sinner, however desperate and deplorable his case may appear to be in his own sense.

1. You see that his first name is a name of glory, greatness, and majesty, THE LORD, THE LORD GOD. This, I say, is a name of great and glorious majesty, and is promised or set forth in the front, to let us know what God is in himself; that he is the infinite, eternal, and unchangeable Being; that he "fills heaven and earth," Jer. xxiii. 24; that "he hath heaven for his throne, and the earth for his footstool," Is. lxvi. 1; that "all the inhabitants of the world are reputed before him but as nothing," Dan. iv. 35, yea, "less than nothing, and vanity," Is. xl. 17. God, in the *first* place, I say, will have us to know what he is in himself, and how we, and all creatures, "do live, and move, and have our being in him," Acts xvii. 28. These, and the like impressions of the glorious majesty of God, are the foundation of all true faith, and of all religious worship and adoration. The soul gets such views and discoveries of the glorious majesty of God, as strikes it with a becoming awe and reverence of him; so that the soul cries out, as Moses, Exod. xvi 11, "Who is like unto thee, O Lord, among the Gods: who is like thee, glorious in holiness, fearful in praises, doing wonders?" Oh! who "shall ascend his holy hill, or abide in his tabernacle?" And like the poor publican, under a sense of sin, and apprehensions of the infinite majesty of God, stands afar off, smites on his breast, and cries, "God be merciful to me a sinner," Luke xviii. 13. But now, though this name of majesty, power, and greatness, be first presented to humble, and abase the soul in its own eyes; yet see what a glorious train of amiable names do follow it, in order to revive the heart of the humble, and the spirit of the contrite one; "The Lord, the Lord God, merciful," &c. It is pleasant to observe how every one of his relative names do answer the soul's case and necessity.

2. MERCIFUL. The case of the poor soul is such, that it is crying out. 'Oh! I am wretched and miserable beyond expression or conception: I am indeed a pitiful object: I am brought low by my sin in Adam, and in my own person; Psal. lxix. 2, "I sink in deep mire, where there is no standing." I know and believe indeed, that Jehovah, the strong and almighty God, is able to keep and deliver me: but what says that to me, since I do not know but his almighty arm may exert itself in my destruction as readily as in my salvation?' Well,

to this the Lord answers, in that name, "I am the Lord God, MERCIFUL." 'If thou be miserable, I am merciful as well as strong: justice is my strange work, my strange act, Is. xxviii. 21, but I delight in mercy, Mic. vii. 18, "My bowels are turned within me, and my repentings are kindled together," Hos. xi. 8, until I get a vent to my mercy?' Pray, Sirs, what is mercy? but a strong bent and inclination in God to do good to and help a sinner in misery. Misery is the very proper object and subject upon which mercy doth work; and therefore, 'O miserable sinner! trust in my mercy flowing out through the blood of my eternal Son.' But a third title is his name,

3. GRACIOUS. May the poor guilty and convinced sinner say, 'I am one of the most miserable creatures upon earth; I am destitute of all grace, of all goodness; I have no qualifications to commend me unto a God of mercy.' Well but, says the Lord, 'I am GRACIOUS. I do not seek any grace, goodness, or qualifications, in the sinner, to commend him to me; but I would have the poor, blind, naked, miserable sinner, to come to get, and not to give; to come and get gold tried in the fire, white raiment, eye-salve, Rev. iii. 18, milk and honey, Is. li. 1, and all grace and goodness from me, *gratis*, freely, "without money, and without price." Do not seek for faith, repentance, love, humility, brokenness of heart, as a price to purchase grace and favour at the hand of God; but come, destitute of all grace, "to the throne of grace, that ye may obtain mercy, and find grace," Heb. iv. 16. But,

4. May the poor convinced and awakened sinner say, 'I have been a presumptuous sinner, and have gone on so long in a tract and trade of sin and rebellion against God, that I am afraid God will endure me no longer; my day of grace is over and gone.' Well but, says the Lord, "I am LONG-SUFFERING: My patience towards sinners is not soon worn out. It is true indeed I did not suffer long the indignities that were done to me by the angels that fell; for that very moment they sinned they were turned out of heaven, and laid up in everlasting chains of darkness, in which they are "reserved unto the judgment of the great day," Jude 6. But this is not my method of procedure towards sinners of Adam's family, whose nature I have assumed, when I passed by the angels that fell. I am not willing that any of them should perish, but that all should come to repentance, 2 Pet. iii. 9. "I have no pleasure in their death, but rather that they turn unto me and live," Ezek. xxxiii. 11. And, therefore, "I wait that I may be gracious," Is. xxx. 18. I stand yet at the door and knock; and if any man, be what he will, will "hear my voice, and open the door, I will come into him, and will sup with him, and he with me," Rev. iii. 20. What is long-suffering! but patience extended and stretched out beyond all expectation, and beyond all deserving. 'If I had had a mind to cut thee off, and cast thee into hell, I have not wanted occasion and opportunity; but I have hitherto borne with all thy folly and wickedness, and to this day "I stand with the outstretched arms of love and mercy, crying, Behold me, behold me," Is. lxv, 1, "Turn ye, turn ye, why will ye die?" Ezek. xxxiii. 2. But,

5. May the poor doubting soul say, 'There may, has been, and is, such an abounding of sin and wickedness with me, that my sin is like unto the great mountains, it is gone up into the heavens, and cries for wrath and vengeance like the sin of Sodom; and therefore I need look for nothing but indignation and wrath.' Well but, says the Lord, Let it be so that thou art abundant in wickedness, my name is ABUNDANT IN GOODNESS. As if he had said, 'Thy wickedness and sinfulness, though it be great, yet it is but the wickedness and sinfulness of a finite creature; but my goodness is the goodness of an infinite God, that can never never be exhausted; and therefore come to me, and get all thy wants supplied, according to my riches in glory, by Christ Jesus. My goodness is such, that I am good even to the evil and unthankful: I make the sun to rise, and the rain to fall, on the evil and on the good, upon the just and unjust, Matth. v. 45. My goodness extends unto all: and therefore come, O come, open thy mouth wide and I will fill it, Psal. lxxxi. 10. Oh! taste and see how good I am, Psal. xxxiv. 8. My treasures are full, and they are open: O, therefore, whosoever will, let him take of my goodness freely. Oh! eat ye that which is good, and let thy soul delight itself in the abundance of my goodness, Is. lv. 2. "I satisfy the desire of the longing soul," Psal. cvii. 9.

6. May the poor soul say, "I can receive no good at the hand of the Lord; for I have an evil heart of unbelief, that calls his truth and faithfulness in question. I see indeed great and precious promises in the word, but I dare not lay claim to them: I doubt and fear that I may not meddle with them; and, when I presume to meddle with them, my unbelieving heart draws back my hand, saying, "His promise fails for evermore:" and thus I lose the benefit of God's promise.' Well, says God, 'To cure thee, O man, of thy unbelief, I present my name to thee, not only as abundant in goodness, but IN TRUTH. My name is faithful and true, Rev. xix, 11, "Righteousness is the girdle of my loins, and faithfulness the girdle of my reins," Is. xi. 5. "It is impossible for me to lie," Tit. i. 2. "My faithfulness is established in the very heavens," Psal. xxxvi. 5. Yea, "heaven and earth shall pass away; but one jot, or one tittle, of my word shall not fall to the ground," Matth. v. 18, and therefore thou mayest, with the greatest safety, trust my word of promise. It is not a thing that I can come and go upon: it is not yea to-day, and nay to-morrow; but it is always yea and amen. 2 Cor. i. 17, 18. And therefore believe the promise; set to the seal to it; for thou canst not put a greater honour upon me, than to set to the seal that I am true, John iii. 33. Therefore, "Believe and see the salvation of God," Is. lii. 10.

7. O, may the poor trembling soul say, 'What if God has shut up his tender mercies in wrath, and so will be favourable no more?' Psal. lxxvii. 7, 9. Unto this it is answered, I KEEP MERCY FOR THOUSANDS, *q. d.* 'I have extended mercy to thousands, that is, innumerable multitudes; and yet my treasures of grace and mercy are as full as ever, and I am as ready to extend my mercy to thousands of persons, yea, thousands of generations, as ever; "Whosoever believes in my name, shall not perish, but have everlasting life,"

John iii. 16. "As the heavens are higher than the earth, so are my thoughts higher than your thoughts," Is. lv. 9.

8. Might the sinner say, 'My sins are so many, they have been so multiplied and highly aggravated, that I fear he will never forgive me.' Unto this the Lord answers, I PARDON INIQUITY, TRANSGRESSION, AND SIN, *i. e.* all manner of sin and provocation that can be thought on; and though your sins be red as scarlet and crimson, I will make them as white as snow, and as wool, Is. i, 18. There is plenteous redemption with me that I may be sought unto; and therefore fear not, only believe; for this is my prerogative, that I love to display, "I, even I, am he that blotteth out thy transgressions for my own sake, and will not remember thy sins," Is. xliii. 25.

Thus you see what a wide door is opened in the New Testament Ark, or what a noble ground of faith is laid in that name of God proclaimed in Moses.

But now, because sinners are ready, like the spider, to suck poison out of this rich declaration of the name of God, merciful and gracious, and to turn his grace unto wantonness, saying, 'If this be the case, we will sin, that grace may abound, Rom. vi. 1, we need not fear the wrath of such a merciful God:" Therefore observe what an awful word immediately follows, WHO WILL BY NO MEANS CLEAR THE GUILTY, *q. d.* 'The design of all this grace and mercy which I have proclaimed, is to lead sinners to repentance, through an apprehension of my mercy in Christ; but if any shall abuse my name, Merciful and Gracious, to encourage themselves in a way of sin and rebellion against my authority, let them know that I will by no means clear such persons: No, no, he "is condemned already, and my wrath abideth on him," John iii. 18, 36. And when "he turns this grace unto wantonness, he but treasures up wrath against the day of wrath, and the revelation of the righteous judgement of God," Rom. ii. 5. And therefore, " Let the wicked forsake his way, and the unrighteous man his thoughts, Is. lv. 7, " and let him return unto the Lord," from this consideration, that "I am the Lord, the Lord God, merciful and gracious; fury is not in me," Is. xxvii. 4. I do not delight in the death of sinners, Ezek. xxxiii. 2, but am ready to shew mercy to thousands. But if he will harden himself in sin because I am merciful and gracious, he will do it to his cost; for " who would set the briars and thorns against me in battle? I would go through them, I would burn them together," Is. xxvii. 4. " But let him take hold of my strength (the man of my right hand), that he may make peace with me, and he shall make peace with me," Is. lv. 7.

HEB. xi. 7.—By faith Noah, being warned of God of things not seen as yet, moved with fear, prepared an ark, to the saving of his house.

THE FIFTH SERMON ON THIS TEXT.

I AM speaking of Christ, the New Testament Ark, into which sinners are to enter, in order to their being saved from the deluge of divine wrath and vengeance. Sirs, I would not wish to have the blood of any soul in this audience, or under my charge, upon my head: and therefore I have been essaying to shew you a way of escape, and for this end I have already essayed to open seven doors by which you may enter by faith into this New Testament Ark. I have yet a few more to open: and O that, while I am opening them, God may persuade and enable you to enter in and be saved.

1st, then, The commission Christ got from his Father, to save and redeem lost sinners of Adam's family, is a pleasant door by which entrance is to be had into the New Testament Ark. He did not take this office unto himself, but was called of God, as was Aaron, Heb. v. 4, Is. xlii. 6, "I, the Lord, have called thee in righteousness, and will hold thine hand, and will help thee." You know, when a man is regularly called or ordained unto any office, it is a sufficient warrant for any man to employ him in his office; and when he is employed, he is obliged to discharge the duties of his office unto those that employ him: Well, Sirs, this is the very case with Christ. And, to clear this, consider these particulars.

1. He was elected unto his office as a Saviour, Is. xlii. 1, "Behold my servant whom I uphold, mine elect, in whom my soul delighteth." Hence he tells us, Prov. viii. 23, That he "was set up from everlasting, from the beginning, or ever the earth was."

2. He was anointed, fitted, and furnished, with all gifts, graces, and endowments, necessary for the discharge of his saving work. Hence he himself declares, Is. lxi. 6, "The spirit of the Lord God is upon me, because the Lord hath anointed me to preach good tidings to the meek." Is. xlii. 5, "I have (says the Father) put my spirit upon him, he shall bring forth judgment to the Gentiles: and accordingly the spirit was given him without measure, John iii. 34, and he received gifts for men, he ascended up on high, Psal. lxviii. 18.

3. His Father actually sent him into the world upon the great errand of redemption, Is. lxi. 1, "He hath sent me to proclaim liberty to the captives, and the opening of the prison to them that were bound, to proclaim the acceptable year of the Lord." A jubilee of release unto all the captives of Sin and Satan, and the day of vengeance of our God, viz.: vengeance upon the old serpent whose head he came to bruise; for, "for this purpose he was manifested, that he might destroy the works of the devil," 1 John, iii. 3.

4. He voluntarily accepted of his Father's commission, to come upon our errand; and with alacrity and cheerfulness came, "leaping upon the mountains, and skipping upon the hills," Cant. ii. 8. He set his face like a flint, Is. l. 7, against all storms that blew upon him, from heaven, earth, and hell; and never fainted nor was discouraged, until he had "finished the work which his Father gave him to do."

5. He opens his commission, and declares himself to be the Sent of God, the great Ambassador of heaven, to negociate in the great affair of peace, pardon, and salvation to lost sinners. John iii. 17, "God sent not his Son into the world to condemn the world, but that the world through him might be saved." John iv. 34, "My meat is to do the will of him that sent me, and to finish his work." John xii. 44, 45, Jesus cried and said, "He that believeth on me, believeth not

on me, but on him that sent me; and he that seeth me, seeth him that sent me.

6. He not only opens his commission, but shews his Father's seal appended to his commission, John vi. 27, "Him hath God the Father sealed." He was solemnly sealed at his solemn inauguration, when baptised by John in Jordan, Matth. iii. at the close, when the heavens opened, and the Spirit of God descended in the likeness of a dove, and his Father testified concerning him, with an audible voice, saying, "This is my beloved Son, in whom I am well pleased." Every miracle he wrought, in raising the dead, opening the eyes of the blind, opening the ears of the deaf, curing all manner of diseases by a touch of his hand, or a word of his mouth, his resurrection from the dead, and pouring out of his spirit upon his disciples in the day of Pentecost, endowing them with power from on high, &c., all these, and many other things, were solemn seals appended to his commission.

7. As he himself was sent and commissioned by his Father, so sends he his apostles and other ministers to proclaim and publish the gospel of the grace of God unto all the world. "As my Father hath sent me, even so send I you," John xx. 21. And what commission gives he them? Mark xvi. 15, "Go ye (says he) unto all the world, and preach the gospel to every creature," Matth. xxviii. at the close. "Go ye therefore and teach all nations, baptising them in the name of the Father, and of the Son, and of the Holy Ghost; teaching them to observe all things whatsoever I have commanded you; and lo I am with you always, even unto the end of the world." Hence "we are ambassadors for Christ, we pray you in Christ's stead, as though God did beseech you by us, be ye reconciled to God," 2 Cor. v. 20. Now, I say, is there not in all this 'a clear and fair ground laid for your believing, or entering into the New Testament Ark?' O, Sirs, ponder Christ's commission from the Father; for this "is the work of God, that ye believe in him whom he hath sent," John vi. 29. See that ye do not refuse him that speaketh, Heb. xii. 25, from heaven, for it is his Father's solemn command, "Hear ye him," Matth. iii. last, *i. e.* believe in his name, for they that turn a deaf ear to him shall perish in the deluge.

2dly, Christ's declared ability and sufficiency to save is another door for faith to enter into the New Testament Ark. No man will readily enter into the ocean upon an insufficient bottom. If one that is on a voyage to a foreign country get the least notice or advice, that such a ship is insufficient, or if he have but a suspicion that it is so, he will turn away from her, and will neither venture his person nor his goods into her. This is the case with every legalist and unbeliever; he has a secret suspicion in his heart, that Christ alone is not sufficient to save him: And therefore he will rather venture his eternal life upon the general mercy of God, or upon the law and the works of the law, upon his own inherent grace, his duties and good qualifications, than upon Christ; or if he does not set Christ aside altogether, he will venture partly upon Christ, and partly upon something done by himself; 'Christ and my faith, Christ and my works and duties, Christ and my obedience, Christ and my tears, prayers, will,

I hope, do my business, and save me from the deluge of God's wrath.' Now, I say, whence comes all this, but from a secret jealousy and suspicion of Christ's ability and sufficiency, and that he alone is not to be lippened unto? And hence, through an evil heart of unbelief, they turn away from him, and lay the stress of their salvation upon this and that, and the other broken plank of their own making and devising, saying with those in Micah vi. 6, " Wherewith shall I come before the Lord? Shall I come before him with burnt-offerings, with calves of a year old? Will the Lord be pleased with thousands of rams?" In a word, until the sinner is fully and thoroughly convinced of the absolute sufficiency of the New Testament Ark, and of his full ability to save, he will never believe in him to the saving of his soul.

Now, to convince you of his ability and sufficiency, will you take the following testimonies concerning him. (1.) take the testimony of God the Father, Psal. lxxxix. 19, " I have laid help upon one that is mighty." (2.) Take Christ's own testimony, Is. lxiii. 1, " I speak in righteousness, and am mighty to save." (3.) Take the testimony of the Holy Ghost, whose office it is to testify of him : " He (says Christ) shall glorify me, for he shall receive of mine, and shall shew it unto you," John xvi. 14, that ye may believe in me. (4.) Take the testimony of all these three witnesses in heaven, together, 1 John v. 10, 11, " This is the record (viz. of the three in one, and one in three), that God hath given to us eternal life, and this life is in his Son." (5.) Take the testimony of the apostle Paul, speaking by the inspiration of the Holy Ghost, Heb. vii. 25, " Wherefore he is able to save them to the uttermost that come unto God by him, seeing he ever liveth to make intercession for them. (6.) Take the testimony of the ransomed in glory, who tell, from their experience, that he alone undertook and accomplished their salvation, Rev. v. 9, " Thou art worthy to take the book, and to open the seven seals thereof; for thou wast slain, and hast redeemed us to God by thy blood." Thus you see there is sufficient ground for your faith to rest upon Christ's ability to save ; and to dispute our doubt of it is to call God a liar, 1 John v. 10, and to call all men liars that ever knew him.

But to illustrate this ground of faith a little further, I will tell you of a fourfold ability and sufficiency that there is in Christ.

1. An ability of merit for obtaining of pardon and acceptance through his obedience unto death. As was already shewed, there are two things the sinner wants in order to restore him to the favour of God, and to his title to eternal life, that was forfeited by his breach of the covenant of works: (1.) Pardon of sin ; and (2.) A perfect law righteousness. Now, both these are to be found in Christ. As to the first, viz. pardon, why this we have in him, for he hath finished transgression and made an end of sin, Dan. ix. 24. As to its condemning power, " he is the Lamb of God which taketh away the sin of the world, John i. 29. " We have redemption in his blood, the forgiveness of sins, according to the riches of his grace," Eph. i. 7. Hence the apostle John declareth, chap. i. 7, " The blood of Jesus Christ his Son, cleanseth us from all sin;" and it is upon the ground

of the satisfaction of Jesus that God declares himself to be the "Lord pardoning iniquity, transgression, and sin," Deut. xxxiv. 7, and promises to be merciful to our unrighteousness, Heb. viii. 12. As to the second, viz. A perfect law righteousness, this is to be had to the full in Christ. for he is "the end of the law for righteousness unto every one that believeth," Rom. x. 4, "He is made sin for us, who knew no sin, that we might be made the righteousness of God in him," 2 Cor. v. 21, "The righteousness of the law is fulfilled in us," Rom. viii. 4, This is that best robe that is put upon the poor prodigal when he comes home, Luke xv. 22, whereby the shame of his nakedness is covered; this is the wedding garment that fits for communion with God, and entitles the soul unto that "inheritance incorruptible, undefiled, and that fadeth not away," 1 Pet. i. 4. So that there is in Christ a fulness of merit for justification.

2. There is in Christ a fulness of wisdom for the soul's instruction and direction in all cases; "for in him are hid all the treasures of wisdom and knowledge," Col. ii. 3. By this Spirit of wisdom and understanding he gives unto fools and babes the knowledge of the "deep things of God, which are hid from the wise and prudent of the world," Matth. xi. 25, compared with 1 Cor. ii. 10. And by his skill and wisdom he directs and guides his poor people through all the dark and difficult steps in their way, until he bring them to glory, and so accomplish that promise, "I will bring the blind by a way that they knew not, I will lead them in paths that they have not known; I will make darkness light before them, and crooked things straight," Is. xlii. 16.

3. There is in him a fulness of strength and ability to bear up the poor soul under all work and warfare that it is called to engage with. Sometimes the poor believer, looking to the poor weak fund of grace within him, is ready to succumb and cry out, 'Alas! such and such work as the Lord carves out for me will be marred in my hand, I am not sufficient to think, to will, to do.' But here, believer, lies an all-sufficient fund of ability, "Thy God hath commanded thy strength," Psal. lxviii. 28, "Then mayest thou be strong in the Lord, and in the power of his might," Eph. vi. 10. "He gives power to the faint, and he increaseth strength to them that have no might," Is. xl. 29. Sometimes again the poor weak believer is ready to faint, because of the many and mighty enemies he has to grapple with; 'Alas! (will he say) I have no might to subdue this or the other strong lust and corruption; it will master me; one day or other I shall fall into the hand of the enemy; Satan supports the power of indwelling sin, so that I have not only flesh and blood, but principalities and powers, spiritual wickednesses in high places to contend with, Eph. vi. 12, I know not what to do.' Well, poor believer, here lies the glory of thy strength, Psal. lxxxix. 17, even in Christ, who has already, in his own person, destroyed sin and Satan, and who has also said, that he will subdue thine iniquities, Mic. vii. 19, "Sin shall not have dominion over you," Rom. vi. 14. And as for Satan, "the God of peace will shortly bruise him under thy feet," Rom. xvi. 20, and mean time his grace shall be sufficient for thee, 1 Cor. xii. 9.

4. There is in him an all-sufficient stock of grace for the supply of all thy wants; for "it hath pleased the Father that in him should all fulness dwell," Col. i. 19, "that out of his fulness all we might receive grace for grace," John i. 16, The grace that is in him, as Mediator, is not in him for himself, but for us poor needy sinners, 1 Cor. i. 30, "He is made of God unto us wisdom, and righteousness, and sanctification, and redemption." "He received gifts for men," Psal. lxviii. 18, that man might be "blessed in him with all spiritual blessings in heavenly things," Eph. i. 3, and therefore men, and the sons of men, are invited to come to him and get their own, for he and all that he is, or has, as Mediator, is for us. O then, "Come, come, come and take of the water of life freely," Rev. xxii. 17.

3*dly*, There is another door of access to the New Testament Ark, that is the door of his good-will that he bears unto fallen man beyond the fallen angels (who are by nature creatures of a higher rank than man; for God made man a little lower than the Angels, Psal. viii. 5.) When the angels left their first state, there was no good-will discovered towards them, yea, on the contrary, they are shut out of heaven to hell, where "they are reserved in everlasting chains under darkness, unto the judgment of the great day," Jude 6, But when man sinned, and fell from the state wherein he was created, what strange work is made for his recovery? Hence is that declaration of the angels at the birth of Christ, "On earth PEACE, GOOD-WILL towards men," Luke ii. 14. He "is not willing that any should perish, but that all should come to repentance," 2 Peter, iii. 9.

Quest. Wherein doth this good-will of God towards man, fallen man, appear? *Answ.* In these few things:

1. Does it not appear in his remembering us in our low estate, Psal. cxxxvi. 23, when we were like the infant cast out into the open field, none to pity or help, yet even then he looked upon us, and our time was the time of love, Ezek. xvi. 5, 9?

2. How did his good-will appear, when, immediately after the fall, the remedy was discovered, Gen. iii. 15, It (viz. the seed of the woman) shall bruise thy head (viz. the serpent's)?" the plaster is at hand to be applied, even before the wound was given by the serpent?

3. Was it not good-will to men upon earth, that he would not trust any angel or archangel with his salvation, but commits it unto his OWN SON, his BELOVED SON, "who is in the form of God," Philip ii. 6, and is fully able for the work?

4. Was it not good-will in the Son of God not only to assume the human nature, but to take our law-place, that law and justice might reach him for our debt? For he "was made of a woman, made under the law," Gal. iv. 4. He was made sin for us, 2 Cor. v. 21. "And he was numbered with the transgressors," Is. liii. 12.

5. Was it not good-will in him to die for our offences, and to rise again for our justification? Rom. v. 25. Greater love than this hath no man, than that a man lay down his life for his friends: "But God commendeth his love to us, in that while we were yet enemies, Christ died for us," John xv. 13, compared with Rom. v. 6-8.

6. Is it not good-will to man, in that when he had finished our re-

demption upon earth, that he should ascend into heaven, to appear in the presence of God for us, Heb. ix. 24, as an Advocate at the high court of justice, Is. liii. last, "He was numbered with the transgressors, and he bare the sin of many, and made intercession for the transgressors," Luke xxiii. 34, 1 John ii. 1, "And if any man sin, we have an Advocate with the Father, Jesus Christ the righteous."

7, Is it not good-will to man upon earth, that he commands the white flag of peace to be lifted up in the view of mankind, and creates the fruit of the lips, peace, peace to him who is afar off, and to him who is near? Is. lvii. 19.

8. Is it not good-will to man, that he makes offer of himself, and of his whole salvation, to sinners? Is. xlvi. 12-13, "Hearken unto me, ye stout-hearted, and far from righteousness, I bring near my righteousness unto you: it shall not be far off, and my salvation shall not tarry."

9. Is it not good-will to man, that when he sees them running unto their ruin, in the broad way that leadeth to eternal destruction, he pursues them, crying, O "turn ye, turn ye, for why will ye die? for, as I live, I have no pleasure in the death of the wicked, but rather that he should turn," Ezek. xxxiii. 11. Oh, how many a cry gives he after Israel! Jer. iii. 1, "Thou hast played the harlot with many lovers, yet return again unto me, saith the Lord," and verse 14, "Turn, O backsliding children, saith the Lord, for I am married unto you."

10. His heart is glad, and heaven rings with joy when a prodigal returns, Luke xv. 23-24, "Let us eat and be merry, for this my son was dead and is alive again; he was lost, and is found. There is joy in heaven among the angels when a sinner is converted, chap. xv. 7-10.

11. His good-will appears in his behaviour when sinners continue obstinate to refuse the offers of his grace, Psal. lxxxi. 13, "O that my people had hearkened unto me." He wept over Jerusalem, saying, Luke xix. 42, "O if thou hadst known, even thou, at least in this thy day, the things which belong unto thy peace!" He enters a protest before heaven and earth, and their blood did not lie at his door, but at their own, Jer. ii. 12-13, "Be astonished, O ye heavens, at this, and be horribly afraid, be ye very desolate, saith the Lord: for my people have committed two evils, they have forsaken me, the Fountain of living waters, and have hewed them out cisterns, broken cisterns, that can hold no water." Thus you see what good-will Christ and his Father bears towards your salvation; and is not this a door by which you may enter into the New Testament Ark, and be saved from the deluge? Oh how justly shall the sinner perish for ever, that despises this good-will, and receives all this grace in vain!

4thly, The command of God, that is laid upon every one that hears the gospel, to believe in Christ, is a blessed door of access into the New Testament Ark, John iii. 23, "This is his commandment, that we should believe on the name of his Son Jesus Christ." Sirs, God has such a good-will towards our salvation, that he has concluded us under a law, and has interposed his authority, enjoining us to believe in the name of his Son; and he has fenced his law with the most awful and terrible threatening in case of disobedience; "He that believeth not is condemned already, because he hath not believed in the name of the only begotten Son of God," John iii. 18; Heb. ii. 3, "How shall we escape if we neglect so great salvation?" chap x. 28-29, "He that despised Moses' law died without mercy, under two or three witnesses; of how much sorer punishment, suppose ye, shall he be thought worthy, who hath trodden under foot the Son of God," chap. vi. 5, "crucified unto themselves the Son of God afresh, and put him to an open shame." Thus you see that the command is peremptory, that you must believe in the name of Christ; you must receive him as the gift of God, otherwise you shall sink in the mighty waters of the deluge of eternal wrath and vengeance, and Christ himself will resent it to the uttermost, if his salvation be slighted; for he will come in flaming fire to take vengeance on all them that know not God, and who obey not this commandment of believing in the name of the only begotten Son of God, 2 Thess. i. 7-8.

Object. 1. 'I am afraid it be presumption in me to believe in and apply Christ.'

Answ. It can never be presumption to obey an express and positive command of God. Is it presumption to pray? Is it presumption to read the word? Is it presumption to hear the word? Is it presumption to sanctify God's name? and is it presumption to remember the Sabbath? You do not reckon it presumption to do any of these, because ye are commanded of God; as little can it be presumption to "believe in Christ, seeing this is his commandment," 1 John, iii. 21.

Object. 2. 'I am such a great sinner, that I am afraid it is not I that is commanded to believe.'

Answ. The command of believing is to all without exception, great sinners, and sinners of a lesser size, Is. i. 8, "Come now, and let us reason together, saith the Lord: Though your sins be as scarlet, they shall be as white as snow; though they be red like crimson, they shall be as wool:" If the command of believing were not to every one, then unbelief would not be their sin; for "where there is no law, there is no transgression," Rom. v. 13. But unbelief is a sin of the deepest dye, and makes every sin else unpardonable, by rejecting the only remedy.

Object. 3. 'You tell us, that we are commanded to believe; and yet at the same time tell us that we want power to believe; that it is the work of God, John vi. 29, and that exceeding great and mighty power of God, that raised Christ from the dead, and must make us to believe,' Eph. i. 19-20.

Answ. It is very true, ye cannot believe; "No man can come to Christ, except the Father draw him," John vi. 44, and yet ye are commanded to believe, not by us, but by that God that commands "things that are not as though they were," Rom. iv. 17, and he commands you, impotent sinners, "dead in sin, to believe in the name of his Son;" that, from a sense of your own impotency, you may turn the work upon himself, as * the Author and Finisher of faith," Heb.

xii. 2, and his command is the vehicle of power: As when he commanded the man with the withered hand, "Stretch forth thine hand." Matth. xii. 13, the poor man minted to obey, and in the mint of obedience he got power to stretch out his hand as he was commanded: So, after his example do ye. Mint at the duty, depending on the power of him who commands you to believe, that he may "fulfil in you all the good pleasure of his goodness, and the work of faith with power," 2 Thess. i. 11.

Object. 4. 'I have essayed and minted to believe, in obedience unto the command, and yet, alas! I am just where I was; I do not find the power of God coming along.'

Answ. Continue in the use of the means of God's appointment, to mint at believing: Continue to hear the word, and mint at mingling faith with it: Continue in prayer: and mint at believing that God will hear you; and in this way wait on the Lord. Remember the poor man that lay at the pool, John v. 5-9, for thirty-eight years, waiting for the troubling of the waters, and at last the Lord came and healed him: So do ye; for "blessed are all they that wait upon him," Psal. xxxvii. 9.

Object. 5. 'But all my labours will be in vain if I be not elected; for it is only they that are ordained to eternal life that will believe, Acts xiii. 48.

Answ. It is true, the election shall obtain, Rom. xi. 7, though others be hardened; but let me tell you, in the matter of believing, you have no more concern with the secret counsels of God, than you have in buying or selling, eating or drinking, or such like common actions of life. If any man should say, I will not open my shop door, because I do not know if God has decreed that I should sell any wares; or, I do not know if God has ordained that any man should buy them: Or, if a man should say, I will neither eat nor drink, because God has fixed the term of my life; I am sure I shall live as long as God has ordained, whatever I do, &c.: Or, I may cast myself down a precipice, or attempt to walk upon the waters, because I shall not perish till God's appointed time come: I say, would you not reckon that man mad, or distracted, that would argue at that rate? Yet the case is the same, when he argues, That he needs not fly to Christ, or enter into the New Testament Ark, because if he be elected to eternal life he shall never perish, whether he believe or not. Sirs, let not the devil and a deceitful heart lead you in among the decrees of God, which are secret; for "the secret things belong unto the Lord our God; but those things which are revealed belong unto us, and to our children," Deut. xxix. 29. Follow commanded duty: believe in the Son of God; and then you shall know your election of God.

Heb. xi. 7.—By faith Noah, being warned of God of things not seen as yet, moved with fear, prepared an ark to the saving of his house.

THE SIXTH SERMON ON THIS TEXT.

THE doctrine taken from the words in their typical and spiritual meaning, was as follows:

"That Christ is the great New Testament ARK, unto which perishing sinners must betake themselves, that they may be saved from the deluge of God's wrath."

The method was:

I. To speak of the deluge of God's wrath, with allusion unto the deluge of waters that destroyed the old world.
II. To speak of the warnings that God gives of the dreadful deluge of his wrath.
III. To speak of Christ as the great New Testament Ark, typified by the ark of Noah.
IV. To cast open the doors of the New Testament Ark.
V. To shew how it is that a sinner actually enters into this Ark by this door.
VI. Proceed to the application of the doctrine.

Having spoken to the first four, I proceed to

V. The *fifth* thing in the method, which was, to speak of the soul's actual entering by these doors into the New Testament Ark.

I find faith sometimes expressed in scripture under the notion of entering, John x. 9, "I am the door: by me if any man enter in, he shall be saved," and Heb. iv. 3, "For we who have believed do enter into rest;" and ver. 7, "Let us therefore fear, lest a promise being left us of entering into his rest, any of you should seem to come short of it." Of the same import is that expression of turning unto Christ as a Strong-hold or Refuge, Zech. ix. 12.

All I shall say upon this head is, to illustrate a little the nature of faith, under the similitude of Noah's entering into the ark, and the creatures that were saved there with him.

1. Then, we see in the text, that Noah was warned of God of his danger before *he prepared an ark*, or fled unto it. Just so is it with sinners in the matter of believing in Christ; God gives the sinner warning of the danger he is in of the wrath to come. As God gave public warning to the old world, by the ministry of Noah, of the approaching deluge: so by the word read and preached, particularly by the preaching of the law, there is warning given to all sinners of the danger they are in of perishing for ever. The voice of God in the law to sinners is, Gal. iii. 10, "Cursed is every one that continueth not in all things which are written in the book of the law to do them." Rom. ii, 8, 9, "Indignation and wrath, tribulation and anguish, upon every soul of man that doth evil." Psal. ix. 17, "The wicked shall be turned into hell, and all the nations that forget God.—The wages of sin is death." Now, these and the like warnings are carried in and brought home to the soul in particular, by the power of the eternal Spirit, before the sinner enter into the New Testament Ark; and the sinner is made to believe the truth of these threatenings: For there is a law of faith, and a particular application of these and the like threatenings, before there be a true gospel faith of the remedy. Hence,

3. You see that Noah was moved with fear before he prepared an ark, or entered thereinto. What was he afraid of? say you. I answer, He was afraid of perishing in the deluge with the rest of the wicked world, (See the text.)

Just so is the case with sinners in the matter of believing, or flying to Christ; they are moved with the fear of an angry God, against whom they have sinned. And hence it is, that the sinner, through the terror of God, and of an awakened conscience, falls a trembling, with the jailor, Acts xvi. 30, and cries, "What shall I do to be saved?" Oh! to whom shall I fly for help, Isa. x. 3. "Who among us shall dwell with the devouring fire? and who among us shall dwell with everlasting burnings?" Is. xxxiii. 14. This is what is commonly called a law-work, which every one that believes hath either in a greater or lesser degree: For "The law is our schoolmaster to lead us unto Christ, that we might be justified by faith," &c., Gal. iii. 24.

3. Noah renounced all the false confidences that the men of the old world betook themselves unto for shelter against the deluge. There is no doubt, but the inhabitants of the old world, when they saw the "windows of heaven opened, and the fountains of the great deep broken up, and the waters increasing and swelling," they would fly to the highest houses or mountains, to save them from the waters of the deluge, in hopes that the waters would stay before they came up where they were: But Noah knew other things; he knew that these were but lying refuges, and that the waters would overtop the highest mountains in the world: And therefore he renounced these vain refuges, and betook himself unto the ark.

Just so is it in the matter of believing in Christ, the poor soul is made to see that "in vain is salvation to be expected from the hills, and from the multitude of mountains," Jer. iii. 23. "That the hail shall sweep away the refuge of lies," Is. xxviii. 17. And the waters shall overflow all these hiding places, which hypocrites, the carnal worldling, or legalist, betake themselves unto: and therefore it flies for refuge unto Christ, that blessed hope set before it, Heb. vi. 18, in the gospel, knowing that there is no name given—whereby to be saved, but by the name of Jesus.

4. Noah believed that the ark (being God's ordinance) was sufficient to save him and his family from the deluge.

So in the matter of believing, Christ is taken up as an all-sufficient Saviour, "able also to save unto the uttermost, all that come unto God by him," Heb. vii. 25; and as he is appointed and ordained of God to be a Saviour every way qualified for the salvation of lost sinners, and made of God "unto us, wisdom, and righteousness, and sanctification, and redemption," 1 Cor. i. 30.

5. God gave to the living creatures (that were to be saved alive in the ark) a certain instinct, which made them to move from all parts of the earth towards the ark, and at last to enter into it.

Just so is it in the matter of believing. God gives an instinct, a supernatural instinct, unto the poor sinner, that makes him restless, until he win Christ, and be found in him, Phil. iii. 8-9. This is nothing else but that drawing power of the word and Spirit of God, whereby the sinner is led to the Rock that is higher than all other refuges; John vi. 44, "No man (says Christ) can come unto me, except the Father which hath sent me draw him;" Hos. xi. 3, "I drew them with cords of a man, with bands of love." You know the bees, before a shower, they, by a certain instinct, fly into the hive: Just so is it here.

6. Noah's faith rested (not in the boards of the ark, but) in God who had appointed him to prepare it.

So in the matter of believing, true faith terminates upon "God—in Christ, reconciling the world to himself," 2 Cor. v. 19. The great design of God in manifesting himself in the flesh, is not that our faith should terminate upon the Man Christ Jesus, but upon God in him. You have a word to this purpose, 1 Pet. i. 21, "Who by him do believe in God, that raised him up from the dead, and gave him glory, that your faith and hope might be in God." So that you see, the scope of the whole work of redemption (through Christ) is to bring us to trust in God, and to place our confidence in him, as a God with us. Sirs, remember that God alone is the object of faith: and if your faith terminate upon any thing inferior to God, Father, Son, and Holy Ghost, it is not saving faith, for it doth not answer the very first command of the law, "Thou shalt have no other gods before me," Exod. xx. 3.

7. When Noah entered into the ark, it was with a resolution to abide there, until the waters of the deluge were abated.

Just so is it here; when a sinner comes by faith unto Christ for refuge, he comes with a design to abide in him, not (like Noah with his ark) for a while, but for ever. The soul in believing cries concerning Christ, "This is my rest for ever, here will I dwell;" Psal. cxxxii. 14. It is the will of Christ that we should abide in him, 1 John ii. 28, "And now little children, abide in him, that when he shall appear, we may have confidence, and not be ashamed, before him at his coming;" John xv. 4-7, "I am the vine; ye are the branches: he that abideth in me, and I in him, the same bringeth forth much fruit: for without me ye can do nothing. If a man abide not in me, he is cast forth as a branch, and is withered, and men gather them, and cast them into the fire, and they are burned. If ye abide in me, and my words abide in you, ye shall ask what ye will, and it shall be done unto you."

VI. The *sixth* thing in the method was to apply this doctrine.

And the only uses I make of the doctrine shall be in a word of trial and exhortation.

Use *first* shall be in a word of trial and examination.

And that which I would have you to try, is, Whether have you got into the New Testament Ark Christ, where alone a sinner can be in safety from the deluge of divine wrath. I remember John the Baptist says unto the Scribes and Pharisees, Matth. iii. 7, "O generation of vipers, who hath warned you to fly from the wrath to come?" So say I to you; have you, upon God's warning, by the word of the law, fled for refuge unto Christ, and taken up your residence and abode in him? I offer these few marks for trial.

1. If ever you fled to the New Testament Ark, you have seen the devouring deluge of God's wrath ready to swallow you up, and you have seen yourselves upon the very brink of perishing for ever in the deep waters, so that you have been made to cry out, Oh "what shall I do to be saved?" Acts xvi. 30.

2. God has broken all your false props and confidences, and made you see they are nothing but lying refuges that would betray you. So was it with Paul at his conversion, what things were gain to him, these he counted loss for Christ, Philip. iii. 7. "Ashur shall not save us," Hos. xiv. 3.

3. You have (by the light of the word and Spirit) got such a discovery of the glory, structure, beauty, and excellency of the New Testament Ark, as has filled you with wonder and admiration at the love, mercy, and grace of God, in providing such an Ark, such a Saviour, 2 Cor. iv. 6, "For God, who commanded the light to shine out of darkness, hath shined in our hearts, to give the light of the knowledge of the glory of God, in the face of Jesus Christ." Oh, will the soul say, at the sight of the Ark Christ, "What hath God wrought?" Numb. xxiii. 23; "This is the Lord's doing, it is wonderful in our eyes," Psal. cxviii. 23; "Without controversy, great is the mystery of godliness, God was manifest in the flesh!" &c., 1 Tim. iii. 16.

4. If ever you entered into the ark, you have seen a reconciled God in the Ark Christ, "For God is in Christ, reconciling the world unto himself," 2 Cor. v. 19. This is the very thing that induces and encourages the soul to enter into it. The poor soul could see nothing before but God a devouring fire to consume it; but, looking to Christ, it sees a smiling God, saying, "This is my beloved Son, in whom I am well pleased," Matth. xvii. 5. O Sirs, this is the very thing that begets faith, love, hope, and confidence, God's love in giving Christ, John iii. 16, "God so loved the world, that he gave his only begotten Son," &c. Now, have you seen God to be love? and have you seen his love manifested in this, that he sent his only begotten Son into the world, that we might live through him? 1 John iv. 9, and has the faith of this love killed your enmity?

5. If you have fled to the New Testament Ark, you will be so well pleased with your new lodging, and your safety therein, that your hearts will be filled with gratitude, and your tongues with the high praises of the Lord, that ever provided such an Ark, and that ever brought you into it. You will sing and say with the church, Micah vii. 18, "Who is a God like unto thee, who pardoneth iniquity, and passeth by the transgression of the remnant of thine heritage;" and with David, Psal. ciii. at the beginning, "Bless the Lord, O my soul, and all that is within me, bless his holy name: Bless the Lord, O my soul, and forget not all his benefits:" and with Israel, when God had brought them through the Red Sea, and delivered them from the hand of the Egyptians, Exod. xv. 11, "I will sing unto the Lord, for he hath triumphed gloriously," &c.

6. If you have ever fled into the Ark, then you will be new creatures; for if any man be in Christ, he is a new creature, old things will pass away, 2 Cor. v. 17. You have got new light in your understanding, a new will and affections, you will not walk according to your old lusts in the flesh, or according to the curse of the world: no, but as the ark and they that were in it were lifted up above the earth upon the waters, towards heaven, so you will not lie grovelling upon the earth, but "seek things that are above, where Christ is," Col. iii. 1.

7. You have got something of the Spirit of Christ: for if any man have not the Spirit of Christ he is none of his," Rom. viii. 9. "But he that is joined unto the Lord, is one spirit," 1 Cor. vi. 17. And his spirit will be in you as " a well of water springing up unto everlasting life," John iv. 14. The Spirit will convince you of sin, &c.

8. If you have fled to the New Testament Ark, you will be concerned to get as many as possible into the Ark with you; and for this end you will be telling them of their danger while out of Christ, and of the great salvation that is to be found in him. How active was Paul, after he came to know Christ, to recommend him to others? Acts ix. 20, &c., compared with Gal. i. 23.

Use *second* shall be of *Exhortation* to all in general.

Is it so that Christ is our great New Testament Ark, to save from the deluge of divine wrath? O then, Sirs, let me beseech and entreat you to consult your own safety, by flying into this blessed Ark, before the waters of the deluge sweep you away into a miserable eternity.

I offer a few motives to stir you up to fly into the Ark.

1. Consider, That there are innumerable multitudes of mankind that are already lost irrecoverably in the deluge of God's wrath, through their not entering into the Ark. The inhabitants of the old world that are said to be in prison, unto whom Noah preached. O what innumerable numbers of men and women have gone down to the sides of the pit since sin entered into the world; " Broad is the way that leadeth to destruction, and many there be that go in thereat," Matth. vii. 13. Now, is it not your interest to take warning from the ruin of so many?

2. Consider, That you must inevitably go the same way, I mean, perish in the deluge, except you enter into the Ark; "For there is none other name under heaven, given amongst men, whereby we must be saved, but by the name of Jesus Christ," Acts iv. 12. It is not your broken planks of a profession of religion, hope in the general mercy of God, your civility. morality, legal righteousness, that will do; God's wrath will stave all these broken planks in pieces: and therefore repair to the ARK Jesus Christ.

3. There is a fixed day, a time set for your entering into the New Testament Ark, which if it be let slip, there will be no entrance into the Ark, but you shall infallibly perish in the deluge. "He that lives for ever, has sworn with his hand lifted up to heaven," that there shall be no more entrance into the Ark. *Quest.* What is the fixed time? *Answ.* It is the day of grace, the day of life, the day of

salvation; if that pass, you are gone for ever: and therefore, "To-day, if you will hear his voice," Psal. xcv. and Heb. iii.

4. The Ark is prepared of God for you, and that at an infinite expense. God has provided a Saviour, Psal. lxxxix. 19, "Help is laid upon one that is mighty," John iii. 16, "God so loved the world, that he gave his only begotten Son, that whosoever believeth in him, should not perish." The Ark is finished, and perfected, and made ready for you: "All things are ready," Matth. xxii. 4.

5. The Ark is at hand, it is near to us, Is. xlvi. at the close, Behold, "I bring near my righteousness, it shall not be far off, and my salvation shall not tarry; and I will place salvation in Zion," &c. "The word is nigh thee, even in thy mouth, and in thy heart: that is the word of faith which we preach," Rom. x. 8.

6. The Ark is ordained for men and women of our stamp, I mean men and women of the human nature: And therefore the call is "to men and the sons of men," Prov. viii. 4. Christ is a Saviour, not for the fallen angels, but for us; "Unto us is this child born," Is. ix. 6, he "is made of God unto us, wisdom, and righteousness, and sanctification, and redemption," 1 Cor. i. 30.

7. Many have already entered, and are saved; an innumerable company, "which no man can number," Rev. vii.

8. The doors of the Ark are cast wide open to you also, together with a promise of safety, "Whosoever believeth shall not perish, but shall have everlasting life," John iii. 16.

9. The great God commands you to enter into the Ark, 1 John iii. 23, "This is his commandment, that we should believe in the name of his Son Jesus Christ."

I conclude with a word to believers who have fled into the Ark.

(1.) By way of comfort.

1. God is with you in the Ark, "For God is in Christ," 2 Cor. v. 19, and he will never leave you, Heb. xii. 5.

2. "Your life is hid with Christ in God," Col. iii. 3, "Because I live, ye shall live also," John xiv. 19.

3. You are freed from condemnation. The law cannot curse you: though man may, yet God will not curse you, Rom. viii. 1.

4. The waters of affliction shall not overwhelm you, Is. xliii. 2, 3: the waves they may dash, but they will turn into foam like the waves of the sea.

5. Death and the grave cannot harm you, "For you are ransomed from the power of both," Hos. xiii. 14.

(2.) A word of counsel to you that are in the Ark.

1. Bless God that provided the Ark.
2. Bless God that brought you into it.
3. Rejoice and glory in the Lord, triumph in him.
4. Live upon Christ, and the provision you find in the Ark.
5. Walk worthy of the Lord, unto all well-pleasing, Col. i. 10.

THE PLANT OF RENOWN.

EZEK. xxxiv. 29.—And I will raise up for them a Plant of Renown.

THE FIRST SERMON ON THIS TEXT.

IF we cast our eyes back upon the foregoing part of this chapter, we shall find a very melancholy scene casting up; we shall find the flock and heritage of God scattered, robbed, and peeled, by the civil and ecclesiastical rulers that were in being at that day: a day much like to the day wherein we live; the ruin of the church of Christ, in all ages and periods of the world, has been owing to combinations betwixt corrupt churchmen and corrupt statesmen. And so you will find it in the preceding part of this chapter: there is a high charge brought in against the shepherds of Israel, and a terrible and awful threatening denounced by the great and chief Shepherd against them, for the bad treatment that the flock of Christ had met with in their hands. However the sheep of Christ may be fleeced, scattered, and spoiled, yet the Lord looks on them: And many great and precious promises are made for their encouragement in that evil day; you may read them at your own leisure, for I must not stay upon them just now: But among all the rest of the promises that are made, Christ is the Chief, Christ is the To-look of the church, whatever trouble she be in. In the 7th chapter of Isaiah, the church had a trembling heart, God's Israel was shaken as ever you saw the leaves of the wood shaken by the wind, by reason of two kings combining against them: well, the Lord tells them, a virgin shall conceive and bear a son, and shall call his name IMMANUEL: But might the church say, what is that to us? what encouragement doth this afford in the present distress? Why, the Messiah is to come of the tribe of Judah, and the family of David; and therefore that tribe and family must be preserved, in order to the accomplishment of that promise. Whatever distance of time, suppose hundreds or thousands of years may intervene before the actual coming of the Messiah, yet the promise of his coming, as it is the ground of your faith for eternal salvation, so it is a security for the present, that the enemy shall not prevail to the total ruin of Judah, and the royal family of David. In all the distresses of the church, Christ is always presented to her in the promise, as the object of her faith, and the ground of her consolation; and accordingly they looked to him in the promises, and were lightened, and their faces were not ashamed. He is here promised under the notion of David; he is promised under the notion of God's Servant; and in the words of the text, he is promised as a renowned Plant, that was to rise in the fulness of time: And blessed be God he has sprung up, and is in heaven already, and has overtopt all his enemies, and all his enemies shall be his footstool.

Here then you have a comfortable promise of the Messiah; where again you may notice, 1*st*, The Promiser, *(I), I will raise up*, &c.

It is a great *(I)* Indeed, it is JEHOVAH in the person of the Father, it was he that in a peculiar manner sent him; "God so loved the world, that he gave his only begotten Son, that whosoever believeth in him should not perish, but have everlasting life." In the fulness of time he sent forth his Son "made of a woman, made under the law, to redeem them that were under the law, that we might receive the adoption of sons." God promised to send him, and accordingly he has actually fulfilled his promise. Again, 2*dly*, We may notice the blessing promised, and that is, a *Plant of Renown:* Christ gets a great many metaphorical names and descriptions in scripture; sometimes he is called a Rose, sometimes he is called a Sun, and sometimes he is called a Door, sometimes he is called the Tree of Life; sometimes he is called one thing, and sometimes another, and he is content to be called any thing to make himself known to us; and here he is called a Plant, and a renowned Plant; but more of this afterwards. But then, 3*dly*, We have the production of this Plant, *I will raise him up.* Hell will endeavour to keep him down, the devil and his angels will endeavour to smother him when he sets his head above ground. So we find Satan sends Herod, and Herod sends the bloody dragoons to murder him when he came into the world. But let hell do its utmost, as it hath done in all ages, and is doing this day to smother that Plant, up it will he; *I will raise him up;* and therefore he shall prosper. But then again, 4*thly*, We may notice here for whom, or for what end, for whose use and benefit it is; *I will raise up (for them) a Plant of renown.* Who these are, you will see by casting your eye on the former part of the chapter, it is for the Lord's flock, his oppressed heritage, that are borne down by wicked rulers, civil and ecclesiastic, *I will raise up for them a Plant of renown,* and he will be their Deliverer.

The doctrine that naturally arises of the verse is in short this.

"That Christ is *a Plant of renown,* of God raising up, for the benefit and advantage of this people, or for their comfort and relief in all their distress: he is a renowned Plant of God raising up."

Now, in discoursing this doctrine, if time and strength would allow, I might.
I. Promise a few things concerning this blessed Plant.
II. I might inquire why he is he called *a Plant of renown?*
III. Speak a little to the raising up of this *Plant.*
IV. Shew you for whom he is raised up. And.
V. Shew you for what end he is raised up. And then.
Lastly, Apply.

I As to the *first* of these, namely, to promise a few things concerning this blessed *Plant.*

1*st,* I would have you to know, what is here attributed and ascribed to Christ, is not to be understood absolutely of him as God, but—

officially, as he is a Mediator and Redeemer. Considering him absolutely as God, this cannot be properly said of him that he was raised up; for he is God co-equal and co-essential with the father; but viewing him as Mediator, he is *a Plant*, as it were, of God's training You will feel from the context, all that is said of Christ has a respect to him as Mediator, that he was to be God's servant, to do his work; in that consideration, he is here called *a Plant*, and *a Plant of renown:* Hence Zacharias, when speaking of him, has a phrase much to the same purpose; "He hath raised up a Horn of salvation for us in the house of his servant David."

Again, 3*dly*, Another thing I would have you to remark is, that this *Plant* is but small and little in the eyes of a blind world. He was little looked upon when he sprung up in his incarnation, and when he was here in a state of humiliation: Men look upon him as a root sprung up out of a dry ground, they saw no comeliness in him why he should be desired; and to this day, though he be in a state of exaltation at the right hand of God, yet he is little thought of, and looked upon by the generality of mankind, and the hearers of the gospel; "He is despised and rejected of men."

But then, 3*dly*, Another thing I would have you to remark is, that however contemptible this *Plant of renown* is in the eyes of a blind world, yet he is the tallest plant in all God's Lebanon: There is not the like of him in it; he as fairer than the children of men, and he is as the apple tree among the trees of the wood; if ever you saw him, ye will be ready to say so too, "whom have I in heaven but thee? and there is none upon the earth that I desire besides thee."

Again, 4*thly*, Another thing I remark is, that this blessed *Plant of renown* was cut down in his death, and sprang up gloriously in his resurrection. The sword of divine justice hewed down this plant upon Mount Calvary, but within three days he sprang up again more glorious, and more beautiful and amiable than ever, and he was "declared to be the Son of God with power, according to the spirit of holiness, by his resurrection from the dead."

Lastly, I would have you to remark, that all the little plants in the garden are ingrafted in this *Plant of renown*; "I am the vine, ye are the branches: he that abideth in me, and I in him, the same bringeth forth much fruit; for without me ye can do nothing. I am like a green fir-tree, from me is thy fruit found." If you be not ingrafted, Sirs, in this *Plant*, you will never grow, and all the trees that are not planted in him are all but weeds. There is a time coming when all the weeds will be plucked up; And therefore take heed that you be ingrafted in him by a faith of God's operation. So much for the *first* thing I proposed.

II. The *second* thing was to show, that he is *a renowned Plant*: He is renowned in heaven, and he is renowned on earth, and will be so: "For his name shall endure for ever." Psal. lxxii. 17.

O he is renowned! for what, say you, is he renowned?

I might here enter upon a very large field; I shall only tell you that he is renowned in his person. There was never the like of him the two natures of God and man are joined together in one in him. Did you ever see that? if you have not seen that, you have not seen the mystery of godliness: He is the most renowned Person in heaven; but he is IMMANUEL, "God manifested in the flesh." Then he is renowned for his pedigree, "Who shall declare his generation?" Considering him as God, his eternal generation from the Father cannot be told: We can tell you he is the only begotten of the Father, but we cannot tell you the manner of generation; it is a secret that God has drawn a veil upon, and it is dangerous to venture into a search of it; and they that have attempted it, have commonly bogged into Arian, Arminian, and Sabellian errors. Considering him as a man, he is sprung of a race of ancient kings, a famous catalogue of them you read of in Matth. i. And who can declare his generation even as a man? For he was born of a virgin, and conceived by the overshadowing power of the Highest. Then he is renowned for his name; he hath a name above every name that can be named whether in this world, or in that which is to come. He is renowned for his wisdom; for all the treasures of wisdom and knowledge are in him. He is renowned for his power; for he is not only the wisdom of God but the power of God; he is the Man of God's right-hand, even the Son of man whom he hath made strong for himself. He is renowned for his veracity and fidelity; for "faithfulness is the girdle of his reins, and righteousness the girdle of his loins." Have you got a word from him? depend upon it, it is a sicker word, it does not fail; the word of the Lord endures for ever, when heaven and earth shall pass away. He is renowned for his righteousness; for he has brought in an everlasting righteousness, whereby the law is magnified and made honourable, and by the imputation of which the guilty transgressors are acquitted: he was made "sin for us, who knew no sin, that we might be made the righteousness of God in him;" that is his name, The Lord our righteousness. He is renowned for his fulness; for all the fulness of the Godhead dwells bodily in him; he is full of grace and truth; full of all created and uncreated excellencies. He is renowned for his love; what but love brought him out of the bosom of the Father to this lower world? what but love made him lay down his life for his people? He is renowned for his liberality; he has a full hand and a free heart, as we use to say; he gives without money and he invites all to come and share of his fulness. He is renowned for his constancy; he is Jesus, the same to-day, yesterday, and for ever: the best of men will fail us when we trust them, they will run like splinters into our hands when we lean upon them; but, Sirs, you will find Christ ay the same, to-day, yesterday, and for ever. And then he is renowned for his authority and dominion; it is great and extends far and wide, whether in heaven above, or in the earth beneath; and his dominion reaches from sea to sea, and from the river unto the ends of the earth; and all the kings of the earth are but his vassals. Thus, I say, Christ in every respect is renowned.

But, here, to keep by the phraseology of the text, he is *a renowned Plant*. Wherein is he renowned?

First, I say, he is renowned for his antiquity; "I was set up from everlasting, from the beginning, or ever the earth was," &c. All the plants in the higher and lower gardens of God are but just upstarts in comparison of him: angels and archangels, and the greatest seraphims, are but of yesterday in comparison of this plant. He is renowned for his antiquity; for he is "The Ancient of days, and everlasting Father," Is. ix.

N. B. Here he was desired to conclude his discourse, in respect the work in the church was over, and that he might give way to another minister that was to preach the evening Sermon.

EZEK. xxxiv. 29—And I will raise up for them a Plant of renown.

THE SECOND SERMON ON THIS TEXT.

I HAD occasion, upon a solemnity of this nature, not long ago, to enter upon these words, but had not time to go far into the import of them: After I had traced the connection of the words a little I took them up in the few following particulars:

1. We have here a great blessing promised unto the church, and that is none other than Christ under the notion of a Prince, and a *Plant of renown*.

2. We have the party by whom this promise is made in the pronoun *(I)*, I JEHOVAH, the eternal God, *I will raise up for them a Plant of renown*.

3. We have the way how this *Plant of renown* is raised; *and I will raise* him up, I that am the great Husbandman of the vineyard, *I will raise up for them*, &c. Then.

4. I noticed the persons to whom the promise is made, *I will raise up for them*, that is, for his church, for his people that are brought into a very low condition, as ye will see by reading the preceding part of the chapter; the flock of Christ were scattered by the shepherds of Israel, they were torn, they were devoured, and under manifold trials; well, what will the Lord do for his flock in that condition? He says, *I will raise up for them a Plant of renown, and they shall hunger no more*.

The observation is much the same with the words themselves;

Namely, "That our Lord Jesus Christ is a *Plant of renown*, of his Father's upbringing; *I will raise up for them a Plant of renown*.

In prosecution of this doctrine, I proposed to observe the order and method following.

I. To premise a few things concerning this blessed Plant.
II. To shew that indeed he is *a Plant of renown*.
III. To speak a little concerning the raising up of this Plant.
IV. Shew for whom he is raised up.
V. Shew for what good, or what benefit and advantage he is raised up. And then,
Lastly, Apply the whole.

As to the *first*, I spoke to it; premised a few things concerning this blessed Plant, and I shall not stay to resume what was said on that head.

I likewise entered upon the *second*, and shewed that Christ is *a Plant of renown* in several respects: I mentioned eleven or twelve particulars wherein Christ is renowned, But I shall not resume these neither.

I shall only tell you a few things wherein this blessed Plant is renowned.

1 In the *first* place, this blessed Plant, he is renowned for his antiquity. There are many other plants in God's garden, as angels seraphims, cherubims, saints militant and triumphant, they are all plants; of God's garden; but they are all but up-starts in comparison of him, for he was set up before ever the earth was; ye will see, that one name of this Plant of renown is, the everlasting Father, or the Father of eternity, as it may be rendered.

2. As he is renowned for his antiquity, so for his beauty, he is the most beautiful Plant in all the garden of God; "I am the Rose of Sharon, and the Lily of the valleys; he is as the apple tree among the trees of the wood:" He is renowned I say, for his beauty, and his glory, for the glory of a God is in him. Is there any glory in his eternal Father? Why, that glory shines in our Immanuel in the very, brightness of it, Heb. i. 3. He is the "brightness of the Father's glory and the express image of his person." Now Sirs, if ever your eyes were opened by the Spirit of God, to take up the glory of this Plant his glory has just dazzled your very eyes; you that never saw any glory in him, you never saw him to this very day. Pray that the light of the glory of God in the face of Jesus Christ may yet shine into your hearts; it would make a heartsome sacrament, if this Plant were displayed in his glory among us. Sirs, have you come to see him in his glory? O give God no rest till he make a discovery of himself to you souls.

3. then, He is renowned for his verdure, for his perpetual greenness. Other plants are fading, you and I are fading plants; "All flesh is grass, and all the goodness thereof is as the flower of the field." He is a tree ever green; he never fades summer nor winter, and shall be ever a green Plant to the saints as it were to eternity. When millions of ages, yea myriads of ages, are past in heaven, he will be as fresh and green to the believer, as when he first saw him, or the first moment the saint entered into glory: Therefore it is, that the songs of the redeemed in glory, are ay new songs, and through eternity will ay be new songs; because they will ay see matter of a new song, and the more they see, they will more wonder at him through eternity. Again.

4. This plant is renowned not only for his verdure, but for his virtue. We read in Rev. xxii. ',That the leaves of the tree of life, were for the healing of the nations," that tree of life is the very same with this *Plant of renown*; the leaves of this plant are for the healing of the nations; and we that are ministers are come this day to scatter the leaves of this tree of life, of this *Plant of renown*; try, if you can

get a leaf of it applied and set home upon your souls, depend upon it, there is virtue in every word of his: Sirs, mingle faith with a word, and you will find it will have the same efficacy with you as it had with the poor woman with the bloody issue, that was healed with a touch of the hem of his garment, who had spent all her living on doctors. O see if ye can find him; I assure you he is here, he is behind the door of every man's heart, Rev. iii. 20. "Behold, I stand (says he) at the door and knock, if any man hear my voice, and open the door, I will come in to him, and will sup with him, and he with me:" and O let him in: there is virtue in him for curing you all, though there were ten thousand millions of you more than there are, there is virtue in him for healing every one of you. But then.

5. This blessed Plant, he is not only renowned for his virtue, but likewise for his fertility: He is not a barren plant; he would not be renowned if he were barren; he brings forth all manner of fruit every month; yea, I may add, every day, every moment. You read in Rev. xxii. of the tree of life, that brings forth twelve manner of fruits every month; that is to say, he brings forth all manner of fruit that is necessary for a poor soul: whatever thy soul stands in need of is to be found in him. See then and gather, see if you can gather some of it: There is the fruit of his incarnation; there is the fruit of his death; there is the fruit of his resurrection: there is the fruit of his ascension; there is the fruit of his intercession, and sitting at the right-hand of God; there is the fruit of his prophetic office; there is the fruit of his priestly office; there is the fruit of his kingly office; there is the fruit of his appearing within the veil; there is the fruit of what he did without the veil, and without the camp, O what fruit is here. Here is wisdom for fools; here is justification for the condemned soul; here is sanctification for the polluted soul, and clothing for the naked: riches for the poor, bread for the hungry, drink for the thirsty; all manner of fruit is here, and we are trying, Sirs, to shake the tree of life among you, and blessed be God they may be gathered. O Sirs, they are dropping among you! O gather, gather, for salvation is in every word that drops from him, for his words are the words of eternal life. But,

6. This blessed Plant is renowned for scent, and pleasant savour. O Sirs, there is such a blessed savour in this *Plant of renown*, as has cast a perfume through all the paradise above; he has cast a perfume through all the church militant, which in Is. v. is called God's vinepard. O Sirs, do ye find any thing of the scent of this *Plant;* I can tell you, if ever you have been made to ken him, it will be so, Cant. i. 4. "Because of the savour of thy ointment thy name is as ointment poured forth, therefore do the virgins love thee." The believer finds a scent about him, he draws a savour from him. What is the design of us ministers but to cast abroad his scent; and it is by this we win souls: and they that cast out and drop the *Plant of renown* out of their sermons, and no wonder their sermons stink, and they shall stink to eternity that throw Christ out of their sermons. The great buisness of ministers is cast forth the scent of Christ to people, I shall read ye a word to this purpose, in 2 Cor. ii. 14—15. "Now

thanks be unto God, which always causeth us to triumph in Christ:" the apostle triumphs in him, and all other honest ministers will just triumph in him too, and all Christians triumph in him that know him; "And maketh manifest the savour of his knowledge by us in every place. For we are unto God a sweet savour of Christ, in them that are saved, and in them that perish. To the one we are "the savour of death unto death, and to the other the savour of life, unto life, and who is sufficient for these things?" Who is able to tell the sweet savour that is in him? But then, again.

7. This blessed *Plant* (in my text) is not only renowned for his savour, but likewise for his shadow, Cant. ii. 3. "I sat down under his shadow with great delight," the shadow of the *Plant of renown*. You are all sitting there or standing, but are you sitting under the *Plant of renown?* Jonah's gourd did him service against the the scorching heat of the sun that was like to take away his life: but, alas, that soon failed him; for God sent a worm and smote it, that it withered; and the worm of death will soon smite and wither you and me; O get in under the shadow of this *Plant of renown*, and ye are secured against death and vindictive wrath for ever: get in under his shadow the shadow of his intercession, the shadow of his power, the shadow of his providence, the shadow of his faithfulness; O sit down under his shadow, and you will find shelter there against all deadly; whatever blasts come, you will find safety there; would you be shadowed from the king of terrors, death is a terror to many, O if you would be shadowed against the awful terrors of death and God's vengeance, get under this shadow, and you are safe.

Again 8, This Plant is renowned for his stature: he is a high Plant, he is a tall Plant. You see the heavens above you, but they are but creeping things in comparison of him, but this glorious Plant, "he is the high and lofty one that inhabits eternity;" you can never see his height. Your eye will look high, and your thought will reach higher; but neither your eye nor your thought will reach unto him. He is taller than all the cedars in the Lebanon of God: "Eye hath not seen, nor hath ear heard, neither hath it entered into the heart of man to think of the height and glory of this Plant of renown." But then,

Lastly, This Plant is renowned for his extent, not only for his stature, but he is a broad Plant. He was planted in the first promise in Paradise, he spread through the Old Testament church, he came the length of filling the land of Judea, but at length this Plant has spread among us, and O that I could spread him among you! and O that I could open the leaves of this Plant, to take you in, he is a broad Plant, he will serve you all. We read of the tree of life being on every side of the river. There is a great river betwixt us and heaven, and that is death, and we are all running to this river of death. As one well observes on the place, this tree is in the middle of the river, he is on this side of time, and he is on that side of time Now this Plant is on both sides of the river. Though you were going to the wastes of America, you will find him there as well as here, if you have but the art of improving him. And this Plant will spread himself through all kingdoms,

Habak. ii. 14. "The earth shall be filled with the knowledge of the glory of the Lord, just as the waters cover the sea." He will not only fill the earth, but the whole heavens throughout eternity. O he is a broad Plant that will extend himself both to heaven and earth! And this shall serve for the *second* thing proposed, namely, to show, that this Plant is indeed a renowned Plant.

III. The *third* thing I proposed in the prosecution of this doctrine was, concerning the raising or upbringing of This Plant.

You see it is no other than the great God that raised up this Plant: I find the great Jehovah glorying in his skill and wisdom, in the raising up of this Plant for the use of the church, Psal. lxxxix. 19, Says the Lord, "I have laid help upon one that is mighty, I have exalted one chosen out of the people. I have raised up David my servant; with my holy oil have I anointed him:" He just glories in it, that he had raised up this glorious *Plant of renown.*

I will tell you a few things with reference to the raising up of this blessed Plant.

1st, He was raised up in the counsel of God's peace from eternity. The Trinity sat in council anent the upbringing of him, "The counsel of peace was between them both," Zech. vi. 13. The Father and the Son agreed upon it, that, in the fulness of time, the Son should come into the world. But then, again,

2dly, He was raised up in the first promise to Adam and Eve. Until this Plant was discovered to them, they were like to run distracted. And indeed, Sirs, if Christless sinners saw where they were, and the wrath of God that is hanging over their heads, they would be ready to run distracted, till a revelation of Christ was made to them. All the promises, all the prophecies, all the types, and all the doctrines of the Old Testament, were the gradual springings of this Plant. But it was under ground, until,

3dly, His actual manifestation in the flesh, when, in the fulness of time, he appeared: "In the fulness of time, God sent forth his Son, made of a woman, made under the law, to redeem them that were under the law, that we might receive the adoption of sons." And then, again,

4thly, This Plant was raised up, even in his death. He was cut off from the land of the living, yet even then he was raised up, even in his very death; when this Plant was cut down on Mount Calvary, his scent and savour ran to the utmost ends of the earth. And what is it but the doctrine of the cross of Christ, that catches sinners unto this very day? These ministers must be the devil's ministers, and not the ministers of Christ, who, instead of preaching a crucified Christ, entertain their hearers with harangues of heathen morality, flourishes of rhetoric, the doctrines of self-love as the principles of religious actions, and the like stuff. Will ever these feed the soul, or convert a soul to Christ? Such ways of preaching may tickle the ear and please the fancy, but can never be the power of God to salvation. I say, it was the doctrine of the cross of Christ that subdued the nations, and that shall be the method of winning souls to Christ to the end of the world. "God forbid (says Paul) that I should glory, save in the cross of our Lord Jesus Christ, by whom the world is crucified to me, and I unto the world." And, writing to the Corinthians, he says, "I desire to know nothing among you but Jesus Christ, and him crucified;" and that will be the way of every faithful minister of Christ. But then, again,

5*thly,* This plant was raised up in his resurrection from the dead. For in his resurrection from the dead he was "declared to be the Son of God with power, by the Spirit of holiness." By the upbringing of this Plant after it was cut down, our hopes began to spring up again: And, Sirs, if this Plant had not sprung up again, our hopes had perished for ever. But "blessed be the God and Father of our Lord Jesus Christ, which, according to his abundant mercy, hath begotten us again unto a lively hope," by the upspringing of this *Plant of renown,* after he was cut down. A living Christ, Sirs, is no small matter, a living Redeemer, our life is just bound up in this *Plant of renown;* because I live, ye shall live also. But then, again,

6*thly,* This *Plant of renown* was raised up higher in his ascension into heaven, when he was set "down on the right hand of the Majesty on high," after he had, by himself, purged our sins: This *Plant of renown,* though he be preached unto us Gentiles in the church militant; yet he is now in person received up into glory, 1 Tim. iii., and is up above in the church triumphant, he is gone up with a shout. O let us sing praises to the *Plant of renown,* for he is gone up on high as our Head, as our God, as our great High Priest, in the higher house.

And then, 7*thly,* He is raised up likewise in the revelation of the everlasting gospel. And thus we are endeavouring to raise him up in the word and sacrament this day, as "Moses lifted up the serpent in the wilderness," John iii. 14, so we are endeavouring to lift up the *Plant of renown,* "That whosoever believeth in him should not perish, but have everlasting life," John iii. 16. O Sirs! I bring this *Plant of renown* to you, I offer him to every one of your hands, and say, Will you have him? O will you take this Plant, and spread his savour among you? He is the Father's elect and delight, and shall not all this company say, It is he in whom my soul delighteth? And O, that every one of this company were saying it from the savoury sense of it upon their hearts! O carry him away with you, carry him in your hearts and foreheads, and let all the world know he is yours, "My beloved is mine, and I am his."

But then, again further, 8*thly,* This *Plant of renown* is raised up in the day of the church's reformation. When the fallen tabernacle of David is reared up, then this Plant appears glorious and beautiful. It is for the honour of Christ that the church be reformed. Alas! we heard a noise of great reformation of late; but where is it? or what doth it amount to? What is there done for Christ? Is there any plant plucked up that he hath not planted? Are any intruders upon Christian congregations by presentations, or sham calls, turned out? Is there any thing done with erroneous professors of divinity, when error is running through the land? O! there are few to stand up for the truth this day, when such persons are let go without a rebuke; yea, without so much as a protest taken by them, who, I am persuaded, are lovers of Christ. Alas! it appears there is little courage for Christ, to whom we owe our all: I say, this *Plant of renown* is raised up in the church's reformation; may it not be said, "This is Zion whom no man seeketh after?" Civil and ecclesiastic authority are studying to bear down Christ, but this Plant will be up upon them, let them tread upon him in his members as they will: His supreme Deity and sovereignty in his church will yet appear; for his Father hath said, "Sit thou at my right hand, until I make thine enemies thy footstool."

But then I might tell you, 9*thly*, That this *Plant of renown* will be raised up at his second coming: And, O Sirs, this *Plant of renown* will then appear in different views, and in different lights! To the saints he will appear in glory, they will lift up their heads and sing: But as for the wicked world, they will see him all in red flames, ready to destroy and devour them: behold, he will come in the clouds, and every eye shall see him; they that have pierced him by error; they that have pierced him by robbing and spoiling his people of the privileges wherewith he hath made them free; these that spoil them of their valuable privileges which he has bought for them with his blood, they will howl and cry in that day; "they who pierced him, and all kindreds of the earth shall wail because of him."

And then, *Lastly*, This *Plant of renown* will be raised up in the songs of the redeemed through endless eternity. The work of all the ransomed in glory will be to raise up the glory of this *Plant of renown* in the highest hallelujahs: "Worthy is the Lamb that was slain, to receive power, and riches, and wisdom, and strength, and honour, and glory, and blessing, to endless evermore." Every bird in every bush will there sing of the glory and beauty of the *Plant of renown*, and he will draw all the millions and myriads that are the inhabitants of the higher house after him; they will be continually highly praising him. Thus you see Christ is a *Plant of renown*, and what way he is raised up.

IV. The *fourth* thing I proposed was, for whom is it that this Plant is raised up?

O, may some poor thing say, was he ever raised up for me? I tell you, Sirs, he was never raised up for the fallen angels; "For he took not on him the nature of angels, but he took on him the seed of Abraham." Our nature was highly honoured at first, but it soon sunk below the beast that perisheth. But the second Adam took our nature upon him, and he hath raised it to a higher dignity than the very angels; for to which of the angels did this honour appertain to be united to the eternal Son of God? So that I say, that this *Plant of renown* is raised up for mankind sinners, not for angel-kind sinners, and every mankind sinner that hears tell of him, should lay claim to him, as in Is. ix. 6. And I advise every one of you mankind sinners to apply it; "Unto us a Son is given, unto us this Child is born, and the government shall be upon his shoulder: And his name shall be called Wonderful, Counsellor, The Mighty God, The everlasting Father, The Prince of Peace;" to us he is given; unto us he is born. I remember the angel, at the birth of Christ, told the shepherds, "I bring you good tidings of great joy, which shall be to all people; for unto you (sinners, not unto us) is born this day, in the city of David, a Saviour, which is Christ the Lord." O Sirs, let all this company receive it as glad tidings of great joy; for I tell you, that this *Plant of renown* is raised up for you, if you have but a heart for to use him. As the firmament is for you, if you will open your eyes, so the Sun of righteousness is for you, if you will open your hearts to him: for the Lord's sake do not refuse him, or else it will not be telling you; you will rue it to eternity. But, say some, are you telling us, that Christ was raised up for all mankind? That is not what I say; but I say, that Christ was revealed to all mankind: I abstract from secret things. Our duty is to go and "preach the gospel to every creature;" therefore, according to our commission, we bring this *Plant of renown* to every creature, whether young or old, every rational creature here; we command you (as you will answer at the bar of the great God, as you will answer at the day of judgment), that you receive this *Plant of renown*. For the Lord's sake do not refuse him; for this is the condemnation, that this *Plant* is brought into the world, and the world will not receive him. Let not the devil nor an unbelieving heart knock off your hands from embracing and receiving him, as offered in this gospel we are preaching. The devil and an unbelieving heart will tell you, your sins are so many, and you have run on such a course of sin, that he cannot belong unto you; but the very thing makes you need Christ is, because you are great sinners. Any of you that needs this *Plant of renown*, I invite you not only to take him home in your hands, in your bibles; but, for the Lord's sake, take him home into your hearts and let him lie there all night between your breasts, saying, "This God is our God for ever and ever, and will be our guide even unto death." If you have got this *Plant of renown*, you will at death just go unto God with a shout, with a song, and say, O death, I defy thee: "O death, where is thy sting? O grave where is thy victory?" what harm canst thou do to me? "For to me to live, is Christ, and to die is gain," gain for endless evermore, because I will win to the immediate enjoyment of God, and abide for ever under this refreshing shadow of this *Plant of renown*.

N. B. I thought to have gone through what I designed on this subject but time and strength will not allow; I shall rather return afterwards, if there be occasion for it.

The Lord bless his word.

Ezek xxxiv. 29 – And I will raise up for them a Plant of renown.

THE THIRD SERMON ON THIS TEXT.

V. THE *fifth* thing is, Why is he raised up, or for what ends and use is this *Plant of renown* raised up by JEHOVAH?

Answ. 1*st* He is raised up as a Redeemer to set the captives of the mighty at liberty. It was a posing question, that would have silenced all mankind, which we have, Is. xlix. 24, "Shall the prey be taken from the mighty, or the lawful captive delivered?" Well, Christ being raised up for this very end, solves the hard question, in the words immediately following. ver. 25. "Thus saith the Lord, even the captives of the mighty shall be taken away, and the prey of the terrible shall be delivered." And if you ask, How doth he this? You have an answer to it, Heb. ii. 14, Col. ii. 14, &c.

2*dly.* He is raised up as a Mediator of the new convenant, to make peace between an offended God, and offending rebellious man, he "makes reconciliation for iniquity," Dan. ix. 24. God was in Christ reconciling the world unto himself, &c. "When we were enemies we were reconciled unto God by the death of his Son." And O, what a great matter is it to be restored to the favour and friendship of that glorious Majesty, to whose wrath we were lying obnoxious, &c.

3*dly.* He is raised up as a Surety, to pay the debt of a company of broken dyvers, and to bind himself under a bond to satisfy justice for their crimes, and that he should reduce them to obedience to their offended Lord. Hence he is called, Heb. vii. 25. "The Surety of a better testament;" and as our Surety he fulfils the law which we had broken, as a covenant, both in its do and die, in our room and stead, and then engages he (by his Spirit) would write the law in their hearts, as a rule, and, by putting his Spirit within them, would cause them to walk in God's statutes.

4*thly,* He is raised up as a renowned Healer, and none-such Physician, Exod. xv. "I am the Lord that healeth thee.." Man, through sin, is become a leper from head to foot, full of wounds, bruises, and putrefying sores, which renders him unfit for any good service, unfit for answering the ends of his creation, to glorify God, or to enjoy him for ever. Well, Christ is raised up for the recovery and health of diseased souls; he has opened up a medicinal well, Zec. xiii. x. that washes from sin and from uncleanness, and, whatever be your malady, we invite you to come to this well, and wash and be clean, like Naaman in the waters of Jordan; O he is all over virtue! his "leaves are for the healing of the nations." And in a particular manner, his commission carries him, to heal the broken in heart, and to bind up all their wounds.

5*thly,* He is raised up as a Witness to tell the truth, or as a prophet to reveal it. We have by the fall lost the knowledge of God and of his truth, and any knowledge of the truth that remains with us by nature, it is detained in unrighteousness. Well, Christ comes to make a revelation of God, and of the things of God unto us; that Christ was raised up for this end, see Deut. xviii. 18. "I will raise them up a Prophet like unto thee, from among their brethren, and will put my words in his mouth, and he shall speak unto them all that I shall command him." But see the awful certification that follows, ver, 19. "Whosoever will not hearken unto my words, that he shall speak in my name, I will require it of him."

6*thly*, He is raised up as a Leader unto the people, We have lost our way to heaven, and Satan was leading all mankind to hell blindfold. But Christ came to shew us the path of life, and to lead us into it, and by his leading, he causes the wayfaring man to walk without erring, "I will bring the blind by a way they know not," &c.

7*thly*, He is raised up as a Commander unto the people, as the Captain of salvation, to fight our battles for us, and to head the armies of God's Israel in their way to glory; And by his skill and conduct, he makes them all conquerors, yea, more than conquerors, at the end of the day, &c.

I might tell you further, that he is raised up as the great High Priest of our profession, that, by one offering, he might for ever perfect them that are sanctified," &c.: As our Advocate with the Father to plead our cause, and to agent our business in heaven: As a Shepherd, to feed his church and people in the wilderness: "He shall feed his flock like a shepherd," &c.; As a prince, to rule them by his word and spirit.; he is the "Prince of peace, and of the increase of his government and peace there shall be no end," &c.; As an everlasting Father, in whom the fatherless family of Adam find mercy, &c,: As a wonderful Counsellor, or to give counsel in all dark and difficult cases. &c.: As a husband and bridegroom, to cherish and comfort his church and people, and accordingly he betrothes her unto him for ever. But these things I do not insist upon. I hasten forward to

VI. The *sixth* thing, which was the application of the doctrine. Is it so that Christ is a *Plant of renown*, raised up by JEHOVAH?

Then, 1*st*, See hence the iniquity and wickedness of these men, who study to derogate from the glory of this renowned Plant. The Arians would darken the renown of this blessed Plant, by denying his supreme Deity, and making him an inferior and dependent being; the Socinians, by denying he had any being before his actual incarnation; the Arminians, by denying his righteousness, and by making the efficacy of his grace to depend upon the will of man and the power of depraved nature. O, Sirs, Christ is not renowned in Scotland this day, either among ministers or professors, as he has sometimes been. "The Head-stone of the corner is rejected," the *Plant of renown* is cast aside, by many ministers in the land; and he is rejected by all that do not really believe in him, &c.

2*dly*, See hence how to know a true and faithful minister of Christ. Some at this day make it a question, whom they shall hear, when there are such divisions, and such a flood of corrupt ministers getting into a church. Why, Sirs, you may know a true minister of Christ, he will have a smell of the *Plant of renown* about him; whether he be in the pulpit or out of it; whether he be in a judicatory, or wherever he be, his great business is to advance the glory of the *Plant of renown*, the smell and savour of his Master will be about him, which the true disciples of Christ will discern.

3dly, See hence whence it is that believers flock to gospel ordinances, where they can get them dispensed by these that bear Christ's commission to dispense them. Why, it is the smell of the *Plant of renown* that draws them thither; hence it is, that his tabernacles are amiable, "and a day in his courts better than a thousand;" why, his scent perfumes these palaces of Zion, as with myrrh, aloes, and cassia, &c.

4thly, See hence why God the Father is called a Husbandman. Why, he is so called with reference unto his raising up this *Plant of renown*, John xv. 1, "I am the true Vine, and my Father is the Husbandman;" he raised him up as the root, and upheld him, and takes branches of the wild olive, and grafts them into him, and makes them fruitful, &c.

5thly, See hence the regard that God hath for his church upon earth, as his own garden. Why, he plants this Tree of life in her, by which she became a new paradise. The tree of life that grew in the earthly paradise, which was the seal and sacrament of the covenant of works, is long since withered and gone; but the tree of life, in the new garden, of God's planting, of which even a sinner may eat, and live for ever, will never wither. O let us admire God's way of grace; for it is full of wonder, in providing this renowned Plant, this new Tree of life for us. His fruit is so far from being forbidden, that it is God's great commandment to all sinners, "to come and eat, and live," &c.

6thly, See hence the excellency of Christ, in his person, nature, offices, and appearances. Why, he is the *Plant of renown*, O Sirs, Christ is such an excellent person, that he is the Renown of the family of heaven and earth; he is the Renown of his Father, for he is "the brightness of his glory." He is the Renown of earth, for by him the human nature is raised up to a higher glory than that of angels; for, even as Mediator, he "hath by inheritance obtained a more excellent name than they." O should not every one of mankind sinners be ready to cry, "O let his name endure for ever, let his name be continued as long as the Sun; for men are blessed in him: and O, blessed be his glorious name for ever, and let the whole earth be filled with his glory?"

7thly, See what makes a land or a church pleasant, a Hephzibah or a Beulah unto the Lord. Why, it is the *Plant of renown* that makes any church or land delectable: If the *Plant of renown* and his interest be thriving in a land or church, it makes her "beautiful for situation, the joy of the whole earth," &c.

8thly, See when it is that a church loses her beauty and glory, and makes defection. Why, it is when Christ loses his savour among her ministers and professors; And when this *Plant of renown* is rejected, God rejects that church, and gives her to the spoil. Sirs, Christ has been long preached in Scotland, but folk have not entertained him by faith, and therefore the Lord, at this day, is threatening to take his Christ altogether away from among us.

9*thly*, See hence how a person may know whether matters be right or wrong, whether he be thriving and prospering in grace, or if he be decaying and going backward. Why, it is aye right with the soul, in whom and with whom Christ is in the ascendant. Is the *Plant of renown* rising or going back with you? If he be rising, then, (1.) He will be raised up in your esteem, as with David, Psal. lxxiii. 25, and Paul, Philip. iii. 8, 9. (2.) In your affection and love, "Whom having not seen, we love," &c., "Lord (says Peter) thou knowest all things, thou knowest I love thee," &c. (3.) He will be raised up in our meditation; every thought will be a captive to his obedience, and our "meditations of him will be sweet, and our souls satisfied as with marrow and fatness, when you remember him, and meditate upon him," &c. (4.) He will be raised up in your talk and walk, they will have a savour of the *Plant of renown*, and the chat and common talk of the world will be tasteless, like the white of an egg, to you. But, O, a talking of Christ, and of his truths, and of the concerns of his glory, will go well down with you. (5.) He will be raised up in your religious worship, both public and private, when you go to prayer, when you go to hear the word, or when you go to a communion table, nothing will please but Christ himself. "O that I knew where I might find him. One thing have I desired, and that will I seek after," &c. (6.) He will be raised up in your wishes and endeavours for the advancement of his kingdom and glory, in as far as your power can go. And whenever his cause comes upon the field, or the cry is made, "Who is on the Lord's side?" You will ay study, in your sphere, to take that side where you think Christ stands, and contend and witness for him, his truths, his ways, and worship, according to your power, &c.

10*thly*, May be by way of lamentation. If Christ be the *Plant of renown*, raised up by his eternal Father, may it not be for matter of lamentation that the *Plant of renown* is in so little request among us at this day, and that there is such a plucking away of the glory of this blessed Plant. Some plucking away the glory of his supreme Deity, as you were hearing, and studying to reduce him among the rank of created and dependent beings: Some plucking at his sovereignty and supremacy, as the alone Head and King of his church; enacting laws inconsistent with, and directly opposite unto these laws that he has given in his word: Some plucking at the "liberty wherewith he has made his people free," by violent intrusions of ministers upon congregations, contrary to scripture pattern, and the covenanted sworn principles of the church of Scotland, inserted in her books of discipline.

O Sirs, if the *Plant of renown* were flourishing in the land, there would not be so many unsavoury plants allowed to grow or come up in his vineyard, as there are at this day. The plant of Popish idolatry is connived at, and on the growing hand, both through Scotland, England, and Ireland. The plant of prelacy, error, and superstition, tolerate, contrary to solemn covenant engagements, which the land lies under; the plant of unsound professors of divinity, poisoning our fountains of learning, and seminaries for the holy ministry; the plant of lax erroneous ministers and preachers, is growing up apace, and filling the land every day. The plant of old malignancy against the power of religion and a covenanted reformation is growing up, especially among a set of pretended Presbyterians, falsely so called. The plant of profanity is flourishing apace, men abandoning themselves unto wickedness, and giving themselves loose reins in drinking, swearing, rioting, whoredom, drunkenness, Sabbath-breaking, and all manner of abominations, burlesquing the scriptures, ridiculing the worship of God, and breaking their profane jests upon the sacred things of God. The plant of ecclesiastical tyranny, which seemed to be nipt a little these two years bygone, is sprouting again as fast as ever, notwithstanding the great cries of a pretended reformation that we heard among a great many ministers and professors in the established church; witness the proceedings of the last Assembly, in the case of Dennie and Traquair, and the entertainment of the petition of the parish of Stow. I say, all these, and many other things that might be insisted upon, evidently declare that the *Plant of renown* is not raised up among us, but rather that his flavour and savour is gone away, in a great measure, from amongst magistrates and ministers, from judicatories and assemblies for worship, and from among the generality of professors and inhabitants of the land. Yea, many come that length, that, like the Gadarenes, they would be well content that Christ were quite departed out of our coasts, that they might with freedom enjoy their swinish lusts: and indeed he seems to be taking his leave of us. But O, what will follow upon his departure? "Woe, woe, also unto them, when I depart from them." See what comes of the vineyard of the Lord of hosts, Is. v. from the beginning, when he departs he takes away the hedge, &c.

11*thly*, Is in a word of exhortation. Is it so that Christ is a *Plant of renown* raised up by JEHOVAH? Then all that bear the name of Christ, especially you who have been entertained at his table, and tasted of his special love and goodness, study to answer God's design, in raising up for us this *Plant of renown*.

Take this in the following particulars, with which I conclude. (1.) Sit down, and rest your weary souls, under the shadow of this renowned Plant, after the example of the spouse, Cant. ii., "I sat down under his shadow with great delight." When you find no rest in the world, by reason of temptations, afflictions, and the working of indwelling corruption, and when you are crying, "O tell me where he maketh his flocks to rest," let your recourse be aye to the *Plant of renown*, for to him "shall the Gentiles seek, and his rest shall be glorious." (2.) I invite you to come and behold the glory and beauty of the *Plant of renown:* "O look unto him, and be saved, all ye ends of the earth." God the Father thinks so meikle of this Plant of his own raising, that he invites the whole world to behold him as the delight of his very soul, Is. xlii. 1, "Behold my Servant whom I uphold, mine Elect in whom my soul delighteth," It is by beholding of his glory, that the work of sanctification, and conformity to the divine image, and the life of religion is maintained and kept up, 2 Cor. iv. last, "All we beholding, as in a glass, the glory of the Lord, are changed into the same image." (3.) Come and feed upon the fruit of this *Plant of renown;* "For his flesh is meat indeed, and his blood is drink indeed." You have been at his table, and perhaps got a meal there, but, Sirs, you would be continually feeding upon him. You see, in the close of the verse, this Plant is raised up to be food to the hungry; "I will raise him up for them, and they shall hunger no more," or be consumed with hunger no more; and therefore be ay feeding upon his fruits, for they are "sweet to the taste, and make the lips of them that are asleep, to speak, like the best wine that goeth down sweetly," &c, (4.) Whenever you find yourselves wounded by temptation, or corruption, or the world, come to the *Plant of renown* for healing, for his "leaves are for the healing of the nations." You have a sweet promise to this purpose, Mal. iv. 2, "To you that fear my name shall the Sun of righteousness arise with healing in his wings; and ye shall go forth, and grow up as calves of the stall," &c. (5.) Let me exhort you, in your sphere, ministers and private Christians, and I would fain take home the exhortation to myself. O let us all join issue with the Father of Christ, in studying to raise up this *Plant of renown,* and to make him more and more renowned, this will be the ambition, and resolution, and endeavour of all that know him. Psal. xlv. at the close, says the church there, "I will make thy name to be remembered in all generations, therefore shall the people praise thee, O Lord, for ever and ever." Let us (that are ministers) preach and proclaim his righteousness and renown, and the glory of his person, in the great congregation. And you (that are the people) O study to commend him by your walk and talk, and the holiness of your conversation, upon all occasions; and, when his cause and interest in the land is in such a sinking condition, let us take a lift of it. Let us lie at a throne of grace, pleading, that he would not forsake the land; but that he would yet return, and be "the glory in the midst of us," Zech. ii. 5.

GOD'S DOVES FLYING TO HIS WINDOWS.

Is. lx. 8.—Who are these that fly as a cloud, and as doves to their windows.

IN the last verse of the preceding chapter, God had made a promise of the continuance of the church upon earth to the uttermost ages of time: "As for me, this is my covenant," &c. Here, in the beginning of this chapter, we have a promise concerning the enlargement of the church under the New Testament, unto the uttermost ends of the earth: Ver. 3, 4, "And the Gentiles shall come to thy light, and kings to the brightness of thy rising. Lift up thine eyes round about, and see; all they gather themselves together, they come

GOD'S DOVES FLYING TO HIS WINDOWS.   303

to thee, thy sons shall come from far, and thy daughters shall be nursed at thy side." We are likewise told, how the church shall be affected with this increase of her numbers and enlargement of her borders. (1.) She will be in a transport of joy upon this account: ver. 5, "Thou shalt see and flow together," &c. (2.) There will be a mixture of fear with this joy; "Thine heart shall fear," as though it were a thing unlawful to join with the Gentiles, &c. (3.) She shall be enlarged with love, so as to leave room for all the Gentile converts. (4.) She shall be struck with surprise and wonder, saying, *Who are these that fly?* &c.

Where four things are considerable. 1. We have a sweet sight that the Old Testament church gets of the state of matters under the New Testament, upon the revelation of Christ in the gospel among the Gentiles. Why, she sees poor souls upon the wing, in great multitudes, flying to a Saviour; and a sweeter sight cannot be seen upon earth, &c. 2. Notice the manner of their flight; they *fly as a cloud, and as doves:* Of which more particularly afterward, when we come to prosecute the doctrine. 3. Notice the term or object of their flight; they fly to the windows for their relief. Like the windows of the ark of Noah, whereat the dove entered, when she could find no place for the sole of her foot, because of the deluge. 4. Notice the pleasant surprise that the prophet of the Old Testament church is put into at this sight. This is implied in the manner of the speech, *(Who are these?)* She is stricken with a pleasant astonishment, to see the sinners of Gentiles, "aliens to the commonwealth of Israel, strangers to the covenant of promise," flocking in to Christ; Christ preached unto the Gentiles, and the Gentiles believing in Christ, being a branch of the great mystery of godliness, 1 Tim. iii. and last.

OBS. That the flight of sinners to a Saviour is a sweet and surprising sight. *Who are these that fly as a cloud?* &c.

The method, through divine assistance shall be,

I. To speak a little of this flight of the sinner to Christ, and shew what it imports.

II. I would speak a little of the manner of their flight: *They fly as a cloud, and as doves.* What may be couched in these metaphors.

III. Speak a little of these windows to which they fly.

IV. Shew that this is a sweet and surprising sight.

V. Apply the whole.

I. The *first* thing is, to speak a little of the flight of a sinner to Christ, the Saviour.

1*st*, Then, This flight supposes that some spiritual life and sensation is given to the sinner; for there can be no flying without life. The sinner is by nature dead in sin, legally dead, and spiritually dead; Eph. ii. 1. "You hath he quickened, who were dead in trespasses and sins." The Spirit of life that is in Christ Jesus enters into the dead soul, and quickens, and gives it at least a sensation of its case, otherwise there can be no flying to Christ.

2dly, This flight supposes or implies an apprehension and fear of danger from a pursuing enemy. The poor soul is made to see danger from the broken law, danger from the sword of justice, the avenger of blood, and thereupon he falls a-trembling, like the jailor, "Sirs, what must I do to be saved?" &c.

3dly, This flight of the soul to Christ implies a renunciation of belief from these lying refuges, in which it had formerly been trusting. The man, in flying to Christ, renounces an empty profession, his common gifts, his common graces, his gospel advances, his law works, his own holiness and righteousness, his tears and prayers; his righteousness cannot profit him, therefore he cries out, "Ashur shall not save us; we will not ride upon horses, neither will we say any more to the work of our hands, Ye are our gods; for in thee the fatherless findeth mercy," Hos. xii. 3. "In vain is salvation hoped for from the hills, and from the multitude of mountains; truly in the Lord our God is the salvation of his people."

4thly, It implies a discovery and uptaking of Christ, and of his salvation, as he is held out in the gospel. A beam of divine light shines into the heart, "even the light of the knowledge of the glory of God in the face (or person) of Jesus Christ," whereby the man sees him to be indeed what the gospel represents him to be, a none-such and incomparable Saviour: one that is the "Man of God's right hand," Psal. lxxv. 17.: "the Man who is God's fellow," Zech. xiii. 7. and therefore mighty to save, &c.

5thly, This flight of the soul to Christ implies the soul's hearty approbation of Christ, and of the way of salvation through Christ, as an ordinance of God calculate for his glory, as well as for his own safety and happiness. O, says the man, "It is indeed a faithful saying, and worthy of all acceptation, that Christ Jesus came into the world to save sinners." I see this method of salvation through the new and living way to be every way worthy of the wisdom of God, and calculate for the manifestation of the glory of his holiness, justice sovereignty, faithfulness, and every other attribute of God, that was lesed by the sin of man; Therefore the man approves of it with his soul, and blesses God that ever found out such a device, &c.

6thly, This flight has in it a strong and ardent desire to be at this Saviour, and to be found in him. "O that I knew where I might find him!" O to be washed with his blood, clothed with his righteousness, sanctified by his Spirit! "Yea, doubtless (says Paul) I count all things but loss, that I may win Christ, and be found in him," &c.

7thly, It implies a hope of winning him, and of being sheltered and saved in him: for, if there be no hope of safety, the man will never flee, and this hope is founded upon the design of the incarnation, &c. the design of the revelation of him in the word &c. the gracious grant made of him in the word, &c. the free promise of life and pardon through him, &c. the calls, and offers, and commands of God to come to him, and the redemption that others have met with, &c.

8thly, A resting and trusting in him, and in him alone, for righteousness, life, peace, pardon, and salvation, to himself in particular

The man does not simply believe that Christ is a Saviour, and that salvation is to be had in him for the elect, or for believers, but he believes in him and on him for his own salvation, Acts. xv. 11. "We believe (or we are persuaded), that through the grace of the Lord Jesus Christ, we shall be saved even as they." We find faith or trust in scripture commonly expressed in word of appropriation and application. The man looks upon Christ as given and offered by God in the gospel; and he says, with Thomas, "My Lord, and my God; or with Paul, "He loved me, and gave himself for me; he is our Lord Jesus Christ." He looks to the God and Father of Christ, and says "He is my God, and my Father, and the Rock of my Salvation," &c. He looks to the covenant of grace and promise sealed with a Redeemer's blood, and cries with David, "This is all my salvation, that he has (in Christ, made or established) with me an everlasting covenant, ordered in all things, and sure," I own indeed that this applying faith is not alike strong in all believers, or yet alike strong in the self same believer at all times; for sad experience makes it evident, that the confidence of faith may be so sadly shaken and staggered through unbelief, temptation, and desertion, as to cry out some times, "Is his mercy clean gone? Hath God forgotten to be gracious? I am cast out of his sight." But then it would be remembered, that although these fits, fears, and staggerings, be in the believer, they are not in his faith, yea, his faith is opposite unto these doubts and fears, and is still fighting against them, "Why are ye fearful, O ye of little faith; Fear not, only believe." And in as far as faith gets the mastery over these doubts and fears, so far will he have of this confidence, as to his own particular claim. Let faith get up its head, and it will speak its own particular leed *, "Abba, Father, doubtless thou art our Father, and our Redeemer, and thy name is from everlasting." Thus you see what this flight is.

II. The *second* thing in the method, is to speak a little to the manner of the soul's flight unto Christ, And this is held out here in the text, under a twofold metaphor; 1*st*, They *fly as a cloud*. 2*dly* They fly *as doves to their windows*.

1*st*, They are here said to fly *as a cloud*. Take this in the particulars following.

1. This points to the multitude of these that should be converted to the faith of Christ, under the New Testament dispensation: For we find a cloud is sometimes expressive of a multitude, Heb. xii. 1, "Seeing we are compassed about with so great a cloud of witnesses." *i. e.* such a great multitude of them, let us lay aside every weight, &c. So here, *Who are these that fly as a cloud?* It says, that as there are innumerable drops of rain, or particles of mist and vapours in a cloud; so under the New Testament, there would be vast numbers and innumerable multitudes, that would take a flight by faith, unto Christ Rev. vii. We shall find, according to the calculation there made, that under the Old Testament they could be summed up; and they are reckoned in whole, out of all the tribes of Israel, to be "a hun-

* Its specific language, or proper and native dialect.

dred and forty-four thousand." But when he comes to speak of the converts among other nations, they are called "an innumerable company which no man can number," ver. 9. This was what the prophet Isaiah foresaw in the verse immediately preceding my text; and likewise, chap. liv. 1. "Sing, O barren, thou that didst not bear, break forth into singing, and cry aloud thou that didst not travail with child: for more are the children of the desolate, than the children of the married wife, saith the Lord." O what a cloud of saints have gone away to heaven since the gospel came to be preached among the Gentiles? And what a cloud of them have gone to heaven out of Scotland, since about two hundred years after the death of Christ, when the gospel came first to be preached among us? It is a sad matter that there should be so few in this generation, in comparison of what was in former days, when the Spirit was poured out from on high! though, blessed be God, there is a pretty number, though few, few, in respect of these that are posting to hell.

2. They *fly as a cloud.* It may signify the unanimity of these converts; they take all one way, like a cloud flying along the heavens they are all joined unto one Head Christ Jesus; they are all knit together in one bond of Christian love: they are all acted by the same Spirit of God and of glory resting on them; they are all clothed with the same robes of imputed and inherent righteousness; they have all one character. they are all heirs of the same inheritance, and they all travel in the same road, the "strait and narrow way that leads unto everlasting life."

3. The *cloud flies* upon the wings of the wind, and what airth soever the wind carries them thither do they go. So all believers are acted, moved, and carried on in their course, by the wind of the influences of the Spirit. When the wind blows, then the clouds accelerate their motion. Just so is it with the believer: If the Spirit be suspended, they lie like a ship wind-bound, they cannot move; but whenever the gale of the heavenly wind blows, then they run the way of God's commandments; hence is that prayer of the spouse, Can. iv. last, "Awake, O north wind, and come, thou south; blow upon my garden, that the spieces thereof may flow out." It was by a gust of this heavenly wind, that the church was made to cry, "Ere ever I was aware, my soul made me as the chariots of Amminadib," &c.

4. They *fly as a cloud.* It says, that there is much of the sovereignty of God, and of the irresistability of his Grace, in the flight of a sinner unto Christ. The clouds are said to be God's chariots, and God's chariot cannot be stopped or hindered in its motion, "Who can hinder the motion of the cloud along the heavens?" No, not all the powers of hell and earth can hinder it: So the work of divine grace in bringing a sinner out of a state of nature into grace; it is the fruit of adorable sovereignty, and he will go on with his work, let devils and men rage, and corruption within do their uttermost to mar and hinder his procedure, "I will take away the stony heart, and I will give the heart of flesh. And who hath resisted his will?" His own arm, that brought about salvation, in a way of purchase, until he could say, "It is finished," will also carry it on in a way of powerful

application; "Thy people shall be willing in the day of thy power: all that the Father giveth me, shall come to me." The work cannot be let which he takes in hand, for the Lord "is a rock, and his work is perfect."

5. *Who are these that fly as a cloud?* It implies, that God's work of grace is of a secret and mysterious nature, It is usual in scripture to express dark and mysterious dispensations by a cloud, "clouds and darkness were round about him," *i. e.* his dispensations were mysterious. So, here, *Who are these that fly as a cloud? i. e.* it is wonderful and mysterious to see how the Lord brings the sinner to take a flight into Christ by faith; God's way in this is a great deep that cannot be searched out; Hence is that of Christ to Nicodemus, John iii. 8' "The wind bloweth where it listeth, and thou hearest the sound thereof, but canst not tell whence it cometh, and whither it goeth," &c.

6. The *clouds* are exhaled out of the earth by the heat of the sun, and raised up above the earth, and mount up towards heaven. Just so, by the warm influences of divine grace, (which are the beams of the Sun of righteousness) the sinner that is lying in the horrible pit, and in a miry clay, and licking up the dust of the earth, is elevate and raised God-ward, and heaven-ward, and made to seek things that are above, Is. xl. 31. "They mount with wings as eagles: Heb. xi. 14 "They seek a better country, that is an heavenly."

7. The clouds, when raised up by the heat of the sun, they are kept up by the mighty power of God. So, believers being brought into a state of grace, they are kept in it "by the power of God, through faith unto salvation." It is he that preserves them in that state; hence believers are called the preserved in Jesus Christ. And as the clouds are in the hand of the Lord, so are all his saints, Deut. xxxiii. 3, "All his saints are in thy hand;" John x. 28. "No man shall pluck them out of my hand;" ver. 29, "My Father, who gave them me, is greater than all, and none is able to pluck them out of my Father's hand," &c.

8. Although the clouds have a louring and dark aspect to the eye, yet they have a blessing in them; they sift down rain upon the earth, which contributes unto its fertility. So God's work of grace on the soul, although it have a dark aspect at the beginning; yet there is a blessing in it in the event, a blessing to the soul when it is landed in Christ; and believers, however ill the world like them, yet they are a blessing unto the world, and contribute to its preservation and fruitfulness. The clouds, you know, pour down rain upon the earth: for believers wherever they come, they study to drop the knowledge of Christ; for the lips of the righteous send many: hence is that of the prophet, Micah v. 7, "The remnant of Jacob shall be in the midst of many people, as a dew from the Lord, as the showers upon the grass, that tarrieth not for man, nor waiteth for the sons of men." And thus you see why they are said to *fly as a cloud.*

2*dly,* They are said to *fly as doves to their windows.* Take the similitude in the following particulars.

1. The dove, you know, is a timorous creature, it is soon frighted.

So believers are timorous of sin, timorous of offending the majesty of God; and therefore they are commonly described to be such as fear the name of the Lord. They are afraid of Satan, that roaring lion, as the doves are afraid of the birds of prey, which would devour and tear them; they are afraid of the snares of the world, and occasions of sin; and therefore they hate the very garments spotted by the flesh.

2. The wings of the dove are its only weapons, it cannot fight, and therefore it flies from the enemy to its windows. So the flight of faith to Christ is the only safety of a believer. Hence they are said to fly "for refuge to the hope set before them." And when the poor believer is tossed with the tempests of affliction, temptation, desertion, persecution, and the workings of a body of sin and death, he is ready to say with David, Psal. lv. 6, "O that I had wings like a dove, for then would I fly away and be at rest."

3. The wings of the dove are very beautiful, they are said to be "covered with silver, and her feathers with yellow gold." So the flight of faith unto Christ is pleasant and delightful unto Christ. He declares himself to be just ravished with it, Cant. iv. 9, "Thou hast ravished my heart, my sister, my spouse, thou hast ravished my heart with one of thine eyes, with one chain of thy neck." When the disciples returned from preaching the gospel among the cities of Israel, and told Christ of many that believed, it is said, he rejoiced in Spirit, &c. It is the pleasure of Christ's heart to have sinners flocking in under the shadow of his wings, and there is joy in heaven, when but one soul flies unto him by faith.

4. The dove is a mournful creature, the remnant of Israel are said to be like doves in the valley, mourning every one for his iniquities. The flight of faith to Christ is penitential, and with weeping for the offence the soul hath done to a God of love. The eye of faith is a weeping eye, Zech. xii. 10, "They shall look upon me whom they have pierced, and mourn," &c.

5. The dove is a simple creature, without art or cunning; we read of the dove's simplicity, and of the serpent's subtilty. So faith is accompanied with a great deal of simplicity, it is the single eye that fills the whole body with light; and believers, when they betake themselves to Christ, they lay aside the wisdom and policy of the flesh. Whenever Paul became a believer, he consulted no more with flesh and blood; they study with simplicity and godly sincerity (not with fleshly wisdom) to have their conversation in the world. Alas! there is little of this at this day, among ministers and professors: little of it among judicatures, where all affairs are managed with carnal policy and wisdom, for pleasing men, especially great men, whatever become of Christ's little ones.

6. The dove is a cleanly creature, and delights much in clean waters and clean places. And so it imports that the flight of faith to Christ, is of a purifying and sanctifying nature. When the soul flies to him, it flies to him to be cleansed from sin, both in the guilt and filth of it. And when the principle of faith is implanted in the soul, it is aye working and wrestling against sin, wherever it finds it, particularly

in the heart; and like the living spring in the well, it is continually working until the mud and filth of sin is wrought out, Acts xv., purifying their hearts by faith.

7. The dove is a social creature, it loves to be in company with its own kind; hence commonly you shall see them flying in flocks. So believers fly and flock together: They do not love to fly with the vulture, the hawk, or the raven, but with their own fraternity. The saints love to be in one another's company; they that fear the Lord associate together, they spake often one to another, Mal. iii. 6.

8. The flight of the dove is swift: and what is swifter than the wings of faith and love, whereby the believer in a moment will mount from earth to heaven? "and enter within the veil, where the fore-runner is for us entered," &c.

9. The dove is a very innocent and harmless creature, it doth injury to none of the other birds; so believers study to "be harmless and blameless, the sons of God without rebuke, in the midst of a crooked and perverse generation." This much for the *second* thing, namely, The manner of the flight, &c.

III. The *third* thing in the method was, to offer a few thoughts anent the *windows* to which the believer flies.

And there are these few things I offer on this head.

1*st*, That God has provided a house for his doves; for windows belong to a house. And what sort of a house, God in his infinite wisdom and love has provided, you may see, Prov. ix. 1, 2, "Wisdom hath builded her house, she hath hewen out her seven pillars." God took up house with man at his creation, but that house fell with the fall of Adam, and the breach of the first covenant; and God and man parted house. But God's heart being full of love to man upon earth, he could not think of a total parting: and therefore, though he broke up family with them for a little, yet he sends his own Son to build him a new house, in which he might take up family again with man; for "he rejoiced in the habitable parts of the earth, and his delights were with the sons of men." And accordingly Christ comes into the world, and lays the foundation of a new house, and it is founded in Zion, and he himself is laid as the foundation of the house, "a tried stone, a precious corner-stone, a sure foundation." And this is a house not for the merit of works, but a house of free mercy, Psal. lxxxix, 3, "I have said, mercy shall be built up for ever," &c.

2*dly*, I remark that there is bield* in this house of mercy that wisdom has built for lost sinners of Adam's family: And therefore the doves here are said to *fly into their windows*. See what bield there is for a sinner here, chased for his life by law, justice, and the devil, Is. xxxii. 2, "a Man (viz. the Man Christ Jesus, the Man of God's right hand, the Master of the house) shall be as a hiding-place from the wind, and a covert from the tempest: as the shadow of a great rock in a weary land." O Sirs, by the revelation of Christ in the church, salvation is placed in Zion, and he bids all the frighted

---

* Shelter or defence.

doves "look unto him and be saved, for he is God, and there is none else besides him.

3dly, I remark that there is light in the house, that God has provided for his doves. For one great use of windows in a house is for letting in the light; the church, the house of God, is a lightsome house, therefore called a valley of vision. Wherever God sets up a church, "the people who sat in darkness see great light: and to them who sat in the land of the shadow of death, light springs up." The light of the Sun of righteousness shines in the church: it shines in the dispensation of the word, and it shines in the manifestation of the Holy Ghost into the hearts of the inhabitants: and therefore all the indwellers of the house are called the "children of the light, and of the day."

4thly, I remark that the windows of this house are open; for the doves do not fly into the windows of a house that are shut. O Sirs, God keeps open doors, and open windows in his house for all comers. Let a sinner come by day or night unto Christ, he is aye welcome: "Come to me who will, I will in no ways cast out."

5thly, That sinners have a claim and title to the Saviour and his salvation, dispensed in the ordinances of the gospel: for they are here said to *fly as doves into their windows*. O Sirs, we tell you, that Christ is your Christ! As the angels, when they preached Christ unto the shepherds, they said unto them, Unto you is born a Saviour; not to us, but unto you is he born; he has not taken our nature upon him, but yours: and therefore he belongs to you, that you may believe, and apply, and use him. Hence the church, Is. ix. 6, cries, "Unto us a child is born, unto us a Son is given," &c.

6thly, That in God's house of mercy, or in the church of Christ, there are a variety of ordinances, wherein the souls of believers may have access to fellowship and communion with him. For it is not here said in the singular number, that they shall *fly as doves to their window*, but, they shall *fly as doves to their windows*.

Now here I will tell you of a few of these windows, by which believers, who are God's doves, do enter upon the wings of faith, to fellowship and communion with the Lord: and these windows are of two kinds, either more private and secret, or more open and public.

1. I say, There are some more private and secret windows of the house, by which the doves do enter into fellowship and communion with the Lord, even in the worst times, when the public doors of the sanctuary are shut, that they can have no access unto them, either through corruption or persecution.

(1.) Then, there is the secret window of meditation. God's doves will enter into his house of mercy here, and have sweet fellowship with him, when none of all the world know anything about it. David, Psal. lxiii., when driven into the wilderness of Judah, when he was driven into a dry and thirsty land, far from the sanctuary or public ordinances, yet he flies into this privy window, and finds sweet entertainment to his soul, ver. 5-7, "My soul shall be satisfied as with marrow and fatness, and my mouth shall praise thee with joyful lips. When I remember thee upon my bed, and meditate on thee in the night watches: because thou hast been my help, therefore in the shadow of thy wings will I rejoice," &c.

(2.) There is the privy window of secret prayer whether it be occasional, ejaculatory, or stated prayer. At this window the believer enters into communion with the Lord, many a time, and is sweetly fed. We find the saints delighting much in this window: No sooner is Paul converted, but immediately it is observed of him, " Behold he prayeth," Acts ix. 14; and David, when speaking of God's doves, Psal. xxiv. 6, calls them the "generation of them that seek the face of Jacob's God." And David himself frequented this window of secret prayer much; seven times a-day he would be hovering about it; and O, but God loves to hear the voice of his doves in prayer! Cant. ii. 14, "O my dove that art in the clefts of the rock, in the secret places of the stairs, let me see thy countenance, let me hear thy voice; for sweet is thy voice, and thy countenance is comely." He invites his doves to come here frequently to this window, and he promises to entertain them, Matth. vii. 7, " Ask and it shall be given you; seek and ye shall find; knock and it shall be opened unto you."

(3.) There is the window of praise, thanksgiving, and singing of psalms, not only in public, in consort with others, but even in private and secret, Eph. v. 19, " Be ye filled with the Spirit: Speaking to yourselves in psalms and hymns and spiritual songs, singing and making melody in your heart to the Lord: Giving thanks always for all things unto God and the Father, in the name of our Lord Jesus Christ." O this window of praise is a pleasant window to the believer, especially when he has met with the Lord, and has been liberally dealt with there, in private or in public ordinances. Then he is ready to say with David, Psal. ciii. 1-4, " Bless the Lord, O my soul, and all that is within me, bless his holy name. Bless the Lord, O my soul, and forget not all his benefits. Who forgiveth all thine iniquities: who healeth all thy diseases. Who redeemeth thy life from destruction: who crowneth thee with loving-kindness and tender mercies."

(4.) There is the private window of reading the scriptures. This Christ has recommended to his doves, and to all men, John v. 39, " Search the scriptures, for in them ye think ye have eternal life, and they are they which testify of me." Many a sweet meal the believer gets, in reading of the word of God, either alone, or in family worship: In this ordinance of God, the Ethiopian eunuch found the Messiah. When the Spirit of the Lord glances into the heart of the believer by any truth or doctrine, or history of the word, he can, in that case, say, that the word of God is " better unto him than gold, yea, than much fine gold, sweeter also than honey, and the honey-comb;" as David declares from his experience, Psal. xix: and Jer. xv. 16, "Thy words were found, and I did eat them, and thy word was unto the joy and rejoicing of mine heart."

(5.) There is the private window of personal or family fasting and humiliation has been much owned of the Lord. This we find recommended by Christ unto his friends and followers, Matth. vi. 17, 18; " But thou, when thou fastest, anoint thine head, and wash thy face, that thou appear not unto men to fast, but unto thy Father which is in secret: And thy Father which seeth in secret shall reward thee openly."

(6.) There is the private window of christian communion and fellowship for conference and prayer, and mutual edification. This has been much owned of the Lord; and God's doves we find in scripture assembling themselves together after this manner, frequently in dark, cloudy, and evil days of general defection, Mal. iii. 16. When men were calling the proud happy, and robbing God, and spoiling his house, it is said, "Then they that feared the Lord spake often one to another, and the Lord hearkened, and heard it; and a book of remembrance was written before him for them that feared the Lord, and that thought upon his name." Thus you see some private windows, &c.

2. There are some of them more open and public windows of God's house, unto which God's doves used to resort in great flocks and companies, which are sometimes called the gates of Zion, or the courts of the great King, where his subjects pay him a public tribute of worship before the world.

(1.) Then, There is the large and open window of preaching the everlasting gospel, calculate for gathering doves unto God's house of mercy: "Go ye into all the world (says Christ), and preach the gospel to every creature." Apostles, prophets, evangelists, pastors, and teachers, they are all set a-work to open this window, and to invite and call sinners to come flocking into Christ by it. By this ordinance of preaching of the gospel, the sound of the voice of Christ is gone to the uttermost ends of the earth; and what are all ministers but the voice (of Christ) crying in the wilderness of this world, to fly into him for safety from the wrath that is to come. Wisdom (Prov. ix. 3-5) "crieth in the tops of the highest places, Whoso is simple, let him turn in hither: As for him that wanteth understanding, she saith to him, Come, eat of my bread, and drink of the wine which I have mingled," &c. Sirs, there is a goodly company of souls gathered at present to this window of gospel preaching. O that all this multitude would rise like a cloud, and fly like doves into Christ, through the window of a preached gospel! We read of three thousand souls added to the church by one sermon, Acts ii. 41. The residue of the Spirit is with Christ; and if there would come the rushing of the mighty wind of the Spirit among this company, there would be a pleasant flight of a cloud of souls to the blessed Mediator.

(2.) There is the public window of baptism, that initiating ordinance, 'which signifies and seals our ingrafting into Christ, and our partaking of the benefits of the new covenant, and our engagement to be the Lord's.'* Sirs, ye are all entered into God's outer house by this window. O do not stay there, but fly in a little further, even into the chambers of presence. The outward seal of God's covenant gives you a right to take hold of the covenant, and of Christ the covenant Head; and I may say to you (who have come in at this window of the visible church), what Paul says concerning the Jews, Rom. ix. 4, "To you belongs the adoption, and the glory, and the

---

* See Assembly's Shorter Catechism, Quest. "What is Baptism?"

covenants, and the giving of the law, and the service of God, and the promises;" and therefore take care that you do not forsake your own mercy; never rest until you get the baptism of the Spirit, as well as the baptism of water, by which ye shall be "sealed unto the day of redemption."

(3.) There is the public window of the sacrament of the Lord's supper, where there is a feast provided for the friends, the doves of Christ. This is the window which we are met here to open for all, who by faith have taken a flight to Christ, offered and presented to them, either in the word read or preached; and therefore we call to all the Lord's doves, "Come and eat, O friends; drink, yea, drink abundantly, O beloved." Here, at this ordinance of the supper, there is meat indeed, and drink indeed, provided, even the flesh and blood of IMMANUEL, God-man, all the blessings of the everlasting covenant. You see the institution of this ordinance, 1 Cor, xi. 23, &c.

(4.) I might tell you of the window of public prayer, wherein the ministers offer up the joint prayers of the church, or God's people unto the Lord; he being God's mouth unto them in preaching, and their mouth unto God in prayer.

(5.) The window of public praise and thanksgiving, when all God's doves join together in offering up the tribute of thanksgiving to him with one mouth, and with one voice and consent, which is an emblem of the work of the triumphant company in glory, who are continually warbling forth the praises of the Redeemer in high hallelujahs, every one crying, "Worthy is the Lamb that was slain."

(6.) There is the window of public fasting and humiliation before the Lord, for public sins, and personal failings and backslidings. Thus we find God's doves frequently employed, especially when there has been grievous provocations in a church, and signs of the Lord's anger and displeasure gone forth. Joel. ii. 15-17, "Blow the trumpet in Zion, sanctify a fast, call a solemn assembly. Gather the people: sanctify the congregation: assemble the elders: gather the children, and those that suck the breast: let the bridegroom go forth of his chamber, and the bride out of her closet. Let the priests, the ministers of the Lord, weep between the porch and the altar, and let them say, Spare thy people, O Lord, and give not thine heritage to reproach," &c.

Thus I have given you six private and secret, and six public windows of the house of God, to which God's doves should be frequently flying, upon the wings of faith, for a meeting with Christ.

IV. The *fourth* thing in the method was to show, that it is a pleasant and surprising sight to see sinners flying to Christ *as a cloud, and as doves to their windows.*

Here I would show, 1*st*, That it is pleasant: 2*dly*, That it is surprising.

1*st*, That it is a pleasant sight: It is pleasant to God the Father, Son, and Holy Ghost, and to all the angels and glorified saints; for there is joy in heaven, when a sinner on earth takes a flight into Christ by faith. It is pleasant to all honest ministers who travail in birth till Christ be formed in sinners; and it is pleasant to God's whole family; all his house rejoices when the prodigal comes home.

I will tell you some things that make it a pleasant sight to see sinners fly into Christ *as doves to their windows.* 1. It cannot but be pleasant, because it is a fulfiling of God's purpose of grace and love from all eternity. He has loved his own with an everlasting love; he loved them when he saw them in their blood. Now, must it not be pleasant to see the election of God obtaining and taking place; to see his everlasting love breaking out in the drawing of his own with loving-kindness? 2. It must be pleasant, because the flight of sinners to Christ is just the travail of Christ's soul, Is. liii., " He shall see of the travail of his soul, and shall be satisfied." It is a satisfaction to Christ to see the fruit of his sore travail, when he said, " Now my soul is exceeding sorrowful, even unto death ;" and what is so pleasant unto Christ himself, cannot but be pleasant unto all that love him. 3. It is the day of his espousals, the day of Christ's marriage and coronation, and therefore must be very pleasant to the bride, and the friends of the Bridegroom, Cant. iii. 11, " Go forth, O ye daughters of Zion, and behold King Solomon with the crown wherewith his mother crowned him in the day of his espousals," &c. 4. Because then the prisoners are released, " the captives of the mighty are taken away, and the prey of the terrible is delivered," &c. 5. It is pleasant, because then the head of the old serpent gets a new bruise, and his works are destroyed more and more, " The strong man is then bound, and spoiled of his goods."

2dly, I come to tell you, that the flight of the sinner to Christ is not only pleasant, but surprising and amazing. And this will appear, if we consider,

1. The state and condition that the sinner is into before he fly to Christ. He is dead in sin, wholly destitute of any principle of spiritual life. Now, is it not surprising to see God shewing wonders among the dead? to see a dead sinner rising, and taking a flight to Christ within the veil? The sinner is afar off; and is it not surprising to see the man that was " afar off, made nigh by the blood of Jesus?" The sinner is by nature full of enmity against God and his Christ, yea, enmity itself: And is it not surprising to see the enmity of the heart broken, and the man brought to a state of peace and reconciliation with God.

2. The flight of the sinner to Christ is surprising, considering the strong opposition that arises against it from within. The ignorance of the mind lies in the way; for we are " alienate from the life of God, through the ignorance that is in us," and it is impossible, while this stands in its power and reign, that ever the sinner can fly to Christ, because faith is founded in knowledge, even " the light of the knowledge of the glory of God in the face of Jesus Christ." The obstinacy and hardness of the heart stands in the way. The will is inflexible, and will bend to nothing but the almighty power of God; and is it not surprising to see this iron sinew bended and made pliable by the rod of the Mediator's strength? &c. The legal bias of the heart opposes the sinner's flight unto Christ: The man is married to

the law as a covenant, and nature can never think of another way of acceptance before God than by doing or working; and is it not surprising to see the sinner that was wedded to the law, and to his own righteousness, crying, "I through the law am dead to the law, that I may live unto God," through the righteousness of Christ; and saying with Paul, "What things were gain to me, these I counted loss for Christ; yea, doubtless, I count all things but dung, that I may win Christ, and be found in him, not having mine own righteousness," &c. Again, the guilt that is upon the conscience opposes the sinner's flight to Christ; for we find a guilty Adam flying from the presence of God; and the natural language of a guilty conscience, when it is awakened, is, O there is no mercy for me, there is no hope of acceptance. Now, is it not surprising to see the sinner, that was flying from God under a sense of guilt, flying to him through Christ, and crying, "Pardon mine iniquity, for it is great," &c. Again, the carnality of the affections lie in the way of the sinner's flight. The man was flying after vanity, and crying, "O, who will shew me any good," who will give me riches, honours, pleasures in a word? This is the natural run of the affections; they spend themselves upon things that cannot profit; and is it not surprising to see the man turning his back upon all these things? saying with Solomon, "All is vanity," and seeking and "setting his affections on things that are above, where Christ is at the right hand of God."

3. The flight of the sinner to Christ is surprising, if we consider how active Satan is to keep the sinner under his power. He is called the strong man, and he keeps the house; he rules in the hearts of the children of disobedience, and leads them about in the chains of their own lusts. Now, is it not surprising to see Christ coming in a day of his power, "spoiling the strong man of his prey;" and not only so, but arming the poor captive of the devil as a soldier under his own banner, to resist that enemy, and put him to flight, and by the shield of faith quenching the fiery darts of the enemy?

4. It is surprising, if we consider the entanglements of an ensnaring world. The devil is called the god of this world, because, ever since the entry of sin, Satan has got so much power over the good things and bad things of it, as that they are all his tools for ruining the souls of sinners, and for detaining them in his service. Hence is it that we see most part of the world dancing to the devil's pipe, and selling their souls for profits, for pleasures, for riches, for honours, and the like. These are just the devil's baits, whereby he trains men and women on, until he has brought them to hell, where he is sure he has them fast through eternity. Now, is it not surprising to see a sinner that has been decoyed and deceived all his days with the things of the world, casting them all behind his back, and trampling on them like the woman, Rev. xii. 1, who hath the moon under her feet, &c.

In a word, is it not surprising to see the dry bones getting life, and flesh, and strength? to see the Ethiopian washed and made whiter than snow? the seed of the serpent that licked the dust taking a flight from earth to heaven?

V. The *fifth* and last thing in the method, was the *Application*.

Use *first* shall be of *inference*, in these following particulars,

1*st*, From what has been said, we may see the usefulness of gospel ordinances, when dispensed in their purity and power. Why, they are just the windows of wisdom's house, by which the soul enters into the presence of God, and enjoys fellowship and communion with him. David, upon this account, esteemed gospel ordinances under the Old Testament, and longed for them, Psal. lxxxiv. 1, "How amiable are thy tabernacles," &c. Ver. 10, "A day in thy courts is better than a thousand," &c.

2*dly*, See hence whence it is that the saints, who have "tasted that the Lord is gracious," do frequent the ordinances of God's appointment. Why, they are God's doves, as they are frequently called in the book of the Song; and is it strange to see doves flocking to their windows? Indeed, the world think it strange to see some travelling far to a sacrament, and are ready to sneer at them as fools for their pains; but let a blind world do their uttermost, God's doves will not be feared from the windows of his house.

3*dly*, See hence the attractive virtue that is in Christ. Why, when he lets out his grace, and love, and glory, he garrs [makes] sinners come flying like a cloud, and like flocks of doves after him, to the windows of his house. "If I be lifted up (says Christ), I will draw all men unto me." O, sweet and victorious is his way of drawing! He draws with the cords of a man, and the bands of love. No wonder when all is considered, though the gathering of the people be unto the blessed Shiloh.

4*thly*, See hence what is the great work of faithful ministers of the gospel. Why, it is just to open the windows of gospel ordinances, and to invite the simple doves, exposed to the fowls of the air, and ravenous birds, to turn in hither to Christ, who is a hiding-place, &c.

5*thly*, See the folly of sinners, yea, of the generality of gospel hearers, who come flying about the windows of gospel ordinances, and yet do not fly in at the windows to Christ himself, by a real faith closing with him. O, how many come to hear the gospel of Christ, who do not close with Christ! and how many come to a communion table, who do not feed upon Christ himself! O, the folly of such is great, when salvation is near unto them, and they so near to salvation, and yet come short of it through unbelief, &c.

6*thly*, See the madness and wickedness of some in our day, who scare God's doves from his windows, and who make the ordinances of God to be abhorred. Some do this by offering the doves unwholesome food of error and heathenish morality, or truth unskilfully prepared. Some scare the doves by their immoralities, and untender walk, like the sons of Eli, &c.; and judicatories, at this day, are scaring and scattering the Lord's doves from their windows, by violent intrusions, whereby they shut both doors and windows of the sanctuary, and then exclaim against the poor doves, that they do not haunt their usual windows. God sees well how his doves, his little ones, are guided at this day; and he knows how to provide his doves, and reckon with those that scatter and fright them. He will, in his own time and way, take these foxes and vultures, which men and judicatories are letting slip through their fingers. The day of vengeance is in his heart, and the year of his redeemed is a-coming, Is. lxiii 4.

7*thly*, See the use both of law and gospel, and how they stand in a sweet subserviency unto the salvation of a soul. Why, by the noise, and thunders, and terrors of the law, God's doves are wakened, and set to the flight from the wrath to come; and this being done, the gospel opens the windows, and casts open the door of access to Christ, crying, " Turn ye to your strong-holds, ye prisoners of hope," Zech. ix. 12: So that Christ being discovered in the gospel, the law becomes a schoolmaster to bring sinners unto Christ, that they may " be justified by faith," Gal. iii. 24, " from all things from which they could not be justified by the law of Moses," Acts xiii. 39. This much by way of inference.

Use *second* may be of *Trial.*

Have you fled to Christ *as doves to their windows?* Many fly to Christ in a way of profession, but, if ever thy soul really took a flight to him upon the wings of faith and love, you may know it by these or the like things.

1*st*, Did ever a thunder-clap from Mount Sinai startle you, and raise you out of your natural security, and put you in a consternation, like a heap of doves at the sight of a gun? So that you was wild, and knew not what to do, or whither to fly for help, like these converts, Acts ii. 37, and the jailor, Acts xvi. 27, and Paul at his conversion, &c.

2*dly*, When, like Noah's dove, you was wandering up and down in your thoughts for a place of rest, got you a discovery of the Ark Christ, and came hovering about the Ark? Our great Noah opened the windows of the Ark, and took thee in with himself, and became a hiding-place unto thee, &c.

3*dly*, If this be the case at thy entry at the window of the Ark, thou hast been made to sing, Psal. cxvi. 7, " Return unto thy rest, O my soul, for the Lord hath dealt bountifully with thee;" or that, Psal. ciii. 4, " He redeemeth my life from destruction, he crowneth me with loving-kindness and tender mercies. Bless the Lord, O my soul; and all that is within me, bless his holy name," &c.

4*thly*, If so, when you took your flight to Christ, you left all idols behind you, crying with Ephraim, " What have I to do any more with idols?" These things you counted gain will be loss in your view. As for sins, even your dearest sins, your right hands and right eyes, you will be careful to cut them off, and pull them out, &c. As for the world you was taken up with, you will cry, Away with it; it is a mere mass of vanity, all vanity and vexation, &c. As for the law, you will be dead to it as a husband, " I through the law am dead to the law." As for your works of righteousness that you gloried in, you will count them dung, and loss, filthy rags, &c. As for the wisdom of the flesh, you will reckon it stark folly and madness, &c. As for your own strength, you will see it to be weakness, " I am not sufficient of my-self," &c. As for your own fulness, you have found it to be nothing but emptiness; and that, instead of being rich and increased with goods, you have seen that you are wretched and miserable, &c.

5thly, If you have really fled to Christ *as doves to their windows,* there are some things you have found in him, which you could never find any where else. 1. Thou hast found the life of thy soul in him: Our "life is hid with Christ in God: He that hath the Son hath life," &c. 2. Thou hast found rest to thy soul in him: Thou triedst to find this and the former in lying refuges, but was aye disappointed in thy expectation, but now, now, thou hast found it according to his promise, Matth. xi., "Come unto me, all ye that labour and are heavy laden, and I will give you rest," O glorious rest! Is. xi. 10. 3. Thou hast found soul health in him, like the woman that spent all her means upon other physicians to no purpose, till she came and touched the hem of Christ's garments, and then the bloody issue was stayed. So can not thou say upon thy coming to Christ; thou foundst his countenance to be thy health; healing is under his wings, Mal. iv. 2, Psal. ciii. 3, He healeth all my diseases, &c. 4. Thou hast found food to thy soul in him: His "flesh is meat indeed, and his blood is drink indeed," &c "O taste and see that the Lord is good," &c. 5. Thou hast found clothing to thy naked soul in him: You was trying, like our first parents, to cover thy nakedness with fig leaves; but now thou castest these away, and taking the skin of the word to cover thee with, which God provided, and upon thy being thus clothed with the righteousness of Christ, thou hast been made to sing that song, Is. lxi. 10, "He hath clothed me with the garments of salvation, he hath covered me with the robe of righteousness," &c. 6. You have found riches, and unsearchable riches, in him, that do not rot in the grave, gold better than the gold of Ophir, to make you up for all eternity. 7. In one word, you have found your God in him, whom you lost in the first Adam; for God is in Christ, and you have found him as your own God: And now you will be ready to say, He is "my God, and I will prepare him an habitation, even the God and Father of our Lord Jesus Christ; and therefore I will exalt him. Our God is the God of salvation," &c.

Use *third* may be of *Consolation* unto God's doves in this dark and evil day, in which their usual windows to which they used to flock, are like to be shut by a set of men and judicatories who should open them, and who should gather God's doves, instead of scattering them.

There are these few things I offer for comfort in an evil day like this.

1*st,* Know for your encouragement. that, when the windows of public ordinances are shut up, either by persecution, violence, or defections, or when you are scared away from them by vultures, or birds of prey, that have got into the house, yet God can let you in to communion with him, by the private and secret windows I mentioned in the doctrinal part. God's doves, though they may be shut out of the kirks, yet they shall not be shut out from fellowship with him, one way or other; no, he will gather unto him them that are sorrowful for the solemn assembly, &c.

2*dly,* God hears the mourning of his doves even when they are driven to the "clefts of the rocks, and secret places of the stairs," Cant. ii. 14, &c.

3dly, God's eye is upon his doves, and he "tells all their wanderings;—the eyes of the Lord are upon the righteous,—and they run to and fro," &c.

4thly, His heart and his affection is set upon his doves, even to a ravishment, Cant. iv. 9, "Thou hast ravished my heart, my sister, my spouse." And this affection is invariable, for he rests in his love, &c.

5thly, The arms of his power and providence are about his doves, and "He covers them with his feathers, and he will hide them in the secret of his tabernacle, when thousands shall fall at their side, and ten thousand at their right-hand. Come, my people, "enter into your chambers, shut the doors about thee," &c.

6thly, Ere it be long, thy soul will take a flight out of this ill world, into the land of rest, the house of many mansions, where thou wilt be at rest for ever.

Use *fourth* might be of *Terror* unto all these that are doing hurt to God's doves at this day.

Some are scaring and frighting them, some are scattering them, some are plucking at their gospel rights and privileges, some plucking at their name with slander, some plucking them out of their dwellings, because they cannot commit themselves into the hands of the birds of prey. I shall only say to you, if there be any such hearing me, as I doubt not but there may be some of them to spy out our liberty on this occasion, 1. "God is jealous for his doves with a great jealousy," Zech. i. 14. 2. He is sore displeased with you for the injuries that are done to them in helping on their affliction, Zech. i. 15. 3. God is preparing a cup for you to drink, and a bitter one, Psal. lxxiv. 8, "In the hand of the Lord there is a cup, and the wine is red," &c. He will render tribulation to them that trouble his doves. God's doves, that are mourning now, shall sing when ye shall mourn; they will be singing in heaven, when ye shall be mourning and howling among devils, &c.

Use *fifth* shall be of *Exhortation:* 1st, To all in general; 2dly, To God's doves in particular.

1st, a word of exhortation to persuade sinners to rise out of the earth like a cloud, and fly like doves unto Christ. O that all this company before me would clap their wings, and take a flight, and never rest until they had fled for refuge to this hope set before them in the gospel! To set you all a-flight, if possible, let me deal with you in a rational way.

1. God commands you to fly to Christ, "This is his commandment, That we should believe on the name of his Son Jesus Christ," &c.

2. He invites you to fly to his Christ, "Behold my servant whom I uphold," &c.

3. He entreats and beseeches you to fly to him, "We pray you in Christ's stead, as though God did beseech you by us, be ye reconciled to God," &c.

4. He expostulates with you, because of your backslidings, to fly to him, "O my people! what have I done unto thee?" &c.

5. He assures you of welcome by his promise, "Come to me who will, I will in no ways cast out," &c. And by his oath, "As I live, I

have no pleasure in the death of the wicked, but rather that the wicked turn from his way and live," &c.

6. All things in his house are ready to give entertainment unto you, behold, "all things are ready, come to the marriage," Proverbs 8th and 9th chapters.

7. Fly, the windows are open, the heart of Christ is open, &c. His arms are open and stretched out, &c. His covenant is open to you to take hold of it, &c.

8. Consider what is behind you. (1.) The roaring lion, ready to devour you. (2.) The curse of the broken law is behind you, &c. (3.) The wrath of God is behind you. O! who knows the power of it? &c.

9. There is no safety for you in heaven nor earth, if you do not fly from sin: "There is no other name under heaven, given among men, whereby we must be saved," &c. "How shall we escape, if we neglect so great a salvation, they that despised Moses' law died without mercy," &c.

10. The time of flying will be gone within a little; no flying out of hell; none to come to you there to cry, "Turn ye to your strong-holds," &c. "He that lives for ever and ever, has sworn, with his hand lifted up to heaven, that time shall be no more," &c. "And therefore to-day, if ye will hear his voice," &c.

11. Fly, or else you will lose your soul for ever; "He that believeth not shall be damned." And "what is a man profited, if he shall gain the whole world, and lose his own soul," &c.

Object 1. 'You bid us fly, but to what purpose, you tell us we are dead in sins?' *Answ.* It is the glory of sovereign grace, to shew wonders to the dead; see what he did among the dry bones, Ezek. xxxvii. 3, &c. Can these dry bones live? Yea, if the Spirit of the Lord breathe upon them, God has bidden prophesy upon the dry bones, to cry to the dead, to arise and fly; and therefore we must do it. And if God would bid me say to the mountains, remove, to the rocks and trees and grass piles, arise and live, I would do it, and I would believe that God would make it effectual.

Object. 2. 'You bid me fly, but alas, I want wings to fly, "O that I had wings like a dove, for then would I fly," &c. *Answ.* If there be a will to fly, and a hearty desire to fly, thou hast got wings: and if you want even that, seek wings from him that bids you fly, for he gives power to the faint, and then they mount up with wings as eagles, &c.

Object. 3. 'I have a load of sin upon my back, I cannot get up.' *Answ.* "Cast thy burden upon the Lord," and if you cannot fly, rest you with your load upon him; for as faith is a flying, so it is a resting, &c.

Object. 4. 'Christ is so far away, that I will never reach him.' *Answ.* Do not say so, for he is near, Rom. x. 8, &c.

Object. 5. 'When I attempt to fly, the devil and the world, and my own heart, pull me back again into the mire, and then I am just where I was.' *Answ.* From that moment that thou makest an attempt to fly to Christ, the devil, the world, and corruption, will be upon thee to harass thee. But though they may do thee many an ill turn, yet they shall never pull thee out of Christ, if once thou hast fled to him, no man " shall pluck them out of my hand, my Father who gave them me is greater than all (says Christ), and none shall pluck them out of my Father's hand." Many a pluck the enemy gives at Christ's doves, but they shall never pluck them away from him.

Quest. You bid me fly like a dove into Christ, and his windows; but will you give me your advice in order to it? *Answ.* 1. Be much in viewing the holiness of the law, and of the Lawgiver, " for it is a schoolmaster to bring us to Christ," &c. 2. Be much in viewing your danger while out of Christ, condemned already, &c. 3. Be much in studying the gospel, Christ in his person, nature, and offices; the freedom of the covenant, and the fulness and suitableness of the gospel remedy, &c. 4. Be persuaded of the Lord's willingness to take you in to himself, at his windows, his bowels sound towards sinners, &c. 5. Cry for the wind of the Spirit to blow, that thereby you may be set a-flight, for he testifies of Christ, and joins the sinner to him, &c. 6. Make a desperate attempt to be at Christ, through the window of prayer, and of faith in prayer; wrestle, cry, seek, and knock, for to such it shall be opened, &c.

2*dly*, The *second* sort I would speak to are believers, who have *fled like a cloud, and as doves to* Christ's *windows.*

1. Bless the Lord that gave you counsel, and did not allow you to sit still in a natural state, within the sea-mark of his wrath, but chased you with his law terrors, and drew you in at his windows to himself. Sing his praise, saying, " Bless the Lord, O my soul," &c. " He brought me up also out of an horrible pit," &c.

2. Have you fled to Christ? Abide in him as in a lodging and dwelling-place: Just as the man-slayer was to abide in the city of refuge, after he had fled to it, and was never to go out of it, until the death of the high priest: and your High Priest never dies; and therefore you are never to be found out of your gospel-refuge, &c.

3. Frequent the windows of his ordinances, both the more secret and retired windows of prayer and meditation, reading, fasting, Christian conference; and those that are more solemn and public, such as word and sacrament, when you can have access: For there it is that Christ feeds his doves, and gives them interviews with himself; and when the public windows are shut, or defiled, or haunted with foxes or birds of prey, that fright, scatter, or tear the doves, be the more frequently resorting unto the more private or secret windows, &c.

4. Have you fled to Christ *like doves to their windows,* and taken up your rest in him: never look back to your old houfs and resorts, your lying refuges, nor look to the general mercy, &c. Never look to an empty profession, &c.; never take up again with the works of the law, &c.; bid all these adieu, never to come back to them again, &c.

5. When, like the dove, you come to pick up any thing that is necessary for you upon earth, do not sit still upon the earth, but away again to your windows, and soar upward toward Christ. " Set your affections upon things above, where Christ is at the right hand of God," &c.

6. Invite others to your windows where you have been entertained, and do what you can to recommend Christ and his way and word and ordinances to them, "O taste and see that the Lord is good," says David, &c.

7. When the Lord has taken you from among the pots, and made you like the wings of a dove covered with the silver and yellow gold of his own Spirit and righteousness. O do not defile your feathers, do not tarnish and blacken your profession with the filth of sin Do not lie down in the puddle with the men of this world: "Be not conformed to this world, but be ye transformed by the renewing of your mind. Let your light so shine before men, that they may see your good works, and glorify your Father which is in heaven."

8. Let God's doves drink the pure and running water of the sanctuary, I mean, keep by the pure word, worship, and ordinances of his appointment, the river of divine truth, gospel doctrine and worship, dispensed in gospel ordinances. Alas! the streams of these rivers do not make glad the city of God, at this day, through many corners of the land. Why, the waters are fouled with the feet of a set of hirelings, intruders, and corrupt and lax ministers, that are forced in upon them; men that are unskilful in the law, men that want the dove-like spirit of Christ, and therefore are incapable of feeding God's doves. Let God's doves be aware of them that foul the waters of the sanctuary, that corrupt the doctrine, discipline, worship, and government, which we in these lands are sworn to maintain and preserve in their purity, Philip. iii. 1, "Beware of dogs, beware of evil workers, beware of the concision," &c.

ACTION SERMON.

CHRIST SET UP FROM EVERLASTING.

Prov. viii, 23. —I was set up from everlasting, from the beginning, or ever the earth was.

THERE are such evident rays of the eternal and supreme Deity of Christ, as also of his personality and essential oneness with the Father, in this passage, as looks the Arians and Socinians, these blasphemers of the Son of God, quite out of countenance, and obliges them, though with great absurdity, to allege, that what is spoken of and by Christ in this chapter, and particularly from ver. 22 to ver. 31, is to be understood of wisdom as one of the attributes of the divine nature. But it is beyond controversy, among all orthodox interpreters, that it is Christ the second person of the glorious Trinity, under the notion of wisdom, that here speaks, as might be cleared from many personal properties, personal acts, and personal words, that are ascribed to him in this passage of scripture, which, for brevity's sake, I cannot insist upon at this time.

The penman of this book was Solomon, "But behold a greater than

Solomon is here," even Christ, "the wisdom of God, and the power of God, in whom all the treasures of wisdom and knowledge are hid." As Solomon had all his wisdom out of this treasure; so being under the conduct of the Spirit of wisdom and revelation, is led, as a type, to speak in the person of his glorious anti-type, as his father David doth frequently in the book of the Psalms, particularly in Psal. xvi. and Psal. xl. 1-22. Christ recommends his dictates in the word unto the children of men, and shews what advantage will accrue to them by the study of the scriptures: agreeable unto what he says, John v. 39, "Search the scriptures, for in them ye think ye have eternal life, and they are they which testify of me." From the 22d verse unto the 31st, in order to engage our faith and trust in him, he elegantly describes the glory of his person, that so we beholding as in a glass, his glory, may be changed into his image. More particularly, (1.) He shews how, from all eternity, he lodged in his Father's arms and bosom, as his beloved Son, in whom he was and is well pleased, ver. 22, "The Lord possessed me in the beginning of his way, before his works of old." (2.) He speaks of his eternal designation unto the great work and service of our redemption, in the words of my text, *I was set up from everlasting,* &c. Where we may notice,

1. The divine person, who is the speaker, in the pronoun, *(I)* I, the eternal Son of God, the glorious Immanuel, the faithful and true Witness. I who am God co-equal with the Father; and who sat as a constituent member of the council of peace, anent the great affair of man's redemption, and therefore cannot but be well acquainted with what was transacted there.

2. The result of that eternal transaction declared with relation to himself, *I was set up, i. e.,* I was, by an act of the divine will, common to all the three persons of the glorious Trinity, Father, Son, and Holy Ghost, elected, set apart, or fore-ordained to the great service of man's redemption. A word parallel unto this, and which casts a light upon the text, you have, Psal. ii. 7, where Christ, speaking of himself, says, "I will declare the decree: the Lord hath said unto me, Thou art my Son, this day have I begotten thee." This is called the Father's will, Psal. xl. 7, 8, "Lo! I come, in the volume of the book, it is written of me, I delight to do thy will."

3. In the words we have the date of the divine council and decree, with relation to our Redeemer, or when he was set up for that service. It bears date from the ancient years of eternity, *I was set up from everlasting, from the beginning, ere ever the earth was.* Here are words that swallow up all finite thought and consideration, it leads us back to an eternity past, and who could ever have told us what was acted in the divine mind and council from all eternity, but he only who is the Alpha, and the Omega, from everlasting to everlasting, God. He *was set up from everlasting, from the beginning, ere ever the earth was.* So much for explaining the words.

DOCT.—"That as Christ is the everlasting God; so, from all eternity, he was fore-ordained and set up for the great service of man's redemption. *I was set up from everlasting,*" &c.

To this purpose is that of the apostle, 1 Pet. i. 20, "He was verily fore-ordained before the foundation of the world, but was manifest in these last times."

The method, through divine assistance, I shall observe, is as follows,

I. To prove that Christ is the everlasting God, and that he *was from the beginning, ere ever the earth was.*

II. Shew what is imported in his being *set up from everlasting.*

III. For what ends and purposes was he *set up.*

IV. Why he, and none else, *was set up* for this end.

V. Make some application of the whole.

I. The *first* thing is to prove, That Christ is the everlasting God, and that he was *from the beginning, ere ever the earth was.*

The Socinians affirm, That he had no being before his actual incarnation. And the Arians, though they allow that he had a being before his incarnation; yet they deny his eternal existence, and consequently make him but a nominal deity, and reduce him among the rank of created beings. Now, in opposition to both these damnable heresies, I shall endeavour to trace a little, the scriptural account of the eternal existence of the Son of God, our glorious Redeemer.

And *first,* that he existed before his incarnation, or his being born of the virgin, is evident from the appearance he made to our first parents in paradise, after the fall, Gen. iii. 15, It, viz. the seed of the woman, shall bruise thy head, viz. the serpent's, explained by the apostle, Heb. ii. 14, That this was God in the person of the Son, intimating his future incarnation, and the design thereof is evident, for God absolutely considered is not a promising but an avenging God, a consuming fire unto the workers of iniquity. And all the promises in him are yea and amen. It is only the Lion of the tribe of Judah, and none else. that opened the book of the divine council anent our redemption. And therefore it was he, and none else, that broke up this seal, and disclosed this secret unto our first parents in paradise.

In like manner, it was he that preached the gospel to Abraham, saying, "In thy seed shall all the nations of the earth be blessed," as is clear from Gal. iii. 8.

We find him executing his threefold mediatorial offices, before ever he came in the flesh: We find him, as a prophet, preaching righteousness unto the great congregation, Psal. xl. 9, "I have preached righteousness in the great congregation: Lo, I have not refrained my lips, O Lord, thou knowest!" And by his Spirit in Noah he preached to the old world, who, because of their disobedience, were shut up in the prison of hell; as we see in 1 Pet. iii. 18-20. We find him acting as the great Priest of his church, before his actual appearance in the flesh, Psal. cx. 4, "The Lord hath sworn, and will not repent, Thou art a Priest for ever after the order of Melchisedeck," and his royal and kingly office is asserted by God the Father, before ever he appeared in the flesh, Psal. ii., "Yet have I set my King upon my holy hill of Zion;" I have done it; it is not a thing to do, but it is done already: I have set him King, &c. And he speaks to him as a person actually existing: "Ask of me, and I shall give thee the heathen for thine inheritance, and the uttermost parts of the earth for thy possession." Thus you see him executing all his offices before he was incarnate.

But I need not stand upon this point, in opposition to the Socinians, seeing we have it from Christ's own mouth, who is the faithful witness, John viii. 58, says he there to the Jews, " Before Abraham was, I am," alluding probably unto that same name he took to himself, when he appeared unto Moses in the bush, and sent him to bring Israel out of Egypt: Go (says he), and tell them, " I AM hath sent me unto you," Exod. iii. 14; a name equivalent unto the name JEHOVAH, which signifies *past, present, and to come*, and distinguishes him from all the dunghill deities of the nations.

But then, *secondly*, let us go back further, even to the creation of the world, and we shall find his existence and agency, in the production of all created beings, John i. 2, 3, " In the beginning was the Word, and the Word was with God, and the Word was God. The same was in the beginning with God. All things were made by him; and without him was not any thing made that was made." He must needs be the everlasting God, who is the Creator of all the ends of the earth. Gen. i. 1, " In the beginning, God created the heaven and the earth;" hence, Psal. cii. 25, " Of old hast thou laid the foundation of the earth; and the heavens are the work of thy hands," &c. Which words are applied unto Christ, Heb. i. 10-12, " Thou, Lord, in the beginning, hast laid the foundation of the earth; and the heavens are the works of thine hands. They shall perish, but thou remainest: and they all shall wax old as doth a garment; and as a vesture shalt thou fold them up, and they shall be changed: But thou art the same, and thy years shall not fail."

Again, *thirdly*, Let us run up to the endless ages before the creation of the world. and we find him existing or ever the earth was, John xviii. 5. He prayeth that he might be glorified with his Father, with the same glory that he had with him before the foundation of the world. Hence he is not only called the mighty God, but the everlasting Father, or the Father of eternity; and Micah v. 2, " His goings forth were from of old, from everlasting." But I need not stand upon this, seeing the very words of the text are so clear as to this matter, " *I was set up from everlasting, from the beginning, or ever the earth was.*" If he were not the everlasting God, he could never have been set up from everlasting, So much for the first thing.

II. The *second* thing proposed was, to enquire, what is imported in his being *set up from everlasting*.

And there are these few things that I take to be imported in this expression.

1st, It supposes the council of peace, or an eternal transaction between the Father and the Son, concerning the redemption of lost sinners; for this is the result of the council here declared by the Son,

I was set up from everlasting. Zech. vi. 13. "The council of peace shall be between them both."

2*dly,* It implies the infinite complacency that the Father and Son had in each other from all eternity. This is more clearly expressed in the verse immediately preceding the text, "The Lord possessed me in the beginning of his ways, before his works of old;" and yet more clearly, ver. 29, 30, "When he appointed the foundations of the earth, then I was by him, as one brought up with him; and I was daily his delight, rejoicing always before him." So Is. xlii. 1, Matth. iii. at the close; chap. xvii. 5.

3*dly,* It implies a divine ordination and decree, whereby he was from eternity elected unto the great service of man's redemption. Hence he is called his Father's Elect, Is. xliii. 1, "Behold my Servant whom I behold, mine Elect, in whom my soul delighteth." So Psal. lxxxix. 19, says God the Father, "I have laid help upon one that is mighty, I have exalted one chosen out of the people;" and, with an eye to this decree of the election of Christ is that fore-cited of the apostle, 1 Pet. i. 20, "Who verily was fore-ordained before the foundation of the world," &c. Though he be God co-equal with the Father, yet he voluntarily came under a decree of election, that so he might be the head of the election among mankind sinners, in whom they are elected unto everlasting life, Eph. i. 4, "He hath chosen us in him, before the foundation of the world."

4*thly, I was set up from everlasting,* it implies, that, in consequence of the decree, he was called of God to undertake the work of redemption, Is. xlii. 6, "I the Lord have called thee in righteousness, and will hold thine hand, and will keep thee, and give thee for a covenant of the people, for a light of the Gentiles." Heb. v. 4, 5, "No man taketh this honour unto himself, but he who is called of God, as was Aaron: So also Christ glorified not himself to be made an high priest, but he that said unto him, Thou art my Son, this day have I begotten thee."

5*thly,* It implies his own voluntary consent to, and compliance with his Father's call: This is of so great moment, that it is registrated in the volume of the book of God, Psal. xl. 7. 8, "Then said I, Lo, I come; in the volume of the book it is written of me: I delight to do thy will, O my God; yea thy law is within my heart." Upon which words the apostle Paul comments, Heb. x. 5—10, applying them to the purpose in hand.

And, upon this voluntary consent of the Son of God, followed a multitude of great promises that the Father made to him. The Father promised to fit him with a human nature, to be personally united to his divine nature: "A body hast thou prepared me; a promise of all needful furniture and assistance in the undertaking, that an immeasurable fulness of the Spirit, and all his gifts, graces, and qualifications, should rest upon him, Is. xi. 2, 3, chap. xlii. liii. 10—12, "The pleasure of the Lord shall prosper in his hand. I will divide him a portion with the great, and he shall divide the spoil with the strong?" That he should see his seed; a seed should serve him, that should be accounted to him for a generation, Psal. xxii. at the close: That he would make his enemies his footstool, and greatly plague all that hated him: And that, when he had drunk of the brook that ran in the way, he should again lift up the head, and be repossessed, even in the human nature, of all that glory which he had with the Father before the world was. Thus you see what is implied in his being set up from everlasting.

But now, before I go on to the third general head, I would here shew, how (in consequence of all this, which was done before the foundation of the world was laid) he was actually set up in time, in the view of lost sinners of Adam's family, whom he came to save and redeem. And,

1. His first appearance was in the promise made to our first parents, of his future incarnation, already mentioned, Gen. iii. 15, which was the only foundation of faith the church had, until the days of Abraham, to whom that promise was renewed, "In thy seed shall all the nations of the earth be blessed, Gen. xxii. 18.

2. He was set up typically, in the view of the church, under the old Testament. What was the meaning of the tabernacle and temple, of all the sacrifices and ceremonies of that economy? They were all intended as shadowy representations of good things to come, upon the actual appearance of the Son of God in our nature.

3. He was set up prophetically, in the prophecies of the prophets, Isaiah, Jeremiah, and the rest; for all the prophets prophesied of him: To him they did all bear witness, and every one of them successively spoke more clearly than another, till John the Baptist came in the spirit and power of Elias, pointing him out with the finger, saying, "Behold the Lamb of God."

4. He was set up personally and actually, in his incarnation, obedience, and death. His birth was celebrated and intimate by a company of angels, saying, "Unto you is born, in the city of David, a Saviour, which is Christ the Lord," and that heavenly anthem, "Glory to God in the highest, and on earth peace, good-will towards men." His inauguration unto his mediatorial work, at his baptism, was celebrated by the opening of the heavens, the descent of the Spirit upon him in the likeness of a dove, and a voice coming from his Father, from heaven, saying, "This is my beloved Son, in whom I am well pleased;" which voice was again repeated at his transfiguration and his passion. His death was celebrated by the rending of the veil of the temple from top to bottom, a quaking of the earth, a rending of the rocks, and a darkening of the sun in the firmament; all importing, that now the finishing stroke was given to the head of the old serpent, and that principalities and powers were spoiled, and the prince of this world cast out of his usurped authority and government.

5. He was set up in a glorious and triumphant way and manner, in his resurrection and ascension; for then he was "declared to be the Son of God with power, according to the Spirit of holiness, by his resurrection from the dead." And when he ascended up "on high, he led captivity captive, and sat down at the right hand of the Majesty on high;" and things in heaven, and things on earth, and things under the earth, being ordered to bow at the name of Jesus,

and every tongue to confess that he is the Lord, to the praise and glory of his Father.

6. He was and is set up declaratively, in the preaching of the everlasting gospel; which is like the pole upon which the brasen serpent was lifted up in the wilderness, by looking unto which the Israelites were cured of the fiery serpents. John iii. 14, 15, says Christ there, "And as Moses lifted up the serpent in the wilderness, even so must the Son of man be lifted up: that whosoever believes in him should not perish, but have eternal life."

7. He is set up sacramentally, in the sacraments of baptism and of the supper, particularly in the last of these, which we are about this day to celebrate. In these symbols and sacramental acts of his own institution, he is evidently set forth crucified before you; and therein we may, as in a glass, discern the Lord's body, which was broken for us, and his blood of the New Testament, which was shed for us. There he is present, though not in a corporal and carnal manner, yet in a symbolical and spiritual manner, saying to his people, "Eat, O friends; drink, yea, drink abundantly, O beloved."

8. He is set up in an efficacious way and manner, in a day of conversion, and in the renewed manifestations of himself to the souls of his people, by the power of his word and Spirit. When he draws by the veil, and makes the light of the knowledge of his glory to shine into the heart, then, O then, Christ is set up in the heart of the sinner; he gets the throne of the heart, and every thought is brought into captivity unto his obedience. What a pleasant upsetting of Christ and his kingdom would it be, to see him going forth, with his bow and sword, in the gospel, travelling in the greatness of his strength, making all the inhabitants of the land to fall under him, every one crying, The Lord is our Judge, the Lord is our King, the Lord is our Lawgiver! O then covenanting work would go on apace, and every one will say to another, "Come, and let us join ourselves unto the Lord, in a perpetual covenant that shall not be forgotten," Jer. 1. 5.

9. Christ will be set up in a glorious and remarkable way and manner, at his second coming, without sin, unto the salvation of his people; for then he will descend from heaven, with a shout, with the voice of the archangel, and the trump of God, when he shall come with clouds, and every eye shall see him. Then shall he be glorified in his saints, and admired in all them that believe, while all the wicked unbelieving world, and kindreds of the earth, shall wail because of him, crying to the rocks and mountains to fall on them, and hide them from the face of him that sits upon the throne, and from the wrath of the Lamb; and the heavens passing away with a mighty noise, the elements melting with fervent heat. So much for the second thing proposed; for all these were in view, when Christ was set up from everlasting.

III. The *third* thing proposed in the method was, to shew for what ends and purposes Christ was *set up from everlasting, from the beginning, or ever the earth was*. I answer in these particulars.

1*st*, He was set up from everlasting, as a Sun to give light unto this lower world, which (through the sin of man) was become like a dungeon of darkness. No sooner had man sinned, but his mind (which before was like a lamp of light, as to the knowledge of God, and of his mind and will), became dark, yea, darkness itself. "Once were ye darkness," says the apostle, speaking of man in his natural state. There is the face of a covering cast over all people, and the veil that is spread over all nations; and, upon this account, this world is called a dark place; and again, these parts of the earth, where Christ is not known, are called the dark places of the earth. But now Christ is and was set up, as a glorious Sun, to enlighten the world in the knowledge of God, and of the way of salvation, hence called the Sun of righteousness, the Light of the world, because he spreads the light of the knowledge of the glory of God among lost sinners of Adam's family, by his Word and Spirit. Hence, when the gospel of Christ, which is the lamp of God's anointed, comes unto a people, they "that sat in darkness see great light, and to them that sat in the region and shadow of death light doth spring up."

2dly, He is set up as a second Adam, the Head of a new covenant of grace and promise. All mankind were lost and ruined in the first Adam, and by the breach of the covenant of works that was made with him as their federal head and representative; so that the curse of that covenant was the only legacy he could bequeath unto his posterity, and under this curse we had lain through all eternity, if God had not raised up for us "a Horn of salvation, in the house of his servant David." Sirs, God had a purpose of love and grace, from all eternity, toward a select company of Adam's family, he pitches upon his own beloved Son, as a new covenant Head, and enters into a covenant of grace with him, to deliver them out of a state of sin and misery, and bring them unto a state of salvation through him, Psal. lxxxix. 3, "I have made a covenant with my chosen, I have sworn unto David my servant," &c. Accordingly Christ, as the second Adam, steps in the room of the first Adam, and fulfils the covenant of works, both as to its precept and penalty; whereby the promise of eternal life made to him, upon condition of perfect obedience, devolves upon him as a second Adam, and he becomes the righteous heir of everlasting life, not only by birth, but also by purchase; and all the promises of the covenant, and all the salvation of the covenant, stand in him. And that moment a sinner quits his holding of the first Adam, and of the law as a covenant, and, by a faith of God's operation, is determined to take hold of Christ, and the covenant whereof he is Head, that moment, I say, he is brought into the bonds of the covenant of grace and promise, according to that which you have, Is. lv. 3, "Hear, and your souls shall live, and I will make an everlasting covenant with you, even the sure mercies of David," &c.

3dly. He was set up from everlasting, as a repairer of breaches between God and man. Whenever man sinned, and joined himself in a confederacy with Satan, the god of this world, the breach between God and man became wide like the sea; death and hell was the penalty of the law; the faithfulness of God was engaged, that "without the shedding of blood there could be no remission of sins." And though all the angels of heaven, and men upon earth, had been sacrificed, and their blood shed, in order to satisfy justice, it would have been rejected; the offence was infinite, with respect to the object of it, and therefore a satisfaction of infinite value behoved to be offered, Psal. xl. 6, Heb. x., Sacrifices and offerings thou wouldst not, viz. of man's providing. Well, then, How shall the breach be repaired? How shall the different claims of mercy and justice be reconciled, with respect to the guilty criminal? Lo, I come, says Christ, I will assume the human nature, and in that nature I will die in the room of the criminal; and in this way I will make peace through the blood of my cross. I will be wounded for their transgressions, and bruised for their iniquities; the chastisement of their peace shall be upon me, and by my stripes they shall be healed; and so justice shall be satisfied, and mercy shall be for ever magnified. 1 Pet. iii. 18, "Christ also hath once suffered for sins, the just for the unjust, (that he might bring us to God)." Thus he is set up as the Repairer of breaches; hence called the Mediator between God and man: and there is no Mediator between God and men, but the man Christ Jesus.

4thly, He is set up as the true temple where God sets his name, and in which alone God is to be worshipped in an acceptable way and manner. The Old Testament tabernacle and temple was but a shadow of Christ, in whom the fulness of the Godhead dwells bodily. And as all the worship of Israel was to be performed in the temple; so all our sacrifices and services are to be offered up in the name of Christ, for he hath made us accepted in the Beloved. In him, as our New Testament Temple, is to be seen the true Shechina, the brightness of the Father's glory, and the express image of his person. Here is the true oracle whereby the mind of God is conveyed unto us, "For no man hath seen God at any time; the only begotten Son, who is in the bosom of the Father, he hath declared him." Here is the true ark where the tables of the law are kept, and in whom the law is magnified and made honourable. In him we have the true mercy-seat and throne of grace, unto which we are called to come with boldness, that we may obtain grace, and find mercy to help in every time of need. Here we have the Priest of our profession ministering in the holy of holies, and appearing in the presence of God for us.

5thly, He is set up as a bridge of communication between God and man, between heaven and earth, by which God comes down to us, and we come up unto him, notwithstanding of the two infinite gulfs of natural and moral distance between him and us. These gulfs were impassible, until Christ, by his incarnation, took away the natural distance; for in him, as IMMANUEL, God and Man meet together in one person: and by his death and satisfaction he removed the moral distance, by taking away the sin of the world; for this end was he manifested, to take away our sin. Now, these two infinite gulfs being removed, God and man meet together in a blessed amity and friendship; and we have "boldness to enter into the holiest by the blood of Jesus." Hence is that of Christ's, John xiv. 16, "I am the way, and the truth, and the life; no man cometh to the Father but by me." This was shadowed by Jacob's dream of the ladder, reaching from heaven unto earth, and the angels of God ascending and descending thereupon; signifying that, through Christ (in whom all the rounds and steps of the ladder are finished) the angels are ministering spirits unto the heirs of salvation, upon the footing of Christ's mediation; and that we have access to God through him. Through him we ascend unto God's holy hill, and abide in his tabernacle.

6*thly*, He is set up as the great gospel city of refuge, typified by the cities of refuge under the law, unto which the manslayer was to fly for safety from the avenger of blood, Heb. vi. 18. Believers are said to fly for refuge, to lay hold upon the hope set before them: justice cries for vengeance: God's broken law cries for vengeance: conscience cries for vengeance: the devil, as God's executioner, cries for vengeance. O the deplorable case and condition of the poor guilty criminal before the revelation of Christ! All refuges fail him: for the hail sweeps away all his refuges of lies, and in this case his hope and strength perishes from the Lord, until God make a discovery of Christ as the city of refuge that he has set open, with a cry from heaven, "Turn ye to your strong-holds, ye prisoners of hope:" Then, O then, the soul flies for refuge as a dove to its windows, and gets in to the clefts of the rock, and abides in the secret place and shadow of the Almighty, saying, O this is my rest, and here will I dwell at ease: "for there is no condemnation to them that are in Christ." Here the poor soul can turn about to law, to justice, to conscience, to the devil, and the world, and say, "Who can lay any thing to my charge? It is God that justifieth, who is he that condemneth?"

7*thly*, He is set up as a mystical brazen serpent in the camp of Israel, in the camp of the visible church, that the poor sinner, finding himself stung by the fiery serpents, sin and Satan, may, by looking unto him, be healed. Hence is that of Christ, John iii. 14, 15, "As Moses lifted up the serpent in the wilderness, even so must the Son of Man be lifted up," &c. The gospel is the pole upon which he is lifted up, in the view of all mankind: for by his commission we preach the gospel unto every creature; and the cry goes forth to the ends of the earth, "Look unto me, and be saved, all the ends of the earth; for I am God, and there is none else." Sirs, the venom of the old serpent has diffused itself through all the powers and faculties of the soul and body; and it is worming out your life; and die you must, unless you cast the eye of faith upon Christ, as the only ordinance of God for your salvation. As the stung Israelite had infallibly died, unless he had looked unto the brazen serpent; so the sinner that does not look by faith unto Christ, the true brazen serpent, shall infallibly die, not the first death only, but also the second: for there is no name, under heaven, given among men, whereby a poor sinner can be saved, but by the name of Jesus: but whosoever believes (in the name of Jesus) shall not perish, but shall have everlasting life."

8*thly*, He is set up as a foundation of hope and help to the lost family of Adam, to build upon for their eternal salvation: Is. xxviii. 16, "Behold, I lay in Zion, for a foundation, a stone, a tried stone, a precious corner stone, a sure foundation: He that believeth shall not make haste, shall not be ashamed or confounded." All other foundations are but foundations of sand, and the house built upon the sand will fall, and great will the fall thereof be; "for other foundation can no man lay than that is laid, which is Jesus Christ." Adam, in innocency, did indeed stand upon another foundation; and, if he had continued there, he would have had obtained life and happiness, by way of pactional debt; but there is no other foundation for a lost sinner to build upon, but the foundation Christ.

9*thly*, He is set up as the end of the law for righteousness to every sinner that believes in him. He has, by his obedience unto death, and the perfect holiness of his nature, brought in an everlasting righteousness, for the justification of the ungodly sinner that believes in him: This is his name, whereby he is called, The Lord our Righteousness, Jer. xxiii. 6: and "what the law could not do, in that it was weak through the flesh, God, sending his own Son, in the likeness of sinful flesh, for sin condemned sin in the flesh, that the righteousness of the law might be fulfilled in us." This is that white raiment Christ counsels us to buy of him, that the shame of our nakedness may not appear. And see how he sets up, or sets out, this righteousness, even to the stout-hearted, and far from righteousness, Is. xlvi. at the close, "I bring near my righteousness; it shall not be far off, and my salvation shall not tarry," &c. And the language of the soul, when it puts on that robe, is that which you find, Is. xlv. at the close, "Surely, shall one say, in the Lord have I righteousness and strength. In the Lord shall all the seed of Israel be justified, and shall glory."

10*thly*, He is set up as a storehouse, out of which the bankrupted and beggared sinners of Adam's family may be supplied with every thing they need: "For it hath pleased the Father, that in him should all fulness dwell; and that, out of his fulness, all we may receive grace for grace." We, who are his ministers and ambassadors, are authorised to cast open the gates of this storehouse, and give full liberty unto all wretched, miserable, blind, poor, and naked sinners, to come and take what they want, without money and without price, Is. lv. 1, Rev. xxii. 17.

11*thly*, To shut up this head at present, he is set up as the salvation of God to all lost sinners. Christ, in scripture, is frequently called "The Salvation of God." Jacob, Gen. xlix. 19. when he is blessing his children, makes a pause, casting his eyes upon the Shiloh that was to spring out of the tribe of Judah, and cries, "I have waited for thy salvation, O Lord." Old Simeon gets Christ, when a babe, in his arms, Luke ii. 29, "Lord, now lettest thou thy servant depart in peace, according to thy word; for mine eyes have seen thy salvation." one him, he who is our God, is the God of salvation. He has wrought, dista still works, manifold salvation in the midst of the earth; salvation manifes in, Matth. i. 22 ! salvation from the curse of the broken law, being re 13 ; salvation from Satan, for he through death destroyed friendship' ii. 14 ; salvation from the sting of death, 1 Cor. xv. 55 ; blood of Jes hell, and the wrath that is to come, 2 Thess. i. 10. So that, whenever a sinner looks unto him by the eye of faith, he may sing that song, Is. xii. 1, 2, "I will praise thee; for though thou wast angry with me, yet thine anger is turned away, and thou comfortedst me. Behold God is my salvation: I will trust, and not be afraid; for the Lord JEHOVAH is my strength and my song, he also is become my salvation."

Thus you see some of these ends and uses for which Christ was *set up from everlasting.*

Many more particulars might be insisted on, if time and strength would allow. I only name some of them.

1. He was set up as our Redeemer, to pay the ransom justice demanded, that we might not go down to the pit.

2. As a Surety, to pay the debts of bankrupts; therefore called, Heb. vii. 22, "The Surety of a better testament."

3. As a Physician, to heal us of all our diseases. With him is the balm in Gilead, and he is the Physician there.

4. As a Shepherd, to gather his Father's flocks unto his fold: Is. xl. 11, "He shall feed his flock like a Shepherd."

5. As a wonderful Counsellor, to give advice in all doubtful cases, Is. ix. 6. So David, Psal. xvi. 7, "I will bless the Lord, who hath given me counsel."

6. As an everlasting Father, in whom the fatherless orphans of Adam's family findeth mercy, Is. ix., Hos. xvi.

7. As the mighty God, that was able to encounter principalities and powers, and to spoil them on his cross, Is. ix.

8. As the Prince of peace, the King of Salem, "I create the fruit of the lips, peace, peace, to him that is afar off," &c.

9. As the Amen, the faithful and true Witness, by whose declaration all controversies are to be decided between God and man, and man and man.

10. As a Guide and Leader, to guide the blind by a way they know not, by his word and Spirit.

11. As a Captain of salvation, or Commander, under whose banner we are to fight our way to heaven, through the armies of hell and earth.

12. As a Bridegroom, with whom we are called to make a match, Is. liv. 6, Hos. ii. 19, 20.

IV. The *fourth* thing in the method was, to enquire into the grounds and reasons why Christ *was set up from everlasting*, for the great work and service of redemption.

Answ. 1. Here we must have recourse unto adorable Sovereignty, because it was his will and pleasure, and say, as Christ said in another case, Matth. xi. 26, "Even so, O Father, for so it seemed good in thy sight."

Answ. 2. Because of the good-will he did bear to man upon earth. Hence this was one of the notes of the song of angels at his birth, Luke ii. 14, "Glory to God in the highest; peace, good-will to man."

Answ. 3. Because of his ability for the undertaking: Psal. lxxxix. 19, "I have (says the Lord) laid help upon one that is mighty." He is the man of God's right hand, and the arm of JEHOVAH was in him and with him

Answ. 4. Because he voluntarily offered himself unto the work and service, as you heard in the first head of the doctrine, Psal. xl. 8, he had a heart to the work: "Thy law (says he) is within my heart," Is. 1. 5.

Answ. 5. Because of his undaunted courage to encounter all difficulties and opposition in the way; hence called "The Lion of the tribe of Judah." See his courageous behaviour, Is. l. 7-9.

Answ. 6. Because from everlasting God foresaw what a revenue of glory would accrue to the crown of heaven, through his mediation, even a greater glory than by all his other works of creation and providence. Hence the first note of the song of angels, Luke ii. 14, is "Glory to God in the highest." *q. d.* All the other works of God praise him; but now we see the highest revenue of glory to be levied out of the strange work of God, in uniting the divine and human natures in that Child that is born in the city of David. And I conceive it was with an eye to this, Is. vi., when they are viewing the personal glory of our Redeemer, cry out, "The whole earth is full of thy glory." As if they had said, 'It is no surprise to us angels to see his glory shining in the heavens; but to see the glory of the only begotten of the Father made flesh, and dwelling among men upon earth, a theatre of sin, rebellion, and misery; this is what indeed strikes us with astonishment and admiration.' I might here let you see how all the divine perfections are glorified to the full in the work of redemption, for which Christ was *set up from everlasting*. But I haste to the

V. And *last* thing proposed which was the application of the doctrine.

Use *first* shall be of *Information*, in the particulars following.

Is it so that Christ was set up from all eternity, for the great work and service of man's redemption?

1. Then, See hence the antiquity and eternity of the love of God towards lost sinners of Adam's family. His love must be from everlasting, because Christ *was set up from everlasting*, as a help meet for us, Psal. lxxxix. 19, "I have laid help upon one that is mighty." I have done it in eternity, before the world was. Hence the eternity of his love is asserted Jer. xxxi. 3, "I have loved thee with an everlasting love." Run back the love of God, we shall never find the beginning of it.

2. See hence, not only the eternity, but the activity of the love of God. It was not an indolent, but an operative love; it was such a love as set his power, his wisdom, and other perfections a-work; and all the persons of the glorious Trinity a-work, to accomplish his purpose of grace and love towards sinners of mankind. So that if the question be put,

What was God doing from all eternity before he created the world? Here you have an answer: The Father and Son possessed one another, "In the beginning of his ways, before his works of old:" and Infinite Wisdom, inspired by infinite and amazing love, set him a-work to lay the plan of our salvation, through his beloved Son: as you see here, *I was set up from everlasting.*

3. See hence that Christ is the great Secretary of Heaven, who is

intimately acquainted with the mind of God, which is unsearchable by any other but himself. For you see here, that he brings forth things that were done in eternity, before ever man or angels had any being, *I was set up from everlasting*. There is a word to this purpose, Matth. xi. 27, "All things are delivered unto me of my Father: and no man knoweth the Son, but the Father; neither knoweth any man the Father, save the Son, and he to whomsoever the Son will reveal him." Sirs, would you know the secrets of heaven, the mysteries of the kingdom, that were hid in God from eternity? Then come to Christ: hear ye him, and he will tell you things, that none in heaven or earth can tell you, but himself: No man hath seen God at any time; the only begotten Son, who is in the bosom of the Father, he hath declared him.

4. See hence the stability and perpetuity of the covenant of grace. Why, Christ *was set up from everlasting*, as the new covenant Head. The covenant was transacted with him, as second Adam, from everlasting, Psal. lxxxix. 3. And the covenant derives its stability from the covenant Head, Psal. lxxxix. 28. "My covenant shall stand fast with him:" and this is the very thing that makes it a sure covenant to us. Hence, Psal. lxxxix. 33, 34, "I will visit their transgression with the rod; nevertheless, my loving-kindness will I not take from him:" and therefore, "my covenant will I not break (viz. with them), nor alter the thing that is gone out of my lips," Is. liv. 9, 12. "For this is as the waters of Noah unto me; for as I have sworn that the waters of Noah should no more go over the earth; so have I sworn that I would not be wroth with thee, nor rebuke thee. For the mountains shall depart, and the hills be removed, but my kindess shall not depart from thee, &c.

5. See the great ground and reason of the stability and perpetuity of the church. Why, it is founded upon the everlasting mountains of the divine decrees and perfections, whereby Christ *was set up from everlasting*, as the basis and foundation upon which she stands. This is the rock upon which he builds his church, and the gates of hell shall never prevail against her. Storms and tempests are raised against her: Tempests of persecution; tempests of error; tempests of divisions and delusions. But what do they all come unto in the issue? Why, they are just like the billows of the sea breaking upon a rock, dashing themselves into foam, while the rock stands immoveable.

6. Was Christ set up from everlasting? Then see hence a good reason why all hands should be at work to exalt him, and set him on high. Why, in so doing, we join with a whole Trinity; whose plot was to set him up from everlasting. Though he be rejected by the generality of builders through England and Ireland, and in Scotland also, there is no matter of that: God, who set him up from everlasting, has made him the Head Stone of the corner; and therefore, however weak and impotent they be, that are bearing testimony for him and his cause, yet they shall prevail. Christ and his cause will aye be uppermost at the end of the day; for he that set him up from everlasting, will have him set up, and his cause maintained through all periods of time, in spite of all the powers of hell and earth.

7. See how it is, that faith pleases God, insomuch that, without it, "It is impossible to please him." Why, faith exalts Christ, whom God *set up from everlasting:* it falls in with the great plot of heaven, and cries, O precious Christ! precious Christ! none but him. Psal. lxviii. 25, "Whom have I in heaven but thee? and there is none upon earth whom I desire besides thee." O says faith he is "my Lord and my God." He is "my God, and I will prepare him an habitation; my Father's God, and I will exalt him. He is indeed fairer than the children of men. As the apple-tree among the trees of the wood. The chiefest among ten thousand; and altogether lovely. This is my Beloved, and this is my Friend, O daughters of Jerusalem." Now, I say, such language of faith cannot but be pleasing unto God, who *set him up from everlasting.* Hence faith is called the very work of God, John vi. 29, "This is the work of God, that ye believe on him whom he hath sent."

8. See the reason why God has such an implacable quarrel against the sin of unbelief, as to declare, John iii. 18, "He that believeth not is condemned already." Why, the reason is, it counteracts the work of God from eternity. God set him *up from everlasting:* But unbelief is for pulling him down, and tramples his blood under foot; crucifies him afresh; it despises and rejects him whom God *set up from everlasting:* And is it any wonder, then, that God is so much offended at the unbeliever? O Sirs, you that reject Christ, and continue in your unbelief, remember that the arrows of God's vengeance will be made drunk with your blood through eternity, for the indignities done to him whom God *set up from everlasting.*

9. See the reason why the pleasure of the Lord has prospered, and shall prosper in his hand, maugre [in spite of] all the opposition of hell and earth. Why, God *set him up from everlasting,* and therefore he has upheld, and will uphold, him. As he has finished redemption in a way of purchase, so he shall finish it in a way of power, "All his enemies shall be his foot-stool," Psal. lxxxix. 23.

> "I will beat down before his face,
>   all his malicious foes;
> I will them greatly plague who do
>   with hatred him oppose."*

His victorious arms shall prosper; he shall ride forth in glory and in majesty; and they shall bow under him, because God hath *set him up from everlasting.* Who then shall ever be able to shake his throne and government, Psal. xi. 1—6, &c.

10. See what good reason we have to celebrate our Christian passover, and to set him up sacramentally, by perpetuating his memory upon earth, until his second coming. This sacrament of the supper is a public owning and confessing him, and his dying love, and glorious achievements in the work of redemption, before God, angels, and men. It is putting honour upon him, and avouching him as our Redeemer, our Mediator, our Prophet, Priest, and King, in the face of

---

* Metre translation received by the Church of Scotland.

the devil and his angels, who are looking on us with vexation: It galls the devil, and stills that enemy and avenger, to see Christ, who bruised his head upon Mount Calvary, exalted and set up among the children of men, at a communion table, Heb. ii. 14, "Through death he destroyed him that had the power of death, and spoiled principalities and powers." How tormenting then must it be to the devil, to see Christ at his table, dividing the spoils among a company of poor sinners, who once in a day were his vassals and bond slaves?

But now let us go on to celebrate actually the memorials of the death of our glorious Immanuel, and to divide the spoils of the victory over sin and Satan, death and hell, which is the great work of the day.

THANKSGIVING SERMON.

ABRAHAM REJOICING TO SEE CHRIST'S DAY AFAR OFF.

John viii. 56.—*Your father Abraham rejoiced to see my day: and he saw it, and was glad.*

THE Jews, as you will see in the preceding part of the chapter, valued themselves exceedingly upon this account, that they were the natural seed and posterity of Abraham, the father of the faithful; and they were offended at our Lord, for comparing himself to Abraham, ver. 52, 53, Our Lord, in the words that I have read, proves that he was greater than Abraham: namely, because Abraham having gotten a promise of the Messiah to come of his lineage, he earnestly desired to see that happy day: And accordingly, though he did not see the real incarnation of the Messiah, yet he got a sight of it by faith, to the unspeakable joy and admiration of his soul: *Your father Abraham rejoiced to see my day: and saw it, and was glad.* In which words we may notice,

1st, Abraham's ambition and desire; he *rejoiced to see my day*.

2dly, Abraham's sight by faith; he saw the day of the Messiah.

3dly, Abraham's frame, which was the fruit of his faith; he *was glad*.

1st, I say, we have the height of Abraham's ambition and desire expressed in these words, *Abraham rejoiced to see my day*. The word *agaliastato* signifies, *he leapt at it*. Though the word commonly is put for rejoicing, yet here, it must rather signify *a transport of desire*, than of joy: Otherwise there would be a tautology in the latter clause of the verse, where it is said again, *He saw it, and was glad*. The notices he had received of the Messiah to come, had raised in him an expectation of something that was so exceeding great, that he reached out and stretched himself forth to see it. He never leapt so much to see the promised land that God was to give to his posterity, as to see the day of the Son of man.

Observe, That they who discern the dawnings of the Sun of righteousness, cannot but wish to see his rising. The mystery of redemption is that which angels desire to look into; much more should we, that are more immediately concerned in it.

2dly, We have Abraham's sight of faith; he *saw it, i. e.* he saw the day of the Messiah; he saw it by the spirit of prophecy, he saw it by the eye of faith acting upon that promise, " In thy seed shall all the nations of the earth be blessed:" And he had his faith confirmed by the sight of Melchisedec, one " made like unto the Son of God, the Priest of the most high God and King of peace and of righteousness:" He saw the angel of the covenant, with two other angels, in the plains of Mamre. And in offering Isaac, and the ram in the room of Isaac, he saw a double type of the great sacrifice that was to be offered up in the fulness of time. And his calling the place Jehovah Jireh, " In the mount of the Lord it shall be seen," says, that he saw something more in it, than others did, which time would produce.

3dly, We have Abraham's frame as the fruit of his faith; he *was glad.* He *was glad* of the Lord's favour and kindness to himself, and of the mercy, grace, and love which he saw God had in store for all the nations of the earth, in the promised seed. But the words will be further cleared, in taking notice of the following observations from them.

Obs. *1st,* That the time of the gospel is the day of Christ, in a way of eminency and excellency.

2dly, That the Old Testament saints breathed and longed much for a sight of the gospel day. and for the actual coming of the great Messiah. Abraham here leapt, as the word signifies, through the strength of desire after it.

3dly, That even the panting desires of the soul after Christ, though he be not enjoyed in a sensible way, are accompanied with a great deal of joy. So Abraham *rejoiced to see my day;* or his desires after it was that which filled him with a holy joy.

4thly, That the breathing or longing desires of the soul after Christ shall not be disappointed. Abraham, though he did not see the Messiah actually manifested in the flesh, yet he got such a sight of him, and his day, as yielded a great deal of satisfaction and joy.

5thly, That faith is the eye of the soul, whereby it takes up Christ, and the glorious blessings that come along with him, as held out in the revelation of the word. So here Abraham saw the day of Christ, by faith acting upon the promises and types of him, that were presented before his view.

6thly, That faith acting upon the promise, will see Christ through many veils, and at a prodigious distance. Thus we are told, Heb. xi. 13, that Abraham, and others, saw the promises of Christ afar off, and they embraced them: Faith is a quick-sighted grace, it takes up things at a vast distance.

7thly, That faith's views and uptakings of Christ fills the soul with joy and gladness. " Whom, having not seen, ye love; in whom, though now ye see him not, yet believing, ye rejoice with joy unspeakable, and full of glory," 1 Pet. i. 8.

I shall abstract from all these doctrines, and discourse a little upon the words themselves. And speak a little,

I. Of the day of Christ.
II. Of faith's views and sight of this day.
III. Of the joy and gladness arising from a sight of this day.
IV. Whence it is, that a sight of Christ, and of the day of Christ, brings such joy and gladness.
V. Apply.

1. The *first* thing is to discourse of the day of Christ. And here I will tell you,

1*st*, of some notable days of the Son of man. 2*dly*, Give you some qualities of the day of Christ. 3*dly*, Some notable sights that are to be seen in his day.

1*st*, I would tell you of some notable days of the Son of man.

1. There is a day of his eternal destination to be your Redeemer. This is a day of more ancient date, than the day of the world's creation; for he was verily fore-ordained before the world was made. "I was set up from everlasting, from the beginning, &c. Of this day the Psalmist speaks, Psal. ii.. "Thou art my Son, this day have I begotten thee. I will declare the decree the Lord hath said unto me." Which decree was fully manifested in his resurrection from the dead, as the apostle Peter shews, Acts ii.: all the prophesies, promises, and types of the Old Testament, were nothing else but so many gradual openings of what were concerted in the council of peace from eternity.

2. There was the day of his actual incarnation, or manifestation in the flesh. When the eternal Son of God was made of a woman, made under the law: This was the most surprising day that ever the world had seen; a more remarkable day than that, when the foundations of the world were laid. This was a day of which a host of angels are dispatched from the throne of glory, to proclaim the glad news to the shepherds, Luke ii., "I bring you good tidings of the great joy, which shall be to all people: for unto you is born this day, in the city of David, a Saviour, which is Christ the Lord."

3. This day of his solemn inauguration and instalment into his mediatory office. This was a day of great solemnity: then the heavens were opened unto him, and a voice issued out from from heaven, saying, "This is my beloved son, in whom I am well pleased?" And the Spirit of the Lord descended on him, in the likeness of a dove; never such an ordination of a minister as this of Christ; for that day he was anointed with the oil of gladness above his fellows.

4. Another notable day of Christ was the day of his oblation or death, when by one offering he for ever perfected them that are sanctified. That day the work of our redemption was perfected in a way of purchase. Hence it was, he cried out, "It is finished, and bowed his head, and gave up the ghost." This day, the little stone cut out of the mountain, which broke in pieces the kings and kingdoms of the earth, was himself broken in pieces, by the heavy hammer of his Father's wrath. Oh! was it not a notable day, when the Father drew his glittering sword from against his only and beloved Son, and bathed

it in his blood for our sins; wounded him for our iniquites, and cried, "Awake, O sword, against the man that is my fellow."

5. The day of resurrection was a notable day; for then, and thereby, was fulfilled the sign of the prophet Jonas, which was the consummating evidence of his Messiah-ship, Rom. i. 4. He was "declared to be the Son of God with power, according to the Spirit of holiness, by the resurrection from the dead." Was it not a remarkable day, when Christ as our Surety having descended into the grave, he came forth again as our Surety, like Samson, carrying the gates and bars of the prison along with him, crying to his friends, "I am he that liveth, and was dead, and behold I am alive for evermore," &c.
'And because I live, ye shall live also." His resurrection is our discharge of the debt, and we are raised up together with him. Christ's resurrection was a greater miracle, than if all the race of Adam had been brought out of the grave in a moment, for he had the heavy stone of the curse of God, and of our sins lying upon him. And who could roll away this "stone from the door of the sepulchre? and yet it is not possible that he should be held therein, He was taken from prison and from judgement."

6. The day of his solemn ascension into heaven, and his sitting "down at the right hand of the majesty on high," Heb. i. 3. There was but little of the solemnity of that day seen by the inhabitants of this world; only the disciples, when upon Mount Olivet, in company with him, they stood gazing up into heaven as he passed out of their sight. But O! it was a day of great solemnity in the eyes of the invisible world of spirits! All the trumpets of heaven sounded, and all the fiery chariots of angels attended him in his passage; "God is gone up with a shout, the Lord with the sound of a trumpet. Sing praises to God, sing praises; sing praises unto our King, sing praises," Psal. xlvii. 5, 6, and lxviii. 17. "The chariots of God are twenty thousand, even thousands of angels: the Lord is among them as in Sinai in the holy place."

7. The day of Pentecost was a remarkable day, when, like a mighty Prince newly come to the throne, he scattered his gifts among his subjects; when, like "the rushing of a mighty wind," the Spirit was poured out from on high, in his miraculous and extraordinary gifts, endowing the apostles and others with the gift of tongues, in order to the propagating and spreading the gospel among all nations of the world; and when some thousands of sinners (several of whom had their hands dipt in the blood of Christ) were converted unto his obedience.

8. The day of his manifestation by the Gospel, especially among the Gentile nations, is a notable day of the Son of man. When the partition wall between Jew and Gentile was broken down Eph. iii. 14,; the old Testament economy unhinged, and the waters of the sanctuary, which were pent up in the typical temple, began to run down to the valley of Shittim and water the uncultivated nations, that were aliens to the commonwealth of Israel; the preaching of the gospel unto the Gentiles was such a notable day of the Son of man, that it is made a great branch "of the mystery of godliness," I Tim. iii. last.

This day was fulfilled the old prophecy of Jacob, that to "Shiloh should the gatherings of the people be," and the promise made to Abraham, "In thy seed shall all the families of the earth be blessed." And that of Isaiah, chap. xi. 10, "There shall be a root of Jesse, which shall stand for an ensign to the people, to it shall the Gentiles seek."

9. The day of his marriage and coronation is a remarkable day of Christ, when the poor sinner, that was in covenant with hell, lying among the pots, under the sentence of death, and the curse of the law, is taken and betrothed unto the Son of God; and he says to it, "Thy Maker is thine Husband, (the Lord of hosts is his name)." That day there is a new crown of glory set upon his head, and a royal diadem put in his hand, "Go forth, O ye daughters of Zion, and behold King Solomon with the crown wherewith his mother crowned him in the day of his espousals, and in the day of the gladness of his heart." This day makes little noise in the world, but it makes a great noise in heaven, "for there is joy in heaven at the conversion of one sinner."

10. The day of the renewed visits that he makes to the soul, in the ordinances of his appointment, word, sacraments, prayer, or meditation; when the soul is made to say, "I sat down under his shadow with great delight. He brought me to the banqueting house, and his banner over me was love," &c.

11. Again, The day of his appearing in the power of his Spirit, in the dispensation of the everlasting gospel, when he goes forth with his bow, and with his sword, conquering and to conquer: pulling down the strong-holds of Satan; destroying the works of the devil, and rearing up his kingdom; reviving and reforming his churches; and sinners flocking in to him, like doves to their windows, and like dew from the womb of the morning.

12. Again, The day of the believer's death is a notable day of Christ, for then it is that he comes with the keys of hell and death in his hand, to usher the poor soul into the house not made with hands, eternal in the heavens; the house of many mansions: according to his promise, "I will come again and receive you to myself, that where I am, there ye may be also."

Lastly, The Day of his second coming will be a notable day, for then he will come without sin to the salvation of all that believe in him. Of this day Christ speaks, when he says, "Look up, and lift up your heads, for your redemption draweth nigh." That day he will descend from heaven with a shout, with the voice of the archangel, and with the trump of God; when the earth will cast forth the dead, and the sea will give up the dead which are in it; and a separation will be made for ever between the sheep and the goats; the wheat and the chaff. Oh, the awful solemnity of that day of Christ! when the heavens, being on fire, "shall be dissolved, the elements shall melt with fervent heat, the earth, and the works that are therein, shall be burnt up." Thus I have given you some notable days of Christ. I shall not positively determine which of those days Abraham had in his view, when he saw the day of Christ: perhaps all of them together: but especially the day of his incarnation, death, resurrection, ascension, and manifestation by the word and spirit, for the salvation of souls.

2dly, I come to give you some of the qualities of the day of Christ.

1. Then, You see in the text, that it is a day of joy and gladness; *Abraham rejoiced to see my day, and he saw it, and was glad;* and no wonder, for he is the consolation of Israel, and gives the oil of joy for mourning. Whenever the day of Christ breaks on a poor soul, though formerly it had been sitting in the region and shadow of death, it lays aside its sackcloth, and girds itself with gladness: so soon as ever he appears, "the shadows of death are turned into the morning." And it cannot miss to be a day of gladness; for,

2. It is a day of light; and truly light is sweet: the darkness of unbelief, the darkness of ignorance, the darkness of error, the darkness of despondency, evanishes, when the day of Christ breaks, just as the clouds and darkness of the night evanishes at the appearance of the sun. And no wonder, for he is the "Light of the world: the Sun of righteousness: the bright and the morning Star, given for a light to enlighten the Gentiles, and the glory of his people Israel."

3. His day is a day of life from the dead. Death spiritual and eternal, as well as death temporal, had been the heritage of all the race of Adam, if Christ had not come; but when he comes, he brings life to a lost world. When he comes in a day of conversion, the soul is "quickened, which was dead in trespasses and sins." And after the dark night of desertion, when he returns to pay a new visit, by the refreshing influences of his Spirit, it is "like life from the dead: I will be as the dew to Israel:" And what then? "They shall revive as the corn." When he comes in the power of his Spirit, the dead "are made to hear the voice of the Son of God." When he comes at the last day, it will be a day of reviving to the bodies of his saints; for he will cry, "Awake and sing, ye that dwell in dust: thy dew is as the dew of herbs, and the earth shall cast out the dead."

4. The day of Christ is a day of vengeance upon sin, Satan, and the world. Our glorious Immanuel, with a view to the day of his appearing in the flesh, and in the power of his word and Spirit, for the ruin of Satan's kingdom, cries, "The day of vengeance is in mine heart:" and accordingly when he comes, he takes vengeance on the old serpent, spoils principalities and powers; and for this end is he manifested, and manifested in the gospel, and manifested savingly to the soul, "to destroy the works of the devil."

5. The day of Christ is a day of jubilee: it is a year of release, Numb. xxv. 10, Deut. xv. 2, wherein he causes open the prison gates, and cries to the prisoners to come forth, and to them that are in darkness, shew yourselves, Is. xlix. 9. Whenever he comes, and makes day break upon a poor soul, though formerly it was bound that it could not move; yet, whenever he comes, I say, the bonds of sin, ignorance, and unbelief drop off, the lame man is made to leap like an hart, and the tongue of the dumb to sing.

6. It is a day of love, Ezek. xvi. 8. "When I passed by thee, thy time was the time of love." By his appearing in the flesh, and his manifestation in the gospel; the kindness and love of God our

Saviour toward man hath indeed appeared in a surprising way. "Herein is love, not that we loved God, but that he loved us," John iv. 10. Whenever he draws near to the soul, he causes a kindly glowing and warming of heart toward himself; "Did not our heart burn within us, while he talked with us by the way, and while he opened to us the scriptures?" Luke xxiv. 32. If he but speak a word to a poor soul, or call it by its name, as he did to Mary, immediately the poor soul will fall under the bonds of his love, and be ready to cry, as she did, Rabboni, my Master; or with Thomas, My Lord, and my God.

7. The day of Christ is a day of peace, it is prophesied, that, "in his day, the very mountains should bring peace to the people," Psal. lxxii. 3. That "men should beat their swords into ploughshares, and their spears into pruning hooks," Is. ii. 4. His name is the Prince of peace: and peace on earth, and good-will towards men, was proclaimed by the angels, whenever he set his foot in this lower world; and whenever he comes and visits a poor soul, he brings in peace with him, and a "peace that passeth all understanding." It is peace like a river: It is righteousness like the waves of the sea. "Peace I leave with you, my peace I give unto you: of the increase of his government and peace there shall be no end."

8. It is a day of salvation: He is given for salvation to all the ends of the earth. When he comes into the world he proclaims, "I that speak in righteousness, mighty to save." The day of his death was the day of purchased salvation. The day of the gospel is the day of proclaimed salvation. This is the day of salvation, this the accepted time: "To-day, if ye will hear his voice, harden not your hearts." The day of conversion is the day of applied salvation; Luke xix. 9, "This day is salvation come to this house." And the day of death, and of his second coming, is the day of completed and perfected salvation.

9. The day of Christ is an everlasting day, a durable day, in which the sun shall never go down. Indeed, in the day of Christ the sun may be eclipsed, but it shall never set with respect to a poor soul, whom he has visited with distinguishing love. No, the day of grace is but the beginning of the day of glory. "The Lord shall be unto thee an everlasting light, and thy God thy glory." So much for the qualities of the day of Christ.

3*dly*, I would tell you of some wonderful and surprising sights that are to be seen, and some great works that are done in the day of Christ.

You have a cluster of the great works that are done in the day of Christ, Dan. ix. from verse 24th to the end of the chapter.

1. A stop is put to the mighty torrent of sin, that had been overflowing the face of the world, like a mighty deluge. We are told, verse 24th, that the Messiah shall finish transgression. The word in the margin is, He shall restrain transgression. Ignorance, atheism, infidelity, and all manner of wickedness, had overflown Jews and Gentiles; as the apostle shews, Rom. i., ii., and iii. Now, by the coming of Christ a stop was put unto this flood of sin: for, by the

preaching of Christ crucified, the Jewish errors and superstitions, and the idolatries and abominations of the Gentile world, are overthrown; and the kingdom of Satan falls down before him, through the nations of the earth, Psal. cxiv. 3, 7, "The sea fled, Jordan was driven back; at the presence of the Lord; at the presence of the God of Jacob.

2. In the day of the Messiah, transgression is ended, verse 24; or, as it reads in the margin, it is sealed up, hid, or covered, out of the sight of God. By sin there is a separation between God and us. Well, Christ comes to make an end of it: To take it out of the way, that so there might be a meeting betwixt God and us again: and he seals it up: He covers it with his blood, so as, though it be sought for, yet it shall never be found: and O, is not this a great work done in the day of Christ.

3. In the day of Christ, verse 24, there is reconciliation made for iniquity; "For God was in Christ, reconciling the world unto himself, not imputing their trespasses unto them," 2 Cor. v. 19. Rom. v. 10, "When we were enemies, we were reconciled to God by the death of his Son." No sooner had man sinned, but red war commenced between God and man, Psal. vii. 2, God is angry with the wicked, and their hearts are enmity against God, And the war had lasted through eternity, if Christ had not come and "made peace by the blood of his cross."

4. In the day of Christ, everlasting righteousness is brought in, verse 24. By the sin of Adam, and the breach of the first covenant, righteousness before God was gone quite out of the world There was indeed something, and that very little, of a moral righteousness to be found in or among some of the heathens; but, as one says, all their shining virtues were but splendid sins. There was nothing of a law righteousness to be found among all the race of mankind; nothing that could answer the law in its spirituality: hence say the psalmist, and the apostle, "there is none righteous, no, not one." But now, Christ brings in an everlasting righteousness into the world by his obedience unto the death. He "magnifies the law, and makes it honourable; and the Lord is well pleased for his righteousness' sake," Rom. viii. 3, 4.

5. In the day of Christ the vision and the prophecy is sealed up: That is, the canon of the scripture is completed; with an awful advertisment to the world, to take care, that none add to, or diminish and take from, the words of the book; under the pain of the wrath of God, Rev. xxii. 18, 19. There you see with what an awful solemnnity the vision and prophecy is sealed: Read, "For I testify unto every man that heareth the words of the prophecy of this book, if any man shall add unto these things, God shall add unto him the plagues that are written in this book: And if any man shall take away from the words of the book of this prophecy, God shall take away his part out of the book of life, and out of the holy city, and from the things which are written in this book."

6. In the day of the Messiah the most holy is anointed; that is Christ himself, who is the holy One of God, Acts iv. 27. "The holy

One of Israel is anointed with the oil of gladness above his fellows.' And Christ may be called the most holy, with allusion unto the place in the temple of Jerusalem, called the "Holy of Holies;" wherein was the Shechina, the visible appearance of the divine presence, from between the cherubims, Exod. xxv. 22. He is our New Testament Holy of the Holies, into which, as kings and priests unto God, we are allowed to enter, and participate of his anointing; I mean, of the Spirit of Christ.

7. In his days the covenant is confirmed with many, verse 25. By his death and blood the covenant of grace and all the promises of it are so ratified and confirmed, that we, without fear of vicious intromission, may intermeddle with the blessings thereof, as goods disponed by a testamentary deed, Heb. ix. 16, 17, "Where a testament is, there must also, of necessity, be the death of the testator. For a testament is of force after men are dead; otherwise it is of no strength at all whilst the testator liveth."

8. He has made the sacrifice and oblation to cease, verse 27, that is he has put an end to these typical sacrifices that were of divine appointment, during the standing of the Old Testament economy, the sacrifice of his own death having come in the room of all these.

Besides these mentioned by Daniel, I will tell you of some other great and wonderful things, that are done in the days of the great Messiah: And O, let all the world wonder at them!

1. In his day the glory of heaven is brought down to earth! And O, what a wonder is here! Christ is the brightness of the Father's glory: and to be sure the brightness of the Father's glory must be the brightest and most glorious thing in heaven: yet this is brought down to the earth, and seen by men upon earth, John i. 14, "The word was made flesh, and we beheld his glory, the glory as of the only begotten of the Father!" Sirs, whatever you think of this; yet I can tell you, that this is the admiration of angels; see how they fall a wondering at it, Is. vi. 3. The seraphim, while they are beholding the glory of God, in the face or person of Christ, they are so stricken with wonder, that they cry, "Holy, holy, holy is the Lord of hosts!" And observe what is added in the close of the verse, "The whole earth is full of his glory!" The seraphim do not say, The whole heavens are full of his glory; for that is no wonder to them, "seeing there can in no wise enter into heaven any thing that defileth:" But that the whole earth should be filled with the glory of an incarnate Deity; that he should come down from heaven, and manifest his glory to a lost world, full of sin and misery, through a veil of flesh, is what the inhabitants of heaven are stricken with wonder at. O Sirs! "The tabernacle of God is with men!" In the days of the Messiah, the glory of heaven is brought down to earth; and is not this a great thing done, in the Messiah's days?

2. In the days of Christ, "the temple of God is opened, and the ark of his testament is to be seen," Rev. xi. last verse. O Sirs! We who live in the days of Christ, have a far better and more glorious temple than ever the church of Israel had, even when their material temple was in its greatest splendour: Christ is the temple! and Oh, God is

in his holy temple; yea, the fulness of the Godhead dwells in him bodily! And the temple is opened in the dispensation of the everlasting gospel; and we have free access into this temple; every bar and impediment that stood in our way of communion with God, is now removed; and we have "boldness to enter into the holiest by the blood of Jesus, by a new and living way which he hath consecrated for us, through the veil, that is to say, his flesh,' Heb. x. 19, 20. And here is to be seen the ark of his testament; the ark was a chest, wherein the two tables of the law were kept, written upon stone. Well, Christ is the true Ark, in whom the law is kept, and kept for ever. The honour, beauty, and glory of it is maintained and preserved by Christ; for he has made it honourable, and magnified it by his obedience unto the death. Oh, is not this a great thing done in the days of the Messiah!

3. In his day paradise is opened; and the new Jerusalem is brought down from God out of heaven, Rev. xx. 10. We lost an earthly paradise by the sin of the first Adam, but we regain a heavenly paradise by the righteousness of the second Adam. Yea, the new Jerusalem is sent down; all the glory of heaven and of a happy eternity are wrapt up in a word of grace; in a covenant of grace. and brought down to us, that we by faith may possess them.

4. A bridge is laid over the infinite gulf of natural and moral distance, between God and man, and the gulf of divine wrath, that cut off our communication with heaven! And by this bridge, a free passage and communication is opened, between God and man; by the bridge of the human nature united to the divine, offered in a sacrifice to justice, we may pass and repass, or "go in and out, and find pasture. The just suffered for the unjust that he might bring us to God." He is the way to the Father, and there is no coming to the Father but by Christ. This is the ladder that Jacob saw, passing between heaven and earth, and the angels ascending and descending upon it. It is upon the footing of the mediation of the Son of God. that the "angels are ministering spirits, sent forth to minister for them who are the heirs of salvation."

5. In the day of the great Messiah, a throne of grace is reared, and proclamations issued out to all the ends of the earth, to come unto it with boldness, for "mercy and grace to help in time of need," Heb. iv. 16. Is. lv. 1, "Ho, every one that thirsteth, come ye to the waters, and he that hath no money, come, buy and eat, yea, come, buy wine and milk, without money and without price." O Sirs, is it not a happiness to live in such halcyon days, that whatever we need, we have it for the asking? For now, since the tribunal of justice is sprinkled by the blood of the Lamb, and turned to a mercy-seat, it is nothing but ask and have, with the King that sits on the throne: "Ask, and it shall be given you; seek, and ye shall find; knock. and it shall be opened unto you. For this is the confidence that we have towards him, that if we ask any thing according to his will, he heareth us." So forward and liberal is he, that he even prevents us with his mercy, before we ask it of him: "Before they call, I will answer; and whiles they are yet speaking, I will hear." And again, "Hitherto

have ye asked nothing; ask, and ye shall receive, that your joy may be full."

6. In the days of the Messiah the true manna is rained upon the children of Israel, in the wilderness of this world. It was a real and continued miracle that God wrought for Israel, in the wilderness, when, instead of feeding them with the product of the earth, he made the heavens to rain down bread among them, about their tent doors, till they came to the promised land. But, O Sirs, this was but a faint shadow of the miraculous way that God takes of feeding our souls, while travelling through the wilderness of this world, unto the promised rest that is above: "My Father (says Christ) giveth you the true bread from heaven." And what is that true bread? It is the flesh and blood of his eternal Son: "This is meat indeed, and drink indeed: and except we eat the flesh, and drink the blood of the Son of man, we have no life in us." This true manna is rained down upon us, in the dispensation of the everlasting gospel. The preaching of an incarnate and crucified Redeemer, brings Christ and his salvation as near to us as ever the manna was brought to Israel, when it fell about their tent doors: yea, we have it in our hands; we have it in our mouths; we have it in our hearts; in the word of faith which we preach.

7. In this day the mystical brazen Serpent is lifted up upon the pole of the everlasting gospel, that poor sinners, who are dying of the sting and poison of the old serpent, may be healed by looking unto it. John iii. 14, 15, "As Moses lifted up the serpent in the wilderness, even so must the Son of man be lifted up; that whosoever believeth in him, should not perish, but have eternal life."

8. In the day of the Messiah, the wells of salvation are opened. "Waters break up in the wilderness, and streams in the desert." It was prophesied, Is. xii. 3 (of the day of Christ), "With joy shall ye draw water out of the wells of salvation:" And I would fain hope that, even in this place, and upon this occasion, that promise has been fulfilled to not a few. The Rock has followed them, and been like rivers of waters in a dry place to their souls; passing through the valley of Baca, they found it a well, the rain also came down and filled the pools of ordinances; according to that promise, Psal. lxxii. 6, "He shall come down like rain upon the mown grass, as showers that water the earth."

9. In his day, beggars are taken from the dunghill and set among princes. This is what is foretold by the prophet David, upon the humiliation of the most high God, Psal. cxiii. 7, 8, "He raiseth up the poor out of the dust, and lifteth the needy out of the dunghill, that he may set him with princes, even with the princes of his people." O what a surprising scene is it, when Christ the Prince of the kings of the earth comes, in a day of power, and takes the poor soul, lying in the dunghill of a natural state, wrapt up in sin and misery, decks it with his own beauty, makes it like "the king's daughter, all glorious within," and verifies that word upon it. Psal. xlv. 9. "Upon thy right hand did stand the queen in gold of Ophir?" The poor

soul even blushes to think of its preferment, of what it is come to, when it looks "unto the Rock whence it was hewn."

10. In the day of the Messiah "the barren woman is made to keep house, and to be a joyful mother of children," Psal. cxiii. 9. The poor Gentile world was a poor barren woman during the Old Testament dispensation; but Oh! now, in the day of the Messiah, she keeps house; or, as it is in the Hebrew, 'she dwells in a house;' she is brought in under the roof of the house of mercy, which shall be built up for ever. And she is made a joyful mother of children: hence is that call given to the Church of God among the Gentiles, under the New Testament, Is. liv. 1, " Sing, O barren, thou that didst not bear, break forth into singing, and cry aloud, thou that didst not travail with child; for more are the children of the desolate, than the children of the married wife, saith the Lord:" The converts unto the Christian faith under the New Testament, among the Gentile nations, are far more numerous than the converts that were made to him among the Jews, under the Old Testament, Rev. vii. 4—9, there is there mention made only of twelve thousand out of every tribe; but among the rest of the nations and languages of the world, there is an innumerable company which no man can number, clothed with the white robes of the imputed and implanted righteousness of Christ, crying, "Salvation to our God that sitteth on the throne, and unto the Lamb, for ever and ever."

11. In the day of the Messiah, not only is the head of the old serpent bruised, but death, the king of terrors, is vanquished, and his destroying or stinging power is removed! The death of Christ was the death of death; his burial and resurrection was the destruction of the grave, Hos. xiii. 14, "I will ransom them from the power of the grave." Our glorious Redeemer having spoiled death and the grave, he proclaims the victory, saying, "I am he that liveth, and was dead; and behold I am alive for evermore, and have the keys of hell and of death," Rev. i. 17.

Thus much for the *first* thing, namely, the day of Christ.

II. The *second* thing in the method was, to speak a little of faith's view, or sight of the day of Christ.—For clearing of this I would have you to know,

1st, That it could not be a sensible corporeal sight of the day of Christ that Abraham had, like that of Simeon, when he "took him up in his arms and blessed God, saying, Lord, now lettest thou thy servant depart in peace, according to thy word, for mine eyes have seen thy salvation." For in Abraham's time Christ was not yet come in the flesh, nor dead: He came not for many hundreds of years after Abraham's days. And therefore,

2dly, It must needs be a sight of his day by faith, which "is the evidence of things not seen, and the substance of things hoped for." Faith is frequently expressed in scripture, under the notion of seeing, or believing in Christ, John vi. 40. "He that seeth the Son, and believeth on him, hath everlasting life." Is. xlv. 22, "Look unto me, and be ye saved, all the ends of the earth;" and in many other places.

What the eye of the body is unto the visible frame of nature, that is faith unto the new world of a gospel revelation; for as it is by the natural eye that we behold the heavens and the earth, sun, moon, and stars, and all other material objects, and the glory of God in them; so it is by faith that we take up the new heavens and the new earth, of which Christ is the glorious Sun of righteousness; hence is that of the apostle, 2 Cor. iii. 18, "All we beholding, as in a glass, the glory of the Lord, are changed into the same image."

Now Abraham's sight of Christ, and of the day of Christ, I conceive it carries these things following in it.

1. It plainly supposes, that Abraham had a revelation of Christ, and of what was to be done in his day, revealed to him in the promise, Gen. xxii. 18, "In thy seed shall all the nations of the earth be blessed:" He had it revealed to him in his type Melchisedec; and in that remarkable trial of his faith, in offering up his son, Isaac. Sirs, without a revelation of Christ, faith could never take him up. The revelation of Christ is to the eye of faith just what the light of the sun is to the eye of the body; take away the light, a man cannot see any thing that is about him; so take away the revelation of the word, we can never see Christ, or the things of Christ. Hence the word is called "a light shining in a dark place"—until the day dawn. So then, Abraham, seeing the day of Christ, supposes he had a revelation of Christ. But, O Sirs, there is a vast difference between the revelation that Abraham had of Christ, and that which we now enjoy under the New Testament! There is as great an odds as there is between break of day and the sun shining in his meridian height and light. But what a shame is it to us, that there should be such a difference between his faith and our faith! Though the discovery he had of Christ was so faint in respect of ours, yet we are told, "That he staggered not at the promise of God through unbelief;" whereas we are staggering almost at every step.

2. Abraham's seeing of the day of Christ, implies an act of the understanding, or a knowledge and uptaking of Christ, suited unto the revelation of him. His seeing of the day of Christ, says, that the light of the revelation had not staid without him, but it had entered into his heart; according to that, 2 Cor. iv. 6, "God, who commanded the light to shine out of darkness, hath shined in our hearts." God, by his Spirit, takes the things of Christ, and he shews them unto us. "Unto you it is given to know the mysteries of the kingdom of heaven."

3. Abraham's seeing of the day of Christ, it has in it an act of delectation, *He saw my day, and was glad.* He was delighted at the sight of the day of Christ, Zech. ix. 9. "Rejoice greatly, O daughter of Zion, shout, O daughter of Jerusalem; behold thy King cometh unto thee, meek, and having salvation!" &c. Oh, with what triumphant delight the spouse expresses her sight of him! Cant. ii. 8. "It is the voice of my beloved: behold he cometh leaping upon the mountains, skipping upon the hills."

4. An act of application and improvement. To be sure when Abraham got that promise of the Messiah, to come of his loins, "In

thy seed shall all the nations of the earth be blessed," he would be ready to say as Jeremiah did, chap. xv. 16. "Thy words were found, and I did eat them; and thy word was unto me the joy and the rejoicing of mine heart." He would no doubt bring it home with particular application to his own soul, saying, surely in this blessed seed have I righteousness and strength, in him will I be justified, and in him alone will I glory, "This is my beloved; and this is my friend."

5. I think it may have in it also, an act of wonder and admiration: He saw the day of Christ, and was surprised with the sight, saying with the apostle, "without controversy, great is the mystery of godliness, God was manifest in the flesh." Thus you see what is implied in that sight that Abraham had of the day of Christ; but especially I think it points at the two principal acts of faith, viz. knowledge and application.

Quest. What are the grounds of the metaphor? or why is faith represented in scripture under the notion of the bodily sight?—I shall endeavour to clear this in the few following particulars.

1. The eye, you know, is a passive recipient kind of an organ: My meaning is this, the eye does not send out a light from itself, nor doth it give and communicate any thing unto the object that it beholds: What do you give or add to the sun, moon, or stars, when you behold them? Your eyes only receive the print or image of them into your mind, without adding any thing unto them.

Just so is it with faith, it does not give or communicate any thing unto God, or Christ, or to what it beholds in the world of grace, but it just takes them up, or takes them in, as they are presented to the soul's view in the light of the revelation. What did the Israelites give unto the brazen serpent when they looked unto it and were healed? As little do we give or add unto Christ, when we look unto him and are saved.

2. The eye of the body is a very assuring sense. What are we more sure of, than of what we see with our eyes? If a man see the light of the sun, all the world will not persuade him but that it is day, or that the sun is up.

So faith is a grace that carries a great deal of certainty in the very nature and bosom of it. Heb. xi. 1, "Now faith is the substance of things hoped for, and the evidence of things not seen." And ver. 13, it is said of the worthies, that they saw "the promises afar off, and were persuaded of them, and embraced them."

3. The eye is a directing organ. The man that has the light of the day, and his eyes open, he will know his way, and is not so ready to stumble and fall into ditches and precipices as a blind man, or one that walks in darkness.

So faith is a directing grace, when by faith we "look unto Jesus, then we run the race that is set before us." We are said "to walk by faith and not by sight."

4. The eye, though it be little, is a very capacious organ. The man that has the light of day, and his eyes open, will see every thing visible; it takes up the whole visible frame of nature.

So faith is a most capacious grace, extending itself to every thing that lies within the vast circuit of the revelation. I own indeed there may be a true faith which takes up but little of the light of revelation at first. Like the eye of an infant, it really takes in the light, and perceives external objects, but with a great deal of weakness and confusion, until it come gradually to more strength; and then it widens and extends itself further and further. Just so is it with the eye of faith : At first the light of knowledge, it is but dim; the man, like an infant, does not see far; but " the path of the just is as the shining light, that shineth more and more unto the perfect day," Prov. iv. 18. As the light and strength of faith grows, it widens itself to take in more of God; more of Christ; more of things that are above, where Christ is. It wades deeper and deeper into the mysteries of the kingdom, until it come to be at last swallowed up in immediate vision.

5. The eye is an impressing organ; what we see with our eyes, leaves an impression upon our minds. If a man look upon the sun for a little, he will find the impression of the sun in his eye, even though he shut it, or though he turn his eye away from it.

Even so faith leaves an impression of the glory of the Sun of righteousness, 2 Cor. iii. 18, " All we, beholding, as in a glass, the glory of the Lord, are changed into the same image."

6. The eye is a very quick sort of an organ, taking up things at a great distance : it will run from the one end of the heavens to the other, in a very trice*, it will mount up to the heavens among the stars, and in a moment will view the whole circuit of the heavens.

So faith is such a quick-sighted grace, it takes up things at a great distance, as the faith of Abraham did here, when he saw the day of Christ afar off. It will in a moment, as it were, look back to an eternity past, and view the everlasting springs of electing and redeeming love, before ever the foundations of the world were laid ; and then, at the same breath, turn itself towards an eternity to come, and take a view of the hidden glories of an invisible world that are within the veil.

7. The eye is a curious piece of work. Naturalists tell us, it is the most curious part of the whole body of man: There is much of the glory, wisdom, and power of the great Creator, to be seen in the formation of the eye of the body.

So faith is a grace that is curiously wrought in the soul. There is more of the power and wisdom of God discovered in the formation of the grace of faith, than in any other part of the new creature. Hence it is he takes one of his blessed names from it, and styles himself " The Author and the Finisher of faith." And as " he fulfils in us all the good pleasure of his goodness," so in a particular manner the " work of faith with power," 2 Thess. i. 11. Yea that same "exceeding great and mighty power of God," which was put forth in the resurrection of Christ from the dead, is said to be exerted in them that believe, Eph. i. 19.

8. The eye of the body is a very tender thing ; it is soon hurt and prejudiced. A very little waff of any thing will do it hurt, and if it

* A moment, or the shortest time wherein one can say, *one, two, three*.

be hurt it will soon weep. And this is the way how it comes to health; it weeps out any dust or mote that gets into it.

Just so is it here, faith is a very tender kind of a grace, it thrives best in a pure conscience. Hence the apostle speaks of "keeping the mystery of the faith in a pure conscience." The living actings of faith are marred by the dust of sin, or the vanities of the world getting into the mind where it is seated. And wherever true faith is, if it be hurt by sin, it vents itself in a way of godly sorrow and repentence, Zech. xii. 10, "They shall look on him whom they have pierced, and mourn:" And as long as there is any thing of the dust of sin cleaves to the soul, faith will aye be venting itself in a way of repentence, and mourning, saying, "Wretched man that I am, who will deliver me from this body of death?" Thus I have given you some account of Abraham's faith, whereby he saw the day of Christ.

III. The *third* thing in the method was, to speak a little of his joy, which was the fruit of his faith. *He saw his day, and was glad.* For clearing of this I offer the few following propositions.

1. There are several sorts of joy men are incident unto.

1st, A natural joy common to all, with the rest of the affections, and is in itself neither good nor bad, and is commonly raised by the actual enjoyment of something loved or desired.

2dly, There is a sensual joy; when the heart is, as it were, soaked and drenched with the delights and pleasures of a present life. Such a joy was that of the rich man, Luke xii. 16—20, who cried, "Soul take thine ease, eat, drink, and be merry, for thou hast goods laid up for many years." See James v. 5.

3dly, There is yet a more criminal, or rather I may call it a devilish joy: When men are so far abandoned of God, as to take pleasure in sin, that abominable thing which God hates; like those who are said to "drink iniquity as the ox that drinketh up the water. To draw iniquity with cords." Rom. i. 32, there we are told of some who not only commit sins, but "have pleasure in them that do them."

4thly, There is a spiritual joy and gladness; so called, because the Spirit of God is the author of it, and spiritual things the object thereof. "Light is sown for the righteous, and gladness for all that are upright in heart." And it is of this last kind of joy that I now speak.

Prop. 2. This spiritual joy is a thing proper and peculiar only to believers in Christ: It will not, it cannot grow in any other soil but a believing heart. The rest of the world are strangers to it, and strangers do not intermeddle with their joy. Indeed a believer may want the exercise of this holy joy; his harp may (through prevailing troubles, temptation, unbelief, and despondency) "be turned into mourning, and his organ into the voice of them that weep." Hence David cries out, "Restore unto me the joys of thy salvation, that the bones which thou hast broken may rejoice." But though a believer may want the exercise of this holy joy, yet,

1st, He has always ground of rejoicing; while Christ lives, while the covenant stands, while the love of God lasts, he can never want ground and matter of rejoicing. Hence,

2dly, He hath always God's call and warrant to rejoice: "Rejoice evermore. Rejoice in the Lord always, and again, I say, rejoice. Rejoice in the Lord, ye righteous, and shout for joy, all ye that are upright in heart."

3dly, He hath always the promise of joy: "Your hearts shall rejoice, and your joy no man taketh from you." The redeemed of the Lord shall return and come to Zion with singing, and everlasting joy shall be upon their heads: They shall obtain gladness and joy, and sorrow and mourning shall flee away." He has promised the oil of joy for mourning.

4thly, They have always the seed of joy in the soul. The seed of God is the seed of joy; yea, their very tears of godly sorrow are the seed of joy: "They that sow in tears shall reap in joy. He that goeth forth and weepeth, bearing precious seed, shall doubtless come again rejoicing, bringing his sheaves with him," Psal. cxxvi. 5, 6.

Prop. 3. This spiritual joy and gladness it hath several ingredients of which it is made up: As,

1st, It includes in it some measure of spiritual health and soundness of mind and spirit. A sick man may have the habit of joy, but the want of health will restrain the exercise of it. Where this joy is, the sun of righteousness has arisen, with some measure of healing under his wings, upon the soul; the broken bones are restored, and set in their joints again.

2dly, It includes some measure of satisfaction, arising from a supply of soul wants. Where there is nothing but want and need, there can be but little of this holy joy. Prov. xiii. 12. "Hope deferred maketh the heart sick." If thy soul be rejoicing in the Lord, it is a sign thou hast got a taste of the marrow and fatness that is to be found in the house of God.

3dly, It has in it a dilatation and enlargement of the heart, that was under bonds and fetters. A man under the bonds and fetters of darkness, unbelief, and despondency, his joy is marred. But O, when his fetters are knocked off, and he brought out of prison, he leaps like an hart. "I will run the way of thy commandments, because thou hast enlarged my heart."

4thly, It has in it something of an internal peace, quiet, and serenity of mind: For where there is no peace, there can be no true joy. The storms of an awakened conscience must be hushed into a pleasant calm where this joy is, through the discovery of a reconciled God, or some beams of his favour; and then the soul cries, as in Psal. cxvi. 7. "Return unto thy rest, O my soul, for the Lord hath dealt bountifully with thee."

5thly, It has in it an elevation of the heart and soul after the Lord Jesus, and things that are above; whereby the soul gets above this weary land, and all the storms, clouds, and tempests thereof. The man mounts up as upon eagles' wings; and ay the higher he ascends, like the lark, he sings the sweeter notes of praise and thanksgiving.

Prop. 4. Of all other joy, this joy of faith is the most glorious and excellent: Which will appear from the following qualities of it.

1st, It is a cordial joy: It pervades the heart and all the corners of the soul; "Your heart shall rejoice, and your joy no man taketh from you. My heart is glad." The joy of the wicked is but skin-deep, it is superficial: "In the midst of laughter the heart is sorry:" But the joy of faith is like the "best new wine, that goeth down sweetly, causing the lips of those that are asleep to speak." Song. vii. 9.

2ndly, It is a hidden and a secret joy. Many a blithe heart has the believer in secret, which the world knows nothing of. His life is a hidden life, hid with Christ in God; and his joy is like his life. The springs of this joy are hidden, it flows out of a secret fountain, even from the throne of God and of the Lamb: The channel of it is hid, even the covenant of grace and promise: The actings of it are hid, and the subject in which it resides.

3dly, It is a strengthening joy. Neh. viii. 10. "The joy of the Lord is your strength;" and no wonder, for faith brings in strong consolation, Heb. vi. 18. This spiritual joy is health to the navel, and marrow to the bones. What appeared insupportable before, now appears to be easy; duties and difficulties in the way are easily vanquished; when the joy of faith comes, the feeble then becomes as David, Zech. xii. 8. and the poor soul becomes like a giant, refreshed with new wine, hearty and strong for battle.

4thly, It is a glorious and unspeakable joy. 1 Pet. i. 8. "Whom having not seen, ye love, in whom, though now ye see him not, yet believing ye rejoice, with joy unspeakable and full of glory," There is only a gradual difference between it and the joy of heaven; and it is so great, that the tongue cannot make language of it, as Paul said of the language of the third heaven, it is unutterable.

5thly, It is a permanent and abiding joy; a joy which the world cannot give, and which the world cannot take away; no, not the severest tortures and persecutions of the world. Hence it is, that the saints have gone to stake, fire and gibbet, with an air of heavenly grace about them. "Your joy no man taketh from you," says Christ. It is but the dawnings of that eternal joy and triumph which the saints shall have above, through an endless eternity.

6thly, It is a matchless, and transcendent, and incomprehensible joy. There are several joys that we read of in scripture, but the joy of faith transcends them all.

1. There is the nuptial joy. The day of marriage is called a day of gladness.

2. There is a joy of children: There is a joy when a man child is born into the world. It was, and is still a valuable mercy, because children are an heritage of the Lord.

3. There is a joy of conquest and victory: "They shall rejoice as men when they divide the spoil," Is. ix. 3.

4. There is a joy of harvest: "They joy before thee according to the joy in harvest." But now, I say, the joy of faith surpasseth them all, for it is unspeakable, and full of glory. "Thou hast put gladness in my heart, more than in the time that their corn and wine increased." This much for the third thing in the method.

IV. The *fourth* thing was, to enquire whence it is that a sight of Christ, and of his day, by faith, fills the soul with joy and gladness.

Ans. 1*st*, This flows from the excellency that faith sees in the day of Christ: "this is a day which the Lord hath made, we will be glad, and rejoice in it." It is a day of light, of life, of salvation, &c. as you heard in the doctrine part.

2*dly*, Because of the many great and excellent things it sees to be done in his day, which are all matter of joy and gladness. In his day the glory of heaven is brought down to earth; the New Testament temple is reared and opened, &c. (for which see the first head.)

3*dly*, Faith, it applies Christ, and all the great blessings of his day: It sits down under his shadow, and tastes the sweets of his fruits; and hence it is that it fills the soul with joy and gladness. Whatever great things we see or hear tell of, we will not be much moved therewith, except we have an interest and concern therein. Now faith it interests the soul in Christ, and all the blessings of his kingdom and administration, and hence it is that it brings such gladness; the language of faith is, "This is our God, we have waited for him," &c.

4*thly*, Faith is the parent of hope, and is the substance of things hoped for, and so it fills with joy. "We rejoice in the hope of the glory of God."

V. The *fifth* thing is the use of the doctrine.

Use *first*, It serves for *Information*, in these few following particulars.

1*st*, From what is said, we may see from whence it was that the Old Testament saints longed so much for the coming of Christ, and the days of the New Testament. O, says the spouse, "Until the day break, and the shadows fly away, turn, my beloved, and be thou like a roe, or a young hart upon the mountains of Bether." All that they had in the type, promise or prophecy, were but shadows and expressions of what was to come.

2*dly*, See hence what a privilege and happiness we are possessed of, whose lot is cast in the day of Christ, the gospel-day which Abraham and other saints rejoiced to see at such a great distance. Christ says to his disciples, while here upon earth, "Blessed are your eyes and ears, for they see and hear those things, which many prophets and righteous men desired to see and hear, and did not see nor hear them."—But yet we, who live in the day of the gospel, see and hear more than the disciples did themselves. They saw the Messiah only in a state of humiliation at that time, like a prince in disguise; but now we see him upon the throne, vested with all power in heaven and in earth. Upon this account, Christ says, that the least in the kingdom of heaven, viz., in the kingdom of the New Testament church, is greater than John the Baptist, who was greater than any that had been born of a woman since the fall of Adam, because he was put in case to say, "Behold the Lamb of God which taketh away the sin of the world."

3*dly*, See hence the misery of unbelieving sinners under the New Testament dispensation. Why, the day is broken, and yet they never saw daylight, "The light shineth in darkness, and the darkness comprehendeth it not." There is an awful word that points at you, 2 Cor. iv. 3. 4. "If our gospel be hid, it is hid to them that are lost; in whom the god of this world hath blinded the minds of them that believe not, lest the light of the glorious gospel of Christ, who is the image of God, should shine into them:" And that word of Christ, John ix. 39. "For judgment I am come into this world; that they who see not might see, and they who see might be made blind."

4thly, See hence whence it is that there is such opposition by hell and its agents at this day, to the settlement of an honest ministry in vacant congregations. Why, they see plainly that, if an honest ministry got into a congregation, the day of Christ would break there, and that would break Satan's kingdom, and his works of darkness in which the ungodly world do delight; and in them is literally fulfilled that word of Christ, John iii. 20., "Every one that doeth evil hateth the light, neither cometh to the light, lest his deeds should be reproved." They know very well that a faithful minister would lift up his voice like a trumpet, and reprove their deeds; and therefore it is that they cannot endure a man that has any thing of the savour of God or religion about him: a hue and cry will presently be raised against him, as a dangerous and turbulent person, one that will make a rent in the church, or turn the world upside down.

5thly, See hence whence it is that believers are called the "children of the light, and of the day:" Why, because they not only live in the day of Christ, but the day-spring has visited them in a saving way; the day has dawned, and the day star has arisen in their hearts, "even the light of the knowledge of the glory of God, in the face of Jesus Christ." And this is the reason why there is a divine light shines in the way and walk of the believer, which is not to be seen about other folk. Their light so shines before men, that they, seeing their good works, glorify their Father which is in heaven.

Use *second* may be of *Trial.*

Sirs, since it is your privilege to live under the day of Christ, I ask you, Has the light of the day ever dawned savingly? If so, then,

1st, The light of it has darkened the light of this world, and all the transient vanities of it, discovering them to be vanity and vexation of spirit; and you will look "not at the things which are seen, but at the things which are not seen."

2dly, The light of it has discovered the abominable nature of sin, so that you will abhor it, and abhor and loathe yourselves because of it, saying, "Behold I am vile." The light of the day of Christ is of a humbling quality, Is. vi. &c.

3dly, If the light of the day of Christ has arisen on you in a saving way your eyes will be turned towards the sun that makes day, I mean Christ, the glorious Sun of righteousness; and you will be so much taken up with him that you will account all things but loss, &c.

4thy, The light of the day of Christ has warmed thy soul with love to the Lord; love to his ordinances, a day in his courts will be better than a thousand; love to his people, they are my delight, the excellent ones of the earth.

Use *third* shall be of *Exhortation.*

Sirs, has your lot fallen in the day of Christ, which Abraham saw by faith, and was glad? Then,

1*st*, Receive the light of the day; entertain the light of the Sun of righteousness. O behold that glorious Sun, that is shining upon you in the dispensation of the gospel! You are as much warranted to make use of the light of the Sun of righteousness, to direct you to glory, as you are warranted to make use of the natural sun, to direct you in your way home to your several abodes. What freer than the light? The beggar has as good a right to use it as the prince upon the throne. So the daylight of the Sun of righteousness, and the blessings of his day, are as free to you as to any man; and, therefore, O do not shut out the light, but entertain and receive it. John viii. 12. "I am the light of the world (says Christ); he that followeth me shall not walk in darkness, but shall have the light of life."

2*dly*, Is this the day of Christ? O then, work while it is day, work out the work of your salvation while the day lasteth, for the night hasteth on, wherein no man can work. And if you ask, What is the work of God? I give you the same answer that Christ gave, and I cannot give you a better, "This is the work of God, that ye believe on him whom he hath sent." The everlasting gospel is preached to all nations, for the obedience of faith. O, for the Lord's sake, believe on the name of the Son of God, for this is his great commandment: this is the foundation of all obedience, and without it you cannot obey one commandment of the law, for 'whatever is not of faith is sin."

3*dly*, Is this the day of Christ? O then, let us be glad, and rejoice therein. This was the practice of Abraham, the father of the faithful, and this will be the practice of all the genuine true-born children of Abraham. Psal. cxviii. 24. "This is the day which the Lord hath made, we will rejoice and be glad in it. O let us rejoice in his person, for he is the glory of mankind, as well as the brightness of his Father's glory. Let us rejoice in him, saying, "To us a Son is given," &c. Let us rejoice in his fulness, suitableness, and excellency, "for such an High Priest became us, who is holy, harmless, undefiled. separate from sinners, &c., who is made of God unto us wisdom, righteousness, sanctification, and redemption." Let us rejoice in the great things that we see actually done in his day, that he has finished transgression, made an end of sin. Let us rejoice to see the glory of heaven brought down to earth, the "Word made flesh, and tabernacling among us." O rejoice and wonder, that the tabernacle of God is with man, that the temple of God is opened; and in the view of all this together, let us join issue with the Church. Is. xii. 3. "Behold, God is my salvation; I will trust, and not be afraid; for the Lord Jehovah is my strength and my song; he also is become my salvation; therefore with joy shall ye draw water out of the wells of salvation."

CHRIST, AS THE BREAKER, OPENING ALL PASSES TO GLORY THAT WERE IMPASSIBLE.

OPENED UP IN THREE SACRAMENTAL SERMONS, FROM.

MICAH ii. 13—The breaker is come up before them; they have broken up, and have passed through the gate, and are gone out by it; and their king shall pass before them, and the Lord (or Jehovah) on the head of them.

WHATEVER literal respect these words may have unto the return of the children of Israel from their Babylonish captivity, through the instrumentality of Cyrus, yet it is generally agreed upon not only by Christian, but even by some Jewish interpreters, that they have a principal and ultimate view unto the glorious Messiah, and the great work of salvation that he was to accomplish in the fulness of time.

The prophet tells us, in the preceding verse, that Christ, as the great Shepherd of Israel, was to gather together the lost sheep of the house of Israel, and would gather a New Testament church to himself; and, by reason of the multitude of converts that should flock unto the ever-blessed Shiloh, the noise and report of their gathering should be heard far and near through the earth. But sense and reason might look on this as a thing altogether impracticable, because of the strong bars that stood in the way, and the great opposition that would be made by hell and earth, to the rearing and gathering the New Testament church; therefore the prophet here prophecies, that Christ should rid the way, and clear the passage, and make mountains as a plain.

In which words we have these three things:

1*st*, The way of the Lord's ransomed opened up by the great Redeemer, *The breaker is come up before them.*

2*dly*, The escape of the ransomed by this way, or the improvement they make of it by faith. This is held forth in these three expressions, *They have broken up—They have passed through the gate—They have gone out by it.*

3*dly*, We have the glorious march of the ransomed under the Redeemer's conduct, as their renowned general, *Their King shall pass before them, and* JEHOVAH *on their head.*

1*st*, I say, we have the passage opened up by the great Redeemer, *The breaker is come up before them.* Where again we have.

1. The designation given to the glorious Messiah, he is called the Breaker. Cyrus was an instrument in the hand of God, for breaking the Babylonish yoke, and so paving a way for the return of Israel into their native land; and herein he was a type of Christ, by whom the yoke of our spiritual captivity under sin and Satan is broken, and a way paved for coming up to the land of rest and

glory that is above of which the earthly Canaan was a corruptible type. Some think that in this expression, there is an allusion unto the he-goat or the ram, which in a storm breaks the way to the rest of the flock. Christ is "given for a leader and commander to the people," and he it is that opens the passage to glory for us, through the storms and tempests of his Father's wrath, and the rage of men and devils. Whatever allusion there may be in this name, yet it is abundantly plain that it is Christ that is intended; for he that is called the Breaker in the beginning of the verse, is called their King, and Jehovah, in the close of it; *their King shall pass before them, and Jehovah on the head of them*: and who can bear this name, or wear the weight and worth of it, but he who has "a name above every name."

2. We have the courageous appearance of the glorious Redeemer in his breaking work. He comes up, he appears upon the field with an undaunted and heroic courage, to encounter enemies and opposition that stood in the way, he sets his face to it, and is not afraid to meet the enemy in the field of battle.

3. We have the party that he heads, or those in whose quarrel this Breaker appears; *He comes up before them.* This being a relative, leads you back to the preceding verse, where we find them set forth under the notion of a flock of sheep; silly, weak, and timorous creatures, that can do nothing in their own defence; the bark of a dog will make ten thousand of them to run. Such weak, helpless creatures are we, when Christ appears for our relief, *The Breaker is come up before them.* As for the other particulars in the verse, it is like we may have occasion to point at them in the sequel of the discourse; at present, I offer this doctrine from the words.

OBSERVE, "That as Christ is the Breaker up of our way to glory, so he comes up before us, for our encouragement as the renowned Captain of salvation."

In discoursing this doctrine, I shall endeavour, through divine assistance.

I. To inquire upon what account Christ is called the Breaker.
II. Speak of the coming up of this Breaker.
III. Inquire into the import of his coming up before his people.
IV. Shew why he acts the part of a Breaker.
V. Apply.

I. The *first* thing is; to inquire into the reason of this name, Why is Christ called the Breaker?

Answ. 1. In general he is so called, because of the great opposition he had to break through, in the glorious undertaking of our redemption, both in the purchase and application of it. The eternal Son of God had a spiritual kingdom to rear up in this lower world, among the lost family of Adam: but before he could effectuate his design, he must break in upon the powers of hell, and overthrow the usurped kingdom of the devil, who, because of his universal empire that he had obtained, is called the god of this world. Accordingly, the first work that the Son of God undertakes, is to bruise or break the head of the Serpent, Gen. iii. 15., *i.e.* to destroy his power or to wrest the government out of his hand: accordingly, when he had finished the work of our redemption upon the cross, he is said to have "spoiled principalities and powers, and made a shew of them openly, triumphing over them in it."

2. Having broken the head of the serpent, he breaks open his prison, and proclaims freedom and liberty unto his prisoners. Had that question been put to all the angels in heaven and men upon earth, which you have. Is. xlix. 24: "Shall the prey be taken from the mighty, or shall the lawful captive be delivered?" it would have silenced them, and put them to an eternal stand. Well, who answers the question? the blessed Breaker that is come up before us, he steps in (ver. 25): "Thus saith the Lord, even the captives of the mighty shall be taken away, and the prey of the terrible shall be delivered; for I will contend with him that contendeth with thee, and I will save thy children." O, Sirs, we had remained eternal captives to Satan, unless the Son of God had undertaken our deliverance, and broken the chains of our captivity. Zech. ix. 11: "As for thee also, by the blood of thy covenant, I have sent forth thy prisoners out of the pit wherein there is no water."

3. He is fitly called the Breaker, because he breaks up a new and living way, by which we have access to God and glory. The old way of the covenant of works was blocked up with so many bars, thorns, woes, and curses, that it was become impassible; none of the fallen race of Adam could enter by that road; but our blessed Goel, our kind Kinsman, comes, and by his obedience unto the death, opens up a new entry or passage, by which we have access to God, and Christ himself is that way. John xiv. 6: "I am the way and the truth, and the life; and there is no coming to the Father but by me." Of this new way cast up by the Breaker that is come up before us, the prophet Isaiah speaks, chap. xxxv. 8-10: "A high-way shall be there, and a way, and it shall be called the way of holiness; the unclean shall not pass over it, but it shall be for those; the wayfaring men, though fools shall not err therein; no lion shall be there, nor any ravenous beast shall go up thereon, it shall not be found there, but the redeemed shall walk there. And the ransomed of the Lord shall return and come to Zion with songs, and everlasting joy upon their heads; they shall obtain joy and gladness, and sorrow and sighing shall flee away."

4. He is called the Breaker, because he breaks through the storms of divine wrath, the rage of men and devils, in order to accomplish our redemption. The justice of God stood in his way with a flaming sword, ready to be sheathed in his bowels; the curse of the broken law rolled mountains in his way: the armies of hell were combined to oppose him in his work, "many bulls compassed him, the strong bulls of Bashan surrounded him; a sea of blood and sufferings presented him upon his undertaking; but such was the love of his

heart, that he breaks through, he forces his way, setting his face as a flint against all discouragements.

5. He may be called the Breaker, because in a day of power he breaks the enmity of our hearts against him; "pulls down the strongholds of iniquity," that Satan has reared up in our hearts, "bringing every thought into captivity unto his obedience." The hearts of the children of men are, by nature, hard as leviathans, Job. xli. 24.: but he breaks it by the hammer of his law. The heart is bolted against him with enmity, unbelief, pride, and prejudices, but these bars he breaks in pieces by the power of his victorious all-conquering grace.

6. He may be called the Breaker, because those who will not bow unto his royal authority, he breaks them in pieces; according to what you have, Psal. ii. 9. "Thou shalt break them as with a rod of iron, thou shalt dash them in pieces as a potter's vessel." And Psal. lxviii. 21. "He will wound the head of his enemies, and the hairy scalp of all them that go on still in their trespasses." Proud Pharoah refuses to bow to his word and commandment, and the Lord breaks him and his numerous host, and sinks them like lead in the mighty waters. He has many breaking judgments at hand, whereby he can destroy whole nations and kingdoms, when they rebel against him, as we see in the ten plagues of Egypt.

7. He may be called the Breaker because of the breaking trials that he many times brings upon his own people and children in this world. "Thou breakest me, says Job (chap. xiv. 14), with breach upon breach, and runnest after me like a giant." Psal. xliv. 19. "Thou hast fore broken us in the place of dragons," &c. And indeed, escape who will, they shall not, if they offend him: "You only have I known of all the families of the earth, therefore I will punish you. If his children forsake my law, and walk not in my judgments, if they break my statutes and keep not my commandments, I will visit their transgression with the rod, and their iniquity with stripes." And O! how breaking is the rod of a father unto his own dear children, when they have provoked him by sin! David was so broken with a sense of God's anger against him, Psal. li. 8. that he is made to complain that his bones were broken: "Make me to hear joy and gladness, that the bones which thou hast broken may rejoice."

8. He may be called the Breaker, because of his breaking judgments and calamities that he brings on a sinful or offending church and nation; such as sword, famine, pestilence, desolation by fire or water, the withdrawing of his Spirit, the withdrawing of the means of grace. You see how the Lord breaks his barren vineyard, Is. v. &c.

II. The *second* thing was, to speak of the upcoming of Christ as the Breaker. I understand it of his coming up to avenge the quarrel of his children and people. Like a mighty champion he takes the field and enters the lists with the powers of hell and earth, in order to avenge the quarrel of his Israel.

You have a description of this renowned Champion, and of his coming up in his church's cause and quarrel, Is. lix. 16—18. "And he saw that there was no man and wondered that there was no intercessor. Therefore his arm brought salvation unto him, and his righteousness, it sustained him. For he put on righteousness as a breastplate and an helmet of salvation upon his head; and he put on the garments of vengeance for clothing, and was clad with zeal as a cloak. According to their deeds, accordingly he will repay, fury to his adversaries, recompense to his enemies, to the islands he will repay recompense." Here I will tell you of some seasonable upcomings of the blessed Breaker, for the help and relief of lost sinners; and then tell you of the manner of his coming up.

1*st*, The blessed Breaker came seasonably up, and appeared in our quarrel, in the council of peace. When the question was put, Who will take the field against the old serpent and his seed, for the help and relief of lost sinners of Adam's family? presently the blessed Breaker appeared in our quarrel, saying, Lo, I come, send me and I will "bruise the head of the serpent," and set the captives at liberty, to the glory of divine justice, and to the eternal honour of his law.

2*dly*, He came up seasonably upon the field, immediately after the fall of man. The prey had no sooner fallen into the hands of the mighty, but the mighty Redeemer steps in upon the enemy, giving him a deadly thrust: With the word of his mouth he slays the wicked one, saying, "It shall bruise thy head, and thou shalt bruise his heel," Gen. iii. 15.; which at once gave a deadly wound to the enemy, and saved the poor prisoner "out of the pit, wherein there is no water." All the appearances of Christ for his church during the Old Testament dispensation, were founded upon the grace of this first promise.

3*dly*, He came up really and personally in his incarnation. What was his whole life in this world, but a continued battering and breaking down of the kingdom of darkness? This was the design of his doctrine, miracles, life, and death; by the preaching of his gospel through the cities of Israel, he saw "Satan fall like lightning from heaven;" by a word spoken; he, in a miraculous manner, threw him out of the souls and bodies of men at once; and by his death he destroyed "him that had the power of death, that is the devil." And with a view unto this, he tells his disciples, "Now is the judgment of this world come; now shall the prince of this world be cast out." And by his resurrection from the dead, and his ascension into heaven, he came up as a victorious and renowned Conqueror from the field of battle, carrying the spoils of sin and Satan, hell and death, along with him: "God is gone up with a shout, the Lord with the sound of a trumpet; twenty thousand chariots of angels attending him, as at Sinai. He ascended up on high, and led captivity captive."

4*thly*, He may be said to come up, or to take the field against the enemy, when he appears in the power of his spirit in the dispensation of the gospel, when he girds his sword on his thigh, and rides prosperously and successfully upon his chariot of truth, dividing a portion with the great, and sharing the spoil with the strong. Oh how terrible is this Breaker unto the powers of hell, when he sends the rod of his strength out of Zion, making a willing people in the day of his armies! When the "armies which are in heaven follow him, whose name is, The WORD of GOD!" When he "smites the nations with the sharp sword that goeth out of his mouth!" While every one that runs may read his name "on his vesture and on his thigh, King of kings, and Lord of Lords."

5*thly*, He may be said to come up in the outward dispensation of his providence, for the relief and deliverance of his church and people, when they are harassed or oppressed in their temporal or spiritual privileges, by men of malignant spirits, who bear rule over them. Thus the Breaker came up seasonably for the relief of Israel in Egypt, when they were groaning under their Egyptian taskmasters, breaking their oppressors and enemies with plague upon plague. Thus he many times came up for their relief, during the government of the judges and kings of Israel. Thus he came up after the seventy years captivity, and broke the Babylonian empire in pieces, to make way for the return of his people to their native land.

6*thly*, He comes up as a mighty Breaker, when he finds religion at under, and has a mind to revive his own work in a backsliding land and church. He comes first and breaks down, before he begins to build up. There is commonly a shaking of nations, before the desire of all nations come, for the building up of Zion. See in what awful majesty the Breaker appears, Hab. iii. in order to the reviving of his work in the midst of the years. The prophet, ver. 2. puts up a prayer, "O Lord, revive thy work in the midst of the years; in the midst of the years make known; in wrath remember mercy." Well, his prayer is heard, God comes for the revival of his work, but his glorious march was so awful, as made the prophet himself to fall a-trembling, ver. 16. "When I heard, my belly trembled, my lips quivered at the voice; rottenness entered into my bones. When he cometh up unto the people, he will invade them with his troops." And yet how sweet and glorious is the issue of that awful dispensation? as you see in the verse following.

7*thly*, He may be said to come up in every display of his grace and love to a particular believer, when he seasonably interposes for the relief of a poor soul, sinking under the burden of sin, temptation, affliction, and desertion. The Breaker comes up seasonably, when he dispels clouds, and lifts up the light of his countenance; when he rebukes the roaring lion, and blunts and breaks his fiery darts; when he says to the poor soul, "Fear not, I am with thee;" when he heartens or animates the poor soul for its work or warfare, saying, "Fear not, thou worm Jacob—I will make thee a new sharp thrashing instrument, having teeth. My grace shall be sufficient for thee."

8*thly*, And O how seasonably does he come up at death, when the poor soul is trembling at the thoughts of going through Jordan, and launching out into a wide eternity? What a sweet upcoming is it, when he says to the soul, as Rev. i. 17. "Fear not, for I am he that liveth and was dead, and behold I am alive for evermore." Thus I have given you some of the seasonable upcomings of the blessed Breaker.

Quest. In what manner doth he come up in our quarrel, to the help of the weak against the mighty?

Answ. 1. He comes up seasonably. All his appearances for the help and relief of his people, have ever been well timed. O how seasonably did he interpose immediately after the fall, when the roaring lion was about to tear the prey, saying as Pharoah, in another case, "I will pursue, I will overtake, I will divide the spoil?" Then indeed he came up and bruised the head of the serpent. How seasonably did he deliver Israel out of Egypt? How seasonably did he turn back their captivity? How seasonably did he interpose for our relief in the land at the late glorious revolution, when we were upon the point of being swallowed up with Antichristian tyranny and darkness? O how seasonably does he come up to the help and relief of the poor soul, when it is upon the point of being swallowed up with temptation, desertion, and affliction? Deut. xxxii. 36. "The Lord shall judge his people, and repent himself for his servants, when he seeth that their power is gone, and there is none shut up or left."

2. He comes up for the help of his church and people solitarily; or he alone comes up. It is his own arm that brings salvation. He stood alone in the glorious work of redemption; "He trode the winepress alone, and of the people there was none with him;" and therefore he alone must bear the glory of it; "Not unto us, O Lord, not unto us, but unto thy name give glory." And when he comes up for the deliverance of his church and people from tyranny and oppression, whatever instruments he may make use of, yet he alone must have the glory, because they are but instruments, and can do no more than the tool without the hand of the workman. Hence is that of the church, Psal. xliv. 3. "They got not the land in possession with their sword, neither did their own arm save them; but thy right hand, thine arm, and the light of thy countenance."

3. He comes up in our quarrel with the greatest alacrity and cheerfulness. He "rejoiced in the habitable parts of the earth, and his delights were with the sons of men." The Sun of righteousness rejoiced to run his race; and like a giant or strong man refreshed with new wine, he gave a shout when he came up into the field of battle: "I have a baptism (says he) to be baptised with, and how am I straitened till it be accomplished."

4. He comes up speedily: he did not linger nor tarry when he came upon his redeeming and saving expedition; no, he flew as it were upon wings, Cant. ii. 8. "Behold he cometh, leaping upon the mountains, and skipping upon the hills."

5. He comes up courageously to his breaking work, challenging all the powers of hell, as it were, to the combat. With what undaunted magnanimity did he set his face to the cause, when he is entering the field! See Is. l. 8. 9. "He is near that justifieth me,

who will contend with me? let us stand together: who is mine adversary? let him come near to me. Behold the Lord God will help me, who is he that shall condemn me? lo, they all shall wax old as a garment; the moth shall eat them up."

6. He comes up victoriously, distributing death and ruin amongst all his and his church's enemies. Victory follows him whithersoever he goes: his enemies being unto him but as briars and thorns entering the lists with a consuming fire. When he whets his glittering sword, and his hand takes hold on judgment, he "renders vengeance unto his enemies, and a reward unto all them that hate him."

7. His coming up to his breaking work is irresistible. Who can stay his hand, or stop him in his march? When Red Seas and Jordans of wrath and vengeance were in his way, this Breaker did break through them; when the armies of earth and hell were in his way, he "trode them in his anger, and trampled them in his fury, and stained all his raiment with their blood." And hence it follows,

8. That the upcoming of the Breaker is with much awful majesty, and astonishing greatness. When he came up upon the field of this world, he struck terror amongst the powers of hell. When they saw the divine majesty and greatness that was about him they cried, "What have we to do with thee, Jesus, thou Son of the most high God, art thou come to torment us before our time?" When he comes up to plead the controversies of Zion, the proud and wicked of the earth, that carried it with a high hand against his church and people, they would then be content to creep into the clefts of the rocks, and caves of the earth, "for fear of the Lord, and for the glory of his majesty," Is. ii. 19. And when is it that they are thus struck with terror? It is when the Lord comes up to his breaking work, as you see in the close of that verse, when he ariseth terribly to shake the earth. So much for the *second* thing, namely, the upcoming of the Breaker.

III. The *third* thing in the method was, to inquire what may be implied in his *coming up before them*?

But before I go on to this, you may readily ask, to whom is it that he comes up?

I answer, 1. As the Shepherd of Israel, he comes up to the sheep of his pasture, to preserve or deliver them from wolves or foxes, that would tear them.

2. He comes up as a captain to his soldiers, to head and lead them on against the armies of the aliens; for he is given for a "Leader and Commander to the people."

3. He comes up as a King to his subjects, or on the head of his armies, to rule and defend, to restrain and conquer all his and their enemies; as in the close of the verse, *their King shall pass before them, and* JEHOVAH *on the head of them.* Thus you see the Breaker comes up to his sheep, his soldiers, and subjects; and whoever they be that are not of that number, the Breaker comes up against them, for they are not on the Lord's side.

Now to come to the question, what is imported in his coming up to them?

1st, It imports, that he has them and their case deeply at heart, that he is heartily engaged in their quarrel; otherwise how would he come up to them as a Breaker? Many that bear the name of shepherds of the flock now-a-days, they have the case of Christ's sheep, his little ones, so little at heart, that they are very easy what come of them, if they get patrons and the great ones of the world pleased. But however little account they make of them, and their rights and privileges, yet the great shepherd has them so near at heart, that he has declared that it were better for such that "a millstone were hanged about their necks, and they cast into the midst of the sea, than that they should offend or hurt one of these little ones." At the coming up of the Breaker, the weight of this woe will be felt, however little account some may make of it now, while they are tearing the flock of Christ in pieces, and forcing them to send up many a heavy complaint to heaven.

2dly, His coming up to them implies, that their passage is hard and difficult, that their way is lined with many hardships, enemies, and difficulties; otherwise why would he come up as Breaker to them? Some think that there is an allusion here to the custom of sending pioneers before the army, to level the way, and to make rough places plain, that the march of the army may not be retarded. Sirs, the way to heaven is an up-the-hill way; it is a thorny and rough way, where we may lay our account with many difficulties and trials: "In the world (says Christ) ye shall have tribulation." It is not a peradventure, but a shall be. Rev. vii. 14. "These are they who came out of great tribulation." But here is your comfort, the Breaker has gone up before us; he has rolled the insuperable mountains of law and justice, sin and wrath, out of the way; and he has left nothing behind to impede our march to glory, but "a few light afflictions which are but for a moment," and shall (through his over-ruling providence) "work for us a far more exceeding and eternal weight of glory."

3dly, His coming up to them implies his authority and right to rule and govern them, as a captain-general has power and authority in the army. I remember what the Lord said unto Joshua, chap. v. 14., when appearing in the form of a man. Joshua asks him, "Art thou for us, or for our adversaries?" "Nay," says he, "But as Captain of the host of the Lord am I now come." So here, the Breaker is come up to them; it implies that he is a head of government unto them, and so it is implied in the close of the verse, *their King shall pass before them, and the Lord on the head of them*. God has set his Christ as his "King upon his holy hill of Zion;" he hath given him to be "Head over all things to the church;" and his name is, THE KING OF KINGS, AND LORD OF LORDS: and accordingly they acknowledge his authority, saying, "The Lord is our King, the Lord is our Judge," &c.

4thly, It implies not only authority, but strength and ability to support it. The Breaker that goes up before them is the mighty, yea, the almighty God: his name is JEHOVAH that is on the head of them: he rides in the heavens by his great name JAH, for the help of his Israel, and in his excellency on the sky. This is he that "weighs the mountains in scales, and the hills in a balance: who metes out the heavens with a span, and comprehendeth the dust of the earth in a measure." Oh! who is able to stand before this mighty Breaker that is come up before them?

5thly, It implies their ignorance and inability to break up their own way. There are two things wherein believers are exceedingly defective, while on their journey to Immanuel's land.

1. They are ignorant of the way, as Thomas said, John xiv. 5. "How can we know the way?" It is a way which lay hid in God, and which none was able to discover, unless Christ had done it. The Breaker is that Lion of the tribe of Judah, that breaks open the seven seals of the book of God's councils anent our redemption. He breaks the seals of the book doctrinally, by revealing the will of God, and bringing life and immortality to light; and practically, by the powerful working of his Spirit, giving us an understanding to know him, that he is the way, the truth, and the life; and in this way, the wayfaring men, though fools, should walk and not err, when the Breaker goes up before them.

2. Inability is another thing incident to the saints while on their way. They want strength to walk in the way when it is revealed. Well, but the Breaker goes up before them, and he "gives power to the faint, and increases strength to them that have no might."

6thly, The Breaker is gone up before them; it implies that he has paved the road, and travelled the way before them as their Leader and Commander. And there are three things especially, wherein Christ goes before his people.

1. In obedience. 2. In suffering. 3. In going through death into glory.

1. He goes before us in obedience, for he himself was made under the law. Although, as to his own person, he was above the law, being the great Lawgiver, yet he submitted to obey it: as a Surety, he submitted to obey it as a covenant; and as a pattern of holiness and obedience, he submitted to it as a rule. Hence he calls us to learn of him, and to take his yoke upon us, particularly the yoke of obedience unto the law, for, says he, "my yoke is easy, and my burden is light." A green yoke is galling and uneasy to the cattle, till it be well worn and used. Well, says Christ, "The yoke of my law, I have made it easy, by using or wearing it before you, I have fulfilled it as a covenant, and obeyed it as a rule, that it may not be uneasy."

2. He goes before us in suffering. "Christ (says the apostle Peter) has suffered for us, leaving us an example, that we should follow his steps," 1. Pet. ii. 21. and chap. iv. 1. "Forasmuch as Christ hath suffered for us in the flesh, arm yourselves likewise with the same mind," viz., that ye may follow him in the same road of suffering. Hence also is that of the apostle, Heb. xii. 2. 3. "Looking unto Jesus, the Author and Finisher of our faith: who, for the

joy that was set before him, endured the cross, despising the shame. Consider him that endured such contradiction of sinners against himself, lest ye be wearied and faint in your minds."

3. The Breaker comes up before us through death, and by entering into glory as our Forerunner. Death, the king of terrors, sometimes looks with such an awful aspect, that the very thoughts of its approaching, is enough to overwhelm us with fear and terror; and the apostle tells us of some, "who, through fear of death are all their lifetime subject to bondage." Well, but how may a poor soul be delivered from the fear of death? Why, here is the antidote; the Breaker has come up before us, through the valley of the shadow of death: he has broken the strength, and pulled out the sting of that formidable all-conquering monarch, by his death and resurrection from the dead. He has shewed us that death is not the end of our course, but a passage into a happy immortality. Hence, he promises that whosoever believes in him, "though he were dead, yet shall he live." And again, he shall not so be devoured of death and the grave, but "he will raise him up at the last day." Thus the apostle argues at large, 1 Cor. xv. 12.—21. Christ has gone before us through death, ver. 20., and become the "first fruits of them that sleep." Had Christ passed into heaven before he died, as Enoch and Elias, we had wanted the great pledge and evidence of a future immortality. But Christ, as the great Captain of our salvation, he suffered, he died, and then entered into his glory; to assure us, that in this road we are to follow him, that we may be with him.

7thly, The Breaker is come up before them; it implies his routing and discomfiting all these enemies that stood in the way of our salvation.

The principal enemies the believer has to grapple with are these, 1. Satan; 2 Sin: 3 The world; and 4. Death. Now, the Breaker, by going up before us, routed and broke the strength of all these enemies.

1. As for Satan, he has bruised his head, and through death destroyed him.

2. As for the world, he has vanquished both its smiling and frowning things: "Be of good comfort (says he), I have overcome the world."

3. As for sin, he has "finished transgression, and made an end of sin; and condemned sin in the flesh." By his sacrifice on the cross, he condemned it as an arch-traitor against heaven.

4. As for death, he entered the territories of the grave, and spoiled it of its power and strength: "O death, I will be thy plague; O grave, I will be thy destruction." These enemies made an attempt upon the Son of God, but they were all foiled in the enterprise. The Breaker that went up before us has broken and shattered them, so that we have no cause to fear them. We see by what Christ hath done, that these enemies are not invincible: that their power is not incontrollable; they were conquered by him as our head and representative in our cause and quarrel; and therefore, we may, by faith, take up and divide the spoils, saying, "Thanks be unto God, which

always causes us to triumph in Christ;" for what was done by the Head, in his own person, shall shortly be done in all the members.

But further, I say, that Christ, by his engaging with these enemies, has quite maimed and disarmed them, and taken away their right to hurt any of his friends and followers. By the breach of the covenant of works, these enemies have a law-right over all the children of men: the curse of the broken law gave Satan a law-right to rule, the world to vex, sin to enslave, death to destroy us, and give us up to hell. All this was contained in that "handwriting which was against us, and contrary to us." But now, I say, Christ upon the cross, tore and cancelled that handwriting, by satisfying justice, and becoming a curse for us; and ever since the devil has no law-right to tempt or molest; the world has no law-right to trouble or molest; sin has no legal dominion, nor death any right to sting or frighten any member of Christ. The inroads that these enemies make upon the believer, they are nothing else, if duly considered, but illegal invasions and usurpations; and a believer in Christ, viewing the death and satisfaction of Christ, whereby he cancelled that handwriting, whenever any of these enemies attack him, he may warrantably look them in the face and say, Where is your warrant in law to trouble or molest me? Your law-right fell to the ground, when my Head and Surety tore the handwriting that was against me. And, you know, whatever power or strength an enemy may have, yet it weakens and dispirits him exceedingly when his law-right is challenged, and he cannot shew it; because, in this case, his actions are but vicious intromissions, and he may be treated as a thief and robber. So then, learn to deal with your enemies upon a law-ground, upon the footing of the death and satisfaction of Jesus Christ, this would both inspire you with courage in your resistance, and dispirit them in their attacks.

8thly, The *Breaker is gone up before them*; it implies, the way to heaven is patent, and that there is no legal bar or impediment to stop or hinder their passage to the land of glory, whither the Breaker is gone up. Christ has come up to us as a surety and representative, and by his obedience to the death, has given complete satisfaction to the law and justice of God, and so has cleared the way of all legal impediments, arising from the breach of the first covenant. Hence it is that believers, through the death and resurrection of Christ, are put in a capacity to challenge all adversaries and accusations, saying, as Rom. viii. 33. 34. "Who shall lay anything to the charge of Gods elect? It is God that justifieth, who is he that condemneth? It is Christ that died, yea, rather that is risen again, who is even at the right hand of God, who also maketh intercession for us." As if the apostle had said, *The Breaker is come up before us*; and therefore, what have we to fear from hell or earth, if the great judge be satisfied?

9thly, The *Breaker is come up before them*; it implies, that whatever dangers, or difficulties, or opposition, be in their way, yet they are in absolute safety under his conduct. When *their King passeth before them, and* JEHOVAH *on the head of them*, what have they to fear? For when he ariseth, all their enemies are scattered. Hence it is that the Lord so frequently checks the unbelieving fears of his people, upon the account of these dangers and enemies they are threatened with in their way, Is. xli. 10. "Fear thou not, for I am with thee, be not dismayed, for I am thy God: I will help thee, yea, I will strengthen thee, yea, I will uphold thee with the right hand of my righteousness." Accordingly, when faith views the presence of a reconciled God in Christ, it contemns and despises the most threatening dangers, Psal. xxiii. 4. Yea, though I pass through the valley of the shadow of death, I will fear no evil, for thou art with me."

IV. The *fourth* thing was, to inquire into the grounds and reasons of this dispensation, why doth Christ break up the way to his people? Why doth he come up upon the field in their quarrel?

Answ. 1*st*, Because they were gifted to him of the Father, as a heritage and possession, Psal. ii. John xvii. "Thine they were, and thou gavest them me." Now Christ makes very much of his Father's gift, they are beloved of him for his Father's sake; and for the sake of his Father who gave him them, he will *break up the way before them.*

2*dly*, Because they are the purchase of his blood, he has bought them from the hand of justice at a dear rate. The blessed Breaker was broken in their quarrel, "He was wounded for their transgressions, and bruised for their iniquity;" and therefore it is no wonder that he comes up in their cause and opens the way to them through the armies of hell.

3*dly*, Because his faithfulness is engaged to lead them in their way through all the difficulties of their pilgrimage, "I will bring the blind by a way they know not," &c. "I will never leave thee, I will never forsake thee; I will contend with him that contendeth with thee, and I will save thy children."

4*thly*, Because he is to give an account of them unto his Father, who gave them to him. "The day comes when Christ will deliver up the kingdom to the Father, that God may be all in all." When the present administration of Christ, as Mediator, comes to an end, Christ will "gather all his elect together," and say "Here am I, and the children whom thou hast given me." Now that he may make a faithful account of them, he will break up their way before them.

5*thly*, Christ breaks up their way, because they cannot break up their own way; "While we were yet without strength, in due time Christ died." Believers are a feeble folk, insufficient of themselves to think or do anything of themselves. Now, the Lord loves "to perfect strength in their weakness, and out of weakness to make strong, for he is a strength to the poor, and a strength to the needy, in their distress."

6*thly*, He breaks their way, and comes up before them, because they trust in him as their Leader and Commander; and he will not betray their trust; no, he will answer the expectation of the poor;

"This poor man cried, and the Lord heard. They looked unto him and were lightened."

7*thly,* He comes up before them as a mighty Breaker, that he "may still the enemy and the avenger:" that he may get amends of Satan for disturbing the creation of God, disordering his works, striking at his Father's image, and making an attempt upon man, whom he had planted as his viceroy in this lower world. Therefore, immediately after the fall, the Lord tells that enemy, that he would bruise his head, break him and all his works in pieces, and so avenge our quarrel upon that usurping enemy; "the day of vengeance (says he) is in mine heart, and the year of my redeemed is come."

8thly, He comes up as a Breaker in their quarrel, because of the near and dear relation that he has come under unto them. He is their Redeemer, and will he not come up in the quarrel of his ransomed ones? He is their everlasting Father, and will he not come up before his children, his seed that the Lord hath given him? Yea, for, "like as a father pitieth his children, so the Lord pitieth them that fear him." He is their Shepherd, and will he not break the way to his flock to follow him? Yea, surely, for he leadeth "Joseph as a flock:—He shall gather the lambs with his arm, he will carry them in his bosom; and shall gently lead those that are with young." He is their Husband and Bridegroom, and will he not take the way through all opposition of hell for his beloved bride, whom he hath betrothed to himself for ever? He is their King, Captain, and General, and will he not appear in the quarrel of his soldiers, and head them in their march to glory? Yea, *their King shall pass before them.* Thus much for opening the words in a doctrinal way.

MICAH ii. 13.—The Breaker is come up before them; they have broken up, and have passed through the gate, and are gone out by it, and their King shall pass before them, and the Lord (or Jehovah) on the head of them.

THE SECOND SERMON ON THIS TEXT.

V. HAVING discussed the doctrinal part in a former discourse, I now proceed to the *Application.*

And the *first* use shall be of *Information.*

From what has been said we may see,

1. Whence is it that the true church of Christ is "terrible as an army with banners." Why, the Breaker is in the midst of her, and comes up before her. When Jehovah is on her head, she cannot miss to be a terror to the gates of hell, and all its auxiliaries. You have a passage to this purpose, in Psal. lxxvi. 1. 2. compared with verses 3. 5. 6. 7 "In Judah is God known; his name is great in Israel. In Salem also is his tabernacle, and his dwelling-place in Zion. There break he the arrows of the bow, the shield and the sword and the battle. Selah. The stout-hearted are spoiled, they

have slept their sleep; and none of the men of might have found their hands. At thy rebuke, O God of Jacob, both the chariot and horse are cast into a dead sleep. Thou, even thou, art to be feared; and who may stand in thy sight when once thou art angry?"

2dly, See hence whence it is, that God's Jerusalem proves a burdensome stone, and they that hurt her do it to their own cost in the issue. Why, the Breaker comes up and appears in the quarrel, in his own time. Some bold strokes are given at this day at the carved work of God's temple, invasions made upon the fundamental rights and privileges of the church, and of God's people, particularly in choosing their own pastors: patrons and corrupt clergymen, and their followers, are peeling and spoiling the spouse of Christ, and "taking away her veil from her." But wait a little, till the Breaker come up, till Jehovah enter the field, and then we will see breach for breach. I read you a word for this, Is. xli. 11. 12. 13, 16. "Behold, all they that were incensed against thee shall be ashamed and confounded; they shall be as nothing, and they that strive with thee shall perish. Thou shalt seek them and shalt not find them, even them that contended with thee; they that war against thee shall be as nothing, and as a thing of nought. For I the Lord thy God will hold thy right hand, saying unto thee, Fear not, I will help thee."

3dly, See hence whence it is that the true church of God at any time falls into the hand of the enemy, though Jehovah be her Head, her Patron, and Protector. Why, the mystery of it lies here, she sins away her Breaker by not following him in the road that he has broken up to her. Christ hath travelled the road, he hath shewed us the way both as to doctrine, discipline, worship, and government. Now, when a visible church doth not follow him, but will needs, like Israel, follow other leaders, and walk after the commandments of men, and manage the affairs of Christ's kingdom, according to the plan of worldly politics, whereby the kingdoms of this world are ruled and governed; in that case she does not follow her King, she practically disowns Jehovah for her Head, and thereupon she is dismantled of her walls of salvation, her chariots and horsemen are gone, and in that case, the "boar out of the wood doth waste her, and the wild beast of the field devours her." The church of Christ can never thrive but by treading the footsteps of Christ, the Breaker, that has gone up before us, he having "left an example, that we should follow his steps.*"

4thly, See hence the most effectual way to stop the course of defection that we have been going into for a considerable tract of time, when religion is very low and languishing; when a corrupt party, or a church are prevailing; when error like a gangrene is prevailing, and the foundations going out of course;" what is the best method in that case to stop the enemy that comes in like a flood? Why, in that case we should call the mighty Breaker that he may again come back to us, for whenever he appears, then the

---

* See more on this subject in my father's Synodical sermon, from Psal. cxviii. "The Stone which the Builders refused, the same is become the Head of the Corner."

enemy that comes in like a flood is driven back, Psal. cxiv. 3. 4. "The sea flies, Jordan is driven back, the mountains skip like rams, and the little hills like lambs." Yea, ver. 7., the very "earth falls a-trembling at the presence of the God of Jacob." Ver. 11, "He turns the rock into standing water, and the flint into a fountain of waters."

5*thly*, See hence whence it is that "the righteous hold on his way, and waxes stronger and stronger," notwithstanding of his having the powers of hell, the world, and indwelling corruption, to wrestle with. Why, here is the reason of it, *the Breaker is gone up before him*, he hath opened his way, he hath Jehovah on his head, as the Captain of his salvation: and hence it is, that "though the archers shoot at him, and grieve him, yet his bow abideth in its strength, and the arms of his hands are made strong, by the hands of the mighty God of Jacob."

Use *second* of this doctrine is of *Trial*.

Is it so that the glorious Redeemer is the Breaker up of the way to glory, and that he comes up as a mighty Champion to fight their battles against the powers of hell and earth? Then, Sirs, may we not cry on this occasion? "Who is on the Lord's side?" Are you for this Breaker, or are you against him? The whole race of Adam are divided between Christ and the devil, they must either be of the seed of the woman, or the seed of the serpent; it will not prove you to be on the Lord's side that you are called Christians, for many that bear that name were never anointed with his Spirit, and "if any man have not the Spirit of Christ, he is none of his." It will not prove you to be on his side, that you have been admitted to a communion table; for many will plead on the day of accounts, "Lord, Lord, we have eaten and drunken in thy presence;" yea, some will be capable to say more, namely, that they "have prophesied in his name, and done many wonderful works in his name;" and yet he will utterly disown them, saying, "Depart from me, ye that work iniquity, I never knew you." And therefore you need some other things to distinguish you from others, or to prove that you are on the side of this mighty Breaker, who came up before the armies of Israel.

Quest. How shall I know whether I be on his side, or against him? In answer unto this question, I shall go no further for marks than the text itself.

1*st*, Then I ask you for trial, have you broken up from your natural bondage and captivity? Every sinner is by nature a captive, a prisoner in chains, held fast in the "gall of bitterness, and under the bond of iniquity." Now, Christ having purchased liberty with his blood, he comes in a gospel dispensation, and "proclaims liberty to the captives, and the opening of the prison to them that are bound." Now, the question that I ask is, Whether has the Lord ever, by the power of his Spirit, determined you to break up and shake off your spiritual fetters? Has the chain of spiritual darkness been broken by the light of the Lord shining into your hearts? Has the chain of enmity been broken by the love of God shed abroad in your hearts by the Holy Ghost. Has the chain of unbelief been broken off, so that now you would give a thousand worlds to be rid of an evil heart of unbelief, that causes you to depart from the living God? Have you broken up from all the unfruitful works of darkness, and be made to say with Ephraim, "What have I to do any more with idols?"

2dly, I ask for trial, Have you *passed through the gate?* For they that follow the Breaker, as they break up, so they *pass through the gate*. And I will tell you of a twofold gate you have readily passed through, if you be followers of Christ.

1. The law-gate. And, 2. The gospel-gate.

(1.) Many pass through the law-gate of conviction, who yet never pass through the gospel-gate of believing in the Son of God. But I do not think there are any adult persons that shall ever pass the gate of the gospel without passing the gate of the law, "for the law is our schoolmaster to bring us unto Christ." So then, I ask you, have you passed the law-gate of conviction, terror, and humiliation? Has Christ, the mighty Breaker, taken the hammer of his law, and broken the rock in pieces? Has he made thee even to fall a-trembling with the jailor? and made you to cry, "What must I do to be saved?" I do not limit the holy One of Israel to any stinted measure of law-work. He acts as a Sovereign, both in dispensing the terrors of his law and the consolations of the gospel. But this I think I may say with safety, that no sinner will ever fly to a Saviour, till he see, that if God mark his iniquity according to the tenor of his law, he cannot stand before him. But, as I said, many go through this gate of law-terrors and conviction, who never go further. Cain, Judas, Felix, and many others, are standing witnesses of the truth of this. And therefore,

(2.) The main inquiry is, whether you have really passed "the strait and narrow way of believing in the Son of God?" Christ is the only gate and door of salvation for a lost sinner, John x. 9. Heb. x. 19. 20. and a believing in him is an entering in at God's door, an entering into God's rest, a state of peace, favour, and fellowship with God. Now, I say, have you entered in at this door by believing in the Lord Jesus Christ? I remember Christ says, "Strait is the gate, and narrow is the way which leadeth unto life, and few there be that find it."

And if you be among these few, I will tell you of two or three things you have left behind you; "For it is easier for a camel to go through the eye of a needle," than for a man to carry them along with him in his passage through this "gate of believing in the Lord Jesus Christ."

1st, You have left self behind you. For, says Christ, "If any man will come after me, let him deny himself," particularly, self-righteousness, or the works of the law, in point of justification and acceptance. This can never go in through the gate; no, no, "Publicans and harlots (says Christ to the self-righteous Pharisees) go in to the kingdom of God before you." So soon as ever Paul passed through this gate, though before he was, "touching the righteousness which is in the law, blameless," yet then he reckoned it but dung.

2dly, You have left your sins and lusts behind you. The narrow gate of salvation will not admit of these neither: so soon as ever a man enters this gate, he cries with Ephraim, " What have I to do any more with idols ? if I have done iniquity I will do so no more." Yea, though they were as dear and near to him as his right hand, and his right eye, he will not spare them: no, he casts them all to the moles and bats, and wages war for ever against every known sin.

3dly, You have left the love of the world; for " if any man love the world, the love of the Father is not in him. The friendship of this world is enmity with God." The love of God and the love of the world cannot reign in the same heart, " No man can serve two masters, we cannot serve God and Mammon." So soon as ever a man passes through this gate he gets the eye of his understanding opened to see that God's verdict of it is true, that it is all vanity and vexation of spirit, And then as he falls out of conceit with the things of this world, as his portion, so he quits the ways and courses of this world, according to that exhortation of the apostle, " Be not conformed to this world, but be ye transformed by the renewing of your mind." And particularly he quits carnal reason and policy as his guide, in the things of Christ, and matters that concern the glory of God, and salvation of his soul. As you see in the apostle Paul, so soon as " it pleased God (says he) to reveal his Son in me, immediately I conferred not with flesh and blood."

4thly. We are told here also, that the followers of Christ, the glorious Breaker, " go out at the gate that he breaks up to them." An expression like this we have, John x. 9. " I am the door: By me, if any man enter in, he shall be saved, and shall go in and out, and find pasture." So soon as the poor soul passes through the gate, he finds some things without the gate, as it were, which he could never find before. I shall instance a few, among many things, he goes out to, " when he passes through the gate."

1. He goes out from darkness unto light : " Ye were sometimes darkness, but now are ye light in the Lord." He gets " the eyes of his understanding opened, to know what is the hope of his calling, and what the riches of the glory of his inheritance in the saints." The man begins to see things that were not seen by him before. He sees the holiness of the law, the majesty of the Lawgiver, the exceeding sinfulness of sin, the glory of Christ, the beauties of holiness, the nothingness of things temporal, and the importance of things everlasting.

2. He goes out from death to life. The man, before he passed this gate, was dead, legally dead, spiritually dead, and every moment in danger of going down to the second death ; but now he enters into life, into a life of justification, having the handwriting cancelled and cross-scored by the blood of the Lamb. " There is no condemnation to them that are in Christ Jesus:" No, they are alive unto God through Christ. He enters into a life of sanctification and holiness.

The man, who before, was wallowing among the pots, gets the beauty of the Lord his God put upon him; whereby he is made to shine like the wings of a dove. He enters into a life of consolation, arising from the intercourse and fellowship that he now finds with the Lord. The light of God's countenance puts more gladness in his heart, "than when corn, and wine, and oil doth abound." In a word, a man no sooner goes out by this gate, than he enters into life eternal. "For he that hath the Son hath life. He that believeth in the Son hath everlasting life." And, like an heir of such inheritance, he carries himself "like a stranger in the earth, looking for a city which hath foundations, whose builder and maker is God."

3. The man goes out from bondage. The bondage of sin, Satan, and the curse, "unto the glorious liberty of the children of God." So that the man does not look on it any longer as a piece of thraldom, like Doeg, to be detained before the Lord in his ordinances. No, no, he is ready to say, Psal. xxvii. 4. "One thing have I desired of the Lord, and that will I seek after, that I may dwell in the house of the Lord all the days of my life, to behold the beauty of the Lord, and to inquire after him in his temple," Psal. lxxxiv. 10. "For a day in thy courts is better than a thousand: I had rather be a doorkeeper in the house of my God, than to dwell in the tents of wickedness." It is no bondage to him to walk in the strict and cleanly ways of holiness. No, he finds sin and the ways of it to bring him under a spirit of bondage; but for the ways of the Lord, they are his delight. He rejoices to work righteousness; and he is ready to say with David, "O that my ways were directed to keep thy statutes! My soul breaketh with the longing that it hath unto thy righteous judgments at all times." But I do not insist further on this use.

MICAH ii. 13.—The Breaker is come up before them; they have broken up, and have passed through the gate, and are gone out by it; and their king shall pass before them, and the Lord (or Jehovah) on the head of them.

THE THIRD SERMON ON THIS TEXT.

Thirdly, A *third* use I make of the doctrine, may be by way of Terror unto all the wicked and ungodly world, who are living in a state of sin and rebellion against God.

This mighty Breaker will take the field against you, and O, when he whets "his glittering sword, and his hand takes hold on judgment, he will render vengeance unto his enemies."

Quest. Who are they that may be ranked among that number of the enemies of Christ, whom he will break as with a rod of iron? I answer,

1st, The great potentates of the earth, who do not employ their power in the service of his kingdom; or who employ their power to the hurt and prejudice of his cause and interest in the world. They are not exempted from his authority, no they must stand on a level with others before this awful Breaker; Psal. ii. 9. "Thou shalt break them with a rod of iron, thou shalt dash them in pieces like a potter's vessel. Be wise now therefore, O ye kings, be instructed, ye judges of the earth." When men of power and authority begin to kick against him, he can, with the greatest ease, be avenged on them, for he "shall cut off the Spirit of princes; he is terrible to the kings of the earth; he pours contempt upon princes, and strikes through kings in the day of his wrath."

2dly, This mighty Breaker will, in his own time, take the field against all unfaithful ministers and shepherds, who, instead of feeding the flock of Christ, feed themselves with the fat; and who, instead of gathering, do scatter the Lord's flock and rule them with rigour and cruelty. To this purpose you may read the whole 34th chapter of Ezekiel, from the beginning to the end, at your own leisure, and see whether or not that passage be applicable to any of us, who are called shepherds at this day.

3dly, The Breaker will take the field against all ignorant persons, who live in darkness in the midst of light; "It is a people of no understanding: therefore he that made them will not have mercy on them, and he that formed them will shew them no favour."

4thly, Against all unbelievers who reject the offers of his grace through Christ: "He that believeth not is condemned already, and the wrath of God abideth on him." He will come "in flaming fire, taking vengeance on all that know not God, and obey not the gospel."

5thly, Against all nominal professors, who rest satisfied with a name to live, whilst dead in sin.

6thly, Against all covenant breakers who deal deceitfully with God or man, in the matter of solemn vows, whether national or personal; a heavy charge, which we in this land may take home, and for which, it is to be feared, God will be avenged on us. "Shall he break the covenant and be delivered?" No, says the Lord, "I will bring a sword upon you, which shall avenge the quarrel of my covenant."

7thly, He will come up as a Breaker against all apostates and backsliders, who seemed to run well in the ways of God, but quickly turn aside, like a deceitful bow, unto crooked ways. Many of you have been lifting up your hands to the most high God at a communion table, making a solemn profession to God, angels, and men, that you will follow the Lord whithersoever he goes. Oh, for the Lord's sake beware of acting a perfidious part with God, like these, Psal. lxxviii. 35. "Who remembered God as their rock, and the high God as their Redeemer, but whose hearts were not right with him, neither were they stedfast in his covenant," ver. 37. For backsliders in heart shall be filled with their own ways. No man putting his hand to God's plough and looking back, is fit for the kingdom of God.

8thly, Against all unclean persons who wallow in the puddle of their abominable lusts, Heb. xiii. 4. "Whoremongers and adulterers God will judge." You are by name and surname excluded out of the kingdom of heaven, 1 Cor. vi. 6—8.

9thly, Against all the proud and haughty ones of the earth, who carry themselves insolently towards others, as if they were not their fellow creatures, or worthy to be set with the dogs of their flock. All who pride themselves in their riches, ornaments, wisdom, honours, or preferments, and are lifted up in their hearts with these or the like things; the Breaker will be upon you with his rod of iron, Is. ii. 11, 12. "The lofty looks of man shall be humbled, and the haughtiness of men shall be bowed down, and the Lord alone shall be exalted in that day. For the day of the Lord of hosts shall be upon every one that is proud and lofty, and upon every one that is lifted up, and he shall be brought low."

10thly, The Breaker will come up against magistrates and elders that do injury to the Lord's vineyard, and spoil his poor people of any rights or liberties that he allows them, whether as men or Christians. See to this purpose, Is. iii. 14, 15, "The Lord will enter into judgment with the ancients of his people, and the princes thereof." That is, the great men that bear rule, and have authority in their hand; "for ye have eaten up the vineyard, the spoil of the poor is in your houses. What mean ye, that ye beat my people to pieces, and grind the faces of the poor, saith the Lord of hosts?" Some that are guilty this way, may perhaps screen themselves with some colour of law; but if any such be hearing me at present, I warn them, in the name of God, that their cobweb pretences will stand them in no stead when the Breaker takes the field against them.

11thly, The Breaker will come up against all such as declare their sin as Sodom, and who, instead of taking with the reproofs of the word, the reproofs of conscience, the reproofs of providence, do harden their hearts as if they would bid heaven a defiance, and, like swine, turn about and rend those who cast the jewel of a reproof before them; "He that being often reproved, hardeneth his neck, shall suddenly be destroyed, and that without remedy. O! consider this, ye that forget God, lest he tear you in pieces, when there is none to deliver you out of his hand."

And because all this and many more evils are prevalent and rampant in the day and generation wherein we live, we have reason to fear, that some breaking calamity or other is at the door; and let none such promise themselves impunity, for there is no escaping the stroke of this awful Breaker; no, no, whither will ye flee from his presence? See an awful lecture to this purpose, Amos ix. 2-6, &c.

That I may, if possible, strike terror into the hearts of a wicked and ungodly world, that they may awake, and flee from the wrath that is to come. I shall take notice of a few breaking engines that this mighty Breaker has at hand, wherewith he can reach a blow unto them.

1. He has a breaking arm. Who has an arm like God? "His right hand and his holy arm hath gotten him the victory" over all his enemies, and will do so to the end of the world.

2. He has a breaking countenance. When he frowns upon a person, or when he lifts up his reconciled countenance upon a soul, he puts more gladness into it than when corn and wine and oil did abound. But, Oh! when he casts down his countenance, and frowns, who is able to bear it? Ps. lxxx. 16. "They perish (says the church) at the rebuke of thy countenance;" and no wonder, for "the pillars of heaven tremble and are astonished at his rebuke."

3. He has a breaking word; "Is not my word a hammer that breaketh the rock in pieces?" Indeed his promising word yields comfort, and is the savour of life. But, Oh! his threatening and condemning word, "it is a breaking hammer and a piercing two-edged sword," and by this sword of his mouth he will slay the wicked. "I have hewed them by the prophets, I have slain them by the words of my mouth."

4. He has a breaking voice. O! "Who can thunder with a voice like him? The voice of the Lord breaketh the cedars, the Lord breaketh the cedars of Lebanon." Oh, when this mighty Breaker shall, at the last day, "descend from heaven with a shout, with the voice of the archangel, and with the trump of God," how will the wicked appear? they will fall "awailing because of him, and begin to cry to the rocks and mountains to fall on them, and cover them from the face of him that sitteth on the throne, and from the wrath of the Lamb."

5. He has a breaking wind; "With the breath of his lips shall he slay the wicked," Is. ix. 4. Ps xviii. 8. "There went up a smoke out of his nostrils, and fire out of his mouth devoured; coals were kindled by it." And by this breath of the Almighty hell fire is kindled, which can never be quenched, Is. xxx. 33. "Tophet is ordained of old; yea, for the king it is prepared, he hath made it deep and large; the pile

thereof is fire and much wood, the breath of the Lord like a stream of brimstone doth kindle it."

6. He has at hand breaking bolts of thunder, whereby he can strike the sinner dead in a very moment; and, if he let fly one of these bolts, who is able to withstand it? Ps. lxxviii. 42. He sent hot thunderbolts amongst the rebellious Egyptians.

7. He has many breaking armies of angels, stars, and plagues at his command, whereby he can punish a rebellious church or nation. If he but hiss for the fly, the locust, the caterpillar, or such like inconsiderable insects, how speedily will they run to avenge his quarrel? as you see in the case of Egypt. Thus, I say, this mighty Breaker does not want abundance of engines; and, therefore, let not the rebellious exalt themselves against him, but let the wicked forsake his way.

Use *fourth* of this doctrine may be by way of *Consolation* and *Encouragement* to believers, under all their discouragements and difficulties, in their way through the waste howling wilderness. There is no dark or difficult step in the way that Christ has not beaten and travelled before you; and, therefore, has sanctified it to you. I shall instance in a few particulars.

1*st*, In general, here is comfort under a multiplicity of troubles and sorrows, like so many billows breaking upon you. *The Breaker is come up before* you in this road. Christ "was a man of sorrows and acquainted with grief. He was oppressed and afflicted;" and, therefore, in bearing the cross, look unto him, and consider him,—lest ye be wearied and faint in your minds. And know, for thy encouragement, "that thy light affliction, which is but for a moment, worketh for thee a far more exceeding and eternal weight of glory. Christ suffered, and then entered into his glory." And so those must "enter the kingdom through many tribulations."

2*dly*, And more particularly, here is comfort in case of temptation. Perhaps the roaring lion seems to be let loose upon thee, his fiery darts of temptation fly thick about thy ears, and thou art ready to say, One day or other I shall fall by the hand of Saul; here is comfort, *the Breaker is come up before* thee in this road, he was in all points tempted like as thou art. You see, Matth. iv., what furious onsets he met with from the tempter; and had he the boldness to make an attempt upon the Leader and Commander, and should the soldiers, the followers, think it strange that he attacks them with the same or the like temptations? And know, for thy comfort, that the enemy had his head bruised, his kingdom and strength ruined, in the attempt he made upon Christ; and he has also promised, Rom. xvi. 20, to tread Satan under thy feet; and, therefore, be of good comfort, and hold on thy way.

3*dly*, Hast thou a load of sin and guilt lying on thee, perhaps crying, "Mine iniquities have gone over mine head, as an heavy burden they are too heavy for me to bear?" Why, here is comfort, the Breaker has gone up before thee, he has the experience of this weight, for "the Lord laid upon him the iniquity of us all," and he has such a tender sympathy with the poor soul that is groaning under a load of sin and guilt, that he bids you "cast thy burden upon the Lord, and he will sustain thee. Come unto me, all ye that labour and are heavy laden, and I will give you rest."

4thly, Here is comfort in case of desertion.

O, may some poor soul say, I am trysted with a hiding God, the Comforter that should relieve my soul is far from me.

Here is relief, *the Breaker is come up before* thee in this way. What black and dark clouds were about him, when he cries, "My God, my God, why hast thou forsaken me?" And such is his sympathy with his poor people in that case, that he has left a promise for their encouragement, that though he may hide for a small moment, and in a little wrath, yet he will return with everlasting kindness. "Weeping may endure for a night, but joy cometh in the morning."

5thly, Here is comfort in case of reproach. Perhaps thy name is pierced through with the sharp arrows of reproach and calumny. Why, the Breaker has travelled this road, he was called "a blasphemer, a wine-bibber, a friend of publicans and sinners," and charged with a correspondence with Beelzebub. What worse can be said of thee? But, besides, let the world blacken thee as they will, the day comes when he will openly acknowledge and acquit thee, and thy name shall be had in everlasting remembrance with him: he will one day bring forth "thy righteousness as the light, and thy judgment as the noonday."

6thly, Art thou deserted and betrayed, forsaken by friends and familiar acquaintances, in whom thou trusted? Why, the Breaker has gone up before thee in this road also; he was betrayed by Judas, and forsaken by all his disciples, they "that did eat bread with him, lifted up their heel against him." But he has told thee for thy encouragement, that, desert or betray thee who will, he will never do it, "I will never leave thee, nor forsake thee;" flames of fire and floods of water shall never separate thee and him.

7thly, Perhaps thou meetest with hard justice, yea, with the greatest injustice from men. Well, *the Breaker is come up before* thee in this road also; for though he did no violence, nor was any deceit in his mouth, yet he was numbered amongst the vilest malefactors, and condemned as such. Although he showed all loyalty to the powers of the earth, and gave the most shining pattern and example of it, yet he was condemned as an enemy to Cæsar, and so he has sanctified that lot to his followers also.

8thly, Perhaps thou art afraid to look death, the king of terrors, in the face, thy heart and flesh shrinks when thou thinkest of going through the dark valley into an unknown world, a bottomless and awful eternity. Well, take courage, *the Breaker is come up before* thee, and, in his up-coming, he has plagued death and destroyed the grave, Hos. xiii. 14. So that the very nature of it is, as it were, altered; that "cup of trembling given him of the Father," is turned into a cup of consolation, by his tasting of death for every man; and therefore, believer, thou mayest lift up thy head when thou seest death making his approaches, and invading that tabernacle of clay, for the day of thy redemption draweth nigh.

Thus you see there is no road thou canst travel in thy journey through this weary wilderness, but the way is already paved and broken up by thy glorious Head and King: And the experience that Christ had of these things unavoidably brings along these two things with it.

1. A tender sympathy with his people in the like cases. He knows the heart of a stranger, for that he himself was a stranger in the earth: in all their afflictions he is afflicted; he is touched with the feeling of our infirmities, being in all points tempted like as we are. And O! how relieving is it to a poor creature in affliction, to have a tender sympathising friend to take a lift of its burden?

2. His experience of this evil brings forth speedy succour; for in "that he himself hath suffered, being tempted, he is able to succour them that are tempted."

But O, say you, the succour is long a-coming.

Answ. It shall not tarry a moment longer than he sees it for his glory and thy good; and therefore take a good heart, it shall come in the best time, and thou shalt be convinced of it when it comes, that it is so: "The vision is yet for an appointed time,—though it tarry, wait for it; for at the end it shall speak, and not lie, because it will surely come, it will not tarry." Do not say that the Lord has forgotten to be gracious because he delays the promised relief; no, woman may forget her sucking child (says he), yet will I not forget thee. Thou art engraven upon the palms of his hands, &c.

Use *fifth* of this text and doctrine shall be of *Exhortation*.

1*st*, To sinners, to the captives of hell, who are yet under the chains of their spiritual captivity.

Has Christ broken in upon the powers of hell? broken up Satan's prison? and broken up the way to heaven and glory? removed all legal bars and impediments out of the way of salvation? Oh: then, let me exhort and call you who are yet in covenant with death, and in an agreement with hell, to shake off the fetters of sin; for this mighty Breaker calls you to come up to him in the way that he has opened, he calls "to the prisoners to come forth, and to them that are in darkness to shew themselves," Is. xlix. 9.

[The prosecution and enforcements of this exhortation are wanting, but may be supplied from the preceding uses of terror to sinners, and encouragement to saints to follow Christ in the character of a Breaker. The reverend author had prepared about a quarter of a sheet to insert here, but his sickness and death ensuing, I was thereby deprived of the same by certain unexpected incidents, which I shall forbear to mention.]

A second word of exhortation is to believers, especially unto believing communicants, who have been getting the seal of the covenant, the pledges of his love, at a communion table.

Is it so that Christ has broken up the way to glory? has he taken the field as our renowned General, to fight our battles against all the opposing powers of hell and earth, and their auxiliaries?

Then let me exhort you to pull up your drooping spirits? take courage and hold on your way, and march to glory; fight the good fight of faith, and persevere therein to the end, maugre all the opposition you may meet with from your spiritual enemies.

I need make use of no other motive to engage your compliance with my exhortation, than what the words of my text afford, *The Breaker is come up before you;* and if you require an authentic commentary upon this, you have it in the close of the verse, *Their King shall pass before them, and Jehovah on the head of them.* There seems to be an allusion unto the march of an army, with their general on their head; or the march of Israel through the wilderness, with the pillar of fire and cloud before them. Where four things may be noticed for your encouragement in your march through the wilderness of this world.

1*st*, Observe your General's name, it is *Jehovah.*
2*dly*, His royal office and relation, he is *their King.*
3*dly*, His proximity or nearness to the army, he is *on their head.*
4*thly*, His majestic mein, conduct, and behaviour, suited to his office and relation.

1*st*, I say, for thy encouragement in thy march and journey to Immanuel's land, through the howling wilderness, take a view of your General's name, it is *Jehovah: The Lord* (or *Jehovah,* as it is in the original) *is on the head of them.* This is not the name of any inferior dependent being; no, it is a name peculiar only to the most high, supreme, and self-existent God, Psal. lxxxiii. 18. "That men may know that thou, whose name alone is JEHOVAH, art the Most High over all the earth." It is "by this name that he rides upon the heavens in the help of his people, and in his excellency on the sky," Deut. xxxiii. 26. The name of a successful and victorious general will inspire the whole army with courage, and strike a terror into the hearts of the enemy. Well, believer, the name of thy General, and the Captain of thy salvation, is JEHOVAH, a name at which every knee must bow, of things in heaven, and things in earth, and things under the earth. All the devils in hell fall a-trembling at the greatness of this name: and therefore take courage, hold on thy way, and resist even unto blood, striving against sin, under the conduct of such a renowned name, saying with the church, Psal. xx. 5. "We will be joyful in thy salvation, and in the name of our God we will set up our banners."

And because we are called and commanded, in our work and warfare to trust in the name of the Lord, and to stay ourselves upon him, as our God; therefore, to encourage faith in this name, I will only give two or three additional epithets that I find affixed to it in scripture.

1. I find him called JEHOVAH T'SIDKENEU, the Lord our Righteousness: Jer. xxiii. 6, "This is his name, whereby he shall be called the LORD OUR RIGHTEOUSNESS." He has, by his active and passive obedience unto the law, brought in everlasting righteousness for our justification, by which righteousness the law is magnified and made honourable, and we, through faith in him, have the righteousness of the law fulfilled in us; and therefore, whenever the law, as a cove-

nant, comes to demand the debt of obedience, as the condition of life, or bends its curse against thee, for the violation of its precepts, thou art to improve the name of thy General, by an applying faith, saying, He is the Lord my righteousness, He was made sin for me, who knew no sin, that I might be made the righteousness of God in him.

2. I find him sometimes called JEHOVAH ROPHI, The Lord thy Healer or Physician, Exod. xv. 26; and therefore, whenever thou findest thyself wounded by the fiery darts of Satan, or the pestilence or contagion of sin, in any shape, affecting thy soul with deadness, darkness, weakness, unbelief, enmity, or be what it will, presently have recourse to thy General, for he is the Captain of salvation, and by looking unto him, thou shall be healed, as Israel was healed in the wilderness, by looking unto the brazen serpent.

3. I find him sometimes called JEHOVAH SHAMMAH, The Lord is there, Ezek. last chapter, last verse; which points at his gracious presence in his church, and among his people. "He is in the midst of her, she shall not be moved; the Lord will help her, and that right early." By his essential presence he fills heaven and earth; and he is present in his church in a way of special grace, for he says of Zion, "This is my rest for ever, here will I dwell; the Lord is there, sitting upon a mercy-seat, to hear, help, and give out liberally to his subjects.

4. He is sometimes designed JEHOVAH-JIREH, The Lord will see or provide, Gen. xxii. 14. This name is a glorious encouragement under any want or strait, whether as to the soul or body, for hereby we are assured, that, "when the poor and needy seek water, and there is none, and their tongue faileth for thirst, the Lord will hear them, the God of Israel will not forsake them," Is. xli. 17.

5. I find him called JEHOVAH-NISSI, The Lord my Banner. Exod. xvii. 15., because he gives a banner unto them that fear him, and they display it because of truth; and when they are allowed access unto him in his ordinances, "they sit down under his shadow with great delight, and his banner over them is love. His name is a banner of war, a banner of victory, a banner of triumph, unto them that trust in it.

2*dly*, We have in the words not only Christ's name, but his office and relation to his people; he is their King, the Captain of their salvation; he is a person of royal authority, and he is installed King of Zion by his Father, Psal. ii. 6. "Yet have I set my King upon my holy hill of Zion. He hath on his vesture, and on his thigh a name written, King of kings and Lord of lords," Rev xix. And that you may admire, and trust, and honour him as a mighty King.

1, Consider the height of his throne; it is the very same throne that the Father sits upon, hence called the throne of God and of the Lamb. When he overcame, he sat down with the Father on his throne, Rev. iii., at the close; and this throne of his is so high and lifted up, that when the angels look up to its height and glory, they are so dazzled that they cover their faces with their wings.

2. Consider the magnificence of his dwelling-place. Other kings

have their royal palaces; but what are they with all their splendour, but piles of dust? Zion's King he inhabits eternity; he dwelleth in the high and holy place, and in light that is inaccessible and full of glory, which no man hath seen, nor can see. O who shall dwell with him in his tabernacle? See an answer, Psal. xxiv. 4.

3. Let us take a view of the splendour of his retinue. "The armies which are in heaven follow him," armies of angels, and the armies of the saints. His court is crowded with attendants, "Ten thousand times ten thousand, and thousands of thousands, minister unto him."

4. Consider the vastness of his revenues; he levies tribute from heaven, earth, and hell. All creatures whatsoever pay a revenue of praise unto him as their great Lord, Rev. vii. 10. The church triumphant cries, "Salvation to our God who sitteth upon the throne, and to the Lamb, for ever and ever." The church militant adore him, saying, "Let the whole earth be filled with his glory." Yea, hell itself must pay a tribute of praise unto his justice, and acknowledge the equity of his administration.

5. Consider the largeness of his dominion, in respect of all persons and places; "His kingdom ruleth over all," Ps. ciii. 19. His kingdom of grace, under the New Testament, extendeth to the heathen, and the uttermost parts of the earth. And in respect of duration, his kingdom is an everlasting kingdom. In a word, he is the "King of kings and Lord of lords, the Prince of the kings of the earth; by him kings reign, and princes decree justice." O who would not follow such a King? who would not desire to be amongst the number of his subjects? who would not desire to espouse his cause against all that dare to invade his prerogatives, as many are doing at this day, by encroaching on the immunities and liberties of his subjects? Do it who will, it will be to their own cost in the issue.

3dly, Another thing here, mighty encouraging to the subjects and followers of this mighty Prince, is his proximity or nearness unto his subjects or soldiers; "He is on the head of them." He is not only a Head of government, or a King, but he is also a Head of influence, such a head as that of the natural body unto the members, which cannot be separated, but must always be where the members are. "God hath given him to be Head over all things unto the church, which is his body." He and they are "joined together by one spirit," Rom. viii., Col. ii. 19. "Not holding the Head, from which all the body, as by joints and bands, having nourishment ministered, and knit together, increaseth with the increase of God."

O what a great matter is this! and how may it inspire believers to hold on their way, and maintain their warfare, that *the Lord*, or Jehovah, *is on the head of them!* There are two or three mighty encouragements that arise hence.

1. If Jehovah be on thy head, he knows well how matters go with his militant members in the field of battle. Do not say therefore, "My way is hid from the Lord, and my judgment is passed over from my God, for his eyes run to and fro through the whole earth." A hair of your head cannot fall to the ground without his knowledge and permission.

2. If Jehovah be on thy head, thou shalt not want what is needful to bear thy charges in thy journey and warfare. The whole army here is provided and maintained upon the expense of the General. More particularly,

(1.) The army must be provided of meat and drink. Well, Jehovah on the head of them will see to this, "Thy bread shall be given thee, and thy water shall be sure. Thy wants shall all be supplied by thy God, according to his riches in glory, by Christ Jesus."

(2.) The army must have clothing. Well, Jehovah on their head will see to that also; he has provided an armoury, wherein hang the shields of the mighty men of war, Eph. vi. You see there what a vast complete stand of armour Jehovah has provided for his soldiers, the shield of faith, the helmet of salvation, the breastplate of righteousness, the girdle of truth, the sword of the Spirit; nothing is wanting there, to offend the enemy, or defend the soul in its warfare.

(3.) The army must have their garrison for winter quarters, where they may be sheltered from stormy wind and tempest. Well, Jehovah on the head of them, he has provided this, yea, he himself is their garrison, their dwelling-place in all generations. He is a hiding-place from the wind, and a covert from the tempest, &c.

(4.) The army must have their orders and directions how to direct their motions, especially in a march. Well, Jehovah on the head of them, he will not let this be wanting either; his "law is a lamp to their feet, and a light unto their path. He hath showed thee, O man, what is good, and what the Lord thy God requireth of thee."

(5.) The sick and wounded in the army must be seen to. Well, Jehovah on the head of them is an experienced Physician, and a tender-hearted Shepherd; he gathers the lambs with his arm, he tenderly bindeth up the wounds of them that are broken in heart, and wounded in spirit. Thus you see what glorious encouragement arises from this, that Jehovah is on the head of them.

4thly, We have here their glorious and victorious march, under the conduct of Jehovah: he passes on before them; where these things are implied:

1. That hereaway [in this earth] believers are not at home, for they are but on a journey; they are like Israel in the wilderness, where they found no city to rest in, no resting-place on this side Jordan; no, they "desire a better country, that is an heavenly."

2. That they are in motion, or making progress towards their rest; for they are passing on, as it is said of the travellers to Zion, Ps. lxxxiv. "They go from strength to strength, every one of them appeareth before God in Zion."

3. That their King and General on their head is well acquainted with their ways, for he passes on before them, as their Leader and Commander; however ignorant or unskilful they are in themselves, yet their Head and King has all the treasures of wisdom and knowledge hid in him, and therefore he will know the way that they take, and the course that they steer; he will not leave them to their own conduct in the wilderness; no, but he will guide them by his counsel, till he hath brought them to glory.

4. That Jehovah, their Head and King, marches in the front, to encounter all opposition, and to rid the passes of their way; and O what enemies dare stand up to oppose them, when Jehovah passes on before them as their King! Surely in him they shall be "conquerors, yea, more than conquerors: Their bow shall abide in its strength, for Jehovah is the strength of Israel, who can neither lie nor repent," 1 Sam. xv. 29.

5. That the church and people of God, while keeping his way, is under his particular protection; he will "hide them in the secret of his tabernacle; they shall abide under the shadow of the Almighty; he shall cover thee with his feathers, and under his wings shalt thou trust; his truth shall be thy shield and buckler.

6. That there is something of particular greatness and majesty in the Lord's appearances in the behalf of his people. Hence they are likened to an army, with an invincible general on their head, which made Balaam to cry out, "How goodly are thy tents, O Jacob! and thy tabernacles, O Israel! He couched, he lay down as a lion, and as a great lion: who shall stir him up?"

Thus you see what glorious encouragement springs out of this word, to animate and hearten believers in their spiritual warfare, *Their King shall pass before them, and Jehovah on the head of them.* But the eye of faith will see infinitely more in them than any thing that I have said, or can say.

I conclude with a few advices, in order to your successful march towards glory, under the conduct of your glorious King and Head, that passes on before you. as the Captain of your salvation.

1*st*, Then, study to be well acquainted with the glorious Breaker that has come up before you, and keep him ever in your view; for the very sight of the Captain inspires the soldiers with courage and valour, that, if he be in their view, they go on their way rejoicing, though hell and death, and armed legions of devils and men were in their way. Hence it is that the saints are called so frequently to look to him in their Christian course and warfare. He calls on them so to do, Is. xlv. 22. "Look unto me, and be ye saved." They encourage one another to this, Heb. xii. 2. "Let us run with patience the race that is set before us, looking unto Jesus, the Author and Finisher of our Faith." And we find them declaring their experience of the profit and advantage of so doing, Psal. xxxiv. 5. "They looked unto him, and were lightened, and their faces were not ashamed." A sight of him inspired them with such undaunted boldness, that they could look all their enemies in the face, without being in the least dismayed.

2*dly*, Study to be well acquainted with the way that he has broken up before you. You have an account of the way by the prophet Isaiah, chap. xxxv. "A high-way shall be there, and a way, and it shall be called the way of holiness; the unclean shall not pass over it, but it shall be for those; the wayfaring men, though fools, shall not err therein." This is none other than the cleanly way of justification and acceptance by faith in the Lord Jesus Christ, which vents and discovers itself in the study of holiness, both in heart and life: So that Christ himself improved by faith, both for justification and sanctification, for righteousness and strength is the high way cast up for us to walk in. "I am the way (says Christ, John xiii. 6.); no man cometh to the Father but by me." Study, I say, to be well acquainted with this way of access, this way of salvation. It is not the way of works, but the way of grace: "By grace are ye saved through faith, and that not of yourselves, it is the gift of God: not of works, lest any man should boast." It is not the nasty way of sin, but the cleanly way of obedience to the law of God; and when you have obeyed, even in the strength of the Lord, you must make mention of his righteousness, even of his only.

3*dly*, Seeing Jehovah is on your head, put on Jehovah's armour, "Put on the whole armour of God," says the apostle, Eph. vi.; where you have also an account of the several pieces of the Christian armour, such as the shield of faith, the helmet of salvation, &c. This is sometimes called the armour of light, because it comes from the Father of lights, the Author of every good gift, and perfect gift; and, because all the pieces of the Christian armour, such as faith, hope, sincerity, and truth, are all founded in light, even "the light of the knowledge of the glory of God, in the face of Jesus Christ;" and because, like bright shining armour, it is beautiful in the eyes of the world; their light shines before men, so that others, seeing their good works, glorify their Father which is in heaven. And, particularly, I would recommend a holy dexterity in handling the sword of the Spirit, which is the word of God; because, by this weapon, your glorious Captain-General battled the enemy, in his encounter with him in the wilderness; and therefore study, like the valiant of King Solomon, to have this "sword girded on your thigh, because of fear in the night."

4*thly*, Observe carefully Jehovah's orders, seeing Jehovah your King is on your head. By the martial law, it is death for a soldier to disobey the orders of his leader and commander. What anarchy and confusion would there be in an army if it were otherwise! O Sirs, seeing your King passes before you, and Jehovah on your head, be sure to do whatever he commands you; he has given forth "his good, his perfect and acceptable will; he hath showed thee what is good, and what the Lord thy God requires of thee." And if kings, parliaments, magistrates, ministers, or be who they will, command or require you to do otherwise than Jehovah has directed you, you have an answer ready at hand, "Whether it be right, in the sight of God, to hearken unto you more than unto God, judge ye."

5*thly*, In following Jehovah as your renowned King and General, be sure to keep the rank and sphere wherein he has put you; for Jehovah is not the author of confusion, but he is a God of order. So soon as an army in battle begins to break their ranks, and to fall into disorder, it is an evidence that they are worsted by the enemy, and therefore great care is taken by a skilful general to keep the soldiers in their proper rank and order. So here, the Captain of salvation will have every one to abide in the vocation in which he is called; he will have magistrates to act under him in their sphere, ministers in theirs, and private Christians in their capacity; and if every one thus study to serve the Lord in their proper station, the whole body of believers shall be edified and built up, and the very women, though they tarry at home, yet they shall divide the spoil.

6thly, Whenever you find yourself distressed by the attacks of the enemy, sin, Satan, or the world, be sure to cry to Jehovah for help, for he is on your head, and passes on before you. This has been the practice of the followers of the Lamb in all ages of the world, Ps. xxxiv. 6. " This poor man cried, and the Lord heard him, and saved him out of all his distresses." You have Jehovah's command so to do, " Call upon me in the day of trouble, I will deliver thee," &c. I can assure you that the cry of one of his soldiers, in distress by the enemy, goes to his heart, and awakens his resentment; how much more when the whole church is crying to heaven, because of the injuries that are done her, either by the wild boars, or else by wolves in sheep's clothing? I can assure you that the Breaker will come up at the cry of his poor people, when they are oppressed, either in their civil or spiritual rights and privileges. I read a lecture to you to that purpose, Psal. xviii. 6. " In my distress I called upon the Lord" (viz., when floods of ungodly men made him afraid, ver. 4). Well, the Breaker takes the field, and see what awful work follows, from ver. 7 to ver. 14.

7thly, Seeing Jehovah is on your head, as your King and the Captain of your salvation, let never his standard fall, if you can keep it up. Jehovah has lifted up his standard in Scotland, beyond many nations of the earth, a standard of pure doctrine, discipline, worship, and government. Attempts are made at this day to pull down this standard, though we lie under the strongest ties, both national and personal, to stand by it.

Some are attempting to pull down the standard of doctrine, particularly by denying the self-existence and supreme deity of the Son of God, our renowned King and Head.

Others are attempting to strike at the government of the church, by a tyrannical and lordly usurpation upon the rights of the Lord's people, in choosing their own pastors.

And some talk of a bill preparing in the Parliament of Britain, whereby a deeper wound is yet to be given to the church of God in this matter; and some say that the hand of J——b is in it.

But be who they will, that act such a part against the known rights and privileges of the subjects of the King of Zion, I pretend to be no extraordinary prophet, yet I think I may warn them, in the name of God, that the Breaker will take the field against them in his own time and way, and recompense tribulation to them that trouble his people.

Meantime, let me exhort the Lord's people, "to stand fast in the liberty wherewith Christ hath made them free, that they be not entangled again with any yoke of bondage," that men would wreathe about their necks; and, in so doing, you have this for your encouragement, the Breaker is come up before you; your King passeth before you, and Jehovah on your head; and if the Lord be for you who can be against you?

ACTION SERMON.

ETHIOPIA STRETCHING OUT HER HANDS TO GOD.

PSAL. lxviii. 31.—*Ethiopia shall soon stretch out her hands unto God.*

THIS psalm was penned, probably, upon the occasion of David's carrying up the ark from the house of Obededom, to the tent he had pitched for it in Mount Zion, whereby was typified the ascension of Christ, and the erection of his spiritual kingdom and government in the world, by the preaching of the everlasting gospel. You see his ascension and exaltation spoken of, ver. 18. "Thou hast ascended on high, thou hast led captivity captive, thou hast received gifts for men, yea, for the rebellious also, that the Lord God might dwell amongst them." And in the following part of the psalm is foretold the erection of his kingdom, over the belly of all opposition that should be made thereunto, either by hell or earth.

The words read (not to insist in the entry) are a declaration of the success of the gospel among the Gentile nations. Ethiopia, Egypt, and other places of the world, would submit unto his royal sceptre, when it should be swayed among them in the dispensation of the gospel, *Princes shall come out of Egypt, Ethiopia shall soon stretch out her hands unto God.* It is only the latter clause I am to speak to: Where,

1st, We have a solemn act of divine worship, and that is, the stretching out of the hands. The actions of the body are the expressions of the actions of the soul or mind, Psal. cxliii. 6. says the psalmist, "I stretch forth my hands unto thee, my soul thirsteth after thee, as a thirsty land, Selah." So Psal. cxli. 2. "Let my prayer be set forth before thee as incense, and the lifting up of my hands as the evening sacrifice." So that the internal worship of the soul is the thing intended by the lifting up of the hands. And in every act of worship, faith, which is the hand of the soul, is the leading and principal part, insomuch that, "without faith, it is impossible to please God.

2dly, We have the object of this worship, or to whom the hand is to be lifted up: it is unto God; to "God in Christ, reconciling the world to himself, not imputing their trespasses unto them." An absolute God cannot be the object of a sinner's faith, hope, trust, and confidence, but on the contrary, the object of his terror and amazement. Hence, like our father Adam, before the revelation of the promised seed, we fly from him, and do not love to retain the knowledge of him in our thoughts; as it is said of the heathen world, Rom. i. 28., who want the knowledge of Christ.

3dly, In the words we may notice, who they are that stretch out their hands unto God; Ethiopia, which may be understood either literally or figuratively. If we take it figuratively, it is to be understood of the Gentile nations in general, a part being put for the whole. God the Father had said to the Son, Psal. ii. "Ask of me, and I shall give thee the heaven for thine inheritance, and the uttermost parts of the earth for thy possession." And accordingly, upon his resurrection and ascension, the gospel came to be preached to the Gentiles, according to the commission given to the apostles, Mark, xvi. 15. "Go ye into all the world, and preach the gospel unto every creature" under heaven, that is, unto all nations of the world, without distinction. And thereupon Ethiopia, with the rest of the Gentile nations, did receive the word of the gospel, and did obeisance unto the Son of God. And how the leaven of the gospel came to be spread unto Ethiopia, in particular, we have some account, Acts, viii. 27. to the close, where we are told of the conversion of the Ethiopian eunuch, by the ministry of Philip, who, after a profession of his faith in Christ, being baptised in his name, went on his way towards his own country, rejoicing; and, no doubt, would spread the glad tidings of salvation through Christ in his own country, some of the fruits whereof are said to remain amongst the Abyssines of Inner Ethiopia unto this day.

4thly, We have the ready and cheerful obedience that is given by Ethiopia or the Gentile nations, unto the call of the gospel; they soon stretch out their hands unto God, that is, they will do it without delay, and with readiness of mind; a literal accomplishment of which you will see, Acts, xiii. 40. 47. 48., where, when the Jews rejected the gospel, the apostle tells them, that seeing they put the word of God from them, "lo, we turn to the Gentiles, for so hath the Lord commanded us, saying, "I have set thee to be a light of the Gentiles, that thou shouldst be for salvation to all the ends of the earth." And then it is added, "And when the Gentiles heard this, they were glad, and glorified the word of the Lord;" that is, they entertained it with a ready mind.

5thly, We have the certainty of the event, they shall stretch out their hands unto God: As if he had said, however firmly they were rooted in their ignorance and idolatry, and other wickednesses, for many ages and generations, yet such shall be the efficacy of the gospel, and the victorious power of grace accompanying it, that they shall give up with their idols, and stretch out their hands in a way of worship and obedience unto the only living and true God. Much to this purpose is that word, Psal. cx. 3. "The Lord shall send the rod of thy strength out of Zion, Rule thou in the midst of thine enemies. Thy people shall be willing in the day of thy power; or (orig.) in the day of thy armies."

From the words thus briefly opened, I offer the following doctrine.

OBSERVE, "That when the gospel is the power of God among a people, they soon stretch forth their hands unto a God in Christ, as their God."

This text, as I told you, is a prediction of the success of the gospel amongst the idolatrous Ethiopians, and other Gentile nations, who had for many generations been stretching out their hands unto strange gods, dunghill deities; yet, whenever the gospel light comes among them, with the power of the Spirit, they turn to the true and living God, and stretch forth the hand unto him. *Ethiopia shall soon stretch out her hands unto God.*

In discoursing this doctrine, I shall, through divine assistance, observe the following method.

1. I would take a view of the condition of sinners without the gospel, or before the grace and power of the gospel reach their hearts.

II. I would speak of the power of the gospel, whereby they are made to stretch out their hands unto God.

III. Of that hand that is stretched out unto God, when they are converted unto him.

IV. Why, or for what end, the hand is stretched out to God.

V. I would inquire whence it is, that the hand is soon stretched out unto God, when the heart is effectually touched by the power of the gospel grace.

VI. Make it evident that when the heart is touched by the power of the gospel, the hand is soon, or without delay, stretched out to God.

VII. And, lastly, Apply.

I. The *first* thing is, to take a view of the condition of sinners without the gospel, or before gospel grace hath reached their hearts.

To clear this I refer you to that description of the state of the Gentile nations, before the gospel came among them, given by the apostle Paul, Eph. ii. 1. 2. 3. 11. 12. " And you hath he quickened, who were dead in trespasses and sins; wherein in time past ye walked according to the course of this world, according to the prince of the power of the air, the spirit that now worketh in the children of disobedience. Among whom also we all had our conversation in times past, in the lusts of our flesh, fulfilling the desires of the flesh and of the mind, and were by nature the children of wrath, even as others." Ver. 11, " Wherefore remember, that ye in times past, being Gentiles in the flesh, who are called uncircumcision, by that which is called circumcision in the flesh made by hands," ver. 12, " That at that time ye were without Christ, being aliens from the commonwealth of Israel, strangers from the covenant of promise, having no hope, and without God in the world." From which it appears, that Ethiopia, Scotland, and all the Gentile nations, and every individual among them, is, by nature, in a most dismal and deplorable condition, without God, the chief good, without Christ, the only Saviour, without hope of salvation, without the true church, where life and immortality alone is brought to light; without God's covenant of promise, which is the only charter of salvation; under the power of sin and Satan, the great enemy of their salvation; and, consequently, in a state of hostility against God. But these things I cannot now stand upon, and therefore proceed to

II. The *second* thing, which was to speak of the power of gospel grace, whereby sinners, like the Ethiopians, are made to stretch out their hands unto God.

There are only these few things I offer upon this head.

1st, The preaching of the everlasting gospel is the great means, of divine institution, for the conversion and salvation of sinners, Rom. i. 16, "The gospel is the power of God to salvation. It hath pleased God, by the foolishness of preaching, to save them that believe."

2dly, This power of God, in and by the gospel, is an exceeding great and mighty power, Eph. i. 18—20, hence called the revelation of his arm, Is. liii. 1, while the creation of the world is but the work of his fingers.

3dly, The way of exerting this power, in and by the gospel, upon the hearts of men, is very deep and mysterious. There is a glorious mystery in the contrivance, a mystery in the purchase, and as great a mystery in the application of our redemption. Hence it is compared unto the motion of the wind about us, which we cannot see, John iii. 8, "The wind bloweth where it listeth, thou hearest the sound thereof, but canst not tell whence it cometh, and whither it goeth."

4thly, It is wholly supernatural. However Arminians and others may boast of their natural powers, yet he who knows what is in man better than man himself, declares "That it is not of him that willeth, nor of him that runneth, but of God who sheweth mercy," Rom. ix. 16. "No man (says Christ, John iv. 44), can come to me, except the Father, which hath sent me, draw him."

5thly, This power is irresistible: nothing can stand against it. When God works, who can let or hinder him? All the power of corruption must give way before this power; the darkness of the mind, the obstinacy of the will, the carnality of the affections, the gates of brass and bars of iron, give way at the presence of the Lord, 2 Cor. x. 4, 5, "The weapons of our warfare are not carnal, but mighty through God," &c.

6thly, Though it be irresistible, yet there is no violence done to the natural powers of the soul. It is true, there is violence done to the strong man of sin and corruption, when a stronger than he binds him, and spoils him of his goods; but no violence is done to the natural powers of the soul by the power of gospel grace. What violence is done to the understanding to fill it with the light of the knowledge of the glory of God? What violence is done to the will to restore it to liberty? What violence is done to the affections of the soul to have them turned away from vanity to centre upon a God in Christ, who is the proper object of love?

7thly, The power of God in the gospel effectuates an universal change upon the soul, without any noise or din. Hence the kingdom of God is said to come without much observation. Conquests among men are with the confused noise of the warrior, and garments rolled in blood; but it is otherwise in God's conquest of sinners, it is in a secret and silent way that his work is done; hence it is compared to the falling of the dew, or to the spreading of leaven in a measure of meal, or the outgoings of the light of the morning, or the growth of the corn and grass, all which are the works of Infinite Power, and done with the greatest silence, and yet all very visible and discernible in their effects and fruits. But I pass this, and go on to the third thing in the method.

III. The *third* thing was, to inquire a little into the import of the phrase, *stretching out the hand to God*, when the heart is touched by the power of gospel grace.

Now, the stretching out of the hand of faith unto the true and living God, it supposes or implies these things following.

1*st*, A revelation of God, and of his mind and will unto the children of men, through Jesus Christ. Whatever discoveries God may make of himself in the works of creation and providence, yet, without a revelation of him, through Christ, in the gospel glass, they will never engage a sinner to stretch out the hand of faith unto him, as we see in the case of the heathens, who, though they knew God, even his eternal power and Godhead, in the things that were made, yet they glorified him not as God. It is only the gospel that is the power of God unto salvation. It is upon the preaching of the gospel, which is the rod of the Mediator's strength, that *Princes come out of Egypt, and Ethiopia stretches out her hand unto God.*

2*dly*, It implies an internal illumination of the heart and mind with the knowledge of the glory of God in the face of Jesus Christ. This is the very spring of a saving conversion unto the true God. Hence Paul, describing his own conversion, gives it in one word, Gal. i. 16. "When it pleased God to reveal his Son in me," immediately his hand that was stretched out against the Lord, in a way of persecution, is stretched forth for the advancement of the kingdom of Christ, 2 Cor. iv. 6, "God, who commanded the light to shine out of darkness, hath shined in our hearts," &c. This is the radical act of faith; hence faith is expressed by it, Is. liii. 11, "By his knowledge shall my righteous Servant justify many." So John xvii. 3, "This is life eternal, that they might know thee the only true God, and Jesus Christ whom thou hast sent."

3*dly*, The stretching out of the hand of faith unto God implies an assent of the soul unto the record of God concerning Christ. The assent of the mind unto anything is frequently expressed by the motion of the hand; so here, *Ethiopia shall stretch out the hand to God*, it implies a setting to his seal that God is true, in the testimony or record that God gives unto Christ in the word of the gospel; they (upon the matter) say with Paul, 1 Tim. i. 15, "This is a faithful saying, and worthy of all acceptation, that Christ Jesus came into the world to save sinners." As the Queen of Sheba said, so will the soul say when it beholds the glory of the true King Solomon, "O it is all true that I heard of Christ, and the half was not told me," &c.

4*thly*, A hearty approbation of the way and method of salvation. When a man stretches out his hand unto God, he upon the matter says, "It is a saying worthy of all acceptation, that Jesus Christ came into the world to save sinners;" O I like it well; it is worthy of infinite Wisdom and Love.

5thly, The lifting up of the hand is an act of admiration. When anything extraordinary occurs, or is told, we are ready to lift up the hand, and say, "O strange! Is it so indeed?" O what ravishing wonder fills the soul, when it by faith beholds the glory of Christ's person and mediation! O, will the man say, "Who is this that cometh from Edom, and with dyed garments from Bozrah? this that is glorious in his apparel, travelling in the greatness of his strength! O who is a God like unto thee, that pardoneth iniquity, and passes by the transgression of the remnant of thy heritage!—Without controversy, great is the mystery of godliness! God was manifest in the flesh!—What is man, that thou art mindful of him?

6thly, Sometimes the lifting up of the hand is an act of renunciation. When a man believes, he, upon the matter, abjures all Christ's rivals, that would usurp the throne of the heart, saying with Ephraim, "What have I to do any more with idols? O Lord our God, other Lords besides thee have had dominion over us, but by thee only will we make mention of thy name." He renounces all his lying refuges and false confidences wherein he had trusted, saying, with returning Israel, Hosea xiv. 3, "Ashur shall not save us, we will not ride upon horses, neither will we say any more to the work of our hands, Ye are our gods; for in thee the fatherless findeth mercy;" and Jer. iii. 23, "Truly in vain is salvation hoped for from the hills, and from the multitude of mountains; truly in the Lord our God only is the salvation of his people."

7thly, It implies an allegiance unto him as our Lord and Sovereign; *Ethiopia shall stretch out her hands to God*—*i.e.*, they shall, upon the discovery of God in man's nature, subject unto his authority, and receive the law from his mouth, saying, "The holy One of Israel is our almighty King. The Lord is our Judge, the Lord is our Lawgiver, the Lord is our King." They kiss the Son, and bow the knee unto him, because he hath "a name which is above every name that can be named."

8thly, The lifting up of the hand is an act of strong and fervent affection, which is a necessary concomitant of faith. When our affections are moved with love, desire, delight, we are ready to express it with the lifting up of the hand. So here, in believing, the will and affections are captivated with the love and loveliness of the blessed Bridegroom. O, will the soul be ready to say, "Thou art fairer than the children of men; He is altogether lovely. Whom have I in heaven but thee?" O, the raised esteem that the soul has of him! and the ardency of affection and desire that the soul has towards him! Is. xxvi. 9, "The desire of our soul is to thee; with my soul have I desired thee in the night, yea, with my spirit within me will I seek thee early."

9thly, The lifting up of the hand is an expression of confidence and trust, *Ethiopia shall stretch out her hands to God*, as if he had said, They shall confide and trust in a reconciled God in Christ; Psal. xxxvi., "How excellent is thy loving kindness, O God! therefore the children of men put their trust under the shadow of thy wings." The language of the soul, when it stretches out the hand to God, as a promising reconciled God, is much like that; Is. xii. 2, "God is my salvation: I will trust, and not be afraid, for the Lord Jehovah is my strength and my song, yea, he also is become my salvation." They trust in the name of the Lord, and his name is their strong tower of defence. Prov. xviii. 10.

10*thly*, The lifting up of the hand is an act of appropriation and application; *Ethiopia shall stretch out the hand to God*, as the Lord their God, and they shall have no other gods before him. Faith is a grace that draws in an infinite God revealing himself in Christ, as the soul's portion and property, as Israel did; Exod. xv. 2, "He is my God, and I will prepare him an habitation, my Father's God, and I will exalt him;" Psal. xlviii. 14, "This God is our God for ever and ever," See Psal. lxxxi. 2. And this appropriation of God goes upon the ground of the grant that is made in and through a second Adam in the new covenant, "I am the Lord thy God. I will say, It is my people; and they shall say, The Lord is my God," Zech. xiii. last.

Lastly, This phrase of stretching out the hand to God implies an open profession of the faith in Christ, before the world, angels, men, and devils, which is sometimes called in Scripture an avouching of the Lord to be our God; and is sometimes done there by a person or people, with the solemnity of lifting up the hand, an ancient form of swearing, Rev. x. 5, 6, when the angel swore by him that liveth for ever and ever, he doth it with his hand lifted up to heaven. So here, *Ethiopia shall soon stretch out her hands unto God*, that is, the inhabitants of Ethiopia, and of the Gentile nations, shall openly profess the God and Father of our Lord Jesus Christ to be their God, and they shall do it with the solemnity of an oath or covenant, as Israel did, Josh. xxiv. 22. When Joshua told them, " Ye are witnesses against yourselves. that ye have chosen you the Lord, to serve him." And in this manner have we, in this land, and neighbouring nations, lifted up our hand to God, declaring him to be our God, and ourselves to be his people, although, alas! these covenants have been scandalously broken, burnt, and in a great measure buried.

IV. The *fourth* thing was, to inquire, for what end, or upon what design, do sinners stretch out their hands unto God, when their hearts are touched by the power of the gospel.

Answer, in the following particulars.

1*st*, They stretch out their hands unto God, as helpless, lost, undone sinners, to a mighty Saviour, to help them out of the horrible pit and miry clay into which they had fallen, by their sin and apostacy in Adam, and in their own persons. When a sinner believes in Christ, he is just like Peter walking upon the waters; the waves and billows of God's wrath are just ready to swallow him up, whereupon he cries, " Lord, save me, I perish;" stretching out the hand to Christ for help. Lord, will the poor sinner say, I heard thy voice in the gospel, saying, "O Israel, thou hast destroyed thyself, but in me is thine help." Thou hast laid help upon one that is mighty, and I lay my help where thou hast laid it.

2*dly,* They stretch out their hands as rebels against Heaven, suing for peace at the hand of their offended Lord and Sovereign. All mankind commenced war against Heaven in the breach of the first covenant; every man by nature is enmity against God, and every sin is an act of rebellion; and, while sinners continue in a state of hostility against God, God is angry with them every day, and he says, he will wound the head of his enemies, and the hairy scalp of them that go on still in their trespasses. Now, when the sinner sees his sin and misery, and danger of falling into the hands of an angry God, he stretches out his hand for peace and reconciliation, because he hears that God is in Christ reconciling the world to himself. He sees the white flag cast out from heaven, with a proclamation, Is. lvii. 19. " I create the fruit of the lips, peace, peace to him that is far off, and to him that is near."

3*dly,* As guilty criminals, condemned in law, to receive the king's pardon and remission, according to the promise, Isa. xliii. 25. " I, even I, am he that blotteth out thy transgressions, for mine own name's sake." Oh! will the man say with David, Psal. cxxx. 3, 4. " If thou, Lord, shouldst mark iniquity, O Lord, who shall stand before thee? But there is forgiveness with thee, that thou mayest be feared." And therefore, " God be merciful to me a sinner!" So David, Psal. li. 1. " According to thy loving kindness, blot out my transgressions."

4*thly,* They stretch out the hand as supplicants (Zeph. iii. 10) and beggars to receive of God's alms. God says in his word, " If any man lack wisdom, let him ask of God, who giveth to all men liberally, and upbraideth not." Well, when the pride and legality of the heart is broken by the power of the gospel, the sinner comes a-begging at the door of grace and mercy, crying for a supply of all his wants. He hears God sits upon a throne of grace, calling the poor, blind, and naked, to come " without money, and without price, to receive grace and mercy to help in a time of need;" and therefore he stretches out the hand in a way of supplication, that God, for Christ's sake, may " supply all his need, according to his riches in glory by Christ Jesus."

5*thly,* The sinner stretches out the hand unto God, as a servant, to work the work of God, and to do whatsoever he commands him. " Lord, what wilt thou have me to do?" Acts ix. 6.

6*thly,* As a soldier to fight the Lord's battles against sin, Satan, and the world: " Oh! do not I hate them, O Lord, that hate thee, and am not I grieved with those that rise up against thee?" Psal. cxxxix. 21.

7*thly,* As a blind creature, that needs to be guided in the way that he knows not. Isa. xlii. 16. " I will bring the blind by a way that they know not." Well, says the poor soul, Lord be a leader unto me, for " good and upright is the Lord, therefore will he teach sinners in the way," Psal. xxv. 8.

8*thly,* As the hand of a distressed child unto a tender-hearted father. No sooner is the heart of a sinner touched by the power of gospel grace but he begins to cry unto God, Abba, Father; Father, help; Father, heal; Father, relieve; and this is what the Lord delights in, and desires, as you see, Jer. iii. 4. " Wilt thou not from this time cry unto me, my Father;" and oh! how are his bowels sensibly touched with this cry; as you see in the case of the prodigal, Luke xv., and of Ephraim, Jer. xxxi. 19. "Is he my dear son?" &c.

9thly, The hand is stretched out as the hand of the bride is stretched out to the bridegroom in marriage. God says in the gospel, "Thy Maker is thine husband; I will betrothe thee unto me for ever." Amen, says the poor soul; a bargain be it; from this time forward, I will call thee *Ishi*, my husband, Hosea ii. 16. And thus that prophecy is fulfilled, Is. xliv. 5. "One shall say, I am the Lord's; and another shall call himself by the name of Jacob; and another shall subscribe with his hand unto the Lord, and surname himself by the name of Israel."

V. The *fifth* thing was, to inquire whence it is that the hand is soon stretched out unto God, when the heart is effectually touched by the power of gospel grace.

Ans. 1st, Because the command of believing, or of stretching out the hand of faith unto God, is peremptory, and admits not of the least delay, 1 John iii. 23. "This is his commandment, that we should believe on the name of his Son, Jesus Christ." From the first moment that this command of the King of kings and Lord of lords was intimate, there has never been one moment of time allowed you to continue in your unbelief; no, "To-day, if ye will hear his voice, harden not your hearts," Psal. xcv. 7 compared with Heb. iii. 7 and iv. 7.

2dly, The sinner, whose heart is touched, is aware of the dangerous condition he is into, before the hand be stretched out unto God in a way of believing. He is convinced that he is condemned already, and that the wrath of God abideth on him; he sees the avenger of blood pursuing him, and ready every moment to seize him, and therefore he will lose no time, but, like Ethiopia, soon stretch out his hand to God.

3dly, They soon stretch out their hands unto God, because God has been long stretching out his hand to them, Rom. x., last, "But to Israel he saith (viz., by Isaiah, chap. lxv. 2.) All day long have I stretched out my hands unto a gainsaying and disobedient people." O, will the soul say, has God's hand been stretched out all day long unto me, and have I been disobedient, and pulled back my hand from him? O, if I have done so wickedly and foolishly, through grace, I will do so no more.

4thly, Because much precious time is already lost in the serving of sin, and the time to come is so uncertain and short, that it cannot be lippened to, Rom. xiii. 12, 13. "And that knowing the time, that now it is high time to awake out of sleep. The night is far spent, the day is at hand; let us therefore cast off the works of darkness, and let us put on the armour of light."

5thly, They soon stretch out their hand to God, because Christ has made them willing in the day of his power; he has made a discovery of his glory, beauty, and excellency, to their souls, whereby their hearts and wills are sweetly bended to an infalling with his own call, Psal. cx. 3. "Thy people shall be willing in the day of thy power;"

and then it immediately follows, "In the beauties of holiness from the womb of the morning; thou hast the dew of thy youth."

6*thly,* They soon stretch out the hand to God, because they are made to see, in gospel light, God's glory, and their own salvation, concerned in the matter. By faith in Jesus Christ, or a ready complying with the gospel call, we at the same time glorify God's faithfulness, power, wisdom, and other perfections; and likewise secure our own eternal salvation; for "whosoever believeth in him shall not perish, but have everlasting life," John iii. 16.

VI. I might here also touch upon the certainty of the event. For here it is not said, Peradventure *Ethiopia* may *stretch out her hands unto God,* no, but it shall be so, *Ethiopia* shall *stretch out her hands unto God.*

Now, the certainty of the event turns upon these four things.

1*st,* Upon the purpose of God, which can never miscarry; "for the counsel of the Lord standeth for ever, the thoughts of his heart unto all generations." His decrees are like mountains of brass that are immoveable; and therefore, says the apostle, Rom. xi. 7. "The election hath obtained it, and the rest were blinded." As many as were ordained to eternal life shall believe, shall stretch out their hands unto God.

2*dly,* Upon the purchase of Christ. God the Father gave a select company of Adam's posterity unto Christ, whom he redeemed, not by corruptible things, such as silver or gold, but by his own precious blood; and of all that the Father gave him, whom he hath bought with such a valuable ransom, he will lose none, but will present them to his Father at the end of the day, saying, "Here am I, and the children whom thou hast given me," Isa. viii. 18, and Heb. ii. 13.

3*dly,* Upon the promise of God recorded in his word, which is nothing else than the extract of the purpose of his heart. He has said, "Ethiopia, and the Gentile world, shall stretch out their hand unto God: Thy people shall be willing in the day of thy power: And all that the Father giveth me shall come unto God." And hath he pledged his faithfulness in the promise, and "will he not do it? Hath he spoken it, and shall it not come to pass?"

4*thly,* Upon the power and efficacy of divine grace, the iron sinew of the obstinate will is bended to an infalling with the offers of Christ, and of salvation through him; and therefore it is, that they quickly and readily stretch out the hand to God.

VII. The *seventh* thing is the use of the doctrine.

Use first shall be of *Information.*

See hence, *first,* the deplorable condition of sinners by nature, before the gospel is preached to them, and before gospel grace call them effectually. Why, like the Ethiopians, they were sitting in darkness, and in the region and shadow of death. Yea, not only they that want the gospel altogether, but they that have it and do not believe it, do not improve the means of grace and salvation, are resembled unto the Ethiopians, Amos ix. 7. "Are ye not as children of the

Ethiopians unto me, O children of Israel? saith the Lord;" no better than heathens and barbarians.

2dly, See hence the efficacy and power of the gospel, when accompanied with the Spirit of God. Why it, as it were, washes and changes the Ethiopian; it makes the sinner, who was stretching out his hands unto strange gods, to stocks and stones, to stretch out his hand unto the only living and true God. It changes the nature of the sinner, and "turns him from darkness unto light, and from the power of Satan unto God," Acts xxvi. 18.

3dly, See hence that God had an ancient kindness for the Gentile nations, and that he had a mind to erect a church among them under the New Testament. Why, here is a prediction of it, *Ethiopia shall stretch out her hands unto God.* God's design of love unto us Gentiles broke out immediately after the flood, in the prophecy of Noah, "God shall enlarge Japhet, and he shall dwell in the tents of Shem;" and in the words of dying Jacob, Gen. xlix. 10, that upon the coming of Shiloh, unto him should the gathering of the people be. He is given for to be a light to enlighten the Gentiles, and for salvation unto all the ends of the earth. "He is set up for an ensign to the nations; to him shall the Gentiles seek, and his rest shall be glorious." O what manner of praise is it that this, and the like ancient prophecies, are now fulfilled, and that our lot is cast in the days of the New Testament, wherein the tabernacle of God is set up among the Gentiles, who were aliens from the commonwealth of Israel during the whole Old Testament dispensation, and that even these isles of the sea are made to wait for his law; and that this day we have opportunity of keeping the solemn feast of his supper! O let us stretch out our hands unto God in a way of praise and thanksgiving, and let "songs be heard from the ends of the earth, even glory, glory to Jesus Christ the righteous," Is. xxiv. 16.

4thly, See from this text and doctrine, that the door of faith and salvation stands wide open to all sorts of sinners, even though they be as black as Ethiopians, through their lying among the pots of sin, yet the grace of the gospel casts a favourable look towards you, as you see, ver. 13 of this psalm where my text lies, "Though ye have lien among the pots, yet (if ye stretch out the hand of faith unto a God in Christ) shall ye be as the wings of a dove covered with silver, and her feathers with yellow gold." See, to this purpose, Is. i. 18; Jer. iii. 1. And, therefore, let no sinner give way unto despairing thoughts, as if the grace and call of the gospel did not concern them, for sinners of all sorts and sizes are called, and have been actually brought unto Christ, who "came not to call the righteous, but sinners to repentance," Matth. ix. 13.

5thly, See from this doctrine the folly and wickedness of the sin of unbelief, which is a drawing back the hand from God, instead of a stretching it out unto him. Hence unbelievers are said to stop the ear, and pull away the shoulder, Zech. vii. 2, "and say unto God, Depart from us, for we desire not the knowledge of thy ways. What is the Almighty that we should serve him?" Job xxi. 14. O how many such are there who sit under the drop of the gospel! Sirs, remember that God will resent such treatment, Prov. i. 24—27, "Because I have called, and ye refused, I have stretched out my hand, and no man regarded; but ye have set at nought all my counsel, and would none of my reproof: I will also laugh at your calamity, I will mock when your fear cometh, when your fear cometh as desolation, and your destruction cometh as a whirlwind, when distress and anguish cometh upon you." The Ethiopians will rise in judgment against all such.

6*thly*, See from this doctrine how the covenant of peace and friendship is established betwixt God and the guilty sinner, in the day of conversion; why God's hand is stretched out all the day long, in the dispensation of the gospel, beseeching rebellious sinners to be reconciled to him, through the death and blood of his Son, whereby his justice is satisfied, 2 Cor. v. 19, compared with Is. lxv. 2. Now, in the day of conversion the sinner, like Ethiopia, stretches out his hand unto God. He casts away the weapons of war against God, and submits unto the offers of peace and reconciliation made in the gospel; he gives the hand unto the Lord, as the expression is, 2 Chron. xxx. 8; where good King Hezekiah, proclaiming the passover to Judah and Israel, exhorts them to yield themselves unto the Lord. The word in the original is, "Give the hand to the Lord." So that, when a sinner believes in Christ, he, as it were, strikes hands with the Lord, upon the footing of the great sacrifice of atonement. And this I take to be the meaning of that word, Psal. l. 5, "Gather my saints together unto me, even those that have made a covenant with me by sacrifice," alluding unto the ancient custom of cutting the sacrifice in twain, and passing between the parts of it, in making covenants between man and man, &c., Gen. xv. 10—17.

7*thly*, See from this doctrine, wherein the essence either of personal or national covenanting with God doth consist. Why, it just lies in following the example of Ethiopia, which stretched out the hand unto God, in a way of faith and solemn profession, that the God of Christ shall be their God, and that the Father of Christ shall be their Father; and that in the strength of the grace that is in Jesus, promised in a new covenant of grace, they will cleave unto him by a personal holy walk and conversation; and that, through grace, they will cleave unto the doctrine, discipline, worship, and government, that he has appointed in his house, in his holy oracles. It must be a strange kind of a spirit, that either sets his people on edge against such covenants, or turns them to an indifferency about the public work and cause of Christ, as if it were not worth the contending for, or suffering for. When God commands us to "contend for the faith delivered to the saints," Jude iii., and to "stand fast in the liberty wherewith Christ hath made us free," Gal. v. 1. It appears evidently to be a plot of hell for burying a testimony for our solemn covenants, and for the reformation of Scotland, and for our encouraging judicatories to go on in their course of backsliding from the Lord, and his work and way.

8*thly*, See hence what is the proper duty of all, but especially of every one that is come up to keep the Lord's passover, even like

Ethiopia, to stretch out the hand to a God in Christ, reconciling the world to himself, by the death and blood of his eternal Son. O, is there any soul in all this company, that will draw back the hand from receiving the Christ of God, his unspeakable gift? He and his righteousness, and whole salvation, is brought to our hand, that ye may receive him, as your own property, for ever. You stand absolutely in need of him; for, without him, you are undone. But I cannot stand at present upon motives.

Object. 1. "You bid me stretch out my hand to God, in order to receive his unspeakable gift; but, alas, I have nothing in my hand, no good to commend me to God."

Ans. Faith (when it comes to receive Christ), it is the beggar's hand, which comes not to give, but to get Christ, and all with him for nothing, Isa. lv. 1. "Ho, every one that thirsteth, come ye to the waters, and he that hath no money; come ye, buy and eat, yea, come, buy wine and milk, without money and without price." Rev. xxii. 17. "And the Spirit and the bride say, Come: And let him that heareth, say, Come: And let him that is athirst come; and whosoever will, let him take the water of life freely."

Object. 2. "My hands are so black with sin, the abominable thing that God hates, that I am ashamed and confounded when I think of stretching out the hand to Christ."

Ans. That moment ye lay hold on Christ, " ye are washed, ye are sanctified, ye are justified in the name of the Lord Jesus, and by the Spirit of our God." See what black hands Peter's hearers had, Acts ii. 23, and iii. 14, 15, when they were reeking with the blood of Christ; yet the promise of life and salvation is tendered to them through Christ, by the apostle, ver. 38. "Repent, and be baptized, every one of you, in the name of Jesus Christ, for the remission of sins; and ye shall receive the gift of the Holy Ghost: For the promise is to you, and to your children."

Object. 3. "My hand is quite withered and impotent, I cannot stretch out my hand, as you bid me."

Ans. If you imagine that it is I only, or any minister, that bids you stretch out the hand of your soul unto God, you quite mistake it; no, it is God himself that bids you stretch out the hand to him, and therefore, out with the withered hand as it is, make the mint, as the poor man did you read of in the gospel, and it shall be restored; for he gives power who commands.

Object. 4. "My heart draws back my hand; when I would do good, evil is present with me; so that, how to perform that which is good I find not."

Ans. If this complaint flow from a conviction of the sin of unbelief, and the prevalency of a body of sin, it is no bad symptom; for we find the apostle Paul, Rom. vii., hath the same complaint concerning himself. And therefore, poor soul, be not discouraged, for he who is the "Author and Finisher of faith, will strengthen thy weak hands, and confirm thy feeble knees."

THE KINGDOM OF GOD WITHIN THE SOUL OF MAN.

LUKE xvii. 21.—For behold the kingdom of God is within you.

THE FIRST SERMON ON THIS TEXT.

THE occasion of these words may be gathered from ver. 20, where you see a question moved by the Pharisees, "When the kingdom of heaven should come?" They had an ill-grounded notion of a temporal kingdom to be reared up by the Messiah; that he would relieve their nation from the Roman yoke, promote the grandeur of their Sanhedrim, make the members of it his peers and princes, his countrymen his life-guard, and all the nations of the world their vassals and tributaries. This, I say, was the carnal notion they framed in their minds of the kingdom of the Messiah; and they are fond to know when that happy time would commence. Unto this question of theirs Christ answers, ver. 20, 21, where he industriously waves their curiosity, as to the time of the Messiah's kingdom, and makes it his business to rectify their mistaken notion, anent the nature of it; and for this end he acquaints them.

1*st*, That the kingdom of the Messiah would have a silent entrance, without worldly pomp and splendour, which was but little regarded by God. And his kingdom cometh not with observation, or outward show and pageantry, as the word in the original may be rendered. When Messiah the Prince cometh into the world, men shall not, like the Athenian newsmongers, be saying of him, Lo, he is here! or Lo, he is there! As when a prince is going with his court from place to place, through his territories, he is in every body's mouth, and they are ready to make it their talk, "The king and his court is in this, or that, or the other place." Christ lets the Pharisees know, that they were but feeding themselves with mere fancies and delusions, while they imagined such things concerning the Messiah and his kingdom.

2*dly*, He lets them know, that the Messiah's empire and government was to be principally established in the heart and soul, where no prince but himself can reign, *For behold the kingdom of God is within you.* Where two or three things are to be considered:

1. The designation given to the Messiah's kingdom. It is called the kingdom of God. Christ, essentially considered, is God co-equal and co-eternal with his Father; and as he and the Father are the same in substance, equal in power and glory,* so they have one and the same kingdom, which ruleth over all. As Mediator, he is his Father's Viceroy; and his great business in this world was to reduce sinner's of Adam's family unto their allegiance to God, from which

---

* Shorter Catechism, quest. 6th.

they had fallen, by the subtlety of Satan, the god of this world, who had drawn them into a confederacy with himself against God.

2. We have the seat of this kingdom of God. It is within you. In the margin it reads, " The kingdom of God is among you ;" and so the meaning is, as if he had said, " You are inquiring after the kingdom of the Messiah, and are not aware that it is already begun to be erected, ever since the commencement of John the Baptist's ministry, who warned you that the kingdom of God was at hand; and now it is already begun. The gospel is preached; the truth of it is confirmed by miracles; the Messiah is already among you, and there are multitudes who already believe in him, and yet you take no notice of all."

But although this sense of the words be very agreeable both to the original and context, yet I shall at present follow the reading of our own translation, *the kingdom of God is within you*, which is also agreeable to the original; and so the meaning is, as if he had said, " You foolishly dream of a temporal kingdom to the Messiah, like that of the kingdoms of this earth; but you mistake it; my kingdom is of a spiritual nature, and it is the glory of my administration, that I do not so much govern the bodies and outward liberties of men, as their hearts and consciences. The principal throne of my kingdom is in the soul, the more noble part of the man."

3. We have the importance of this matter, in the note of attention, Behold; as if he had said, " Your error, with respect to the Messiah's kingdom, is of a dangerous tendency, and, if persisted in, will certainly terminate in your rejection of the true Messiah, and the ruin of the whole Jewish church and nation; and therefore attend to what I say concerning the spirituality of my kingdom, as a thing of the last consequence; *for behold the kingdom of God is within you*. If I do not reign in your hearts, by the power of my grace and spirit, you can have no benefit by my administration."

The doctrine I mention is this, " That the kingdom of Christ in this world is of a spiritual nature, and is principally seated in the heart and soul within man;" *The kingdom of God is within you.*

We find Christ asserting this, when before the bar of Pilate, to be judged for his life, John xviii. 36, " My kingdom (says he) is not of this world: If my kingdom were of this world, then would my servants fight, that I should not be delivered to the Jews: But now is my kingdom not from hence." As if he had said, " Thou hast no reason to entertain any jealousy of my kingdom and government, as though it had any tendency to hurt or disturb Cæsar's government; for it is wholly spiritual, relating to the hearts and souls of the children of men, to reduce them to their obedience and duty they owe, both to God and to one another." Accordingly we find that, through the whole of the Scriptures, his dealings are with the heart or inward man, Psal. li. 6, " Thou desirest truth in the inward parts; and in the hidden part thou shalt make me to know wisdom." " My son (says the Lord by Solomon) give me thine heart." He stands at the door of the heart and knocks; and it is the everlasting doors of the heart that are summoned, with so much solemnity, to be lifted up unto him, Psal. xxiv. 7. But I do not stand farther, at present, in the confirmation of a truth so plain. It will be further evident in the prosecution of the doctrine, which, through divine assistance, I shall attempt in the following order and method.

I. I would inquire a little into the situation and government of the heart, before the kingdom of God come to be erected.
II. I would inquire a little into the nature of this kingdom of God, that is said to be within us.
III. Why it gets the designation of a *kingdom,* and the *kingdom of God.*
IV. How, or after what way, this kingdom comes to be erected.
V. Give some qualities of this kingdom of God.
VI. Show how much the face of affairs within is changed to the better, when the kingdom of God is reared up.
VII. Make some application of the whole.

I. The *first* thing is to inquire a little into the melancholy situation of the soul, or of the inward man, before the kingdom of God be reared up by the power of divine grace.

In general then you would know that, before the kingdom of God come to be within us, our hearts are just a cage of unclean birds. I will tell you of some sad guests that are within doors, before the kingdom of God be set up in the heart.

1st, The devil is within. There are few bodily, but many spiritual possessions in our day, for he rules and " works in the hearts of the children of disobedience," Eph. iii. 2. He sits as commander in chief there, and he says to one lust of the heart, Go, and it goes; and to another, Come, and it comes, to do him service, and promote his interest in the world. Some, when cast into a passion, and injured by their neighbour, are ready to say, " The devil is in such or such a person." Although such a way of speaking discovers little of the fear of God, yet it is a certain truth, of every unconverted person, the devil is really in him; he reigns and rules in the hearts of the children of disobedience. It is his mint and forge, where he frames all his engines for dishonouring God in this visible world. Hence he that commits sin is said to be of the devil. They are his brats and offspring, the seed of the old serpent, " Ye are of your father the devil," for ye do his work, says Christ, speaking of the Jews.

2dly, The world and its vanities are within before the kingdom of God come to be within, Eccles. iii. 11, says Solomon, concerning the natural man, whose portion is in this life; " Also he hath set the world in their hearts;" that is, God, in a way of righteous judgment, gives up men unto sensual and earthly affections, so that the serpent's curse cleaves to them, Gen. iii. 14, " Upon thy belly shalt thou go, and dust shalt thou eat." The man is sensual, not having the Spirit of God, but the spirit of this world, which makes him to lie grovelling among the dust of the earth, feeding himself with ashes, which are rank poison to his soul, " for to be carnally minded is death," Rom. viii. 6.

3dly, All the rotten stuff of a depraved nature is within; every imagination of the thoughts of the heart is evil only, and continually evil. Wickedness, yea, desperate wickedness, is within the heart, before the kingdom of God be reared up there. Atheism lodges there; "for the fool hath said in his heart that there is no God." Enmity against God lodges there; "The carnal mind is enmity against God, and is not subject to the law of God, neither indeed can be." Pride is within, which is just the poison of the old serpent, that he infused into our nature; "The wicked, through the pride of his heart, will not seek after God," Psal. x. 4. What but the pride of the heart keeps sinners from submitting to the righteousness of Christ, and going about, with the Jews, to establish their own righteousness? What but the pride of the heart makes the sinner, like Laodicea, to imagine that he is "rich, and increased with goods, and stands in need of nothing?" What but pride makes them to say to God, "Depart from us, for we desire not the knowledge of thy ways? What is the Almighty that we should serve him?" Job xxi. 14, 15. "We ourselves are lords, and will come no more unto thee." Unbelief, which calls God a liar, is within, in its full reign, before the kingdom of God come to be set up. O, how much need of that caution, Heb. iii. 12, "Take heed, brethren, lest there be in any of you an evil heart of unbelief, in departing from the living God." It is because of the universal ascendant that the sin of unbelief has among sinners under the gospel, that the complaint is so often repeated, "Who hath believed our report?" The darkness of hellish ignorance is within; by nature "we are alienated from the life of God, through the ignorance that is in us."

Not to multiply particulars upon this head, the heart, as Christ informs us, is the very source of all wickedness that is perpetrated upon the face of the earth; for "out of it proceed evil thoughts, murders, adulteries," perjury, and all manner of profanity, Mark vii. 21. It is first acted in the heart before it be acted in the life; hence is that exhortation unto Jerusalem, which every one may apply, "O Jerusalem, wash thine heart from wickedness, that thou mayst be saved; how long shall vain thoughts lodge within thee?"

Thus I have given you a short view of what is within doors, before the kingdom of God come to be within.

II. The *second* thing is to show, what is this *kingdom of God* which he sets up in the heart and soul of man, which is so full of wickedness by nature.

For understanding this you would know that God is said to have a fourfold kingdom—his kingdom of nature, his kingdom of providence, his kingdom of grace here, and his kingdom of glory hereafter.

1st, His kingdom of nature. When God gave a being unto this world, and all the creatures that are in it, he appointed them certain laws, whereby they were to be governed unto the ends he had before him, in giving them a being. Thus, as the God of nature, he gives laws unto the celestial luminaries of sun, moon, and stars, to observe their annual and diurnal motions. And by the same laws of nature, the "birds of the air, the beasts of the field, the fish of the sea, and all that passeth through the paths of the seas," are guided unto their proper ends, with as great order and regularity, as though they were inspired with reasonable souls. By these laws of the God of nature, seed time and harvest, summer and winter, day and night, observe their seasons. This I say is called God's kingdom of nature.

2dly, There is his kingdom of providence, whereby he upholds and governs all his creatures, and all their actions, making them subservient to his own glorious design. And here his government is not tied so down to the laws of nature, but he can counteract them whenever he has a mind; he can invert the order of nature, and stop and countermand his creatures from following their natural course, as when he stopped the motion of the sun in the days of Joshua, and made it return back in the days of Hezekiah; when he restrained the fire from consuming the three children, and the lions from tearing Daniel; and made the waters of the Red Sea to stand up in heaps till Israel had passed through, and the waters of Jordan to run back to their fountains. There is not any creature but is under the command of his providential kingdom and government. This his kingdom "ruleth over all things in heaven, and things on earth, and things under the earth;" angels, men, and devils, and all creatures above or below do his pleasure.

3dly, There is this kingdom of his grace, where he erects his throne of grace, and displays the riches of his grace and love among the children of men, which is just the church militant.

4thly, His kingdom of glory, or church triumphant in heaven, where he reigns among saints and angels for ever.

Now, it is the *third*—viz., his kingdom of grace—that I now speak of. Now, God's kingdom of grace in this world, it is divided into that which is visible and invisible.

1. God's visible kingdom of grace is either universal, consisting of all through the world, that have a credible profession of faith in Christ, and subjection to him, as their Judge, King, and Lawgiver; or it is more particular, consisting of a society of men, professing the name of Christ in a nation, in a province, in a country, or yet in a particular family; for we read of the church of God in a house or family. But then,

2. We are to consider that God has his invisible kingdom, made up only of real believers, who are joined to the Lord Jesus as their Prophet, Priest, and King, not only by the bond of an outward profession, but by an inward participation of his Spirit of faith. This invisible kingdom, I say, is made up of believers only, and they are called his invisible church or kingdom, because his government is principally seated in the hidden man of the heart, which is not obvious to the ocular inspection and observation, but only as the fruits of his internal government in the heart flow out in the life and walk; and hence it is that Christ here says, *The kingdom of God is within you.* And by it I understand the work of grace in the heart of a sinner, whereby every faculty and power, both of soul and body,

which naturally were in rebellion against God, are new moulded, and brought in subjection unto the Lord. The darkness of the mind is made to give way to "the light of the glory of God in the face of Jesus Christ;" the rebellion of the will to yield unto God's will of grace, precept, and providence; the affections, which were scattered among a thousand vanities, are made to centre upon God in Christ, as their proper and ultimate object.

Now, this kingdom within the soul, it is described to us variously in Scripture by the Spirit of God. I shall name a few of these scriptural characters of it, because we can have no right notions of divine and supernatural things, except we regulate our conceptions of them by the revelation of the word.

(1.) Then, it is sometimes called, a being born again, John iii. 6. "Except a man be born again, he cannot enter into the kingdom of God." This was such a mystery unto Nicodemus, that he says, though a master in Israel, "Can a man be born when he is old? Can he enter the second time into his mother's womb, and be born?" As in the natural birth, the child is brought out of the dark cell of its mother's belly, into this roomy and lightsome world, and that with much pain and travail; so in the new birth the sinner is brought out of the dark vault of nature, where it never saw the sun, into a world of grace, where the Lord is its everlasting light; and this cannot be accomplished without violence done unto corrupted nature, which occasioneth for the most part violent throws and pangs, like these of a travailing woman.

(2.) I find it sometimes called a new creation, 2 Cor. v. 17. Our natures are so miserably marred by the fall, that when God comes to erect his kingdom within us, he finds no pre-existent matter out of which to form it; and therefore the same creating power that was put forth in framing of the heavens, and laying the foundations of the earth, must be put forth in rearing up his kingdom in the soul.

(3.) Sometimes it is expressed by a liberating of the captive from his bondage and prison in which he is shut up, Isa. lxi. 1.

The sinner is led captive by Satan at his will; he has the cords and bonds of iniquity wreathed about the poor soul, and has him shut up in a dungeon of darkness, that he cannot see his sin and slavery, or the way of his escape. Now, when Christ, the Captain of salvation, comes by his word and Spirit, to rear up the kingdom of God in the soul, he breaks in pieces the fetters of captivity; he says to the prisoners, Come forth, and to him that sits in darkness, shew thyself. And whom the Son thus makes free, they are free indeed, preferred unto the glorious liberty of the children of God.

(4.) It is called a revealing of Christ in the soul, Gal. i. 15, 16. "It pleased God to reveal his Son in me. The vail and face of covering is rent, and the light of the knowledge of the glory of God in the face of Jesus Christ shines into the heart," whereby the man, that was formerly darkness, becomes light in the Lord. And in this light of the Lord, the man, who was blind, is made to see light clearly, insomuch, that he wonders at every thing in the revelation of the word, especially he falls a-wondering at the glory of Christ's person and undertaking, saying, "Without controversy, great is the mystery of godliness: God was manifested in the flesh." He wonders at the glory of the divine attributes and perfections displayed in his person and work, saying, "Who is a God like unto thee?" Micah vii. 18.

(5.) It is called a-being joined to the Lord; he that "is joined unto the Lord is one spirit." The man now begins to hold Christ as a new Head of influence and government. He quits the first Adam as a covenant head, and becomes dead to all expectation of life and righteousness by Adam's covenant, and is married to a better husband. He quits the devil as his head and ruler, the old head of apostacy and rebellion, and joins himself to the Lord Jesus as his Head, and holds him as a Head from whom, as by joints and bands, he has nourishment ministered, whereby he is made to increase with the increase of God, Col. ii. 19.

(6.) It is sometimes called a resurrection, Eph. ii. 1: the sinner is dead in trespasses and sins, and behold he stinketh, as it is said of Lazarus, John xi. 39. He is quite putrefied in the grave of sin, "no soundness in him, from the sole of the foot, even unto the head," no principle of life; but when God comes to set up his kingdom within, the spirit of life which is in Christ Jesus, enters, and makes him a partaker of the first resurrection; the dry bones are made to live, by the blowing of the four winds of the influences of the Holy Ghost.

(7.) It is sometimes called God's workmanship; ye are "his workmanship, created in Christ Jesus unto good works," Eph. ii. 10, and Philip. i. 6; it is called a good work, "He that hath begun a good work in you, will perform it until the day of Jesus Christ." The erection of this spiritual kingdom in the soul is the work of God, it carries the peculiar stamp of God upon it; and it is a good work, because it is a work whereby the ruins of the fall of Adam are repaired, and the image of God is restored, &c.

Many other names are given in Scripture unto this kingdom of God in the soul; for instance, it is called a being dead to the law, and a being married unto Christ. Sometimes a being drawn with the cords of a man, and bands of love. Sometimes the baptism of the Holy Ghost. Sometimes an opening of the eyes of the blind, and a turning from darkness unto light. Sometimes a being saved, and called with an holy calling. Sometimes an opening of the heart; a lifting up of the everlasting gates to Christ. Sometimes a circumcising the heart to love the Lord. These, I say, and many other scriptural accounts we have of it, and here it is called *the kingdom of God within* a man. Which brings me to

THE SECOND SERMON ON THIS TEXT.

III. THE *third* thing proposed, which was, to inquire why this kingdom of grace in the heart is called a *kingdom*, and *the kingdom of God*.

1st, A kingdom, you know, is the common residence of the king.

So the renewed heart is the residence of "the King eternal, immortal, and invisible, the only wise God." Isa. lvii. 15. "Thus saith the high and lofty One that inhabiteth eternity, whose name is holy, I dwell in the high and holy place," unto which no man can approach, and "with him also that is of a contrite and humble spirit, to revive the spirit of the humble, and to revive the heart of the contrite ones." The gracious soul is built up "an inhabitation of God through the Spirit; I will dwell in them, and I will walk in them, saith the Lord." The expression is amazing, it imports a fixed residence, and that with wonderful pleasure and satisfaction.

2dly, A kingdom has its laws by which it is governed.

So in the heart of the believer the law of God is established; "I will put my law in their inward parts, and write it in their hearts," Jer. xxxi. 34. It is said of the righteous man, "The law of his God is in his heart, none of his steps shall slide," Psal. xxxvii. 31. The grace of God doth not teach or lead to lawless liberty in sin; no, but it teaches to deny "all ungodliness and worldly lusts, and to walk soberly, righteously, and godly, in this present world." Indeed the doctrine of grace floating in the head, may possibly lead men of corrupt hearts, through their own mistaken notions of the grace of God, to argue as some did in the apostle's days, "Let us sin, that grace may abound." But the grace of God, when it fastens upon the heart, it teaches to deny all ungodliness. And how doth it teach this? But by engraving the law of God in the heart, or by casting the heart into that mould of holiness that the law of God requires, and then the man delights "in the law of the Lord after the inward man;" and having a transcript of the law within, obedience to it in the outward walk becomes just the man's element, so that he "rejoices and works righteousness, and remembers the Lord in his ways; my soul breaketh for the longing that it hath unto thy righteous judgments at all times," Psal. cxix. 20.

3dly, A kingdom hath its courts of equity, where right and wrong are determined.

So there is a court of justice established in the spiritual kingdom which is set up within, I mean the court of conscience informed and instructed. The law of God being written on the heart by the finger of the eternal Spirit, conscience, God's deputy, reads and understands it, and either accuses or excuses, according as his actions are agreeable or disagreeable unto the law of God, which he has given him as the rule of his obedience. It is true there is something like this to be found in the Heathen, and men who are yet in a natural state, as you see, Rom. ii. But when the kingdom of God comes to be set up in the soul, the great Lord of the court he purges it from dead works, whereby it had been defiled and stupified, supports the authority of his own deputy, renews his commission, and commands every action of the heart or life to be strictly tried and examined at its bar, declaring, that what conscience, according to his law, binds on earth, shall be bound in heaven, and what it approves on earth shall be approved in heaven. And hence comes that tenderness of heart and life that is to be found among those that are truly exercised unto godliness, which the world are ready to ridicule, under the notion of needless nicety, and precise singularity, and what not; and are ready to think it strange that they run not with them unto the same courses of riot or defection. Why, the matter is this, the man is afraid if he walk as others do, he shall transgress the law of God which he finds in his heart, and so be arraigned and condemned before the bar of his own conscience, and have the sentence ratified in heaven by the Lord of the conscience; and before he run the risk of a condemning conscience, and a frowning God, he would rather have all the world glooming and looking down, well knowing that the smiles of the world and their mirth and jollity will do him little service when under the challenges of an awakened conscience, and the terror of an angry God; whereas, if God and his deputy approve of him in his way, he is capable to rejoice in tribulation, distress, famine, nakedness, and all outward misery, saying with Paul, "Our rejoicing is this, the testimony of our conscience, that in simplicity and godly sincerity, not in fleshly wisdom, but by the grace of God, we have had our conversation in the world."

4thly, A kingdom hath its treasury and storehouse. We frequently hear of the public treasures of the king.

So this spiritual kingdom of God that is within has its storehouse; but, with this difference, that the stores of other kingdoms are within them, but the storehouse of this invisible kingdom lies without it, namely, in Christ, who is the Head of the kingdom; for, it hath "pleased the Father, that in him should all fulness dwell,—that out of his fulness we should receive grace for grace," Col. i. 19, John i. 16. And herein lies one of the principal differences between God's way, with Adam in innocency, under a covenant of works, and his way with believers under a covenant of grace. God gave Adam the flock in his own hand, with a promise of life if he improved it, and a threatening of death and eternal ruin if he lost and spent it; but, in the covenant of grace, God will not trust man with the flock, but he has laid it in the hand of Christ, as the Head of the new covenant, and the promise of life is not made to us directly, but to him, and all that embrace him by a faith of his own operation; for "this is the record that God hath given unto us eternal life, and this life is in his Son, and he that hath the Son, hath life," 1 John v. 11, 12.

5thly, A kidgdom commonly has its enemies, both foreign and intestine, with whom it wages war.

Just so is it with the kingdom of God reared up in the heart by the power of divine grace. It has foreign enemies with whom it is continually grappling. Satan, the god of this world, and all his auxiliaries, "the lust of the flesh, the lust of the eye, and the pride of life," are continually at war to ruin it. Hence is that of the apostle, "We wrestle not against flesh and blood only, but against principalities and powers, against the rulers of the darkness of this world, against spiritual wickednesses in high places." And then this kingdom is at war with the intestine enemy of indwelling sin, remaining atheism, remaining enmity, unbelief, pride, carnality, hypocrisy; these lie lurking in the secret corners of the soul, waiting all opportunities to betray it into the hand of the devil and the world from without; and therefore the poor believer is obliged to keep even his own heart with all diligence. Many a hot battle has the grace of God within, with indwelling corruption, when none in all the world knows it; "the flesh lusteth against the Spirit, and the Spirit against the flesh, and these two are contrary the one to the other;" which made the apostle Paul to cry, "I find a law in my members, warring against the law of my mind, and bringing me into captivity to the law of sin which is in my members. O wretched man that I am, who shall deliver me from the body of this death."

6thly, A kingdom hath its magazines for military provision. We read of David's armoury in the kingdom of Israel, where did hang the shields of the mighty.

So this kingdom of grace within has its armoury, from which it is furnished with weapons, and all necessary provision for carrying on the war against Satan, the world, and indwelling corruption; and the armoury of this kingdom is none other than the word of God, Eph. vi. 11. We read of the whole armour of God, whereby we are enabled to stand against the wiles of Satan. There we are directed, ver. 14, to have our loins girt about with truth, God's own girdle, for "truth is the girdle of his loins and reins;" the righteousness of Christ revealed in the gospel is to be our breastplate, to defend against all charges and accusations from the devil, the world, or an accusing conscience. Our feet, ver. 15, are to be shod with the gospel of peace, which is the preparation against the rough and thorny paths we may travel in, following the Lamb whithersoever he goes; and then, ver. 16, faith fraughted with the belief of the word, is a shield that defends the soul against all the fiery darts of Satan. The hope of salvation, ver. 17, and "immortality brought to light in the gospel, is a helmet that defends the head against all the showers of temptation that may come from the devil, and the world. And the word of God, skilfully managed in the hand of faith, is the sword of the Spirit's furnishing, which both defends the soul and offends the enemy, and puts him to flight. Thus this kingdom has its armoury.

7thly, A kingdom has its confederates, with whom it is in league, offensive and defensive.

So has this spiritual kingdom of God in the soul: God himself in

Christ is its great and glorious Confederate. At the same time that he disannuls the man's covenant with hell, and his agreement with death, he makes with him an "everlasting covenant, even the sure mercies of David," Jer. xxxii. 40, "I will make an everlasting covenant with them, that I will not turn away from them, to do them good; but I will put my fear in their hearts, that they shall not depart from me." By virtue of this covenant, he is engaged to be their "God for ever, and their Guide even unto death;" to go with them "through fire and water; to strengthen, help, and uphold them with the right hand of his righteousness:" whatever battle they are engaged in, to stand at their right hand, to save them "from them that would condemn their soul:" and whatever piece of work or duty he calls them to, to work in them "both to will and to do of his own good pleasure;" and that he "will never, never, never leave nor forsake them." And thus you see upon what account the work of grace in the soul is called a kingdom. Like a kingdom it is the residence of the great King; it has laws by which it is governed, it has a court of equity where all iniquity is condemned, it has its treasury that is inexhaustible; it has its wars, foreign and domestic, it has its magazines for military provision, and its confederates with whom it is in league, even a reconciled God in Christ, who makes "a covenant for them with the beasts of the field, and with the fowls of heaven, and with the creeping things of the ground," Hos. ii. 18.

LUKE xvii. 21. — For behold the kingdom of God is within you.

THE THIRD SERMON ON THIS TEXT.

IV. THE *fourth* thing was, to inquire how this kingdom comes to be erected in the soul.

The apostle, we find, gives an account of this, 2 Cor. x. 4, 5, under the notion of a great king, with his armies, invading an enemy's country, laying siege unto his strongholds, reducing them by force of arms unto his obedience; "The weapons of our warfare are not carnal, but mighty through God to the pulling down of strong holds, casting down imaginations, and every high thing that exalteth itself against the knowledge of God, and bringing into captivity every thought to the obedience of Christ." Where, to illustrate the matter in hand, we may notice these few things.

1st, The state and condition of the heart and soul of man, when God, by the power of his Word and Spirit, comes to make an attack upon it, in order to establish his kingdom; it is in a state of hostility, fortified as with strong holds, walls, and high towers and bulwarks, against all attacks that may be made upon it. Unbelief, ignorance, pride, self-conceit, carnal wisdom and policy, and the like, they are the strong holds that the devil has reared up in the heart of man against God, and against the power of his word; through the power of natural corruption, the sinner is so depraved that he is wholly in the devil's interest, in covenant with death, and in an agreement with hell. And hence it comes that, when ministers of the gospel, according to their commission, begin to mount the batteries of the law against their corruptions, and come close home to them, to hit their beloved idols, crying aloud, and not sparing them, they are ready to storm and rage, accounting them their enemies.

2*dly*, We may notice the designation given to our work, who are ministers of the gospel. It is called a warfare, and, if we be true to our trust, faithful to God and to the souls of men, we may lay our account with many a hot battle with the lusts and corruptions of men. And hence it is that we shall commonly find faithful ministers of Christ, the very butt of the malice of hell and its emissaries; the strength of battle is against them, commonly in a day of persecution; they may resolve with it to have all the engines of hell employed to ruin them and their ministry. Sometimes, and commonly, the enemy attempts to ruin their name and character by reproach and calumny, in order to render their ministry useless. Sometimes they contradict and attempt to weaken it by nibbling at their doctrine, as the Pharisees did at the doctrine of Christ himself. Sometimes harassing them with prosecutions before their courts, for disobedience unto their iniquitous laws, as the Jewish Sanhedrim did the apostles of Christ, Acts iii. and iv. Sometimes persecuting them even unto the very death, as we see frequently verified in Christ, and many of his prophets, under the Old, and also under the New Testament. Why, what is the matter that faithful ministers are thus the butt of the world's malice? Why, the matter is, they are engaged in a warfare against the lusts and corruptions of the world, and by their testimony they torment them that dwell upon the earth; and therefore they "make war against the witnesses (Rev. xi. 7), and go about to kill them, and cast out their names as evil, and their dead bodies in the streets," that they may be rid of them, and of their testimony both; and because of these and the like hardships they meet with, they are sometimes, through the weakness of nature, put to cry with Jeremiah, "Wo is me, my mother, that thou hast born me a man of strife, and a man of contention unto the whole earth," Jer. xv. 10.

3*dly*, We have the design of this warfare that ministers of the gospel are employed in. It is not to destroy the persons, or ruin the worldly interests of men, but to save their souls, by rescuing them from the slavery and bondage of Satan, and their own lusts, and bring them into the glorious liberty of the sons of God; or, as the apostle expresses it in the close of the fifth verse, "to bring every thought into captivity unto the obedience of Christ." Sinners are the devil's captives, led about by him in the chains of their own lusts: and so much are they in love with the devil's slavery, that every imagination of the thoughts of their heart is evil only, and continually evil. Now, the design of our warfare, as ministers of Christ, is to proclaim liberty unto the captives, to free them from their slavery, and to reduce them unto their ancient allegiance and obedience unto the King of kings and Lord of lords. And for this end we set the trumpet of the law to our mouth, to warn sinners of their danger, if they continue in the devil's service, and to emit the joyful sound of the gospel trumpet, proclaiming the glorious fulness, suitableness, and excellency of Christ, and the love of God to lost sinners through him; that, by these cords of a man, and bands of love, we may bring " every thought of their heart into captivity to the obedience of Christ, and of God in him, as their only Judge, King, Saviour, and Lawgiver," Is. xxxiii. 22.

4thly, We have the weapons that ministers of the gospel are to make use of in invading Satan's kingdom, in order to the rescue of his prisoners and captives; negatively they are not carnal, not physically carnal. We are not commanded by our great Master to advance or carry on the warfare of his kingdom, with the Popish and Mahometan weapons of fire and sword. Christ never taught his followers to make use of the force of arms, to dethrone kings, and overturn kingdoms, in order to set up his government in the world. When Peter drew the sword on his behalf, he orders him to put it up, for all " they that draw the sword shall perish with the sword." And as the weapons of our warfare are not physically, so are they not morally carnal; that is, the conquest of souls unto the obedience of Christ, is not carried on by the wisdom of words, high strains of oratory or of human eloquence, like some preachers in our day, who go to the pulpit under a pretence of preaching Christ crucified, and instead of that study to tickle the ears and fancies of men with a jingle of fine words, dry heathenish harangues of morality, or at best mere legal stuff, turning the gospel of Christ, with their conditions and qualifications, into a new-fashioned covenant of works, just like the Pharisees of old, who took away the key of knowledge, and instead of opening the gospel door of salvation to poor perishing sinners, shut it up, and would " neither enter in themselves, nor suffer others to enter in," who had a desire after it. I say Christ's kingdom in the heart was never advanced by such weapons as these. The weapons that faithful ministers make use of are not carnal but spiritual; namely, the " word of God, which is the sword of the Spirit," Heb. iv. 12. " The word of God is quick and powerful, and sharper than any two-edged sword, piercing even to the dividing asunder of soul and spirit, and of the joints and marrow, and is a discerner of the thoughts and intents of the heart." Both law and gospel are comprehended under the notion of the sword, or these are the two edges thereof.

1. The law preached in its spirituality and extent, rigour and severity, is an engine to be made use of for battering down the devil's kingdom. Indeed, there is a way of preaching the law that will never harm the kingdom of Satan; Seneca's and Plato's morals never converted any to Christianity. The Pharisees preached the law to the people, but then they pared off the spirituality of it, and confined themselves to the bare letter, which made men to imagine that they might be saved by their own obedience, and thus they settled them upon a sandy foundation. The way of preaching the law, so as to pull down Satan's strong holds, is to preach it as Christ himself preached,

particularly in his sermon upon the mount, by entering into its spirituality, as ransacking the souls and consciences of men, and showing how, by the least sinful thought or word, they become thereby liable unto eternal wrath and vengeance, according to that of the apostle, Gal. iii. 10, "Cursed is every one that continueth not in all things which are written in the book of the law to do them." By this way of preaching the law, men become dead to the law, sin becomes exceeding sinful, it revives and appears in its native hellish hue, whereby the sinner dies to all conceit of his own ability, strength, or righteousness, and thus it is a schoolmaster to lead us unto Christ, that we may be justified by faith.

2. Another weapon or edge of the sword of the word of God, is the gospel of the grace of God through an incarnate God, a crucified Christ. "We preach Christ crucified (says the apostle), to the Jews a stumbling block, and to the Greeks foolishness; but to them which are called, both Jews and Greeks, Christ the power of God, and the wisdom of God." "I determined not to know anything among you (says Paul to the Corinthians), save Jesus Christ, and him crucified." By this weapon it was that the apostles of Christ invaded the devil's kingdom of darkness, whereby the idols of the heathen nations were brought down, the devil's oracles silenced, his slaves and votaries brought over to the obedience of Christ, and the Mosaic economy unhinged; and it is nothing but a vain chimera and imagination of men's brains, destitute of the true knowledge of religion and Christianity, who think they advance the interest of Christ in the souls of men by any other means. Now, we are told here that these weapons of law and gospel are mighty through God. It is not they are mighty through our eloquence, or through the excellency of the instrument; no, no, Paul may plant, and Apollos water, but it is God that gives the increase; all depends upon the concurring efficacy of the Spirit of the Lord: "Not by might, nor by power of man, but by my Spirit, saith the Lord of hosts," Zech. iv, 6. "He puts the treasure in earthen vessels, that the excellency of the power may be of God and not of man," 2 Cor. iv. 7.

3. We may notice the glorious effects produced by these weapons of the word, the artillery of Christ's kingdom. What execution do they by the Spirit of God? "They pull down strong holds; they cast down imaginations, and every high thing that exalteth itself against the knowledge of God, and bring every thought into captivity to the obedience of Christ." Where again briefly we may notice

(1.) The great end aimed at by the artillery of the gospel, committed into the hands of ministers and ambassadors of Christ. It is twofold:

[1.] To convey the knowledge of God; and [2.] To bring them to the obedience of Christ.

[1.] I say, to bring them to the knowledge of God: "For this is life eternal, to know the only true God, and Jesus Christ whom he hath sent." Sinners have lost all saving knowledge of God, of his nature, of his will, of his perfections, insomuch that they are alienated from the life of God, through the ignorance that is in them. Now, the design of the gospel revelation is to make God known as he is in

Christ, reconciling the world unto himself; to publish his name to be "the Lord God, merciful and gracious, forgiving iniquity, and transgression, and sin," that so knowing the excellency of his loving kindness, they may be engaged to "put their trust under the shadow of his wings."

[2.] Another end of the gospel revelation is to bring sinners unto the obedience of Christ, and of God in him. God has set his Christ as King in his holy hill of Zion ; he has appointed all flesh to hear and obey him, to receive the law, and all the discoveries of the mind of God, from him. It is his will "that all men should honour the Son, even as they honour the Father;" and for this end he hath "highly exalted him, and given him a name which is above every name, that at (or in) the name of Jesus, every knee should bow, of things in heaven and things in earth, and things under the earth ; and that every tongue should confess that Jesus Christ is Lord, to the glory of his eternal Father," Phil. ii. 9—11. Now, when these designs of the gospel revelation are obtained, the victory is the Lord's, and the kingdom of God is reared up in the soul. But,

(2.) We may notice the strong opposition that lies in the way of the sinner's being brought to the knowledge of God, and obedience of Christ. Why, there are strong holds, imaginations, high things, and swarms of disobedient thoughts.

[1.] By strong holds, I think we are principally to understand original sin, which is called strong holds in the plural number, because it is seated in every faculty and affection, and because of the many fastnesses that original sin has in the heart, so that, when it is beat out of one lying refuge, it retires and lurks in another ; and it is called strong because of its advantageous situation, even in the very heart, Rom. vii. 20—23, called "sin that dwells in us ; a law in our members." It is seated in the darkened mind, deceitful heart, obstinate will, seared conscience, irregular passions and affections. It is strong, being founded in our natures, conveyed by natural generation, " I was shapen in iniquity, and in sin did my mother conceive me ;" strong because of its impenetrable nature, called therefore a heart of stone, proof against attacks either from mercy or judgment ; "Thou hast stricken them, but they have not grieved, thou hast consumed them, but they refused to receive correction; they made their faces harder than a rock ; they refused to return," Jer. v. 3.

Again [2.] In the heart of man there are imaginations or reasonings that oppose themselves unto the erection of the spiritual kingdom in the heart. When God's method of grace and salvation is revealed ; when the mystery of a Trinity of persons in one God, the mystery of the union of the two natures in the person of Christ, the mystery of regeneration and sanctification by the Spirit of Christ, and of justification by imputed righteousness without the works of the law, the mystery of the life of faith on the Son of God, and of union to him by faith, and of receiving out of his fulness grace for grace ; I say, upon hearing of these, and the like supernatural mysteries, carnal reason is ready to start up and say, How can these things be ? They cannot go down with corrupt reason, the wisdom of God is foolishness unto man, and hence it comes that we have got a set of preachers in our day who explode all the supernatural mysteries of the gospel; they make their own corrupted reason the standard of revelation, and whatever their reason cannot comprehend, that must be set aside as a piece of enthusiastic nonsense, or mystical divinity, that nobody can comprehend: these professing themselves to be wise, they become fools. A rational religion, as Mr Thomas Halyburton observes, is like to be the ruin of religion in our day and generation.

Again [3.] The apostle tells us here of high things in the heart, that exalt themselves against the knowledge of God, and the entrance of this spiritual kingdom; by which I understand principally the pride, vanity, and self-conceit of the heart of man by nature, which is ready to vent itself in language like that of Laodicea, Rev. iii. 17, "I am rich, and increased with goods, and have need of nothing;" or, like that of the proud Pharisee, Luke xviii., "God, I thank thee that I am not as other men are: I fast twice in the week, I give tithes of all that I possess." Every man in a natural state sits mounted upon an imaginary throne of self-conceit. He is conceited of his own wisdom, though he be born like a wild ass's colt; conceited of his own righteousness by the law, though it be no better than filthy rags; conceited of his own strength and ability to do what is pleasing to God, although he "be not sufficient of himself to think a good thought;" conceited of his own fulness, though he "be wretched, miserable, blind, poor, and naked;" conceited of his own purity and holiness, clean in his own eyes, though he be not washed from his iniquity. These are high things that stand in the way of the erection of the kingdom of God in the soul.

[4.] There are swarms of rebellious thoughts every day, and hour, and moment, bullering up from the source of corruption in the heart; and these taking up their lodging in the soul, every thought and imagination being evil only, and continually evil; every thought of the natural heart which is enmity against God being an act of rebellion against the authority of Christ. So you see what strong opposition there is in the heart against the erection of this kingdom.

(5.) We may notice what execution is done in a day of power upon all these, when Christ comes to set up his throne; strongholds are pulled down, imaginations and reasonings are cast down at the foot of divine revelation, high and proud conceits are levelled, and rebellious thoughts reduced to the obedience of Christ. Take up the scope of this in the following particulars, relating to the way of erecting and maintaining the kingdom of God in the souls or hearts of men.

[1.] Then, God by the power of his Spirit, accompanying the revelation of the word, batters and shakes the foundation of the strongholds of sin and self in the heart; insomuch, that the rocky heart, which before seemed impenetrable, begins to shake and quake within the man, and, through a sense and apprehension of the wrath of God, begins to cry, "What shall I do to be saved? Is not my word a hammer, saith the Lord, to break the rock in pieces?" Jer. xxiii. 29.

[2.] A window is opened, as it were, in the dark vault of the mind, whereby a beam of light is let in, and there is a twofold beam that shines into the heart.

1. A beam of law-light, whereby the vermin of hell that is in the soul, is discovered, and the wrath of an infinite God ready to fall down and grind it into powder.

2. A beam of gospel-light, discovering Christ in his glorious fulness and excellency, every way suited unto the soul's necessity, 2 Cor. iv. 6, 7, " God, who commanded the light to shine out of darkness, hath shined in our hearts, to give the light of the knowledge of the glory of God, in the face of Jesus Christ."

[3.] Christ being discovered, the heart is summoned to surrender and open unto him, as " the Lord of hosts, the King of glory, the Lord mighty in battle," Psal. xxiv. 7; upon which the iron sinew of the will gives way, the gates of brass, and bars of iron, whereby the heart was shut against the Lord, are all broken in pieces by the arm of Jehovah, and the soul is so willing to entertain him, that it cries, as Psal. cxviii., " Open unto him the gates of righteousness, for blessed is he that cometh in the name of the Lord to save us."

[4.] Christ, by his Spirit, comes in and takes possession of the heart, as his temple and dwelling-place, saying of it, as he said of Zion of old, " This is my rest, here will I dwell," Ezek. xxxvi. 27, " I will put my Spirit within them." And thus we are built up an "habitation of God through the Spirit: If any man open unto me, I will come in, and will sup with him, and he with me."

[5.] Being come into the heart, he repairs the breaches and ruins that had been made upon it by sin and Satan while in their possession; he proceeds to garnish and deck his dwelling-place with his own furniture, so that the soul which had lien among the pots, becomes " as the wings of a dove covered with silver, and her feathers with yellow gold ;" and like the " King's daughter, all glorious within," Psal. lxviii. 13, and xlv. 13.

[6.] Satan, and sin, and self being dethroned, a new government is erected, Christ is set up and proclaimed King; his laws intimate, and not only intimate, but, as I said before, written and engraven on the heart, as with a pen of iron. The law of faith to be believed, and the law of commandments to be obeyed, as the only rule of life, unto every one of which the soul says, Amen. O this and that, and the other precept or promise, " is a faithful saying, worthy of all acceptation," 1 Tim. i. 15.

[7.] The soul being thus conquered and captivated to the obedience of Christ, is admitted to new privileges and immunities, some of which are presently possessed, and others secured by the oath of God and his gracious promise. Sin is presently pardoned, its debt paid, and all former obligations to wrath cancelled, " I, even I, am he that blotteth out thy transgressions, for mine own sake." The man's person is accepted by virtue of his union with Christ, the Lord our Righteousness, Eph. i. 6, " He hath made us accepted in the beloved." He has a new name given him; formerly his name was a child of the devil, a transgressor from the womb; but now he gets the new name of a son, a child of God, and this is an " everlasting name, that shall never be cut off," Isa. lvi. 5, "As many as received him, to them gave he power to become the sons of God;" he becomes an heir of the kingdom, "If sons, then heirs, heirs of God, and joint heirs with Christ." Now God says to the man, "All are yours, and ye are Christ's, and Christ is God's: He is admitted to fellowship and communion with God, Father, Son, and Holy Ghost; I will sup with him, and he with me." The Lord says to the man, "Eat, O friend, drink, yea, drink abundantly, O beloved." The soul is brought "into the banquetting house, and God's banner over it is love;" and it can say in some measure "Now verily my fellowship is with the Father, and with the Son Christ Jesus." A royal guard is set about the soul, the guard of the divine attributes, and a guard of angels for his defence, "As the mountains are round about Jerusalem, so the Lord is about that soul; henceforth, even for ever, the angel of the Lord encampeth round about them that fear him." He has the earnest and pledge of the inheritance of glory given him, "In whom also, after that ye believed, ye were sealed with the holy Spirit of promise, which is the earnest of our inheritance."

[8.] War (as you heard) is proclaimed against all other lords and lovers, but Christ himself, and they treated as usurpers and invaders of his kingdom and privileges. "Do not I hate them, O Lord, that hate thee? and am not I grieved with those that rise up against thee? I hate them with perfect hatred; I count them mine enemies." And thus Christ, as a glorious Conqueror, having got possession, he keeps possession of the heart and soul to the very end, saying, "I will never leave thee nor forsake thee; be thou confident of this very thing, that he which hath begun a good work in thee, will perform it until the day of Jesus Christ," when he shall present thee before his Father, without "spot or wrinkle, or any such thing." And so much for the manner of erecting this kingdom of God in the soul.

LUKE xvii. 21.—For behold the kingdom of God is within you.

THE FOURTH SERMON ON THIS TEXT.

V. THE *fifth* thing in the method was to give you some of the excellent qualities and properties of this kingdom of God in the heart.

You have four of them in a cluster, Rom. xiv. 17, where the apostle tells us, "that the kingdom of God is not meat and drink, but righteousness and peace, and joy in the Holy Ghost."

1*st*, He lets us understand, that this kingdom is not of a carnal, but of a spiritual nature; for it is not meat and drink. The men of the world, whose portion is in this life, their cry indeed is, "What shall we eat? what shall we drink? wherewith shall we be clothed?—Who will show us any of this world's good?" But the man who has the kingdom of God within him, is taken up with things spiritual and eternal; he looks not at "things that are seen, but at things that are not seen." He has meat to eat that the world knows not of; for the food of this kingdom is the hidden manna; he "eats the flesh and drinks the blood of the Son of man." The glorious mystery of the incarnation and satisfaction of Christ, viewed and applied by faith, affords him many a sweet meal that the world knows nothing about.

2*dly*, The apostle tells us that it is a kingdom of righteousness. Wherever God reigns, "righteousness and judgment are the habitation of his throne." When he comes into the heart of a sinner, he makes him to submit unto the imputed righteousness of Christ, calling and owning him by that sweet name, Jer. xxxiii. 6, "This is his name whereby he shall be called, The Lord our Righteousness." And then by his Spirit he implants a principle of inherent righteousness for sanctification, which influences the man to the study of holiness in all manner of conversation, so that holiness to the Lord becomes the beautiful badge and livery of the kingdom, Psal. cx. 3.

3*dly*, It is a peaceable kingdom, or rather a kingdom of peace; the "kingdom of God is not meat and drink, but righteousness and peace." These are sweetly connected together, Is. xxxii. 17, "The work of righteousness shall be peace, and the effect of righteousness shall be quietness and assurance for ever." What a calm does it bring into the soul, when, upon the imputation of the righteousness of Christ, God says to the soul, "There is now therefore no condemnation to him that is in Christ Jesus; because the righteousness of the law is fulfilled in him;" all the storms of law terrors are then hushed into a pleasant calm; and what serenity and tranquillity doth it yield to the soul, when it is helped, with simplicity and godly sincerity, to have its conversation in the world, Psal. cxix. 165, "Great peace have they which love thy law;" Gal. vi. 16, "As many as walk according to this rule, peace be on them, and mercy, and upon the Israel of God. Their peace is like a river, and their righteousness like the waves of the sea." This peace is so great a part of the kingdom of God within, that we find the saints in Scripture refusing to throw it up; no, to please the greatest potentates, as in the case of the three children, Dan. iii. 4. And when through untenderness at any time they have been left to di·turb the peace of the kingdom of God within them, they would give a world to have it recovered; as we see in the case of David, Psal. li. He had broken the peace of the kingdom of God within him, by his murder and adultery, in the case of Bathsheba and Uriah. Well, how doth he roar and cry, as if his bones had been all out of joint, Psal. li. 8, xxxii. 3, 4.

4*thly*, It is a very joyful kingdom; "The kingdom of God is not meat and drink, but righteousness and peace, and joy in the Holy Ghost." While this kingdom, I mean the work of grace in the heart, is in a prosperous condition, and is maintained in its purity and power, there is an air of joy and pleasure to be seen through every corner of the kingdom, and the joy of the soul is like the joy of harvest, or the joy of them that divide the spoil, upon the back of a victory. While the streams of the pure river of the water of life, that proceedeth out of the throne of God and of the Lamb, waters the soul, the kingdom of God within is glad, Psal xlvi. 4, and its joy is such as adds no sorrow;

in the midst of the joy of the wicked their heart is sorrowful, and their triumph is short, for a moment. But it is otherwise here, there is perpetual ground of joy and triumph, to them that have the kingdom of God within them. Hence are these and the like commands and calls to the righteous, "Be glad in the Lord, and rejoice ye righteous: and shout for joy all ye that are upright in heart; rejoice evermore, and again I say rejoice." Unto these I add,

5*thly*, That it is a hidden and mysterious kingdom, therefore called "the hidden man of the heart," 1 Pet. iii. 4. The way of its erection is a mystery, as Christ tells Nicodemus, John iii. 8, "The wind bloweth where it listeth, and thou hearest the sound thereof, but canst not tell whence it cometh, and whither it goeth; so is every one that is born of the Spirit." The way of its subsistence and preservation is a mystery, for it is maintained by an invisible communication between Christ in heaven and the poor soul upon earth; this kingdom "holds the Head Christ, from which all the body as by joints and bands having nourishment ministered, and knit together, increaseth with the increase of God." The affairs of this kingdom are such a mystery unto a blind world, that they just wonder at the believer what he is doing, while he is pursuing the interests of the kingdom of God within him, "I am a wonder unto many (says David), but God is my strong refuge;" and indeed they are set for signs and wonders in Israel at this day, Is. viii. 18.

6*thly*, It is a very pleasant and delectable kingdom, exceeding glorious and beautiful; and no wonder, for it is just "the beauty of the Lord our God upon the soul," Psal. xlv. 13. "The King's daughter is all glorious within; her clothing is of wrought gold." The Spirit of God takes the glory of Christ, decks the soul with it, 2 Cor. iii. 18, "We all with open face, beholding as in a glass the glory of the Lord, are changed into the same image, from glory to glory, even as by the Spirit of the Lord." Ye have a very lofty account of the glory of this spiritual kingdom, Is. liv., even when it is covered with affliction, and tossed with the winds and waves of adversity and trouble; when the world can see no form or comeliness about it, ver. 11, 12, "Behold I will lay thy stones with fair colours, and lay thy foundations with sapphires; and I will make thy windows of agates, and thy gates of carbuncles, and all thy borders of pleasant stones."

7*thly*, It is an honourable kingdom; and no wonder, for it is the kingdom of God. There is a greater tribute of honour and glory levied to him out of this kingdom than from all the world beside, "This people have I formed for myself, they shall shew forth my praise." Hence believers are called trees of righteousness, the planting of the Lord, in whom he will be glorified; and that soul that has the kingdom of God within it, becomes truly honourable. They are made "kings and priests unto God—a chosen generation, a royal priesthood, a peculiar people—the excellent ones of the earth," and more excellent by far than the rest of the world, Is. xliii. 3, 4, "Ever since thou wast precious in my sight, thou hast been honourable; and I have loved thee, therefore will I give men for thee, and people for thy life; I gave Egypt for thy ransom, Ethiopia and Seba for thee."

8*thly*, It is a most expensive and dear bought kingdom unto the Son of God; it cost him the travail of his soul before it could be reared up in the heart. Every grain of grace wrought in the soul by the Spirit of the Lord is the purchase of blood, and that not common blood, but of the best blood of the whole creation; "We are not redeemed by corruptible things, such as silver and gold, but with the precious blood of Christ; the redemption of the soul is precious," and had ceased for ever, unless this ransom had been found for it.

9*thly*, It is a thriving and flourishing kingdom; "the righteous shall flourish like the palm tree, he shall grow like the cedar in Lebanon," Psal. xcii. 12. It is true, indeed, this kingdom doth not always flourish and grow in a sensible way and manner, for it is most oppressed and borne down with the strength of temptation, affliction, and trouble; hell and earth are continually seeking to stifle and suppress it; but yet it is habitually flourishing, for out of weakness it becomes strong. The great King, he rules so dexterously in this kingdom, that he makes the very attacks of the enemy subservient to, yea, and all crushing dispensations to resolve in the advantage of the true interests of this kingdom, according to his promise, Rom. viii. 28.

10*thly*, It is a lasting, and an everlasting kingdom; and no wonder, for it is the *kingdom of God*. The everlasting God is the King of this kingdom, and "his kingdom is an everlasting kingdom, and his dominion that which shall not be destroyed," Dan. vii. It is built upon an everlasting foundation, even Christ the "Rock of ages—a Stone, a tried Stone, a precious corner Stone, a sure foundation;" and if this foundation could be destroyed, what should the righteous do? Its charter is an everlasting covenant, Jer. xxxii. 40, "I will make an everlasting covenant with them." It is surrounded with walls that are everlasting, even the perfections of an infinite God which are round about it, as the mountains are about Jerusalem. Thus I have given you some of the qualities of this spiritual and invisible kingdom of God that is within the soul of the believer.

VI. The *sixth* thing was to show how much the face of affairs is changed to the better by the erection of the kingdom of God in the soul.

I have much prevented myself as to this, by what is already said upon the former head. I only add that, by the erection of this new kingdom, the government is quite altered from what it was before. For,

1*st*, There is a new King upon the throne of the heart. Christ, "the King of kings, the Prince of the kings of the earth," rules where Satan had his seat; and O, what a happy change is this! the Prince of life to reign in stead of the god of this world, &c.

2*dly*, There are new laws introduced into the kingdom; "the law of the Spirit of life in Christ Jesus," instead of the law of sin and death. Sin gave laws to the soul, and was wholly under its command, but now the man is under the law to Christ, 1 Cor. ix. 21.

3*dly*, New liberty is brought in, instead of former bondage. The man was under bondage to sin, Satan, the world, the curse, death; but now he is made free by the Son, and so he is free indeed, advanced to the "glorious liberty of the sons of God." Liberty to serve the Lord, and to run the way of his commandments, &c., Psal. cxix. 32.

4*thly*, There is a new light introduced, instead of former darkness, therefore said to be "translated from the power of darkness into God's marvellous light;" the Sun of righteousness arises, and the Lord becomes the man's everlasting light, and his God his glory, Isa. lx. 19.

5*thly*, The man gets a new spirit, "Not the spirit of the world, but the Spirit which is of God, whereby he knows the things that are freely given him of God; (it is said of Caleb and Joshua, that they were men of another spirit than the rest of the wicked Israelites), "a spirit of wisdom and revelation, a spirit of grace and supplication," Zech. xii. 10.

6*thly*, The man gets a new will, instead of the rebellious will and iron sinew; he is made willing to fall in with the will of God; "Lord, what wilt thou have me to do?" Acts ix. 6.

7*thly*, A new object of trust and confidence is set up in the soul. Formerly he trusted in an arm of flesh, but now he trusts in the living God; formerly he trusted in lying refuges, but now he trusts only in the foundation God hath laid in Zion, Isa. xxviii. 16.

8*thly*, A new hope. Formerly he hoped in a thing of nought, but now with Israel, his hope is in the name of the Lord, in a God in Christ, and he flees for refuge unto the hope set before him in the gospel, and his hope, like an anchor, "enters into that within the vail, whither the Forerunner is for us entered," Heb. vi. 18, 19.

9*thly*, He gets a new love to the Lord, instead of former enmity against God; so that he can say in some measure of sincerity, that he "loves the Lord his God with all his heart,—soul,—strength,—and mind." He himself delights in the Lord, and the "desire of his soul is unto his name, and the remembrance of him," Isa. xxvi. 8.

10*thly*, There is just a new heart given the man when the kingdom of God is set up. The heart before was a stony rocky heart, that would not yield either to the word or rod of God. But now he has got the heart of flesh, Ezek. xxxvi. 26, "A new heart also will I give you, and a new Spirit will I put within you." And from hence it is, that the thoughts of the heart take a new turn. The thoughts which wandered after every vanity, do now run after God, after the living God. So that the man can say in some measure, "My meditations of him are sweet, and I will be glad in the Lord: When I remember thee upon my bed, and meditate on thee in the night watches, my soul shall be satisfied as with marrow and fatness." Thus you see there is a wonderful change effected by the erection of this kingdom of God in the soul.

VII. The *seventh* thing in the method was, the *Application* of the whole.

And the *first* use may be of *Information* in the particulars following.

1*st*, Hence see the riches of God's love, and the freedom of his grace in erecting his kingdom in the worst part of the whole creation of God, even in the heart of a sinner, which is deceitful above all things and desperately wicked;" the very seat of sin and Satan, pride, enmity, unbelief. O the freedom of his grace! "His ways are not as our ways, nor his thoughts as our thoughts." Is this the manner of man? No, it is a way peculiar unto God himself.

2dly, See hence whence it is that believers are so highly valued beyond the rest of the world in God's esteem, and why he has such a care of them beyond others. He will reprove kings for their sakes. He will give men for them, and people for their life. He adjusts the whole of gospel ordinances for their edification; gives "apostles, prophets, evangelists, pastors, teachers, for perfecting them." He calculates and adjusts the whole of his providential administrations for their advantage, Deut. xxxiii. 28, "He rides upon the heaven in their help, and in his excellency on the sky." Why, what is the matter that there is such ado about them beyond others? Why? the matter is this, *the kingdom of God is within them;* and ye know a king levels the whole of his administration for the benefit of his kingdom.

3dly, See hence the error of these who prefer the world's great ones to Christ's little ones, in the administration of the affairs of his visible kingdom upon earth. Why, it must be a dangerous error to set aside these, and denude them of the privileges of the kingdom, who have the kingdom of God within them; and prefer these, who perhaps have the devil, and the world, and sin reigning in their hearts, because providence has given them something of the pelf of this world beyond their neighbours. Who so fit to choose officers in the kingdom of Christ, as they that have *the kingdom of God within?* I fear there will be a sad reckoning ere all be done, for the injuries that are done to these whom "God has chosen, rich in faith, and heirs of the kingdom," however poor they be in this world. Perhaps some may be thinking there is no need of such discourse now, after what has been done of late; but, Sirs, I own I am of another mind, and will be so, through grace, till I see the foxes taken that have spoiled, and still are spoiling, the vines, Cant. ii. 15.

4thly, See hence the difference between Christ's kingdom and the kingdoms of this world. Why, other kings rule over the bodies and states of men; but Christ's kingdom relates to the spirit and conscience; and they that impose any thing on the subjects of Christ, that is inconsistent with his laws and liberties, they invade the prerogative of Christ, they impose upon his kingdom, and they that do so will pay for it. "It were better for them that a millstone were hanged about their neck, and they cast into the midst of the sea," than to offend these that have the kingdom of God within them. He will resent it, Luke xvii. 2.

5thly, See hence that heart religion is a thing that God principally regards, Psal. li. 6, "Thou desirest truth in the inward parts." Sirs, all our flourish of a profession, our reading, hearing, communicating, is but the offering of swine's blood on God's altar, without this, see Isa. i. 11-14, Psal. lxxviii. 35-37.

6thly, See hence a good reason why the saints of God should walk circumspectly, and "be holy in all manner of conversation." Why, they should watch and pray, and stand upon their guard against all sin in heart and life, and avoid all appearance of evil. Why, *the kingdom of God is within them;* and have they not good reason to watch and be upon their guard against every thing that may disturb or disquiet the peace of the kingdom. The peace of a kingdom is a most valuable blessing. O Sirs, be upon your guard against all sin, in whatever shape it may appear and present itself, for it will break the peace of the kingdom of God, and if any parley be entertained with these enemies, he will make all the kingdom tremble with his frowns.

7*thly*, See why faithful ministers do travel in birth for the conversion of sinners. Why, they are concerned to have the kingdom of Satan overturned, and the kingdom of God reared up in the souls of their hearers.

8*thly*, See hence whence it is that the saints and faithful ministers of Christ will stand up for the prerogatives of Christ, and the privileges of his subjects, upon their utmost peril. Why, *the kingdom of God is within them,* and therefore they cannot but be zealous for their King, and his prerogatives. Some folk now-a-days are come that length, as to think and say, that these worthies who suffered in the late times of persecution, died as a company of fools, when they would not redeem their lives, by saying, "God save the king." Would you know what was the matter with them? Why, by acts of parliament, the prerogative of Zion's King was taken, and set upon the head of King Charles and King James, and they declared, "In all causes, not only civil, but ecclesiastical, head." And they could not find freedom in their consciences, to pray that God might save a man in his usurpations upon the prerogatives of Christ the King of Zion, whose kingdom they had within them, especially when they knew the enemy would interpret their praying in these terms, a praying for their prosperity and success in such a wicked way. Sirs, they who now-a-days talk at that rate, know little of true tenderness of conscience, or of true zeal for the glory of Christ, as the alone Head and King of his church.

9*thly*, See hence the true spring of reformation in a church or land, and the true spring also of defection and backsliding. Why, when the Spirit of the Lord erects the kingdom of God within, especially in the hearts of magistrates or ministers, men of power and influence; then reformation work goes on apace, men then put to their hands heartily to the building up of Zion; every one then is ready to lend a lift to help up with the Head-stone of the corner. But when the kingdom of God is not within, men lose heart and hand to the work of the Lord, and fall a-work to daub with carnal wisdom and policy, which quite spoils and mars the building, instead of furthering it. What was it that made parliaments, and assemblies, and people of all ranks go so clean to work about the year 1638, and the year that followed it, to advance a work of reformation, and to engage themselves by solemn covenant to maintain it? And what makes the work go on so slowly now? Why, if folk, especially men of influence and power, had the kingdom of God within them, which, alas! is much wanting now-a-days, otherwise there would not be so much daubing with untempered mortar as there is. O Sirs, if ever ye would see the Lord's work thrive again in the land, pray that the same Spirit may be poured out from on high, that he may lay the foundation of the work by setting up his kingdom in the heart of kings, nobles, gentry, ministers, elders, and all ranks of people in the land; and then the hearts of the children will be turned to their fathers, and we may expect to see the church of Christ in this land, "looking forth as the morning, fair as the moon, clear as the sun, and terrible as an army with banners, Cant. vi. 10.

10*thly*, See hence a good reason why honest people who have a real principle of grace, cannot submit unto the ministry of intruders, who enter the house of God some other way than by the door of a lawful call and ordination; and why they scruple to join with these that take such men by the hand, or help them and encourage them in their intrusions. Why, folk that have the kingdom of God within them, they cannot think of committing the custody of the kingdom of God, and the concerns thereof, unto men who want the King's call and commission; and they can never think that they who thrust themselves into the priest's office for a piece of bread, will be much concerned to build up and advance either Christ's invisible kingdom within, or his visible kingdom. I fear there are too many foul fingers about matters of this kind among us at this day, and if the coat fit any that are now hearing me, let them put it on.

11*thly*, See hence the true spring and foundation of zeal for the public cause and interest of Christ; why, it is laid in the erection of the kingdom of God within the soul. Whence is it that the zeal of God's house doth eat up some of the saints? Whence is it that they prefer Jerusalem to their chief joy, and are ready to sacrifice their worldly all for the public cause of Christ in the land or place where they live? Why, the spring of their zeal lies here, they have got the kingdom of God within them; and, Sirs, allow me freely to tell you, that it is good to be zealously affected in a good thing; it is good to be on the Lord's side, in so far as you know his cause; but beware of laying stress upon this, that you are upon the right side of the question; for folk may have a zeal of God, and yet that zeal not be according to knowledge, and therefore will but go a short way in the Lord's reckoning. Folk may cry, "The temple of the Lord, the temple of the Lord, the temple of the Lord are these," and make a great ado and noise about the public interests of the church, and yet want an inward principle and an outward practice correspondent unto such a profession, the Lord declares that such are but "a smoke in his nose, a fire that burneth all the day."

A second use of this doctrine may be of *trial* and *examination*.[*]

---

[*] For this, see Sermon on Psal. lxxxix. 2, "Mercy shall be built up for ever."

THE KINGDOM OF GOD WITHIN THE SOUL OF MAN.

LUKE xvii. 21.—For behold the kingdom of God is within you.

THE FIFTH SERMON ON THIS TEXT.

I PROCEED now to the *third* use of this doctrine, namely, of *Exhortation*.

1*st*, To all in general.

Is it so that God has a spiritual and invisible kingdom in the hearts and souls of his people? Then, Sirs, let me exhort you to make way for the entry of the "Messiah, the Prince, the Lord of hosts, the King of glory," that he may rear up the kingdom of God within you. "His kingdom (he hath declared) is not of this world, it is seated in the heart and soul; and, Sirs, we that are ministers of the gospel come as the heralds of this great King, summoning you to surrender, and cast open the everlasting gates of your souls unto him. Perhaps some of you may think the ministers' words are but wind, it is a vain summons without authority; but, Sirs, the sound of our Master's feet is behind us; and therefore, if you will not hear us, hear himself speaking, and remember that his words are directed to every soul, young and old, within these walls. Psal. xxiv. 17, " Lift up your heads, O ye gates, and be ye lift up, ye everlasting doors, and the King of glory shall come in." The summons is repeated and doubled again, ver. 9, " Lift up your heads, O ye gates, even lift them up, ye everlasting doors, and the King of glory shall come in." And, in case you ask his name, in whose authority we summon you, saying, " Who is this King?" see an answer to that inquiry, ver. 8-10, "The Lord strong and mighty, the Lord mighty in battle. The Lord of hosts, he is the King of glory, Selah." See if you dare sit his summons; if you do, remember it will be to your cost, and upon your peril.

But now, to illustrate this exhortation a little, and enforce it, I shall obviate and answer a few questions, that may be readily moved upon such a summons.

Quest. What is it that you call us to, when you require us, in the name of Christ, to lift up the gates of our souls and hearts to him?

I answer, this lifting up the everlasting gates of the heart to the Lord is one of the expressions of faith; hence we are told, when Lydia believed, the Lord opened her heart while Paul preached, Acts xvi. 14, Rev. iii. 20, says the Lord there unto Laodicea, " Behold I stand at the door, and knock; if any man hear my voice, and open the door, I will come in to him, and will sup with him, and he with me." So here, believing in Christ is called a lifting up of the gates or doors of the heart to the King of glory. Now, there is a two or threefold door that is opened to Christ, when a sinner believes in him.

1st, The door of the mind or understanding must be opened to know him, and apprehend the way of salvation through him. Hence faith is not a blind but a seeing grace. "Look unto me, and be ye saved. Thine eyes shall see the king in his beauty." The eye of the mind is shut and blinded by Satan the god of this world, but in believing it is opened to " behold the beauty of the Lord, and the excellency of our God."

2. The door of the will is opened, so as to fall in with him as a Prophet, Priest, and King, for "wisdom, righteousness, and sanctification." Psal. cx. 3, "Thy people shall be willing in the day of thy power." The will, in believing, embraces the revelation made of him, and by him, in the word; as a Prophet, submits unto his righteousness, as its only defence against the charge of the holy law, and receives the law from his mouth, as its only King and Lawgiver.

3. The door of the affections is cast open unto him. The love, the joy, the delight, and desire of the soul must centre and terminate upon him as the supreme good, and upmaking all of the soul, saying, " Whom have I in heaven but thee? and there is none upon earth that I desire besides thee." So that, when we call you to lift up the everlasting gates to the King of glory, we call you to surrender your whole souls unto him, understanding, will, and affections; and, in your doing so, he comes in and sets up his kingdom within you.

Now, because we deal not with stocks and stones, but with intelligent and rational beings, therefore we must deal with you by rational arguments, to cast open the doors of your hearts unto the Lord Jesus, for it is in this way that he persuades and enables the soul to entertain him. And, O Sirs, look up to the Lord, that the concurring power of his Spirit may come along with what is said.

1. Then, will you consider who he is that calls for entry? It is none other than the "Lord of hosts, the Lord mighty in battle; he who doth according to his will in the army of heaven, and among the inhabitants of the earth." But lest this awful and terrible name should make you afraid, take a view of his name, as it is proclaimed, Exod. xxxiv. 6, "The Lord passed by before him, and proclaimed, The Lord, the Lord God merciful and gracious, long-suffering, and abundant in goodness and truth, keeping mercy for thousands, forgiving iniquity, and transgression, and sin." O Sirs, that which fortifies the enmity of the heart against God is ignorance of that revelation that he has made of himself from a throne of grace, or as he is in Christ. We conceive of him as an implacable and inexorable Deity, and, by conceiving of him thus, natural enmity against God is fortified, and our minds quite alienated from him, through the ignorance of God; he is "in Christ, reconciling the world to himself." Sirs, whenever God is seen, and taken up in the gospel glass, he is seen to be a God of grace, mercy, love, and every way amiable; and it is the view of this that makes the heart to open to him. Hence it is that God is at so great pains, in the word, to take off the prejudices that sinners have taken up against him, by wrapping himself up in our nature, in the person of the eternal Son, and by declaring, under the

solemnity of an oath, that he bears no ill will to us; "As I live, saith the Lord God, I have no pleasure in the death of the wicked."

2. Consider in what quality or capacity he comes in, when the everlasting doors of the heart are opened to him. He comes in the capacity of a lawful proprietor. Sin, Satan, and the world are but intruders; the heart is God's property; it was his seat before sin entered, why then should he not have his own? He comes in the quality of a Protector; and, as a King, he is obliged to protect his kingdom in the soul. He protects the soul against all challenges and accusations from the law, saying, there is no condemnation against this man. He protects against the roaring lion that seeks to devour you; "the God of peace shall tread Satan under your feet." He protects against the malice of the world; "In the world ye shall have tribulation, but in me ye shall have peace. Be of good comfort, I have overcome the world." He comes in the quality of a rich Provisor; "All things are yours: my God shall supply all your needs, according to his riches in glory, by Christ Jesus." He comes in the quality of a wise Manager, bidding you cast all your cares on him. The King takes the burden of all the affairs of the kingdom upon himself.

3. Consider the advantages that shall accrue to you by casting open the everlasting doors to the King of glory. Why, he will set up his kingdom within you. I told you, in the doctrinal part, what sort of a kingdom it is that he rears up in the soul. In a word, the King of glory will dwell in you, and walk in you; he will be to you a Father, and all the privileges of children shall be yours; "The Lord God is a sun and shield; the Lord will give grace and glory; no good thing will he withhold from them that walk uprightly."

4. Consider the extreme danger of refusing to open unto him, till you get the kingdom of glory within you. (1.) You are under the power of darkness; there is just a hell of darkness in the soul till Christ be admitted. (2.) You are dead in sin, under the absolute power and reign of it. (3.) You are under the dominion of Satan, the god of this world; he has a law-right to tempt you here, and torment you hereafter. (4.) You are under the curse of God, and the wrath of God abides on you; and how will you bear that burden?

5. Consider how fond he is to have his kingdom set up within you, and how loth he is to take a refusal. (1.) He calls for access. "Open unto me. My son, give me thine heart." (2.) He knocks, and repeats his knocks and calls. See how often they are repeated, Is. lv. 1—13. (3.) He waits for a good answer from the sinner, waits that he may be gracious, and waits till his locks are wet. He, as it were, is content to reason the matter with sinners, and to answer all their objections.

Object. 1. Says the sinner, I am such a guilty sinner, and my sins so aggravated, that he will never come in to set up his kingdom in my heart. *Ans.* Why, says the Lord, "Though your sins be as scarlet, they shall be as white as snow; though they be red, like crimson, they shall be as wool. I, even I am he that blotteth out thy transgressions for mine own sake, and will not remember thy sins."

Object. 2. Says the sinner, I am wretched, miserable, blind, poor, and naked. *Ans.* Why, says the Lord, that shall be no impediment, 'I counsel thee to buy of me gold tried in the fire, that thou mayest be rich, and white raiment, that thou mayest be clothed, and that the shame of thy nakedness do not appear, and anoint thine eyes with eye salve, that thou mayest see."

Object. 3. To what purpose is all this? I have no power to open my heart unto him. *Ans.* "It is he that works both to will and to do." If thou wilt, thou shalt not want power. The blame in Scripture is laid upon the will: "I would, and ye would not," Matth. xxiii. 37.

Object. 4. My will, indeed, is like an iron sinew, like a stone that will not yield. *Ans.* Well, in this case plead the promise, Ezek. xxxvi. 26, "I will take away the stony heart out of your flesh, and I will give you an heart of flesh;" and that promise, Psal. cx. 3, "Thy people shall be willing in the day of thy power."

Object. 5. What if I be not elected? *Ans.* That is none of your business; at first instance, yield your hearts unto him, and ye shall know your election, and that he has indeed "loved you with an everlasting love."

I shall conclude this exhortation with a few advices. Would you have the kingdom of God within you? Then,

1. Be convinced that the devil has his kingdom within you by nature, and that every thought and imagination of your heart is evil. The flaw lies here: Folk imagine they have good hearts towards God, till they be convinced that they are desperately wicked, and until ——— I despair that ever you will get any good by the gospel. That vain imagination must be brought down; and for this end be much in studying the law in its holiness and spirituality.

2. Receive and entertain the word of the King, for this is the King's chariot of state in which he makes his entry; we receive the Spirit by the hearing of faith: this is the weapon whereby he subdues rebels.

3. Be much in viewing the glory of Christ, for at the sight of him the heart opens. "We, beholding as in a glass the glory of the Lord, are changed into the same image, from glory to glory, even as by the Spirit of the Lord."

4. Put up that petition he has put in thy mouth, "Thy kingdom come." O, he is ready to hear the petition which he himself dictates, and believe that he will hear it, because it is of his own compiling. O wrestle, and wrestle by faith fixed on his promise.

5. Put the key of the heart in his own hand, and plead earnestly that he may give it a turn, and press and urge him with his own word of promise, Psal. cx. 3. "Thy people shall be willing in the day of thy power." Sirs, do not stand out under a pretence of inability, for he is so ready to enter into thy heart, and set up his kingdom within thee, that he is willing to take the whole work on himself; he makes the duty ours, but he makes the work his own. "Work

out the work of your salvation with fear and trembling; for it is God that worketh in you both to will and to do of his own good pleasure," Phil. ii. 12. 13.

Secondly, I come to offer a word to believers who have the kingdom of God within them. You, who by the power of the eternal word and Spirit of Christ, have been determined to submit to the authority of him whom God has set as King in his holy hill of Zion, saying, "The Lord is my King, the Lord is my Judge, the Lord is my Lawgiver." Have the strongholds of thy understanding, will, and affection, been brought into captivity unto the obedience of Christ? Is this the case? Then I offer you (1.) a word of consolation; (2.) Of advice and exhortation.

1*st*, A word of consolation and encouragement to you who have *the kingdom of God within you.* Here is ground of consolation that, as his visible kingdom in the world shall be perpetual to the end of time, so his invisible kingdom, or work of grace in thy heart, is an everlasting kingdom, and "his dominion that which shall never be destroyed." Hell and earth may invade it, and indwelling sin may make insurrection, but the "gates of hell shall never prevail against it," to destroy it utterly. And I will tell you of some securities or strong bulwarks, whereby this kingdom in the heart is preserved.

1. Then, it is secured by the unalterable love of God, "The mountains shall depart, and the hills be removed, but my kindness shall not depart from thee." The sense of his love may be withdrawn, so far as the soul may cry, "The Lord hath forsaken me, and my Lord hath forgotten me;" but that shall not be, "for he rests in his love, and changes not."

2. The purpose of God is a noble security for the preservation of this *kingdom of God within you*, Rom. viii. 28. They are said to be called according to his purpose, the erection of the kingdom of God in the heart is just the execution of the decree, "Whom he did predestinate, them he also called. And we are predestinate to be conformed to the image of his Son." Now, is it possible that the purpose of God can be frustrate? No, no, "The counsel of the Lord shall stand." The golden chain of salvation cannot be broken, or one of the links of it be loosed," Rom. viii. 30, "Whom he did predestinate, them he also called; and whom he called, them he also justified; and whom he justified, them he also glorified."

3. The indenture that the Son of God entered into with his Father, from eternity, in the counsel of peace, secures this spiritual kingdom. When God the Father gave a company of the lost race of Adam unto Christ, he engaged that he would set up his kingdom within them, repair his image, carry on the work of sanctification in them, till he had made them meet for glory; and that at the last day he would deliver up the kingdom to his Father, and say, Here am I, and the children thou hast given me; here I present them without spot, or wrinkle, or any such thing. And God the Father, upon this engagement and undertaking of his Son, promised that he should "prolong his days, and the pleasure of the Lord should prosper in his hand."

So that the counsel of peace between the Father and Son must come to nought, before this kingdom of God can be destroyed."

4. The blood and righteousness of Christ secures this kingdom. Christ has purchased a church for himself. Before he could, by his word and Spirit, take possession of one soul in all Adam's family, he behoved, as their Surety, to fulfil the precept, and to underly the penalty of the law, and to pour out his soul unto death. He comes to the kingdom and government by the expense of his royal blood, and is it to be supposed that his kingdom, which he has bought with the blood of his heart, shall be ruined by sin, Satan, or the world, if he have an arm to defend it? No, no, I will give unto them eternal life, and they shall never perish, neither shall any man be able to pluck them out of my hand. And this he speaks of his sheep, for whom he laid down his life, John x. 15 and 28 compared.

5. The covenant of grace and promise secures this kingdom of God within you. This covenant is well ordered in all things, and sure, and contains all the salvation of his people. "The covenant of my peace shall never be removed. My covenant I will not break, nor alter the thing that is gone out of my lips." See how the work of grace is secured by this covenant, Jer. xxxii. 39, "And I will give them one heart and one way, that they may fear me for ever." Ver. 40, "And I will make an everlasting covenant with them, that I will not turn away from them to do them good; but I will put my fear in their hearts, that they shall not depart from me."

6. The effectual call that the Lord gave thee when he called thee unto his kingdom and glory. He called thee from the power of darkness, and translated thee unto the kingdom of his dear Son; and this call secures the possession of this kingdom of God within thee, for his gifts and callings are without repentance; and how can it be otherwise, seeing he calls them according to his purpose.

7. Thy union with Christ, believer, secures the preservation and the perfecting of this kingdom. The whole mystical body of Christ, and every particular member of it shall be perfected; "neither death, nor life, nor things present, nor things to come, shall separate" between you and him; not one stone shall be turned off the foundation God hath laid in Zion; the mortar by which the stones of the building are knit to the foundation, is so well tempered, and he and they are so cemented together, that hell shall never prevail to loose any one of them; no, God's building shall never be demolished.

8. The new name that God has given thee secures the kingdom of God, the work of grace in the soul. He has given to you who have received him the right, power, or privilege, of being called the sons of God, and this is a perpetual name that shall never be razed. Isa. lvi. 5, 6, "To them that take hold of his covenant he gives a name, and a place within his walls, even an everlasting name, that shall never be cut off." The Son abideth in the house for ever; although the servant may be turned out at term day, yet so shall not the son, who is an heir.

9. The seal of the Spirit secures *the kingdom of God within you*, Eph. iv. 30. Believers are said to be sealed unto the day of redemp-

tion. A seal is either (1.) For secrecy; what men would have kept secret they set their seal upon it; and therefore it is a violation of the laws of society, for any man to break up a sealed letter, but he to whom it is directed. (2.) A seal is used for distinction; merchants seal their goods that they may be known to be their own. (3.) A seal is used for security; charters have the king's seal for further security; and in this respect believers "are sealed unto the day of redemption," he hath "sealed us, and given us the earnest of his Spirit." So Eph. i. 13, 14, "After that ye believed, ye were sealed with that Holy Spirit of promise, which is the earnest of our inheritance." Now, this security of the seal of the Spirit is inviolable; for "the foundation of God standeth sure, having this seal, the Lord knoweth them that are his."

10. The life of Christ secures this *kingdom of God within you*; "Because I live, ye shall live also." It is not so much the believer that lives, as Christ that lives in him. The life of Christ in heaven is employed for the security of the work of grace in thy soul. Believer, he lives in heaven as thy Head, thy Husband, thy Redeemer, thy Advocate with the Father, and he has all power in heaven and in earth for this end, that he might be in a capacity to preserve his kingdom of grace; therefore, says the apostle, "When Christ who is our life shall appear, then shall ye also appear with him in glory," Col. iii. 4.

11. The power of God secures this *kingdom of God within you*, John x. 29, "My Father which gave them me is greater than all, and none is able to pluck them out of my Father's hand." Rom. xiv. 24, He (viz. the believer that has the kingdom of God within him) shall be holden up, for God is able to make him stand. As if he had said, The power of God is so much engaged for the preservation of the work of grace, that it shall never perish, if God's arms be able to maintain it. 2 Tim. i. 12, "I know whom I have believed, and I am persuaded that he is able to keep that which I have committed unto him against that day." 1 Pet. i. 5, "We are kept by the power of God through faith unto salvation." And therefore, believer, thou mayest sing and say, as Jude xxiv., "Now, unto him who is able to keep us from falling, and to present us faultless before the presence of his glory with exceeding joy, to the only wise God our Saviour, be glory and majesty, dominion and power, both now and ever, Amen."

But I need not insist on particulars here; all the attributes of God, and the glory of each of them, is concerned in perfecting and preserving this spiritual kingdom. The mercy of God that gave birth unto it; the wisdom of God that contrived it; the faithfulness of God, yea, his holiness is laid in pawn for the preservation of it; yea, the very justice of God is concerned in the preservation of this kingdom; for justice having received complete satisfaction from the Surety, much obliges—to take care for the preservation of this kingdom, for which the ransom of blood was paid. So that you see how well this spiritual kingdom is secured against all attempts made for its ruin; and is not this unspeakable ground of consolation to you, who have the foundation of it laid in your souls by the Spirit of the Lord? The apostle speaks of it as a glorious ground of consolation to the Philippians, chap. i. 6, "Being confident of this very thing, that he which hath begun a good work in you, will perform it until the day of Jesus Christ."

2dly, A word of exhortation or counsel to you who have *the kingdom of God within you*.

1. See that you answer the motto of the kingdom, HOLINESS UNTO THE LORD. "Let your light so shine before men, that they may see your good works, and glorify your Father which is in heaven." Beware of giving the enemy occasion to blaspheme God, and the work of grace by your untenderness.

2. See that upon every occasion, and in all societies, ye be loyal to your King, wherever you see his laws violate, his name profaned, his authority invaded, or his cause trampled on. Strike in for the honour of your King; "be not partakers with the unfruitful works of darkness, but rather reprove them. Come up to the help of the Lord against the mighty."

3. Wage war with all the enemies of the King, either within you or without you. Say not a confederacy with sin or with sinners; "for we wrestle not against flesh or blood, but against principalities, against powers, against the rulers of the darkness of this world, against spiritual wickedness in high places." Do not fear your enemies, for they will flee, and your King will bear the charges of the war.

4. Keep and guard all the avenues of *the kingdom of God within you*. "Watch and pray that you enter not into temptation." Watch the eyes, "I made a covenant with mine eyes. Turn away mine eyes from beholding vanity." Watch the ears, watch the tongue, and "keep thy heart with all diligence, for out of it are the issues of life. —Be sober, be vigilant, for your adversary the devil, as a roaring lion, walketh about, seeking whom he may devour."

5. Observe the laws of the kingdom as your rule, "As many as walk according to this rule, peace be on them, and mercy, and upon the Israel of God," Gal. vi. 16.

6. Contend for the liberties of the kingdom, even of the visible kingdom of Christ without you, for the loss of this will do great hurt to *the kingdom of God within you*. Gal. v. 1, "Stand fast in the liberty wherewith Christ hath made you free;" freedom from sin, freedom from the law as a covenant, freedom from the world and yoke of bondage, inconsistent with Christian liberty, is the purchase of blood.

7. Keep a correspondence with all that are loyal to our King, and have his kingdom within them, especially in a day of defection and backsliding. Mal. iii. 16, "Then they that feared the Lord, spake often one to another, and the Lord hearkened and heard it, and a book of remembrance was written before him, for them that feared the Lord, and that thought upon his name."

GOSPEL TREASURE IN EARTHEN VESSELS.

2 Cor. iv. 7.—*But we have this treasure in earthen vessels, that the excellency of the power may be of God, and not of us.*

TO gain time, I shall not insist upon the preceding context, however material, but come directly to the words themselves. Where we may notice the following particulars.

1. The connection of the words with what went before, in the aversative particle *but; But we have this treasure in earthen vessels,* &c. The apostle had been speaking great and honourable things of the gospel, which he and the rest of the apostles preached, calling it "the glorious gospel of Christ, who is the image of the invisible God," ver. 4, 6. He had showed that there was the same almighty power exerted in and by the gospel in their own and others conversion, as was put forth in the old creation, when God commanded light to shine out of darkness. Now, that none might attribute this efficacy of the gospel unto the apostles, or other instruments that preached it, he immediately adds, *But we have this treasure in earthen vessels, that the excellency of the power may be of God, and not of us.* Q. d. The very reverse of this imagination is God's design in intrusting us with the dispensation of the gospel, even that his own power might be the more illustriously manifested.

2. We have the designation given unto the gospel of the grace of God; a *treasure*. There are two sorts of treasures we read of in Scripture, and the whole world is taken up either with the one or the other, viz., an earthly or a heavenly treasure; the men of the world, whose portion is in this life, are taken up about the first; but real converts, or true believers, are taken up with the last, according to that word of Christ, Matth. vi. 19, 20, "Lay not up for yourselves treasures upon earth, where moth and rust doth corrupt, and where thieves break through and steal. But lay up for yourselves treasures in heaven, where neither moth nor rust doth corrupt, and where thieves do not break through nor steal." It is the last, viz., the heavenly treasure, that the apostle here speaks of. Why the gospel of God's grace is expressed under the notion of a *treasure* you may hear afterwards.

3. We have the vehicle of this treasure, or the weak means or instruments by which this treasure is conveyed unto God's visible family, it is *in earthen vessels*. Ministers of the gospel are so called, that none may think of them above what is meet; we, who are earthen vessels, cry to men of the same mould with us, as Jer. xxii. 29, "O earth, earth, earth, hear the word of the Lord." You and we are earth in our original, earth in our daily support, and earth in our

end, for dust shall return to the dust. God sees it fit that men that are sprung of earth should be served in earthen vessels.

4. We have the reason why God will have the treasure of the gospel conveyed in such earthen vessels, viz., "That the excellency of the power may be of God, and not of us;" that is, in a word, that the whole glory of the conversion of sinners, and edification of saints unto eternal life, might be ascribed, not to us, who are utterly insufficient of ourselves to think or do any thing as of ourselves, but unto God alone, who chooses such weak means, that no flesh may glory in his presence.

The doctrine is much the same with the words, viz., "That God will have the treasure of his gospel conveyed to his church and people in earthen vessels, that all men may know, that the excellency of its power for conversion and salvation to be of himself, and not of man."

Through divine assistance, I shall observe the following method.
I. Speak a little of the gospel treasure.
II. Of the earthen vessels by which it is conveyed to God's family.
III. Of the excellent power of God, which attends the dispensation of this treasure.
IV. Show that the excellency of the divine power is illustriously manifested in the conveyance of the treasure of gospel grace in such a way.
V. Make application of the whole.

I. I begin with the *first* of these, namely, to speak a little of the gospel-treasure. And here I shall show, 1. What is imported in its being called a treasure. 2. Present you with some parcels of this treasure, for it is impossible to bring it all forth to open view, in regard it is unsearchable.

As to the *first*, What is imported in this designation given to the gospel, while it is called a treasure? To this I answer in these particulars.

1. A treasure consists of something very valuable, for what men do not value, they do not reckon it a treasure. What so valuable as the gospel of the grace of God! O, says David, "How precious unto me are the words of thy mouth! they are better to me than thousands of gold and of silver." Every precept, every promise, every truth of God, is a precious jewel which we are to buy at any rate, but to sell at no rate. "Wisdom's merchandise is better than the merchandise of silver, and the gain thereof than fine gold. They that know the value of it will prefer it unto all the treasures of this world, and take joyfully the spoiling of their goods, rather than part with the least hoof of gospel truth; yea, they will not love their life unto the death, in comparison of the gospel-treasure; hence we are commanded to "contend earnestly for the faith once delivered unto the saints."

2. A treasure consists in something that is very useful and profitable unto the life of men in the world; men never reckon that to be

their treasure which is of no use to them. O, what so profitable unto the immortal soul, as that which brings life and immortality to light to them! "It is profitable for doctrine, for reproof, for correction, for instruction in righteousness; and the man of God is made perfect thereby, thoroughly furnished unto all good works," 2 Tim. iii. 15—17.

3. A treasure consists of something very rare; what is common to everybody is not reckoned a treasure. What so rare as the gospel, even as to the external revelation of it? It is not a thing common to every nation; Psal. cxlvii. 19, 20, "He sheweth his word unto Jacob, his statutes and his judgments unto Israel. He hath not dealt so with any nation." The greatest part of the world at this day know nothing of the gospel-treasure; and among these nations to whom it is come, how few are they that enjoy it in its purity! There is but little gospel to be heard in many of the pulpits through Britain. I have lately seen sermons printed, and highly applauded by some, where there is not one grain weight of the gospel-treasure from the beginning to the end, no more than in the writings of Plato, Seneca, and Cicero. And even where the gospel is preached in purity, how few are they that really receive and entertain it by faith!

4. A treasure commonly lies deep and hid in the earth. They that are in quest of the gospel-treasure must dig for it before they find it, therefore called by Christ "a treasure hid in the field." The field where it lies is the word of God; and they who would find it, they are directed to "seek it as silver, and to search for it as for a hid treasure," Prov. ii. 4. Hence our Lord, to the same purpose, exhorts us to "search the Scriptures, for in them we think to have eternal life, and they are they which testify of me," John v. 39.

5. A treasure implies great abundance of these valuable and profitable things; a man that has but a small quantity of money cannot be said properly to have a treasure. David and Solomon, and other kings, had their treasures, wherein there was great abundance of riches. Well, the gospel it opens a mine of riches which have no bottom; Eph. iii. 8, says Paul, "I preach among the Gentiles the unsearchable riches of Christ." Here there is fulness, all fulness, yea, all the fulness of the Godhead; riches which eye hath not seen, ear hath not heard, neither hath it entered into the heart of man to conceive. "But God hath revealed them unto us by his Spirit," says the apostle, 1 Cor. ii. 9, 10.

6. A treasure implies not only abundance of great and good things, but that they are substantial and durable. Men make no account of the treasures of snow, which melt away and perish. Such are all earthly treasures, they perish in the very using; riches make to themselves wings, and fly away like an eagle, mounting up to heaven till she be quite out of sight. We read of a rich man in the gospel, who, when he had filled his barns with corn, and his coffers with money, said to himself, "Soul, take thine ease, for there is goods laid up for many years." But where were his treasures, when God said to him, "Thou fool, this night thy soul shall be taken from thee, and whose shall these things be?" Yea, worldly treasures frequently melt away

before they are taken out of this world, as we see in the case of Job, who, though to-day he was the richest man in the East, yet to-morrow he became poor to a proverb. But now the treasures of the gospel are durable and substantial; Prov. viii. 21, says Christ, the essential Wisdom of God, " I will cause those that love me to inherit substance, and I will fill all their treasures." This is indeed a treasure to be desired, because it endureth for ever; moth and rust do not corrupt it, and thieves break not through to steal it. So much for the import of the expression, why the gospel is called a treasure.

2dly, I go on to bring forth some of the gospel-treasure, that you may know what it is. But here there are two things I would advertise you of before I proceed. (1.) That it is so great that the tongues of men or angels cannot declare it fully; it has not entered into the heart of man to conceive how great it is; so that it is only some little glimpse of it we can give you from Scripture revelation. (2.) You must not look upon this treasure as a thing you have no concern in, for it is all your own; therefore, while we are telling you of it, you must put to the hand of faith, and apply and appropriate it to yourselves; for " things revealed belong unto you and your children; and unto you is the word of this salvation sent. The promise is unto you and to your children, and to all that are afar off." And therefore mingle faith with what you are to hear, that so you may be enriched for eternity. Well, say you, tell us what this gospel-treasure is, bring it out of the earthen vessels, that we may see and know it.

Well then, *first*, In general, I tell you that Jesus Christ is the Alpha and the Omega, the sum and substance of the gospel-treasure. Christ is all in all; and if you win Christ, you win the whole treasure of the gospel that I speak of. Says Paul, Phil. iii. 8, " Yea doubtless, I count all things but loss for the excellency of the knowledge of Christ Jesus my Lord; for whom I have suffered the loss of all things, and do count them but dung that I may win Christ." And when he went up and down the world from nation to nation, scattering the gospel-treasure among them, what was the amount of it but Christ? Eph. iii 8, " Unto me, who am less than the least of all saints, is this grace given, that I should preach among the Gentiles the unsearchable riches of Christ." 1 Cor. i. 23, 24, " We preach Christ crucified, unto the Jews a stumbling-block, and unto the Greeks foolishness; but unto them which are called, both Jews and Greeks, Christ the power of God, and the wisdom of God." And chap. ii. 2, " I determined not to know any thing amongst you, save Jesus Christ, and him crucified." Col. i. 27, 28, " God would make known what is the riches of the glory of this mystery among the Gentiles, which is Christ in you (margin. amongst you), the hope of glory; whom we preach," &c. Thus, I say, the sum total of the gospel-treasure is Christ; and no wonder, for God is in Christ, who is the alone adequate portion of the rational and immortal soul; " It hath pleased the Father, that in Christ should all fulness dwell, that out of his fulness all we might receive grace for grace," Col. i. 19, chap. ii. 9, compared with John i. 16. But, say you, we would hear something more particularly anent this gospel-treasure. Well, then, I shall tell you of some rich and valuable things to be found in the treasure of the gospel.

1. Then, of all things in the world life is the most valuable. It was a true saying of the father of lies, "Skin for skin, yea, all that a man hath will he give for his life." The mariner will heave overboard into the sea all his most valuable goods and commodities that he has with him to save his life. And if the life of the body be so valuable, what must the life of the soul be? Matth. xvi. 26, "What is a man profited, if he shall gain the whole world, and lose his own soul? Or what can a man give in exchange for his soul?" The redemption of the soul is precious, and ceaseth for ever as to any ransom that man can give for it. Well, Sirs, we tell you that the life and salvation of the precious soul is to be found in this gospel-treasure; if a man give but the hearing of faith unto this gospel, his soul shall live, Is. lv. 3. The gospel is called a word of life, and a word of salvation, Acts xiii. 26, and chap. v. 20, "Go (says the angel unto the apostles who were imprisoned), stand and speak in the temple to the people all the words of this life." And whoever he be that believeth the report of the gospel concerning Christ, he shall not perish, but have everlasting life, John iii. 14—16.

2. Next unto life, light is the most sweet and valuable thing in this world. What a melancholy unheartsome habitation would this world be if it wanted the sun in the firmament! "Truly light is sweet, and it is a pleasant thing for the eyes to behold the sun." Well, the gospel brings a more valuable light unto the world then the light of the sun in the firmament, even that light which discovers another world, and a far better world than this is, "for life and immortality is brought to light by the gospel." Wherever the gospel comes, "the people which sat in darkness are made to see a great light; and to them which sat in the region of the shadow of death, light doth spring up," Matth. iv. 16; and John viii. 12, says Christ, "I am the light of the world: he that followeth me shall not walk in darkness, but shall have the light of light." And where this light of the gospel shines into the heart, it is just a prelude of the light of glory.

3. In this gospel-treasure is to be found a treasure of wisdom, whereby the foolish and simple sinner is made wise to salvation. "In Christ (whom we preach) are hid all the treasures of wisdom and knowledge;" and he is made of God unto us wisdom. David found such a measure of wisdom and knowledge in this treasure, that he had more understanding than the ancients, and more wisdom than all his teachers; by the gospel revelation these things are brought to light unto babes, that are hid from the wise and the prudent of this world. See a lecture of the excellency of the gospel wisdom, Job xxviii. 12—23, "It cannot be gotten for gold, neither shall silver be weighed for the price thereof. No mention shall be made of coral, or of pearls: for the price of wisdom is above rubies. The topaz of Ethiopia shall not equal it, neither shall it be valued with pure gold. God only understandeth the way thereof, and he knoweth the place thereof."

4. In this gospel-treasure is to be found that crown of glory which fell from Adam's head that day that he sinned against God, 2 Cor.

iii. ult., "All we with open face, beholding as in a glass (viz. the glass of the gospel revelation) the glory of the Lord, are changed into the same image, from glory to glory, as by the Spirit of the Lord." Christ is the image of the invisible God, and the brightness of his Father's glory; and, by beholding his glory in the gospel, we come to be renewed in knowledge after the image of him that created us at first, 2 Cor. iv. 4-6.

5. The gospel opens a treasure of "fine linen, pure and white, which is the righteousness of the saints," Rev. xix. 8. The judicious Durham upon that place observes, that by this righteousness of the saints, is to be understood the imputed righteousness of Christ, which he proves by several arguments. This is that white raiment which Christ counsels Laodicea to buy of him, that the shame of her nakedness might not appear, Rev. iii. 18. This, I say, we bring forth, and bring near unto you in the gospel revelation, Rom. i. 16, 17, "I am not ashamed of the gospel of Christ: for it is the power of God unto salvation, to every one that believeth. For therein is the righteousness of God revealed from faith to faith." Come then, O naked sinners, and buy white raiment, robes of righteousness, garments of salvation, without money and without price, for it is a gifted righteousness, Rom. v. 17.

6. Here is a treasure of quickening, cleansing, adorning, strengthening, and sanctifying influences of the Holy Ghost; for we receive the Spirit, not by the works of the law, but by the hearing of faith. Christ is a head of influence, who received the Spirit above measure, that he might communicate the Spirit and all his influences unto his mystical body; and the gospel is the channel of conveyance; hence, by the great and precious promises, we are made partakers of the divine nature. These places of the world, where the gospel is not preached, they are like unto the mountains of Gilboa, upon which nothing of the rain or dew of the Holy Ghost descends.

7. Here, in this gospel, is a treasure of noble securities for every thing needful, either for life or godliness, for time or eternity. The gospel-covenant is a large charter under the seal of Heaven, for the whole inheritance of glory, and all that pertains thereunto; and the promises of the covenant are so many particular clauses of the charter, whereby this, and that, and the other blessing is secured, and all these yea and amen in Christ. It is "an everlasting covenant, well ordered in all things, and sure. The mountains shall depart, and the hills be removed, but my kindnes shall not depart from thee, neither shall the covenant of my peace be removed, saith the Lord, that hath mercy on thee," Isa. liv. 10.

8. In this gospel you have a treasure of sovereign medicines and antidotes against all these spiritual and soul diseases unto which we are subjected since the fall of Adam. Here are the leaves of the tree of life, which are ordained for the healing of the nations, Psal. cvii. 20, "He sent forth his word and healed them." We bring you glad tidings of great joy, that there is balm in Gilead, and a Physician there of unerring skill, and who saves to the uttermost all that come unto him, and will employ him, let their case be never so des-

perate, or the diseases never so obstinate against all other remedies; he opens the blind eyes, he makes the lame man to leap like a hart, and the tongue of the dumb to sing; yea, the very dead are made to hear the voice of Gilead's Physician, and so are made alive, John v. 25.

9. In this gospel there is laid open a treasure of great and glorious mysteries, that were hid in God from all eternity. The Lion of the tribe of Judah hath opened the book, and loosed the seven seals thereof, which none in heaven or in earth were capable to do but himself; and now, under the New Testament, by the commandment of the everlasting God, these hid mysteries are published unto all nations for the obedience of faith, Rom. xvi. 25, 26, Col. i. 26, 27. In this gospel there is a revelation of the mystery of the Trinity, three in one, and one in three; the mystery of the incarnation of the eternal Son of God; "And without controversy great is the mystery of godliness; God manifested in the flesh;" the mystery of the death and satisfaction of Christ, whereby the sword of justice, being bathed in his blood, is put up again in its scabbard, and the anger of God turned away from us; the mystery of his resurrection from the dead, whereby he was justified in the Spirit, and the debt we were owing to law and justice discharged; the mystery of his ascension unto heaven, as our Forerunner, whereby the way to glory is opened for us through the territories of the Prince of the power of the air; the mystery of his intercession, whereby our acceptance with God is procured. And all accusations and charges against us are repelled. The gospel brings to light the mystery of the new birth, whereby we are initiated into the kingdom of heaven; the mystery of justification by the imputation of his righteousness unto us, whereby the righteousness of the law comes to be fulfilled in every one that believes; the mystery of our adoption into God's family, whereby the heirs of hell and wrath are put among the children; the mystery of our sanctification by the Spirit of Christ, whereby we are made meet to be partakers of the inheritance of the saints in light. These and the like mysteries are opened in the everlasting gospel, which flesh and blood cannot know, and cannot receive, because they are spiritually discerned.

10. In this gospel-treasure is to be found stores of meat, meat for the hungry, and drink for the thirsty soul, meat indeed and drink indeed. The incarnation and satisfaction of the Son of God, apprehended by faith, is that hidden manna which the world are strangers to. Of this banquet we read, Is. xxv. 6, "In this mountain shall the Lord of hosts make unto all people a feast of fat things, a feast of wines on the lees, of fat things full of marrow, of wines on the lees well refined." A tasting of this food satisfies the longing soul so much, that it hungers no more after the swine husks which the world feed upon. See the open invitation given to all people to come unto this gospel-banquet, Is. lv. 1, "Ho, every one that thirsteth, come ye to the waters," &c. Prov. viii. 4, "Unto you, O men, do I call, and my voice is to the sons of men. Come, eat of my bread, and drink of the wine which I have mingled," see Prov. ix. 1—6.

11. Here in this gospel is a treasure of rich spoils, which Christ the

Captain of our salvation took from the enemy, when he spoiled him upon the field of battle, and triumphed over principalities and powers. Here is the head of the dragon, that old serpent the devil, the destroyer of mankind, which Christ gives to be meat to them that inhabit the wilderness. Here is the hand-writing of the curse of the law, which was contrary unto us, and which gave Satan a law-power over us, retired and cancelled, Col. ii. 14. Here are the keys of hell and death, which Christ took by main force from the jailor; Rev. i. 18, "I am he that liveth, and was dead; and behold, I am alive for evermore, Amen; and have the keys of hell and of death." Here is death itself disarmed of its sting, and the grave of its victory, so as you may triumph over it as a vanquished enemy, saying, "O death, where is thy sting? O grave, where is thy victory? Thanks be to God, which giveth us the victory, through our Lord Jesus Christ." All these spoils Christ took from the enemy, when of the people there was none with him; and yet, like the women that tarried at home, he makes us to divide the spoil; and thus the promise of the Father is fulfilled, Isa. liii. 12, "I will divide him a portion with the great, and he shall divide the spoil with the strong."

12. In this gospel are brought forth all the riches and glory of Immanuel's land, that lies on the other side of the Jordan of death. The new Jerusalem, with all its splendour and glory, is brought down from God out of heaven in the dispensation of the gospel, Rev. xxi. 1—3, and from ver. 10—21, we have a map of the celestial Jerusalem, unto which the redeemed from among men shall be admitted, when they have finished their work and pilgrimage in this lower world. Thus you see what rich treasures the gospel brings unto sinners. Oh, how fitly then is it called "the glorious gospel of the blessed God, which is committed to our trust," 1 Tim. i. 11. Thus much for the *first* general head.

II. The *second* thing in the method was, to speak a little of the *earthen vessels*, wherein the gospel-treasure is brought or conveyed to God's family; for, says the apostle here, *We have this treasure in earthen vessels.* By which, as I said in the opening of the words, we are to understand ministers of the gospel, unto whom he says, "Go ye into all the world, and preach the gospel to every creature." Now, as to this designation given unto ministers of the gospel, there are only two or three questions I would propose and answer.

Quest. 1. What may be imported in this designation of *earthen vessels?*

Answ. (1.) It says that God is the great Potter, who forms all the vessels of his house, whether they be vessels of cups, or vessels of flagons, vessels of lesser or of greater quantity; he forms them all for himself, that they may show forth his glory. (2.) It says that ministers of the gospel are ordained, not for their own use, but for the benefit of the church, even as vessels are for the use of the family. Christ himself, as Mediator and High Priest of our profession, is ordained for men in things pertaining to God; and so are all ministers and ordinances dispensed by them, for the use and benefit of the church; Eph. iv. 11, 12, "When he ascended up on high, he gave some apostles, and some prophets, and some evangelists, and some pastors and teachers, for the perfecting of the saints, for the work of the ministry, for the edifying of the body of Christ. (3.) While ministers of the gospel are called earthen vessels, it says that they are but mortal men, even as others are; they are sprung of earth, and their foundation is of the dust, and unto dust shall they return; Zech. i. 5, "Our fathers, where are they? and the prophets, do they live for ever?" (4.) It says that God will have his church served, not by the ministry of angels, but by men of their own mould and make, that his terror may not make them afraid, as when the law was delivered at Mount Sinai, Heb. xii. 18, 19.

Quest. 2. Whence have these earthen vessels this rich treasure of the gospel, or how come they by it?

Ans. The earthen vessels have all their treasure out of the large storehouse of a Redeemer's fulness. All edifying and saving gifts and graces are committed unto Christ by his Father, as the King, Head, and Lawgiver of his church; he received gifts for men, and accordingly gives gifts unto men, Psal. lxviii. 18, compared with Eph. iv. 11. When Christ calls any man to the work of the gospel, he will not send him a warfare upon his own charges; no. As a king when he sends his ambassadors into foreign courts, they are not allowed to go upon their own private charges and expenses, but upon the charges of the king, whose ambassadors they are. Just so here; the glorious King of Zion, when he sends his ambassadors into this lower world, he bids them spend not upon their own, but upon his credit; and in this case they shall lack for nothing that is needful, as the disciples found when he sent them to preach the gospel through the cities of Israel. Many a time, when they come forth to preach the everlasting gospel unto people, and begin to look in unto the clay vessels, we can see nothing there but weakness and emptiness, notwithstanding of all our study and preparation; and in this case are ready to conclude, we have nothing to bring forth unto the church for its edification, and that we shall be a discredit to the gospel and religion. But O, how doth our glorious Master many times baffle our unbelieving fears, and, for his own glory, conveys in a secret way the treasure of the gospel into the earthen vessels, for the edification of his members! As the milk is put within the mother's breast for the sake of the babe, so is the sincere milk of the word put, as it were, into our breasts, for the benefit of the babes of grace. It is observable, 2 Cor. v. 19, where in our translation the words run, "He hath committed unto us the word of reconciliation;" as on the margin, in the original, it runs, "He hath put in us the word of reconciliation." Thus he puts the treasure in the earthen vessels, in the way of trust, for the use of others. As the king's almoner is intrusted with the king's bounty and charity, for the use of the poor, that he may distribute it to them according to need, so ministers they are almoners of the King of Zion, they have the gospel-treasure committed to them, for the benefit of the poor; for "to the poor the gospel is preached." And well may we spend, when we have the unsearchable riches of Christ as our fund to go upon; the more we spend, the more we have to spend, for by scattering our stock increases.

Quest. 3. For what reason will God have the gospel-treasure conveyed in the earthen vessels?

Unto this you have an answer in the words of the text, *We have this treasure in earthen vessels, that the excellency of the power may be of God, and not of us.* But this leads to,

III. The *third* thing in the general method, which was, to speak a little of that excellent power which accompanies the dispensation of the gospel. This power is frequently spoken of in Scripture, sometimes in proper, sometimes in metaphorical terms. So, Rom. i. 16, the gospel is called "the power of God unto salvation." 1 Thess. i. 5, "Our gospel came not unto you in word only, but also in power, and in the Holy Ghost." Sometimes it is expressed metaphorically, and thus the gospel is called "the rod of the Mediator's strength," and "he makes a willing people in the day of his power," Psal. cx. 2, 3. See liii. 1, it is called a "revelation of the arm of Jehovah." Sometimes it is expressed by "Christ's going forth like a mighty Conqueror, riding upon a white horse, conquering, and to conquer," Rev. vi. 2, Psal. xlv. 4, 5. But to illustrate the excellency of that power of God, that is exerted towards sinners and saints, in the dispensation of the gospel through poor earthen vessels, I shall essay to do two things. 1. I shall give you some of the excellent properties; 2. Some of the excellent effects thereof.

1*st*, Let us take a view of the qualities of this power, and from thence the excellency of the whole will appear.

1. Then, it is wholly divine and supernatural, it is mighty through God. Arminians may talk of the power of their own will, as they have a mind, to convert themselves; the Scriptures of truth inform us, that the power of a whole Trinity is employed in the work of a sinner's conversion. The power of the Father is put forth in it, as Christ declares, John vi. 44, "No man can come to me, except the Father which hath sent me draw him." The power of the eternal Son is exerted, John xii. 32, "And I, if I be lifted up from the earth, will draw all men unto me." The power of the Father and the Son is exerted by the Holy Ghost, the third Person of the Trinity. Hence, Tit. iii. 5, we are said to be "saved by the washing of regeneration, and the renewing of the Holy Ghost." So that Arminians, who talk of the power of their own will to convert, believe, to repent, &c., they invade the prerogative of a whole Trinity, and contradict the record of God, by which we are assured that "it is not of him that willeth, or of him that runneth, but of God that sheweth mercy;" and that "it is God which worketh in us, both to will and to do, of his own good pleasure." So that it is a divine power. And hence it follows,

2. That it is an exceeding great and mighty power. A greater power is exerted in the formation of the new creature in the heart, by the instrumentality of the gospel, than in the creation of the world; hence the last is called the work of his finger, but the other of his almighty arm. The apostle tells us that the same almighty power

that was put forth in the resurrection of Christ from the dead, is exerted towards them that believe. He "fulfilleth in us the whole good pleasure of his goodness, and the work of faith with power;" and the apostle, in the place just now cited, he tells us that it is not only power, but greatness of power, exceeding greatness of power, greatness of almighty power, exerted and put forth in the resurrection of Christ from the dead; which plainly shows the resurrection of Christ to be a greater miracle than if all the race of Adam had been raised out of the grave in a moment. Christ was incarcerated or shut up in the prison of the grave as our Surety, "the Lord having laid on him the iniquities of us all;" and therefore the grave of Christ was locked up by the hand of justice, that laid him in prison for our debt. The curse of the broken law lay as a dreadful weight upon his grave; a weight that all men on earth, and angels in heaven, would never have been able to poise with their united strength. O what infinite power then did it require to raise up Christ from the dead under all this weight! Yet that same almighty power of God, that raised up Christ from the dead, is exerted and put forth towards sinners, in bringing them to believe; and when brought to believe, they must be "kept by the power of God through faith unto salvation."

3. Hence it follows that it is an irresistible power that accompanies the dispensation of the gospel-treasure. There was mighty opposition made to the work of our salvation, in the purchase thereof; hell and earth combined against the Lord and against his Anointed, but on he went, travailling in the greatness of his strength, through all opposition, till he could say, "It is finished." In like manner, when redemption is to be applied, there is mighty opposition made by the powers of hell; the devil studieth to secure his captive by might and main, he fortifies his strong holds against the approaches of divine grace, such as the darkness of the mind, the obstinacy of the will, the carnality of the affections; but when the day of power comes, God makes all these gates of brass and bars of iron to give way; for who can stay his almighty hand, when he says, "The lawful captive shall be delivered, and the prey taken from the terrible?" the strong fetters of the soul's captivity fall off, and "whom the Son makes free, they are free indeed." Thus, I say, the power of God accompanying the gospel is victorious and irresistible.

4. Although it be so, yet this power is exerted in a most sweet and agreeable manner, without any sort of violence done to the natural powers and faculties of the rational soul. I own indeed there is violence done to the corruption of nature; but no violence done to the soul, or its natural powers. The whole powers of the soul were lamed and dislocated by the fall; the understanding darkened, the will perverted from its original rectitude and conformity to the will of God; the affections turned away from God, the chief good, and misplaced upon the creature instead of the Creator; and these corrupt inclinations of the soul rule and govern, instead of the understanding, in all its actions. Now, when the power of God is put forth by the gospel, for the soul's renovation, "all old things are done away, and all things are made new;" every power of the soul is set, as it were, in its pro-

per joint; the mind or understanding is "delivered from the power of darkness, and renewed in knowledge after the image of him that created him;" the will is delivered from its enmity against God, and brought in a due subordination to the will of God, manifested in his promises, precepts, or providences; the affections are turned off from following sin and vanity, and made to centre on God himself, the adequate portion of the rational soul; and all the inferior powers of the soul, subordinated to the understanding, enlightened by the word and Spirit of God. Now, what violence is done to the soul in all this? It is nothing else but a restoring the soul, in some measure, to its primitive rectitude, when it dropt out of the creating hand, which cannot but be most agreeable unto the natural powers of the soul; and therefore the bones that were broken by sin, they are made to rejoice.

5. The excellency of this power appears from this, that all this work is done in a secret, silent, and mysterious way, without any outward noise or observation. When men do any considerable work, particularly when they make conquests, it is "with the confused noise of the warrior, and garments rolled in blood." When kings and great men are going in procession through their territories, it is with much observation, and the common cry is, Lo, he is here, or Lo, he is there; but when God sets up his kingdom within the soul, it is with no such observation, and therefore compared to the falling of dew, the springing of grass and corn, the growth of trees and plants; the almighty power of God is in every one of these, but this power is executed without any noise or din. Just so it is in the work of grace upon the soul; there is an exceeding great and mighty power put forth, but it operates in a secret, silent, and mysterious manner, discernible more in its effects than the manner of its operation; hence Christ, speaking of the new birth, compares the operation of the Spirit unto the indiscernible motion of the air or wind, John iii. 8, "The wind bloweth where it listeth, and thou hearest the sound thereof, but canst not tell whence it cometh, and whither it goeth: so is every one that is born of the Spirit."

2*dly*, Let us take a view of the excellency of this power that accompanies the gospel in a day of power, in the effects thereof, which are indeed wonderful and surprising, a few of which I shall name.

1. Such is the excellency of this power, that thereby a new creature is produced and brought forth out of the barren womb of nothing; for creation is the production of something out of that which had no existence, which nothing but almighty power can effect; yet by the dispensation of the gospel-treasure this is effected, a new creature is formed, and brought into a new heaven and a new earth, wherein dwelleth righteousness, Eph. ii. 10, "We are his workmanship, created in Christ Jesus;" and all this by the word of truth, James i. 18.

2. By the excellency of this power, life is brought out of death; for the conversion of a sinner is the resurrection of the dead soul, Eph. ii. 1, "You hath he quickened who were dead in trespasses and sins." When we go to preach the gospel, we find the valley of vision lying full of dry bones, scattered about the devouring mouth of the grave, and we are ready to put that question, "Can these dry bones live?"

Yet the Lord sometimes lets us see that he can show wonders among the dead, for, by the voice of Christ in the gospel, dead sinners are made alive, John v. 25. If he but say to a dead soul, as he did to Lazarus, "Come forth out of thy grave," immediately the first resurrection is accomplished, and so the second death shall have no power over that soul.

3. By this power of God in the gospel, light is brought out of darkness. The mind of man by nature is not only dark, but darkness; "Once were ye darkness, but now are ye light in the Lord." As, in the old creation, darkness was upon the face of the deep, so is the darkness of ignorance, unbelief, error, and prejudice, upon the face of the soul; but when God says, "Let there be light," immediately the light of the knowledge of the glory of God, in the face of Jesus Christ, translates the soul from darkness unto a marvellous light, 2 Cor. iv. 6.

4. Such is the excellency of this power, that thereby beauty and order is brought out of deformity and confusion, as was already hinted, "Though ye have lain among the pots, yet shall ye be as the wings of a dove covered with silver, and her feathers with yellow gold."

5. By this power of God in the gospel, a new temple and habitation is reared out of the dark quarry of nature, and stones raised up to be children of Abraham, Eph. ii. ult,, "Ye are built up an habitation of God through the Spirit."

Not to multiply particulars, by this power of God in the gospel, the enmity of the heart against God is slain, and the sinner is so far reconciled unto God, that he is made to love the Lord his God with all his heart, soul, strength, and mind. By this almighty power, the prodigal that was in a far country, feeding upon husks with the swine, is brought home to his Father's house, and reinstated in all the privileges of children. By the power of God accompanying the gospel, the poor man, that was oppressed with poverty, is taken out of the dunghill and set among princes, and made an heir of God, and a joint-heir with Christ. The strong man is bound by a stronger than he, and spoiled of his goods; the strong holds of Satan are pulled down, the high imaginations of the heart, that exalt themselves against the knowledge of God, are levelled, and every thought brought into captivity unto the obedience of Christ; the lawful captive is delivered, and the prey taken from the terrible. Thus I have given you a little glimpse of the excellency of the power of God accompanying the gospel, from its properties and effects.

IV. The *fourth* thing in the method was, to show how the excellency of this power comes to be displayed, by the conveyance of the gospel-treasure in earthen vessels. In answer, I shall not dwell upon this; only it is to be observed that it is God's ordinary way to exert his almighty power in the accomplishment of his greatest works, by means which the rational world would think should prove utterly ineffectual. When the great fabric of heaven and earth are brought into being, it is done with a simple word, "By the word of the Lord were the heavens made; and all the host of them by the breath of his mouth." When the pride of Pharaoh and the strength of Egypt is to be broken, when Israel is to be brought out of bondage, and the Red Sea divided, it is effected by the stretching out of the rod of God in the hand of Moses. When the strong walls of Jericho are to be brought down, it shall not be done by engines of war, such as battering rams, but by the simple sounding of ram's horns, and a shout from the camp of Israel. When the host of the Midianitish army is to be discomfited, God will not have it done by thirty thousand, but he will have these reduced to three hundred; and that three hundred shall not draw a sword, but only blow their trumpets, break their pitchers, and hold their lamps in their hands, crying, " The sword of the Lord, and of Gideon ;" and thereupon the Midianitish army is made to melt away, and every man made to sheath his sword in his neighbour's bowels. What was the plot of Heaven in making such insignificant contemptible means to produce such glorious effects ? The plain reason is, that his own arm and power might be the more conspicuous, and that Israel might know that it was not their own bow or sword that saved them, but God's right hand and his holy arm that gave them the victory. In like manner, when God is to set up the kingdom of the Messiah in the world, and to overthrow Satan's kingdom of darkness, he passes by the plodding politicians, the learned philosophers, and elegant orators of the world, and pitches upon twelve poor fishermen, who had no other language than their mother tongue, no other education but the making and mending of their nets ; and, in endowing them with power from on high, whereby they were made capable of propagating the gospel in all the languages of the known world, and the working all manner of miracles for the confirmation of the truth of their doctrine, whereby Satan's kingdom was made to fall like lightning from heaven; the idolatries of the nations, in which they had been rooted for many ages and generations; the devil's oracles amongst them are silenced; the Mosaical economy, which had been of divine authority, is unhinged; the Roman empire, the power of which had been employed to extirpate Christianity, is made to yield unto the sceptre of a crucified Jesus. In like manner, when God is to set up his kingdom in the heart, he will do it by earthen vessels, fraughted with the treasure of gospel truth and grace. Now, what is the design of God in all this, but *that the excellency of the power may appear to be of him and not of man?* The apostle elegantly descants upon this subject, 1 Cor. i. 26—31, " For ye see your calling, brethren, how that not many wise men after the flesh, not many mighty, not many noble are called. But God hath chosen the foolish things of the world, to confound the wise ; and God hath chosen the weak things of the world, to confound the things which are mighty: and base things of the world, and things which are despised, hath God chosen, yea, and things which are not, to bring to nought things that are. The design of all this is, ' That no flesh should glory in his presence, but that he that glorieth, may glory in the Lord alone.' " And so much shall serve for the illustration of the text and doctrine. I proceed now to

The *Application*. And I shall endeavour to dispatch all the application I intend at this time in a few inferences.

Inf. 1. See hence what an excellent and enriching blessing the gospel is, when received in a way of believing; it is a *treasure*, and the best treasure ever a people were possessed of; they are indeed a blessed people that know God in a practical way and manner.

Here it may be asked, Wherein lies the excellency of the gospel-treasure? This was cleared in the doctrinal part; but to what was said I shall add,

1st, It is a celestial and heavenly treasure; it is one of these "good and perfect gifts that come down from above, from the Father of lights, with whom is no variableness, neither shadow of turning." The law is a thing known, in a great measure, by the light of nature; but the gospel is a thing wholly supernatural, both as to the objective and subjective revelation of it.

2dly, It is a spiritual and soul-satisfying treasure. And O how valuable must that treasure be, that enriches the soul, and brings it to life and immortality! Let a man be possessed of all the riches of the East and West Indies, yet while he is destitute or ignorant of the gospel-treasure, Laodicea's character may be affixed to him, " wretched, miserable, poor, and blind, and naked."

3dly, The gospel-treasure the more that a man hath of it, he is always the more humble and denied. Quite contrary to this is the effect of men's possessing worldly treasures; no sooner do some men get a little of the world scraped together, by hook or crook, but they are swelled with pride, and look with an air of contempt and disdain upon others, that are not come their length, as to worldly substance. But, I say, the gospel-treasure hath a quite different effect; for the more a man hath of it, the less doth he think of himself, in comparison of others, as you see it was with the great apostle Paul. Who had more of the gospel-treasure than he? and yet, says he, Eph. iii. 8, " Unto me, who am less than the least of all saints, is this grace given, that I should preach among the Gentiles the unsearchable riches of Christ."

4thly, Though it be a humbling, yet it is really a soul ennobling treasure. The man by having the gospel-treasure hid in his heart, it lifts him from among the common lay of mankind, and sets him among the excellent ones of the earth; it sets him among princes, and among the heirs of the kingdom of heaven; it endows the man with a princely spirit, insomuch that he looks with contempt upon this dunghill-world, and his affections are set a flight after things that are above, where Christ is at the right hand of God. " We look not at the things which are seen, but at the things which are not seen: for the things which are seen are temporal, but the things which are not seen are eternal."

5thly, As was above hinted, the gospel-treasure is durable, abiding, and everlasting; it goes along with a man, through death, which twins him of all his other worldly treasures; Psal. xlix. 16, 17, " Be not thou afraid when one is made rich, when the glory of his house is increased. For when he dieth, he shall carry nothing away: his glory shall not descend after him." But the gospel-treasure is of such a nature, and so well secured, that neither death, nor life, nor things present, nor things to come, shall ever be able to spoil him of it, Rom. viii. at the close.

Well then, Sirs, if the gospel be such a valuable treasure, for the Lord's sake, study to secure it, that your souls may be enriched for ever. *Quest.* How shall we secure it? *Answ.* It is by faith's setting to the seal unto the record of God concerning his Son Jesus Christ. *Quest.* What is the record of God? See this answered, 1 John v. 11, "This is the record of God, that God hath given to us (sinners of mankind) eternal life, and this life is in his Son: and he that hath the Son, hath life." That moment a man sets to his seal to this record of God, as a faithful saying, and worthy of all acceptation, he is secured of all the riches of Christ, which are unsearchable.

Inf. 2. Hath God put this treasure into earthen vessels, as ministers of the gospel are here called? Then see hence how worthy of reception and entertainment a faithful minister of the gospel is; why, although he be but an earthen vessel, yet he brings a glorious treasure along with him unto the people to whom he is sent. Solomon tells us, that "a man's gift makes room for him;" much more he that brings a treasure of gifts. That minister who brings Christ, and all the treasures of heaven along with him, is worthy of all reception, according to that, Rom. x. 15, "How beautiful are the feet of them that preach the gospel of peace, and bring glad tidings of good things!" Although ministers be spoke of by this diminutive character of earthen vessels, yet there are several great and honourable titles and designations given them in Scripture, which plainly show the reception that they are worthy of. Every sent minister of Christ is "the messenger of the Lord of hosts," Mal. ii. 7. A messenger sent from the Lord of all the hosts of heaven, earth, and hell, ought to be entertained, and it is dangerous to maltreat him. Ministers are called the ambassadors of Christ, 2 Cor. v. 20, "Now, then, we are ambassadors for Christ, as though God did beseech you by us: we pray you in Christ's stead, be ye reconciled to God." Ministers of the gospel are called ambassadors, with allusion to the practice of princes, who sent their ambassadors into foreign courts; and the ambassador represents the person of the king that sent him; and if any injury be done to the ambassador, it is reckoned a dishonour done to his great master. The ambassadors of kings, they are send unto foreign courts, to negotiate the affairs of peace, of trade, or of marriage; and in all these respects ministers are ambassadors from the high court of heaven. For,

1*st*, They are sent to negotiate a peace between God and man. They preach the gospel of peace; they have the word of reconciliation committed to them, "As though God did beseech you by us, we pray you to be reconciled to him." We come to cast out the white flag of peace from heaven, to a company of rebels, and to assure you, upon the oath of God that sent us, that he hath no pleasure in your death, but rather that you turn to him and live; and therefore we cry to you, "Turn ye, turn ye, for why will ye die?" We come with the olive branch in our mouths, to let you know that the deluge of God's wrath, that was breaking out against all mankind, is subdued, and that his anger is turned away, through the death and satisfaction of his eternal Son; and therefore, he who hath created our lips, hath ordained us to cry, "Peace, peace to them that are afar off." For this very end, the ministry of reconciliation is committed to us, viz., "That God was in Christ, reconciling the world unto himself, not imputing their trespasses unto them;" although, alas! we that are the ambassadors of peace, may apply that word with respect to the generality of our hearers, Is. xxxiii. 7., "The ambassadors of peace weep bitterly." And why do they weep, but because their Master's offers of peace are rejected, and the ambassadors of peace are maltreated? On this account we follow the example of Christ with respect unto Jerusalem; when he beheld the city, he wept over it, saying, "O Jerusalem, Jerusalem, thou that killest the prophets, and stonest them which are sent unto thee: O that thou, even thou, in this thy day, hadst known the things which belong unto thy peace!"

2*ndly*, Ministers of the gospel are not only ambassadors of peace, but the ambassadors for trade. In time of war between nations, trade fails and ceases; but when peace is proclaimed, trade comes to be open again. As we have a commission to proclaim peace, so likewise we are ordained to tell you that there is a free trade opened unto Emmanuel's land; and to tell you that the commodities of that heavenly country are infinitely better than all the riches, commodities, or accommodations of this present world; and therefore we come to encourage you to carry on a commerce, and to cry from the tops of the high places, that the market of heaven is opened, Is. lv. 1. "Ho, every one that thirsteth, come ye to the waters, and he that hath no money, let him come, buy wine and milk, without money and without price." This is the same with Christ's counsel unto Laodicea, Rev. iii. 18. "I counsel thee to buy of me gold tried in the fire, that thou mayest be rich; and white raiment that thou mayest be clothed, and that the shame of thy nakedness do not appear; and anoint thine eyes with eye-salve that thou mayest see." Sirs, we tell you that you may drive an advantageous trade with heaven, that the commodities thereof are cheap goods, and durable, and the King of that heavenly country guarantees your trade against all enemies that may annoy you. You that are merchants, when you trade with foreign countries in this world, your ships are in danger of being seized by Turkish galleys, or Algerine robbers and pirates, or the like: but you shall not be in any such danger, if you drive a trade with the heavenly country; the King whose name is "the Lord of hosts, and Lord of glory," hath given his parole of honour that your trade shall be protected by him, Is. xxxiii. 21., "The glorious Lord shall be unto us a place of broad rivers and streams; wherein shall go no galley with oars, neither shall gallant ship pass thereby." And therefore, dear sirs, we beseech you to set this heavenly trade on foot.

3*dly*, Ministers are ambassadors from heaven for carrying on a marriage with the King's Son. He had a purpose of marriage from all eternity, between his own beloved Son, and a bride that he had chosen for him in Adam's tribe and family; he was set up and fore-ordained as the Bridegroom of souls from everlasting: from the beginning, ere ever the earth was. The heart of the Bridegroom, and of his royal Father, was so much set upon the match, that infinite power and wisdom, inspired with infinite love, are set a work to remove all impediments that obstructed the match. For,

(1.) Because there was an infinite natural distance between the divine and human natures, therefore the Son of God he came into our tribe, and was made of a woman, his Father prepared a body for him, which accordingly he did put on, in the fulness of time; and thus he comes, as it were, upon a level with the bride, saying, "Thy Maker is thine Husband, whose name is "the Lord of Hosts. I will betrothe thee unto me for ever, yea, I will betrothe thee unto me in righteousness, and in judgment, and in loving kindness, and in mercies. I will even betrothe thee unto me in faithfulness, and thou shalt know the Lord," Hos. ii. 19. 20.

(2) Because the bride was drowned in debt to law and justice, and under the curse and condemnation of the first covenant, and so at an infinite moral, as well as natural distance; therefore the Bridegroom, in order to accomplish the match, becomes Surety for the payment of her debt; and accordingly, "the Lord laid on him the iniquities of us all: and it was exacted of him and he answered for it, without opening his mouth until he could say, It is finished. He having paid the debt, tears the bond and handwriting that was against us with the nails of his cross, and brings forth the discharge of the debt in his resurrection from the dead; for "he died for our offences, and rose again for our justification."

(3.) Because the bride was a prisoner, by the order of justice, under the hand of the jailor and executioner, therefore he comes and spoils principalities and powers, and triumphs over them in his cross; upon the footing of his satisfactory obedience unto the death, he commands the prisoner to be dismissed and the captive bride to be set at liberty; Zech. ix. 11., "As for thee also, by the blood of the covenant, I have sent forth thy prisoners out of the pit, wherein is no water." Thus the lawful captive is delivered, and the prey taken from the terrible.

(4.) Because the bride is in a distant country, afar off, ignorant of the Bridegroom and his glory, therefore he sends his ministers as his ambassadors, to declare his glorious fulness and sufficiency, and how willing he is to have the match accomplished, and what he hath done and suffered in order to bring it about. Ministers are called "the friends of the Bridegroom, who stand and hear him, and rejoice greatly because of the Bridegroom's voice; and their joy is fulfilled when the happy match takes place, John iii. 29.

(5.) Because such is the enmity and alienation of the heart of the bride from the match, that all moral suasion proves utterly ineffectual, therefore the Bridegroom comes in a day of power, and by manifesting himself to her, in the glory of his person and mediation, and by touching the iron sinew of her obstinate will with the rod of his strength, makes her willing in the day of his power, and thus gains the consent of the bride, upon which she cries out, I am the Lord's, and will be called by his name: Hos. ii. 16., "Thou shalt call me Ishi, and shalt call me no more Baali.'

Thus you see that faithful ministers, however they be clay vessels, yet they are ambassadors from heaven, to carry on a peace, an advantageous trade, and an honorable match with the King's Son. And doth it not follow from all this, that a faithful minister of Christ is worthy of all reception and entertainment.

Inf. 3. See from this doctrine, the folly and madness of a great many professed Christians and gospel-hearers, who prefer lumber and trash unto the precious treasure of the gospel, freely and fully offered unto them.

Some prefer their worldly wealth, profits, pleasures, and honours of this life, to all the profits, pleasures, and honours of religion and true godliness. The cry of the generality is, "Who will shew us any of this world's good? what shall we eat? what shall we drink? wherewithal shall we be clothed?" But as for the eternal treasures of the gospel, they have no regard to them, they care for none of these things. I have known some in this place, who, some years ago had a promising appearance of religion, and seemed to run well, but plunging themselves in the mire of worldly affairs, and grasping after the riches of this world, have ever since run backward in religion, instead of going forward; so that we may say of them as Paul did of Demas, "He hath forsaken me, having loved this present world;" and in such is fulfilled that word of the apostle, 1 Tim. vi. 9. 10., "But they that will be rich fall into temptation, and a snare, and into many foolish and hurtful lusts; which drown men in destruction and perdition. For the love of money is the root of all evil; which, while some coveted after, they have erred from the faith, and pierced themselves through with many sorrows."

Some again (and very commonly it is so with those of whom I spoke last), they prefer a jingle of words, a flourish of heathen morality, unto the gospel of Christ; they choose rather to have their ears tickled with the words of men's wisdom, than to have their hearts touched, and their souls fed and nourished with the plain and simple truths of the everlasting gospel. They that are of this spirit they plainly declare that their palate is vitiate with some dreadful soul-distemper or other, their understandings are darkened, and their affections taken up with some other thing than precious Christ, and his unsearchable riches. And I may say of such ministers as entertain their hearers with the flourishes of rhetoric and moral harangues, instead of preaching Christ, and the supernatural mysteries of Christianity, whatever be their character among their votaries, they are ministers of Satan, transforming themselves into ministers of Christ, and that awful word is but too applicable to them and their abettors, Matth. xv. 14., "They are blind guides; and if the blind lead the blind, both shall fall into the ditch."

Much of a kin with these, are they who set a great value upon their own righteousness by the law preferring the same unto the imputed righteousness of the Lord Jesus Christ, and all the riches and treasures of the gospel. Many gospel hearers, they are married unto the law as an husband, and with the Jews go about to establish their own righteousness, and will not submit unto the righteousness of God. Some, perhaps, may have very orthodox heads, while yet they have legal hearts; and thus they seek righteousness, not directly, "but as it were by the works of the law," Rom. ix. 32. They were never really "dead to the law by the body of Christ, that they might be married to a better Husband, even to him who is raised from the dead:" and therefore can never bring forth fruit acceptable to God: but Ephraim's character is applicable to them, "They are empty vines, bringing forth fruit unto themselves."

Now, of all such I may say, as Christ says of self-conceited Laodicea, who imagined herself to be rich and increased with goods, and that she stood in need of nothing, that, in reality, they are but "wretched, and miserable, and poor, and blind, and naked;" you are feeding upon ashes; a deceived heart hath turned you aside, that you cannot deliver your soul, nor say, Is there not a lie in my right hand? But what a melancholy pass will you be found into, when you shall be laid and weighed in God's balances, and that awful hand-writing come forth against you, "MENE, TEKEL, Thou art weighed in the balances, and art found wanting!" And therefore observe how God expostulates with you, because of your folly in preferring your own counters unto the gospel gold and treasure, Isa. lv. 2, "Wherefore do ye spend your money for that which is not bread? and your labour for that which satisfieth not?" And see how he appeals unto the very heavens to bear testimony for him against your madness, Jer. ii. 12, 13, "Be astonished, O ye heavens, at this, and be horribly afraid; be ye very desolate, saith the Lord. For my people have committed two great evils: they have forsaken me the fountain of living waters, and hewed them out cisterns, broken cisterns, that can hold no water."

Inf. 4. Are ministers of the gospel earthen vessels, whereby the gospel-treasure is conveyed to God's family? This serves to inform us,

1*st*, Of the wonderful and amazing condescension of God towards poor sinners of Adam's family; it is out of pity to us that he conveys the treasure in earthen vessels of the like mould with yourselves. When God spake immediately, or by the ministry of angels, at Mount Sinai, unto Israel, the whole camp fell a-trembling, and so terrible was the sight, that Moses himself said, "I exceedingly fear and quake," Heb. xii. 19—21. The apostle John, Rev. xxii. 8, 9, when he had a message delivered to him by an angel of heaven, he was ready to fall into idolatry, or angel-worship, until the angel said to him, "Se thou do it not; for I am thy fellow-servant, and of thy brethren the prophets, and of them which keep the sayings of this book; worship God." Thus you see, that when God conveys the gospel of his grace unto you by earthen vessels, he thereby suits himself unto the weakness and imbecility of man in his fallen estate.

2dly, See hence that death is in the marriage knot between ministers and their people, as well as between husband and wife. When a people get a minister from the Lord, they are to lay their account with the want of him in God's appointed time, the earthen vessel must return again unto the earth; " Your fathers, where are they? and the prophets, do they live for ever?" But though your faithful ministers die, yet their words do not die with them; no, " the word of the Lord endureth for ever;" it takes fast hold of you, as it did of your fathers, and will go either to heaven or to hell with you; it will either be " the savour of life unto life, or the savour of death unto death."

3dly, See also that the ministers of Christ are but tender ware, and had need to be tenderly handled; for an earthen vessel is soon staved, and broken into shells, and then it is of no more use. Your ministers are men of like passions and infirmities of body and mind like yourselves, and stand much in need of your sympathy, especially considering that the strength of battle from hell and earth is against them. What dashing and harsh treatment some of these earthen vessels have met with in Stirling, is pretty well known: some of them have been stoned, some have had their hoary hairs brought to the grave with sorrow, and another had been cast out of the legal synagogue and maintenance, for bearing testimony against the sins of the place, and the tyranny and defection of the judicatories of the Church of Scotland. These things I mention, not out of resentment, but that I may be found a faithful witness for the Lord against the sins of the place; the magistrates and town-council of Stirling must answer unto God for what they have done in this matter. All that I shall say upon the head is, with my royal Master, when they were taking away his life, " Father, forgive them, for they know not what they do;" and with the proto-martyr Stephen, when they were stoning him to death, and when he was going out of time into eternity, " Lord, lay not this sin unto their charge."

Inf. 5. See from this text and doctrine what it is makes (1.) an able, and (2.) a successful minister of the gospel.

As to the *first.* the apostle says of himself, and his brethren in the same office, that " God hath made them able ministers of the New Testament, 2 Cor. iii. 6. Now, if it be asked, What it is that makes a man an able minister of the New Testament? the answer is, When he hath his earthen vessel well stored and plenished with the treasure of that gospel grace and truth that comes by Christ Jesus, such an one is called, by Christ himself, " a scribe well instructed in the kingdom of God; he is like an householder, who brings forth out of his treasure things new and old," for the edification of the church of God, Matth. xiii. 52. He hath " milk for babes, and strong meat for them that are of riper age." But,

2dly, This text also lets us see what it is that makes a man a successful minister of the New Testament. Many able ministers have had but very little success, as we see in the case of Isaiah, chap. liii. 1, " Who hath believed our report?" and chap. xlix. 4, " I have laboured in vain, I have spent my strength for nought, and in vain;

for Israel is not gathered;" and Christ himself, in the days of his humiliation, says, with reference unto the Jews unto whom he preached, "We have piped unto you, but ye have not danced; we have mourned unto you, but ye have not lamented." What, then, say you, makes a minister successful? You have the answer in the words of the text, it is the excellent power of God going along with the dispensation of the gospel-treasure, and the "excellency of the power is of God, and not of us," 1 Cor. iii. 6, "Paul planted, and Apollos watered; but God gave the increase." Some folk are ready to think all is well enough if they get ministers endowed with flourishing gifts; but people had little need to rest there, for although you had Paul, or Apollos, yea, Christ himself in the flesh, to preach to you, all would not do without the power of God coming along; and therefore, it highly concerns such, who regard the edification and salvation of their own soul, to be much at a throne of grace, pleading earnestly with the Lord, that he "in whom are hid all the treasures of wisdom and knowledge," may not only fill the earthen vessel with the treasure of the gospel, but that the gospel may "come to them, not in word only, but also in power, and in the Holy Ghost; for the weapons of our warfare are mighty only through God to the pulling down of strong holds," 2 Cor. x. 4, 5.

The *last* inference I draw from this text and doctrine is this, Hence we may see the nature of that work we are just now to go about. What is the ordination of a minister, but just the consecration or dedication of an earthen vessel to the service of the church of Christ, which is the house of the living God, that therein, or thereby, the treasure of the gospel may be conveyed unto the whole family? which dedication, according to Scripture warrant, is to be done by "fasting and prayer, and the laying on of the hands of the presbytery," Acts xiv. 23, compared with 1 Tim. iv. 14, which work we shall now proceed to, referring the further application of this doctrine to some other occasion.

[The preceding Sermon was preached at the Ordination of the Rev. James Erskine as one of the Associate Ministers of the Gospel at Stirling, 22d January 1752.]

THE CHARACTER OF A FAITHFUL MINISTER OF CHRIST.

A Sermon, preached immediately after the foresaid Ordination, by James Fisher, Minister of the Gospel in the Associate Congregation at Glasgow.

Col. i. 7.—*Epaphras, who is for you a faithful minister of Christ.*

IT tends much to the interest of religion that people love and esteem their pastors, and entertain honourable sentiments of them; for, if once a minister comes to be despised by his flock, his usefulness among them is over, and his doctrine, however agreeable to the form of sound words, will not be edifying to them; it is therefore the apostle's design, in the words of our reading, to cultivate the regard of the Colossians to Epaphras, their ordinary pastor, by giving him the just commendation and favourable character which he deserved, *As ye have learned of Epaphras our dear fellow-servant, who is for you a faithful minister of Christ.*

Passing that part of the character of Epaphras, which respects his relation to the apostle, as *a dear fellow-servant;* in the branch of the verse which we have read, as the subject of discourse, namely, *Who is for you a faithful minister of Christ*, you have a threefold commendation of him. 1. From his office or calling, a *minister of Christ*, 2. From his fidelity in the discharge of that office, a faithful minister of Christ. 3. From the scope and end of his ministry among the Colossians, it is for you, that is, for your good, for your salvation. The design of the whole of this commendation is, that the Colossians might honour and esteem Epaphras for his work's sake; so that we take up the scope of the words in the following

DOCT. "That faithful ministers of Christ, who aim at the edification and salvation of the people among whom they labour in the work of the ministry, ought to be honoured and esteemed by them." 1 Thess. v. 12, 13. "We beseech you, brethren, to know them which labour among you, and are over you in the Lord, and admonish you; and to esteem them very highly in love for their work's sake."

In discoursing this subject; we shall essay,
I. To inquire into the scripture-account of the character and duty of a faithful minister of Christ.
II. Give the reasons why such ministers ought to be honoured and esteemed by the people among whom they labour.
III. Deduce a few inferences for application.

I. The *first* thing is, to inquire into the scripture-account of the character and duty of a faithful minister of Christ.

1. He is one who speaks the things which become sound doctrine, as the apostle exhorts Titus, chap. ii. 1. "But speak thou the things which become sound doctrine." That doctrine is sound, which is a link of that chain of truth, revealed in the holy scriptures; for there is such a close concatenation or linking together of the truths of God, and such a beautiful harmony among them all, that no error whatsoever can at any rate be soldered with them, any more than clay can be incorporated with gold. We speak then the words which become sound doctrine, when we make all the divine perfections to harmonize in the contrivance of our redemption, when we give unto Christ in all the things the pre-eminence, and when we lay the pride of sinful men in the dust. And in order to our thus speaking the things which become sound doctrine, it is necessary that we be well acquainted with the holy scriptures, with approven systems of divinity, and particularly with our own standards, our excellent Confession of Faith, and catechisms, which may well be called forms of sound words.

2. A faithful minister of Christ is one, who is set for the defence of

the gospel, as Paul was Phil. i. 17. "I am set (says he) for the defence of the gospel." There is nothing more warmly inculcate in scripture, than the defence of gospel-truths, Prov. xxiii. 23. "Buy the truth, and sell it not." Phil. i. 27. "Stand fast in one spirit, with one mind, striving together for the faith of the gospel." Heb. x. 23. "Let us hold fast the profession of our faith without wavering." Jude, ver. 3. "It was needful for me to exhort you (says that apostle), that ye should earnestly contend for the faith which was once delivered unto the saints." And in order to the defence of the gospel, it is necessary that we be established in the present truth, as the expression is, 2 Pet. i. 12.; that is, in the truths presently controverted, or which are the present subject of debate. And indeed, it is most lamentable, that in our day there are scarce any of the peculiar doctrines of Christianity, which are not impugned and called in question by men of corrupt minds, and destitute of the truth; such as, the divine authority of the scriptures; the imputation of Adam's first sin to his posterity; the universal corruption and depravation of our nature; the irresistible power and efficacy of the grace of God; the distinct personality and supreme deity of the Son and Holy Ghost; the reality of the incarnation of Christ, or his assuming a holy human nature to his divine person; the absolute perfection and infinite worth of his satisfaction in our room; the necessity of the imputation of his surety-righteousness for our justification; the free election of some to eternal life; the perseverance of the saints; and the eternity of hell torments; with many other important points which might be mentioned. There are others again, who profess to own all the above truths, who yet so blend the law and the gospel, that they make the covenant of grace little better than another edition of the covenant of works; confound the sinner's sanctification with his justification; cry up the necessity of previous good qualifications in order to coming to Christ; and are for leaning on something wrought in them, or done by them, as the ground in less or more of their acceptance before God. And with respect to the government of Christ's house, alas! the generality of the present age seem to be agreed, that it is a matter of mere indifferency and moonshine, whether a person be of the Episcopalian, Independent, or Presbyterial way of thinking about it; although it is the declared principle of this church, founded on the word of God, solemnly sworn unto and sealed by the blood of many of the Lord's witnesses, That the spiritual power and authority, derived from Christ the alone Head, for the edification of his church, is lodged, neither in the hand of the civil magistrate, nor in the community of the faithful, as they call them, but in church officers, ministers and elders acting in parity, and judicatories subordinate to one another. Now, we say that a faithful minister of Christ is set for the defence of the gospel, namely, both for the defence of gospel-truth, and likewise of the hedge of government, which the glorious Head hath set about it.

3. A faithful minister of Christ is one who does not shun to declare to his hearers all the counsel of God, as Paul testifies of himself to the elders of Ephesus, Acts xx. 27., "I have not shunned to declare unto you all the counsel of God." He does not say that he

actually declared unto them the counsel of God, but only that he did not shun to declare it all. For as we know only in part, and prophecy but in part, it is not to be supposed, that all the truths of God, which are comprehended in the unfathomable depth of divine revelation, could be brought forth by any, or even by all that ever preached the gospel; for if the world itself could not contain the books that might be written of Christ, as the apostle John asserts, then all that ever were in the world (the Son of God only excepted) could never exhaust all that might be said, upon what is contained within the volume of God's book; as may appear in some measure from the vast number of commentaries, treatises, and sermons, published and unpublished, these seventeen hundred and fifty years bygone, besides all the lectures of the Old Testament prophets; and yet the half of what might be said has not been told. Well, then, not to shun to declare all the counsel of God, is to keep back no truth which we know from our hearers; it is, to the utmost of our capacity and knowledge, to bring forth, what, we think, as before God, will be most for their spiritual profiting, in the proper season of it, either for instructing the ignorant, and awakening the secure, strengthening of the weak, recovering of these that are gone astray; or for comforting the mourners in Zion, and raising up these that are bowed down under spiritual distress of any kind; and thus studying rightly to divide the Word of God, and give every one their portion of meat in due season, so as that none may be soothed or flattered in their sin upon the one hand, or that any get occasion for desponding fears on the other.

4. A faithful minister of Christ is one that gives attendance to reading and meditation on what he delivers, according to the Apostle's advice to Timothy, 1 Epist. iv. 13, 15, "Give attendance to reading; meditate upon these things;" that is, study them before hand. The Apostle had advised him, in another place, to stir up the gift that was in him, which could not be done without reading and meditation; and if close application to study was enjoined to an Evangelist of uncommon endowments, it must be much more our duty now, when the extraordinary gifts of the Spirit are ceased, to digest into order and method what we are to deliver in public, and not to entertain our people with that which costs us nothing.

5. A faithful minister of Christ is one who seeks to find out acceptable words. This was Solomon's study, Eccl. xii. 10, "The preacher sought to find out acceptable words;" on the margin, *words of delight.* We should endeavour to deliver the truths of God in such a plain and easy manner, as that the weak and ignorant may understand them, shunning all crabbed and bombastic expressions on the one hand, and course and clumsy ones on the other. The Scripture style is by far the smoothest, and at the same time the most elegant for the pulpit; and the more fully we understand any doctrine, the more able will we be to deliver it plainly unto others.

6. A faithful minister of Christ is one who takes heed to himself, as well as to his doctrine, lest, when he preach Christ to others he himself be a cast-away. It is given as one of the characters and qualifications of a minister, that he be *holy*, Tit. i. 8. For a

minister may have both gifts and learning, and likewise some measure of success, and yet want grace, as is plain enough in these who preached Christ out of envy and strife, Phil. i. 15. And yet grace is a very material branch of the ministerial character; for without this we can have no experience on our own souls of the truths we preach to others, nor can we have true sympathy with those who are in any spiritual distress; without grace we can never be in case to say with the Apostle, 2 Cor. i. 3, 4, "Blessed be God, even the Father of our Lord Jesus Christ, who comforteth us in all our tribulations, that we may be able to comfort them which are in any trouble, by the comfort wherewith we ourselves are comforted of God. Again, as a minister is to take heed to himself by inquiring into the state of his own soul, so likewise is he to take heed to his outward walk, to be "an example to believers, in word, in conversation, in charity, in spirit, in faith, in purity." as the Apostle exhorts Timothy, 1 Epist. iv. 12. Examples sometimes do good, where precepts are of little force. It were good for us who are ministers, if we could say in some measure with the Apostle, Phil. iv. 9, "Those things which ye have both learned, and received, and heard, and seen in me, do." As we are to beseech others, that they receive not the grace of God in vain, so we should take special care to give no offence in anything, that the ministry be not blamed, but essay to practise ourselves what we preach unto others, and thus in some degree make proof of our ministry.

7. As a faithful minister of Christ will take heed to himself, so likewise to the particular flock over which the Holy Ghost hath made him an overseer. For, although every minister has a relation to the Church universal, yet he has a more special concern in that particular flock among whom he is called to labour in the work of the ministry. He is to be instant among them, in season and out of season, sparing no pains nor labour in the discharge of his ministerial duty, being glad to spend and be spent, watching for their souls, as one that must give an account; for a faithful minister studies to give a daily account of the state of his flock to the Lord Jesus: if they are flourishing and thriving, he gives an account of them in a way of rejoicing, and blessing him for the outlettings of his grace unto them: if they are languishing or decaying, or guilty of any miscarriages, he gives an account thereof in a way of mourning and sorrowing before the Lord. In a word, a faithful minister of Christ is one who endeavours singly to eye the glory of his Lord and Master in all his ministrations, to be wholly devoted to his service, and the good of the souls committed to his trust; he carries his people upon his breast before the Lord, and has an inward heart concern for their spiritual and eternal welfare. He is one who preaches not himself, but Christ Jesus the Lord, and who determines to know nothing among his people, but Christ, and him crucified. He is one who sees himself to be an unprofitable servant, and that his sufficiency stands only in the Lord; for indeed "who is sufficient for these things?"

II. The *second* thing proposed was, to give the reasons why faithful ministers of Christ ought to be honoured and esteemed by the people among whom they labour.

1. They ought to be esteemed for the sake of him whose message they bear. They are ambassadors for Christ, 2 Cor. v. 20. They receive their commission and authority from him, John xx. 21, "As my father hath sent me, even so send I you." Matth. xxviii. 18, 19, "All power is given unto me in heaven and in earth. Go ye, therefore, and teach all nations—and lo, I am with you always." Ambassadors have their honour and respect according to the rank of their masters who send them; the greater the prince be, the more honourable his messenger. Ministers of the gospel are the ambassadors of the King of kings, and Lord of lords, who has a name given him above every name; and you cannot despise the messenger if you honour the Master that sends him, Matth. x. 40, says Christ, "He that receiveth you receiveth me."

2. Faithful ministers of Christ ought to be esteemed for their work's sake, or for the sake of the message itself which they bear. It is a message of peace, Rom. x. 15, "How beautiful are the feet of them that preach the gospel of peace, and bring glad tidings of good things!" And how wonderful is it, that the God against whom we have sinned should proclaim peace on earth, and good will towards men! A minister's message is a treaty of marriage with the King's Son; and how amazing is it, that our Maker should be our Husband, that he should say to such guilty rebels as we are, "I will betrothe thee unto me for ever!" It is a message for a free commerce and trade with heaven; and surely that must be a gainful trade, which brings in the richest treasure at no expense; for here all the riches of heaven are to be had, and yet no money required for the purchase, Isa. lv. 1, "Ho, every one that thirsteth, come ye to the waters," &c. So that faithful ministers are to be honoured, both on Christ's account who sends them, and on account of the message which they bring from him, which, as it is a treaty of peace, marriage, and traffic, you heard at large explained in the preceding discourse; and therefore I insist not further upon it, but proceed to deduce a few inferences from what has been said.

1, then. Hence, see that a gospel ministry is of divine institution. Epaphras is here called a *minister of Christ*, which plainly says that he had his commission from him. That a gospel ministry is of divine institution is plain from the express designation of some to that office by our Lord Jesus; *he ordained twelve*, and afterwards appointed *other seventy also*, to labour in his harvest; and though it should be said that these were extraordinary officers, yet the same glorious Lord, who gave some to be apostles, prophets, and evangelists, gave some also to be pastors and teachers, with an express order to "commit the Word to faithful men, who shall be able to teach others also."

2. Hence, see that the office of the ministry is perpetually useful and necessary. What Epaphras was to the Colosssians, other ministers will, through grace, be unto other churches, till the end of time; he was a faithful minister for them, that is, for their profit, for their good. Ordinances are perpetually necessary in the church, and

therefore there must be a ministry to dispense them, as is evident from the promise of Christ's presence with his ministers, in teaching and baptizing to the end of the world. The ends for which a gospel ministry is appointed are perpetually necessary; the elect are to be gathered, the mouths of the gainsayers are to be stopped, the saints are to be edified and established till they all come in the unity of the faith, and of the knowledge of the Son of God, to a perfect man, to the measure of the stature of the fulness of Christ.

3. Hence, see that a corrupt erroneous ministry is one of the worst of plagues; for in this case people are destroyed for lack of knowledge. The Apostle Peter tells us, 2 Epist. ii. 1, that "there were false prophets among the people, even as there shall be false teachers among you, who privily shall bring in damnable heresies, and many shall follow their pernicious ways." This is sadly verified at the present day, in this poor church and land, which is now crammed with a lax and corrupt ministry, intruded upon the heritage of God; and, alas! the generality of the people are, like Issachar, "couching under the burden."

4. Hence, see that the removal of the gospel is a sore judgment: "Wo unto you (saith God) if I depart from you. Where there is no vision, the people perish." A famine of hearing the Word of the Lord is unspeakably worse than a famine of natural bread, Amos viii. 11.

4. If ministers are faithful in the discharge of their office, people will have much to account for those who despise their message, for they who despise them despise him that sent them; and "how shall we escape, if we neglect this great salvation?"

Any further application of this subject shall be in a word of *Exhortation*, first to the minister presently ordained, and then to the people over whom he has the charge; this task having been laid on me by your aged pastor, who, if his strength had permitted him, should have done it, it being an usual branch of an ordination sermon.

1st, then, I shall essay to speak a word unto the brother presently ordained.

R. D. B.

You are now ordained a minister of Christ, and it is your duty and mine to study that we be faithful ones.

1. Be faithful, in the first place, to your Lord and Master, whose message you bear; see that you keep close to the instructions which he has given you in his Word, that you may be in case to say to your people, what Paul did to the Corinthians, "I have received of the Lord that which also I delivered unto you." For you are to hear the Word at his mouth, and to give warning from him.

2. Let these you labour among see that you are in earnest about your Master's business, that your heart is so intent upon it, that nothing will give you satisfaction, unless they deal kindly with your Master, by believing the gospel report concerning him, as the gift of God for salvation to all the ends of the earth.

3. Let nothing bribe or scare you from the faithful discharge of your trust; let neither the fear nor favour, frowns nor flatteries of

people hinder you from declaring the counsel of God unto them. See if you can attain to say, in some measure, as it is, 1 Thess. ii. 4-5, "As we were allowed of God to be put in trust with the gospel, even so we speak, not as pleasing men, but God, who trieth our hearts. For neither at any time used we flattering words, as ye know, nor a cloak of covetousness. God is witness, nor of men sought we glory."

4. If you be a faithful minister of Christ, you must lay your account with much opposition in your work; you must not imagine that you will always sail before the wind; you will meet with storms from Satan, from wicked men, and even perhaps from good men themselves. Satan will be at your right hand to disturb you, both in your closet, and in the pulpit; at one time striving to blow you up with self-estimation, and at another, to sink you in the depth of discouragement. As for wicked men, the more faithful you are, the more of their wrath and fury will you draw upon yourself. And even good men may have sometimes unreasonable schemes, which they want to pursue to unwarrantable heights, and which if you oppose, as you are bound in faithfulness to do, you may meet with abundance of resentment from them likewise. So that, if you are a faithful minister, you must lay your account with opposition on all hands. "Behold (says Christ) I send you forth as sheep in the midst of wolves," Matth. x. 16.

5. Remember that the faithful discharge of your ministry is a most laborious work, such labour as frequently makes old age and youth to meet together. The Jews took Christ to be fifty years old (John viii. 57) when he was little above thirty. The most other callings are only an exercise to nature, but a minister's work spends his vital spirits, and makes him like the candle, to waste, while he is shining; hence are ministers compared to soldiers, and watchmen, who are exposed both to hard labour and great danger.

6. As you would desire to be a faithful minister of Christ, be sure to look for furniture, for the whole of your work, from the hands of the glorious Head, who has received gifts for men. As the Apostle says to Timothy (2 Epistle ii. 1) so say I to you, "Thou therefore, my son, be strong in the grace that is in Christ Jesus." Though your work be laborious and difficult, yet he sends none a warfare upon their own charges. In the use of appointed means, trust that his grace shall be sufficient for you, and that his strength shall be made perfect in weakness. Fasten therefore upon the promises of his presence, for your support and through-bearing, under all difficulties, "Lo, I am with you always. Fear not to go down to Egypt, for I will go down with thee, and I will also surely bring thee up again," Gen. xlvi. 4.

7. *Lastly.* Next unto the promised presence and aid of the glorious Head, it may be a considerable encouragement unto you, that you are called to take part of this ministry, with an aged and experienced servant of Jesus Christ, who will always be ready to give you his best advice; and to be sure your entire harmony, mutual love, and joint counsels will contribute much to strengthen your hands, as colleagues, in this part of the Lord's vineyard.

D. B.

I conclude what I have to say to you with repeating a few of the advices the Apostle gives to Timothy. Well then, "Refuse profane and old wives' fables, and exercise thyself to godliness.—I charge thee (says the Apostle) before God, and the Lord Jesus Christ, and the elect angels, that thou observe these things, without preferring one before another, doing nothing by partiality.—Follow after righteousness, godliness, faith, love, patience, meekness. Fight the good fight of faith, lay hold on eternal life, whereunto thou art also called.—Be not ashamed of the testimony of our Lord.—Hold fast the form of sound words.—Endure hardness as a good soldier of Jesus Christ. —Study to shew thyself approved unto God, a workman that needeth not to be ashamed, rightly dividing the word of truth.—Flee also youthful lusts, but follow after righteousness, faith, charity, peace, with them that call on the Lord out of a pure heart,—Be gentle unto all men, apt to teach, patient, in meekness instructing those that oppose themselves.—Preach the Word, be instant in season, out of season; reprove, rebuke, exhort with all long-suffering and doctrine —Watch thou in all things, endure afflictions, make full proof of thy ministry." And, finally.—"Give thyself wholly to these things that thy profiting may appear unto all.—Continue in them, for, in doing this, thou shalt both save thyself and them that hear thee." These and several other instructions, necessary to ministers, both for teaching and ruling their flocks, are to be found in the Epistles to Timothy and Titus, which you and I, and every other minister, ought to be frequently perusing, as we would be found faithful ministers of Christ, I come now, in the

Second place, To speak a word to you of this congregation.

My dear friends,—Your eyes do this day see your teachers, and I trust that God has, according to his promise, given you pastors according to his heart, who shall feed you with knowledge and understanding. You are at present privileged with two of them, when some corners have not so much as one: and, to be sure, of them to whom much is given much will be required.

One of your pastors is stooping under the infirmities of old age, having laboured about fifty years in the Lord's vineyard, and about twenty years thereof among you. O beware of bringing his gray hairs with sorrow to the grave, by rejecting the counsel of God against yourselves, and refusing to receive the message which he brings you from the mouth of God. If in Christ Jesus he has begotten any of you, through the gospel (as I hope has been the case with not a few), then he will have " no greater joy than to hear that his children walk in truth," as the expression is, 3 John 4 ; and if he can say with Paul (1 Thess. ii. at the close), " What is our hope, or joy, or crown of rejoicing ? Are not even ye in the presence of our Lord Jesus Christ, at His coming ? For ye are our glory and joy."

Your other pastor as to years is but a youth; and with reference to him I would say unto you, as Paul said with reference to Timothy, " Let no man despise his youth." Remember that David was but a youth or stripling (as Saul calls him) when he encountered Goliah the Philistine ; yet because he went out against him in the name of the Lord of hosts, " the God of the armies of Israel," he came off the field a conqueror. Jeremiah was called to be a prophet or teacher in his youth, as appears from the first chapter of his prophecy, and yet the Lord fitted that young prophet for the difficult task that was put into his hand.

There are only a few things I would say to you with respect to your duty towards both your ministers.

1. If your ministers should be faithful in declaring the Lord's mind, then you ought to be ready and willing to believe and practise it. It is a sad charge which the Lord lays against Ezekiel's hearers, chap. xxxiii. 31, "They sit before thee as my people, and they hear thy words, but they do them not, for with their mouth they shew much love, but their heart goeth after their covetousness." If you remain barren and unfruitful under such means of grace as you enjoy, it will be more tolerable for hundreds of congregations than for you, in regard they are not so highly privileged.

2. The more faithful your ministers are in point of sin and duty, the welcomer ought their message to be unto you. Some cannot endure to be touched upon the sore heel, or to have the sinfulness of their practices laid in broad-band before them; but if matters be right with you, the closer your ministers come to your consciences by the word, the more searching and trying their sermons be, the more will you love both their persons and doctrine: "Search me, O God (says the Psalmist), and know my heart: try me, and know my thoughts; and see if there be any wicked way in me," Ps. cxxxix. at the close.

3. Pray much for your ministers, that utterance may be given them, that they may open their mouth boldly, and make known the mystery of the gospel. The more you pray for them, the more profit you may expect under their ministry. If you have any spiritual wants to supply, or soul-perplexing doubts to solve; if you be under the prevalency of any temptation, from which you want to be delivered; in a word, if you be desiring the sincere milk of the word, that you may live thereby, then you will certainly be employed in prayer, that your ministers may be directed to speak a word in season unto you, and that the power of the Lord may come along therewith, for conviction or consolation, as your need requires.

4. If you would desire the faithfulness of your ministers to be useful unto you, be sure to keep them in their own room; do not expect from them what you are to receive only from the Lord himself. Remember that the "treasure is in earthen vessels, that the excellency of the power may be of God, and not of us," as you were hearing by the former speaker. But, at the same time, though you are not to idolize your ministers, yet a more peculiar love is due from you to them than to any else. Though you ought to love all the faithful ministers of Christ, yet a more special love is due to your own pastors, who labour in word and doctrine among you, as is clear from the forecited, 1 Thess. v. 12, "Know them that labour among you, and are over you in the Lord, and admonish you; and esteem them very highly in love for their work's sake." And, Heb. xiii. 17, "Obey them that have the rule over you, and submit yourselves; for they watch for your souls, as they that must give an account, that they may do it with joy, and not with grief."

I conclude with that prayer of the Apostles, 2 Cor. ix. 10, "Now he that ministereth seed to the sower, both minister bread for your food, and multiply your seed sown, and increase the fruits of your righteousness." Which is founded upon that promise, Isaiah lv. 10, 11, For as the rain cometh down, and the snow from heaven, and returneth not thither, but watereth the earth, and maketh it bring forth and bud, that it may give seed to the sower, and bread to the eater; so shall my word be that goeth forth out of my mouth; it shall not return unto me void, but it shall accomplish that which I please (or which is well pleasing unto me), and it shall prosper in the thing whereto I sent it."

CHRIST IN THE CLOUDS COMING TO JUDGMENT.

A Sermon by the Rev. Mr Ebenezer Erskine.

MATTH. xvi. 37.—Then shall he reward every man according to his works.

THE text gives us an account of the day of doom, which is the last day of assize, wherein every man shall be tried at the bar of God's justice, and every man shall then and there receive according to his works, whether they be good, or whether they be evil.

I shall not trouble myself or you with the terrors of this day, because I have no time, but will proceed.

It is most certain the day of judgment will come, and that it will be dreadful to all the wicked. But seeing these things must be, what sort of persons ought we to be in all manner of conversation, always looking for the coming of Christ, at whose coming the sun shall be darkened, and the moon shall not give her light, the stars shall fall from heaven, the powers of heaven shall be shaken, the elements shall melt with fervent heat. Who can hear all this, and not be wonderfully dismayed? O who dares eat, drink, or sleep, or take a minute's rest? Be sure, that day shall come. "O awake, ye drunkards! and weep, all ye drinkers of wine! because of the new wine! for it shall be pulled from your mouth. Gird yourselves and lament, ye priests! howl, ye ministers of the altar! Alas! the sore terrible day of the Lord is at hand."

DOCT. "This is a gospel truth, that Christ, who came into the world in the form of a servant, will one day come as a judge, attended with his holy angels.

And if this be so, then, *first*, for an use of exhortation.

1st, Let us all be warned, and, while we have time, provide for that day; yet, the weather is fair, we may frame an ark to save us from the flood; yet are the angels at the gate of Sodom, and yet Is Jonah in the streets of Nineveh; yet the prophet laments, crying, "O Judah! how shall I entreat thee?" Yea, the Apostle prays, nay, we pray you in Christ's stead, that you be reconciled unto God. But here a question will arise, How will Christ appear?

I answer,—He who, as a man, once appeared to be judged, will then appear to judge all mankind. Consider this, ye that are going to the bar, what a dreadful sight will this be to the faithless Jews, stubborn Gentiles, and wicked Christians, when every eye shall see him, and they also that pierced him? This is the man, shall they say, that was crucified for us, and again crucified by us. Why, alas! every sin is a cross, and every oath is a spear; and when that day is come, you must behold the Man, whom thus you do crucify by your daily sin; sure this will be a fearful sight. Where is the bloody swearer, that can tear his wounds, heart, and blood? At that day, all these words will appear, the heart be visible, and the body and the blood be sensible of good and evil: then shall the fearful voice proceed from his throne, Where is the blood thou spilled? Here is the woful and terrible judgment, when thou that art the murderer shall see the slain Man be thy judge. What favours canst thou think to expect at his hand, whom thou hast so vilely and treacherously used by thy daily sins? Be sure, the Son of man will come, as it is written, "but woe unto that man by whom the Son of man is betrayed; it had been better for that man he had never been born," Matth. xxvi. 24.

As Christ shall appear in the form of a man, so this Man shall appear in a glorious form. O sinner, look about you, the Judge is coming: a fire devours before him, and behind him a flame burns: on every side the people tremble, and all faces shall gather blackness. Here is a change indeed! He that was at the bar now sits on the throne, and that for ever and ever. Then, Christ stood as a lamb before Pilate: now, Pilate stands as a malefactor before Christ. He that was made the footstool of his enemies, must now judge, till he has made his enemies his footstool. Where shall they run? and how shall they seek the clefts of the rocks and hollow places? The glory of his majesty will kindle a flame, while the heavens and the earth shall flee away from the presence of the powerful Judge.

But if here be the Judge, where is the guard? Behold him coming from above with great power and glory! Would you know his habit? He is indeed clothed with majesty? Would you know his attendants? They are an host of holy angels; nay, yet a much longer train, even the souls of the saints descending from their imperial seats, and attending the Lamb with great glory. Never was there any judge lord of such a circuit: His footstool is in the clouds, his feet are in the rainbow; his judges are saints, his officers angels and archangels. The trumpet proclaims a silence, whilst a just sentence cometh from his mouth upon all the world. Thus you see the assize begun. "I beheld till the throne was cast down (saith the prophet), and the Ancient of days did sit, whose garments were white as snow, and the hair of his head like pure wool; his throne was like the fiery flame, and the wheels as burning fire," Daniel vii. 9.

This is the Judge, whose coming is so fearful, and ushered in by a fiery cloud, and apparelled in snowy white, carried in his circuit on burning wheels, and attended with thousands of thousands. O, ye Jews, behold the Man whom before ye crucified as a malefactor! behold him on his throne, whom ye said his disciples had stolen away by night out of his grave! Matth. xxviii. 13. Behold him in his majesty, him upon whom you would not look in his humility! This is he at whose appearance the kindreds of the earth shall mourn. Such a shout of fury follows the sight of his majesty, that the vaults shall echo, the hills resound, the earth shall shake, the heavens shall pass away, and be turned to confusion. Then shall the wicked mourn, then shall they weep and wail, yet their tears shall not serve their turn; their sins past betray them, and their shame condemns them, and their torments to come confound them: Thus shall the wicked bewail their miserable, hapless, unfortunate birth, and cursed end. O fearful Judge! terrible as an army with banners! The kings of the earth shall be astonished, and every eye shall see this Judge, and tremble at his sight. Lo, but conceive the guilty prisoner come to his trial. Will not the red robes of this Judge make his heart bleed, for his blood shed? Thus have I shewed you how Christ will appear in a glorious manner.

1. Think now, O sinner, what shall be thy reward, when thou shalt meet this Judge. The adulterer for a while may flatter beauty, the swearers grace their words with oaths, the drunkards kiss their cups, and thank their bodily healths, till they drink their souls to ruin; but let them remember, "for all these things God will bring them into judgment." A sad comfort in the end. How shall the adulterer satisfy lust, when he lies on a bed of flames? The swearer shall have enough of wounds and blood, when the devil shall torture his body and rack his soul in hell. The drunkard shall have plenty of his cups, when scalding lead shall be poured down his throat, and his breath draw flames of fire instead of air. As is thy sin, so is thy punishment; this Judge will give just measure in the balance of his indignation and wrath.

For comfort to all that are the Judge's favourites, now is the day (if ye are God's servants) that Satan shall be trodden under your feet, and you, with your Master Christ, shall be carried into the holy of holies. You may remember how all the men of God, in their greatest anguish here below, have fetched comfort from the eyes of faith. It was at this mountain Job rejoiced, being cast on the dunghill, that his Redeemer lived, and that he should see him at the last day stand on the earth. So likewise the evangelist John longed and cried, "Come, Lord Jesus, come quickly," Rev. xxii. 20. "Now, little children, abide in him, that, when he shall appear, we may have confidence, and not be ashamed at his coming. And this is the promise that he hath promised us, even eternal life." 1 John ii. 28, 29. But I proceed.

The persons to be judged are a world of men, good and bad, elect and reprobate.

(1.) There is a summons, and this every man must hear, and this shall be the voice of the last trumpet. "Arise, ye dead, and come to judgment." O what a fearful and terrible voice will this be to all the wicked? How will they tremble at his voice, which makes the earth to tremble? Even at this voice the graves of the dead shall be opened, and every soul re-united to its own body; the dark pit of hell shall be shaken, when the dreadful soul shall leave its place of terror, and once more re-enter into its stinking carrion, to receive a greater condemnation. John v. 28, 29. The voice of Christ is a powerful and strong voice; "The dead shall hear his voice, and they shall come forth, they that have done good unto the resurrection of life, and they that have done evil to the resurrection of condemnation."

Thus much for the summons, you hear it given, and every man must appear. Death must now give back all that he hath taken from the world. What a ghastly and shocking sight shall this be, to see all the graves open, and to see dead men arise out of their graves, and the scattered flying on the wings of the wind, till they meet together in one body, Ezek. xxxvii. 6, "The dry bones shall live." Behold, the power of God Almighty, out of the grave and the dust of the earth, from these chambers of death and darkness, shall raise the bodies of the buried, Rev. xx. 12, 13. "I saw the dead (saith St. John), small and great, stand before God; and the sea gave up the dead which were in it; and death and hell delivered up the dead that were in them: and they were judged every man according to his works." He that said to corruption, Thou art my father; and to the worm, Thou art my sister and mother, said also "I know that my Redeemer liveth, and mine eyes shall behold him." O good God! how wonderful is thy power! Joel iii. 11, 12, "Assemble yourselves, and come all ye heathen to the valley of Jehosaphat, for there will I sit to judge all the heathen round about."

Thus have you an account of the dead being raised; they are all brought together, and now must we put them asunder; the sheep shall be put on the right hand, and the goats on the left hand. And now see the parties thus summoned, raised, gathered, and set apart. Is not here a world of men to be judged all in one day? All tongues, all nations and people of the earth, shall appear in one day. We shall then behold each son of Adam, and Adam shall then see all his posterity. Consider this, ye that are high and low, rich and poor, one with another, "for with God there is no respect of persons." Hark, O beggar, petitions are out of date, yet thou needest not fear, for thou shalt have justice done thee this day. All causes shall be heard, and thou, though ever so poor, and even despised in the world, must with the rest receive thy sentence. Hark, O farmer! now are the lives and leases together finished; this day is the new harvest of the judge, who gathers in his wheat, and burns up his chaff with fire unquenchable; no bribes, no prayers, no tears; but as thou hast done, so thou art sentenced. Hark, O landlord! where is thy purchase to thee and thy heirs for ever? This day makes an end of all; and unhappy were thy soul, if thou hadst not better land than a barren rock, to cover and shelter thee from the presence of the Judge. Hark, O Captain, how vain is the hope of man to be saved by the multitude of an host. Thou hast commanded all the armies of the earth and hell, yet canst thou not resist the power of heaven. Hark, the trumpet sounds, and the alarm summons thee; thou must appear. All must appear, the beggar, the farmer, the captain, the prince, and the greatest potentates of the world; nay, all shall receive their reward according to their deserts.

(2.) This is for terror to the wicked: every man must appear. O that every man would but think of it! Would you know the man that shall at this day be blessed? It is he that thinks on this day, and prepares for it. O then, I beseech you, meditate every day, that you and every man must one day appear before the Judge of the quick and dead, and receive according to your works.

And now, having brought the prisoners to their trial, I must tell you how this trial must be,—for your works. Faith justifies, but it is by works we are judged. Mistake me not, he shall be judged according to his works, as being the best witness of his inward righteousness. But, the better to acquaint you with this trial, we come to consider,—

1. How all men's works shall be manifested to us.
2. How all men's works shall be examined by God.

1. Of the manifestation of every man's works, Rev. xx. 12. "I saw the dead, small and great (saith St. John) stand before God, and the books were opened; and another book was opened, which is the book of life; and the dead were judged out of these things which were written in the books, according to their works." Remember this, O forgetful sinner, thou mayest commit sin after sin, and multiply your sins; but be sure God keeps a just account, and none of your sins, though ever so secret, shall be forgot. There is a book of God's memory; it is called a book of remembrance, Mal. iii. 16, "A book of remembrance was written before God, for them that feared the Lord, and called upon his name." This is that which manifests all secrets; this is that which reveals all doings, whether good or evil. In these records are found at large Abel's sacrifice and Cain's murder, Absalom's rebellion and David's devotion, the Jews' cruelty and the prophets' innocency. Nothing shall be hid when this book is opened, for all may run and read it. "God will bring every man into judgment, with every secret thing, whether it be good, or whether it be evil," Eccles. xii. 14. Wail, ye wicked, and tremble in astonishment. Now your closet sins must be disclosed, and your private faults laid open.

Imprimis. For adultery, envy, blasphemy, drunkenness, oaths, violence, murder, Sabbath-breaking, lying, and every other sin, from the beginning to the end, from your birth to your death, the total sum is eternal death and damnation. But there is another book, that shall give a more fearful evidence than the former, and the secretary in the soul of man. No man can commit a sin, but the soul that is privy to the fact will write it in this book. What a woeful case will thy poor heart then be in! What a strong terror of trembling must it then stand possessed with, when this book shall be opened, and thy sins revealed? This book is now perhaps shut up and sealed; but in the day of judgment it shall be opened, and what will be the evidence that will be brought in? There is a private session to be held in the breast of every sinner; the memory is the record, truth is the law, damnation is the judgment, hell is the prison, devils are the jailors, and conscience both the witness and the judge to pass sentence upon thee. What hopes can he have at the general assize, whose conscience hath condemned him before he appears? Consider this, O thou impenitent sinner!

But yet there is another book we read of, and that is the book of life, wherein are written all the names of God's elect, from the beginning of the world unto the end thereof. This is the precious book of heaven, wherein if we be registrated, not all the powers of darkness, death, or devils, can blot us out again. Therefore, to make some useful applications,

1*st.* Consider now, O sinner, what books one day must be set before thee. The time will come when every word of thy mouth, every glance of thy eye, every moment of thy time, every sermon thou hast heard, every thing thou hast left undone, all shall be seen, and laid open before men, angels, and devils; thou shalt then and there be horribly and everlastingly ashamed. Never go about then to commit sin, though ever so secretly, though at midnight, and all the doors locked about thee, yet at this great day it shall be brought to light.

2*dly.* As you intend the good of your souls, amend your lives, call yourselves to an account, while it is called to-day; search and examine all your thoughts, words, and deeds, prostrate yourselves before God, with broken and bleeding affections; pray that your name may be written in the book of life; and if you do so, God is not unrighteous to forget your labour of love, and all your good works; for at that great day the book shall be opened, our works manifested, and, as we have done, so we must be rewarded; for then shall he reward every man according to his works. But a little to recal ourselves.

The prisoners are tried, the verdict brought in, the indictments are found, and the Judge now sits upon life and death, even ready with sparkling eyes to pronounce the sentence, The Lord grant, that, when this day comes, the sentence may be for us, and we be saved, to our everlasting comfort. O now hold up your heads, all ye saints of the most high God, for this shall be a blessed day for you: for then shall ye hear the sweet heavenly voice of Christ, saying, "Come ye blessed of my Father, inherit the kingdom prepared for you." I cannot express what joy it will be to the righteous, when they shall hear Christ say, Come, ye blessed soul, who hath been bathed in repenting tears. Here is a sentence able to revive the dead, much more the afflicted. Are you sorrowing for your sins, leave it awhile, and meditate with me on this ensuing melody. Hark! yonder is the choir of angels sounding to the Judge, while he is pronouncing thy sentence. Now is the day of your coronation; now shall ye be made perfectly happy, and that for ever. Come, saith Christ, you that have suffered for me, now you shall have your reward; you shall have your souls filled to the brim with joy, such as is unspeakable, and full of glory.

But I must return to the left hand, and shew another crew, prepared for another sentence. And O what a terrible sentence will that be, which will make all ears glow and tingle. "His lips (saith the prophet) are full of indignation, and his tongue like a consuming fire," Isa. xxx. 27. What fire is so hot as that fiery sentence, Matth. xxv. 41, " Depart from me, ye cursed, into everlasting fire, prepared for the devil and his angels."

1. They must depart. This seems nothing to the wicked. Now they are content to be gone; they have much more delight in sin than in God's service. But whither must they go? "From me." If from me, then from all my mercies, my glory, and my salvation? But whither, O Lord, shall the cursed go, that depart from thee? Into what haven shall they arrive? What master shall they serve? It is thought a great punishment to be banished from our native soils? What then is it to be banished from the almighty God? But whither must they go? Into everlasting fire. O what bed is this! no feathers but fire, no friends but furies, no ease but fetters, no daylight but darkness, no clocks to pass away the time, but endless eternity, fire eternal, always burning, and never dying. O who can endure everlasting flame! it shall not be quenched night or day; the smoke thereof shall go up for ever and ever. The wicked shall be crowded together, like bricks in a fiery furnace. But for whom was this fire prepared? For the devil and his angels. These must be your companions. The last sentence is now pronounced. What: Go (who?) ye cursed, into everlasting fire, to crews of devils. O take heed, that you live in the fear of God, lest that, leaving his service, he give you this reward, "Depart from me ye cursed," &c.

2. Consider, then, what fearful trembling will seize on your souls, that have their sentence for eternal flames: O which way will they turn? How will they escape the Almighty's wrath? To go backward is impossible, to go forward is intolerable. Whose help will they crave? God is their Judge, heaven their foe; the saints deride them, angels hate them. Good Lord, what a world of miseries hath seized on miserable souls. Their executioners are devils, the dungeon hell; the earth stands open, and the furnace burning, ready to receive you. O how will these poor souls quake and tremble! Every part of their body will bear a part in their doleful ditty; eyes weeping, hands wringing, breasts beating, hearts aching, with voices crying. Now, O man of the earth, what shall thy wealth avail thee; one drop of water, to cool thy tongue in the flames, is worth more than all the pleasures of the world.

Thus you have heard the sentence of the just and wicked; and the Judge is risen from his glorious seat. The saints guard him along, and the sentenced prisoners are delivered to the jailors; shrieks of horror shall be heard. What woes and lamentations shall be uttered, when devils and reprobates, and all the damned crew of hell, shall be driven into hell, never to return. Down they go howling, shrieking, and gnashing their teeth: The world leaves them, the earth forsakes them, hell entertains them; there they must live, and yet not live nor die; but dying live, and living die.

O miserable must these be, if the drowning of the world, the swallowing up of Korah, and the burning of Sodom with brimstone, were attended with such terror and hideous outcries; how infinitely, to all possibility of conceit, and trembling of that red fiery day; in a word, what wailing, weeping, roaring, and yelling, filling both heaven, earth, and hell! O most miserable wretches, Matth. xxii. 12. "Take them away, and cast them into utter darkness: there shall be weeping and gnashing of teeth." A darkness indeed! They must for ever be debarred from the light of heaven. Sunshine never peeps within these walls, nothing is there but smoke and darkness; and such is the portion of sinners, and the reward of the wicked.

THE WORD OF SALVATION.

Acts. xii. 16.—To you is the word of this salvation sent.

PAUL is here preaching Christ Jesus in the chapter; and in this verse he makes application of his sermon to his hearers, and that very close. More particularly in the words you may notice, (1.) The nature of the gospel described, it is the word of salvation. (2.) The indorsement or direction, shewing to whom it is directed or sent, *To you, &c.* you men and brethren, you Jews or Gentiles, to whom it is preached.

Observe, That the gospel, as a word of salvation, is sent to every sinner that hears it.

Before I proceed to speak to this doctrine, I would obviate an objection that may be made against it.

Object. Is not the gospel-call here limited to them that fear God in the text?

Ans. 1. If by these that fear God, is to be understood religious people, into whose hearts God hath put his fear, these are the persons that will most of all welcome the word of salvation, because they see most their need of it; but the gospel message is not here limited to them, and others excluded; no, the Apostle here speaks to all his auditory, both gracious and graceless, as appears not only in this text, "Men and brethren, children of the flock of Abraham, to you is the word of this salvation sent," but also in the application of this sermon to the graceless as well as to the gracious, ver. 40. 41.; compared with the two preceding verses.

2. There is a fear of God that is the fruit of conviction, and a fear of God that is the fruit of conversion; the former is by the law, the latter is by the gospel. It is like, that the former is specially meant here, for at this time the word was with power; it struck an awe and dread upon the Apostle's auditory And though no sinner, no, not the most stupid that hears the gospel, is excluded from the call thereof, so as it can be said, the word of salvation is not sent to him; no, no, it is sent to every one, yet none but such as fear God, so far as to be filled with an awe and dread of God speaking to them in the word, and with a conviction of sin, and of their need of this salvation, none but such will receive and welcome the word of this salvation; for if they have no fear of God, and of his wrath, no sense of sin, and of their deserving damnation, they will not value, but slight and despise the word of sal-

vation. This text, therefore, doth not limit the word of salvation, as sent only to them that fear God, but only points out the manner and method wherein this word of salvation comes to be received and entertained, and how it will not be received by these that have nothing of the fear and dread of God upon them.

3. These that are awakened to any sense of sin, and fear and dread of God, are the persons that are most ready themselves, as if the word of salvation were not sent to them; therefore these, in a particular manner, are mentioned, and encouraged to take it to themselves, because they are afraid to apply the word. Others that are called will not come. And they that have this fear upon them, have a will, but want courage; and therefore the Lord says to them, as it were, Fear not to come, *for to you is the word of this salvation sent.*

4. That the word of salvation is sent to all, even to them, who, through the want of the fear of God, reject it, is plain both from this text and context, compared with other scriptures. See the commission, Mark xvi. 15. "Go ye into all the world, and preach the gospel to every creature." Isa. xlvi. 12. "Hearken to me, ye stout hearted, that are far from righteousness." Rev. iii. 20. "Behold, I stand at the door, and knock: if any man hear my voice, and open the door, I will come in to him," &c., any man, be what he will. In short, the word of salvation, importing all salvation necessary, looks to all sinners that need this salvation. The gospel would not be glad news to all people, if any sinner were excluded.

Hence the call is to all the ends of the earth, "Look unto me, and be ye saved:" Hence the call also is, "Whosoever will, let him come, and take of the water of life freely." And again, "To you, O men, do I call, and my voice is to the sons of men." &c. "Ho, every one that thirsteth, come to the waters," &c.

In prosecuting the observation, we shall observe the following method.
I. I shall speak a little of this salvation.
II. Of the word of salvation.
III. Of the sending of this word.
IV. Make application.

I. We shall speak a little of this salvation, and consider what it supposes, and what it implies.

1*st.* What it supposes, namely, misery. Our miserable state by nature, is a state of alienation and estrangement from God. We are without God, and are "alienated from the life of God; aliens from the commonwealth of Israel." It is a state of enmity: "The carnal mind is enmity against God;" we are in actual rebellion against Him. It is a state of darkness and ignorance; we are "destroyed for lack of knowledge:" A state of bondage to sin, Satan, the world, and divers lusts; we are fettered and in prison, led captive. It is a state of impotence: we are by nature without strength; we cannot so much as ask deliverance; we are not sufficient of ourselves to think any thing as of ourselves. It is a destitute state, a pit wherein there is no water, a comfortless state, a bewildered state, a cursed and condemned state; for "he that believeth not is condemned already:" He that believeth not the gospel is condemned already by the law: "Cursed is every one that continueth not in all things that are written in the book of the law, to do them." It is a state of death, spiritual death, and legal death.

2dly. What does salvation imply? It implies the whole redemption, purchased by Christ, and the whole of the application of it by the Spirit. It is salvation from a state of estrangement to a state of acquaintance with God; from enmity to peace and reconciliation; from darkness to light; from bondage to liberty. It includes pardon and justification, adoption and filiation, sanctification of nature, heart, and way, communion with God; afterward a glorious resurrection of the body, and eternal life and glory, in being for ever with the Lord.

II. The *second* head proposed was, to speak of the word of salvation which I may do by answering these four questions.

Quest. 1. What is the word of salvation?

Ans. Not the law, but the gospel; that is that which is the power of God to salvation, Rom. i. 16. Whatever discovers Christ, and salvation through Him, is the gospel.

Quest. 2. Why is it called the word of salvation?

Ans. Because it discovers salvation, it describes salvation, it conveys salvation, as a charter does an estate, or as a testament does a legacy; it offers salvation, it establishes a connection between faith and salvation to all mankind sinners; for "He that believeth shall be saved;" and because it is the organ or instrument by which the Spirit applies salvation.

Quest. 3. How does the word operate in the hand of the Spirit, when believed unto salvation?

Ans. It operates as seed cast into the ground. It operates as rain and dew: "My doctrine shall drop as dew" As the light; "They that sat in darkness saw a great light; It is a light shining in a dark place:" As fire; "Is not my word like a fire?" As water, as wind, as a seal imprinting the divine nature: As a glass, through which we see God's glory: As balm for healing; "He sent his word, and healed them.

Quest. 4. What are the qualities of this word of salvation?

Ans. 1. It is a divine word; "the word of God." God, Father, Son, and Holy Ghost, is the Author of it. Hence the gospel is called "the gospel of God," Rom. i. 1. and xv. 2. 16. 2. It is a word of God in Christ, Heb i. I, 2, and ii. 3. It is secured "in the hands of a Mediator, yea, and amen in him." It is given to us by Christ, and sealed in his blood; "This is the New Testament in my blood." 3. It is a gracious word of God in Christ; it is free; it does not move upon our goodness or badness; our goodness does not further, nor our badness hinder it. It is a word that comes from pure grace, and springs from his free mercy, who is the God of all grace. It is such a gracious word, that it contains all grace. Hence, 4. It is a complete word, containing all our salvation; for it contains God in it, Christ in it, and the Spirit in it. It contains a righteousness in it, founding a legal title to life eternal, namely, the obedience of Christ; and a legal security from eternal death, namely, the satisfaction and death of the Surety. It contains all the parts of life, and may well be called the word of life; life in the beginning of it in regeneration; "Of his own will begat he us by the word of truth." The life of justification; we are justified in believing and receiving of Christ our righteousness, as offered in the word. The life of sanctification, the life of consolation, the life of glory hereafter. 5. It is a sure word; "the sure mercies of David;" sure, and more sure than a voice from heaven, such as even that which the disciples heard on the mount, 2 Pet. i. 19. "We have a more sure word of prophecy," &c. 6. It is a gracious, complete, sure word of God in Christ to sinners, as well as to saints; it is to sinners of Adam's family, for it presents a remedy for their malady. This leads to,

III. The *third* head proposed, namely, to speak of the sending of this word. Here it may be inquired from whom, by whom, to whom it is sent, and for what purpose.

1st, From whom is it sent? *Ans.* It is a word of salvation, sent from the God of salvation, to whom belong the issues from death; and it carries the impress of himself upon it. As the word is God's word, so it is of God's sending; "He sent his word, and healed them," Psal. cvii. 20.

2dly, By whom is it sent? *Ans.* Not by angels, but by men; "We are ambassadors for Christ," 2 Cor. v. 20, It is true, God sent his word first by Christ; "He so loved the world, that he sent his only-begotten Son," &c. Then Christ sends it by men, that we may not be afraid at his appearance, as Israel were of old; "We have this treasure in earthen vessels," 2 Cor. iv. 7.

3dly, To whom is it that he sent this word of salvation? *Ans.* To all sinners that hear it. Whosoever look to the word of salvation, will find it looking to them, Gen. xii. 3. What was the gospel preached to Abraham? "In thee, or in thy seed, shall all the families of the earth be blessed." Is not this a word of salvation to us also? It includes all, so as every sinner may take hold of it. See John iii. 16. I Tim. i. 15. Christ came to call sinners to repentance. See Prov. i. 20. Isa. xlvi. 12. It is a word that suits the case of sinners; and therefore, if it be inquired,

4thly, For what purpose is it sent to sinners? *Ans.* For the same purpose that a healing remedy is sent to a deadly malady; for Christ comes in the word, and is presented there, "for wisdom, righteousness, sanctification, and redemption;" 1 Cor. i. 30, and Rev. iii, 17, 18. More particularly, it is sent as a word of pardon to the condemned sinner; "I, even I, am he that blotteth out thy transgressions, for my own name's sake." Hence may every condemned sinner take hold of it, saying, This word is sent to me. It is sent as a word of peace to the rebellious sinner, saying, "Christ hath received gifts for men, even for the rebellious." O I am a rebel, may the sinner say, here is a word for me: It is sent as a word of life to the dead; The hour cometh, and now is, when the dead shall hear the voice of the Son of God, and they that hear shall live;" as a word of liberty to the captives; "The Spirit of the Lord God is upon me, because he hath anointed me to proclaim liberty to the captives, and the opening of the prison to them that are bound," &c.: as a word of healing for the diseased; for the word says,

"I am the Lord that healeth thee:" As a word of cleansing, or a cleansing word for the polluted; "I will sprinkle you with clean water," &c.: As a word of direction to the bewildered; "I will lead the blind by a way they know not," &c.: As a refreshing word to the weary; The Lord God hath given me the tongue of the learned, to speak a word in season to him that is weary:" As a comforting word to the disconsolate; it brings in the good news of the river, the streams whereof make glad the city of God, and of Christ the consolation of Israel: As a drawing word, and a strengthening word to the powerless soul, saying, "He giveth power to the faint, and to them that have no might he increaseth strength. Thy people shall be willing in the day of thy power. When I am lifted up, I will draw all men after me." It is sent, in short, as a word of salvation, and all sort of salvation and redemption to the lost soul, saying, "Christ came to seek and to save that which was lost; and that we are not redeemed with corruptible things, such as silver and gold, but with the precious blood of Christ."

IV. The *last* head proposed was, to make application. Is it so, that the gospel, as a word of salvation, is sent to every sinner that hears it? Then,

1*st*, Hence see the kindness of God in Christ to sinners of mankind. Why hath he made such a difference between sinning men and sinning angels? There was never a word of salvation sent to angels that sinned; no, they are reserved in chains to the judgment of the great day; but to you, "O men, do I call, and my voice is to the sons of men; *to you is the word of this salvation sent.*

2*dly*, See what a valuable book the Bible is, which contains this word of salvation. O how ought we to search the scriptures! for in them we think, and think aright when we do so, that we have eternal life and salvation conveyed to us. Why? They testify of Christ; and we ought especially to search out the words of eternal life, the words of salvation that lie there.

3*dly*, Hence see what a valuable blessing the gospel is, and the dispensation thereof, and how welcome a gospel ministry should be unto us; "How beautiful upon the mountains are the feet of them that preach the gospel of peace!" Rom. x. 15, that publish the word of salvation. How sad is it when the gospel-ministers have not beautiful feet, when they defile their feet by steppping into the puddle of defection and corruption, and so make poor souls to nauseate the very gospel preached by them; and how sad is it when these that profess to preach the gospel of peace, have their feet defiled in the puddle of error! How desirable is it, when they have both the gospel of peace in their mouth, and beautiful shoes upon their feet, and are shod with the preparation of the gospel of peace, and with a gospel conversation, declining to walk with others in a course of defection!

4*thly*, Hence see the inexcuseableness of unbelief in rejecting the gospel, since it is sent to every one that hears it. Men have no cloak for their unbelief, no ground to say, This word of salvation is not sent to me; yea, it is sent to thee, whosoever thou art; it is a rope cast down for thy drowning soul to grip to.

5thly, Hence see how culpable they are that straiten the door, and hamper the call of the gospel, saying in effect, if you have not such marks, it is not you; it is only upon such and such terms that it is to you. This is to make the gospel no gospel. It is as if Christ came to save saints, but not to save sinners. They contradict the very design of the gospel, which is a word of salvation to sinners of all sorts and sizes. *To you is the word of this salvation sent.* To you, O sinner, is the door of salvation opened. Whatever straitens this door, whatever doctrines you may hear that hamper the gospel-offer, and tend to make you suppose, that there is no room for you, no access for you, you may suspect that either to be no gospel doctrine, or that has such a legal mixture accompanying it, as you ought to shun like the devil, because it would keep you back from Christ and salvation.

6thly, Hence see the ground of God's controversy at this day, together with an antidote against the errors and evils of the day. The great ground of God's controversy, at this day, with the generation we live among, is their rejecting the word of salvation. Wherefore is he now speaking in wrath and war, but because we will not hearken to him speaking in mercy. Scotland hath been deaf to the word of God, and to the warnings of God. Judicatories have been deaf to the word of God, to the word of salvation, calling them to reform, and return to the Lord; deaf to any testimony lifted up for reformation: and the whole land hath been deaf to the voice of God in the gospel. And what if God now thunder and roar out of Zion, and say, you shall hear at the deafest side; if you will not hear the voice of the word, you shall hear the voice of the sword. O what is the quarrel? Why, God says, "This is my beloved Son, hear ye him:" No, but we refuse to hear him. General Assemblies have refused to hear him; they give ear more to a patron, or a great man, and give more obedience to him, than to the voice of Christ. He said, "Feed my sheep, feed my lambs:" No, say they; but let them be worried with wolves, rather than displease and offend men of rank and power. How justly may the Lord say to such, "Go to the gods whom ye have served," and see if they can deliver you in the day of death, or in the day of wrath.

See here also an antidote against many errors of the day. Here is an antidote against enthusiastic delusions, viz., if we take the word of God for the rule and the warrant of faith, and of every particular duty. Some will say, we must wait for the Spirit being poured out; and till the Spirit comes, there is no doing; therefore we may sit still, and do nothing, either in the matter of our salvation-work, or generation work, either in personal or public work. Why, here is a delusion, here is enthusiasm, to make the Spirit the rule of faith and duty, and not the word of God. When God spake to Moses at the Red Sea, saying, "Speak to the people that they go forward." What! go forward, might unbelief say, into the sea, and be all drowned! Nay, stay till we see the water divided. No, says God, "Speak to the people that they go forward!" and in going forward at the word and call of God, making his call and word the rule of faith and duty, in this way they were to find the sea divided before them. To wait upon God's working, either outwardly or inwardly, without answering the call of his word, and going forward in the way of duty, is to wait without a warrant; it is a delusion, a tempting of God. You are to mint at believing the word of salvation sent to you. The people we call Quakers say, they ought not to pray till the Spirit moves them, making the inward motions of the Spirit, and not the word of God, the rule of duty. Thus it is no wonder that they be misled by a delusive spirit; for the word of God is the sword of the Spirit, and though we cannot fight without the Spirit, yet the Spirit will not fight for those, or with those, that will not take his sword in their hand; though we can do nothing without the Spirit, yet the Spirit will do nothing without the word. But if once we take the sword of the Spirit in our hand, I mean, take the word for our rule, and mint at duty, and at the work of believing, which is the work of God, according to the direction of the word of God; then, and not till then, are you to expect God will work powerfully; for out of his own road he will not, namely, if you turn away your ear from hearing his word, or if he do, he will bring you to this road before he do any thing more.

Here also see an antidote against all, or most of all the errors of the age wherein we live. Here is an antidote against all practical error, against all profanity, looseness, and luxury, whoredom, and debauchery, that have been long running down, like a mighty stream, through all ranks of persons, from the throne to the dunghill, in every corner of the land. What would remead these evils? Even the receiving of this salvation that is sent in the gospel to us. Unbelief in rejecting this salvation, which is a salvation from all sin as well as misery; this unbelief in slighting the Saviour and salvation, is the root of all the looseness and profanity in the age. Men do not see this root that lies hid under ground. Here is an antidote against the deism of the age. Why do men undervalue the scriptures, and deny the necessity of divine supernatural revelation? Even because they reject the word of salvation, they do not see that the gospel only is the word of salvation, and that there is no salvation but in the faith of it; but the faith of this word would cure the deism of the age. Here is an antidote against Arminianism; for salvation comes not of the free will of man, but of the free grace of God, in a word of salvation sent to us. Here is an antidote against Arianism. Would any soul deny the supreme deity of Christ, and his proper divinity, if they believed, that with him are the words of eternal life, and that a word from his mouth is a word of salvation? Isa. xlv. 22. "Look unto me, and be ye saved, all the ends of the earth; for I am God, and there is none else." Here is an antidote against Antinomianism; for by this salvation we are not saved to sin and to wickedness, and break the law of God; but saved from sin and wickedness. The gospel being a word of complete salvation, the grace of God therein appears to all men, teaching effectively what the law does perceptively, namely, to deny ungodliness and wordly lusts, and to live soberly, righteously, and godly, in this present evil world. Here is an antidote against legalism, or Neonomianism, as some call it, which turns the gospel to a new law, and the covenant of grace, as it were, to a covenant of works. This text and doctrine shews, that we are not saved by a work, but by a word; not by any work of ours, but by a word sent from God to us, even *a word of salvation:* "Not by works of righteousness which we have done, but according to his mercy he saved us," Tit. iii. 5. See 2 Tim. i. 9. Here also is an antidote against ignorant preachers of the gospel, that confound the marks of faith with the grounds of faith, or the evidences of faith with the warrant of faith, or the condition of the covenant with the qualities of the covenanted, as if the gospel call were only to saints, or to sinners so and so qualified; and so, leading men in to themselves for a ground of faith, instead of leading them out of themselves to Christ, exhibited to them in a word of salvation sent to them. The gospel method of salvation is the reverse of all legal schemes in the world. The legal strain supposes always some good quality about the sinner, before he be allowed to meddle with the word of salvation, and so shuts the door of the gospel, which it pretends to open. But the gospel strain brings the word of salvation freely to every sinner's door, and supposes him to be destitute of all good qualities whatsoever, and leaves no room to any sinner to say, I am not allowed to come in.

7*thly*, Hence see how much it concerns all and every one, to try and examine what entertainment they have given the word of salvation that is sent to them. Have you received it, or not, in a saving way?

1. Have you received it as the word of God, the word by way of eminency, the word of God in Christ. 1 Thess. ii. 13. and received it not as the word of man, of this or that man; but, as it is in truth, the word of God? &c.

2. Have you received it as the word of salvation, or as a faithful saying, and worthy of all acceptation, both as a truth and as a good? This reception of it supposes a view you have of your being a lost sinner welcoming a saviour.

3. Have you received it as the word of this salvation; a present salvation, a particular salvation? This particular salvation from sin and wrath that you need, this near salvation; "I bring near my righteousness to the stout-hearted, and far from righteousness; my salvation shall not tarry," Is. xlvi. 12. 13. this great salvation, this purchased salvation, this promised salvation, this offered salvation, presently offered, Faith fixes on something present. You need not say, Rom. x. 6—8. "Who will ascend to heaven, &c. the word is nigh," &c. Again,

4. Have you received it as a sent salvation, as God's send, as God's gift, sent by the hand of his ambassadors, sent freely and sovereignly, without your seeking after it, sent out of the storehouse of divine grace.

Have you received it as sent to sinners, to sinners in general? For here is glad tidings of great joy to all people. "Upon this mountain shall the Lord of hosts make unto all people a feast of fat things, of wines on the lees," &c. Is. xxvi. 6.

6. Have you received it as sent unto you in particular? To you, sinners, says the general dispensation: To thee, sinner, in particular, says the particular offer: "Whosoever will, let him come." Hast thou then received it, as sent to thee, though a guilty sinner; to thee, though a vile sinner? Hast thou entertained it with a me, me, of particular application, saying, Here is an offer to me, a gift to me, a

promise from heaven to me? Hast thou found thyself called by name, and said, I am warranted to take hold of Christ, and the salvation he brings with him, in this word of salvation; and even so I take him at his word, "Lord, I believe, help thou my unbelief?" Have you hereupon found the virtue of this word, as a word of salvation, saving you from your doubts and fears, saving you from your bonds and fetters, saving you from your helpless and hopeless condition, and making you to hope for complete salvation from sin and misery? Have you found salvation begun in the faith of the word of salvation, and being begotten to a lively hope thereby? And does this hope begin to purify your heart, and this faith begin to work by love to God, and hatred of sin, and of yourself for sin? And is your continual recourse to this word of salvation, or to the promise of God in Christ, for all your salvation?

8*thly*, Hence see what matter of joy and praise believers have, who have been determined thus to entertain the word of salvation; for when the word of salvation is received through grace, then the work of salvation is begun: and you need be in no uneasiness now, though you be called to work out the work of your salvation with fear and trembling; because it is God that worketh in you both to will and to do. He that hath begun the good work in you, will perfect it unto the day of the Lord. The word of salvation may be unto thee, O believer, the word of consolation all the days of your life: for it is a word of salvation not only from the sinful state and miserable state you were in, but it is a word of salvation also bringing the good news of salvation in every case; salvation from the devil, the world and the flesh; salvation and deliverance from the hands of all your enemies; salvation from the sting of death, salvation from the terror of judgment, salvation from the curse of the law, and from the guilt of all your sins; salvation not only from all evil, but salvation to eternal life, for the word of salvation you have received and entertained through grace, contains all the words of eternal life. The word of salvation is the word of life for you, when under deadness, and the word of liberty for you, when under bondage; a word of rest for you when under weariness; a word of relief for you, when under distress of whatsoever sort. It is a word of salvation confirmed with the oaths of God, "That by two immutable things, in which it is impossible for God to lie, they might have strong consolation, who have fled for refuge to lay hold on the hope set before them.

9*thly*, Hence see matter for terror to those that neglect this great salvation that is sent to them by this word. "How shall they escape who neglect so great a salvation," and a salvation come so near to them? O sinner, it is a salvation sent to your house, and will you reject it? salvation sent to your soul; a word of salvation sent to your hand to receive it, and will you reject it? a word of salvation sent to your ear, saying, "But hear, and your soul shall live:" A word of salvation sent to your heart, and by it God is knocking at the door of your heart: O will you refuse him that speaketh from heaven? See Heb. xii. 25. If you will not hear God's word of grace in the gospel, saying, "To you is the word of this salvation sent;" you must lay your account to hear his word of wrath in the law, saying, yea, swearing in his wrath, that you shall not enter into his rest. If you have no fear of God, as it is in the verse where my text lies; if you shall never be persuaded to fear the Lord, and his goodness manifested in the word of salvation sent to you, you must lay your account to fear the Lord and his wrath, manifested in the word of condemnation, which the law pronounces against them that believe not the gospel, John iii. 18. "He that believeth not is condemned already." And there is no escaping this sentence of condemnation, but by receiving the word of salvation.

10*thly*. Hence, see how much it is the interest of every one to receive, and entertain, and welcome this word of salvation. "O hear, that your souls may live." Hear the joyful sound of salvation, O lost perishing sinner, before the door of mercy be shut, and the day of grace be over. Consider,

1. What sort of a salvation is offered to you. It is a spiritual salvation, the salvation of the immortal soul. "What shall a man profit, though he gain the whole world, if he lose his own soul?" If you would not lose and ruin your souls, O receive the word of salvation. It is a costly salvation, it comes running in the channel of the blood of Christ. It is brought to your hand, and free to you, however dear bought by the Redeemer. You have nothing to pay for it; the price of it is paid already; the condition is fulfilled. It is a complete salvation, salvation from every thing you need to be saved from; salvation from unbelief, enmity, atheism, heart-hardness, heart-deadness, and every thing that you make an objection against receiving of this salvation. You say you cannot believe, you cannot repent, but you would be saved from your unbelief and impenitence? This, and all the other branches of salvation is sent to you, when the word of salvation is sent. Will you welcome a Saviour to save you from all, to be wisdom, and righteousness, and sanctification, and redemption, and all to you? It is an everlasting salvation. Would you be happy after death, and have an eternity of happiness? Life and immortality is brought to light by this word of salvation. O poor dying sinner, consider what an everlasting salvation this is.

2. Consider what need thou hast of this salvation. Thou hast a dark mind, and needest salvation from that darkness and ignorance. Thou hast a guilty conscience, and needest salvation from that guilt. Thou hast a hard heart, and needest salvation from that hardness. Thou hast a powerful and strong corruption, and needest salvation from that. Thou hast a corrupt nature, and needest salvation from that. Thou hast many heart-plagues, and needest salvation from these plagues, and healing. Behold all this salvation, and infinitely more comes with the word of salvation; no salvation thou needest is excepted. Thy need is great, death is at hand, judgment at hand : "Now is the accepted time, now is the day of salvation." There will be no word in the day of judgment to sinners, but a word of condemnation, "Depart from me, ye cursed, into everlasting fire, prepared for the devil and his angels." But now, in the day of salvation, is sent to you this word of salvation; now, now is the day, and perhaps now, or never.

3. Consider what a firm ground this word of salvation is for faith

to believe upon. It is the word of God, the God that cannot lie. It is ratified by an oath of God. It is a word confirmed by the blood of the Son of God. It is a word attested by the Three that bear record in heaven. It is a word spoken by the inspiration of the Spirit of God, "He that hath ears to hear, let him hear what the Spirit saith to the churches. The Spirit and the bride say, "Come;" come and hear this word of salvation; come and believe; come and apply to thyself what is offered to thee.

4. Consider the good warrant you have to intermeddle with this word of salvation. It is sent to you on purpose that you may believe it with application to yourself; and that every one of you, thou man, thou woman, may take it home to thy own heart; for to thee is the word of salvation sent. To thee is this love letter sent from heaven. Read the indorsement, and see if it be not to thee. It is backed to thee, O guilty sinner, saying, Christ came to save sinners. It is backed to thee, O inhabitant of the earth, that art not yet in hell; "Look to me, and be ye saved, all the ends of the earth." It is backed to thee, O scorner, that hast hitherto been a mocker of God and godliness, Prov. i. 20. 22. 23. It is backed to thee, O rebellious sinner. If thou wert excepted, all mankind would be so. Behold Christ hath ascended up on high, led captivity captive, and received gifts for men, even for the rebellious, that God the Lord might dwell among them. It is backed to thee, O black and bloody sinner, Isa. xviii. "Come now, and let us reason together, saith the Lord; though your sins be as scarlet, they shall be white as snow; though they be red like crimson, they shall be as wool." It is backed to thee, O sinner that art thirsting after other things than Christ, Isa. lv. 1. 2. "Ho everyone that thirsteth, come. Wherefore spend ye your money for that which is not bread?" &c. Wherefore do ye thirst and pant after other things that cannot give you satisfaction? Yea, it is backed for thee O unhumbled, unconvinced sinner. Say not, that cannot concern thee, because thou art not convinced of thy sin. O, the word of salvation comes even to thee also, Rev. iii. 18. "I counsel thee to buy of me gold tried in the fire," &c. even thee, that, as in the preceding verse, art saying that thou art rich and increased with goods, and stand in need of nothing; and knowest not, that thou art wretched, and miserable, and poor, and blind, and naked. Unconcerned sinner, to thee, even to thee, is the word of this salvation sent. Is this love-letter backed for thee? O then, know, that though you have no will, you have a warrant to receive it, and Christ in it. If you reject this word of salvation, it is either because you will not, or dare not, or cannot receive it.

If you say you will not take it to you, then remember you are willingly subscribing your own doom. And I take instruments against you, that you will not have salvation, you will not come to Christ that you may have life; you are preferring some base lust to the Lord of glory, and so preferring, of consequence, damnation to salvation, death to life.

If it be not a will of obstinacy, but impotency, saying, O if my will were subdued; behold the word of salvation comes with salvation from that plague of unwillingness, saying, "Thy people shall be willing in the day of thy power." And *to you is the word of this salvation sent*, that you may welcome it; and so far as you welcome it, so far are you willing.

If you say you dare not take the word to yourself as a word of salvation to you; why dare you not do what God offers you? How durst you sin against God when he forbade you? And now you dare not take his word for your salvation when he bids you! How durst you venture on his fury against his command? And now you dare not venture on his favour, through Christ, at his call and command. Was it not enough to offend his justice? and will you venture now to slight his mercy? This is worse than all your former sins, to refuse salvation that he offers from the guilt of all.

If you say you cannot, because of utter impotency; that shall be no stop. You cannot believe, you cannot come to Christ; but as the word of salvation is sent to you, so salvation is come to you, because you cannot come to it. The Saviour is come to you, because you cannot come to him. Are you for him? The word of salvation is a word of power; and drawing power is in it, to draw you that cannot come. "When I am lifted up, I will draw all men after me." Are you willing to be drawn? Then the word of salvation hath so far taken effect upon you, as to remove your unwillingness, and to make you willing. Look for another pull of omnipotency; for the word of salvation is a word of omnipotency; it is the almighty word of the almighty God. Saving power, drawing power, is in it. Welcome it as such, and in due time you shall be able as well as willing. Your faith is not to be acted in the sense of self-ability and sufficiency, but in the sense of self-inability and insufficiency. Our sufficiency is of God, salvation is of God, "All things are of God," 2 Cor. v. 18. " who hath given to us the ministry of reconciliation," and given to you this word of salvation : and it contains all your salvation. And if any part of it were left to you, it would not contain all your salvation. What you cannot do, this salvation can: therefore receive it, and bless God for it, that *to you is the word of this salvation sent.*

END OF THE SERMONS.

THE

BELIEVER'S JOINTURE.

The Believer's perfect beauty, free acceptance, and full security, through the imputation of Christ's perfect righteousness, though imparted grace be imperfect.

O HAPPY soul, JEHOVAH's bride,
   The Lamb's beloved spouse,
Strong consolation's flowing tide
   Thy Husband thee allows.
In thee, though, like thy father's race,
   By nature black as hell ;
Yet now, so beautify'd by grace,
   Thy Husband loves to dwell,
Fair as the moon thy robes appear,
   While graces are in dress :
Clear as the sun, while found to wear
   Thy Husband's righteousness.
Thy moon-like graces, changing much,
   Have here and there a spot :
Thy sun-like glory is not such,
   Thy Husband changes not.
Thy white and ruddy vesture fair
   Outvies the rosy leaf ;
For 'mong ten thousand beauties rare
   Thy Husband is the chief.
Cloth'd with the sun, thy robes of light
   The morning rays outshine ;
The lamps of heaven are not so bright,
   Thy Husband decks thee fine.
Though hellish smoke thy duties stain,
   And sin deform thee quite,
Thy Surety's merit makes thee clean,
   Thy Husband's beauty white.
Thy pray'rs and tears, nor pure, nor good,
   But vile and loathsome seem ;
Yet gain, by dipping in his blood,
   Thy Husband's high esteem.
No fear thou starve, though wants be great,
   In him thou art complete :
Thy hungry soul may hopeful wait,
   Thy Husband gives thee meat.
Thy money, merit, pow'r, and pelf,
   Were squander'd by thy fall ;
Yet, having nothing in thyself,
   Thy Husband is thy all.
Law precepts, threats, may both beset
   To crave of thee their due ;
But justice for thy double debt
   Thy Husband did pursue.
Though justice stern as much belong
   As mercy to a God ;
Yet justice suffer'd here no wrong,
   Thy Husband's back was broad.
He bore the load of wrath alone,
   That mercy might take vent ;
Heav'n's pointed arrows all upon
   Thy Husband's heart were spent.
No partial pay could justice still,
   No farthing was retrench'd ;
Vengeance exacted all, until
   Thy Husband all advanc'd.
He paid in liquid golden red,
   Each mite the law requir'd,
Till, with a loud, 'Tis finished,
   Thy Husband's breath expir'd.
No process more the law can 'tent ;
   Thou stand'st without its verge,
And may'st at pleasure now present
   Thy Husband's full discharge.
Though new-contracted guilt beget
   New fears of divine ire ;
Yet fear thou not, though drown'd in debt,
   Thy Husband is the payer.
God might in rigour thee indite
   Of highest crimes and flaws ;
But on thy head no curse can light,
   Thy Husband is the cause.

Christ the Believer's Friend, Prophet, Priest, King, Defence, Guide, Guard, Help, and Healer.

DEAR soul, when all the human race
   Lay welt'ring in their gore,
Vast numbers in that dismal case
   Thy Husband passed o'er.
But pray, why did he thousands pass,
   And set his heart on thee ?
The deep, the searchless reason was,
   Thy Husband's love is free.
The forms of favour, names of grace,
   And offices of love,
He bears for thee, with open face,
   Thy Husband's kindness prove.

'Gainst darkness black, and error blind,
  Thou hast a sun and shield ;
And to reveal the Father's mind,
  Thy Husband-Prophet seal'd.
He likewise, to procure thy peace,
  And save from sin's arrest,
Resign'd himself a sacrifice ;
  Thy Husband is thy Priest.
And that he might thy will subject,
  And sweetly captive bring,
Thy sins subdue, his throne erect,
  Thy Husband is thy King.
Though num'rous and assaulting foes,
  Thy joyful peace may mar,
And thou a thousand battles lose,
  Thy Husband wins the war.
Hell's forces, which thy mind appal,
  His arm can soon dispatch ;
How strong soe'er, yet for them all
  Thy Husband's more than match.
Though secret lusts with hid contest,
  By heavy groans reveal'd,
And devil's rage : yet, do their best,
  Thy Husband keeps the field.
When in desertion's ev'ning dark,
  Thy steps are apt to slide,
His conduct seek, his counsel mark,
  Thy Husband is thy guide.
In doubts, renouncing self-conceit,
  His word and Spirit prize :
He never counsel'd wrong as yet,
  Thy Husband is so wise.
When weak, thy refuge seest at hand,
  Yet cannot run the length ;
'Tis present pow'r to understand
  Thy Husband is thy strength.
When shaking storms annoy thy heart,
  His word commands a calm :
When bleeding wounds to ease thy smart,
  Thy Husband's blood is balm.
Trust creatures, nor to help thy thrall,
  Nor to assuage thy grief ;
Use means, but look beyond them all,
  Thy Husband's thy relief.
If Heav'n prescribes a bitter drug,
  Fret not with froward will ;
This carriage may thy cure prorogue ;
  Thy Husband wants no skill.
He sees the sore, he knows the cure
  Will most adapted be;
'Tis then most reasonable, sure,
  Thy Husband choose for thee.
Friendship is in his chastisements,
  And favour in his frowns ;
Thence judge not then, in heavy plaints,
  Thy Husband thee disowns.
The deeper his sharp lancet go,
  In ripping up thy wound,
The more thy healing shall unto
  Thy Husband's praise redound.

Christ the Believer's wonderful Physician and wealthy Friend.

KIND Jesus empties whom he'll fill,
  Casts down whom he will raise ;
He quickens whom he seeks to kill ;
  Thy Husband thus gets praise,
When awful rods are in his hand,
  There's mercy in his mind ;
When clouds upon his brow do stand,
  Thy Husband's heart is kind.
In various changes to and fro,
  He'll ever constant prove ;
Nor can his kindness come and go,
  Thy Husband's name is Love.
His friends in most afflicted lot
  His favour most have felt ;
For when they're try'd in furnace hot,
  Thy Husband's bowels melt.
When he his bride or wounds or heals,
  Heart-kindness does him move ;
And wraps in frowns, as well as smiles,
  Thy Husband's lasting love.
In's hand no cure could ever fail,
  Though of a hopeless state,
He can in desp'rate cases heal,
  Thy Husband's art's so great.
The medicine he did prepare
  Can't fail to work for good :
O balsam pow'rful, precious, rare,
  Thy Husband's sacred blood ;
Which freely from his broached breast
  Gush'd out like pent-up fire.
His cures are best, his wages least,
  Thy Husband takes no hire.
Thou hast no worth, no might, no good,
  His favour to procure :
But sees his store, his pow'r, his blood ;
  Thy Husband's never poor.
Himself he humbled wondrously
  Once to the lowest pitch,
That bankrupts through his poverty
  Thy Husband might enrich.
His treasure is more excellent
  Than hills of Ophir gold ;
In telling store were ages spent,
  Thy Husband's can't be told.
All things that fly on wings of fame,
  Compar'd with this, are dross ;
For searchless riches in his name
  Thy Husband's doth ingross.
The great IMMANUEL, God-Man,
  Includes such store divine ;
Angels and saints will never scan
  Thy Husband's golden mine.
He's full of grace and truth indeed,
  Of Spirit, merit, might ;
Of all the wealth that bankrupts need
  Thy Husband's heir by right.
Though heav'n's his throne, he came from thence
  To seek and save the lost :

Whatever be the vast expense,
  Thy Husband's at the cost.
Pleas'd to expend each drop of blood,
  That fill'd his royal veins,
He frank the sacred victim stood;
  Thy Husband spar'd no pains.
His cost immense was in thy place,
  Thy freedom cost his thrall;
Thy glory cost him deep disgrace,
  Thy Husband paid for all.

The Believer's safety under the covert of Christ's atoning blood and powerful intercession.

WHEN Heav'n proclaim'd hot war and wrath,
  And sin increas'd the strife;
By rich obedience unto death,
  Thy Husband bought thy life.
The charges could not be abridg'd
  But on these noble terms.
Which all that prize are hugg'd amidst
  Thy Husband's folded arms.
When law condemns, and justice too
  To prison would thee hale;
As sureties kind for bankrupts do,
  Thy Husband offers bail.
God on these terms is reconcil'd,
  And thou his heart hast won;
In Christ thou art his favour'd child,
  Thy Husband is his Son.
Vindictive wrath is whole appeas'd,
  Thou need'st not then be mov'd;
In Jesus always he's well pleas'd,
  Thy Husband's his *Belov'd.*
What can be laid unto thy charge,
  When God does not condemn?
Bills of complaint though foes enlarge,
  Thy Husband answers them.
When fear thy guilty mind confounds,
  Full comfort this may yield;
Thy ransom-bill with blood and wounds
  Thy Husband kind has seal'd.
His promise is the fair extract
  Thou hast at hand to shew;
Stern justice can no more exact,
  Thy Husband paid its due.

No terms he left thee to fulfil,
  No clog to mar thy faith;
His bond is sign'd, his latter-will
  Thy Husband's seal'd by death.
The great condition of the band
  Of promise and of bliss,
Is wrought by him, and brought to hand,
  Thy Husband's righteousness.
When therefore press'd in time of need
  To sue the promis'd good,
Thou hast no more to do but plead
  Thy Husband's sealing blood.
This can thee more to God commend,
  And cloudy wrath dispel,
Than e'er thy sinning could offend;
  Thy Husband vanquish'd hell.
When vengeance seems, for broken laws,
  To light on thee with dread,
Let Christ be umpire of thy cause;
  Thy Husband well can plead.
He pleads his righteousness, that brought
  All rents the law would crave;
Whate'er its precepts, threat'nings, sought,
  Thy Husband fully gave.
Did holiness in precepts stand,
  And for perfection call,
Justice in threat'nings death demand?
  Thy Husband gave it all.
His blood the fiery law did quench,
  Its summon need not scare;
Tho't cite thee to Heav'n's awful bench,
  Thy Husband's at the bar.
This Advocate has much to say,
  His clients need not fear;
For God the Father hears him ay,
  Thy Husband hath his ear.
A cause fail'd never in his hand,
  So strong his pleading is;
His Father grants his whole demand,
  Thy Husband's will is his.
Hell-forces may all rendezvous,
  Accusers may combine;
Yet fear thou not who art his spouse,
  Thy Husband's cause is thine.
By solemn oath JEHOVAH did
  His priesthood ratify;
Let earth and hell then counterplead,
  Thy Husband gains the plea.

www.ingramcontent.com/pod-product-compliance
Lightning Source LLC
Chambersburg PA
CBHW021423300426
44114CB00010B/618